T0214144

Lecture Notes in Computer Science 12788

More information about this subseries at http://www.springer.com/series/7409

Abbas Moallem (Ed.)

HCI for Cybersecurity, Privacy and Trust

Third International Conference, HCI-CPT 2021
Held as Part of the 23rd HCI International Conference, HCII 2021
Virtual Event, July 24–29, 2021
Proceedings

 Springer

Editor
Abbas Moallem
San Jose State University
San Jose, CA, USA

ISSN 0302-9743   ISSN 1611-3349 (electronic)
Lecture Notes in Computer Science
ISBN 978-3-030-77391-5   ISBN 978-3-030-77392-2   (eBook)
https://doi.org/10.1007/978-3-030-77392-2

LNCS Sublibrary: SL3 – Information Systems and Applications, incl. Internet/Web, and HCI

This Springer imprint is published by the registered company Springer Nature Switzerland AG
The registered company address is: Gewerbestrasse 11, 6330 Cham, Switzerland

Foreword

Human-Computer Interaction (HCI) is acquiring an ever-increasing scientific and industrial importance, and having more impact on people's everyday life, as an ever-growing number of human activities are progressively moving from the physical to the digital world. This process, which has been ongoing for some time now, has been dramatically accelerated by the COVID-19 pandemic. The HCI International (HCII) conference series, held yearly, aims to respond to the compelling need to advance the exchange of knowledge and research and development efforts on the human aspects of design and use of computing systems.

The 23rd International Conference on Human-Computer Interaction, HCI International 2021 (HCII 2021), was planned to be held at the Washington Hilton Hotel, Washington DC, USA, during July 24–29, 2021. Due to the COVID-19 pandemic and with everyone's health and safety in mind, HCII 2021 was organized and run as a virtual conference. It incorporated the 21 thematic areas and affiliated conferences listed on the following page.

A total of 5222 individuals from academia, research institutes, industry, and governmental agencies from 81 countries submitted contributions, and 1276 papers and 241 posters were included in the proceedings to appear just before the start of the conference. The contributions thoroughly cover the entire field of HCI, addressing major advances in knowledge and effective use of computers in a variety of application areas. These papers provide academics, researchers, engineers, scientists, practitioners, and students with state-of-the-art information on the most recent advances in HCI. The volumes constituting the set of proceedings to appear before the start of the conference are listed in the following pages.

The HCI International (HCII) conference also offers the option of 'Late Breaking Work' which applies both for papers and posters, and the corresponding volume(s) of the proceedings will appear after the conference. Full papers will be included in the 'HCII 2021 - Late Breaking Papers' volumes of the proceedings to be published in the Springer LNCS series, while 'Poster Extended Abstracts' will be included as short research papers in the 'HCII 2021 - Late Breaking Posters' volumes to be published in the Springer CCIS series.

The present volume contains papers submitted and presented in the context of the 3rd International Conference on HCI for Cybersecurity, Privacy and Trust (HCI-CPT 2021), an affiliated conference to HCII 2021. I would like to thank the Chair, Abbas Moallem, for his invaluable contribution to its organization and the preparation of the proceedings, as well as the members of the Program Board for their contributions and support. This year, the HCI-CPT affiliated conference has focused on topics related to usable security, security and privacy by design, user behavior analysis in cybersecurity, and security and privacy awareness.

I would also like to thank the Program Board Chairs and the members of the Program Boards of all thematic areas and affiliated conferences for their contribution towards the highest scientific quality and overall success of the HCI International 2021 conference.

This conference would not have been possible without the continuous and unwavering support and advice of Gavriel Salvendy, founder, General Chair Emeritus, and Scientific Advisor. For his outstanding efforts, I would like to express my appreciation to Abbas Moallem, Communications Chair and Editor of HCI International News.

July 2021   Constantine Stephanidis

HCI International 2021 Thematic Areas and Affiliated Conferences

Thematic Areas

- HCI: Human-Computer Interaction
- HIMI: Human Interface and the Management of Information

Affiliated Conferences

- EPCE: 18th International Conference on Engineering Psychology and Cognitive Ergonomics
- UAHCI: 15th International Conference on Universal Access in Human-Computer Interaction
- VAMR: 13th International Conference on Virtual, Augmented and Mixed Reality
- CCD: 13th International Conference on Cross-Cultural Design
- SCSM: 13th International Conference on Social Computing and Social Media
- AC: 15th International Conference on Augmented Cognition
- DHM: 12th International Conference on Digital Human Modeling and Applications in Health, Safety, Ergonomics and Risk Management
- DUXU: 10th International Conference on Design, User Experience, and Usability
- DAPI: 9th International Conference on Distributed, Ambient and Pervasive Interactions
- HCIBGO: 8th International Conference on HCI in Business, Government and Organizations
- LCT: 8th International Conference on Learning and Collaboration Technologies
- ITAP: 7th International Conference on Human Aspects of IT for the Aged Population
- HCI-CPT: 3rd International Conference on HCI for Cybersecurity, Privacy and Trust
- HCI-Games: 3rd International Conference on HCI in Games
- MobiTAS: 3rd International Conference on HCI in Mobility, Transport and Automotive Systems
- AIS: 3rd International Conference on Adaptive Instructional Systems
- C&C: 9th International Conference on Culture and Computing
- MOBILE: 2nd International Conference on Design, Operation and Evaluation of Mobile Communications
- AI-HCI: 2nd International Conference on Artificial Intelligence in HCI

List of Conference Proceedings Volumes Appearing Before the Conference

1. LNCS 12762, Human-Computer Interaction: Theory, Methods and Tools (Part I), edited by Masaaki Kurosu
2. LNCS 12763, Human-Computer Interaction: Interaction Techniques and Novel Applications (Part II), edited by Masaaki Kurosu
3. LNCS 12764, Human-Computer Interaction: Design and User Experience Case Studies (Part III), edited by Masaaki Kurosu
4. LNCS 12765, Human Interface and the Management of Information: Information Presentation and Visualization (Part I), edited by Sakae Yamamoto and Hirohiko Mori
5. LNCS 12766, Human Interface and the Management of Information: Information-rich and Intelligent Environments (Part II), edited by Sakae Yamamoto and Hirohiko Mori
6. LNAI 12767, Engineering Psychology and Cognitive Ergonomics, edited by Don Harris and Wen-Chin Li
7. LNCS 12768, Universal Access in Human-Computer Interaction: Design Methods and User Experience (Part I), edited by Margherita Antona and Constantine Stephanidis
8. LNCS 12769, Universal Access in Human-Computer Interaction: Access to Media, Learning and Assistive Environments (Part II), edited by Margherita Antona and Constantine Stephanidis
9. LNCS 12770, Virtual, Augmented and Mixed Reality, edited by Jessie Y. C. Chen and Gino Fragomeni
10. LNCS 12771, Cross-Cultural Design: Experience and Product Design Across Cultures (Part I), edited by P. L. Patrick Rau
11. LNCS 12772, Cross-Cultural Design: Applications in Arts, Learning, Well-being, and Social Development (Part II), edited by P. L. Patrick Rau
12. LNCS 12773, Cross-Cultural Design: Applications in Cultural Heritage, Tourism, Autonomous Vehicles, and Intelligent Agents (Part III), edited by P. L. Patrick Rau
13. LNCS 12774, Social Computing and Social Media: Experience Design and Social Network Analysis (Part I), edited by Gabriele Meiselwitz
14. LNCS 12775, Social Computing and Social Media: Applications in Marketing, Learning, and Health (Part II), edited by Gabriele Meiselwitz
15. LNAI 12776, Augmented Cognition, edited by Dylan D. Schmorrow and Cali M. Fidopiastis
16. LNCS 12777, Digital Human Modeling and Applications in Health, Safety, Ergonomics and Risk Management: Human Body, Motion and Behavior (Part I), edited by Vincent G. Duffy
17. LNCS 12778, Digital Human Modeling and Applications in Health, Safety, Ergonomics and Risk Management: AI, Product and Service (Part II), edited by Vincent G. Duffy

38. CCIS 1420, HCI International 2021 Posters - Part II, edited by Constantine Stephanidis, Margherita Antona, and Stavroula Ntoa
39. CCIS 1421, HCI International 2021 Posters - Part III, edited by Constantine Stephanidis, Margherita Antona, and Stavroula Ntoa

http://2021.hci.international/proceedings

3rd International Conference on HCI for Cybersecurity, Privacy and Trust (HCI-CPT 2021)

Program Board Chair: **Abbas Moallem,** *San Jose State University, USA*

- Mohd Anwar, USA
- Phoebe M. Asquith, UK
- Xavier Bellekens, UK
- Jorge Bernal Bernabe, Spain
- Ulku Clark, USA
- Emily Collins, UK
- Francisco Corella, USA
- April Edwards, USA
- Timothy French, UK
- Steven Furnell, UK
- Robert Gutzwiller, USA
- Nathan Lau, USA
- Heather Molyneaux, Canada
- Phillip L. Morgan, UK
- Jason Nurse, UK
- Hossein Sarrafzadeh, USA
- Adam Wójtowicz, Poland
- Daniel Wilusz, Poland
- Sherali Zeadally, USA

The full list with the Program Board Chairs and the members of the Program Boards of all thematic areas and affiliated conferences is available online at:

http://www.hci.international/board-members-2021.php

HCI International 2022

The 24th International Conference on Human-Computer Interaction, HCI International 2022, will be held jointly with the affiliated conferences at the Gothia Towers Hotel and Swedish Exhibition & Congress Centre, Gothenburg, Sweden, June 26 – July 1, 2022. It will cover a broad spectrum of themes related to Human-Computer Interaction, including theoretical issues, methods, tools, processes, and case studies in HCI design, as well as novel interaction techniques, interfaces, and applications. The proceedings will be published by Springer. More information will be available on the conference website: http://2022.hci.international/:

General Chair
Prof. Constantine Stephanidis
University of Crete and ICS-FORTH
Heraklion, Crete, Greece
Email: general_chair@hcii2022.org

http://2022.hci.international/

Contents

User Behavior Analysis in Cybersecurity

Security and Privacy Awareness

Usable Security

Authentication Management of Home IoT Devices

Aniqa Alam[1]($\boxtimes$), Heather Molyneaux[2], and Elizabeth Stobert[1]

[1] Carleton University, Ottawa, Canada
{aniqa.bintealam,elizabeth.stobert}@carleton.ca
[2] National Research Council of Canada (NRC), Ottawa, Canada
heather.molyneaux@nrc-cnrc.gc.ca

Abstract. The number of IoT devices in the home has been increasing rapidly. With the popularity comes different security vulnerabilities. One of the main causes for some vulnerabilities is users' weak password management strategies. In this paper, we explored end-users' password management for home IoT devices. We conducted a literature survey examining previous works on security and privacy concerns of home IoT devices and password management. We also conducted an online survey with 93 home IoT device users to determine their security and privacy concerns, authentication management, and feature preferences for a new authentication management tool. We found out that our participants were very concerned about security/privacy issues, but they followed insecure security steps in practice. However, they were found to be welcoming towards a new security tool for managing their passwords. We used the findings to suggest design principles for the design of an authentication management tool for home IoT devices.

Keywords: Usable security · Home IoT · Password management

1 Introduction

The usage of Internet of Things (IoT) devices in home environments has been increasing rapidly, with technology companies frequently introducing new products and features. By some estimates, there will be around 375.3 million smart home devices in 2024 [4]. As their popularity has soared, cybersecurity researchers have identified security and privacy concerns with smart home IoT devices, including vulnerable and unreliable devices, over-privileged application usage, and different viral attacks [48].

An Important aspect of IoT security is users' ability to manage the security and privacy of their devices. Text-based passwords are the most widely used authentication mechanism for home IoT devices, largely due to their simplicity and familiarity [15]. However, creating and managing strong passwords in the home IoT environment is challenging for users. Users often keep the insecure default passwords of their IoT devices due to both a lack of security awareness,

© Crown 2021
A. Moallem (Ed.): HCII 2021, LNCS 12788, pp. 3–21, 2021.
https://doi.org/10.1007/978-3-030-77392-2_1

and the difficulty of changing those passwords. Another password management issue arising for IoT is that users face memorability issues when they need to remember multiple strong passwords for different devices, such as WiFi passwords, mobile device passwords that they use to set up their IoT devices, and device-specific passwords (e.g., to access device settings). Additionally, recommended setups, such as having guest WiFi, can place additional password burdens on the management of IoT devices. Finally, home IoT devices are often used in co-housing situations (such as a family home), and this may require maintaining several passwords to ensure multiple access. The scale of the authentication management tasks increases with the number of home IoT devices in a household. To date, little work has been done to explore end user's authentication management strategies for home IoT devices, and there are no existing tools to assist users with authentication management in the home IoT environment.

Previous studies of authentication management in non-IoT contexts have found that the cognitive burden of password management leads users to frequently create predictable and weak passwords and reuse them across multiple accounts, which hampers security [25]. These insecure password practices are also prevalent in the context of home IoT devices [15]. Different solutions have been suggested and implemented to help users create secure passwords, including password meters, stringent password policies, and several alternatives to text-based passwords to increase memorability (e.g., graphical passwords) [7,21,43]. Still, a universal usable solution to the password problem has yet to be developed.

To investigate how users cope with the challenges of managing their home IoT security, we conducted an online survey of 93 home IoT users to use in developing a tool to support IoT authentication management (Sect. 3). We found in our survey that most users are managing a fairly small number of devices, but that they are concerned about a variety of aspects of security and privacy, and would welcome features for additional tool support in their IoT security management task. Together with a survey of the literature on security and privacy concerns for home IoT devices, we present a set of design principles for tools to help users manage their home IoT authentication tasks.

2   Background

Home Internet of Things (IoT) devices that are physical objects designed for use in home environments that have networked interconnection that collects and transmits data over the internet [49]. We define a "smart home" as a home containing home IoT devices. Although some smart home devices can function on a local network [12], we will consider only internet-connected devices in this study.

Users can control, monitor, and access home IoT devices remotely using mobile phones, tablets, and web applications [12]. Popular home IoT devices include thermostats (e.g., Nest[1]), lightbulbs (e.g., Philips Hue[2]), outlets, door

---

[1] https://store.google.com/us/product/nest_learning_thermostat_3rd_gen.

[2] https://www.philips-hue.com/en-us.

locks, motion sensors, TV streaming devices, smart assistants (e.g., Google Home, Amazon Echo), and indoor/outdoor security cameras [13]. In addition to the features enabled by their connectedness, these devices can be used to enable home automation. For instance, a smart thermostat automatically adjusts the temperature, or the smart lights get turned on/off based on motion sensor readings [48]. With the rise of the smart home hubs such as Samsung SmartThings and Apple Homekit, end users are empowered to have centralized control for devices that may come from different manufacturers [13,48].

Some IoT devices connect to the internet directly through home WiFi networks [48]. Other devices connect through a centralized hub; communication between IoT devices and the hub is usually through low energy protocols (e.g., Zigbee and Z-wave) [14]. The hub is connected to the home's router and acts as a bridge to connect IoT devices with the internet [14]. In cloud-based integration, all the information on the devices and the user's commands are transmitted through the cloud [48]. Cloud services also expose APIs for controlling devices over HTTP, and services like IFTTT[3] use these APIs to connect with the IoT devices [48].

2.1 Security and Privacy Issues in Home IoT Devices

IoT security and privacy research has focused on security and privacy risks due to pairing and discovery protocols that leak information about devices in the home [46], insecure and improper information flow and leakage [38,42], vulnerabilities in the devices that can allow an attacker to remotely spy on users [11,31], and the difficulties of patching networked devices [47,49]. With the increased number of IoT devices, ransomware, and malware attacks on IoT devices have also increased at a higher rate [26]. There have been multiple attacks in smart home environments, such as the 2016 Mirai DDoS attack [48,49,51], the Net thermostat glitch that disrupted temperature [3], the baby monitor and smart camera hack [19], and improper information access and recording by smart TV [33].

Smart homes are also prone to access threats, which refer to the loss of confidentiality in keys or passwords that leads to unauthorized system access [23]. Poor password management practices, such as password reuse, is one of the main causes of these attacks. In an example attack, a malicious actor might tamper with control information, allowing an unauthenticated system status may convince the house controller that there is an emergency situation, and that doors and windows should be opened [23].

Furthermore, most IoT devices lack screens and keyboards, which restricts users' ability to directly enter authentication credentials on devices [16]. Therefore, users have to use a separate device (e.g., smartphone/tablet/computer) for authentication, which leads users to manage yet more passwords. Alternative entry mechanisms, such as speaking passwords to voice assistants, often have insecurities [16].

---

[3] https://ifttt.com.

Previous research has created a number of solutions to security and privacy concerns for home IoT devices. Tian et al. [37] developed a platform named SmartAuth that automatically collects security-related information from third-party apps and performs automatic operations based on context. User studies of SmartAuth showed that it helped end users avoid significantly more overprivileged third-party applications. Seymour et al. [32] developed a privacy assistant named Aretha, combining a network disaggregator, a personal tutor, and a firewall to increase users' control over knowledge and mechanisms of smart home devices [32]. Simpson et al. [34] developed a centralized, hub-based, security manager for smart home devices that intercepts all network communications to identify and protect vulnerable devices by applying available security patches. Novo [30] proposes a new architecture based on blockchain technology for access management in scalable IoT scenarios. Jan et al. [20] propose a mutual authentication scheme for IoT systems where both the client and server encrypt and exchange payloads to mutual authenticate.

2.2 Usability of Home IoT Security

User studies of home IoT devices have mainly focus on user's threat models, satisfaction, negative experiences, and motivation [10,44]. However, there has been no study exploring how users manage their passwords in smart homes.

Alqhatani et al. [1] studied users' understanding of privacy on IoT devices. They found that users were mostly unaware of the privacy controls on their devices, and complained about the lack of options to adjust their desired level of privacy. Zeng et al. [48] identified gaps in security threat models due to a lack of technical understanding of smart home devices, which often lead to limited awareness and concern for some security issues. He et al. [18] investigated users' negative experiences with smart homes. They found that the users were unable to distinguish between a power outage and system failure of their devices.

Brush et al. [5] surveyed users and found that end users were mostly concerned about the security of devices that provided physical security (e.g., smart door locks and cameras). Naeini et al. [29] found that users' home IoT privacy preferences are diverse and context-dependent; for instance, users were less comfortable collecting biometrics than environmental data (e.g., room temperature). Worthy et al. [45] identified trust as a critical factor in IoT technology acceptance.

Ur et al. [40] investigated an Internet-connected lighting system, bathroom scale, and door lock and found out that none of the devices gave a usable way to delegate accesses. All the devices also lacked a proper monitoring system meaning it was impossible to understand who has accessed the devices. Mennicken et al. [28] found that most smart homes have only one technical user who configures IoT devices, while other residents use them passively.

Security and privacy concerns have also been explored in the context of household robots [6,8] and smart toys [27]. It is evident that device type plays an important role in end user security and privacy attitudes. Privacy issues in smart home technologies that assist senior citizens have also been studied, and these studies indicate that senior citizens may require different security tools for better usability [9, 38].

2.3 Authentication Challenges in Multi-user Smart Home Devices

Most smart home devices rely on usernames and passwords for authentication [17]. Using passwords creates usability and security challenges for configuring and maintaining home IoT devices. The password problem is worsened for smart home devices, as most IoT devices do not have any user interface [17]. Besides, the social, cultural, and legal relations between people living in the same home affect how people share their home IoT devices, which in turn impacts the usability of the authentication to those devices [35]. As a result, password-sharing and multiple access are required, but these needs are highly contextual. In this section, we will discuss such authentication management related challenges of home IoT devices.

Passwords for Home IoT Devices. Text-based passwords are the most widely used authentication method, and they bring with them various usability and security challenges, including memorability [17]. The majority of home IoT devices use traditional text-based passwords for authentication. Various alternatives to text-based passwords (e.g., audio-based authentication, biometric authentication, camera-based authentication, and token-based authentication) have been studied, but users have been found to prefer traditional passwords over other alternatives [17].

Home IoT devices have a variety of authentication needs, including device passwords (to authenticate access to the device), passwords for other services (e.g., WiFi), and pairing passwords (e.g., Bluetooth). For instance, remote access to Philips Hue requires creating a password-protected account that enables access via a website or a smartphone's data network [40]. The Z-Wave smart door lock controller can be remotely accessed by creating an account on the manufacturer's website, which grants the ability to monitor lock status, lock/unlock the door, and add/delete access codes [40]. Although passwords play an essential role in various smart home devices, very little work has been done to ensure secure password management in the smart home context.

People exercise poor password practices and reuse passwords across various accounts. Users choose predictable passwords, even for relatively essential accounts. As a result, accounts are vulnerable to online guessing attacks where attackers guess what the user's password might be using common and personal information [25]. These issues and risks are also applicable in the context of smart home device authentication. Moreover, the lack of security affordances on IoT devices effectively encourages users to neglect security, turning off authentication, or leaving default passwords in place. The most likely risks related to password compromise of smart home devices are stealing information from home applications and sensors, and gaining unauthorized access to IoT device functionality [37].

Previous research has suggested that the implementation of strong data-driven feedback during password creation may help users to create strong passwords [39]. In more recent work, Maclean and Ophoff [25] found that the users understand quite a lot of the characteristics of strong and weak passwords and suggested that the application of the "nudge" function may work effectively to create strong passwords. Yu et al. [47] proposed a network middlebox that would enforce users to use a new administrator-chosen password to access smart camera's management interface. However, such a solution may face several usability problems including memorability of the passwords. One widely suggested and approved solution to better password behavior is password managers, which generate and store strong passwords of different accounts, but traditional password managers are not designed to manage IoT device passwords.

Sharing and Multi-access Authentication. Security and privacy are different in smart homes because they are multi-user and multi-device systems that require shared and multiple access controls to be usable [49]. However, the current smart home setup is usually not well designed for shared and multiple users. In particular, usable access control mechanisms are often missing. For instance, some smart lighting systems offer only one role; therefore, the owner has to share her/his authentication details or the device where the app is installed to delegate full access to other users [40]. Moreover, the guests cannot control the lights over a smartphone's data connection even if they are located near the lights; they need to be connected to the same WiFi network that the device is connected to [40]. Such problems hint at the necessity of both role-based and context-based access control mechanisms. Changing contexts can also initiate password sharing [35]. For instance, Locasto, Massimi, and DePasquale [24] found that people may share passwords and account information at the end of their life. Similarly, people may stop sharing passwords in case of divorce/termination of relationships [35]. These cases are also applicable in smart home environments.

IoT device data sharing is highly contextual, and previous studies suggest that people do not usually want to share their home information. Financial incentives are found to be one of the principal motivations for sharing data [1]. For instance, participants in one study were willing to share IoT device data to home insurance companies for monetary incentives in the future [2]. Whether people will share home IoT data or not depends on a variety of factors such as the type of data recorded, the location where it is recorded, whom the data is shared with, the perceived value of the data, and benefits provided by services using that data [36]. Naeini et al. [29] and Lee and Kobsa [22] found that people are highly concerned when their home data is collected. Zheng et al. [51] found that users are concerned about data monitoring by specific external entities (e.g., government, manufacturers, internet service providers, and advertisers). However, they still use the devices because of the convenience they get from the device and those entities.

The majority of home IoT devices lack a usable access control policy specifications that considers particular users and contexts to permit access to resources and authenticates users [16]. For example, additional users of Net Thermostat either have full or no access to all of the thermostat's capabilities [16]. However, the nature of the multi-user home IoT domain requires multi-access control and authentication to be usable and secure. Some devices offer slightly better access control (e.g., on Apple HomeKit, one can invite additional users, restricting them to: full control, view-only control, local or remote control), but more contextual factors (e.g., relationships, device capabilities and environment) should be applied to access control and authentication policies [16].

He et al. [16] identified desired access-control rules for home IoT devices considering both relationships and devices' capabilities. In their approach, an individual device's capability dictates access control. For instance, users would be willing to allow others to play music using voice assistant controls, but would not want to let them order things online using the same mechanism. The authors also identified relationship dimensions in the home context. For instance, users were found to be willing to provide full access to the spouse but limited access to children based on their age. Similarly, distant family members got more access than babysitters or neighbors. The authors acknowledged that the relationship context might vary depending on the social and cultural values; therefore, there should be flexibility in configuring the access control of different home IoT devices. Similarly, Geeng et al. [13] identified that relationship-based access control depends on trust and power dynamics, which can change over time. Zeng et al. [49] tested the usability of a prototype smart home app having several types of multi-access control mechanisms with seven households; however, they found that users have weaker preferences for such features due to the set-up and interface complexity, tradeoff with control flexibility, and not acknowledging social norms. Authentication management and sharing were not addressed in the prototype.

3   Study

To investigate the authentication management strategies of smart home IoT users, we conducted an online survey. We were interested in exploring three aspects of users' experiences with home IoT: (1) users' security and privacy concerns, (2) authentication behaviors and sharing preferences, and (3) their features preferences for tools to help manage home IoT devices. Our study was reviewed and cleared by NRC's Research Ethics Board.

3.1   Survey Structure

We conducted pilot tests with four participants and edited our survey according to their feedback. Our final survey had 64 questions, including two eligibility questions. Our survey questions consisted of single/multiple choice, 5-point Likert scale questions with the "do not know" option, and open-ended questions.

Our survey questions were structured into four parts. In the first part, we asked users about their demographics. This section included questions about participants' gender, age, education, security/privacy knowledge, and type of home

IoT devices they use. In the second part, we focused on users' data-sharing practices, and concerns about data privacy and security. For example, participants were asked if they share information recorded by home IoT devices, what type of data they share and with whom, and the reasons behind sharing that data. We also asked them how concerned they are about security and privacy issues regarding home IoT devices, including the perceived risk level of different control mechanisms. In the third part of the study, we asked participants how they manage the passwords of their IoT devices. We asked them how many IoT device passwords they need to remember, how often they change their passwords, and their password reuse behaviors. In the final part of the survey, we asked respondents about the features they would like to have in a tool for home IoT management, and the potential feasibility of password management tools for this task.

3.2   Participants

We recruited survey respondents through Prolific.co, an online crowdsourcing research recruitment platform. To participate in our study, participants needed to be English-speaking, at least 18 years of age, and have at least one home IoT device. Our survey took participants an average of 18 min to complete, and we paid participants GBP 3.00.

A total of 112 people completed the full survey, but 19 surveys were found not to meet the recruitment criteria, leaving us with a total of 93 survey responses. Of these 93 respondents, 65% participants identified themselves as male, 34% as female and 1% as non-binary. They ranged in age from 19–64 years old, but the vast majority (89%) of our participants were aged between 19 to 24 years.

Accordingly, 56% of our participants reported having only completed high school. The remainder of the participants had other post-secondary degrees, including 14% with a graduate degree. 29% participants reported that they had a computer science degree. Participants generally rated themselves as knowledgeable about computers; 51% participants marked their computer skill as "experienced". However, the majority of participants rated their security (57%) and privacy (55%) knowledge as "average". 13% of participants marked their security knowledge as "below average or low" and 17% of participants identified themselves in the "below average or low" in terms of privacy knowledge.

4   Results

Our survey participants used a variety of home IoT devices to control their home appliances directly from their smartphones/computers (Table 1).

The majority (67%) of our participants had one or two IoT devices in their home. The rest of the participants had more than two IoT devices, and 8% reported having five or more IoT devices. 51% of participants marked that they had been using home IoT devices for more than one year, and the remaining participants said that they had used IoT devices for less than one year. In our

Table 1. Number of participants using each Home IoT devices

IoT device name	Total	Percentage
Smart light	29	31%
Intelligent personal assistant	37	40%
Smart thermostat	13	14%
Smart camera	16	17%
Smart power outlets and switches	6	6%
Smart hub	19	20%
Door lock	3	3%
Smoke detector	13	14%

survey, we defined primary users as the users who own and configure the IoT devices and 65% of participants reported that they were the primary user of their home IoT devices. However, 31% of participants reported that they never change their IoT device settings.

4.1 Security and Data Privacy Concern

Participants used a 5-point Likert scale to react to five concerns regarding IoT privacy and security issues (Fig. 1), and privacy and security attacks (Fig. 2).

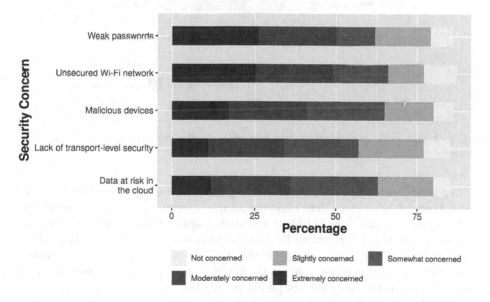

Fig. 1. Likert scale responses for participants' reaction to specific security concerns in home IoT devices.

They also used a 5-point Likert scale to report their perceived risk levels of the different behaviors to access IoT devices.

When we asked about security concerns (Fig. 1), our participants said they were extremely concerned about weak passwords (30%) and insecure Wifi networks (28%), and were moderately concerned about malicious devices (27%) and transport-level security (26%). However, they marked that they were only somewhat concerned about cloud security (30%).

Regarding security attacks (Fig. 2 to home IoT devices, participants reported being extremely concerned about audio recording (35%), password hacking (34%), and spying at home (22%); and moderately concerned about data collection and mining (36%), network attacks on local devices (29%), adversarial remote control (22%), and network mapping (24%). The majority of the participants (28%) were reported being somewhat concerned about re-pairing devices.

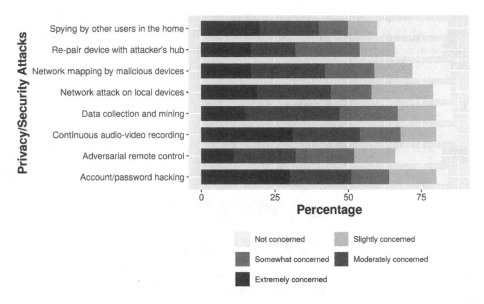

Fig. 2. Likert scale responses for participants' reaction to specific security attacks concerns in home IoT devices.

We asked participants to report their perceptions of the sensitivity of different types of IoT device data and control mechanisms. Participants rated the authority to lock the door (47%) and read the input of the door lock (37%) as extremely sensitive information. Reading motion sensors (31%) was considered moderately sensitive. Turning on/off the light (21%), adjusting the bedroom light (21%), and adjusting the lights in shared spaces (21%) were considered as somewhat sensitive. Respondents perceived reading the device's battery levels was a slightly sensitive (31%) issue.

20% of our participants reported that they share their IoT data with other users, primarily their family (78%), friends (47%), or on social media (8%).

Supporting families to maintain a healthy lifestyle (45%), convenience (30%), and mutual encouragement (25%) were the main reasons for sharing their data. The remaining 80% of our participants reported that they do not share their IoT device data with anyone. However, when we asked participants why they do not share their IoT device data, most of them replied either they did not have the need to share, or they did not have anyone to share their data with. Quoting one of our participants:

"I didn't even have a chance yet, no one asked me for it [IoT device data]"

It appears that some users do not think that sharing IoT device information would be particularly sensitive, and they may end up sharing the information in case necessity arises. A few of the participants mentioned security and privacy as the reasons for not sharing their device data; however, such responses were rare (2%).

4.2   Password Management of Home IoT Devices

As the largest proportion of participants reported that they had two IoT devices in their home, most (32%) participants also reported that they had to manage two passwords for operating their IoT devices. 18% of participants mentioned managing six passwords for their smart home. We also asked participants about what other types of passwords they needed to remember on a daily basis. In addition to IoT device-specific passwords, participants reported managing their home Wifi passwords (73%), IoT device passwords (56%), smartphone lock passwords (52%), apple ID (29%), pairing passwords (26%), and tablet lock passwords (13%) for operating IoT devices.

Our participants mentioned using insecure strategies to remember their passwords. 60% of participants reported that they try to remember their passwords in their heads. 23% of participants reported that they write their passwords down on paper, and 13% reported storing them on their mobile phones. Only 10% of participants use password managers to securely store their passwords.

Similarly, password reuse was frequently reported by our participants. Among the participants who reuse their passwords, 64% of them partially reuse passwords, 22% participants completely reuse passwords, and 14% of them follow a mixed mechanism (sometimes reusing passwords completely and sometimes partially). 80% of participants said that they routinely changed default passwords, but 48% of participants said that they never subsequently changed their passwords.

4.3   Features for Home IoT Password Management

In the final part of the survey, we asked participants about what kind of features they would potentially like to see in a software tool to assist in managing authentication for home IoT devices. The majority (59%) of participants expressed a preference for a mobile application tool, and wanted the affordances of mobile authentication to be available for the application (44% wanted fingerprint-based authentication and 36% marked text-based passwords as their first preference). The majority of the participants (70%) also marked that they would like to have two-factor authentication in such a tool. Figure 3 shows participants' desirability ratings for different features.

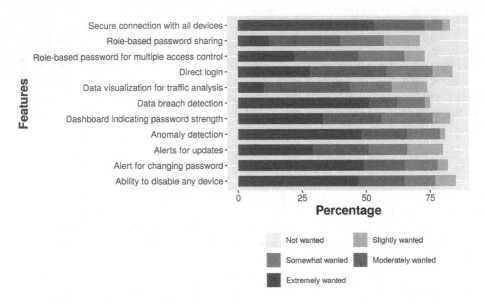

Fig. 3. Likert scale responses for participants' preferences to a password manager for home IoT devices.

We presented a few scenarios to our participants, and then asked questions about when they would want to receive notifications in such cases. Participants said that they want to be notified in real-time when new devices are added to the system (68%), when other users add a new user (65%), and when anomalies are detected (74%). However, they want only daily notification about the availability of critical updates (31%) and detection of data collection (28%). The majority (47%) of our participants said that they would want to see a weekly summary report, and 37% of participants wanted to see summary reports every month.

Our participants reported that they would like to let their spouse and parents perform different security-related tasks (e.g., add/delete/change a user profile, access control conditions, passwords, privacy preferences etc.) on the IoT management tool. Most of the respondents (86%) said they would not let any non-family members perform such actions, and this seemed to be because the majority of our participants trust their family members and believe that their family members will not spy on them using IoT devices.

5   Discussion

We conducted a survey of 93 home IoT users to ask about their security management practices and concerns. We found that these users were security conscious,
but were not necessarily taking the correct steps to protect themselves, their
devices, and their information. For instance, our participants reported being very
concerned about password hacking, but also reported poor password hygiene,
including password reuse and infrequent password changes.

Another trend we found in our data was that users seemed to have inaccurate
beliefs about password management. The majority of our users reported reusing
passwords across multiple accounts, and reported that they do this to cope
with the difficulty of remembering multiple passwords. However, a number of
participants seemed to have the alarming understanding that reusing passwords
(partially or completely) is a good security practice. One participant wrote:

> "[I reuse passwords] because they are safe."

Similar to previous password studies [41], some of our participants described
a clear reuse strategy for coping with the demands of home IoT passwords. They
reuse their passwords based on the importance of their devices. As one of our
participants described:

> "I completely reuse password to less important devices and partially reuse
> to more important IoT."

However, our study did not give us any insight into how users consider and
evaluate the importance of their home IoT devices.

The IoT users that we surveyed were clear that there were different levels
of trust for different groups of users of their home IoT. In particular, participants expressed greater comfort sharing IoT devices with family members. The
majority of our participants said that they are not concerned about spying by
family members. They reported trusting their spouses with most IoT device control access, but said they might not give all kinds of access to children or parents. Participants reported that they would not give access to their IoT devices
to non-relatives; however, situations may arise when they might have to (e.g.,
babysitter).

Finally, our survey results showed strong support for software tools to aid in
the management of home IoT devices. Our participants reported a keen interest in having a authentication management tool for home IoT devices. They
expressed concerns about IoT device security, and described how they are trying
to ensure security in their own (often insecure) ways. They seemed to welcome
towards a security tool for better security management, and expressed preferences for a large variety of features. They are looking for a complete and usable
solution that addresses the usability and security problems in IoT devices they
need to deal with day to day life (for instance, fear of data leakage, password
hacking etc.).

5.1   Design Guidelines for an IoT Password Management Tool

Password managers are widely regarded as one of the most secure methods of securing passwords for end users. Based on the findings of our literature review and survey, we suggest that the development of a password management tool specifically targeted to home IoT devices could greatly assist users in becoming aware of and managing security problems.

Based on our literature analysis and survey results, we identified four recommendations for the design of a usable password management tool for home IoT devices:

User Control. We found that users like to have control over their password management tools. Therefore, password management tools should give users full authority to customize privacy and security preferences easily. The user interface should be developed in such a way that the users can navigate security configuration easily.

Besides single user control, the design should also consider multiple user control due to the nature of smart homes. Access control policies should consider the relationship, device capability, and environmental context. Access control should be flexible, and there should be mechanisms to consider social norms [49]. A role-based password sharing option should be included in a usable way. Primary users should also have the role-based authority to enable/disable the devices remotely.

Awareness. Our survey analysis suggests that the users want to be notified/alerted about insecure behaviors and security/privacy breaches in real-time. We recommend incorporating such features to make the output from this security tool more meaningful to the users.

We also recommend improving user awareness and control through careful user interface design. Data-driven feedback while creating passwords can help users create stronger passwords [39]. There should be an option to empower users to make better password choices by educating them about guessing attacks using digital infographic posters and interactive comics [50].

Our results find that not all passwords are of equal importance to users. We recommend that password management tools should allow users to identify the importance level for each password and behave accordingly to warn the users. Nudges could be incorporated to "warn" users for insecure password behaviors [49].

Transparency. One of the primary reasons users do not use security tools (e.g., password managers) is that they do not trust the third-party app. As one of our participants said:

> "I do not trust companies that create such password managers, I am afraid that my passwords will leak, whether during an attack, or through corruption, or by selling data to companies."

One approach to earn users' trust is to be transparent. For instance, a possible strategy can be to provide information regarding what the app is doing [48] and how it is protecting the data. The tool should also notify users in case of data collection to ensure transparency.

Strong Security Features. Our survey suggests that the participants want strong security features, such as two-factor authentication. Participants expressed concern about recovery options for master passwords. Our study finds that the users trust and prefer both fingerprint authentication and text-based authentication compared to other methods. As one of our participants stated:

> "The fingerprint is the obvious #1 choice for me... It's the most convenient and secure method of accessing the master password. A text-based traditional password follows - just because I have a strong belief in the security and complexity of my password. Facial recognition is good, but it can be tricked by a photograph. Also, it usually doesn't work as well as expected. Graphical passwords are too much gimmick for me. Gestures are not reliable. Audio-based passwords are bad because everyone could hear you speak your password out loud."

However, further research is required to examine the reliability and usability of various authentication options.

5.2   Limitations and Future Work

Our study provides a first exploration into the topic of end user password management for home IoT devices. Our results suggest that home IoT users are security conscious, but that they are in need of centralized tool support for managing the authentication concerns that accompany their smart home setups.

We had difficulty recruiting a representative sample of users for this survey. Although IoT is spiking in popularity, the majority of our participants had only a small number of devices in their homes, which we think may have affected the way in which they cope with the demands of managing their IoT devices. Additionally, our participants were mainly very young, and in a few cases it was clear that they were not able to fully implement smart home features in homes that they did not control (such as a parents' home or shared accommodation).

In the future, we plan to re-run the study with a more diverse user base with at least a few IoT devices. We will conduct a comparative analysis of our data to understand whether there is any impact of demographic and culture on password management. We plan to use the findings of this study to design a prototype, and we also plan to test its usability with participants from different demographics and cultures.

6   Conclusion

There are increasing numbers of IoT devices in the home, but users lack support for their security and privacy concerns in managing these devices. As the popularity of these devices gains, so too does the scale of the management task, necessitating the development of strategies and tools to support users.

In this work, we explored the problems surrounding password management for home IoT devices for end users. We surveyed 93 home IoT users, and found that although people are concerned about the security and privacy of their home IoT devices, they also have misconceptions about how to protect these devices and the information they track.

We suggest that tool support is needed to help users manage the growing authentication management task for home IoT devices, which can encompass a variety of different kinds of users and passwords. Our study showed that users were interested in having a variety of features in such a tool, and we suggest that some kind of password manager could be used to support both authentication management but also awareness of threats and access control in a single location.

Finally, based on our analysis of the literature and our survey data, we identified and proposed four design principles for a usable password management tool for home IoT devices: user control, awareness, transparency, and strong security features. Ours is an initial study of authentication management for home IoT devices. We found that users lack support for these tasks, and in future we plan to use our findings and design recommendations to design a password management tool specifically geared to home IoT management.

References

1. Alqhatani, A., Lipford, H.R.: There is nothing that I need to keep secret: sharing practices and concerns of wearable fitness data. In: Fifteenth Symposium on Usable Privacy and Security (SOUPS 2019) (2019)
2. Behm, S., Deetjen, U., Kaniyar, S., Methner, N., Münstermann, B.: Digital ecosystems for insurers: Opportunities through the internet of things. McKinsey (Feb 2019)
3. Bilton, N.: Nest thermostat glitch leaves users in the cold. The New York Times (Jan 2016)
4. Blumtritt, C.: Smart Home - Number of Households in the Segment Smart Home Worldwide 2024 (2020). www.statista.com/forecasts/887613/number-of-smart-homes-in-thesmart-home-market-worldwide
5. Brush, A.B., Lee, B., Mahajan, R., Agarwal, S., Saroiu, S., Dixon, C.: Home automation in the wild: challenges and opportunities. In: proceedings of the SIGCHI Conference on Human Factors in Computing Systems, pp. 2115–2124 (2011)
6. Butler, D.J., Huang, J., Roesner, F., Cakmak, M.: The privacy-utility tradeoff for remotely teleoperated robots. In: Proceedings of the Tenth Annual ACM/IEEE International Conference on Human-Robot Interaction, pp. 27–34 (2015)
7. De Carné de Carnavalet, X., Mannan, M.: From very weak to very strong: analyzing password-strength meters. In: Network and Distributed System Security Symposium (NDSS 2014). Internet Society (2014)
8. Choe, E.K., Consolvo, S., Jung, J., Harrison, B., Patel, S.N., Kientz, J.A.: Investigating receptiveness to sensing and inference in the home using sensor proxies. In: Proceedings of the 2012 ACM Conference on Ubiquitous Computing, pp. 61–70 (2012)

9. Courtney, K.L., Demeris, G., Rantz, M., Skubic, M.: Needing smart home technologies: the perspectives of older adults in continuing care retirement communities (2008)
10. Demeure, A., Caffiau, S., Elias, E., Roux, C.: Building and using home automation systems: a field study. In: Díaz, P., Pipek, V., Ardito, C., Jensen, C., Aedo, I., Boden, A. (eds.) IS-EUD 2015. LNCS, vol. 9083, pp. 125–140. Springer, Cham (2015). https://doi.org/10.1007/978-3-319-18425-8_9
11. Denning, T., Kohno, T., Levy, H.M.: Computer security and the modern home. Commun. ACM **56**(1), 94–103 (2013)
12. El-Hajj, M., Fadlallah, A., Chamoun, M., Serrhouchni, A.: A survey of internet of things (IoT) authentication schemes. Sensors **19**(5), 1141 (2019)
13. Geeng, C., Roesner, F.: Who's in control? interactions in multi-user smart homes. In: Proceedings of the 2019 CHI Conference on Human Factors in Computing Systems, pp. 1–13 (2019)
14. Geneiatakis, D., Kounelis, I., Neisse, R., Nai-Fovino, I., Steri, G., Baldini, G.: Security and privacy issues for an IoT based smart home. In: 2017 40th International Convention on Information and Communication Technology, Electronics and Microelectronics (MIPRO), pp. 1292–1297. IEEE (2017)
15. Haney, J.M., Furman, S.M., Acar, Y.: Smart home security and privacy mitigations: consumer perceptions, practices, and challenges. In: Moallem, A. (ed.) HCII 2020. LNCS, vol. 12210, pp. 393–411. Springer, Cham (2020). https://doi.org/10.1007/978-3-030-50309-3_26
16. He, W., et al.: Rethinking access control and authentication for the home internet of things (IoT). In: 27th USENIX Security Symposium (USENIX Security 18), pp. 255–272 (2018)
17. He, W., Hainline, J., Padhi, R., Ur, B.: Clap on, clap off: usability of authentication methods in the smart home. In: Proceedings of the Interactive Workshop on the Human Aspect of Smarthome Security and Privacy (2018)
18. He, W., Martinez, J., Padhi, R., Zhang, L., Ur, B.: When smart devices are stupid: negative experiences using home smart devices. In: 2019 IEEE Security and Privacy Workshops (SPW), pp. 150–155. IEEE (2019)
19. Hill, K.: 'baby monitor hack'could happen to 40,000 other foscam users (2013)
20. Jan, M.A., Khan, F., Alam, M., Usman, M.: A payload-based mutual authentication scheme for internet of things. Future Gener. Comput. Syst. **92**, 1028–1039 (2019)
21. Komanduri, S., et al.: Of passwords and people: measuring the effect of password-composition policies. In: Proceedings of the Sigchi Conference on Human Factors in Computing Systems, pp. 2595–2604 (2011)
22. Lee, H., Kobsa, A.: Understanding user privacy in internet of things environments. In: 2016 IEEE 3rd World Forum on Internet of Things (WF-IoT), pp. 407–412. IEEE (2016)
23. Lin, H., Bergmann, N.W.: IoT privacy and security challenges for smart home environments. Information **7**(3), 44 (2016)
24. Locasto, M.E., Massimi, M., DePasquale, P.J.: Security and privacy considerations in digital death. In: Proceedings of the 2011 New Security Paradigms Workshop, pp. 1–10 (2011)
25. Maclean, R., Ophoff, J.: Determining key factors that lead to the adoption of password managers. In: 2018 International Conference on Intelligent and Innovative Computing Applications (ICONIC), pp. 1–7. IEEE (2018)
26. McLean, A.: IoT malware and ransomware attacks on the incline: Intel security (2015)

27. McReynolds, E., Hubbard, S., Lau, T., Saraf, A., Cakmak, M., Roesner, F.: Toys that listen: a study of parents, children, and internet-connected toys. In: Proceedings of the 2017 CHI Conference on Human Factors in Computing Systems, pp. 5197–5207 (2017)
28. Mennicken, S., Huang, E.M.: Hacking the natural habitat: an in-the-wild study of smart homes, their development, and the people who live in them. In: Kay, J., Lukowicz, P., Tokuda, H., Olivier, P., Krüger, A. (eds.) Pervasive 2012. LNCS, vol. 7319, pp. 143–160. Springer, Heidelberg (2012). https://doi.org/10.1007/978-3-642-31205-2_10
29. Naeini, P.E., et al.: Privacy expectations and preferences in an IoT world. In: Thirteenth Symposium on Usable Privacy and Security (SOUPS 2017), pp. 399–412 (2017)
30. Novo, O.: Blockchain meets IoT: an architecture for scalable access management in IoT. IEEE Internet Things J. 5(2), 1184–1195 (2018)
31. Oluwafemi, T., Kohno, T., Gupta, S., Patel, S.: Experimental security analyses of non-networked compact fluorescent lamps: a case study of home automation security. In: LASER 2013, pp. 13–24 (2013)
32. Seymour, W., Kraemer, M.J., Binns, R., Van Kleek, M.: Informing the design of privacy-empowering tools for the connected home. In: Proceedings of the 2020 CHI Conference on Human Factors in Computing Systems, pp. 1–14 (2020)
33. Shane, S., Rosenberg, M., Lehren, A.W.: WikiLeaks releases trove of alleged CIA hacking documents. New York Times (2017)
34. Simpson, A.K., Roesner, F., Kohno, T.: Securing vulnerable home IoT devices with an in-hub security manager. In: 2017 IEEE International Conference on Pervasive Computing and Communications Workshops (PerCom Workshops), pp. 551–556. IEEE (2017)
35. Stobert, E., Biddle, R.: Authentication in the home. Proc. HUPS (2013)
36. Tabassum, M., Kosinski, T., Lipford, H.R.: "I don't own the data": end user perceptions of smart home device data practices and risks. In: Fifteenth Symposium on Usable Privacy and Security (SOUPS 2019) (2019)
37. Tian, Y., et al.: Smartauth: user-centered authorization for the internet of things. In: 26th USENIX Security Symposium (USENIX Security 2017), pp. 361–378 (2017)
38. Townsend, D., Knoefel, F., Goubran, R.: Privacy versus autonomy: a tradeoff model for smart home monitoring technologies. In: 2011 Annual International Conference of the IEEE Engineering in Medicine and Biology Society, pp. 4749–4752. IEEE (2011)
39. Ur, B., et al.: Design and evaluation of a data-driven password meter. In: Proceedings of the 2017 CHI Conference on Human Factors in Computing Systems, pp. 3775–3786 (2017)
40. Ur, B., Jung, J., Schechter, S.: The current state of access control for smart devices in homes. In: Workshop on Home Usable Privacy and Security (HUPS), vol. 29, pp. 209–218. HUPS 2014 (2013)
41. Ur, B., et al.: "I added'!'at the end to make it secure": observing password creation in the lab. In: Eleventh Symposium On Usable Privacy and Security (SOUPS 2015), pp. 123–140 (2015)
42. Wang, Q., Hassan, W.U., Bates, A., Gunter, C.: Fear and logging in the internet of things. In: Network and Distributed Systems Symposium (2018)
43. Wheeler, D.L.: zxcvbn: low-budget password strength estimation. In: 25th USENIX Security Symposium (USENIX Security 2016), pp. 157–173 (2016)

44. Woo, J.B., Lim, Y.K.: User experience in do-it-yourself-style smart homes. In: Proceedings of the 2015 ACM International Joint Conference on Pervasive and Ubiquitous Computing, pp. 779–790 (2015)
45. Worthy, P., Matthews, B., Viller, S.: Trust me: doubts and concerns living with the internet of things. In: Proceedings of the 2016 ACM Conference on Designing Interactive Systems, pp. 427–434 (2016)
46. Wu, D.J., Taly, A., Shankar, A., Boneh, D.: Privacy, discovery, and authentication for the internet of things. In: Askoxylakis, I., Ioannidis, S., Katsikas, S., Meadows, C. (eds.) ESORICS 2016, Part II. LNCS, vol. 9879, pp. 301–319. Springer, Cham (2016). https://doi.org/10.1007/978-3-319-45741-3_16
47. Yu, T., Sekar, V., Seshan, S., Agarwal, Y., Xu, C.: Handling a trillion (unfixable) flaws on a billion devices: rethinking network security for the internet-of-things. In: Proceedings of the 14th ACM Workshop on Hot Topics in Networks, pp. 1–7 (2015)
48. Zeng, E., Mare, S., Roesner, F.: End user security and privacy concerns with smart homes. In: Thirteenth Symposium on Usable Privacy and Security (SOUPS 2017), pp. 65–80 (2017)
49. Zeng, E., Roesner, F.: Understanding and improving security and privacy in multi-user smart homes: a design exploration and in-home user study. In: 28th USENIX Security Symposium (USENIX Security 19), pp. 159–176 (2019)
50. Zhang-Kennedy, L., Chiasson, S., Biddle, R.: Password advice shouldn't be boring: visualizing password guessing attacks. In: 2013 APWG eCrime Researchers Summit, pp. 1–11. IEEE (2013)
51. Zheng, S., Apthorpe, N., Chetty, M., Feamster, N.: User perceptions of smart home IoT privacy. Proc. ACM Hum. Comput. Interact. 2(CSCW), 1–20 (2018)

Emics and Etics of Usable Security: Culturally-Specific or Culturally-Universal?

Aniqa Alam, Robert Biddle, and Elizabeth Stobert[✉]

Carleton University, Ottawa, Canada
{aniqa.bintealam,robert.biddle,elizabeth.stobert}@carleton.ca

Abstract. This paper explores how cultural attitudes and practices affect the design and usability of security software. Cultural differences cause users from eastern and western cultures to behave differently and sometimes insecurely with the same security tools because of dissimilar beliefs and understanding. Using the *emics-etics* framework to guide our examination of cultural differences, we review the literature on three areas of security: software piracy, password sharing, and mobile device sharing. We suggest that security tools need to acknowledge *emics*, or insider, perspectives to become culturally inclusive. We propose how security software and business strategies can be designed to create culturally appropriate security tools.

Keywords: Usable security · Cultural factor · Technology sharing

1 Introduction

With the rapid growth of interconnected computer systems and applications, almost all users are affected daily by computer security. Computer security requires actions to protect data and resources from accidental or malicious acts [26]. Today, the security community has generally accepted the importance of human factors in security, acknowledging that security needs to be usable to be secure [68].

It is typically accepted in usable security research to consider security systems as culturally universal. Security systems and their ecosystems of use are usually Euro-centric and developed by asserting the norms and practices of imagined (western) users [34]. The usability of security systems is frequently only tested with western users or users living in the west. By doing so, the presumption is that "Johnny" [83] from the USA would behave the same way with the system as "Johnny" from Bangladesh would. However, previous studies and theories emphasize the consequences of cultural differences in the uptake and use of technologies, including security software [15,24,30].

In this work, we question the cultural universality of security systems, arguing that security systems should include culture-specific mechanisms to be usable

© Springer Nature Switzerland AG 2021
A. Moallem (Ed.): HCII 2021, LNCS 12788, pp. 22–40, 2021.
https://doi.org/10.1007/978-3-030-77392-2_2

and culturally appropriate. The current cybersecurity ecosystem creates a new structure of domination, which is exercised through owning, designing, and controlling security software – constituting a new form of digital colonization [46]. We argue that without understanding culture-specific mechanisms, including social, political, and economic conditions that affect users' behaviors, security systems will continue to embed unequal treatments and weaken usability.

We propose a framework, *emics-etics for usable security*, which characterizes differences in understanding a culture from the viewers' perspectives: that of viewers who live in a culture (*emics*) and that of those who live outside the culture (*etics*). In this paper, we conduct an extensive literature review and use our framework to analyze how current security systems lead users in non-western countries to behave in ways that are normally flagged as harmful by security researchers. We focused on three specific areas of security that frequently show cultural differences: software piracy, password sharing, and mobile device sharing. For our review, we categorized work based on how the participants of the studies (or countries of focus) have experienced the socio-economic and political consequences of digital colonialism [46].

Our literature survey suggests that following an emics approach for designing and evaluating security systems will lead to address problems arising from western ethnocentrism in usable security. Analyzing three security problems from an emics perspective, we highlight the importance of an emics approach, and suggest some of the problems caused by sharing could be solved by considering social and cultural practices as the center of security designs [71] and vendors' business strategies.

2 Emics-Etics Framework for Usable Security: A Culture-Centric Framework to Address Usability Problems with Security Tools

To incorporate cultural factors in security systems, we first need to understand what culture is. Although culture does not have any widely-accepted specific definition, one of the most frequently cited approaches defines it as "patterns, explicit and implicit, of and for behaviour acquired and transmitted by symbols, constituting the distinctive achievements of human groups ... [and] ideas and their attached values" [44, p.181]. In other words, culture refers to what a group or society believes to be true that forms some common values and norms [6]. People's perceived values and norms define what they will consider good or bad and acceptable or unacceptable, which creates a set of rules about behaving and performing tasks [6]. Cultures can consist at different levels and sizes; for instance, "western culture," "US culture," "gang culture," and even "family culture" [6].

There have been different culture-centric frameworks proposed for incorporating a range of methodological possibilities to understand a variety of topics [18]. One of the most widely used frameworks for investigating cross-cultural issues is known as *emics-etics* [17,48,60,80]. In this work we have applied this framework to identify the implications of cultural differences in usable security.

Historically, the terms emics and etics were derived first in linguistic analysis [60]. The term *emics* is adapted from phonemics, and refers to the sounds that are specific to a particular language in a particular culture [20]. The term *etics* is adapted from phonetics, and refers to sounds that are the same in all languages [20]. The emics (within culture) and etics (outside of culture) concepts are also widely used as cross-cultural framework. They are considered as two *standpoints* from which human observers can describe culturally-specific (emics) and culturally-universal (etics) human behaviours [43].

An emics analytical standpoint is internal and holistic, and can distinguish and understand the intrinsic cultural values of a society [43]. On the other hand, an etics analytical standpoint is external or alien, and often misunderstands and misrepresents the *other* cultural values due to a lack of a frame of reference [18]. For example, an etics perspective on credential sharing would criticize users for sharing their banking passwords with family members, but an emics perspective would recognize the gender roles that limit the ability of women in the Kingdom of Saudi Arabia (KSA) to independently visit banks, leading them to share their passwords with trusted male relatives [5].

For our review, we categorized literature works based on how the participants of the studies (or countries of focus) have experienced the consequences of digital colonialism [46] – the east (digitally colonized) and the west (digital colonizers). The west refers to the countries that possess (or have historically possessed) dominating technological power and current sources of geopolitical and cultural epistemic inequalities. The eastern countries experience the consequences of these epistemic inequalities.

This paper uses the terms "east" and "west" beyond their geographic meaning and cultural differences to symbolize cultural and intra-country inequalities. The terms are relative to each other, meaning one country is considered as west in respect to the countries it dominates or vice-versa. For instance, the USA, Canada, and the UK would be considered to have colonizing power in respect to countries like Bangladesh, India, and Pakistan, although historically, Canada and the US were also colonized by the British.

Strategic essentialism [73] refers to how minority or ethnic groups create a temporary/long-term sense of collective identity setting aside their cultural differences [23]. For instance, many cultural, religious, and linguistic groups in India come together as "Indian" in terms of their common colonization by the British [23]. This notion is essential for collective political movements and feminist studies. However, for our work, we argue for the impossibility of essentialism in the context of security design and acknowledge intra-country cultural differences. For instance, by our definition, Australian Aboriginal groups are considered as east (digitally colonized), although Australia as a country is considered as the west (digital colonizer). Due to the scarcity of literature, we could not incorporate many examples of this aspect. However, our study provides guidelines to understand and incorporate similar cases in the future.

Based on the available literature, we have considered Bangladesh, Pakistan, India, China, Singapore, Thailand, Malaysia, Uganda, Kenya, KSA, Australian Aboriginal groups and Maori people of New Zealand as examples of eastern cultures. We have considered the USA, Canada, Australia, New Zealand, Finland, Slovenia and the UK as examples of western cultures.

3 When Security *Emics* Meets *Etics*: Culture-Specific Security Challenges

To examine the role of culture in the usability of security systems, we conducted a literature review to find long-term trends in some culture-specific security problems. We focused on three specific areas that frequently show cultural differences: software piracy, password sharing, and mobile device sharing. We chose these three topics based on the fact that they frequently show cultural differences, but also because they represent a substantial cross-section of research in usable security, and encompass work relating to malware (software piracy), authentication (password sharing), and privacy (mobile phone sharing). For each area, we examined:

1. What are the security problems, and what are the reasons for them?
2. What are the etics approaches and the problems with these approaches?
3. What are the emics approaches that offer solutions to these problems?

3.1 Software Piracy

Software piracy has long been a problem in information technology. It refers to the distribution of counterfeit software at a lower price than the original product, and the illegal file-sharing of copyrighted software among peers [29]. Even though software piracy has been identified as an important concern since at least 1990 [59]; piracy has yet to disappear and is still prevalent around the world. According to a 2018 Business Software Alliance report, 37% of all software on personal computers is unlicensed [19]. In 2017, there were approximately 300 billion global visits to piracy websites [58] and it is roughly estimated that every third copy of Microsoft's Windows operating system is pirated [10].

Security Implications of Piracy. Software piracy introduces security dependencies among interconnected systems in the network environment of the vendors [10]. If software vendors restrict unlicensed copies from downloading security patches to combat piracy, they may end up creating a large population of unpatched hosts on the internet, who are susceptible to get infected and spread malware in the entire network [10,56]. For this reason, in 2005 Microsoft had to cancel its program designed to restrict downloading security updates in pirated Windows XP [54].

End users of pirated software are always at risk. They cannot access post-sale technical support, which is available to paid users [45]. In 2003, the "Blaster" worm was an example of users' vulnerability from using pirated software. In this attack, devices running unlicensed Windows XP were forced to be disconnected from the internet since the security patch to prevent the virus was only available for registered users [45]. The attack affected around 48,000 computers running Windows XP and Windows 2000. Despite the foreseeable risks that the use of pirated software poses, the practice is still rampant in many countries.

In addition to security risks, software piracy also causes substantial monetary loss to software vendors. In 2017, businesses lost an estimated USD 16.4 billion in the Asia Pacific from unlicensed software [19]. Sometimes, the users/distributors of pirated software illegally sell unauthorized copies of original software at a lower price and become a competitor of the producer [12].

Etics of Piracy. The etics approach to preventing piracy provides generalized solutions from a western perspective. Because these strategies are not tailored to the cultural circumstances of eastern countries, they have been ineffective and piracy rates have remained high in eastern countries. For instance, piracy rates in India, Indonesia, Malaysia, China, Korea, Singapore, Bangladesh, Nigeria, Ethiopia, Lebanon, Brazil and Vietnam are higher than in any western countries [4].

The lack of clear legal frameworks and weak enforcement in the east compared with the west is widely considered as the major contributing factor for this situation [29,40]. For example, in China, piracy laws are hardly enforced even though these laws are nominally quite strict [29]. Similarly, in a 2019 study of software use in Ethiopia, one participant described local attitudes towards piracy law as "illegal, but not serious" [1].

The etics approach to understand and solve piracy usually implies that economic development, moral education, robust legal frameworks, and less government corruption would lead to a reduction of software piracy [11]. Digital rights management (DRM) technologies like blockchain and machine learning are used to eradicate software piracy [7].

Emics of Piracy. The emics approach considers culturally-specific values to understand software piracy practice in eastern countries. For instance, the standards of intellectual property rights and protection are rooted in western values of liberalism and individual rights [75]. Such blanket policies may not be effective in eastern cultures as they contrast with eastern users' collective values [22,32]. For example, American students were found to have more positive attitudes towards copyright law, whereas Singaporean students were more affected by the importance of family and community values [76].

In eastern countries, there is typically no active social consensus that digital piracy is unethical or illegal [7]. Individuals believe software piracy does not cause any direct harm to the copyright owner [84]. These culture-specific beliefs also may lead to higher levels of piracy. The victims of piracy—western software companies—are also perceived as monopolistic colonial corporations that are not proximate to the pirated software users; therefore, the concentration of effect is impersonal and rather low [39, 47, 77]. Also, the original software prices are inflated resulting in massive profits for the copyright owner [7]. As a result, eastern users perceive the price as inequitable and a justification of their piracy behaviour [29].

Gender roles and religion also have impacts on piracy attitudes. For instance, Indonesian and Bangladeshi men have a more positive attitude towards digital piracy than women [31, 79]. Another study found that being religious in Australia makes users less likely to approve piracy; however, non-religious people in Australia and religious consumers in Indonesia have more positive attitudes towards software piracy [9].

Piracy also occurs in western countries; however, the reasons for piracy are significantly different than in the east. For instance, studies in Slovenia, Portugal and Finland found that past behaviour, subjective knowledge, and enjoyment have the strongest effect on the piracy intention. Perceived consequences and normative beliefs work as determinants of piracy intention [41, 42, 52].

The emics approach would suggest that the price of the software should be lowered to be affordable by digitally colonized countries [62]. One approach is for software companies to give away free samples to reduce piracy. Microsoft's initiative to give Windows Starter Edition, a discounted version of the operating system, to users in Thailand and Malaysia, is an example of such a strategy [29]. Religious and family education may also work effectively to discourage individuals' privacy practices.

3.2 Password Sharing

Almost everyone in the world needs to interact with passwords multiple times daily, but passwords are a problematic system with numerous flaws. One of the least addressed issues with password systems is that they do not have any provision for safe password sharing. Passwords are designed to be inherently private and secret, disregarding the fact that in some cultures, social norms and family values *require* them to be shared. As a result, people frequently share their passwords for banking, social media, and entertainment accounts [5, 37] following insecure procedures: writing them down on paper, or sending them through SMS, email and social media.

Security Implications of Password Sharing. Password sharing causes harm to both business owners and individuals. When a malicious user obtains passwords as a result of password sharing, it can result in credential fraud, account compromise, monetary loss, and cyberbullying [53]. According to Parks Associates, the pay-TV industry was projected to lose USD 6.6 billion in revenue from password sharing and movie piracy in 2019, and the number could grow to USD 9 billion by 2024 [27]. In 2010, Kingdom of Saudi Arabia suffered the seventh-highest incident of security breaches, although they had only 0.007% of internet users in the world [5]. One of the identified causes is password sharing behaviours among co-workers and family members [5].

Etics of Password Sharing. The etics approach considers password sharing a bad habit and a harmful behaviour for security and provides technological and policy-based solutions to mitigate this behaviour. Frequent password resets and the use of biometrics are some common suggestions to limit this behaviour [27]. For instance, Mandujano and Soto propose a system for tracking keystrokes so that it can limit access if the keystroke dynamics are changed when used by different users [49]. One commonly cited advantage of graphical authentication systems is that they are more challenging to describe and share because they are not simple text strings [14]. Password policies can also be designed to decrease password sharing [70].

Emics of Password Sharing. The emics approach considers that people share their passwords with extended family and friends due to cultural expectations and necessity. It suggests developing technological tools and policies for secure password sharing. Although people from both eastern and western countries share their passwords, their cultural beliefs are different, requiring different approaches to address them.

Banking password regulations are treated as universal but developed based on western individualist cultural values [5]. An emics approach considers that some clauses of these regulations contradict the religious and cultural role of women in some conservative communities. For instance, the primary religion of KSA is Islam (97% of the total population is Muslim), and women in KSA usually do not participate in public life without a mahram (permitted male acquaintance). The policy regarding safeguarding banking accounts in KSA states that "banks are responsible for providing secure and safe systems and services for their customers unless the customer fails to safeguard their account user number or password and divulges it to a third party" [5, p. 299]. Such a policy essentially makes it harder for women to access banking facilities when bankers are all male. Women also hesitate to go to ATM booths and withdraw money as it is not culturally acceptable to go there alone. As a coping strategy, they usually share their bank card and PIN with their mahrams, which violates the password policies but allows them to participate in society.

The emics approach also considers family values in some cultures which situate parents in esteemed positions. As a result, parents are culturally expected to know (adult) children's monetary status including banking passwords. For instance, both men and women in KSA believe that fathers should know the banking passwords of their children as they have 'rights' over their children's money [5]. However, it is also acknowledged that gender plays an important role in such sharing. For instance, women in KSA share their passwords because their fathers monitor and safeguard their finances even after their marriages, whereas men give banking access to their fathers out of respect. If men wish to revoke such access, they are perceived as 'mature' in the family, rather than secretive.

There has been limited work on password sharing in other eastern cultures; however, family values and parent-children relationship in many eastern countries follow a similar pattern to KSA. On the contrary, family values are often different in western cultures. For instance, although parents usually know the passwords of their children when they are young; it becomes a case of family negotiation when they become teenagers [37]. Both eastern and western children may know the passwords of their parents or grandparents only if the parents or grandparents cannot set or remember their passwords themselves [5,37].

Sharing passwords is common among couples from both eastern and western cultures. In eastern countries, password sharing among couples is considered as a 'need to know' rooted in mutual trust and convenience [5]. In KSA, men often manage both of the partners' accounts since women do not have access everywhere. In almost all households, wives are financially dependent on husbands. Therefore, husbands usually inform their wives/children/mother of their banking credentials and asset information in case of emergency. On the other hand, the main reasons for sharing passwords among couples in western cultures are the convenience and distribution of household work [71]. Often, only one partner manages the accounts for both irrespective of gender. Having a joint account is common in the west, and rare in eastern cultures.

Colonial banking authentication systems and legislation also do not acknowledge cultural practices like money and property sharing among extended family members. In turn, this hampers the banking accessibility of different minority groups and cultures. In rural and remote Aboriginal and Torres Strait Islander communities in Australia, people usually share bank cards and PINs with both family members and clan members [65,69]. In New Zealand, Maori people usually share ownership of property; but banking systems do not allow them to access loans with shared property [35]. Some members of the Ngukurr Aboriginal people of the Northern Territory in Australia share their banking cards and PINs with their school-going children so that they do not get "shamed" in front of the non-Aboriginal community for not having enough money [69].

Another common practice in Australian Aboriginal communities is "book-up": a system to take a small and short term loans from stores, taxis, hawkers, and airlines by sharing debit cards along with PIN as a security check [72]. The book-up process carries clear risks, but without this process, short term credit would be otherwise unavailable [66].

The banking authentication system also does not give any solution for areas (both in the east and west) where physical banking is inaccessible. For instance, in the Torres Strait Island communities, there are 17 inhabited islands but only one island (Thursday Island) with a bank [71]. To access the banking facilities from other islands, people usually have to book tickets, prepare to stay overnight and spend around AUD 250–300 depending on the season. Hence, as a matter of survival, when one person from a remote island goes to Thursday Island, they do everyone's shopping and other business by taking their bank cards and PINs [71].

People from both cultures share passwords of their official personal computers and library access with colleagues and friends [38]. In family settings, other than sharing WiFi passwords or the subscriptions passwords (e.g., Netflix), people are often found to share email credentials with family to check emails in case of emergency (such as, travel) [37,82]. However, further research is needed to understand cultural differences in such sharing. For instance, because of family values in eastern cultures, adult children might not feel comfortable sharing Netflix accounts with parents and elder relatives.

Considering culture-specific behaviours, family values, gender and religious norms, an emics approach would not discard the importance of password sharing. Rather it would suggest developing culture-centric password sharing tools and appropriate password policies to enable secure password sharing [71].

3.3 Mobile Phone Sharing

One of the benefits of mobile phones is to generate and store content (e.g., photos, audio files, video files, and messages) and share them with social contacts. The usage dimensions of mobile phones have also expanded: people can now use them as their mini computers [36]. However, the security model of the mobile phones is still binary (locked/unlocked) as they are primarily designed to be private devices following the "one account, one user" privacy model [36,67]. In practice, mobile devices are shared for various reasons, which challenges this definition and architecture [2,36,63,67], and weakens security.

Security and Privacy Concerns of Mobile Phone Sharing. Mobile sharing causes both privacy and security issues. In 2012, around 12% of US mobile phone owners reported experiencing unauthorized access that they perceived as a violation of their privacy [16]. Another self-reported anonymous survey found that around 31% of participants had accessed someone else's phone without any permission [50]. One of the most common privacy invasion scenarios is when parents, siblings, friends, relatives, and strangers ask to use the owner's phone for a specific task (e.g., taking a photo, playing a game, or making an emergency call) and then browse through the personal data [3,21]. Mobile device sharing may lead to leaks of private information, as well as changes to data, both intentional (e.g., writing a text message as an impostor) or unintentional (e.g., deleting contents and changing app settings) [28].

Etics of Mobile Device Sharing. Current mobile authentication mechanisms have not evolved much for tackling the above-mentioned security issues. As a result, the majority of the users are forced to follow the "all or nothing" approach in terms of their data when they share their phones [28]. An etics approach considers mobile devices as personal and understands that unlock authentication is sufficient for managing unauthorized access by strangers. However, the unlock authentication mechanism fails to efficiently manage access by known users [21], especially when device sharing is a cultural norm [3].

One approach to addressing mobile device privacy is to enable multiple user accounts. Multiple user access was introduced in Android version 4.2 (API 17) in November 2012, and restricted profiles were introduced in version 4.3 (API 18) in July 2013 [64]. Using multiple user accounts, the device owner can create, delete, and modify secondary accounts [61]. Secondary accounts are password-protected, and the secondary account holder cannot view the device owner's data, nor make changes in the device (e.g., update and download apps) but can use the owner-selected apps [64]. However, this mechanism has not been found to be usable in different eastern cultures. It should also be noted that this feature has never been introduced on devices running iOS, further restricting the usefulness of this alternative for many users.

Emics of Mobile Phone Sharing. Cultural expectation plays a vital role in how users from both eastern and western cultures perceive privacy. Personal space and privacy concepts are well-accepted in the west, but are a foreign concept in eastern cultures. As a result, we can see from an emics approach that Android's multi-access authentication may violate trust in family settings, as the very existence of such a feature implies there is something to hide, which is unacceptable [67].

Our emics approach understands cultural expectations in device sharing among parents and children. For instance, all family members often charge their phones in the same place, and children can access their parents' accounts anytime, even after owning mobile phones by themselves [74]. The father figure usually bears the mobile phone cost of everyone in the family [74]; hence, it is perceived as normal if the children make phone calls from their parent's phones or vice-versa. A study of Pakistani users found that women's (mother figure's) devices are usually considered by default as a "family device" [67]. Some women from Bangladesh reported that their children used their phone for playing games and watching videos; however, children usually did not touch their father's phone. Parents usually have unlimited access to their adult children's devices. If parents want to check their children's mobile devices, children usually comply to uphold the image of being "good" [67]. However, being open to monitoring is performative, and parents sometimes secretly spy on their children's usage [67].

In western cultures, minor children who do not own mobile devices usually get access to their parents' mobile phones. Adult children get access to their parents' devices only in case of necessity or accident. For instance, if the parents are not technologically-adept, adult children often offer technical support and manage accounts for their parents [51]. Parents sometimes monitor their minor children's browsing histories when they share the same devices [51]. However, parents usually do not tell their children about this.

Couples from both cultures share devices but gender plays an important role in sharing. In eastern cultures, both of the partners check each other's phones, but the wife typically does so in secret. The husband does it openly because of culturally-accepted gender superiority [67]. Sometimes, monitoring is viewed as coercive. For example, some women from Bangladesh reported that their husbands installed spyware for tracking their usage [67]. They reported feeling upset and described their coping strategy, which is to call their parents using colleagues' and friends' mobile devices [67]. In the west, couples share their devices because of proximity and convenience. For instance, while watching TV, one person may use their partner's mobile device to play games just because it was nearer [51]. Partners also answer calls or access devices to help navigate when the other person is driving [51].

In rural and underdeveloped areas in the east, mobile devices are shared with family, friends, and neighbors because of lack of affordability. In rural parts of Kenya, only wealthy families can usually afford a mobile device [57]. In these households, the device owner (usually the male head of the family), becomes the tech-savvy user and performs tasks on behalf of others [67]. This situation also gives rise to small businesses: for people who cannot afford a mobile device, they can pay to use the device to communicate [25]. Similarly, in some parts of rural Uganda, mobile money is used to pay for goods and services [81]. These services are unusual in the west.

Considering family values, gender role, and economic conditions, an emics approach would suggest culture-centric multiple access mechanisms for enabling secure device sharing in day-to-day life.

4   Discussion

Usable security is difficult to achieve, and there is always room for improvement in security. One of the impediments to increasing the usability of security systems is the practice of western ethnocentrism while designing security tools that results in digital domination. We applied our proposed emics-etics framework to explore cultural-centric security issues, and analyzed related works about three security challenges written on both eastern and western cultures. We identified flaws in current security solutions that stem from following an etics approach, and provided some culture-specific suggestions using emics to solve them. A summary of our findings is presented in Table 1.

Our discussion is divided into three sections. In the first section, we describe the importance of sharing in eastern cultures and the remaining sections explain how both technology and business can leverage such sharing attitudes to increase security for eastern users.

4.1   Sharing as Cultural Norm and Necessity

A common theme that arose in all three areas of our analysis was sharing, and issues arising from the cultural understanding that relationships should be prized above individuals in some cultures. As we have seen, shared/pirated software creates the possibility of malware attacks on end-users' devices. Password sharing may result in identity theft, account compromise, and monetary loss. Private information may be leaked, manipulated, or used negatively as a consequence of mobile device sharing. However, people still share despite the possibilities of privacy and security risks.

Our emics analysis of eastern cultures reveals that sharing is a cultural norm and necessity. Culturally, people are expected to share technology within family

Table 1. Summary of solution approaches to security problems.

Security problem	Etics approach	Emics approach
Software and OS Piracy	– Legal frameworks in eastern countries need to be strict – Law enforcement in eastern countries needs to be strong – Less corrupt governments would strengthen both legal frameworks and law enforcement – People should be taught that piracy is morally wrong – Impact of *globalization* may reduce piracy in the long run	– Concept of *intellectual property rights* is 'foreign' to eastern people – Software sharing is a socially accepted norm – Software prices should be cheaper in eastern countries – *Collective morality* does not consider piracy a 'wrong' deed because it does not create any direct harm to anyone – Technology sharing is considered a part of the 'community well-being' as not everyone can afford software/product – Gender and religion have impact on piracy
Password sharing	– Password sharing is dangerous for security – Technical solutions are required so that people cannot share passwords – Legal frameworks should limit password sharing – Strict password policies limiting password sharing should be applied	– Password sharing is a cultural norm • Family members share passwords with each other because of trust, power role, convenience, and social expectation • Gender norms do not always allow women to access banking and other services – Family expectations, geographical disadvantages and lack of infrastructural facilities create necessities of sharing password
Mobile device sharing	– Mobile devices are designed for personal usage only – Unauthorized device sharing violates users' privacy – Technical frameworks are required for secure device sharing. For example, • Android's Multiple Access Mechanism for multiple accounts • Software for hiding private files	– Authorized/unauthorized device sharing among family, friends, colleagues, and community is culturally accepted – People share devices because of trust, necessity and social expectation Android's Multiple Access framework does not work in east because it is not accepted to "openly" hide information from family – Mobile device sharing with community is required because not everyone can afford a mobile phone

and community spheres. On the other hand, sharing becomes a necessity when sharing is the only way to access services. As a result, the trade-off between sharing and security/privacy threats becomes obvious when sharing offers convenience and security threats mostly remain theoretical.

Security designers tend to overlook the fact that sharing is inevitable in eastern cultures. In our analysis, we termed such attitudes as etics, because they are formed by western ethnocentrism – an assumption that western cultural practices are ideal, which leads to the interpretation of another culture from outside. We propose our emics approach to integrate cultural relativism in security environments by understanding the importance of culture-specific practices.

Our emics-etics analysis shows that some of the problems caused by sharing could be solved by accepting sharing-related culture-specific expectations and practices in security solutions. We envision a culturally-inclusive security environment where etics will be ideally applied to find out universal components, whereas emics will validate the claimed universality of them. In our work, we do not mean to imply that universal components do not exist (for example, the memorability problems of passwords appear to be culturally universal), only that we cannot treat all security problems and solutions as universal and independent of culture.

4.2 Sharing in Business Strategy

After understanding the socio-economic situation of the east, it is evident that sharing technology is socially accepted. We suggest that software and OS vendors need to accept and plan for sharing in their business models. Subscription sharing has already been introduced in different products. One of the most common and successful examples is Netflix, which is found to be popular among eastern cultures [13]. Netflix, the leading internet entertainment provider, allows playing up to four screens simultaneously on the same subscription. In 2016, the CEO of Netflix acknowledged the realities of password sharing "...password sharing is something you have to learn to live with because there is so much legitimate password sharing..." [8, p. 1]. Netflix's shared subscription model helped reduce movie piracy [78]. It is still a growth company with around 167 million total subscriptions in 2019 [33].

We propose that operating system and software vendors follow the same strategy where the user is able to share the registration key with a limited number of family and friends. Microsoft 365 (previously known as Office 365) has started to offer shared subscriptions under the plan named "Microsoft 365 Family," which allows six people to share the same account [55]. We speculate that the shared subscription model may work effectively to encourage users not to use pirated software, thereby reducing security risks.

Similarly, we also propose that a shared subscription model could help increase the popularity of under-adopted security tools. For instance, password managers, tools that generate and store passwords securely, are highly encouraged by security experts, but few people use them. We suggest that the ability to share subscriptions for such tools might also be able to be leveraged to attract new users to these tools. This model could also be applied to other subscription-based security tools, such as anti-virus software.

4.3 Sharing in Technology Tools

Our emics-etics analysis of different security problems suggests that current authentication systems and mobile device architectures do not provide secure sharing, but that technology sharing is a norm in some cultures. We propose that enabling secure sharing in technology tools could increase their usability. For instance, role-based sharing can be implemented in authentication systems and access control mechanisms.

Authentication systems should have multiple password sharing options. The owner's password should be the primary password. All the secondary passwords would have society based family roles for personalizing action control. For instance, if the wife shared a secondary password with her husband, he would not be able to withdraw cash over a certain amount set or monitor all transaction history. We assume that it will be hard for users to memorize all the secondary passwords for every shared account. Therefore, we propose that a culture-centric password manager could be developed to store and securely share passwords.

We also suggest that mobile devices should be designed to have culturally-sensitive role-based multiple access mechanisms. Owners should be able to customize different roles' access to hide/unhide data and applications. We also suggest to provide a mechanism that obscures from the person with whom the device is shared that they are accessing a filtered account. For instance, an eastern daughter might choose to hide some applications/data from her father but if he found out that she was hiding her data, it would cause mistrust and bad consequences. Nirapod [3] is an example of such a prototype tool that offers hidden multiple access using a secondary password but users faced password memorability problems while using it. Further studies required to make such tool usable in everyday life.

5 Conclusion

In this paper, we present a cross-cultural literature review using our emics-etics framework for usable security to highlight the differences between eastern and western cultures regarding security beliefs, understanding, and practices. Our study finds significant cultural differences in security attitudes, and we suggest that cultural factors (e.g., trust, family values, and social norms) must be considered while designing and developing security mechanisms.

We also discussed some suggestions, design considerations, and challenges for security system designers to consider when designing universal security tools. Our findings contribute a new cross-cultural framework for understanding and evaluating cultural practices and a set of suggestions for accommodating cultural knowledge to design and develop culturally appropriate security tools.

This work is an initial phase of a bigger research project. In future, we plan to conduct cross-cultural studies to evaluate how our suggestions play out in accommodating cultural differences. We plan to test our proposed systems empirically by conducting user studies with people from different cultures. Our emics-etics framework suggests a promising approach to considering cultural differences for security, analyzing failures, and suggesting new ways forward.

References

1. Adem, A.M.: Software piracy understanding, challenges, detection and prevention in higher education students of Ethiopia. Daagu Int. J. Basic Appl. Res.-DIJBAR **1**(2), (38–46) 22(11) (2019)
2. Ahmed, S.I., Haque, M.R., Chen, J., Dell, N.: Digital privacy challenges with shared mobile phone use in Bangladesh. In: Proceedings of the ACM on Human-Computer Interaction 1 (CSCW), pp. 1–20 (2017)
3. Ahmed, S.I., Haque, M.R., Haider, I., Chen, J., Dell, N.: "Everyone Has Some Personal Stuff" designing to support digital privacy with shared mobile phone use in Bangladesh. In: Proceedings of the 2019 CHI Conference on Human Factors in Computing Systems, pp. 1–13 (2019)
4. Aleassa, H., Pearson, J.M., McClurg, S.: Investigating software piracy in Jordan: an extension of the theory of reasoned action. J. Bus. Ethics **98**(4), 663–676 (2011)
5. Alghamdi, D., Flechais, I., Jirotka, M.: Security practices for households bank customers in the Kingdom of Saudi Arabia. In: Eleventh Symposium On Usable Privacy and Security (SOUPS 2015), pp. 297–308 (2015)
6. Altman, I., Chemers, M.M.: Culture and environment, No. 2, CUP Archive (1984). https://s3.amazonaws.com/ipri2018/IPRI2018_MAL.pdf
7. Amirullah, A., Ravindran, M.: Digital Piracy in Malaysia
8. Balakrishnan, A.: Your shared Netflix password is safe, the CEO says (2016). https://www.cnbc.com/2016/10/17/your-shared-netflix-password-is-safe-the-ceo-says.html. Accessed 08 May 2020
9. Arli, D., Pekerti, A.: Who is more ethical? cross-cultural comparison of consumer ethics between religious and non-religious consumers. J. Consum. Behav. **16**(1), 82–98 (2017)
10. August, T., Tunca, T.I.: Let the pirates patch? an economic analysis of software security patch restrictions. Inf. Syst. Res. **19**(1), 48–70 (2008)
11. Banerjee, D., Khalid, A.M., Sturm, J.E.: Socio-economic development and software piracy: an empirical assessment. Appl. Econ. **37**(18), 2091–2097 (2005)
12. Banerjee, D.S.: Software piracy: a strategic analysis and policy instruments. Int. J. Ind. Organ. **21**(1), 97–127 (2003)
13. Choudhury, B.: Netflix Reigns As South East Asian viewership surges under lockdown (2020). https://www.forbes.com/sites/bedatrichoudhury/2020/04/21/netflix-reigns-as-south-east-asian-viewership-surges-under-lockdown/#54a7a03219b6. Accessed 01 May 2020
14. Biddle, R., Chiasson, S., Van Oorschot, P.C.: Graphical passwords: learning from the first twelve years. ACM Comput. Surv. (CSUR) **44**(4), 1–41 (2012)
15. Boas, F.: Race, Language, and Culture. University of Chicago Press, Chicago (1982)
16. Boyles, J.L., Smith, A., Madden, M.: Privacy and data management on mobile devices. Pew Internet Am. Life Project **4**, 1–19 (2012)
17. Brislin, R.W.: Cross-cultural Encounters, Face-to-face Interaction: Face-to-face Interaction. Pergamon Press (1981)
18. Brislin, R.W.: Cross-cultural research in psychology. Annu. Rev. Psychol. **34**(1), 363–400 (1983)

19. BSA: Software management: Security imperative, business opportunity (2018). https://www.muso.com/magazine/global-piracy-increases-throughout-2017-muso-reveals/. Accessed 08 May 2020
20. Buckley, P.J., Chapman, M., Clegg, J., Gajewska-De Mattos, H.: A linguistic and philosophical analysis of emic and etic and their use in international business research. Manag. Int. Rev. **54**(3), 307–324 (2014)
21. Cornejo, R., Brewer, R., Edasis, C., Piper, A.M.: Vulnerability, sharing, and privacy: analyzing art therapy for older adults with dementia. In: Proceedings of the 19th ACM Conference on Computer-Supported Cooperative Work & Social Computing, pp. 1572–1583 (2016)
22. Donaldson, T.: Values in tension: Ethics away from home (1996)
23. Dourish, P.: HCI and environmental sustainability: the politics of design and the design of politics. In: Proceedings of the 8th ACM Conference on Designing Interactive Systems, pp. 1–10 (2010)
24. Dourish, P., Bell, G.: Divining a Digital Future: Mess and Mythology in Ubiquitous Computing. MIT Press, Cambridge (2011)
25. Egelman, S., Jain, S., Portnoff, R.S., Liao, K., Consolvo, S., Wagner, D.: Are you ready to lock? In: Proceedings of the 2014 ACM SIGSAC Conference on Computer and Communications Security, pp. 750–761 (2014)
26. Garfinkel, S., Lipford, H.R.: Usable security: history, themes, and challenges. Synth. Lectures Inf. Secur. Privacy Trust **5**(2), 1–124 (2014)
27. Smith, G.: Netflix, HBO and cable giants are coming for password cheats: password resets and thumbprints are among the tactics being considered (2019). https://www.bloomberg.com/news/articles/2019-11-08/netflix-hbo-and-cable-giants-are-coming-for-password-cheats. Accessed 30 Nov 2019
28. Hang, A., Von Zezschwitz, E., De Luca, A., Hussmann, H.: Too much information! user attitudes towards smartphone sharing. In: Proceedings of the 7th Nordic Conference on Human-Computer Interaction: Making Sense Through Design, pp. 284–287 (2012)
29. Hill, C.W.: Digital piracy: causes, consequences, and strategic responses. Asia Pacific J. Manag. **24**(1), 9–25 (2007)
30. Hofstede, G., Hofstede, G.J., Minkov, M.: Cultures and organizations: Software of the mind, vol. 2. Citeseer (2005)
31. Hossain, A., Das, A.K., Mim, N.T., Hoque, J., Tuhin, R.A.: Software piracy: factors and profiling. In: 2019 2nd International Conference on Applied Information Technology and Innovation (ICAITI), pp. 213–219. IEEE (2019)
32. Husted, B.W.: The impact of national culture on software piracy. J. Bus. Ethics **26**(3), 197–211 (2000)
33. Collins, J.: Netflix's business model does not work (2020). https://www.forbes.com/sites/jimcollins/2020/01/22/netflixs-business-model-does-not-work/#1f6c97822ccd. Accessed 08 May 2020
34. Jonas, A., Burrell, J.: Friction, snake oil, and weird countries: cybersecurity systems could deepen global inequality through regional blocking. Big Data Soc. **6**(1), 2053951719835238 (2019)
35. Kake, J.: Rebuilding the Kāinga: Lessons from Te Ao Hurihuri. Bridget Williams Books (2019)
36. Karlson, A.K., Brush, A.B., Schechter, S.: Can I borrow your phone? Understanding concerns when sharing mobile phones. In: Proceedings of the SIGCHI Conference on Human Factors in Computing Systems, pp. 1647–1650 (2009)
37. Kaye, J.: Self-reported password sharing strategies. In: Proceedings of the SIGCHI Conference on Human Factors in Computing Systems, pp. 2619–2622. ACM (2011)

38. Kayes, I., Iamnitchi, A.: Aegis: a semantic implementation of privacy as contextual integrity in social ecosystems. In: 2013 Eleventh Annual Conference on Privacy, Security and Trust, pp. 88–97. IEEE (2013)

39. Kini, R.B., Ramakrishna, H.V., Vijayaraman, B.S.: Shaping of moral intensity regarding software piracy: a comparison between Thailand and US students. J. Bus. Ethics **49**(1), 91–104 (2004)

40. Koay, K.Y., Tjiptono, F., Sandhu, M.S.: Digital piracy among consumers in a developing economy: a comparison of multiple theory-based models. J. Retail. Consum. Serv. **55**, 102075 (2020)

41. Koklič, M.K.: Digital piracy among adults in Solvenia: an application of the theory if interpersonal behaviour. Econ. Bus. Rev. **18**(2), 135–150 (2016)

42. Korhonen, J.: Software piracy among university students (2017)

43. Kraay, J.N.: Emics, etics, and meaning, an exploration. Philosophia Reformata **41**(1–2), 49–71 (1976)

44. Kroeber, A.L., Kluckhohn, C.: Culture: A critical review of concepts and definitions. Harvard University, Papers. Peabody Museum of Archaeology & Ethnology (1952)

45. Kwan, S.S.K., Jaisingh, J., Tam, K.Y.: Risk of using pirated software and its impact on software protection strategies. Decision Support Systems

46. Kwet, M.: Digital colonialism: US empire and the new imperialism in the Global South. Race Class **60**(4), 3–26 (2019)

47. Logsdon, J.M., Thompson, J.K., Reid, R.A.: Software piracy: is it related to level of moral judgment? J. Bus. Ethics **13**(11), 849–857 (1994)

48. Lonner, W.J.: Issues in cross-cultural psychology. Perspectives in cross-cultural psychology, pp. 17–45 (1979)

49. Mandujano, S., Soto, R.: Deterring password sharing: user authentication via fuzzy c-means clustering applied to keystroke biometric data. In: Proceedings of the Fifth Mexican International Conference in Computer Science, 2004, ENC 2004, pp. 181–187. IEEE (2004)

50. Marques, D., Muslukhov, I., Guerreiro, T., Carriço, L., Beznosov, K.: Snooping on mobile phones: prevalence and trends. In: Twelfth Symposium on Usable Privacy and Security (SOUPS 2016), pp. 159–174 (2016)

51. Matthews, T., Liao, K., Turner, A., Berkovich, M., Reeder, R., Consolvo, S.: "She'll just grab any device that's closer" a study of everyday device & account sharing in households. In: Proceedings of the 2016 CHI Conference on Human Factors in Computing Systems, pp. 5921–5932 (2016)

52. Meireles, R., Campos, P.: Digital piracy: factors that influence the intention to pirate-a structural equation model approach. Int. J. Hum.-Comput. Interac. **35**(12), 1046–1060 (2019)

53. Meter, D.J., Bauman, S.: When sharing is a bad idea: the effects of online social network engagement and sharing passwords with friends on cyberbullying involvement. Cyberpsychol. Behav. Soc. Netw. **18**(8), 437–442 (2015)

54. Microsoft: Microsoft to implement worldwide anti-piracy initiative (2005). https://news.microsoft.com/2005/01/26/microsoft-to-implement-worldwide-anti-piracy-initiative/. Accessed 08 May 2020

55. Microsoft: Microsoft 365 for home: Find the right solution for you (2020). https://www.microsoft.com/en-ca/microsoft-365/compare-all-microsoft-365-products?&activetab=tab:primaryr1?activetab=tab:primaryr1. Accessed 08 May 2020

56. Moore, D., Shannon, C., Claffy, K.: Code-red: a case study on the spread and victims of an internet worm. In: Proceedings of the 2nd ACM SIGCOMM Workshop on Internet Measurment, pp. 273–284 (2002)
57. Murphy, L.L., Priebe, A.E.: "My co-wife can borrow my mobile phone!" gendered geographies of cell phone usage and significance for rural kenyans. Gend. Technol. Dev. **15**(1), 1–23 (2011)
58. MUSO: Global Piracy Increases throughout 2017, MUSO Reveals (2018). https://www.bsa.org/media/Files/StudiesDownload/. Accessed 08 May 2020
59. Naumovich, G., Memon, N.: Preventing piracy, reverse engineering, and tampering. Computer **36**(7), 64–71 (2003)
60. Pike, K.L.: Language in relation to a unified theory of the structure of human behavior, vol. 24. Walter de Gruyter GmbH & co KG (2015)
61. Pixel Phone Help: Change guest and user setting (2020). https://support.google.com/pixelphone/answer/2865944. Accessed 08 May 2020
62. Png, I.P., Chen, Y.N.: Software pricing and copyright: enforcement against end-users. Available at SSRN 165228 (1999)
63. Rangaswamy, N., Singh, S.: Personalizing the shared mobile phone. In: International Conference on Internationalization, Design and Global Development, pp. 395–403. Springer (2009)
64. Ratazzi, P., Aafer, Y., Ahlawat, A., Hao, H., Wang, Y., Du, W.: A systematic security evaluation of android's multi-user framework. arXiv preprint arXiv:1410.7752 (2014)
65. Reay, M.: Being black: Aboriginal cultures in "settled" Australia. Aboriginal Studies Press (1988)
66. Renouf, G.: Book up. A Report for the Australian Securities and Investments Commission, NSW, Australia, Some Consumer Problems (2002)
67. Sambasivan, N., et al.: "Privacy is not for me, it's for those rich women": performative privacy practices on mobile phones by women in South Asia. In: Fourteenth Symposium on Usable Privacy and Security (SOUPS 2018), pp. 127–142 (2018)
68. Sasse, M.A.: Computer security: Anatomy of a usability disaster, and a plan for recovery (2003)
69. Senior, K., Bern, J.E., Perkins, D.: Variation in material wellbeing in a welfare based economy. University of Wollongong, South East Arnhem Land Collaborative Research Project (2002)
70. Shay, R., et al.: Encountering stronger password requirements: user attitudes and behaviors. In: Proceedings of the Sixth Symposium on Usable Privacy and Security, pp. 1–20 (2010)
71. Singh, S., Cabraal, A., Demosthenous, C., Astbrink, G., Furlong, M.: Password sharing: implications for security design based on social practice. In: Proceedings of the SIGCHI Conference on Human Factors in Computing Systems, pp. 895–904. ACM (2007)
72. Singh, S., Cabraal, A., Demosthenous, C., Astbrink, G., Furlong, M.: Security design based on social and cultural practice: sharing of passwords. In: International Conference on Usability and Internationalization, pp. 476–485. Springer (2007)
73. Spivak, G.C.: In other worlds: Essays in cultural politics. Routledge (2012)
74. Steenson, M., Donner, J.: Beyond the personal and private: modes of mobile phone sharing in urban India. Reconstruction Space Time Mob. Commun. Prac. **1**, 231–250 (2009)
75. Steidlmeier, P.: The moral legitimacy of intellectual property claims: American business and developing country perspectives. J. Bus. Ethics **12**(2), 157–164 (1993)

76. Swinyard, W.R., Rinne, H., Kau, A.K.: The morality of software piracy: a cross-cultural analysis. J. Bus. Ethics **9**(8), 655–664 (1990)
77. Tan, B.: Understanding consumer ethical decision making with respect to purchase of pirated software. J. Consum. Mark. **19**(2), 96–111 (2002)
78. The Telegraph: Internet piracy falls to record lows amid rise of Spotify and Netflix (2016). https://www.telegraph.co.uk/technology/2016/07/04/internet-piracy-falls-to-record-lows-amid-rise-of-spotify-and-ne/. Accessed 08 May 2020
79. Tjiptono, F., Arli, D.: Gender and digital privacy: examining determinants of attitude toward digital piracy among youths in an emerging market. Int. J. Consum. Stud. **40**(2), 168–178 (2016)
80. Triandis, H.C.: Reflections on trends in cross-cultural research. J. Cross Cult. Psychol. **11**(1), 35–58 (1980)
81. Vokes, R.: Before the call: mobile phones, exchange relations, and social change in South-Western Uganda. Ethnos **83**(2), 274–290 (2018)
82. Watson, H., Moju-Igbene, E., Kumari, A., Das, S.: "We Hold Each Other Accountable": unpacking how social groups approach cybersecurity and privacy together. In: Proceedings of the 2020 CHI Conference on Human Factors in Computing Systems, pp. 1–12 (2020)
83. Whitten, A., Tygar, J.D.: Why Johnny can't encrypt: a usability evaluation of PGP 5.0. In: USENIX Security Symposium, vol. 348, pp. 169–184 (1999)
84. Yu, S.: Digital piracy justification: Asian students versus American students. Int. Crim. Justice Rev. **23**(2), 185–196 (2013)

Development of a Novice-Friendly Representation of Camouflaged Boolean Networks

Salsabil Hamadache[1,2(✉)] and Malte Elson[1,2]

[1] Psychology of Human Technology Interaction, Faculty of Psychology, Ruhr University Bochum, Universtitätsstr. 150, 44801 Bochum, Germany
[2] Horst Görtz Institute for IT Security, Ruhr University Bochum, Bochum, Germany
`{salsabil.hamadache,malte.elson}@ruhr-uni-bochum.de`

Abstract. Psychological research has established that the way problems are represented affects mental models that are activated, the strategies a solver might employ to solve the problem, and the problem solving success. In the education of IT-related subjects, such as computer science or IT security, problems are often complex and overwhelming for first-year studies. We suggest that providing problems to student in depictive instead of descriptive representations may yield more successful problem solving and will test this hypothesis in the field of Boolean logic. More precisely, we have developed a representation of Boolean networks that we expect to be better suited for novices to work on than the traditional, abstract representation. De-camouflaging, the process of determining the identities of concealed logic gates within a network, will serve as a task by which the usefulness of our representation will be tested. Naïve participants will thus solve de-camouflaging tasks on both our novel, depictive, representation as well as the traditional, descriptive, representation. In our talk at the International Conference on Human-Computer-Interaction, we will report in how far the two representations differentially affect problem solving success, strategies used, and the subjective experience of participants working on this task.

Keywords: Logic gates · Camouflaging · Reverse engineering · Obfuscation

1 Introduction

IT specialists are highly in demand, yet many students of IT-related subjects find themselves overwhelmed by the difficulty of their study contents [1, 2]. Establishing why certain tasks are especially hard may yield useful hints for educators working to improve prospective professionals' education and is thus a promising field of research. This paper aims to contribute to this objective by developing a representation format that affects success in reverse engineering Boolean networks.

A. Moallem (Ed.): HCII 2021, LNCS 12788, pp. 41–49, 2021.
https://doi.org/10.1007/978-3-030-77392-2_3

1.1 Past Research

Psychological research has long established that different representations of the same problem affect whether individuals can solve it and how they proceed in doing so [3]. This insight has been used in the development of curricula, particularly in the fields of math and physics, since many students struggle when building a mental model of problems in this domain [1]. Little research has, however, been performed in the field of Computer Science, and even less in the subfield of Boolean logic, which combines mathematical and technical elements. Before past research is overviewed, we outline a few basic concepts:

(Complex) Problem Solving. Problem solving is psychologically defined as the application of cognitive operations to reach a desired goal state from an initial state [4]. Problems that are complex are, further, dynamic, in transparent, and have barriers making them impossible to solve only by applying routine actions. Instead, it is necessary for solvers to plan, strategize, and dynamically adapt plans and actions in reaction to the problem state.

Academic education often consists of clearly defined, portioned problems, which is why many students fail when confronted with problems that are ill-defined, ambiguous, or highly complex [5].

For example, students may succeed in performing mathematical operations, as long as they are not concealed by a complex task description, but as soon as they take the form of real-life narratives with possibly superfluous information and interconnected pieces requiring multi-step approaches, they might fail.

The Effect of Representation. In order to facilitate problem solving, one might offer students multiple different representations of the same problem that highlight different aspects. The idea hereby is that different aspects of a problem can be highlighted and thus be drawn into the focus of the solver. Moreover, different representations can provide distinctive functions to the solver. For example, an image can lead to computational offloading as it displays aspects that would otherwise be needed to be held in one's working memory [3].

Problem representations can be either depictive or descriptive. Descriptions can hereby take the form of texts, formulas, or symbols. Depictive representations are usually figures, i.e. pictures or diagrams. They are actually intended to display the concepts as they are, instead of symbolizing or abstracting them [3].

Due to this disparity, representations activate different mental models and different strategies and may moderate success.

Various studies have investigated the effects of depictive vs. descriptive representations and differences between representations of the same category. For example, researchers have compared text-based vs. equation-based displays of mathematical concepts [6], diagrams vs. texts in physics [7], and the presence of one vs. several combinations of both depictive and descriptive representations [1]. The overall results of this research are that learners usually prefer concrete over abstract representations and that depictions are better suited to draw inferences than descriptions [3]. One reason for this result is that for individuals who have difficulties grasping the contents of the problem, translating abstract representations, particularly symbols, formulas and equations, into a mental model of the concepts that they can cognitively work with, requires additional cognitive effort. In contrast, if the representation enables them to grasp the problem, they can fully focus their cognitive capacity on solving the problem itself [7].

1.2 Present Research

We suspect that this process of translating the representation into a correct mental concept is particularly hard task for Boolean logic. Two observations lead us to this assumption:

1. Basic Boolean operations are omnipresent in our everyday lives - We regularly perform AND and OR, even XOR operations without explicitly referring to them as such, while at the same time.
2. students routinely fail to perform even the most basic Boolean operations within the context of computer science studies at university [1, 2].

There is thus an obvious discrepancy between the mental representation of Boolean operators that students build when following courses on Boolean logic, and the Boolean logic they regularly use in their everyday life. This might be due to the fact that Boolean logic education heavily relies on symbolic representations:

Boolean Logic and Gate Networks. In Boolean logic, binary inputs are transformed into a single binary output according to defined rules (operations). These inputs are usually described by letters (e.g. A NOR B; I1 NAND I2), while the operations themselves are described by means of symbols (e.g. v for or and ∧ for and). Additionally, in digital networks, each Boolean operator has yet another symbol (see Fig. 1). It is thus possible that first-year students fail at grasping Boolean logic not because of the complexity of the mental operations that need be performed, but rather because of their representation conventions in higher education curricula We thus suggest an alternative representation for Boolean logic gates that offers a concrete depiction instead of an abstract, symbolic description. To test whether our representation actually facilitates real life problem solving, we designed a study in which participants reverse-engineer a Boolean network in which some gate identities were camouflaged. We chose this design for two reasons:

1. This type of reverse engineering, in the context of hardware, has already been conceptualized as a complex problem solving process [8].
2. Past research suggest that some applications of reverse engineering do not require previous experience [9]: Students with no experience on digital systems, computer science, or hardware technology have been able to reverse engineer simple electrical circuits.

The Task at Hand. Sometimes, gate identities are hidden using obfuscation methods. Obfuscation is the process of actively disguising parts of a system from potential adversaries. Applied on the digital networks of a system, obfuscation takes the form of camouflaging: Boolean gates' identities are hereby concealed such that reverse engineers cannot easily determine the function of the network. Obfuscated logic gates can perform the function of either NOR, XOR, or NAND gates, thus testing every possibility for every camouflaged gate would result in 3^n attempts, n being the number of camouflaged gates in a network. Given the dimensions of a system, this can lead to a significant delay in the reverse engineering process, if adversaries do not move beyond the naïve strategy of brute-forcing, i.e. testing all possible identities for all camouflaged gates. Hence, adversaries have developed strategies to accelerate the de-camouflaging of Boolean networks [10]. We are interested in precisely these strategies and therefore picked the de-camouflaging of Boolean networks as the task that needs to be performed by participants in order to test our novel representation. We hereby follow the path set by [8] and [11,12], who have conducted several studies with the goal of developing so-called cognitive obfuscations based on psychological insights into reverse engineering strategies and cognitive processes involved, while also investigating educational research questions relating to the teaching and learning of reverse engineering [13]. Preliminary findings by Wiesen and Becker indicate that novices are indeed able to learn to de-camouflage Boolean networks.

1.3 Hypotheses

We hypothesize that our concrete, depictive representation will invite naïve participants to activate more useful mental models compared to the traditional representation. We thus expect that they will report that the familiar concept of liquids flowing through pipes (see Fig. 2), which requires no specific prior knowledge or training, enables them to focus their cognitive effort on the Boolean operations rather than on the attempt to translate the symbols used to describe them (Fig. 1). This will lead to better performance on the depictive compared to the descriptive representation.

We will investigate the problem solving processes of naïve participants in an exploratory manner and hope to yield valuable insights into the mental models they develop throughout the process.

2 Development Process

We used LiveCode to implement an interactive platform in which de-camouflaging can be practiced (see Fig. 1). Users can enter 0 or 1 into the fields next to inputs I1 through I6. These will then be transformed by the gates displayed in the image, such that 0 and 1 appear in the output fields on the right. This way, the identities of the two hidden gates can be deduced.

Three Boolean networks, each with eight gates, six inputs, and two outputs have been developed. They include NAND, NOR, NOT, OR and hidden gates. The latter are either functionally equivalent to NOR, NAND, or XOR gates. Each of the three networks is displayed once in the conventional representation as in Fig. 1, and once in our newly developed representation (see Fig. 2) in a fully randomized within-subject experimental design. Even though users will thus seemingly work on the same network twice, the problem solving and solution will differ because the correct identities of the hidden gates will differ.

Differences Between the Two Representations. As outlined above, research has shown that depictive representations helped participants to make inferences compared to descriptions. We thus developed a depictive representation to overcome the difficulty of mentally mapping abstract Boolean operations onto one's own understanding of Boolean combinations. To enable participants to activate a concrete and useful mental image, we chose the flow of liquid through pipes. We meticulously mapped one representation onto the other, such that the general layout or the functionality of the valves (or gates) does not differ. A positive input of 1 in the depictive representation stands for the presence of poison in the liquid. Boolean gates can then either clear the liquid of the poison or combine two inflowing liquids in different ways (see Table 1). Because free recall of the operations after just one short introduction seems to be unlikely, we have chosen to label the gates in every item. Even though the descriptions are as similar as possible in the two representations, the ones labeling the descriptive representation remain abstract while the ones in the pipe representation refer to the concrete depiction to maintain the main manipulation we are interested in investigating. Note that camouflaged gates are always depicted as grey/metallic buttons on the pipes to not provide false hints towards their identity resembling another colored button (see Fig. 2).

Table 1. Depictive analogies of Boolean operators

Operation	Depiction
NOT	Removing poison from inflowing liquid
OR	"Mixing", i.e. if either or both inflowing liquids are poisonous, so is the outflowing liquid1
NAND	Adding poison if none or one of the incoming liquids are poisonous, removing the poison if both are
NOR	Adding poison if none of the incoming liquids are poisonous, and removing it if either of them or both are

To enable naïve participants to work on these networks, a short introductory course on Boolean logic has been developed. In it, Boolean operations, the idea of symbolizing operations, and the idea of several Boolean gates building larger networks, are introduced. The concepts of binary inputs and outputs and the fact that one gate's output can be another's input are also discussed. The course and the web tool will be published on the Open Science Framework (https://bit.ly/2N17Bkl).

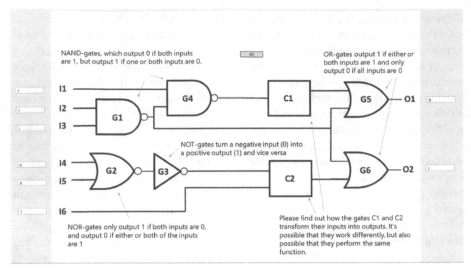

Fig. 1. Boolean network as traditionally illustrated. With explanations for novices to consult. C1 and C2 are obfuscated and need to be identified.

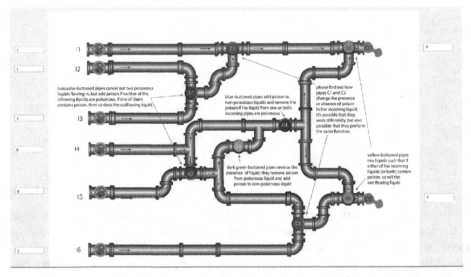

Fig. 2. Boolean network representation developed by the authors. With explanations for novices to consult. C1 and C2 are obfuscated and need to be identified.

3   Study Method

3.1   Participants

Naïve individuals ($N = 50$) without any previous experience in IT-related topics will be recruited using the study recruitment platform Prolific within a larger research project (https://osf.io/wtvks/). We will recruit a sample consisting of adults with an academic degree residing in the United Kingdom. IT-related professions or educational background will serve as exclusion criteria.

3.2 Procedure

Participants will be informed about the purpose of the study and asked for consent and voluntary participation. They will report demographics and complete the introductory course provided by us. They will then receive a test item consisting of a network with four gates (of which one is obfuscated) three inputs, and one output. They are then asked to pick the correct identity among the available choices (NOR, NAND, and XOR). To determine the correct solution, they will be invited to manipulate the inputs (thus insert 0 or 1 in the respective input fields) and observe the output to deduce the network's behaviour. They will receive 20 min to solve this task; and will be allowed to consult the introductory course while working on this task. After the time runs out, participants will be asked if they understood the concepts of Boolean logic, obfuscated networks, and de-obfuscation. They will be asked whether they guessed and depending on the answer on this question together with the correctness of their answer, two scenarios emerge:

(1) The participant does not appear to have obtained the necessary understanding and has picked the wrong answer; or confirms that he has guessed. In this case, the participant will be compensated for participating in this pre-study and not be considered for the main study.
(2) The participant solves the task correctly and indicates that he has understood the introductory course and the task at hand. In this case, he will be compensated for participating in this pre-study and will receive an invitation to participate in the main study.

Main Study. In the main study, participants will receive six networks in a random order. Three of these networks will be displayed in our novel representation, while three will be represented in the conventional manner (see Figs. 1 and 2, respectively). They will receive 12 min for each of the items; and will not receive any feedback on their performance. After solving all 6 items, they will receive questions covering the differential effect of the representation. They will thus be asked to indicate which representation they preferred, which they considered more suited for novices to work on this task on, and whether they thought that they solved more items of one or the other type correctly. Moreover, they will be asked if they were able to develop strategies throughout the experiment or used the brute-force strategy for all items.

4   Results and Implications

Because this is an on-going project, we will report our results in our talk at the 23rd International Conference on Human-Computer Interaction. We will report how participants reacted on the two different representations and whether differences also emerged in behavioural data (e.g. success rate, time needed to solve items, strategy use), even though this is secondary to our main interest of yielding insights into the processes and strategies of our participants. Importantly, we will also discuss implications for the education of Boolean logic and hardware development in computer science and IT security curricula.

Limitations. As outlined above, we carefully ensured that the networks differ mainly on the dimension that we hypothesize will have an effect, i.e. on whether it is depictive or descriptive. If they differ on other dimensions as well, it is necessary to rule out that these differences are causally linked to the differences we will detect.

Most importantly, the representations are alike in their general layout, the number of input and outputs of gates, and even the identity of the gates. However, the depictive representation is displayed in color because only this way could we avoid using yet another set of symbols to define them. It is however unlikely that adults prefer this representation over the other solely on the basis that one is colourful while the other is not. Moreover, we tried to label the gate's functionalities in similar ways while still describing them concretely (i.e. talking about what happens to the liquid once it passes through a gate) vs. in an abstract way (thus talking about 0 s and 1 s and how they are transformed, without any detail as to how or why this transformation is induced by the respective gate). We will thus be unable to rule out that effects will not only be due to the representation itself but may also be caused by the different labeling.

5 Conclusions and Future Research

This paper has introduced the idea of creating a representation of Boolean logic networks that are easily explained to novices and may probably even facilitate complex problem solving tasks such as de-camouflaging.

If our results corroborate our hypotheses, educators may consider developing similar representations themselves to first work with concrete depictions before moving on to abstract descriptions. Possibly, this will help students to master both challenges: understanding Boolean logic itself and understand how Boolean logic can be represented using symbols or formulas. Future research could compare differences between existing representations of Boolean concepts, e.g. Venn Diagrams vs. Truth Tables. However, these kinds of representations are already often used for educational purposes in introductory courses but are limited to few inputs as they get less useful the larger the network. Our representation can be used for any network size and any number of inputs, gates, and outputs.

Another objective of future research may be to test these representations in other tasks instead of de-obfuscation. For example, another task that can be practiced by means of these networks is formulating equations such as $O = (I1 \vee I2) \wedge I3$. This, too, is a difficult problem once networks grow in size, even though it is not a complex problem as defined by [5] as it is static rather than dynamic.

References

1. Ott, N., et al.: Multiple symbolic representations: the combination of formula and text supports problem solving in the mathematical field of propositional logic. Learn. Instr. **58**, 88–105 (2018)
2. Herman, G.L., et al.: Describing the what and why of students' difficulties in Boolean logic. ACM Trans. Comput. Educ. (TOCE) **12**(1), 1–28 (2012)
3. Ainsworth, S.: DeFT: a conceptual framework for considering learning with multiple representations. Learn. Instr. **16**(3), 183–198 (2006)
4. Csapó, B., Funke, J.: The nature of problem solving. OECD (2017). Author, F., Author, S.: Title of a proceedings paper. In: Editor, F., Editor, S. (eds.) CONFERENCE 2016, LNCS, vol. 9999, pp. 1–13. Springer, Heidelberg (2016)
5. Dörner, D., Funke, J.: Complex problem solving: what it is and what it is not. Front. Psychol. **8**, 1153 (2017)
6. Dee-Lucas, D., Larkin, J.H.: Equations in scientific Proofs: Effects on comprehension (1991)
7. ChanLin, L.: Formats and prior knowledge on learning in a computer-based lesson. J. Comput. Assisted Learn. **17**(4), 409–419 (2001)
8. Fyrbiak, M., et al.: Hardware reverse engineering: overview and open challenges. In: 2017 IEEE 2nd International Verification and Security Workshop (IVSW). IEEE (2017)
9. Lee, N.Y.L., Johnson-Laird, P.N.: A theory of reverse engineering and its application to Boolean systems. J. Cogn. Psychol. **25**(4), 365–389 (2013)
10. Forte, D., Bhunia, S., Tehranipoor, M.M. (eds.): Hardware Protection Through Obfuscation. Springer, Cham (2017). https://doi.org/10.1007/978-3-319-49019-9
11. Wiesen, C., et al.: Towards cognitive obfuscation: impeding hardware reverse engineering based on psychological insights. In: Proceedings of the 24th Asia and South Pacific Design Automation Conference (2019)
12. Becker, S., et al.: An exploratory study of hardware reverse engineering—technical and cognitive processes. In: Sixteenth Symposium on Usable Privacy and Security (SOUPS 2020) (2020)
13. Wiesen, C., et al.: Teaching hardware reverse engineering: educational guidelines and practical insights. In: 2018 IEEE International Conference on Teaching, Assessment, and Learning for Engineering (TALE). IEEE (2018)

Testing Facial Recognition Software for Young Adults and Adolescents: An Integrative Review

Aimee Kendall Roundtree[(⊠)] [iD]

Texas State University, San Marcos, TX 78666, USA
`akr@txstate.edu`

Abstract. This integrative review synthesizes research findings from 2008 to 2020 on facial recognition software deployed for young adult and adolescent populations. The aim is to determine the extent to which tests deem these technologies effective, and the extent to which test design considers potential human factors and inherent ethical issues. The review answers the following questions: How are such applications tested? What are the strengths and weaknesses of test design? And what human factors issues do the tests address or implicate? Facial recognition software for this group primarily used experimental design but failed to meet sampling standards necessary for validating and generalizing findings. The software tested, study design, and topics covered left lingering questions about the potential clinical and ethical applications of the technology. They also overwhelmingly did not address the complexities of facial change over time and ethnicities that confound the accuracy of facial recognition software. Facial recognition bodes promising, but human factors could improve their development.

Keywords: Facial recognition software · Adolescents · Young adults · User experience · Usability · Integrative review

1 Introduction

This integrative review synthesizes research findings from 2008 to 2020 on facial recognition software as it is deployed for young adult and adolescent populations. The aim is to determine the extent to which tests deem these technologies effective, and the extent to which test design considers potential human factors and ethical issues inherent in deployments of the software for this group. The review answers the following questions: How are these applications tested? What are the strengths and weaknesses of test design? And what human factors issues do the tests address or implicate?

The original version of this chapter was revised: caption of table 1 and several mistakes in Sections 2 and 3 have been corrected. The correction to this chapter is available at
https://doi.org/10.1007/978-3-030-77392-2_31

A. Moallem (Ed.): HCII 2021, LNCS 12788, pp. 50–65, 2021.
https://doi.org/10.1007/978-3-030-77392-2_4

1.1 Pervasiveness

Facial recognition software has been deployed to help with the responsibility of supervising adolescents and young adults. Summer camps use apps such as Bunk1 and Waldo Photos, for example, to allow parents to monitor their children's activities each day [1, 2]. Both require parents to upload sample images to provide machine learning algorithms a baseline for recognizing children. Then video sensors positioned around camp allow parents to track their child's activities. Another company released FINE, which the company calls an empathy engine and platform for tracking emotional wellness, even for preteens and teens. FINE, or Feeling Insecure Nervous Emotional, is said to be a technology designed to play an active role in supporting mental wellness by predicting sadness and depression with facial expression and AI and digital technology [3]. In India, to reduce the number of cases of missing or abducted young adults, police recently launched the software to help trace children using public surveillance technology [4]. These applications promise to improve childcare provision, well-being, and education.

1.2 Lingering Questions

Still, questions linger regarding the user experience, legality, and ethics of using the software for monitoring young adults [5]. There are uncertainties about how facial recognition impacts human factors such as infringements on rights, privacy, and liberties and human resources and labor impacted by automation and technologies that perpetuate bias and exclusion. The Federal Trade Commission is considering updates to the online child privacy rules to deem children's faces, voices, and other biometric data as "personal information" protected under Federal law [6]. Questions of ownership pose an ethical challenge. Are voices and faces personal information? The digital and open nature of the internet gives long life and wide dissemination to photos and recordings that can be easily edited, manipulated, and used in unintended ways, such as facial profiling and data mining. When parents voluntarily upload images of children online, they usher them into this complex tangle of problems [7]. Ownership is also a point of contention. Social media companies write transferable, royalty- free, worldwide license to use images as they see fit for as long as they see fit. Facial recognition software combined with corporate data mining might infringe on privacy for children whose images are posted often [8]. These issues require thought and care during the design and testing stages of software.

Take, for example, the case of the New York Police Department, who has used the technology to compare crime scene images with juvenile mugshots for about four years. Per the NYPD, if a positive match is detected, it would not be the sole grounds upon which an arrest is made [9]. Reports suggest that they have done so without full disclosure, oversight, or awareness of civilian and civil rights groups [10]. Other departments and cities have had more public debates over the deployment of facial recognition in this population. The New York State Department of Education delayed for privacy reasons one school district's use of facial recognition in school settings. San Francisco citizens, uneasy about potential abuse, blocked city agencies from using facial recognition. Detroit citizens complain about the accuracy of facial recognition software deployed there, particularly because the software has been shown to have lower accuracy identifying darker skinned subjects [9, 10]. Fears about the accuracy of facial recognition software strain implementation.

What compounds these problems is that technology has a higher risk of false matches in younger faces. The National Institute of Standards and Technology evaluates facial recognition algorithms for accuracy; they reported that several facial recognition algorithms have a higher rate of mistaken matches among children and other subjects across long-term aging, as well as subjects with injuries [11, 12]. The error rate was highest in young children but also noticeable in ages 10 to 16. Photos kept for several years are outdated and might further degrade facial recognition comparisons and accuracy [9, 10]. Children's faces change substantially between ages 10 and 19; facial recognition software must accurately account for rapid development and change in facial features over time [13–15]. Furthermore, the judicial system handles juveniles differently; therefore, a deployment of facial recognition technology must abide long standing differentiations in policy and precedent affording them more privacy and protection than adult suspects [9, 10]. These issues require thorough consideration during the design and testing stages of the product life cycle.

1.3 Answering Questions with User Testing

These lingering questions require attention and answers. User testing is essential for answering such questions. User testing is vital for improving software design. According to the Institute of Electrical and Electronic Engineers (IEEE), post product launch, developers spend 50 percent of their time reworking software to fix problems that could have been avoided by preliminary testing [16]. However, product, usability, and user experience research and testing on products and interventions for children is difficult to design for many reasons. Some studies suggest that children and their parents welcome participation in testing [17]. Motivating factors include benefits for the children, altruism, trust in research, relation to researchers. However, fear of risks, distrust in research, logistical aspects, daily life disruptions, and feeling like a "guinea pig" are deterrents [17]. Populations that are young, less educated, ethnic minorities, and at or below the poverty line also face barriers to participating in testing [18]. Finally, the representativeness and power of the sample size matters in terms of generalizing findings. Some user testing standards suggest that testing five participants can expose many of the problems with software [19, 20]. However, many studies refute this finding by demonstrating that testing five participants does not yield enough prospective problems, nor can it uncover complex problems [21–24]. Furthermore, in terms of making software for clinical, legal, or other applications affecting life and livelihood, a higher standard of sample power including more participants may be required, particularly when necessary for research design, such as in the case of controlled trials and predictive statistical analyses.

2 Methods

An integrative review involves using research databases to compile and synthesize in a systematic way the literature published on a topic. The integrative review allows researchers to integrate both qualitative and quantitative findings [25]. For this integrative review, study characteristics included peer reviewed research articles and excluded theses and books. They also included studies published in English language only published from 2008 to 2020. I searched Scopus, Web of Science, PubMed, ERIC, IEEE Xplore, Springer Link. Science Direct, Google Scholar, ACM, and JSTOR to identify sources, and I was limited by library holdings by way of accessing the full text versions of the articles. Search terms included facial recognition, adolescent, teen, university, student, and young adult (root words). Database previews, article abstracts, and titles were searched and screened for eligibility. Once eligible studies were screened, I read the entire article to discern their content and findings. Articles that did not discuss facial recognition software were eliminated. All paragraphs that developed arguments or main points about ethical dynamics, and their article characteristics, were collected in a spreadsheet for analysis and synthesis. Inductive content analysis was used to identify main findings [26–28]. Inductive content analysis helped reduce and group data to find main insights and findings per article.

3   Results

The studies revealed overall potential for facial recognition deployed in young adult and adolescent populations. However, important limitations persist.

3.1   Included Studies

Table 1 displays a flow chart of included studies. The search yielded 92 studies, most of which were eliminated because they were repeats (n = 29); they did not report findings of facial recognition technology, software, or applications (n = 26); they used numerical validation and did not include in the validation process participants who served as raters (n = 15); they included only a small sample of young adults in a larger sample of older adults (n = 10); or they were not available from the university library (n = 2). Ten studies remained for inclusion in the study.

Table 1. Inclusion/Exclusion.

Criterion	n (92 total)
Repeat or no access	31
No tech or software	26
No participant raters	15
Age range issues	10
Included	10

3.2   Study Participants

Table 2 shows that the articles included a total of 1551 participants ranging in age from newborn to 33. Cohorts and subgroups ranged in size from n = 51 to n = 500. Five of the studies discussed facial recognition as it pertains to identifying medical conditions such as dysmorphia and related disabilities such as autism. Two discussed facial recognition as it pertains to identifying an ethnic group or age estimation [29, 30]. Only one tested this population for educational value [32]. Some included a few participants who were not adolescents or young adults between the ages 10 to 20 [29–31, 33, 34, 36, 38]. Six did not report ethnicity [29, 32–34, 36, 38]. Two included homogeneous samples [29, 37]. See Table 2.

Table 2. Participant demographics.

Authors	Aim	n	Sample
Akinlolu [29]	Ethnic	300	150 males and 150 females, ages 15–33 years
Borges et al. [30]	Biometrics	500	500 F, 500 M, 5 age groups (6, 10, 14, 18, 22 years old). Diverse ancestry
Harley et al. [31]	Age estimate	67	82.1% F. Mean age 21.00 (SD = 1.90). Mean GPA 3.14 (SD = 0.69). White (74.60%). Sr. year (40.30%). Math/engineering (10.4%). Social sciences (21.00%). Sciences (32.80%). Business (9.00%). Arts (7.50%). 54% prior bio experience. Mean pretest 78% (SD = 0.15)
Martinez- Monseny et al. [32]	Learner emotion	57	31 patients (13 females, 18 males; mean age: 11.5 years; SD: 4.7 years; range: 4–19). 26 comparable healthy controls (12 females, 14 males; mean age 9 years; SD 3.8 years; range: 3– 18)
Mishima et al. [33]	Dysmorphia	108	74 patients w/47 congenital dysmorphic syndromes. 34 patients w/Down syndrome. Ages newborn to 25 yrs
Narayanan et al. [34]	Dysmorphia	51	51 patients (28 males, age 11 d-18 y) with a facial phenotype and a proven genetic diagnosis, including 15 with chromosomal abnormalities and 36 with single gene disorders

(*continued*)

Table 2. (*continued*)

Authors	Aim	n	Sample
Novello et al. [35]	Dysmorphia	85	31 photos. 14 males. ages 12 to 20. 4 groups (ages 12– 14, n = 5; 15–16, n = 6; 17–18, n = 8; 19–20, n = 12). Most Caucasian. Black (n = 1), mixed (n = 3). 54 adolescent judges ages 12–17 (M = 14.95, SD = 1.60, 59.3% female) rated photos
Patzelt et al. [36]	Emotion	100	Raters age > 16. 60 women (mean SD 29.3). 40 men (mean SD 26.4). Occupation: DDS n = 31; DStud n = 36; MD n = 14; Stud n = 9; Other n = 10. Visual analog scale
Vorravanpreecha et al. [37]	Attractiveness	170	30 photos of Thai children w/down syndrome age 2 mos-11 yrs. 140 non-DS children (94 unaffected controls; 46 other syndrome controls)
Yitzhak et al. [38]	Disability recognition	113	8 photo actors (four F, ages 24–28). 105 UG raters (73.3% F; median age 23.7; SD ± 2.9)

3.3 Study Methods

See Table 3 for details. Bold indicates the main points of the summary of methods details.

Table 3. Study methods

Authors	Design	Details
Akinlolu [29]	Algorithm training	Akinlolu-Raji **image- processing algorithm** for forensic face recognition developed using a modified row method. Facial width, total face height, short forehead height, long forehead height, upper face height, nasal bridge length, nose height, morphological face height, and lower face height computed
Borges et al. [30]	Experimental design	Frontal facial images acquired. 28 frontal facial **landmarks marked**. 40 features, in relation to landmark distances and the iris diameter, determined the most relevant features for the **classification task**. Receiver operating characteristic (ROC) curves plotted to verify accuracy

(*continued*)

Table 3. (*continued*)

Authors	Design	Details
Harley et al. [31]	Validation study	Videos of facial expressions captured analyzed using automatic **facial recognition software** (FaceReader 5.0, Q- Sensor 2.0). Learners' physiological **arousal was recorded** using Affectiva's Q- Sensor 2.0 electrodermal activity measurement bracelet
Martinez- Monseny et al. [32]	Controlled trial	**Computer-assisted recognition tool trained**. Evaluation of dysmorphic features (DFs). **Simple categorization** correlated w/ clinical, neurological scores & neuroimaging
Mishima et al. [33]	Validation study	Facial photographs uploaded to **software**. Results **compared with** the molecular **diagnosis**
Narayanan et al. [34]	Controlled trial	Annotated age, sex, ethnicity (all Southeast Asian). Uploaded photographs. **2D image analysis** pathway with face detection and discarding background. Measurement of multiple lengths, angles, and ratios between 130 points within the face. Output vectors aggregated for a ranked list of 30 possible **syndrome matches** from most to least likely, based on gestalt and annotated feature scores
Novello et al. [35]	Validation study	Image acquisition 2.5 h each. Photos taken in 23 situations and expression. Expert judges eliminated and rated photos. 101 independent judges rated the pictures' emotion. Microsoft Emotion API rated photos. 54 adolescent judges rated photos
Patzelt et al. [36]	Validation study	**PhotoGenic** evaluated attractiveness. **Statistics** estimated participant attractiveness scores
Vorravanpreecha et al. [37]	Controlled trial	**Face detection** and discarding background, followed by **measurement of multiple variables** (lengths, angles, and ratios) between 130 points within the face. Aggregated for ranked list of 30 possible syndrome matches
Yitzhak et al. [38]	Validation study	**Software classifier** and raters shown emotional photos. **Ratings and agreement** analyzed using statistical methods

Table 3 summarizes study methods. Four used experimental design where they tested subgroups and controls [30, 32, 34, 37]. Five were validation studies testing software performance and accuracy as it pertains to actual diagnoses or conditions, particularly comparing human versus computer ratings [31, 33, 35, 36, 38]. Measurements included six studies that tracked some form of internal validity to evaluate identification effectiveness or accuracy [29, 30, 32, 34, 36, 37]. Four tracked external validity by way of human raters, physiological response, or other external data point [31, 33, 35, 38].

Although all studies collected their own prospective archives of images to test, six studies were retrospective, insofar as it included applications that used preexisting databases images [31–34, 36, 37].

Two of the studies tested proprietary software [31, 36]. Two acquired their own images rather than use preexisting data sets [34, 35]. Four studies reported training processes in addition to running accuracy tests [30, 32, 34, 37]. And two enlisted human coders alongside software codes for validation [35, 38].

3.4 Study Findings

Table 4 presents study findings. All studies found some degree of accuracy. More points of comparison increased accuracy [30, 32]. However, some studies reported problems

with performance, such as inability to generalize sub-samples due to insufficient variability and distinctiveness for the features [29, 38], facial features and parameters that
yielded insignificant differentiation [32], false positives and negatives, as well as unde-
tected positives [31, 33, 34, 37]. None of the articles that tested apps factored usability or
the user experience or satisfaction into the analysis. None of the studies considered the
ethics of the applications. None of the studies discussing possible medical applications
discussed the ethics of such applications for diagnoses. None of the studies requested
user feedback from the industries that might use the software, nor did they consult participants in the age group in question or ask them about the usability, user experience,
or ethics of the proposed applications. Two studies factored facial change over time into
the software evaluation and analysis [30, 34].

Overall, all studies reported that the software had capability for high discrimination,
but with wide variability. Software ranged from 50% to 98% accurate or more accurate
than another software in comparison [30, 32–34, 36]. Results reveal that the more features
under consideration, the better [30]. But the studies show how facial recognition proved
less accurate in same sex samples and samples of small age range [39]. Examination of
some facial features proved more accurate than others [32]. Some forms of dysmorphia
were harder to detect than others [33]. Some software was more accurate than others
and less accurate than human coding [31, 35]. Some software was deemed inaccurate
about a fourth of the time and inconsistent with human coders [34, 36].

Table 4. Study findings.

Authors	Findings
Akinlolu [29]	**Quantitative**: Selected proportions were more discriminative for younger ages (i.e. < 10, and < 14), than for < 18. High values in all. Dividing the samples to classify approaching in separate only males (500) or females (500), or yet in short intervals ($6 < $ age < 10, $10 < $ age < 14, $14 < $ age < 18, $18 < $ age < 22) dropped accuracy 22% on average for the new classes. **Qualitative**: None.
Borges et al. [30]	**Quantitative**: 68-pt caricatures $=$ significant improvements in identity discrimination relative to veridical. About 50% as effective as the 147-pt caricatures. **Qualitative**: None
Harley et al. [31]	**Qualitative**: High agreement btwn facial & self-report data (75.6%). Low btwn facial & Q-Sensor data. Tightly coupled relationship does not always exist btwn emotional response components. **Qualitative**: None

(*continued*)

Table 4. (*continued*)

Authors	Findings
Martinez- Monseny et al. [32]	**Quantitative**: Statistically nonsignificant lower mean value (P > 0.05) in 12.5% of parameters. Lower face height in Yoruba males compared to females. Higher % ratios of long forehead height & nose height to total face height. Lower % ratio of lower face height to total face height in males compared to females. FI = 91.8 in males & 91.4 in females. **Qualitative**: None
Mishima et al. [33]	**Quantitative**: Failed 4/74 dysmorphia pts. 13–21 of 70 dysmorphia pts wrong trained. For 85.7% (42/49) the correct syndrome was identified within the top 10 list. Down syndrome (DS) highest-ranking condition for youngest (newborn to 25) facial images of DS patients. For DS pts 20 or older, it ranked first or second highest DS 82.2% (14/17) & 100% (17/17) of the pts using images taken from 20 to 40 years. **Qualitative**: None
Narayanan et al. [34]	**Quantitative**: Software = correct diagnoses for 37 pts (72.5%). Predicted top 10 evals (70.2%). 14 patients (27%). No correct diagnosis. **Qualitative**: None
Novello et al. [35]	**Quantitative**: Expert & adolescent judges agreed 100%. Independent judges, 75.9% (fear)-98% (happiness). Software accurately identified all but one. SD = 0.04 (happiness) to SD = 10.07 (disgust). **Qualitative**: None
Patzelt et al. [36]	**Quantitative**: PhotoGenic mean SD attractiveness score: 6.4 ± 1.2 (6.3 ± 0.8 smiling, 6.6 ± 1.5 neutral). Raters mean SD score was 4.9 ± 1.8 (4.9 ± 1.9 smiling), 4.8 ± 1.8 neutral. Overall diff. 1.6 ± 0.4 (P < .001). **Qualitative**: None
Vorravanpreecha et al. [37]	**Quantitative**: All 30 DS = DS in the top 10 matches. 27 in the first ranking. 18 non-DS recognized as DS. **Qualitative**: None
Yitzhak et al. [38]	**Quantitative**: Software classified prototypical expressions. Poor w/subtle expressions. Human expert face coders validated. Subtle stimuli lacked sufficient facial details. Agreement: 0.63, 0.79 & 0.70. **Qualitative**: None

3.5 Study Limitations

The studies considered their own limitations and potential for future work. The studies made calls for additional variables and conditions [29, 31, 35–38], larger and more complex samples [30, 33–35], time frame adjustments [31, 32], clinician involvement [33, 34], and more sample integrity and control [32, 33] (Table 5).

One study [35] factored in participant fatigue and rater protocol design as a limitation. The same study was the only one to mention racial homogeneity as a limitation. One study [37] also warned that clinician expertise is crucial in using the software. They also admitted their own limitations such as small sample size [30, 33–36], limitations of detection and reliability [29, 32, 36, 37], limitations factoring in context of facial expressions [31, 38], and archive quality [33, 35, 38]. Only one admitted the limitation of sample homogeneity [35]. Only three studies reported adverse events [35] or controversies using facial recognition for the intended purposes [36, 37].

Table 5. Study limitations.

Authors	Future work	Limitations
Akinlolu [29]	Biological determination of ancestral origins might provide definitive and representative anthropometric data of Nigerian ethnic groups and help determine the true nature of the heterogeneity, ethnic diversity	Biological determination of ancestral origins of subjects was not included
Borges et al. [30]	Further studies with more data of individuals (males and females balanced) in shorter (e.g., one and two years) intervals of age	Larger samples are necessary to evaluate reliability
Harley et al. [31]	Use additional physiological, behavioral modalities (e.g., heart rate and posture). In more high-stakes or engaging environments that elicit higher arousal levels. Use multi- level modeling to examine agreement over time	Contextual limitations on EDA levels and potential appraisals of task value
Martinez- Monseny et al. [32]	Longitudinal samples to confirm whether, in severe groups, lipodystrophy and inverted nipples, neurological involvement will be greater	No patients with the same pair of pathogenic variants. Unclear impact of presence of polymorphisms in other genes
Mishima et al. [33]	Consultation with clinical geneticists is essential	Sample size and quality control of facial images. Lack of info about the Face2Gene internal training data set
Narayanan et al. [34]	Deep phenotyping for next generation sequencing era to help classification of variants and clinical significance	Descriptive and limited in terms of the number of patients

(*continued*)

Table 5. (*continued*)

Authors	Future work	Limitations
Novello et al. [35]	Determine if specific characteristics mean greater expressiveness. Increase the number of posing individuals and phenomenological diversity. More ambiguous pictures	Similar videos for younger and older teens. Volunteer fatigue. Forced- choice options, filtering, and prototypical expressions might have inflated accuracy rates. Racial diversity difficult to meet
Patzelt et al. [36]	Further studies with larger sample sizes and different ages, occupations, and ethnicities. Measure influence of skin color pigmentation, and makeup	The reliability of attractiveness evaluation has been controversial. Small sample size of only 10 participants and 100 raters
Vorravanpreecha et al. [37]	Further studies on other genetic syndromes/ethnicities being identified by software algorithms	App cannot replace clinicians' knowledge. Not a replacement for a well-trained clinician
Yitzhak et al. [38]	More exact cues for recognizing subtle, malleable, non- prototypical expressions. Dynamic information	Actors re-enacted. Emotions and not spontaneous expressions. Isolated faces not real-life expressions with body and voice

3.6   Study Quality

Reporting quality was low in most of the studies. All were missing some form of information or another, such as follows: approval by ethics, human subjects, or institutional review board committees [29, 31]; sufficient demographic details about exact numbers of participants per age group [29–31, 33, 36, 38] or ethnicity [29, 32–34, 36, 38]; and information about conflicts of interest or acknowledgment of funding and participant contribution [36, 38]. The articles had a relatively high field-weighted citation impact (FWCI). The global mean of the FWCI is 1.0. Therefore, an FWCI of 1.50 means that the article was cited 50% more than the world average. The articles ranged from 0 to 4.43 FWCI. However, most of the articles were cited rarely (0 to 9 times). One was cited often and had a high FWCI [31]. Two studies did not publish photos of young adults and adolescents from their samples [31, 37]. Two included photos with some facial parts redacted or cropped [29, 32]. Most of the studies included full photos of the faces of young adults and adolescents with no redacting [30, 32–36, 38]. Five of the studies were published in ethnically diverse countries, relatively speaking, including the United States [35–38] and India [34]. Others were published in relatively ethnically homogeneous countries. See Table 6.

Table 6. Study quality.

Authors	IRB	FWCI	Cite	Country	CoI	Photos
Akinlolu [29]	No	0	0	Taiwan	Yes	Redact
Borges et al. [30]	Yes	1.2	4	Netherlands	Yes	Full
Harley et al. [31]	No	4.43	71	UK	Yes	None
Martinez- Monseny et al. [32]	Yes	1.6	4	UK	Yes	Redact
Mishima et al. [33]	Yes	3.34	8	Germany	Yes	Full
Narayanan et al. [34]	Yes	0.94	1	India	Yes	Full
Novello et al. [35]	Yes	1.25	5	US	Yes	Full
Patzelt et al. [36]	Yes	0	1	US	No	Full
Vorravanpreecha et al. [37]	Yes	1.33	8	US	Yes	None
Yitzhak et al. [38]	Yes	1.37	9	US	No	Full

4 Conclusion

This integrative review revealed that the field sorely needs much more research into facial recognition software for young adults and adolescents. Facial recognition software often used experimental design but failed to meet sampling standards necessary for validating and generalizing findings. The software tested, study design, and topics covered left lingering questions about the potential clinical and social applications of the technology. They also overwhelmingly did not address the complexities of facial change over time that confounds the accuracy of facial recognition software. Study design yielded retrospective and confirmatory findings, insofar as the facial recognition software was mostly deployed to predict pre-existing diagnoses and ethnicities. However, the literature did not specify to what end facial recognition software would be deployed prescriptively, nor did it sufficiently address the ethical challenges that practical applications present.

Of the peer-reviewed articles making some reference to the subject matter, only a few provided relevant and sufficient detail. Of the studies that met inclusion criteria, the combined sample of 1551 participants could not undergo rigorous meta-analysis because insufficient reporting of details about the exact numbers of participants in key subgroups. Furthermore, samples were often homogeneous, thereby making it difficult to generalize the findings beyond the relatively small subsets of subgroups included in the studies. These factors are important to consider because they impact the extent to which findings can be safely and reliably generalized. Therefore, while all studies reported moderate to high levels of facial recognition accuracy, the small sample size and (in two cases) lack of experimental design preclude generalizing those accuracy measures to the larger population. Furthermore, limitations of testing design also call into question the validity of the accuracy findings themselves. If the findings are indicative of the small participant sample, then the findings cannot account for the myriad variations and differentiations present in the general population. This finding is important because five of the studies covered medical and social topics such as disability and ethnicity, where generalizations made from poorly designed tests may find their way into clinical practice and political policy that might negatively impact young adults and adolescents. What were reported as marginal or insignificant percentages of false positives and false negatives, when tabulated across the general population, might negatively impact hundreds of thousands of lives.

Other aspects of research design also posed a problem. Most samples were ethnically homogeneous. On one hand, homogeneous studies of non-white ethnic groups were meant as a corrective to studies of facial recognition software originally tested on white participants, which skewed the accuracy and reliability toward white populations and, on the other side, skewed false positives and false negatives toward populations of color. On the other hand, only a few studies included participants with darker skin. More research is needed that investigates the interaction of the two most common confounders as it pertains to facial recognition software: different shades of skin and facial change over time. No studies testing products currently on the market included user experience or usability research. Such feedback would be important for selecting and confirming test design. Studies where facial recognition was deployed to identify disability were designed retrospectively, wherein prior diagnoses were obtained and used to confirm computer diagnoses. Application for prospective diagnoses may not be prudent, given this limitation. User experience and usability feedback can give a more well-rounded and evidence-based picture of potential applications. It would strengthen and make more ethical and reliable findings that integrate feedback from the clinicians and patient populations whose lives and practice would be impacted by the software.

Some aspects of the ethics of study reporting were also questionable. Although 8 of the 10 studies did seek and obtain approval by institutional review boards or ethics committees, as well as acknowledgements and conflicts of interest, most of the studies presented several full photos of the faces of young adults and adolescents with no redacting. Technically, publishing the photos might have been permitted by the IRB, and they also might have been approved by the participants or the participants' care providers themselves. Even in this case, the aggregation of facial photos, particularly in the case of participants with visible disabilities, presented the possibility of readers being able to use Google Photo or other image search tools to reverse engineer these photos and find the identities of these young adults and adolescents. Visual research ethical guidelines recommend that researchers anonymize and redact photos as much as possible in ways that protect the personal information of participants [40, 41]. Visual research ethical guidelines also consider people's faces and voices as their personal information, given the fact that digital files make compromising identity easier. Visual research ethical guidelines also recommend that images of vulnerable populations such as adolescents be protected further behind firewalls that require verification to access. In the past, aggregating and reducing people by physical features for the purpose of categorizing differences in them without taking care to protect their personhood, volition, and autonomy have been used for pernicious and unethical ends, such as eugenics and race science [43–46]. Therefore, it is important to conduct and report research in this area in ways that respect participants as much as possible.

Overall, there is some potential for facial recognition products for young adults and adolescents, particularly for medical purposes. The aggregate data across 1551 participants found that facial recognition software exhibited some degree of internal and external validity by comparison to prior diagnoses. However, external validity was rarely established between software and human raters, which would provide more verisimilitude. Furthermore, human raters of all expertise (from young adults themselves to the teachers and clinicians who will use the software) should also be enlisted to provide usability and user experience feedback, which none of the studies gathered. Asking users and samples of target populations about the ethical and practical implications of the software could improve design. The studies show how more variables help with software accuracy. Varying study design to include more longitudinal controlled trials as well as user experience research might render the studies more reliable and citable in the research community. More studies are in order that investigate more complex variables and more attention paid to facial change over time and differences in ethnicity. Future studies should avoid existing study limitations, such as small and homogeneous samples and protocols that fatigue participants or bias raters. Finally, future studies should take more care in reporting sufficient details for replication, validation, and syntheses by systematic and integrative reviews.

Acknowledgments. The project was funded by the NEC Foundation.

References

1. Barrett, L.: Ban facial recognition technologies for children-and for everyone else. BUJ Sci. Tech. L. **26**, 223 (2020)
2. Cushing, T.: They Grow Up So Fast These Days: Facial Recognition. Tech Edition, Techdirt (2019). https://www.techdirt.com/articles/20190803/19564942711/they- grow-up-so-fast-these-days-facial- recognition-tech-edition.shtml, Accessed 1 July 2020
3. GlobalLogic, Inc.: Method Introduces FINE Empathy Engine: A Platform for Tracking Emotional Wellness (2018). https://www.businesswire.com/news/home/20181002005412/en/Method-Introduces-FINE-Empathy-Engine-Platform-Tracking. Accessed 1 July 2020
4. Shrangi, V., Shahba, D.N.: Police data reveals the most unsafe areas for kids in Delhi. Hindustan Times, 26 November 2018. https://www.hindustantimes.com/delhi-news/police-data-reveals-the-most-unsafe-areas-for-kids-in-delhi/story-bsfyZ6sUqCvyN3n4uE. Accessed 1 July 2020
5. De La Garza, A.: Meet the researchers working to make sure artificial intelligence is a force for good. time, 23 August 2019. https://time.com/5659788/ai-good/. Accessed 1 July 2020
6. Brown, N., Blickensderfer, S.: Even the Games Have Eyes: Data Privacy and Gaming. The National Law Review, 13 March 2019. https://www.natlawreview.com/article/even-games-have-eyes-data-privacy-and-gaming-podcast. Accessed 1 July 2020
7. Kruzel, J.: Language Bullies, Obama's Syria Problem, and RG3. Slate (2013). https://slate.com/news-and-politics/2013/09/language-bullies-onion-humor-and-rg3-the-weeks-most-interesting-slate-stories.html, Accessed 1 July 2020
8. Evans, S. From the baby book to Facebook. Mail & Guardian (2014). https://mg.co.za/article/2014-12-22-from-the-baby-book-to-facebook/, Accessed 1 July 2020
9. Goldstein, J., Watkins, A.: She Was Arrested at 14. Then Her Photo Went to a Facial Recognition. New York Times (2019)

10. Goldstein J., Watkins A.: In New York, Police Computers Scan Faces, Some as Young as 11. New York Times, 2 August 2019. https://blendle.com/i/the-new-york-times/in-new-york-police-computers-scan-faces-some-as-young-as-11/bnl-newyorktimes-20190802–1_6. Accessed 2 July 2020
11. Grother, K. P., Ngan, M., Hanaoka, K.: Ongoing face recognition vendor test (FRVT). National Institute of Standards and Technology (2018). https://nvlpubs.nist.gov/nistpubs/ir/2018/NIST. IR.8238.pdf. Accessed 1 July 2020
12. Grother, K.P., Ngan, M., Hanaoka, K.: Ongoing face recognition vendor test (FRVT). national Institute of Standards and Technology (2019). https://www.nist.gov/system/files/documents/ 2019/11/20/frvt_report_2019_11_19_0.pdf. Accessed 01 July 2020
13. Bishara, S.E.: Facial and dental changes in adolescents and their clinical implications. Angle Orthodontist **70**(6), 471–483 (2000)
14. Suri, S., Ross, R.B., Tompson, B.D.: Craniofacial morphology and adolescent facial growth in Pierre Robin sequence. Am. J. Orthod. Dentofac. Orthop. **137**(6), 763–774 (2010)
15. Darwis, W. E., Messer, L. B., Thomas, C.D.: Assessing growth and development of the facial profile. Pediatric Dentistry **25**(2), 103–108 (2003)
16. Charette, R.N.: Why software fails [software failure]. IEEE Spectrum 42(9), 42-49 (2005)(2003).
17. Tromp, K., Zwaan, C., van de Vathorst, S.: Motivations of children and their parents to participate in drug research: a systematic review. Eur. J. Pediatrics **175**(5), 599–612 (2016). https://doi.org/10.1007/s00431-016-2715-9
18. Robinson, L., Adair, P., Coffey, M., Harris, R., Burnside, G.: Identifying the participant characteristics that predict recruitment and retention of participants to RCTs involving children: a systematic review. Trials **17**(1), 1–17 (2016)
19. Nielsen, J.: How many test users in a usability study. Nielsen Norman Group, 4(06) (2012). https://www.nngroup.com/articles/how-many-test-users/#:~:text=If%20you% 20want%20a%20single,users%20in%20a%20usability%20study. Accessed 1 July 2020
20. Nielsen, J., Landauer, T.K.: A mathematical model of the finding of usability problems. In: Proceedings of the INTERACT 1993 and CHI'93 Conference on Human factors in computing systems, pp. 206–213, May 1993
21. Faulkner, L.: Beyond the five-user assumption: Benefits of increased sample sizes in usability testing. Behav. Res. Methods, Instrum. Comput. **35**(3), 379–383 (2003)
22. Perfetti, C., Landesman, L.: Eight is not enough. Center UIE, 19 June 2001. https://articles. uie.com/eight_is_not_enough/. Accessed 1 July 2020
23. Spool, J., Schroeder, W.: Testing web sites: Five users is nowhere near enough. CHI'01 extended abstracts on Human factors in computing systems, pp. 285- 286 2001, March).
24. Virzi, R.A.: Refining the test phase of usability evaluation: how many subjects is enough? Hum. Factors **34**(4), 457–468 (1992)
25. Whittemore, R., Knafl, K.: The integrative review: updated methodology. J. Adv. Nurs. **52**(5), 546–553 (2005)
26. Waldherr, A., Wehden, L. O., Stoltenberg, D., Miltner, P., Ostner, S., Pfetsch, B.: Inductive codebook development for content analysis: Combining automated and manual methods. In: Forum Qualitative Sozialforschung/Forum: Qualitative Social Research, vol. 20(1), January 2019
27. Kyngäs, H.: Inductive content analysis. the Application of Content Analysis in Nursing Science Research, pp. 13–21. Springer, Cham (2020)
28. Vears, D.: Gillam, L: The boundaries of inductive content analysis: where are they and why does it matter? Int. J. Qualit. Methods **15**(1), 13–21 (2016)
29. Akinlolu, A.A.: Facial biometrics of Yorubas of Nigeria using Akinlolu-Raji image-processing algorithm. J. Med. Sci. **36**(2), 39 (2016)

30. Borges, D.L., Vidal, F.B., Flores, M.R., Melani, R.F., Guimar, M.A., Machado, C.E.: Photoanthropometric face iridial proportions for age estimation: an investigation using features selected via a joint mutual information criterion. Forensic Sci. Int. **284**, 9–14 (2018)
31. Harley, J.M., Bouchet, F., Hussain, M.S., Azevedo, R., Calvo, R.: A multi- componential analysis of emotions during complex learning with an intelligent multi- agent system. Comput. Hum. Behav. **48**, 615–625 (2015)
32. Martinez-Monseny, A., et al.: From gestalt to gene: early predictive dysmorphic features of PMM2-CDG. J. Med. Genetics **56**(4), 236–245 (2019)
33. Mishima, H., et al.: Evaluation of Face2Gene using facial images of patients with congenital dysmorphic syndromes recruited in Japan. J. Hum. Genetics **64**(8), 789–794 (2019)
34. Narayanan, D.L., Ranganath, P., Aggarwal, S., Dalal, A., Phadke, S.R., Mandal, K.: Computer-aided facial analysis in diagnosing dysmorphic syndromes in Indian children. Indian Pediatrics **56**(12), 1017–1019 (2019)
35. Novello, B., Renner, A., Maurer, G., Musse, S., Arteche, A.: Development of the youth emotion picture set. Perception **47**(10–11), 1029–1042 (2018)
36. Patzelt, S. B., Schaible, L. K., Stampf, S., Kohal, R. J.: Software-based evaluation of human age: a pilot study. J. Esthetic Restorative Dentistry **27**(2), 100–110 (2015)
37. Vorravanpreecha, N., Lertboonnum, T., Rodjanadit, R., Sriplienchan, P., Rojnueangnit, K.: Studying Down syndrome recognition probabilities in Thai children with de-identified computer-aided facial analysis. Am. J. Med. Genet. Part A **176**(9), 1935–1940 (2018)
38. Vorravanpreecha, N., Lertboonnum, T., Rodjanadit, R., Sriplienchan, P., Rojnueangnit,
39. Yitzhak, N., et al.: Gently does it: humans outperform a software classifier in recognizing subtle, nonstereotypical facial expressions. Emotion **17**(8), 1187 (2017)
40. Emmison, M., Smith, P., Mayall, M.: Ethics in visual rhetoric. Researching the Visual. Sage, pp. 7–17 (2014)
41. Cox, S., Drew, S., Guillemin, M., Howell, C., Warr, D., Waycott, J.: Guidelines for Ethical Visual Research Methods. The University of Melbourne (2014). https://vrc.org.au/guidelines-for-ethical-visual-research-methods
42. Elks, M.A.: Three illusions in clinical photographs of the feeble-minded during the eugenics era. In: The Routledge History of Disability, pp. 394–420. Routledge (2017)
43. Elks, M.A.: Visual rhetoric: photographs of the feeble-minded during the eugenics era, 1900–1930 (1992)
44. Ehret, U.: Catholicism and Judaism in the catholic defense against Alfred Rosenberg, 1934–1938: anti-jewish images in an age of race science. Eur. Hist. Quart. **40**(1), 35–56 (2010)
45. Bogdan, R.: Citizen Portraits: Photos of People with Disabilities as Personal keepsakes. In: Introduction to Qualitative Research Methods, pp. 289–311, Wiley (2016)
46. Hodl, K.: The Black body and the Jewish body: a comparison of medical images. Patterns Prejudice **36**(1), 17–34 (2002)

Eye Gaze and Interaction Differences of Holistic Versus Analytic Users in Image-Recognition Human Interaction Proof Schemes

Pantelitsa Leonidou[1], Argyris Constantinides[1,2], Marios Belk[1,3(✉)], Christos Fidas[4], and Andreas Pitsillides[1]

[1] University of Cyprus, Nicosia, Cyprus
{pleoni02,cspitsil}@cs.ucy.ac.cy
[2] Cognitive UX Ltd., Nicosia, Cyprus
argyris@cognitiveux.com
[3] Cognitive UX GmbH, Heidelberg, Germany
belk@cognitiveux.com
[4] University of Patras, Patras, Greece
fidas@upatras.gr

Abstract. Image-recognition Human Interaction Proof (HIP) schemes are widely used security defense mechanisms that are utilized by service providers to determine whether a human user is interacting with their system and not malicious software. Inspired by recent research, which underpins the necessity for designing user-centered HIPs, this paper examines, in the frame of an accredited cognitive style theory (Field Dependence-Independence – FD-I), whether human cognitive differences in visual information processing affect users' visual behavior when interacting with an image-recognition HIP challenge. For doing so, we conducted an eye tracking study ($n = 46$) in which users solved an image-recognition HIP challenge. Analysis of users' interactions and eye gaze data revealed differences in users' visual behavior and interactions between Holistic and Analytic users within image-recognition HIP tasks. Findings underpin the added value of considering users' cognitive processing differences in the design of adaptive and adaptable HIP security schemes.

Keywords: Image-recognition CAPTCHA · Human interaction proof schemes · Human cognitive differences · Eye tracking study

1 Introduction

Human Interaction Proof (HIP) schemes (or Completely Automated Public Turing Test to tell Computers and Humans Apart - CAPTCHA) are common and widely used security defense mechanisms in online services [1]. HIP schemes require users to prove that a human user is interacting with the system and not a malicious software through a challenge-response test, aiming to keep online services protected from malicious automated software agents [2]. The design of an efficient and effective HIP scheme is an

© Springer Nature Switzerland AG 2021
A. Moallem (Ed.): HCII 2021, LNCS 12788, pp. 66–75, 2021.
https://doi.org/10.1007/978-3-030-77392-2_5

inevitable tradeoff between usability and security. Increasing the HIP's challenge difficulty leads to improved security of the mechanism, however, usability is significantly decreased [3, 4, 24, 30]. Therefore, numerous works focused on providing a better tradeoff between usability and security of these mechanisms [24–36]. Current HIP implementations can be broadly categorized as *text-recognition HIP schemes*, which require users to recognize a set of distorted textual characters, and *image-recognition HIP schemes*, which require users to solve image puzzle problems (*e.g.*, identify a set of images among a larger set) [5].

Nowadays, one of the most commonly used HIP schemes is Google's reCAPTCHA (Fig. 1) [6], which aims to minimize users' cognitive burden through implicit user interaction data collection methods. In particular, the mechanism uses intelligent techniques to analyze the users' interaction data on a given Website to implicitly infer that a human interacts with the service without asking the user to solve a challenge-response test. Nonetheless, in cases in which the mechanism is not confident on the data accuracy, a fallback image-recognition task must be solved by the user. This fallback task typically splits an image into a 3 × 3 grid, and asks the user to select the segments of the grid that contains the requested information (*e.g.*, cars, traffic lights, cats, etc.).

Fig. 1. Google's reCAPTCHA [6] mechanism.

Research Motivation. From a cognitive processing perspective, the image-recognition HIP task requires visual information processing, and research indicates individual differences in such information processing, which suggest that individuals have an inherent and preferred mode of processing information either *holistically (globally)* or *analytically (locally)* [9, 10]. Among a plethora of cognitive processing differences theories, this work focuses on the field dependence-independence cognitive style theory [10], which is an accredited and widely applied model [11–15] that highlights human cognitive differences into *Field Dependent (or Holistic)* and *Field Independent (or Analytic)*. Evidence suggests that Holistic and Analytic individuals have differences in visual perception and visual information processing [7, 10–15]. While Holistic individuals view the perceptual field as a whole and are not attentive to detail, Analytic individuals view the information presented by their visual field as a collection of parts and tend to experience items as separate from their backgrounds.

Given that such human cognitive differences exist, we believe that current "one-size-fits-all" approaches employed in image-recognition fallback HIP schemes might favor a certain type of cognitive style group (Holistic *vs.* Analytic). Hence, in this paper, we investigate whether human cognitive differences of visually processing information influence users' visual behavior when interacting with an image-recognition HIP task. For doing so, we conducted an eye tracking study ($n = 46$) in which users solved an image-recognition HIP task. Analysis of results revealed several main effects of human cognitive differences towards user interaction and visual behavior in image-recognition HIP schemes.

2 User Study

2.1 Research Questions

RQ_1. Are there differences in time to solve the image-recognition HIP challenge between Holistic and Analytic users?
RQ_2. Are there differences in time to explore the image-recognition HIP between Holistic and Analytic users?
RQ_3. Are there differences in users' visual behavior while exploring and solving the image-recognition HIP challenge between Holistic and Analytic users?

2.2 Study Instruments

Image-Recognition HIP Mechanism. We developed a Web-based image-recognition HIP mechanism (Fig. 2), in which an image is segmented in a grid of 3×3 smaller parts. The instructions of the task are displayed above the grid and the submit button is displayed below the grid. Users are asked to select all squares that contain the requested information (*e.g.*, a window) in order to solve the challenge. Then, users are requested to click on the submit button to validate their solution. If the provided solution is incorrect, an error message is displayed to instruct users to retry.

Apparatus. The study was conducted using an All-in-One HP personal computer with a 24" monitor at a screen resolution of 1920×1080 pixels. To capture the eye gaze metrics, we used the Gazepoint GP3 video-based eye tracker [16]. No equipment was attached to the participants.

Eye Gaze Metrics. Following common practices, we selected fixation count as suggested in [8, 17], which is the total number of fixations during which the eyes of a user focus on a certain item within the surroundings.

Human Cognitive Factor Elicitation. Users' holistic and analytic characteristics were measured through the Group Embedded Figures Test (GEFT) [18], which is a widely accredited and validated paper-and-pencil test [11–15]. The test measures the user's ability to find common geometric shapes in a larger design. The GEFT consists of 25 items. In each item, a simple geometric figure is embedded within a complex pattern, and participants are required to identify the simple figure by drawing it with a pencil over the complex figure. Based on a widely applied cut-off score, participants that solve less than 12 items are considered to have a holistic cognitive style, while participants that solve greater than or equal to 12 items are considered to have an analytic cognitive style.

Fig. 2. An example image-recognition HIP challenge.

2.3   Sampling and Procedure

Participants. We recruited 46 participants that were undergraduate university students. We note that two users were outliers and did not have sufficient eye tracking measures, and were thus excluded from the analysis, resulting in a final dataset of 44 users. To increase the internal validity of the study, we recruited participants that had no prior experience with image-recognition HIP schemes, as assessed by a post-study interview.

Experimental Design and Procedure. We adopted the University's human research protocol that takes into consideration users' privacy, confidentiality and anonymity. All participants performed the task in a quiet lab room with only the researcher present. To avoid any experimental bias effects, no details regarding the research objective were revealed to the participants until the end of the study. The user study involved the following steps: *i*) participants were informed that the data collected during interaction with the HIP mechanism would be stored anonymously and would be used only for research purposes; *ii*) users signed a consent form and completed a questionnaire on demographics; *iii*) an eye-calibration process followed; and *iv*) participants were then requested to solve an image-recognition HIP challenge in order to access an online service. Aiming to increase ecological validity of the user study, we applied the HIP challenge as a secondary task of user interaction. Finally, a post-study interview was conducted to get further insights on the users' interactions and experiences with the HIP scheme.

3   Analysis of Results

Data are mean ± standard deviation, unless otherwise stated. There were two significant outliers in the data that were excluded from the analysis, as assessed by inspection of a boxplot. Figures 3, 4 and 5 illustrate the summary of results; the times to solve the image-based challenge, the times to explore the image-based challenge, and the number of fixations during user interaction with the image-based challenge respectively.

3.1   Differences in Time to the Solve Image-Recognition HIP Challenge Between Holistic and Analytic Users

To investigate RQ_1, an independent-samples t-test was run to determine if there were differences in time to solve the HIP task between Holistic and Analytic users (Fig. 3). There was homogeneity of variances, as assessed by Levene's test for equality of variances ($p = .058$). Results revealed that Analytic users needed more time to solve the HIP task (9.78 ± 5.45 s) than Holistic users (8.3 ± 3.6 s), however this difference was not statistically significant with a difference of 1.47 s (95% CI, −4.25 to 1.29), $t(42) = -1.077, p = .28$.

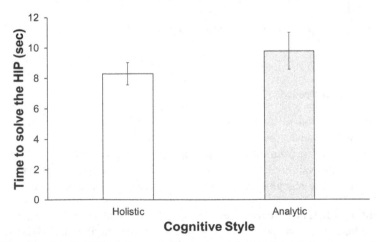

Fig. 3. Time to solve the HIP challenge indicating a tendency of Analytic users requiring more time to solve the challenge compared to Holistic users.

3.2 Differences in Time to Visually Explore the Image During Solving the Image-Recognition HIP Challenge Between Holistic and Analytic Users

To investigate RQ_2, an independent-samples t-test was run to determine if there were differences in time to visually explore the image between Holistic and Analytic users (Fig. 4). There was homogeneity of variances, as assessed by Levene's test for equality of variances ($p = .246$). In line with time to solve, results revealed that Analytic users spent more time to explore the image (7.33 ± 4.09 s) than Holistic users (5.19 ± 2.95 s), a statistically significant difference of 2.13 s (95% CI, -4.28 to 10.75), $t(42) = -2.008$, $p = .051$.

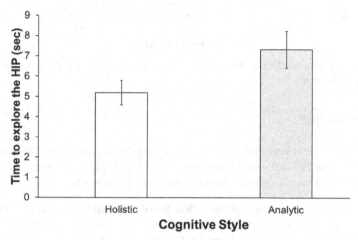

Fig. 4. Time to explore the HIP challenge indicating that Analytic users require more time to visually explore the challenge compared to Holistic users.

3.3 Differences in Eye Gaze Behavior During Solving the Image-Recognition HIP Challenge Between Holistic and Analytic Users

To investigate RQ_3, we conducted two analyses with the number of total fixations and number of revisits on fixations as the dependent variables. We first investigated whether there were differences in total number of fixations between Holistic and Analytic users (Fig. 5). A Welch test was run due to the assumption of homogeneity of variances being violated ($p = .001$). Results revealed that Analytic users generated more fixations while exploring the image (29.45 ± 14.31) than Holistic users (20.2 ± 6.48), a statistically significant difference of 9.24 (95% CI, -15.81 to -2.66), $t(25.448) = -2.669, p = .013$. We further run a Welch t-test to determine if there were differences in number of AOI (Areas of Interest) revisits between Holistic and Analytic users due to the assumption of homogeneity of variances being violated ($p < .001$). Results revealed that Analytic users had more AOI revisits while exploring the image (17.65 ± 10.84) than Holistic users 10.12 ± 4.36, a statistically significant difference of 7.52 (95% CI, -12.4 to -2.64), $t(24.114) = -2.911, p = .008$.

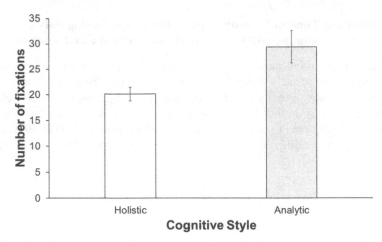

Fig. 5. Number of generated fixations indicating that Analytic users produce significantly more fixations than Holistic users.

4 Main Findings

The analysis of results revealed several main effects of human cognitive differences (holistic *vs.* analytic) towards user interaction and visual behavior of image-recognition HIP schemes. Next, we summarize the main findings of the study.

Finding A. Analytic users required more time to solve the image-recognition HIP challenge compared to Holistic users (95% CI, -4.25 to 1.29; $t(42) = -077, p = .28$), which can be attributed to their analytical approach in information processing since Analytic users visually explored and processed more attention points compared to the Holistic users.

Finding B. Analytic users spent significantly more time to visually explore the image-recognition HIP challenge compared to Holistic users (95% CI, -4.28 to 10.75; $t(42) = -2.008, p = .051$). Such a finding is in line with [11], which suggested similar effects in image-recognition graphical authentication schemes.

Finding C. Analytic users fixated cumulatively on more attention points (95% CI, -15.81 to -2.66; $t(25.448) = -2.669, p = .013$) and had a significantly higher fixation count on attention point revisits than Holistic users (95% CI, -12.4 to -2.64), $t(24.114) = -2.911, p = .008$). This can be explained by their analytical approach in visual information processing, and hence generated more fixations than Holistic users who followed a more global approach in viewing the image grid.

5 Conclusions and Future Work

This paper presents the results of a cognitive-centered research endeavor, which investigated human cognitive differences in information processing and their effects on users' visual behavior and interaction in image-recognition HIP schemes. For this purpose, an eye tracking study was designed, which entailed a psychometric-based survey for eliciting the users' cognitive processing characteristics, and an ecological valid interaction scenario with an image-recognition HIP task.

The findings underpin the value of considering human cognitive differences as an important human factor, in both design and run-time, to implement more effective HIP mechanisms and to avoid deploying image-recognition HIP schemes that unintentionally favor a specific group of users based on the designer's decisions. Specifically, results revealed that Analytic users spent more time to interact and explore the image-recognition HIPs, as well as generated significantly more fixations during interaction compared to Holistic users, which can be explained by the Analytic users' inherent way of processing information using local information processing streams and paying more attention to detail.

Despite our efforts to keep the validity of the study, some design aspects of the experiment introduce limitations. First, we used a specific background image. Although users' choices may be affected by the content and complexity of the image [22, 23], we provided images of the most widely used image categories (depicting a specific scenery and people [19–21]). Expansion of our research will consider a greater variety of image categories in order to increase the validity of the study. Moreover, considering the controlled in-lab nature of the eye tracking study, the users' visual behavior and performance might have been influenced, however, no such comment was received from our participants at the informal discussions that followed the task completion.

Acknowledgements. This research has been partially funded by the EU Horizon 2020 Grant 826278 "Securing Medical Data in Smart Patient-Centric Healthcare Systems" (Serums), and the Research and Innovation Foundation (Project DiversePass: COMPLEMENTARY/0916/0182).

References

1. von Ahn, L., Blum, M., Langford, J.: Telling humans and computers apart automatically. Commun. ACM **47**, 56–60 (2004)
2. Chellapilla, K., Larson, K., Simard, P., Czerwinski, M., 2005. Designing human friendly human interaction proofs (HIPs). In: ACM CHI 2005, pp. 711–720. ACM (2005)
3. Golle, P.: Machine learning attacks against the Asirra CAPTCHA. In: ACM Conference on Computer and Communications Security (CCS 2008), pp. 535–542. ACM (2008)
4. Bursztein, E., Martin, M., Mitchell, J.: Text-based CAPTCHA strengths and weaknesses. In: ACM Computer and Communications Security (CCS 2011), pp. 125–138. ACM (2011)
5. Belk, M., Fidas, C., Germanakos, P., Samaras, G.: Do human cognitive differences in information processing affect preference and performance of captcha? J. Hum.-Comput. Stud. **84**, 1–18 (2015)
6. reCAPTCHA. Online: https://www.google.com/recaptcha/about
7. Constantinides, A., Pietron, A., Belk, M., Fidas, C., Han, T., Pitsillides, A.: A cross-cultural perspective for personalizing picture passwords. In: ACM User Modeling, Adaptation and Personalization (UMAP 2020), pp. 43–52. ACM (2020)

8. Constantinides, A., Fidas, C., Belk, M., Pietron, A.M., Han, T., Pitsillides, A.: From hot-spots towards experience-spots: leveraging on users' sociocultural experiences to enhance security in cued-recall graphical authentication. Int. J. Hum.-Comput. Stud., 149 (2021). https://doi.org/10.1016/j.ijhcs.2021.102602
9. Davidoff, J., Fonteneau, E., Fagot, J.: Local and global processing: observations from a remote culture. Cognition **108**(3), 702–709 (2008)
10. Witkin, H.A., Moore, C.A., Goodenough, D.R., Cox, P.W.: Field–dependent and field–independent cognitive styles and their educational implications. ETS Res. Bull. Series **2**, 1–64 (1975)
11. Belk, M., Fidas, C., Katsini, C., Avouris, N., Samaras, G.: Effects of human cognitive differences on interaction and visual behavior in graphical user authentication. In: Bernhaupt, R., Dalvi, G., Joshi, A., K. Balkrishan, D., O'Neill, J., Winckler, M. (eds.) INTERACT 2017. LNCS, vol. 10515, pp. 287–296. Springer, Cham (2017). https://doi.org/10.1007/978-3-319-67687-6_19
12. Hong, J., Hwang, M., Tam, K., Lai, Y., Liu, L.: Effects of cognitive style on digital jigsaw puzzle performance: a GridWare analysis. Comput. Hum. Behav. **28**(3), 920–928 (2012)
13. Rittschof, K.A.: Field dependence-independence as visuospatial and executive functioning in working memory: implications for instructional systems design and research. Educ. Technol. Res. Dev. **58**(1), 99–114 (2010)
14. Angeli, C., Valanides, N., Kirschner, P.: Field dependence-independence and instructional-design effects on learners' performance with a computer-modeling tool. Comput. Hum. Behav. **25**(6), 1355–1366 (2009)
15. Belk, M., Fidas, C., Germanakos, P., Samaras, G.: The interplay between humans, technology and user authentication: a cognitive processing perspective. Comput. Hum. Behav. **76**, 184–200 (2017)
16. GP3 Eye Tracker. Online. https://www.gazept.com
17. Constantinides, A., Belk, M., Fidas, C., Pitsillides, A.: On the accuracy of eye gaze-driven classifiers for predicting image content familiarity in graphical passwords. In: ACM UMAP 2019, pp. 201–205. ACM (2019)
18. Witkin, H.A., Oltman, P., Raskin, E., Karp, S.: A Manual for the Embedded Figures Test. Consulting Psychologists Press, Palo Alto, CA (1971)
19. Alt, F., Schneegass, S., Shirazi, A.S., Hassib, M., Bulling, A.: Graphical passwords in the wild: understanding how users choose pictures and passwords in image-based authentication schemes. In: ACM MobileHCI 2015, pp. 316–322 (2015)
20. Dunphy, P., Yan, J.: Do background images improve draw a secret graphical passwords? In: ACM Computer and Communications Security, pp. 36–47. ACM (2007)
21. Zhao, Z., Ahn, G., Hu, H.: Picture Gesture Authentication: Empirical Analysis, Automated Attacks, and Scheme Evaluation. Journal of ACM Transactions on Information and System Security (TISSEC) 17, 4, Article 14, 37 pages (2015)
22. Wiedenbeck, S., Waters, J., Birget, J.C., Brodskiy, A., Memon, N.: Authentication using graphical passwords: Effects of tolerance and image choice. In: ACM Symposium on Usable privacy and security, pp. 1–12. ACM (2005)
23. Katsini, C., Fidas, C., Raptis, G. E., Belk, M., Samaras, G., Avouris, N.: Influences of human cognition and visual behavior on password strength during picture password composition. In: CHI 2018, p. 87. ACM (2018)
24. Fidas, C., Voyiatzis, A., Avouris, N.: On the necessity of user-friendly CAPTCHA. In: ACM CHI 2011, pp. 2623–2626. ACM (2011)
25. Belk, M., Germanakos, P., Fidas, C., Holzinger, A., Samaras, G.: Towards the personalization of CAPTCHA mechanisms based on individual differences in cognitive processing. Springer Human Factors in Computing and Informatics (SouthCHI 2013), Springer-Verlag, pp. 409–426 (2013)

26. Belk, M., Fidas, C., Germanakos, P., Samaras, G.: Do cognitive styles of users affect preference and performance related to CAPTCHA challenges? In: CHI 2012 Extended Abstracts on Human Factors in Computing Systems (CHI EA 2012), pp. 1487–1492. ACM (2012)

27. Elson, J., Douceur, J., Howell, J., Saul, J.: Asirra: a CAPTCHA that Exploits interest-aligned manual image categorization. In: Proceedings of the International Conference on Computer and Communications Security (CCS 2007), pp. 366–374. ACM (2007)

28. Belk, M., Germanakos, P., Fidas, C., Spanoudis, G., Samaras, G.: Studying the Effect of Human Cognition on Text and Image Recognition CAPTCHA Mechanisms. HCI **27**, 71–79 (2013)

29. Vikram, S., Fan, Y., Gu, G.: SEMAGE: a new image-based two-factor CAPTCHA. In: ACM Conference on Computer Security Applications (CCS 2011), pp. 237–246. ACM (2011)

30. Fidas, C., Hussmann, H., Belk, M., Samaras, G.: IHIP: towards a user centric individual human interaction proof framework. In: CHI '15 Extended Abstracts on Human Factors in Computing Systems (CHI EA '15), pp. 2235–2240. ACM (2015)

31. Gossweiler, R., Kamvar, M., Baluja, S.: What's up CAPTCHA?: a CAPTCHA based on image orientation. In: ACM World Wide Web (WWW 2009), pp. 841–850. ACM (2009)

32. Tanthavech, N., Nimkoompai, A.: CAPTCHA: Impact of website security on user experience. In: Proceedings of the 2019 4th International Conference on Intelligent Information Technology (ICIIT 2019), pp. 37–41. ACM (2019)

33. Sim, T., Nejati, H., Chua, J.: Face recognition CAPTCHA made difficult. In: Proceedings of the 23rd International Conference on World Wide Web (WWW 2014 Companion), pp. 379–380. ACM (2014)

34. Shishkin, A., Bezzubtseva, A., Fedorova, V., Drutsa, A., Gusev, G.: Text recognition using anonymous CAPTCHA answers. In: ACM Web Search and Data Mining (WSDM 2020), pp. 537–545. ACM (2020)

35. Lazar, J., et al.: The SoundsRight CAPTCHA: an improved approach to audio human interaction proofs for blind users. In: ACM Conference on Human Factors in Computing Systems (CHI 2012), pp. 2267–2276. ACM (2012)

36. Jiang, N., Tian, F.: A novel gesture-based CAPTCHA design for smart devices. In: BCS Human Computer Interaction Conference (BCS-HCI '13). BCS Learning & Development Ltd., Swindon, GBR, Article 49, pp. 1–5 (2013)

Risk Assessment of "Ostrich ZIP"

Michihiro Nakayama and Akira Kanaoka[✉]

Toho University, Miyama 2-2-1, Funabashi Chiba 274–8510, Japan
akira.kanaoka@is.sci.toho-u.ac.jp

Abstract. When sending highly confidential information by e-mail, there is a method of attaching a ZIP file encrypted with a password to the e-mail, and then sending the password for decryption separately by e-mail, which is the same channel. We named this method "Ostrich ZIP". While Ostrich ZIP method is used to protect information through encryption and to prevent misdirection, its meaning is sometimes questioned. However, it is difficult to say that these discussions have been organized. In this paper, the advantages, disadvantages, and threats of Ostrich ZIP are summarized based on these discussions, and the current situation is clarified by surveying the environment related to Ostrich ZIP. In addition, we construct an information leakage event model for file sharing when sending and receiving e-mails, and evaluate and discuss the information leakage risk of ostrich ZIP and alternative measures based on the model. Finally, the background of the use of the ostrich ZIP is discussed from institutional and other perspectives, adding another perspective along with the information leakage risk results. This paper will be provided as a comprehensive risk assessment of the ostrich ZIP.

Keywords: Encrypted ZIP · Passwords

1 Introduction

Information sharing has become an indispensable part of social activities using PCs, smartphones, and the Internet. In sharing information, we do not need to discuss the importance of delivering information to the right person and disclosing information only to the right person.

E-mail has been used as a channel for information sharing for a long time. It is achieved by attaching electronic files saved or created on a PC or smartphone to the e-mail. Since the SMTP used to send and receive e-mails does not have its data protection mechanism, the contents can be viewed by a third party. A protection mechanism must be applied to the data being sent and received separately to protect the information.

One way to protect email attachments is to use ZIP, an archive format that combines multiple files into a single file. ZIP is widely used because it supports compression and encryption of archived contents. Various operating systems support archive decompression as a standard feature, making it convenient to use without installing special applications.

© Springer Nature Switzerland AG 2021
A. Moallem (Ed.): HCII 2021, LNCS 12788, pp. 76–90, 2021.
https://doi.org/10.1007/978-3-030-77392-2_6

When protecting data in file sharing via e-mail, a ZIP file encrypted using this encryption function is sometimes used. Such a ZIP file will be referred to as an encrypted ZIP file in this paper. This file is encrypted, so a key is required to decrypt it. It is common for ZIP files to be encrypted with a password as the key. When an encrypted ZIP file is attached to an e-mail, the key to decrypt it must be shared somehow. The password, which is the key for its decryption, is often sent separately in plain text in another email on the same channel. While this method of sending an encrypted ZIP file as an attachment to an e-mail and sending the decryption password in a separate e-mail is widely used, many doubts about its data protection have been raised.

In this method, passwords are sent through the same channel, and passwords are sent separately near the e-mail with the encrypted ZIP attached. It is imagined that the level of data protection by encryption is lower than what is expected because the key protection is not sufficient. Many of the users of this method are aware of this low level of data protection. Still, they use it because of their organization's rules, the requirements of the recipient organization, and social requirements. We believe that they are operating under the Ostrich Policy, which means escape from reality or self-deception. We call this method the "Ostrich ZIP".

While Ostrich ZIP's advantages and disadvantages have been discussed from various viewpoints, it is difficult to say that there is any literature that organizes them. Therefore, in this paper, we first organize these discussions and clarify the advantages, disadvantages, and threats. Then, Ostrich ZIP's current status is surveyed for typical OSs, software, and Web services. Then, we propose an information leakage event model for file sharing when sending and receiving e-mails, evaluate the information leakage risk of ostrich ZIP and alternative measures based on the proposed model, and compare and discuss the results.

2   Organizing the Ostrich ZIP Discussion

There are already many criticisms of the Ostrich ZIP [1–4]. On the other hand, these criticisms cover multiple viewpoints and are not the same criticism. Therefore, it has not been sufficiently organized, including risk assessment. In this study, we will first conduct a literature review, including academic literature, a survey of discussions on the Web to organize the ostrich ZIP debate, and then organize the advantages and disadvantages, threats, and background to its use, alternative methods, and risk assessment listed therein.

2.1   Literature Review

The literature review was conducted using the free word search function of CiNii[1]. We selected "misdirection," "encrypted e-mail," and "information leak prevention e-mail" as keywords for the search. A total of 136 documents were obtained from the search using each search keyword, but there were no academic discussions about this study.

---

[1] https://ci.nii.ac.jp/.

2.2   Web Survey

In the survey using Web search, we used Google search. We selected "encrypted ZIP file separate mail," "encrypted ZIP sending later," and "ZIP file business with password" as keywords and searched. The keywords were set to Japanese, and only Japanese web pages were used for the survey. As a result of the search, many results were obtained, of which the contents were carefully examined. The contents of 11 articles, in particular, were organized.

2.3   Advantages of Ostrich ZIP

The advantages of Ostrich ZIP obtained as a result of the survey include "countermeasures against erroneous transmissions (10 cases)," "reduction of the risk of information leaks by password protection (3 cases)," "use of only e-mail and ZIP files and no need to introduce new technology (1 case)," "reduction of the risk of route eavesdropping by separate delivery (1 case)," and "support for AES encryption of ZIP specifications (1 case)". Based on the above, we identified the following advantages of the ostrich ZIP. The merits of the effect are not discussed here.

– Countermeasures against missending: Opportunity to notice missending when sending passwords separately
– Eavesdropping prevention: Data protection with encrypted ZIP makes sense for eavesdropping prevention
– Environment-independent: Extraction of encrypted ZIP files is less dependent on the environment

2.4   Disadvantages of Ostrich ZIP

As the disadvantages of ostrich ZIP obtained from the survey, the following were cited: "the anti-tapping effect is weak due to the use of the same channel (4 cases)," "the anti-missending effect of the automatic ostrich ZIP file support is weak (2 cases)," "vulnerability of the ZIP specification (2 cases)," "encryption makes security scanning on the mail server impossible (2 cases)," and "eavesdropping by the server (1 case)". Based on these, we put the advantages of Ostrich ZIP as follows. As with the advantages, the merits of the effect are not discussed here.

– The Dangers of Email Eavesdropping
– Decrease in the significance of using the same channel to prevent miscommunication
– Low strength of encrypted ZIP files

The point that security scan becomes impossible is not a disadvantage of Ostrich ZIP because it covers not only Ostrich ZIP but also multiple methods such as encrypted ZIP files, mail encryption by PGP or S/MIME, and the use of file sharing services such as online storage services. E-mail eavesdropping by the server was likewise determined not to be an inherent disadvantage of Ostrich ZIP.

2.5   The Ostrich ZIP Threats

Two threats to the ostrich ZIP were identified as a result of the survey.

– Eavesdropping by a malicious third party
– Missending of e-mail

2.6   Background of Ostrich ZIP Usage

7 of the 11 Web articles mentioned "meeting the PrivacyMark[2] and ISMS certi-fication" as the background of using the Ostrich ZIP obtained as a result of the survey.

2.7   Alternative Methods for Ostrich ZIP

As the alternative methods of ostrich ZIP obtained from the survey, "PGP or S/MIME (3 cases)", "Online storage service (3 cases)", "Automation of ostrich ZIP (1 case)", "Tell the password by phone (1 case)", "Mail the password (1 case)", "Give the password in person (1 case)" were listed. Based on these results, we put the alternative methods to ostrich ZIP as follows. The merits of the effect are not discussed here.

– PGP and S/MIME
– Sending passwords through a different route
– File sharing services, online storage services
– Automatic ostrich ZIP

The method that automatically encrypts ZIP processing of the attached file and sends the password is called automatic ostrich ZIP.

3   Survey on the Current Status of the Ostrich ZIP

In this section, we investigated the surrounding environment related to the ostrich ZIP as a material to explore the background of the ostrich ZIP. In this section, a survey of the surrounding environment related to the Ostrich ZIP is conducted as a material to explore the background of the ostrich zip's use.

3.1   Specification

The ZIP specification is provided by PKWARE and has been standardized as ISO/IEC 21320-1:2015. The encryption is based on the symmetric key crypto-graphic algorithm Traditional PKWARE Encryption (TPE), which was later modified to allow other cryptographic algorithms such as AES.

TPEs are already known to be vulnerable, and it has been reported that they can be easily decrypted in a commercial environment by running the open-source software Hashcat on a GPU-equipped computer [5].

---

[2] The PrivacyMark is a reputable privacy-centric certification in Japan. https://privacymark.org/.

Table 1. Results of survey on the actual status of ZIP files encrypted by OS

OS	Generation	Default algorithm	Expansion	OS Details
Windows	✓	–	Only TPE	Windows10 pro
macOS		TPE	Only TPE	macOS Mojave 10.14.6
Raspbian OS		TPE	Only TPE	Linux4.14.98-v7, Raspbian OS: 9.8

3.2 Encrypted ZIP Support in Typical Environments

One of the advantages of Ostrich ZIP was its environment-independence. Here, the results of a survey on how encrypted ZIPs are supported in typical environments are reported.

Support by OS. Windows 10, Mac OS X, and Raspbian OS were selected as the target operating systems, and encrypted ZIP creation, decompression, and the default encryption algorithm at the time of creation were investigated. In the case of generation, it was investigated whether it was possible to generate encrypted ZIPs without installing any special software after installation. The cryptographic algorithm information used in the generated encrypted ZIP was obtained from the ZIP file's binary data. For decompression, two types of encrypted ZIP files (encrypted with TPE and encrypted with AES) were prepared in advance, and it was investigated whether decompression was possible for each. Since the Raspbian OS usually has zip software installed at the time of installation, the generation and decompression were investigated using this software.

The results are shown in Table 1. It can be seen that in both OS environments, only TPE is deployed.

A survey was also conducted on iOS and Android OS, which are the leading operating systems used in mobile devices. For the mobile OS, it was investigated whether it was possible to generate encrypted ZIPs. It was confirmed that it was not possible to generate encrypted ZIPs in both the Android 7.0 environment and iOS 13.2.

Typical Software Support. It was investigated whether it is possible to create encrypted ZIPs for four typical e-mail software (Microsoft Outlook 2016 16.0.4266.1001, Mozilla Thunderbird 68.2.2, Apple Mail 12.4, and Becky! Internet Mail 2.74.03). As a result, it was confirmed that none of the software had the function to generate encrypted ZIPs.

Support by Typical Webmail Services. E-mail is increasingly being used by Web services via browsers. Therefore, it was investigated whether it is possible to create encrypted ZIPs for the representative web services, Google's Gmail and Yahoo! The survey was conducted on November 13, 2019. As a result, it was confirmed that there is no function to generate encrypted ZIPs for either service.

3.3 Automatic Ostrich ZIP

The ostrich ZIP requires both the sender and receiver to perform the encryption and decryption process, which is more burdensome than sending and receiving plaintext e-mail. A mechanism can reduce the burden on the sender by automatically encrypting and decrypting the attached file and sending the password. We call it automatic ostrich ZIP.

There are several services and solutions for automatic ostrich ZIP. Depending on the type of automation, there are three main types of automated ostrich ZIPs: gateway ostrich ZIPs, client ostrich ZIPs, and mail server ostrich ZIPs.

Gateway-type automatic ostrich ZIP is a device or service dedicated to encrypted ZIP between the mail server and the sender. Client-based automatic ostrich ZIP automatically performs encrypted ZIP by installing it in the sender's environment. A mail server type automatic ostrich ZIP includes a function to perform automatic ostrich ZIP.

In our research, we found 10 automatic ostrich ZIP solutions. 6 of them were gateway type, 2 were client type, and 2 were mail server type. Besides, 4 of the 10 solutions claimed to support cryptographic algorithm changes.

We also investigated the encryption algorithms of 10 types of e-mails that the authors had received, which were supposed to have been sent by automatic ostrich ZIP. The encrypted ZIP files sent by the same sender were counted as one type. The results showed that all of them were encrypted by TPE.

4 Model of Information Leakage Events in File Sharing During E-Mail Sending and Receiving

To evaluate Ostrich ZIP's risk, an information leakage event model for file sharing during e-mail sending and receiving is proposed, which enables evaluation, including alternative methods. In proposing the model, the threats are limited to information leakage during e-mail transmission and reception, based on the advantages and disadvantages of ostrich ZIP that have been discussed.

First, the events related to information leakage via e-mail are listed and named. Second, the probability of information leakage in various e-mail usage situations, including Ostrich ZIP and alternatives, is represented using combinations of events. Finally, the probability models are simplified, and the probability of information leakage for each method is compared by entering actual values.

4.1 Events Related to Information Leakage via E-Mail

Table 2 shows the events related to information leakage by e-mail. Each event is based on "missending" and "eavesdropping," which were raised as threats of the Ostrich ZIP. Authors examined and listed the events where missending and eavesdropping could occur between sending and receiving e-mail. Each event was assigned an event ID from a to i.

Table 2. Information leakage events by e-mail including ostrich ZIP

Event ID	Information leakage event by e-mail
a	Missending
b	Eavesdropping on mail server
c	Eavesdropping on communication channels
d	Eavesdropping from outside the mail server or communication channel
e	Be aware of missending when sending passwords separately
f	Decryption of encrypted ZIP files by malicious third parties
g	Missending e-mail and sending the password to the erroneous recipient through a different channel
h	Incorrectly selecting a publickey, and its owner is the same as the user to whom the mail was sent in error
i	Incorrectly selecting a user who is allowed to access cloud storage, and that user is the same as the user to whom the mail was sent in error

4.2   Situation of E-Mail Use and Incidents of Information Leakage

Table 3 shows the situations of e-mail use and the events of information leakage under these situations, evaluated as a combination of events.

For the e-mail usage situation, the authors listed in advance factors such as the presence or absence of attachment protection, file sharing methods The presence or absence of communication channel encryption, and the usage situation was subdivided according to each difference. For each usage situation, the events that cause information leakage were represented by the combination of events from a to i listed in Table 2.

4.3   Event Model and Simplified Probability of Leakage Occurrence for Each Leakage Case

Next, the probability of each leakage case defined in Table 3 is examined. Each of the events listed in Table 2 cannot be considered to occur independently It is difficult to calculate the probability of occurrence of each leakage case. However, we believe that even a simplified model has a particular significance, so the simplified probability is obtained by assuming that each event's occurrence is independent. The equations for each leak occurrence case and probability are shown in Table 4.

Table 3. Status of e-mail use and cases of information leakage

Case ID	E-mail usage	Event
1	Send attachments without encryption + without SSL/TLS	$a \cup b \cup c \cup d$
2	Send attachments without encryption + SSL/TLS	$a \cup b \cup d$
3	Send as ostrich zip + no SSL/TLS	$(e^- \cap (a \cup b \cup c \cup d)) \cup (e \cap f \cap (b \cup c \cup d))$
4	Send as ostrich zip + with SSL/TLS	$(e^- \cap (a \cup b \cup d)) \cup (e \cap f \cap (b \cup d))$
5	Send with auto ostrich zip + nc SSL/TLS	$a \cup b \cup c \cup d$
6	Send as auto-ostrich ZIP + SSL/TLS available	$a \cup b \cup d$
7	Send encrypted ZIP passwords via alternative channels (SMS, mail, phone) + SSL/TLS available	$(a \cap g) \cup (f \cap (b \cup d))$
8	Sending encrypted mails by PGP and S/MIME + SSL/TLS available	$a \cap h$
9	Send shared URL and password for link protection in a single email + SSL/TLS	$a \cup b \cup d$
10	Send the shared URL and password for link protection in separate emails + SSL/TLS	$e^- \cap (a \cup b \cup d)$
11	Send shared URLs and passwords for link protection via a separate route from email + SSL/TLS	$a \cap g$
12	Send shared URL and password (link protected + encrypted ZIP) in a single email + SSL/TLS	$a \cup b \cup d$
13	Send shared URL and password (link protected + encrypted ZIP) via email + SSL/TLS respectively	$e^- \cap (a \cup b \cup d)$
14	Send shared URL (without link protection) and encrypted ZIP password in a single email + SSL/TLS	$a \cup b \cup d$
15	Send shared URL (without link protection) and encrypted ZIP password respectively by email + SSL/TLS	$e^- \cap (a \cup b \cup d) \cup (e \cap f \cap (b \cup d))$
16	Send shared URLs (without link protection) and encrypted ZIP passwords via a separate route from email + SSL/TLS	$(a \cap h) \cup (f \cap (b \cup d))$
17	Send shared URLs (without link protection) in a single email + SSL/TLS	$a \cup b \cup d$
18	Online storage with access control + encrypted ZIP password sent by email + SSL/TLS	$a \cap i$

Table 4. Event model and simplified probability of leakage for each leakage case

Case ID	Event	Probability of an event occurring
1	$a \cup b \cup c \cup d$	$P(a) + P(b) + P(c) + P(d)$
2	$a \cup b \cup d$	$P(a) + P(b) + P(d)$
3	$(e^- \cap (a \cup b \cup c \cup d)) \cup (e \cap f \cap (b \cup c \cup d))$	$P(e^-)(P(a) + P(b) + P(c) + P(d)) + P(e)P(f)(P(b) + P(c) + P(d))$
4	$(e^- \cap (a \cup b \cup d)) \cup (e \cap f \cap (b \cup d))$	$P(e^-)(P(a) + P(b) + P(d)) + P(e)P(f)(P(b) + P(d))$
5	$a \cup b \cup c \cup d$	$P(a) + P(b) + P(c) + P(d)$
6	$a \cup b \cup d$	$P(a) + P(b) + P(d)$
7	$(a \cap g) \cup (f \cap (b \cup d))$	$P(a)P(g) + P(f)(P(b) + P(d))$
8	$a \cap h$	$P(a)P(h)$
9	$a \cup b \cup d$	$P(a) + P(b) + P(d)$
10	$e^- \cap (a \cup b \cup d)$	$P(e^-)(P(a) + P(b) + P(d))$
11	$a \cap g$	$P(a)P(g)$
12	$a \cup b \cup d$	$P(a) + P(b) + P(d)$
13	$e^- \cap (a \cup b \cup d)$	$P(e^-)(P(a) + P(b) + P(d))$
14	$a \cup b \cup d$	$P(a) + P(b) + P(d)$
15	$e^- \cap (a \cup b \cup d) \cup (e \cap f \cap (b \cup d))$	$P(e^-)(P(a) + P(b) + P(d)) + P(e)P(f)(P(b) + P(d))$
16	$(a \cap h) \cup (f \cap (b \cup d))$	$P(a)P(h) + P(f)(P(b) + P(d))$
17	$a \cup b \cup d$	$P(a) + P(b) + P(d)$
18	$a \cap i$	$P(a)P(i)$

5   Leakage Risk Assessment Using Event Models

In this section, the risks of Ostrich ZIP and its alternatives are evaluated by defining specific numerical values for the occurrence probability of each event and obtaining the occurrence probability of each case for the simplified probability formula obtained in Table 4.

It is difficult to obtain the true value of the occurrence probability of each event, and it is also difficult to obtain an approximate or guess value that can serve as an indicator. Therefore, the authors decided to set the values based on their considerations. However, the values set by the authors could not eliminate bias. Therefore, the set of probability values prepared by the authors is used as a baseline, and a set of probability values that consider situations where the attacker has an advantage compared to the baseline, and a set of probability values that show a strong effect of Ostrich ZIP are prepared, and by comparing them, the risks of the ostrich ZIP and alternatives are compared. The three sets of probability values are shown in Table 5.

Table 6 shows the three sets of probability values. In situations where the attacker has an advantage, the probability values of events c "Eavesdropping on communication channels" and f "Decryption of encrypted ZIP files by malicious third parties" were increased. On the other hand, in the situation where Ostrich ZIP is effective, the probability of event e "Be aware of missending when sending passwords separately" is increased and the probability of event f "Decryption of encrypted ZIP files by malicious third parties" is decreased. Table 6 shows the probability of occurrence of each leakage case obtained by these values.

Comparing the probability of a leak occurring in Case 3 "Sending with ostrich ZIP + no SSL/TLS" and Case 4 "Sending with ostrich ZIP + SSL/TLS", there is no significant difference between the baseline value set of 0.0109 and 0.0100. It is assumed that the application of SSL/TLS to the communication channel prevents the occurrence of event c, but it is shown that the effect is not strong.

For the valid set of numbers, the results are 0.0056 and 0.0111, and if we assume that the ostrich ZIP is valid, the difference in probability itself is small, but it is almost double the value, which can be said to be an obvious result.

There is a difference in automating the generation and sending of passwords between Case 4 "Sending by ostrich ZIP + with SSL/TLS" and Case 6 "Sending by automatic ostrich ZIP + with SSL/TLS". It can be seen that there is no significant difference in the probability of a leak, 0.0100 and 0.0111 in the baseline set of values. Also, the probability of information leakage in case 6, "Sending with automatic ostrich ZIP + SSL/TLS", is the same as that in case 6, "Sending attachments without encryption + SSL/TLS". In the proposed model, there is no change in the risk of information leakage, indicating that auto-ostrich ZIP is not effective against information leakage in e-mail sending and receiving.

Compared to Case 4, "Sending encrypted ZIP + SSL/TLS", there is a difference between Case 7, "Sending encrypted ZIP + SSL/TLS", which uses encrypted ZIP, and Case 4, "Sending encrypted ZIP + SSL/TLS", in that the password for decryption is sent through a different route. Looking at the probability of leakage, we can see that there is a difference of 0.0001 and 0.0100 in the baseline set of values. This value is about 1/100, indicating that sending passwords through a different route is highly effective. In the same way, we can see that the probability of a leak occurring in case 11, "Sending a shared URL and password for link protection via a separate route from e-mail + SSL/TLS," and case 16, "Sending a shared URL (without link protection) and encrypted ZIP password via a separate route from e-mail + SSL/TLS," in which passwords, etc. are sent via a separate route, are smaller than the other cases. The probability of occurrence is small compared to other cases, indicating that sending the password through a separate route is highly effective.

There is a difference between the case 8 "Sending encrypted mails with PGP and S/MIME + SSL/TLS" and the case 4 "Sending encrypted mails with ostrich ZIP + SSL/TLS" in that a different method is used for encryption. Looking at the probability of leakage, we can see that there is a difference between 0.001

Table 5. Probability of occurrence for each event

Event ID	Baseline	Attacker advantage	Ostrich ZIP advantage
a	0.01	0.01	0.01
b	0.0001	0.0001	0.0001
c	0.001	0.01	0.001
d	0.001	0.001	0.001
e	0.1	0.1	0.5
f	0.01	1.0	0.001
g	0.01	0.01	0.01
h	0.1	0.1	0.1
i	0.1	0.1	0.1

Table 6. Probability of occurrence of each leakage case

Case ID	Baseline	Attacker advantage	Ostrich ZIP advantage
1	0.0121	0.0211	0.0121
2	0.0111	0.0111	0.0111
3	0.0109	0.0201	0.0061
4	0.0100	0.0101	0.0056
5	0.0121	0.0211	0.0121
6	0.0111	0.0111	0.0111
7	0.0001	0.0012	0.0001
8	0.001	0.0010	0.001
9	0.0111	0.0111	0.0111
10	0.0100	0.0100	0.0056
11	0.0001	0.0001	0.0001
12	0.0111	0.0111	0.0111
13	0.0100	0.0100	0.0056
14	0.0111	0.0111	0.0111
15	0.0100	0.0101	0.0056
16	0.0010	0.0021	0.0010
17	0.0111	0.0111	0.0111
18	0.001	0.0010	0.001

and 0.0100 in the baseline set of values. The value is about 1/10, indicating that adopting a different method for encryption is highly effective.

There is a difference between the case 10 "Sending the shared URL and the password for link protection in separate e-mails + SSL/TLS" and the case 4 "Sending the file in ostrich ZIP + SSL/TLS" in that a different method such as online storage is used for file sharing. However, the fact that the file sharing information and its protection password are sent by e-mail is similar. Looking at the probability of a leak, we can see that there is almost no difference between the baseline value set of 0.010 and 0.0100. Incident Case 11, "Sending the shared URL and password for link protection through a separate route from e-mail + SSL/TLS," which has a similar sharing method to Incident Case 10, has a difference in that the password is shared through a separate route, but the difference in the probability of leakage is large, 0.100 and 0.0001. At the same time, file sharing via URLs, such as online storage, is not very effective as an information leakage countermeasure when sending and receiving e-mail.

6   Discussion

6.1   Information Leakage Risk and Usability

The model shows that sending passwords through a separate channel is highly effective against the risk of information leakage. However, sending passwords through a different channel is burdensome for both the sender and the receiver. It is not easy to agree in advance on which channel to use as a separate one, considering that the operational policies of each organization may restrict the use of software and services.

The use of encryption methods other than ZIP, such as PGP and S/MIME, has been highly effective, but these methods are highly dependent on the environment, and it is expected that there will still be many users who cannot use them. For example, Gmail and Yahoo! Mail do not support PGP or S/MIME.

Even if PGP and S/MIME are adopted in various software and services and made available to both senders and receivers, the difficulty of appropriate encryption will remain. In the field of usable security, the difficulty of appropriate encryption by end users has been an issue for a long time, and various approaches have been studied but have not yet reached a fundamental solution.

In the case of encryption using public key cryptography, the main problem is the appropriate selection of the recipient's public key by the sender. If the service or software supports the automatic selection of the recipient's public key linked to the e-mail address, the user's public key for the wrong e-mail address will be automatically selected when the wrong e-mail address is selected, and the erroneously sent user will be able to decrypt the information.

The environment-independence of the method is important from the viewpoint of usability, and it is not easy either.

6.2   Discontinuation of the Use of TPE and the Effect of AES Support in Various Environments

Our survey showed that although various operating systems can deploy encrypted ZIPs without installing additional software, the only supported encryption algorithm is TPE.

In the comparison of the probability of leakage, it was shown that the use of other cryptographic methods such as PGP and S/MIME made a difference in the probability of leakage, but the set of probability values was set on the assumption that TPE was used. However, the set of probability values was set on the assumption that TPE is used. If we assume that AES is used and TPE is abolished, the probability of event f "Decryption of encrypted ZIP files by malicious third parties" can be greatly reduced, and the probability of information leakage in the related occurrence cases can be reduced. However, even if the probability of occurrence of event f is reduced, the probability of occurrence of event e, whether the sender notices the erroneous transmission or not, is strongly related to the occurrence of information leakage in the case of sending passwords by e-mail, and thus does not make a significant difference.

6.3   Control of Information

File sharing through shared URLs, such as online storage services, was shown to be not significantly different from ostrich ZIP in terms of the risk of information leakage. However, online storage services have other advantages. The sender who set up the file sharing has the right to control the file sharing settings even after the file sharing information is sent. If we consider the risk of information leaks occurring and the risk of information leaks spreading as two different things, file sharing via shared URLs has the effect of suppressing the latter. In addition, file sharing through the use of a browser is highly environment-independent and is unlikely to cause usability problems.

Although the main focus of this paper is on the risk of information leakage, when considered from a different point of view, shared URLs can be a good general measure compared to ostrich ZIP.

6.4   Reasons for Adopting Ostrich ZIP and Current Status

The acquisition of Privacy Mark and ISMS certification was cited as the reason behind the use of Ostrich ZIP. In the Guidelines for the Implementation of Personal Information Protection Management Systems based on JIS Q 15001:2006 [6], it is stated that

> When sending and receiving personal information in the form of e-mail attachments, measures are taken to ensure confidentiality, such as encryption and password locks.

is a desirable method for "countermeasures during the transfer and communication of personal information". The fact that this exists as a background can be seen.

However, JIS Q 15001 was revised in 2017, and the revised Guidebook on Countermeasures to Standards [7] does not contain the same description. It is believed that there is no longer a strong rationale for obtaining Privacy Mark or ISMS certification as a reason for adoption.

6.5   Overseas Trends

It has been said that Ostrich ZIP is only used in Japan and is not commonly used overseas [8].

In our survey, we did not find any examples of Ostrich ZIP being used overseas. On the other hand, we did find that there are cases where encrypted ZIPs are being used in e-mails. Matthew Green's tweet on Twitter [9] reported that U.S. Senator Ron Wyden had asked NIST to set up a standard technology for sending and receiving secure files [10], which would replace file-sharing over e-mail using encrypted ZIP. The tweet expressed hope that it would replace file-sharing over email with encrypted ZIPs. The tweets were followed by tweets of approval, suggesting that encrypted ZIPs are being used to share files via e-mail overseas.

7   Conclusion

In this paper, we named the method of "sending an encrypted ZIP file as an attachment to an e-mail, and sending the decryption password in a separate e-mail" as Ostrich ZIP, and organized its advantages and disadvantages, threats, background of use, and alternative methods as a comprehensive risk assessment. This paper gives us a bird's eye view of the current situation, because this kind of organization has not been sufficiently organized.

In addition, a model of information leakage event occurrence was proposed focusing on information leakage during e-mail sending and receiving. Using the proposed model, cases of information leakage were identified, and the probability of occurrence of each case was estimated and the risk of information leakage was compared among the cases. The results show that the risk of information leakage of Ostrich ZIP itself is not significant compared to other cases, and that using other encryption methods and sending secret information such as passwords through other channels are more effective.

The clarification of the risk of information leakage allowed for further discussion. Therefore, we added considerations based on usability, social background, and overseas trends. These showed that the usefulness of Ostrich ZIP is not high, and that the use of shared URLs represented by online storage services, which are not much different from Ostrich ZIP in terms of information leakage risk, has advantages in terms of information control.

Ostrich ZIP is already widely used in many organizations, and it is not easy to change the rules defined in the past. It is hoped that the small technical advantages and reduced social demands of the ostrich ZIP shown in this paper will help to change the rules.

References

1. KImura, T.: Thinking about secure file sending and receiving between organizations - what is the purpose of encrypted ZIP? Internet Week 2016. https://www.nic.ad. jp/ja/materials/iw/2016/proceedings/t17/t17-kimura.pdf (2016). (Japanese)

2. Nomura, Y.: Do you really need encryption on that email? Okayama Information and Communication Technology Study Group. https://www.slideshare.net/nomlab/ss-85329306 (2017). (Japanese)
3. Sawatari, A.: Work Game - Is that "natural" necessary nowadays? Gijutsu-Hyohron (2019). (Japanese)
4. Uehara, T.: Why do we attach zip files with passwords to emails? Column No. 595, Institute of Digital Forensics (2019). https://digitalforensic.jp/2019/12/23/column595/ (Japanese)
5. @hashcat (2019). https://twitter.com/hashcat/status/1129441728761610242
6. JIPDEC PrivacyMark Promotion Center: Guidelines for the implementation of personal information protection management systems based on JIS Q 15001:2006. JSA Press (2010). (Japanese)
7. Uchikawa, K.: Guidebook for Implementing and Implementing a Personal Information Protection Management System for JIS Q 15001:2017. JSA Press (2018). (Japanese)
8. Ogawa, D.: I'll send you the password after that. Why it's not used at all in the U.S. and Europe, ITmedia Enterprise (2015). https://www.itmedia.co.jp/enterprise/articles/1509/18/news016.html
9. @matthew_d_green. https://twitter.com/matthew_d_green/status/1141430884459044864
10. Wyden, R.: https://www.wyden.senate.gov/imo/media/doc/061919%20Wyden%20Sensitive%20Data%20Transmission%20Best%20Practices%20Letter%20to%20NIST.pdf

Identity Recognition Based on the Hierarchical Behavior Characteristics of Network Users

Biao Wang[✉], Zhengang Zhai, Bingtao Gao, and Li Zhang

The Thirty-Sixth Research Institute of China Electronic Technology Group Corporation, Jiaxing, China
{wangb,gaobt}@jec.com.cn

Abstract. The core idea of ensuring network system security is identity recognition of the user. However, how to identify hackers after breaking through the existing system access control mechanism is still an important problem to be resolved. Therefore, this paper proposes an identity recognition method based on hierarchical behavior characteristics of network users. Behavior of network user was divided into interactive behavior characteristic and mouse behavior characteristic. After characteristics fusion, the Random Forest (RF) method was used to construct the user's identification model. And the identification results of single level behavior characteristics were compared with the results of this paper. The results show that the average True Acceptance Rate (TAR) and False Acceptance Rate (FAR) of 8 users' identity recognition were 82.73% and 7.26%, respectively, which is better than the identification result of single level behavior characteristics. This study provides a new idea for identity recognition based on user behavior. Combining the user's macro interaction behavior characteristics and micro mouse behavior characteristics in a short time or with a small amount of data can better identify users. This adds a layer of security protection for network security.

Keywords: Interactive behavior characteristics · Mouse behavior characteristics · Characteristics fusion · RF · Network user

1 Introduction

Nowadays, the Internet has penetrated into all aspects of people's daily life. Users carry out instant messaging, online reading, online office, online shopping, online takeout, online payment, online entertainment and many other activities. However, the Internet is a double-edged sword. People are facing many information security issues while enjoying the convenience brought by the Internet. For example, in April 2019, Toyota's server was hacked, resulting in the disclosure of sales information of 3.1 million customers [1]. How to identify hackers after breaking through the existing system access control mechanism is still an important problem to be resolved.

The core idea of ensuring network system security and user online security is identity recognition of the user. At present, most websites and apps log in through their accounts and passwords to identify users [2]. This method is very convenient, but it has shortcomings such as easy leakage or memory confusion. In order to further strengthen identity

© Springer Nature Switzerland AG 2021
A. Moallem (Ed.): HCII 2021, LNCS 12788, pp. 91–102, 2021.
https://doi.org/10.1007/978-3-030-77392-2_7

recognition of the user, people add verification codes (text messages, letters, graphics) for the second identification. In addition, identity recognition can also be carried out through possessions (such as ID cards, tokens), but there is a risk of loss or forgery. Then, identity recognition based on biometrics (such as fingerprints) solves these problems [3, 4]. This method is liked by more and more people, but requires additional equipment. All of the above are the identity recognition mechanisms performed during login. However, in most cases, people leave the computer unattended for a short or longer period of time after unlocking the computer, such as going to the toilet, drinking water, or simply leaving the computer for some reason without turning off the computer. During this period, illegal users can directly perform operations on the computer beyond the identity recognition during login, such as stealing information or malicious attacks. This means that the identity certificate provided by the user when logging into the network has now become invalid, and the identity of the illegal user has not been effectively identified.

With the rapid development of the Internet, the network environment faced by users has become more complex. For example, a user's online operation may be in a web environment or on a mobile terminal. Today's users tend to use multiple devices. Big data analysis of network user behavior is currently a very popular research field [5]. Identity recognition based on user behavior characteristics can be better applied in complex network environments.

Currently, most researchers used the mouse and keyboard behavior data of network users to identify users [6, 7]. For example, Bailey and Okolica et al. constructed a user behavior biometric system by integrating data from the keyboard, mouse, and user interface (GUI) of network users [8]. The results tested for more than 31 users were 2.10% False Acceptance Rate (FAR) and 2.24% False Rejection Rate (FRR). Biometric system can identify users from three dimensions of user behavior to achieve high accuracy. It also means that human behavior in the network environment should also have a unique behavior pattern, and its online behavior only matches its own behavior pattern [9]. However, the biometric system also requires more user behavior data, which also means that the system requires a long time for the user to perform identity recognition. If the hacker cannot be identified in a short time after breaking through the system access control mechanism, it will cause a lot of losses to the user. However, it is difficult to identify users through short-term user behaviors. Therefore, this study takes the network user's operation behavior in the main page after the software account login as the research object, and tries to combine the user's macro interaction behavior characteristics and micro mouse behavior characteristics to realize the identity recognition of users in a short time.

2   Literature Review

2.1   Research on Identity Recognition Based on Network User Behavior

From behavioral science research, we know that everyone in the real world has different psychological and physical states to form unique behavior patterns [10]. In the process of human-computer interaction, network users carry out a series of activities through mouse, keyboard and other devices in the network environment, which means that the online behavior data of network users contains unique psychological and physiological information of users. Moreover, the user's online behavior takes place actively throughout process of user's human-computer interaction, which provides continuous identity recognition after initial login, and effectively solves the problem of identity recognition after hackers break through the existing system access control mechanism. In addition, the identity recognition technology based on user behavior does not require additional hardware equipment.

Some researchers considered user authentication from the typing mode of text strings entered by network users on the keyboard [11]. The purely identity recognition based on the keystroke dynamics of human behavior biological characteristics does not require any other devices and equipment, but still need to consider the impact of the type of keyboard equipment and the length of the text string. With the upgrading of smart devices, mobile devices and touch screen devices have been used in large numbers [12]. The touch text input of the soft keyboard, which is similar to the text input of keystrokes, also brings new research challenges. However, from the results of testing some users' touch screen operation behaviors and verifying their identity to 99% [13], the research can be a reliable method for user authentication. In addition, some researchers have conducted mouse dynamics studies from the mouse behavior of network users, showing the feasibility of static authentication [14]. Subsequently, the researchers designed experiments and collected user mouse behavior data, and then extracted mouse features based on the basic mouse movements (including time, coordinate points, clicks, etc.), such as direction, velocity, etc. for user identification [15]. Hu T and Niu W proposed a method that can completely retain all basic mouse operations and use deep learning for user authentication [16]. They mapped the mouse dynamic behavior into pictures and trained the image datasets through the CNN network to create a classification models to achieve user identity authentication. These methods currently require more user behavior data or longer time, and cannot identify users quickly.

2.2 Classifiers Used in Existing Research

Different classifiers are used in existing research based on user behavior modeling, and some researchers compare the effects of the two classifiers [17]. Previous studies proposed static authentication based on the dynamics of mouse gestures, and analyzed the user's mouse gestures based on the neural network (ANN) classifier. The final results were 5.26% false acceptance rate, 4.59% false rejection rate and 26.9 s test time [18]. Compared with the existing mouse dynamics method, this method has been optimized in terms of verification samples and accuracy. The results show that the proposed method is more effective in the authentication of free text keystroke dynamics and keystroke spectrum analysis using neural network as the main classifier [19], and achieves a very small equal error rate (EER), ranging from 2.13% to 4.1%. Shen C, Cai Z, Liu X, etc. [20] used the nearest neighbor (NN) and support vector machine (SVM) to model the dynamic process of the mouse moving track after power transformation. The results show that the extracted mouse interaction behavior features play a good role in the two classifiers. Penny Chong [21] classified mouse movement sequences by deep learning architecture, which simplifies feature extraction process, and the architecture has outperformed other machine learning methods [22]. Although there are differences between various machine learning algorithms [23], they can all achieve a high degree of distinction between individual differences in different application environments.

Therefore, this paper considers the hierarchical behavior characteristics of network users to realize user identity recognition, so as to solve the problem of identity recognition after hackers break through the existing system access control mechanism.

3   Methodology

3.1   Research on Hierarchical Behavior Characteristics of Network Users

In the process of human-computer interaction, human behavior is continuous. People turn on the computer switch button and other things according to their behavior intention, and then operate in the network environment through the mouse, keyboard and other input devices, such as web page access and end, mouse movement, click, browse and a series of behaviors. The behavior of network users is the behavior effect produced by users completing their own goals and needs in the network environment, and is affected by the users' psychological and physiological attributes. For example, users form their own goals based on their needs, interests, and values. And the user has a certain understanding of the interactive system, has a certain memory of the interactive system, and is familiar with the fixed structure and hierarchy of the website or system, and will quickly form behavioral intentions in the brain to determine the specific steps of the operation, and then waiting for execution. Finally, the muscle reflection of the user determines the degree and efficiency of the behavior execution process.

The behavior of the network user is derived from the user's session process, as shown in Fig. 1. Different types of interactive devices, systems and browsers are selected by different users, and the time point of conversation is selected according to their own work and rest habits. In the process of human-computer interaction, the user visits the website page, the browsing time or the size of the browsing window according to their own preferences, purposes and habits. At the same time, the mouse behavior of network users is accompanied by the user's session process. Users may have one or more interaction processes in a day. The content of the session changes with the purpose of user interaction, but the architecture of the website has not changed, thereby generating a large amount of repetitive behavior data. In this paper, therefore, user behavior characteristics are extracted from the psychological and physiological aspects of network users in the process of human-computer interaction, and they were divided into two levels: interaction behavior characteristics (Level I) reflect users' psychology and usage habits, and mouse behavior characteristics (Level II) reflect unique physiological characteristics of the user.

Analysis of Interactive Behavior Characteristics
Due to the different life, work schedule, and preferences of users, their interactive behavior characteristics are also different from each other, such as the time point of user login account, page stay time, page browsing percentage, page browsing window aspect ratio, browsing frequency, etc. Next, the website log data of several users were analyzed and compared.

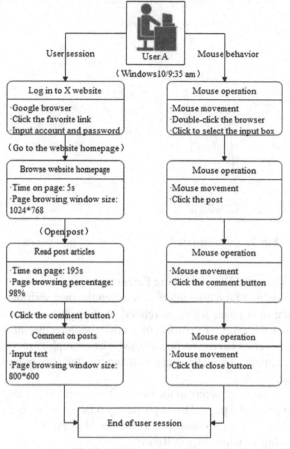

Fig. 1. User's session process

(1) Time Point of User Login Account

Each user logs in to the account according to his own schedule, work goals and other factors. Therefore, the time point of each user's login account is different. First, the frequency of each user's daily login time point was analyzed in hours (as shown in the left picture of Fig. 2). The log-in frequency of 4 users between 0:00 and 7:00 is almost 0, mainly during the period of 8–11 o'clock, 15–17 o'clock, and 19–21 o'clock, which is consistent with people's lives schedule. It can be seen from the figure that the time points of the login accounts of user A and user B are very close, the frequency of user C is low, and user D is mainly in the time period from 15:00 to 17:00.

Secondly, the frequency of each user's weekly login time point was analyzed with days as the unit of measurement (as shown in the right picture of Fig. 2). The daily login frequency of 4 users showed differences. As shown in the figure, the frequency of user A is relatively average, user C is concentrated on Tuesday and Thursday, user B is mainly on working days, and user D is mainly on the last three days of each week.

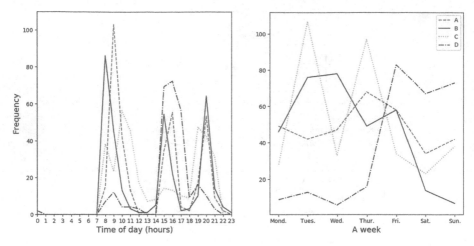

Fig. 2. Comparison of user login account time points

(2) Page Stay Time and Page Browsing Percentage

Page stay time refers to the time interval between the user visiting the current page and jumping to the next page, which is related to the user's information needs and interests. Combined with the information of website architecture and content, users' preferences and interaction habits can be reflected. For example, users quickly leave the first-level page that interacts with the website structure, and stay more interested in the content of the page.

Page browsing percentage refers to the ratio of the height of the page viewed by the user to the total height of the page. This is positively related to the page stay time. It can also indirectly reflect the user's habits such as the speed of browsing content.

(3) Page Browsing Window Aspect Ratio

The page browsing window is the browser window during human-computer interaction, and users can adjust the window size according to their own habits. This feature reflects the user's personal habits and preferences. For example, user B basically uses the default window size of the browser. User A also uses the browser's default window size most of the time, but sometimes adjusts the window size, which is not fixed. User C adjusts the window size and fixes the aspect ratio of the window to achieve the most comfortable browsing state. User D prefers full-screen browsing.

Analysis of Mouse Behavior Characteristics

In the process of human-computer interaction, due to the differences in the user's physiological state and the habit of using the mouse, the mouse behavior characteristics (such as the velocity, acceleration, angle, angular velocity of mouse movement) are also different from each other. Different arm muscle load and carpal tunnel pressure of network users may lead to different velocity and acceleration of mouse movement, which also be reflected in the accuracy and effectiveness of users clicking the button. The wrist posture of the user grabbing the mouse may be related to the angle of the mouse movement. Although the user's mouse behavior is indirectly affected by the user's mental state and operational familiarity, the mouse behavior characteristics tend to be stable within a certain period of time. The user's mouse behavior can be analyzed through the mouse coordinate points recorded in time series in the UI interface. The following is a quantitative analysis of the typical mouse behavior characteristics of several users.

(1) Time of Mouse Click and Double Click

The time of mouse click and double click refers to the time interval for the user to complete a single click or double click operation. As shown in the upper picture of Fig. 3, a user's mouse click time is stable for 20 mouse clicks in different time periods. As shown in the below picture of Fig. 3, there is a difference in the time interval between two users' mouse double-clicks, and the double-click speed of user A is faster than user B.

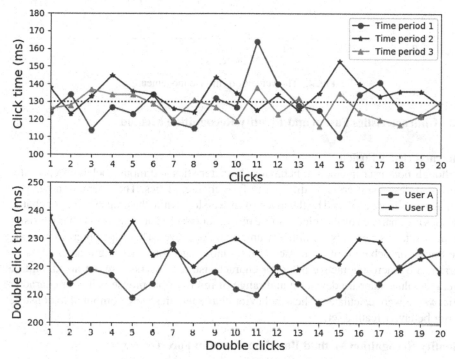

Fig. 3. Time of mouse click and double click

(2) The Velocity of Mouse Movement

The mouse movement tracks of the two users were analyzed and divided into left or right movement. Then the average velocity of each mouse movement sequence was calculated. As shown in Fig. 4, the user's mouse moves to the right faster than to the left. Generally speaking, the average velocity of user B is faster than user A.

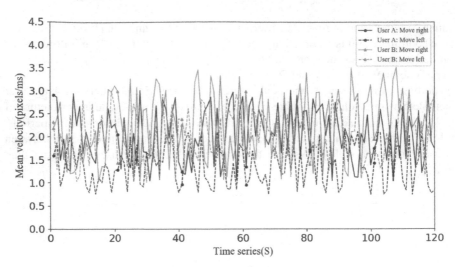

Fig. 4. The velocity of mouse movement

3.2   Characteristics Fusion and Identity Recognition Methods

Characteristics Fusion
Although both user interaction behavior characteristics and mouse behavior characteristics can describe users, it is difficult to fuse characteristics. The interaction behavior
characteristics are analyzed by the macro user web log, while the mouse behavior characteristics are analyzed by the micro mouse movement track. The behavioral characteristics
of the two levels cannot be completely unified on one level. This paper, therefore, taking
the operation behavior of each user in the main page after each login account as the
carrier, the macro interactive behavior characteristics of users were extracted, and the
average value, standard deviation and range of microscopic mouse behavior characteristics value were calculated. These behavior characteristics were combined to construct
a user behavior feature set.

Identity Recognition Method Based on Random Forest
The essence of identity recognition based on hierarchical behavior characteristics of
network users is to confirm whether the current behavior characteristics belong to the
users who claim to be a certain identity, which means that this is a binary classification problem. Random forest (RF) has a very good effect in dealing with classification
problems of high-dimensional features. Therefore, this paper chooses the RF method to
construct the user's identification model. RF is a collection of tree classifiers $\{h(x, k), k = 1,...\}$, each decision tree is a classifier and there is no correlation between decision
trees. The algorithm steps of RF are described as follows:

Input: training data set $D_1 = \{(x_1, y_1), (x_2, y_2)... (x_n, y_n)\}$, test data set $D_2 = \{(x_1, y_1), (x_2, y_2)... (x_n, y_n)\}$, the important parameters m and k of RF;

(1)   RF uses bootstrap method to randomly extract n samples from the training data set
      N to generate a new training sample set $D_{i,(i=1,...)}$;

(2) The CART algorithm is used to construct a single decision tree of the training set D_1. The calculation principle of node splitting during tree growth is the calculation of Gini coefficient;

(3) The growth of a single decision tree ends;

(4) Return;

(5) Repeat the above two steps m times, that is to generate m decision trees to form a random forest without pruning;

(6) Return;

(7) For the test data, the probability of the class of unknown samples is calculated, and vote by a single decision tree to determine the output result;

(8) End.

4 Experimental Analysis and Results

4.1 Experimental Analysis

In this paper, experimental analysis was carried out to verify the effectiveness of the proposed method. Three months of data from 8 users on the A website were collected for analysis. The user behavior characteristics set was obtained through the aforementioned data cleaning, feature calculation, feature fusion and other processes. Then, the behavioral feature sets of 8 users were cross-divided, and the data of each user was a legitimate user as well as an illegal user of others, so as to realize the effectiveness of identity recognition. All data was divided into two parts using a random sample extraction method: training set (70%) and test set (30%). Finally, the random forest (RF) algorithm was used to construct the identity model of each user. In addition, random forest algorithm was used to build user identity model based on interaction behavior characteristics and user identity model based on mouse behavior characteristics. The identification results of single level behavior characteristics were compared with the results of this paper.

In this paper, two evaluation indexes, True Acceptance Rate (TAR: the probability that a legitimate user is correctly predicted as a legitimate user) and False Acceptance Rate (FAR: the probability that an illegal user is incorrectly predicted as a legitimate user), were used to describe the experimental results.

4.2 Results

The confusion matrix of 8 users' identification results based on the behavior characteristics of level I, level II and level I + II was obtained by random forest classifier. Then, the TAR and FAR of the identification of 8 users in three states were calculated, as shown in Table 1. The results show that the average TAR and FAR of 8 users' identity recognition were 82.73% and 7.26%, respectively. However, the average TAR and FAR of identity recognition based on interactive behavior characteristics was 65.28% and 14.86%, respectively; the average TAR and FAR of identity recognition based on mouse behavior characteristics was 72.33% and 11.25%, respectively. In general, the method proposed in this paper is better than the identification result of single level behavior characteristics.

Table 1. Results of user identity recognition

Participant number	Level I + II		Level I		Level II	
	TAR	FAR	TAR	FAR	TAR	FAR
1	0.903	0.0622	0.654	0.1552	0.714	0.1133
2	0.819	0.0743	0.749	0.1299	0.769	0.1247
3	0.767	0.0852	0.623	0.1433	0.759	0.0977
4	0.774	0.0796	0.562	0.1667	0.56	0.1425
5	0.953	0.0615	0.703	0.1548	0.704	0.1269
6	0.828	0.0728	0.518	0.1535	0.731	0.1099
7	0.741	0.0767	0.691	0.1469	0.746	0.0963
8	0.833	0.0683	0.723	0.1383	0.804	0.0885

5   Limitations and Future Work

Three limitations of this study are noted. First, this paper collected the data of 8 users, and divided the data into different levels to construct a user identification model. Since the random forest classifier needs to use the data of legal users and illegal users for training, the training process determines the accuracy of the classifier. In this paper, when constructing the classifier for each user, the illegal user data in the training data includes the data of the other seven users, and the amount of data is equal to the legitimate user data, which is to avoid the impact of data imbalance. This means that for each user, the other seven users are illegal. Therefore, the data of 8 users is sufficient to train the model, and the verification of the identity recognition model is also effective. However, for a large and complex network system, more user data is needed to train the model to avoid overfitting. And the result of a small sample size may contain contingency. Assuming that there are N illegal users, the possibility of having a high degree of similarity with legitimate users among the N illegal users will increase. In the future research, we will increase the number of research objects and use more samples to prove the universality of the results.

Second, this paper compared the identification results of single level behavior characteristics with the results of this study. But for single level behavior characteristics, this method contains more characteristic attributes, which may have an impact on the results. In the future research, multi-dimensional comparison is attempted to improve the reliability of the results.

Third, this study only used the random forest classification algorithm, without further comparative analysis of the classification results. Random forest has been proved to be over fitted in some noisy classification or regression problems. Moreover, the influence of some noise data on the classification results is still unclear. In the future research, we will try to further optimize the random forest algorithm, or use different classifiers and prediction methods for comparative analysis to improve the accuracy of the identification model.

6 Conclusions

The core idea of ensuring network system security is identity recognition of the user. However, how to identify hackers after breaking through the existing system access control mechanism is still an important problem to be resolved. Therefore, this study takes the network user's operation behavior in the main page after the software account login as the research object, and tries to combine the user's macro interaction behavior characteristics and micro mouse behavior characteristics to realize the identity recognition of users in a short time.

The results show that the average TAR and FAR of 8 users' identity recognition were 82.73% and 7.26%, respectively. However, the average TAR and FAR of identity recognition based on interactive behavior characteristics was 65.28% and 14.86%, respectively; the average TAR and FAR of identity recognition based on mouse behavior characteristics was 72.33% and 11.25%, respectively. In general, the method proposed in this paper was better than the identification result of single level behavior characteristics. This study provides a new idea for identity recognition based on user behavior. Combining the user's macro interaction behavior characteristics and micro mouse behavior characteristics in a short time or with a small amount of data can better identify users. This adds a layer of security protection for network security.

References

1. New Toyota Data Breach Exposes Personal Information of 3.1 Million Customers [EB/OL]. https://www.cpomagazine.com/cyber-security/new-toyota-data-breach-exposes-personal-information-of-3-1-million-customers/. Accessed 09 Apr 2019
2. Biddle, R., Mannan, M., Van Oorschot, P.C., et al.: User study, analysis, and usable security of passwords based on digital objects. IEEE Trans. Inf. Forensics Secur. **6**(3), 970–979 (2011)
3. Wang, Y., Hu, J.: Global ridge orientation modeling for partial fingerprint identification. IEEE Trans. Pattern Anal. Mach. Intell. **33**(1), 72–87 (2011)
4. Jing, X., Li, S., Zhang, D., Lan, C., Yang, J.: Optimal subset-division based discrimination and its kernelization for face and palmprint recognition. Pattern Recogn. **45**(10), 3590–3602 (2012)
5. Mengyao, X., Yan, F., Wang, B., Yi, S., Yi, Q., Xiong, S.: Construction of network user behavior spectrum in big data environment. In: Li, K., Fei, M., Dajun, D., Yang, Z., Yang, D. (eds.) Intelligent Computing and Internet of Things, pp. 133–143. SpringerS, Singapore (2018). https://doi.org/10.1007/978-981-13-2384-3_13
6. Buriro, A., Crispo, B., Conti, M.: Answer authentication: a bimodal behavioral biometric-based user authentication scheme for smartphones. J. Inf. Secur. Appl. **44**, 89–103 (2019)
7. Shen, C., Cai, Z., Guan, X., et al.: User authentication through mouse dynamics. IEEE Trans. Inf. Forensics Secur. **8**(1), 16–30 (2012)
8. Bailey, K.O., Okolica, J.S., Peterson, G.L.: User identification and authentication using multimodal behavioral biometrics. Comput. Secur. **43**, 77–89 (2014)
9. Yi, Q., Xiong, S., Wang, B., et al.: Identification of trusted interactive behavior based on mouse behavior considering web user's emotions. Int. J. Ind. Ergon. **76**, 102903 (2020)
10. Wieman, H.N.: The unique in human behavior. Psychol. Rev. **29**(6), 414 (1922)
11. Kang, P., Cho, S.: Keystroke dynamics-based user authentication using long and free text strings from various input devices. Inf. Sci. **308**, 72–93 (2015)

12. Salem, A., Obaidat, M.S.: A novel security scheme for behavioral authentication systems based on keystroke dynamics. Secur. Priv. **2**(2), e64 (2019)
13. Damopoulos, D., Kambourakis, G., Gritzalis, S.: From key loggers to touch loggers: take the rough with the smooth. Comput. Secur. **32**, 102–114 (2013)
14. Everitt, R.A.J., McOwan, P.W.: Java-based internet biometric authentication system. IEEE Trans. Pattern Anal. Mach. Intell. **25**(9), 1166–1172 (2003)
15. Zheng, N., Paloski, A., Wang, H.: An efficient user verification system via mouse movements. In: ACM Conference on Computer & Communications Security. ACM (2011)
16. Hu, T., Niu, W., Zhang, X., et al.: An insider threat detection approach based on mouse dynamics and deep learning. Secur. Commun. Netw. **2019**, 1–12 (2019)
17. Kołakowska, A.: Usefulness of keystroke dynamics features in user authentication and emotion recognition. In: Hippe, Z.S., Kulikowski, J.L., Mroczek, T. (eds.) Human-Computer Systems Interaction. AISC, vol. 551, pp. 42–52. Springer, Cham (2018). https://doi.org/10.1007/978-3-319-62120-3_4
18. Sayed, B., Traoré, I., Woungang, I., et al.: Biometric authentication using mouse gesture dynamics. IEEE Syst. J. **7**(2), 262–274 (2013)
19. Alpar, O.: Frequency spectrograms for biometric keystroke authentication using neural network based classifier. Knowl. Based Syst. **116**, 163–171 (2017)
20. Shen, C., Cai, Z., Liu, X., et al.: Mouse identity: modeling mouse-interaction behavior for a user verification system. IEEE Trans. Hum. Mach. Syst. **46**(5), 734–748 (2016)
21. Chong, P., Elovici, Y., Binder, A.: User authentication based on mouse dynamics using deep neural networks: a comprehensive study. IEEE Trans. Inf. Forensics Secur. **15**, 1086–1101 (2019)
22. Nguyen, T.T., Armitage, G.: A survey of techniques for internet traffic classification using machine learning. IEEE Commun. Surv. Tut. **10**(4), 56–76 (2009)
23. Hämäläinen, W., Vinni, M.: Classifiers for educational data mining. In: Handbook of Educational Data Mining. Chapman & Hall/CRC Data Mining and Knowledge Discovery Series, pp. 57–71 (2011)

Security Analysis of Transaction Authorization Methods for Next Generation Electronic Payment Services

Daniel Wilusz[✉] [ID] and Adam Wójtowicz [ID]

Department of Information Technology, Poznań University of Economics and Business,
al. Niepodległości 10, 61-875 Poznań, Poland
{wilusz,awojtow}@kti.ue.poznan.pl

Abstract. Real-world and ubiquitous human-computer interactions require payment processes that have to be instant, convenient and interoperable. However, these functional requirements are in opposition to one of the most significant non-functional requirement: security of the payment process. A number of various attacks on confidentiality of payment or payer data, integrity, authenticity and non-repudiation of payment transaction, as well as on availability of the payment service are reported. Next generation electronic payment services utilize wide range of payment authorization methods. Security analysis of authorization methods described in this paper includes four sequential phases. The first one is identification of relevant authorization methods related to payment authorization in various scenarios. The second one is identification of classes of vulnerabilities and threats that are, or potentially can be, related to transaction authorization processes. The third phase comprises analysis of risks resulting from possible impact of the threats on the authorization methods. The fourth phase covers identification of all types of countermeasures that can be applied against risks identified in the previous phase. The result of presented work can be useful in a number of risk analysis scenarios. Especially in those, where security of composed system is analyzed, which means a system that supports a number of assets, electronic payments methods, and countermeasures or security controls in various scenarios when they are simultaneously used and interact with each other.

Keywords: Cybersecurity · Transaction authorization · Security analysis

1 Introduction

Nowadays, in both cyber and physical spaces users more and more often spontaneously interact with various electronic services. To be useful for commercial applications, these interactions require availability of instant, convenient and interoperable payment processes. However, these functional requirements are in opposition to one of the most significant non-functional requirement: security of the payment process. A number of various attacks on confidentiality of payment or payer data, integrity, authenticity and

© Springer Nature Switzerland AG 2021
A. Moallem (Ed.): HCII 2021, LNCS 12788, pp. 103–119, 2021.
https://doi.org/10.1007/978-3-030-77392-2_8

non-repudiation of payment transaction, as well as on availability of the payment service are reported.

Next generation electronic payment services utilize wide range of payment authorization methods. These methods can be classified to the following categories: secret, encryption and biometrics based. Secret based methods include presentation to the verifier a secret combination of characters or predefined alphanumeric identifier. A secret can be also used to generate deterministic encryption key, that is used to get access to resources (e.g. PKCS 5 Password based Encryption Standard or BIP-39 mnemonic seed phrase). Secrets can be reusable or one time (one time password, OTP). OTP is valid for single payment authorization only. Encryption based methods include the interactive protocols, e.g., challenge-response protocol. In some challenge-response protocols, the payer proves the knowledge about a secret but does not reveal it during transaction authorization, e.g., digital signature schemes. Biometric methods are based on the characteristics of the payer, e.g., physiological attributes of human body or behavioral characteristics of the user. The payment authorization involves various execution environments, e.g., dedicated software (e.g., mobile app, web browser plugin), dedicated hardware (e.g., hardware security module, cold wallet, security token) or web service. The next generation electronic payment services may use a mix of authorization methods and environments, e.g., multifactor or out-of-band (OOB). Multifactor authorization uses at least two of four factors to authenticate a user: user knowledge (e.g. password), user possession (e.g. smartcard), individual characteristics of the user (e.g. fingerprint) or user location. The combination of payment authorization methods may depend on the payment context, e.g., mutual trust, payment risk level, device availability, or application scenario: cyber or physical. Each combination of these methods and environments influences the level of payment security breach risk [30, 32].

Security analysis of electronic payment methods described in this paper includes four sequential phases. The first one is identification of relevant authorization methods related to payment authorization in various scenarios. The second one is identification of classes of vulnerabilities and threats that are, or potentially can be, related to transaction authorization processes. The third phase comprises analysis of risks resulting from possible impact of the threats (identified in phase two) on the authorization methods (identified in phase one). The fourth phase covers identification of all types of countermeasures that can be potentially applied against risks identified in phase three. A single countermeasure can mitigate a number of various risks, and a single risk can be mitigated by a number of various countermeasures. In this phase also risk mitigation with the countermeasures is briefly analyzed.

The result of presented work can be useful in a number of risk analysis scenarios. Especially in those, where security of composed system is analyzed, which means a system that supports a number of assets, electronic payments methods, and countermeasures or security controls in various scenarios when they are simultaneously used and interact with each other.

A number of prior works on security of transaction authorization process have been published. However all of them have their shortcomings. The report [18] takes technical perspective of a software developer and is too low-level. In turn, the paper [11] takes more formal approach, however is a bit outdated, not comprehensive enough, and is focused more on general online banking security than particularly on transaction authorization process. Similarly, the interesting report [16] is not comprehensive enough. Therefore there is a need for comprehensive security analysis for emerging transaction authorization methods.

2 Emerging Transaction Authorization Methods

Next generation electronic payment systems employ technologies (e.g. blockchain databases, biometric authentication, hardware security modules as for 2021) that are not common in the financial sector, to process payment transactions. Examples of next generation payment systems are: Ethereum, Apple Pay or Mastercard Biometric Card.

The presented analysis is focused on transaction authorization as opposed to user authentication or user identification before transaction. However, in some transaction authorization methods these actions are combined together or difficult to separate, thus in such cases the aggregated methods are also the subject of the analysis.

Transaction authorization methods that have status of state-of-the-art popular methods or emerging new methods have been described in this section; obsolete methods or methods that are rarely used for transaction authorization purposes have been omitted. The authorization methods classification presented in Sect. 2 intentionally reflects end-user perspective or human-computer interaction perspective, as opposed to system security perspective presented in Sect. 4 and 5. In other words, our selection has been designed to reflect user choice of methods that he/she is faced with when choosing or configuring the service.

Also it is assumed that selected authorization methods have state-of-the-art security mechanisms applied; any additional custom security functionalities that can be applied to those methods are listed in countermeasure list in Sect. 5 and can be combined with standard methods as it has been described in Sect. 5.

M1: Password
Password is a memorized secret that can be presented to authorize a transaction. Password usually takes the form of character string, passphrase or PIN number, that can be automatically generated by the software or composed by the user.

M2: One Time Password
One time password (OTP) is an authorization method that for each transaction requires a unique password generated solely for the purpose of that transaction. OTP cannot be used repeatedly both during the same session and between sessions [22]. For passive adversaries, one-time passwords are the solution to the challenge of eavesdropped fixed passwords [14]. The one time passwords can be distributed as a pre-shared list [14], generated by an electronic token [11, 23], generated by software (Time-based One Time Password - TOTP codes) [16] or sent by external service via out of bound channel (c.f. Sect. 5, C4).

M2.1: Shared Lists
Shared password list usually takes the form of a card or scratch card containing a numbered list of one-time passwords. When authorizing a transaction, the system requests the user to enter the one time password found on the list under a specific number.

M2.2: Hardware Tokenizer
Hardware token is a standalone device that generates one time passwords to authorize transactions. After entering a PIN, the user reads the OTP from the device's display and inputs it into transaction authorization interface.

M2.3: Software Tokenizer (TOTP)
Software tokenizer is a software implementation of the TOTP algorithm that generates OTP based on current time and pre-shared secret.

M2.4: OTP Sent Via Out of Band Channel
OTP Sent to the user via out of band channel (e.g. SMS message) contains additional data, such as a recipient of the transaction, an amount, and a description, which makes it more difficult to launch a phishing attack.

M3: Digital Signature
In the context of transaction authorization, digital signature is a cryptographic proof of transaction integrity and authenticity. The digital signature is produced by a signing algorithm that takes both the cryptographic private key of the subject and the message as an input. The digital signature is verified by a verifying algorithm that takes the digital signature to be verified, the cryptographic public key of the subject and the message as an input. The private and public keys of the subject are produced by the subject using key generation algorithm, with the private key required to remain a secret [25]. A transaction is authorized if the submitted digital signature of transaction has been correctly verified using a public key of the user authorizing the transaction. Public key algorithms can be vulnerable to man-in-the-middle attack, especially when public keys are not authenticated. To bind the user identity with a public key, the public key certificate is used [19].

M4: Public Key Certificate
Public key certificate is a document that consists of a data part and a signature part. The data part contains a public key of the subject and the data identifying the subject. The signature part consists of the digital signature of a certification authority on the data part, thus associating the data part with the identity of the subject [14, 19]. In case the private key is compromised, lost by the user, or invalidated, the certificate should be revoked [19]. Certificate revocation is a process to ensure that particular certificate is no longer used to validate the identity of the private key owner [1]. Many methods have been proposed to revoke a certificate, e.g., certificate revocation list (CRL), online certificate status protocol (OCSP), short-lived certificates. It is noteworthy that according to CAP theory, it is impossible to design a distributed system to revoke a certificate immediately [23]. Public key infrastructure is a distributed environment consisting of hardware, software, people, and procedures that enables the creation, distribution, use, storage, and revocation of public key certificates [5].

M5: Biometrics
Biometrics is a method for automated identification based on acquiring biological or behavioral characteristics of an individual [10, 21]. Biometric features have properties of universality, individuality, permanence, collectability and performance. Biometric authentication consists of three steps: acquisition of biometric data with the sensor,

converting the data to digital pattern, and comparison of the pattern with a reference pattern. Biometrics can be used for: user identification (one-to-many model, e.g. to identify mobile user for the remote service); or user verification (one-to-one model, e.g. to verify whether it is the owner who tries to unlock the device). There is no "perfect" biometrics: it is usually a trade-off between security, convenience, invasiveness and cost.

M5.1: Fingerprints

Factors affecting quality of fingerprints acquisition include: injuries, dirt, humidity, skin tensility, pattern location and orientation. The following acquisition technologies are used: optical sensors which are cheap but easy to circumvent and dirt sensitive; capacitive sensors which are dirt and humidity sensitive; thermal sensors which are temperature sensitive; and ultrasonic sensors which are expensive but hard to circumvent and they analyze not only fingerprints but also finger physical properties, such as blood vessels.

M5.2: Face

Face biometrics usage is unobtrusive for users due to ease of data collecting with regular camera. Algorithms can compare face geometry (geometrical relations between selected details) or vectors describing whole face images. 3D face models are used to recognize faces from the different angles, and to make successful attack more difficult. Following factors have impact on the quality of recognition: lighting, camera parameters, glasses, clothes, aging and other face changes, mimics, twins, children, relatives. Contrary to regular image face IR image or thermogram is resistant to variable lighting conditions or other image changes, but specific camera has to be used. Active infrared (IR) uses short wavelength IR light to illuminate an area of interest, some of the IR energy is reflected back to camera and interpreted to generate an image. In turn, thermal imaging uses mid- or long wavelength IR energy. Thermal images are passive, only sense differences in heat, thus challenges include: variable nose and mouth temperatures caused by respiration, glasses blocking thermal imaging, and image is dependent on intensive physical activity, or eating.

M5.3: Voice

Voice recognition is easy to apply in mobile devices, because of built-in sound processing, filtering, speaker, microphone; recognition technology is mature. Authentication can be performed according to one of four schemes: fixed phrase, phrase send by the system (each time new), freely chosen phrase, conversation which verifies both knowledge and voice (two factors). Factors that affect quality of the voice recognition include: background noise, human emotional state, aging, or respiratory diseases. Other problems include: confidentiality and convenience in public places; user privacy (nationality, sex, age).

M5.4: Iris

Iris image can be acquired with regular camera or near infrared scan. The structure of the iris is analyzed, not the color. Iris templates have strong uniqueness, low false acceptance rate (FAR), low computational power requirements. Since eye pupil constantly adapts itself to changing light conditions, advanced iris-based techniques can distinguish real eye from the its static image used by an attacker. The emerging technologies include: long-distance recognition or combination of iris and face recognition in single process.

Problems include: face distance, lightning, movement, glasses, and sensitivity to high quality photograph attacks or contact-lens attacks.

M5.5: Finger/Palm Veins
Finger/palm veins recognition is one of the most accurate biometric authentication methods. It is based on vascular patterns formed by the blood vessels located inside the human body (inside the finger or whole palm). Patterns are considered to be unique for each individual and even among the different fingers of a given person [8]. It is the least privacy intrusive biometrics, since it is hard to collect samples without ones acceptance. Other advantages include: data acquisition speed, recognition reliability, pattern persistence during lifetime, and high security. The accuracy of the scanning process can be decreased by light sources, specific kind of dirt, and finger position.

M6: Hardware Security Keys
Hardware security keys have been developed to generate and store authorization data in secure manner. Hardware security keys may support wide range of cryptographic protocols such as key generation, encryption/decryption, digital signature, OTP generation etc. Cold wallets are off-line hardware storage for cryptocurrency private keys. Since cold wallets are offline most of the time and since they require physical access and PIN confirmation to make payments, it is difficult to compromise them.

M7: Smartcards
Smartcard is an ISO/IEC 7816 standard compliant card equipped with a microprocessor to perform transaction authorization. The smartcard microprocessor is compliant with various cryptographic protocols.

M8: Device Registration
Device registration allows to limit access to the transaction authorization system only to pre-registered devices. It takes advantage of hardware/software fingerprinting combined with identification through secret data.

3   Threats to Transaction Authorization

In this section, the potential threats related to use of transaction authorization methods have been classified into main groups. As in the case of authorization method classification (Sect. 2), the threat selection and classification is perceived also from human-computer interaction perspective. The list of threats that have been analyzed includes threats that are focused on front-end security: client device, client software, or authorization attributes stored and input by the user. The goal of these threats is to attack user security or privacy in various possible ways. This analysis tries to comprehensively list all of them. The list does not contain server side threats (e.g. web application-level attacks such as cross site scripting, SQL injection or session hijacking) nor low level communication threats (e.g. network traffic sniffing, spoofing, man in the middle attacks), since the analyzed methods do not introduce any variance to such threats.

T1: Threats to Authorization Attributes Through Guessing
In order to perform a transaction by unauthorized party, authorization attributes such as passwords, or biometric patterns can become a target of remote attacks on their

confidentiality. It includes brute force or dictionary attacks on user credentials. The attack can be automated or semi-automated. Nowadays the passwords are recommended to be hashed. Despite the difficulty of reversing the hash function and computing the password from the hash value, there are methods that allow an adversary to deduce the password. The adversary can select likely passwords, calculate the hash value, and compare it to the value stored in the system [17]. Another method of attacking hashed passwords is to use rainbow tables. Using tables containing the text and its hash value makes the password discovery attack computationally much faster (at the cost of increasing the memory space to store the values of rainbow table) [3]. To make the rainbow table attack infeasible, salted passwords are applied [17].

T2: Threats to Confidentiality of Authorization Attributes Through SIM Swap Scam
SIM swap scam relies on malicious taking control over a user's cell phone service identified by a given number by fraudsters in order to obtain OTPs and security messages that are sent to that cell phone user for transaction authorization [9].

T3: Threats to Confidentiality of Authorization Attributes Through Phishing Attacks
Phishing is defined as a deceptive, online attempt performed by an adversary to obtain confidential information such as passwords, one time passwords, biometric samples, certificates, in order to authorize transactions [12, 23].

T4: Threats to Confidentiality of Authorization Attributes in Physical Spaces
Many knowledge-based factors are susceptible to eavesdropping while being input to the device in public physical spaces, e.g., with surveillance high resolution cameras. As for biometric attributes, not all are as difficult to collect without one's knowledge or permission as vein patterns or electrocardiogram patterns. Biometric samples such as face images, fingerprints (left frequently, e.g., on a glass), or various behavioral biometrics are relatively easy to collect without user knowledge. Subsequently they can be used to instantly infer additional information (e.g. emotional state from face images or voice samples) and take advantage of them (e.g. in dynamic marketing applications), or in order to perform an attack on the transaction authenticity. Collecting one's biometric samples can be followed by preparing fake authenticators imitating corresponding parts of the human body (artificial finger, face mask, high resolution iris image, etc.), in order to conduct unauthorized transaction authorization [31].

T5: Remote Device Control
In this threat an attacker remotely takes full or partial control over an end-user device. The device is controlled with malware that has administrative privileges at victim machine, with malware that resides in the web browser in man-in-the-browser scenario, or with key logger that eavesdrops user keystrokes, e.g., while user types password. The infection of the malware can be performed in various scenarios such as based on social-engineering (Trojan horse) or based on exploitation of software security hole. The process of infection itself is out of the scope of this analysis.

T6: Unauthorized Physical Access to the Device
Unauthorized physical access may result in taking the control over the device to perform actions in the name of legitimate user of the device, which include network activity, transaction authorization attempts or removing activity evidences.

T7: Threats to Transaction Authenticity Through System False Acceptance

Practical limitation of a great majority of biometric access control systems results from the existence of non-zero false acceptance rate (FAR). Biometric systems usually allow their managers to adjust sensitivity level and find an optimal trade-off between FAR, false reject rate (FRR) and other recognition parameters for a given application. However, the adjustment rarely allows these rates to be reduced to zero, especially in large-scale systems. False acceptances followed by unauthorized transaction confirmation (intentional or accidental) are inherent risks that cannot be omitted.

T8: Threats to System Security After Authorization Attribute Compromise

As opposed to conventional authenticators such as passwords, once the biometric sample or template is eavesdropped or disclosed by an attacker, the countermeasures are not straightforward. Compromised password, digital certificate or credit card data can be effectively revoked and reissued. In case of a biometric pattern reflecting an immutable attribute of a person's body, the act of eavesdropping on the pattern has permanent consequences. Despite obvious advantages, the fact that biometric patterns are immutable over time can also introduce privacy-related risks beyond just compromising the system [31]. Potentially, there are many circumstances in which a user might want to change his or her identifier, but its biological uniqueness persists even though the sample as well the template are recoded to different digital representations. Revocation or cancellation is possible only in specific cases with a priori use of special techniques of cancellable biometrics and/or biometric cryptosystems [21, 29].

T9: Threats to Confidentiality of User-Related Sensitive Information

Privacy risks are higher in biometric authorization systems than in conventional systems because of the continuous mode in which some biometric systems operate. Some biometric applications require always-recording feature which can disclose sensitive data such as personal images, or enterprise intellectual property. This threat is related mostly to temporal and spatial accumulation of raw visual or audio data.

Moreover, authorization attributes can encode the properties of parts of human body (e.g. physiological biometrics) or some human behavior (e.g. behavioral biometrics). It is relatively easy for access control systems designed for acquiring the biometric samples and processing the encoded templates, to perform additional analysis of templates or sample data, and infer information describing users based on these data. The information may refer not only to the body, or medical condition of the user, but it can even be used to estimate cultural or social characteristics of the user. For example voice sequences can reveal language spoken (nationality), accent (cultural/social characteristics), age, gender, emotional state. Face images or 3D head models can reveal medical condition, age, gender, race, estimated cultural/social characteristics, emotional state. Biometrics such as iris, vein patterns, electrocardiogram patterns, behavioral biometrics such as gait can reveal medical condition. Behavioral biometrics such as style of typing or style of touchscreen usage can reveal, directly or indirectly, privacy-sensitive input [31].

T10: Threats to User Anonymity (Confidentiality of User Identity)

The presence of identifiers, even if they are not originally referring to any sensitive data in the system, makes it possible to bind a person's virtual identity (anonymous or pseudonymous) used in cyberspace with his or her real-world identity, or to bind several persons' virtual identities with each other. Moreover, some identifiers could be used not only to bind identities themselves, but also to bind data and metadata describing actions of a particular user authenticated in various distributed services if service providers collude. In emerging ubiquitous services which are naturally decentralized and untrusted on the one hand, and require new seamless and convenient access control methods on the other, this threat is of special significance. Threats to privacy through data cross-analysis include also privacy risks following from cross-analysis of voluntary biometric databases created for user verification purposes with mandatory screening databases [31].

T11: Loss of Authorization Credentials
A user can lose authorization credentials in a number of ways. A user may lose a data storage such as a one-time code card, hardware security key, or a mobile device with a repository of such data. The previously mentioned storage media may also become damaged or failed. Access to authorization credentials may not be possible due to media not being supported by updated hardware or software.

4   Risk Analysis

In this phase of the analysis, possible impact of the threats (identified in Sect. 3) on the authorization methods (identified in Sect. 2) is presented. Rows in Table 1 represent authorization methods (M1–M8) while columns in Table 1 represent threats (T1–T11). Risk identifier present at the intersection of the given row and column means the given methods is vulnerable to the given threat. The risks identifiers are used in Sect. 5, where countermeasures mitigating the risks are described.

The results of the analysis presented in Table 1 are explained by threat for particular methods below:

- Threat T1, namely authorization attribute guessing (automated or semi-automated), affects passwords method (M1) obviously if user chooses short, weak, dictionary-based, or reused character string for password. Also T1 affects biometric methods (M5.1-M5.5) especially if biometrical attribute uniqueness is not high, which can be true for attributes such as face (M5.2) or voice (M5.3).
- Threat T2, SIM swap scam, is limited to the use of the mobile network as a channel for OOB authorization, so it mainly affects the method M2. This threat also affects the M8 authorization method, which requires a registered device, but only if a phone number is required for authorization, as opposed to the identifier specific to the device itself.
- Unlike the previous threat, the threat T3, phishing attacks, affects a number of authentication methods. In particular, all password-based methods are vulnerable (R1_3-R2.3_3), with the exception of M2.4_4, which in addition to the one-time password provides the user with detailed information about the transaction being authorized. In the case of biometric authorization methods, a phishing attack can result in the interception of biometric data samples (R5.1_3-R5.5_3).
- Threat T4 applies to all authentication methods that involve user interactions through the UI. All typed passwords can be recorded as one inputs them in public (R1_4-R2.4_4) and biometric features, except blood vessel patterns (M5.5), can be captured by various surveillance techniques (R5.1_4-R5.4_4).

Table 1. Results of the risk analysis. Authorization methods are in rows, threats are in columns, risks are in table cells.

	T1	T2	T3	T4	T5	T6	T7	T8	T9	T10	T11
M1	R1_1		R1_3	R1_4	R1_5						R1_11
M2.1			R2.1_3	R2.1_4	R2.1_5						R2.1_11
M2.2			R2.2_3	R2.2_4	R2.2_5						R2.2_11
M2.3			R2.3_3	R2.3_4	R2.3_5	R2.3_6					R2.3_11
M2.4		R2.4_2		R2.4_4							R2.4_11
M3					R3_5	R3_6		R3_8			R3_11
M4					R4_5	R4_6				R4_10	R4_11
M5.1	R5.1_1		R5.1_3	R5.1_4	R5.1_5			R5.1_8		R5.1_10	
M5.2	R5.2_1		R5.2_3	R5.2_4	R5.2_5		R5.2_7	R5.2_8	R5.2_9	R5.2_10	
M5.3	R5.3_1		R5.3_3	R5.3_4	R5.3_5		R5.3_7	R5.3_8	R5.3_9	R5.3_10	
M5.4	R5.4_1		R5.4_3	R5.4_4	R5.4_5			R5.4_8	R5.4_9	R5.4_10	
M5.5	R5.5_1		R5.5_3		R5.5_5			R5.5_8	R5.5_9	R5.5_10	
M6											R6_11
M7										R7_10	R7_11
M8		R8_2			R8_5	R8_6				R8_10	R8_11

- Threat T5, remote device control, is very severe, as a majority of authentication methods are susceptible. Methods employing devices that are independent of the device under the adversary's control (M2.4, M6, M7) show resilience.
- Threat T6, gaining physical access to the device, mainly affects authentication methods based on the possession factor, which is stored on the user device that the adversary physically accesses (R2.3_6, R3_6, R4_6, R8_6).
- Threat T7, authorization system's false acceptance, is specific to biometric attributes that are not characterized by high uniqueness level, such as face or voice (R5.2_7, R5.3_7).
- Threat T8 affects those methods for which compromised authorization data cannot be revoked. In most cases, this threat applies to biometric methods for which the compromised biometric pattern cannot be revoked because it is an inherent characteristic of the user (R5.1_8-R5.5_8). In turn, if the private key used in cryptocurrency system is compromised, its revocation is impossible, because the stored cryptocurrency is permanently bound to it (R3_8). The only solution left for the user is to transfer the funds to another address, hoping to get ahead of the adversary.
- Threat T9 is strongly related to user privacy, which applies only to biometric authentication methods (R5.2_9-R5.5_9). Fingerprints are an exception as it is difficult to infer sensitive information from this feature.
- Threat T10 to confidentiality of user identity occurs when the specific authorization data is used across multiple services. Linking authorization data from multiple services (even with anonymous access) can reveal user identity. Authorization methods based on biometrics are particularly susceptible to this threat (R5.1_10-R5.5_10).
- Threat T11 applies to any method that uses devices or items that may be lost or information that may be forgotten or deleted. Only biometric methods show resilience to this threat.

5   Countermeasures

C1: Secure Hardware Storage of Authorization Secret
Cryptographic keys are vulnerable to eavesdropping while cryptographic operations are performed in the device memory. This constitutes a motivation to use cryptography dedicated security processor [27]. Hardware security module (HSM) is a physically secure, tamper-resistant security system that provides a wide range of cryptographic functions to secure transactions [28]. Examples of HSM are trusted platform modules (TPM), U2F security keys and smart cards.

The use of USB security keys allows encryption keys and certificates to be stored within dedicated microchip, which means that they do not leave the device even when cryptographic operations are performed. It can reduce the risks (R3_5, R4_5, R8_5) of an adversary taking control over the device (e.g. via malware installed on the computer), due to the requirement for the user to manually authorize each transaction with USB security key interaction. HSM can significantly reduce the risk (R2.3_6, R3_6, R4_6, R8_6) associated with unauthorized physical access of an adversary to a device, as HSM integration with a host device enables disk encryption and controls booting option, including hard disk integrity check.

C2: Partial Password

Partial password is the input from a user to a challenge-response protocol, in which each time a user attempts to log in, he or she is presented with a challenge in which characters from random password positions must be entered. The types of attacks applied to a simple password also apply to a partial password, but the adversary must collect more data to launch a successful attack [12, 15].

A partial password reduces the risk (R1_4) associated with password threats such as recording during typing. The risk (R1_3, R1_5) associated with phishing attacks and device takeover (e.g., by malware) is also reduced because it requires the adversary to repeat the attack multiple times before learning the full password. Partial password has ambiguous impact on risk related to automated password guessing (R1_1): it makes technical layer of an attack harder but computational layer easier.

C3: OOB Authorization Channel

Out of band (OOB) is a separate communication channel for transaction authorization [13]. OOB security relies on the independence of the separate channels to prevent both from being compromised simultaneously [23].

The OOB authorization channel reduces the risks (R1_5, R2.1_5, R2.2_5, R2.3_5, R5.1_5, R5.2_5, R5.3_5, R5.4_5, R5.5_5) of unauthorized transaction authorization caused by an adversary taking control over the device, as it prevents the adversary from reading messages incoming to another device (not controlled by an adversary) through a different channel or outgoing from another device through a different channel.

C4: Distributed Architecture

A design solution that allows reduction of some of the privacy-related risks is a shift towards "distributed architecture". In this solution, biometric templates are stored in an encrypted form within devices (e.g., smartcard or mobile device) over which a user has full control. Each device has a biometric sensor built-in. User identification, authentication or transaction authorization is performed locally by comparing the acquired sample with the stored template (according to more robust verification instead of identification scheme). Some applications [6] demonstrate that such an approach is possible to implement and effective from the privacy perspective. However, unfortunately the current dominant trend is just the opposite – to store and process as much data as possible in the cloud-based, centralized manner that is potentially privacy destroying [31].

Avoiding centralized storage of biometric templates mitigates risks to confidentiality of user-related sensitive information (R5.2_9, R5.3_9, R5.4_9, R5.5_9), and to user anonymity (R5.1_10, R5.2_10, R5.3_10, R5.4_10, R5.5_10).

C5: Cancelable Biometrics

Cancelable biometrics protects a user biometric characteristics by using transformed or distorted biometric data to create biometrics based template. The compromised biometric templates do not allow biometric trait recovery [21, 33]. Cancelable biometrics must meet the following requirements: revocability, irreversibility, diversity, unlinkability. Revocability allows for easy revocation and reissuance if the template is compromised [4, 26]. Irreversibility makes it computationally difficult to reconstruct the original biometric pattern from stored reference data [4, 21, 26]. Diversity requires a large number of protected templates from the same biometric trait because the same cancelable templates cannot be used in different applications [4, 21, 26]. Unlinkability means that knowledge of one template generated from a biometric feature cannot provide additional knowledge of other templates generated from that feature [21, 26].

Revocable biometrics reduces system security risks (R5.1_8, R5.2_8, R5.3_8, R5.4_8, R5.5_8) related to compromised authorization data due to application of revocable transformed biometric patterns. As the transformed biometric patterns do not reveal biometric characteristics cancellable biometrics reduces the risks (R5.2_9, R5.3_9, R5.4_9, R5.5_9). Due to unlinkability of these patterns, the risks related to revealing user sensitive data and risks (R5.1_10, R5.2_10, R5.3_10, R5.4_10, R5.5_10) to user anonymity are mitigated.

C6: Liveness Detection

Liveness detection addresses the significant challenge to biometrics that is related to resistance to attacks with fake authenticator. The examples of this countermeasure include: pulse in finger, or heartbeat for fingerprint or vein biometrics; eye blinking or pupil changes for iris or face biometrics.

Liveness detection reduces the risks of an adversary authorizing a transaction based on captured (R5.1_4, R5.2_4, R5.3_4, R5.4_4) or automatically generated (R5.1_1, R5.2_1, R5.3_1, R5.4_1, R5.5_1) biometric patterns because authorization requires not only the pattern, but also other relevant vital signs of the user (e.g., finger blood flow, eye micro movements, head movements, etc.). Although liveness detection can indeed reduce the likelihood of success of the attacks, it introduces new privacy-related risk, since it increases the amount of sensitive data that is collected in a continuous manner (R5.2_9, R5.3_9, R5.4_9, R5.5_9).

C7: Biometric Cryptosystem

Biometric cryptosystem uses biometric traits to generate cryptographic keys [29]. In such a system a cryptographic key is generated each time the user wants to use it. As the biometric traits are fixed, only the helper data are required to reconstruct the cryptographic key. Biometric cryptosystem can be developed to act as public biometric infrastructure with certified biometric based public-private key pairs [10].

Biometric cryptosystem reduces security risks (R5.1_8, R5.2_8, R5.3_8, R5.4_8, R5.5_8) related to compromised authorization data due to application of revocable certificates. As the public-private key pairs do not reveal biometric characteristics it reduces the risks (R5.2_9, R5.3_9, R5.4_9, R5.5_9) of revealing user sensitive data.

C8: Mnemonic Phrase

Mnemonic phrase is a list of random words, that is used to calculate seed in order to generate deterministic cryptographic key [24]. The example of mnemonic phrase generation algorithm and seed generation algorithm is included in BIP 39 [7].

Application of the mnemonic phrase reduces the risks (R3_11, R4_11, R6_11) of losing cryptographic keys, as it allows for their deterministic recovery from a word list.

C9: Virtual Keyboard

A virtual keyboard is a software that acts as a keyboard, with the user selecting characters by pointing them on the device screen [20]. This solution partially reduces the risk (R1_5) of an adversary intercepting characters of password typed on the computer using a key logger.

C10: Device Identification
Device identification involves restricting access to transaction authorization interface by filtering out devices based on their attributes (e.g. location, operating system, web browser, network address). This solution implies that authorization data is not enough to successfully authorize a transaction, but a specific device is also needed. In such a situation, the adversary must intercept not only the authorization data, but also the user device and even gain access to the user local network.

The use of device identification mitigates or compensates the risks associated with: automated credentials guessing (R1_1, R5.1_1, R5.2_1, R5.3_1, R5.4_1, R5.5_1), SIM swap scam (R2.4_2, R8_2), phishing attack (R1_3-R2.3_3, R5.1_3-R5.5_3), confidentiality of authorization attributes in physical spaces (R1_4-R2.4_4, R5.1_4-R5.4_4), and transaction authenticity through false acceptance (R5.2_7, R5.3_7).

C11: Authorization Credentials Dependent on Transaction Attributes
Authorization credentials that are dependent on transaction attributes are generated dynamically by taking the transaction attributes as an input in order to bind the authorization credential with transaction details. Such solution can be applied to one time password generation and reduces the risks (R2.2_3, R2.3_3, R2.2_5, R2.3_5) caused by intercepted authorization data.

C12: Multimodal Biometric System
Multimodal biometric systems combine multiple biometrical recognizers. They have been developed to reduce the FAR and FRR (R5.2_7, R5.3_7). Also they have been developed to increase the user convenience, since the modalities can be chosen dynamically according to their availability and suitability in the given context. However, they increase the possibility of data cross-analysis accompanied by the associated increased risks of privacy breach (R5.2_9, R5.3_9, R5.4_9, R5.5_9).

C13: Multifactor Transaction Authorization
Multifactor transaction authorization requires the user to use at least two different types of evidence in order to authorize transaction. Four different types of evidence can be distinguished: knowledge, possession, inherent and location [16]. Multifactor transaction authorization still may show vulnerability to man-in-the-middle attack, so it is proposed to introduce separate communication channels for factors [23].

Multifactor transaction authorization reduces the vulnerability risks with varying degrees of strength. Simply introducing a second factor does not necessarily reduce the total risk. Threats that are particularly difficult to eliminate with multifactor approach are phishing and social engineering: an adversary may persuade a user to disclose various authorization factors and to perform various actions ultimately leading to the authorization of an unwanted transaction. The choice of the second authorization factor must be preceded by a risk analysis of both transaction authorization methods. The Table 1 may be helpful in making such choices. From the content of the mentioned table it can be showed as an example that a good pair of authorization factors are a one-time password sent by SMS combined with biometrics based on the finger vein pattern, as they share no common threats.

6 Conclusions

The presented security analysis of transaction authorization methods takes into account many factors posing risks to the analyzed methods and allows to draw useful conclusions. First, using authorization methods combined can significantly reduce the risk of threats, but only in cases when those methods are selected not to share common threats (e.g. M5.1 and M6, or M2.4 and M5.5). Second, not all identified risks can be reduced by the countermeasures (e.g. R3_8, R8_10, R7_11), and even if they can the residual risk remains (e.g. C2 for R1_4). Next, the countermeasures should be selected carefully, as they may introduce new risks (e.g. C6 can increase R5.2_9, or C12 can increase R5.3_7). Finally, the number of threats to an authorization method does not correspond to the ease of reducing the risks associated with this method. For example M3 is vulnerable only to four risks, but they include the risk R3_8 that is hard to reduce in the context of the cryptocurrencies. The risk analysis presented in Sect. 4 and the list of countermeasures from Sect. 5 can be useful for selecting authorization methods and appropriate countermeasures when designing a transaction authorization mechanism.

The future work includes more detailed risk analysis:

- analysis of cases in which combining a number of no-risk threats on a single method can produce high-risk;
- probability estimation for each risk;
- impact estimation for each risk;
- for each risk analysis how each countermeasure can affect risk impact and risk probability.

References

1. Adams, C.: Certificate revocation. In: van Tilborg H.C.A., Jajodia, S. (eds.) Encyclopedia of Cryptography and Security. Springer, Boston, MA (2011). https://doi.org/10.1007/978-1-4419-5906-5_71
2. Brose, G.: Password. In: van Tilborg, H.C.A., Jajodia, S. (eds.) Encyclopedia of Cryptography and Security. Springer, Boston, MA (2011). https://doi.org/10.1007/978-1-4419-5906-5_213
3. Brose, G.: Rainbow tables. In: van Tilborg, H.C.A., Jajodia, S. (eds.) Encyclopedia of Cryptography and Security. Springer, Boston, MA (2011). https://doi.org/10.1007/978-1-4419-5906-5_219
4. Cimato, S., Sassi, R., Scotti, F.: Biometric privacy. In: Jajodia, S., Samarati, P., Yung, M. (eds.) Encyclopedia of Cryptography, Security and Privacy. Springer, Berlin, Heidelberg (2021). https://doi.org/10.1007/978-3-642-27739-9_734-2
5. De Soete, M.: PKI. In: van Tilborg, H.C.A., Jajodia, S. (eds.) Encyclopedia of Cryptography and Security. Springer, Boston, MA (2011). https://doi.org/10.1007/978-1-4419-5906-5_301
6. Fido Alliance: How FIDO Works? https://fidoalliance.org/how-fido-works/
7. Garreau, M.: Ethereum 201: Mnemonics (2020). https://wolovim.medium.com/ethereum-201-mnemonics-bb01a9108c38
8. Gomez-Barrero, M.: Finger vein. In: Jajodia, S., Samarati, P., Yung, M. (eds.) Encyclopedia of Cryptography, Security and Privacy. Springer, Berlin, Heidelberg (2021). https://doi.org/10.1007/978-3-642-27739-9_1487-1

9. Jordaan, L., von Solms, B.: A biometrics-based solution to combat SIM swap fraud. In: Camenisch, Jan, Kisimov, Valentin, Dubovitskaya, Maria (eds.) iNetSec 2010. LNCS, vol. 6555, pp. 70–87. Springer, Heidelberg (2011). https://doi.org/10.1007/978-3-642-19228-9_7

10. Kaga, Y., Matsuda, Y., Takahashi, K., Nagasaka, A.: Biometric authentication platform for a safe, secure, and convenient society. Hitachi Rev. **64**(8), 473 (2015)

11. Laerte, P., Holtz, M., David, B., Deus, F., de Sousa Junior, R.: A formal classification of internet banking attacks and vulnerabilities. Int. J. Comput. Sci. Inf. Technol. **3** (2011). https://doi.org/10.5121/ijcsit.2011.3113

12. Laudon, K.C., Traver, C.G.: E-commerce: Business, Technology, Society. Pearson, London (2016)

13. Latvala, S., Sethi, M., Aura, T.: evaluation of out-of-band channels for IoT security. SN Comput. Sci. **1**(1), 1–17 (2019). https://doi.org/10.1007/s42979-019-0018-8

14. Menezes, A.J., Van Oorschot, P.C., Vanstone, S.A.: Handbook of applied cryptography. CRC press, Boca Raton (2001)

15. Mourouzis, T., Wojcik, M., Komninos, N.: On the security evaluation of partial password implementations. arXiv preprint arXiv:1701.00104 (2016)

16. OWASP: Multifactor Authentication Cheat Sheet. https://cheatsheetseries.owasp.org/cheats heets/Multifactor_Authentication_Cheat_Sheet.html

17. OWASP: Password Storage Cheat Sheet. https://cheatsheetseries.owasp.org/cheatsheets/Pas sword_Storage_Cheat_Sheet.html

18. OWASP: Transaction Authorization Cheat Sheet. https://cheatsheetseries.owasp.org/cheats heets/Transaction_Authorization_Cheat_Sheet.html

19. Paar, C., Pelzl, J.: Key establishment. In: Understanding Cryptography. Springer, Berlin (2010). https://doi.org/10.1007/978-3-642-04101-3_13

20. PCMag, virtual keyboard. https://www.pcmag.com/encyclopedia/term/virtual-keyboard

21. Rathgeb, C., Uhl, A.: A survey on biometric cryptosystems and cancelable biometrics. EURASIP J. Info. Secur. **2011**, 3 (2011). https://doi.org/10.1186/1687-417X-2011-3

22. Rayes, M.O.: One-time password. In: van Tilborg, H.C.A., Jajodia, S. (eds.) Encyclopedia of Cryptography and Security. Springer, Boston, MA (2011). https://doi.org/10.1007/978-1-4419-5906-5_785

23. Rosenberg, B. (ed.): Handbook of financial cryptography and security. CRC Press, Boca Raton (2010)

24. Rusnak, P.: Mnemonic code for generating deterministic keys (2013). https://github.com/bit coin/bips/blob/master/bip-0039.mediawiki

25. Sako, K.: Digital signature schemes. In: van Tilborg, H.C.A., Jajodia, S. (eds.) Encyclopedia of Cryptography and Security. Springer, Boston, MA (2011). https://doi.org/10.1007/978-1-4419-5906-5_17

26. Scholarpedia, Cancelable biometrics. https://www.scholarpedia.org/article/Cancelable_biom etrics

27. Smith, S.W.: Secure coprocessor. In: van Tilborg, H.C.A., Jajodia, S. (eds.) Encyclopedia of Cryptography and Security. Springer, Boston, MA (2011). https://doi.org/10.1007/978-1-4419-5906-5_495

28. Sustek, L.: Hardware security module. In: van Tilborg, H.C.A., Jajodia, S. (eds.) Encyclopedia of Cryptography and Security. Springer, Boston, MA (2011). https://doi.org/10.1007/978-1-4419-5906-5_509

29. Uhl, A., Rathgeb, C.: Biometric encryption. In: Jajodia, S., Samarati, P., Yung, M. (eds.) Encyclopedia of Cryptography, Security and Privacy. Springer, Berlin (2021). https://doi.org/10.1007/978-3-642-27739-9_1519-1

30. Wilusz, D., Wójtowicz, A.: Securing cryptoasset insurance services with multisignatures. In: Herrero, Á., et al. (eds.) 13th International Conference on Computational Intelligence in Security for Information Systems (CISIS 2020). Advances in Intelligent Systems and Computing, vol. 1267. Springer, Cham (2021). https://doi.org/10.1007/978-3-030-57805-3_4
31. Wójtowicz, A., Cellary, W.: New challenges for user privacy in cyberspace. Human-computer interaction and cybersecurity handbook, pp. 77–96. Taylor & Francis Group, Boca Raton (2019)
32. Wójtowicz, A., Chmielewski J.: Technical feasibility of context-aware passive payment authorization for physical points of sale. In: Personal and Ubiquitous Computing, vol. 21, issue 6, pp. 1113–1125. Springer London (2017). https://doi.org/10.1007/s00779-017-1035-z,
33. Yang, W., Hu, J., Wang, S.: A finger-vein based cancellable bio-cryptosystem. In: Lopez, Javier, Huang, Xinyi, Sandhu, Ravi (eds.) NSS 2013. LNCS, vol. 7873, pp. 784–790. Springer, Heidelberg (2013). https://doi.org/10.1007/978-3-642-38631-2_71

Security and Privacy by Design

Beyond Murphy's Law: Applying Wider Human Factors Behavioural Science Approaches in Cyber-Security Resilience

An Applied Practice Case Study Discussing Approaches to Assessing Human Factors Vulnerabilities in Cyber-Security Systems

Nicola Fairburn[✉], Andrew Shelton[✉], Frances Ackroyd[✉], and Rachel Selfe[✉]

Atkins Ltd, A Member of the SNC-Lavalin Group, London, England
{Nicola.fairburn,Andrew.shelton,Frances.ackroyd,
Rachel.selfe}@atkinsglobal.com

Abstract. Traditional approaches to cyber-security resilience, assuring the overall socio-technical system is secure from immediate known attacks and routes to potential future attacks, have relied on three pillars of people, process, and technology.

In any complex socio-technical system, human behaviour can disrupt the secure and efficient running of the system with risk accumulating through individual and system-wide errors and compromised security behaviours that may be exploited by actors with malicious intent.

Practitioners' experience and use of different assessment methods and approaches to establish cyber-security vulnerabilities and risk are evaluated. Qualitative and quantitative methods and data are used for different stages of investigations in order to derive risk assessments and access contextual experience for further analyses. Organisational security culture and development approaches along with safety assessment methods are discussed in this case study to understand how well the people, the system, and the organisation interact.

Cyber-security Human Factors practice draws on other application areas such as safety, usability, behaviours and culture to progressively assess security posture; the benefits of each approach are discussed.

This study identifies the most effective methods for vulnerability identification and risk assessment, with focus on modelling large, dynamic and complex socio-technical systems, to be those which identify cultural factors with impact on human-system interactions.

Keywords: Human factors · Cyber-security · Behavioural science · Organisational culture · Security culture · Cyber- resilience · Socio-technical · Safety assessment · Climate · Behavioral · Organizational culture · Socio-behavioural · Sociotechnical

1 Introduction

Traditional approaches to cyber-security resilience, that is assuring the overall socio-technical system is secure from immediate known attacks and routes to potential future

© Springer Nature Switzerland AG 2021
A. Moallem (Ed.): HCII 2021, LNCS 12788, pp. 123–138, 2021.
https://doi.org/10.1007/978-3-030-77392-2_9

attacks, have relied on three pillars of people, process, and technology. Historically greater emphasis has been placed on technology solutions with reduced attention placed on the human element; now human behaviours, culture and organisational human factors are considered in every cyber-resilience improvement programme.

There are multiple different understandings of 'human factors' (HF). The International Ergonomics Association (IEA) defines human factors as '…the scientific discipline of interactions among humans and other elements of a system, and the profession that applies theory, principles, data and methods to design in order to optimize human well-being and overall system performance' [1]. Part of these human-system interactions involve understanding the drivers for behaviours e.g. the capability, opportunity and motivation. It also involves; ensuring the design supports the needs of the user, identifying where the user will find the system complex to interact with, ensuring the design minimises the likelihood of human error and ensuring the design maximises the opportunities for error tolerance.

In any complex socio-technical system, the significant risk of certain "human factors" disrupting the secure and efficient running of the system is now widely recognised. The accumulated effect of individual and system-wide human errors and compromised security behaviours lead to vulnerabilities that may be exploited by threat actors, or attackers, with malicious intent. Identifying those vulnerabilities; assessing the risk arising from them; and evidencing the argument for making improvements is critical to developing cyber-resilience.

Within safety, James Reason's (1997) [2] 'Swiss Cheese' model of accident causation is used in risk analysis and risk management, where the risk of a hazard causing harm in the system is reduced as layers of defence are added. For straightforward security compromises, where layers of defence prevent the risk from developing, this model still applies to security, as demonstrated in Fig. 1.

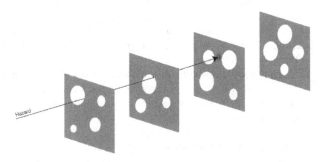

Fig. 1. Multiple defensive layers of security prevent hazards becoming incidents.

However, in cyber-security a threat actor seeks to attack targeted systems and can manipulate these layers to exploit any vulnerabilities within the wider socio-technical system to create an attack path. Furthermore, rather than a linear path of circumstantial failure, threat actors can actively weave their way through defences to engineer a system failure as demonstrated in Fig. 2.

Fig. 2. Manipulation of vulnerabilities by a threat actor.

The Murphy's law adage stresses that 'what can go wrong will go wrong', with acknowledgement that it is often considered in reality as a case of 'what can go wrong might go wrong at some point'. However, in cyber-security assurance it is necessary to go beyond Murphy's law as 'what can go wrong will be actively sought out and manipulated to make it go wrong'.

When considering 'the human' and human behaviour in a large, complex socio-technical system, a distinction should be made between the different roles adopted by humans as 'end-users', attackers, defenders and bystanders. While the threats posed by individual threat actors, with the intention of actively creating and exploiting vulnerabilities, are well-documented, they can be emphasised at the expense of potential vulnerabilities posed by humans in the system carrying out their everyday work tasks.

In order to understand the human-centred activities a key element of the investigation activities focused on the day-to-day tasks of all humans in the organisation as they interact with the system. Drawing on both goal-orientated and social interactions enables the identification of vulnerabilities which can be exploited by the threat actors, and recommendation of human-centred mitigations to increase security.

From working within high-hazard domains, HF have a pedigree in understanding and identifying the potential vulnerabilities within a system, in sharing knowledge across domains, and transferring best practices to create a more rigorous cyber-security process.

Comparisons have been made across both safety and cyber-security, drawing on HF practitioner experience. On the surface, safety hazards and cyber-attack paths look very different and the processes used to identify the underlying vulnerabilities within the system are also different. A cyber threat is often perceived as an adversary deliberately targeting a system, however that is not the only way to assess vulnerabilities in a cyber-security context. As stated by Dekker [4] "…people in safety critical jobs are generally motivated to stay alive, to keep their passengers, their patients, their customers alive. They do not go out of their way to deliver overdoses; to fly into mountainsides…". The majority of people want to do a good job both in a cyber-security and safety context. One of the most striking similarities within both domains is the requirement to understand the human element of risk and what drives risky behaviours. Most people do not intend to undertake risky security behaviour, but multiple factors can influence their actions such as time pressure, outdated system or task design, or deliberate manipulation through social engineering, all of which can result in workarounds, lapses and behaviour that leads to people unintentionally compromising security.

As HF practitioners, assessing the human cyber risks within a system requires a shift in focus from the malicious outsider threat, to incorporating a wider focus to include social engineering, organisational culture and system design that can create the opportunity for attack paths.

In the socio-technical system of interest it is the vulnerabilities that are sought out. In terms of cyber-security, a vulnerability is an element of the system which has the potential to be exploited as part of an attack path, and is assessed with an associated risk of compromise.

1.1 Case Study

This paper introduces the case study activities experienced by the authors and their organisation with a number of clients in different sectors. It explores the overlaps and differences from across domains and discusses how this knowledge can be applied to a risk investigation to identify the widest set of human-based and system vulnerabilities. The method and processes described draw upon existing best practices in technical, cyber-security and behavioural science safety approaches into one homogenised methodology.

Cyber-security investigations have been conducted into a variety of systems, ranging from single technology applications, for example an app on a mobile phone, to multiple inter-related systems, with interactions from multiple parties, based in different locations. For the purpose of this paper, an example transactional system 'System 1' is accessed and interacted with from two office sites, and the investigation scope is identified accordingly, as shown in Fig. 3.

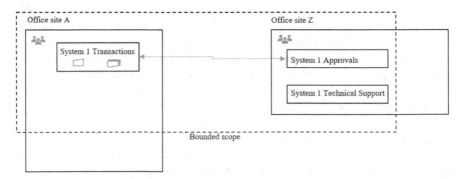

Fig. 3. Example diagram showing System 1 usage across office sites A and Z.

People and processes are intrinsically interwoven with technology throughout its design, manufacture, installation, use and maintenance, and ultimately disposal. Cyber-security risk is therefore assessed for each of these stages, and for all interactions, within the socio-technical system in order to identify vulnerabilities which could enable an adversary to gain access to the information contained within. In the example above, authorised access to System 1's transactions by users in office sites A and Z would be examined, along with the cases where System 1 users required approval by senior users, or needed technical support in order to complete a transaction. In addition, unauthorized use of System 1's connection between office sites, would also be a plausible vulnerability line of enquiry. Note that other systems and interactions in both office sites are beyond the scope boundary of this investigation.

2   Recognised HF Approaches

Human Factors practitioners adopt a human-centred approach to work across different industries, and working with multi-disciplinary teams. This wide range of work allows us valuable access to a range of tools and techniques. The following sections draw upon and pull together experience of utilising HF processes within the technology domain, the safety domain, behavioural science and cultural assessment and following a human-centred assessment approach. Collating best practice from each of these domains has allowed the creation of a bespoke approach for cyber-security HF investigations to date, combining the best techniques from across multiple domains in high hazard industries.

2.1   HF Adoption of Formal Cyber-Security Methods

When investigating an organisation's security defences against a potential cyber-security attack, it is important that the system is considered in its entirety and that potential vulnerabilities are assessed from the mindset of an attacker. This section outlines the existing methods and practices drawn on by HF and cyber-security domain experts for investigating and identifying cyber-security vulnerabilities.

The aim of the reviews, investigations and assessments is to develop an accurate, 'real world' view of the socio-technical system. These are required to produce a detailed analysis of the vulnerabilities which may lie within. The focal point of an investigation could be narrow, such as a piece of technical equipment, or broad, such as an establishment or group of people.

A typical security project is divided into phases namely: Familiarisation & Modelling, Investigation, Analysis and Risk Assessment. These phases are demonstrated in Fig. 4 and outlined below.

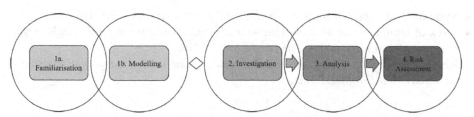

Fig. 4. Typical phases of a cyber-security investigation.

Familiarisation and Modelling

The aim of the initial phases of the investigation is to gain a primary understanding of the socio-technical system under investigation by gathering existing technical and process material, and engaging stakeholders. It is important to confirm the scope of the process and the boundaries of the socio-technical system that will be explored, and ultimately analysed.

Modelling provides a central focal point for all information found to date and reflects the initial high-level analysis of the critical components within the system, this allows the team to discuss identified high level impacts associated with those components.

Investigation

Investigation of a socio-technical system is planned and conducted in order to progressively discover and identify likely areas of potential vulnerablity. After initial identification, further qualification through deep dive exploration of all candidate areas reveals the extent of the vulnerabilities that may exist. Data is collected through a range of quantitative and qualitative methods and analysed to evaluate technical security assurance, along with security and organisational culture. As the data accumulates, a developed picture of the initial assessment outcomes and the potential impacts of vulnerabilities on the system as a whole, is made.

Analysis and Risk Assessment

During the 'Analysis' phase the accumulated data is analysed from the perspective of an adversary in order to establish how the vulnerabilities could be exploited and manipulated into potential attack paths to infiltrate the system. Following this, risks are quantified during the 'Risk Assessment' phase according to their liklihood of occurance and the impact on the organisaiton. Again this overlaps with, and leads directly into, the next phase where risk mitigation strategies are formulated and proposed.

2.2   HF Practitioner Experience

In undertaking HF activities on complex systems, HF practitioners are experienced in the application of structured, rigorous methodologies, and providing strong substantiation arguments in support of safety and security cases which are presented to regulators. This experience afforded the opportunity to select, learn and create best practice in translating methods, and rigour to new domains such as cyber-security assurance. The following outlines some of our learning:

- System scope – *the importance of bounding the system that is being assessed.*
- Work-as-imagined and work-as-done – *the identification of the differences which can appear between work-as-imagined and work-as-done.*
- Risk and Resilience – *The likelihood that some form of unintended outcome will have an impact on the organisation.*

System Scope

It is important to ensure the scope of the system is fully bounded and the practitioner assessing the system, fully understands how the system is used, by means of developing a task analysis to identify human interaction with the system under investigation. For example, a technical system may have limited human interactions compared with a site which may have multiple digital systems within scope. From experience gained in the cyber-security domain, a system of systems approach has been adopted looking at the individual technological system and the context in which it operates. The system of system approach proposed here incorporates the features of a typical HF system of systems approach but goes beyond it in order to evaluate the scope of the accumulated risk and attack paths. Therefore, to undertake a successful cyber investigation the scope of the system should be clearly defined and the human interactions within the system understood and documented.

Work Done vs Work Imagined

From investigating human error, a significant part of the HF input is to review, understand and analyse how work is intended to be carried out ('work-as-imagined') compared with how work is conducted in reality ('work-as-done') [3]. This approach involves utilising task analyses, hierarchical and tabular task analysis (HTA,TTA) for example, behavioural and system modelling, and engagement with end-users through interviews and focus groups. In addition, observations are carried out to review 'work-as-done', including any workarounds to cyber-security procedures that may pose a greater risk. Evaluating the differences and variation between work-as-done and work-as-imagined, will help the client's understanding of the interaction of many factors in the overall system, such as organisational pressure, poorly written or out of date procedures, and inadequate training to name a few. As will be discussed later, the gaps between 'work-as-done' and 'work-as-imagined' are a good indicator of where system weaknesses or potential vulnerabilities may lie that could be exploited by an adversary.

Risk and Resilience

Definitions of risk in cyber-security vary; for the purposes of this case study, it can be conceived as a form of unintended outcome that has the ability to impact the mission, whether in a commercial or defence environment. These impacts are loss of: finance, reputation, operational capability and, in some contexts, loss of life.

The risks of cyber-security attack paths and vulnerabilities being exploited are established against a standard risk matrix of risks, the impact of the unintended outcomes, and the likelihood. The level of risk however varies for each case and for maximum effectiveness, is aligned with the risk appetite of the organisation. Some may have a conservative, low security risk-appetite whereas others may be more risk tolerant in a security context. The risk-benefit analysis (RBA) is therefore unique for each organisation and system.

Furthermore there may be a set of risks associated to system 'A', for instance a mobile phone, which may be deemed to be acceptable, and another set of risks associated to system 'B', let's say a server room, which are also deemed to be acceptable. However, when the mobile phone is in the server room the accumulated risks of the larger, combined, systems will be different, and may become unacceptable. In this context a system of systems approach can be recognised and the importance of clearly defining the boundaries of the targeted system and the scope of the investigation at the outset are highlighted.

2.3 Culture

In order to understand how well the people and systems in an organisation interact, it is increasingly important to recognize and assess how the organisational and security environment affects the operation of work done and work-as-imagined. Organisational cultures where blame is high for security breaches or those where operational focus is consistently prioritized over security issues, could be exploited as potential vulnerabilities.

By collecting data on both the security culture and organisational culture throughout the investigation process and timeframe, it is possible to standardize some responses as a basis for assessing risk, and to identify anomalous areas for further in-depth interviews. This is achieved through incorporating questions and commentary into all interviews, surveys, observed group discussions and tasks, and making use of security culture questionnaires and pulse surveys for climate. In addition, organisational change and development methods can be utilized to improve the security implications of cultural factors. Furthermore, readiness or baseline assessments of the impact of cultural factors can then be incorporated into an overall strategy for cultural change development.

Expected human-computer interactions, flows of information and security decision-making points can be identified on the socio-technical systems model, even where complex systems are in use. Identifying cultural factors that alter or interrupt those interactions, information or decisions across the breadth of the target system yielded effective vulnerability identification and risk assessment. These models and factors are then overlaid with complementary security data using robust assessment frameworks developed for the organisation.

Qualitative and quantitative methods and data were used for different stages of the investigation in order to derive risk assessments and access contextual experience for further analyses. For example, exposure to the risk of social engineering was assessed using 'direct' questions, whereas expectations of blame for an incident was asked 'indirectly' with opportunities to comment.

The primary focus of the approach is to assess the impact of cultural factors on cybersecurity risk, Potential vulnerabilities can be exploited in a direct attack on an identified cultural weakness, or by engineering the situation to take advantage of cultural factors.

In activities that focus on modelling large, dynamic and complex socio-technical systems, identifying cultural factors that affect human interactions across the breadth of the system were most effective for vulnerability identification and risk assessment.

2.4 Safety Assurance Applied to Security

Safety assurance is a formal and systematic process which aims to demonstrate that an organisation, functional system, plant or process are tolerably safe. Safety assurance can result in risks being effectively managed and lead to improved system performance.

HF forms an integral part of the safety assurance process. With HF specialists working alongside safety specialists to help to ensure the 'human' element of risk is identified and effectively managed throughout the safety assurance process.

HF are integrated into safety assurance in multiple industries such as aviation, nuclear, defence and rail. Some of the worst major accidents have highlighted the complex role of the 'human' within the wider complex socio-technical systems. These major accidents have helped to demonstrate the combination of system failures and human failures perfectly aligning to result in some of the worst disasters (for example, Piper Alpha, Chernobyl and Herald of the Free Enterprise). Having HF effectively integrated within the safety assurance process can help to identify human failure within the complex socio-technical system where the human is an integral part of the complex system and come up with effective mitigation solutions to minimise the likelihood of human error from occurring.

Providing HF safety assurance within a complex socio-technical system is detailed and a proportionate approach must be adapted depending on the level of 'risk' involved. A typical approach to HF safety assurance is presented in Fig. 5. This approach is systematic, detailed and can be time consuming. Focusing HF efforts in the areas of highest risk such as safety-critical, safety-related or complex tasks ensures efforts are proportionate to the risk. Once the overall set of these tasks are identified, task analysis is conducted on each to analyse the task detail undertaken by operators and maintainers. Error analysis is conducted to identify credible human error. The extent to which human errors are quantified with the derivation of human error probabilities (HEPs) depends on the requirements from the safety case. Regardless of whether it is done numerically or quantitatively, HF practitioners indicate the likelihood of error occurrence and identify the performance shaping factors (PSFs) that will make that error more or less likely to occur.

A key part of the process is to identify opportunities to mitigate the human error. The 'as low as reasonably practicable' (ALARP) approach is adopted within HF safety assurance. Therefore, whilst eliminating human error is the preference (based on the ERICPD[1]), several factors are considered including cost of proposed change, consequence and likelihood of the error occurring. One option, which is used particularity within operational plants where engineered changes are more costly, is to derive procedural controls such as human-based safety claims (HBSCs) to protect against system and human error. Procedural controls rely on operators or maintainers to form a key layer of defence against an unintended consequence (see Fig. 1 to highlight layers of defence against an unintended consequence). Therefore, any HBSCs made will need to be qualitatively substantiated to ensure the necessary arrangements are in place to demonstrate that the HBSCs form a reliable layer of defence against an unintended consequence.

This HF assurance approach utilizes a number of HF tools and techniques, including hierarchical and tabular task analysis (HTA,TTA), error analysis, walk-throughs and talk-throughs with operators and maintainers, desk top reviews of documentation such as operating procedures, derivation of HEPs and qualitative substantiation of HBSCs. These HF tools and techniques are not unique to HF safety assurance and can be utilised across any domain to support HF assessment work. In addition, whilst this traditional

---

[1] Eliminate, Reduce, Isolate, Control, Personal Protective Equipment and Discipline.

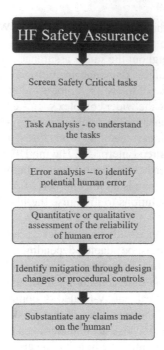

Fig. 5. A typical HF safety assurance process.

approach to HF safety assurance has been presented here this approach can be adapted to suit a range of different domains such as cyber-security to ensure HF are integrated and 'human' remains a key focus in identifying human failures or vulnerabilities and any potential defence and solution can be delivered consistently and reliably.

3   Methods

From the previous sections it is apparent that there are multiple HF qualitative and quantitative methods available for HF practitioners to use when undertaking a cyber-security review. The following section outlines the process utilised by HF for cyber-security investigations drawing upon the knowledge and techniques applied across wider domains. It should be recognized the process defined below is iterative throughout, with further investigation or analysis being conducted as required, until all parties are satisfied that the socio-technical system has been analysed in full (Fig. 6).

Familiarisation
Assurances of stakeholder and user confidentiality are made during initial contact in this stage. As outlined in Sect. 2.1 the output of the familiarization stage summarises the 'what and why' of the existing socio-technical system as well as any vulnerabilities that immediately emerge.

The methods that are used include literature reviews and internal briefings, as well as reviews of security processes, procedures and documentation regarding the existing

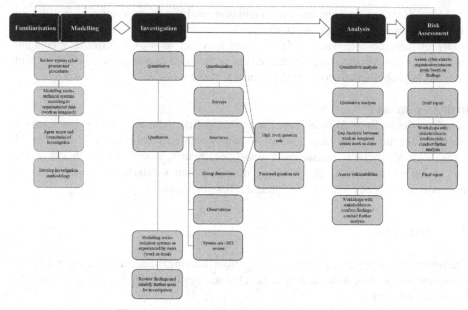

Fig. 6. Cyber-security HF investigation process.

systems. The reviews include training records, cyber-security training, organisational charts and technical processes in order to establish the 'work-as-imagined' and facilitate the development of investigation strategies unique to that system.

Modelling
Human-system interactions are identified to develop the initial socio-technical model which will act as a baseline for the investigation which is updated as the process evolves. The methods used include; task analysis, system modelling and behaviour modelling.

Investigation
All interactions are examined using a number of methods including quantitative questionnaires and surveys along with qualitative interviews, discussions and observations of behaviours, work environment and system use which could include assessments of usability and human computer interaction (HCI).

After the initial engagement, thematic analysis is conducted in order to prepare a focused question set developed to encapsulate themes enabling further exploration in subsequent engagements. The data produced is used to build up a picture of how the socio-technical system actually operates and where potential vulnerabilities may lie.

Analysis
Wider practitioner experience is employed to create a full understanding of the data set by applying theory, skills, knowledge and expertise along with external application of guidance, standards and recommended good practice. Utilising a number of human factors methods enables a comprehensive overview of system vulnerabilities to be captured.

Methods include quantitative and qualitative analysis of interviews as well as gap analysis between identified 'work-as-imagined' and 'work-as-done' processes. The emergent gaps indicate where vulnerabilities may lie, such as security shortcuts and workarounds, as processes are not carried out as intended. Workshops may be held with users and stakeholders to confirm the accuracy of the models.

Risk Assessment
Based on the findings from accumulated investigation data, the overall risk matrix is evaluated for impact and likelihood of human-system vulnerabilities leading to attack paths. Methods include: human risks assessment matrix, assessed individually and as part of the wider system. The resulting matrix is then validated across the team for inter-rater consistency and socio-technical risk mitigations.

4 Discussion

The following section discusses the findings from utilising the defined process to identify vulnerabilities within a defined system. This section has been broken down into the following subsections.

The Different Humans in the System
In large, complex cyber-security socio-technical environments, it is important to consider the full range of different human roles and tasks, rather than honing in on one group. Behaviours vary for different humans in the system depending on whether they are attacker, defender, or end-users of systems with either specific tasks, or occasional use. By expanding the perspective beyond the traditional focus of preventing the harm caused by threat actors alone, the security and day-to-day work behaviours can be placed at the centre of a resilient cyber-security system.

Beyond the 'Technology-only' Approach
By adopting a broad HF-led human-centred approach, vulnerabilities and risks can be identified earlier than a technology-first approach would yield. Even in the most technologically complex environments, there are always some human task-related interactions that contribute to vulnerabilities.

Earlier Engagement, Wider System Scope
In early practitioner activities, HF were invited, after the initial project engagement, to review problems that were deemed beyond the bounds of the technical system. This resulted in the need to ask questions of the wider socio-technical system retrospectively, in order to identify the causes of vulnerabilities rooted in social and cultural issues. Wider understanding of the impact of human factors on the system have been incorporated into further developments of the models since, that reflect the full scope of the socio-technical system, not just the technical element.

A lesson learned from practice was that understandings of the user task could have been further developed earlier in the process, depending on the system scope, which would have helped when assessing risk.

4.1 Iterative Model Development and Validation

Building models and assurance arguments from which to generate further areas of investigation and risk mitigations, provided artefacts for discussion and feedback at stakeholder workshops. In addition, ongoing validation of re-usable instruments and tools for future investigations and to evidence recommendations were evaluated and reviewed with teams. This construction of models and validation with stakeholders can be an iterative process depending on project design. The accuracy of the model needs to be agreed and accepted by all parties, with sufficient evidence to explain differences to key stakeholders. Further data collection to confirm this accuracy of models and to eradicate discrepancies may be required at times. On other occasions, evidence may surprise individuals within the organisations being assessed who take a more macro view of operations and processes, when micro system intricacies are identified of which they may have been unaware.

4.2 Integrating Cyber and HF Approaches

A key to the success of the investigation practice set out in this study has been the adoption of cyber-security domain expertise and the integration of HF processes into the cyber-security investigation team, in order to fully assess the risks within complex socio-technical systems. HF, as a discipline, have a long standing history of successfully integrating into receptive multidisciplinary teams, for example working closely with safety specialists as part of safety assurance activities; and now a close one-team approach with cyber-security domain teams. Integrated contributions to potential vulnerabilities, system and attack path modelling, and risk assessments were produced as a collaborative effort across disciplines.

Initially the scope of some clients' work allowed for limited integration activities, but it was important for HF to be a fully integrated part of the cyber team in order to elicit the relevant information from end-users. Effort was put into integration and collaboration activity, ensuring that HF maintained an independence but contributed practices which would support and complement the exercise as a whole. For example, HF introduced the development of a consistent, transparent positive investigation environment, where people were able to speak out, aware of the exercise ethics, confidentiality and actions for their reports, which has been critical to the success of each investigation.

Terminology Presents a Barrier
Another reason for ensuring participants were put at ease was because it was found that some cyber-security terms and the general use of 'cyber' could be confusing for participants outside the security domain. The term 'cyber' wasn't generally understood, it was too ambiguous and somewhat misleading when in reality, the process was to analyse a complex socio-technical system. More problematic still was the term 'investigation', which immediately implied wrongdoing and that a perpetrator was being sought out. It was important to overcome these barriers for the participants to invest fully in the process.

Introduction of HF Ethics to Investigations
The importance of clear ethical briefings was highlighted to all investigation teams, and to participating interviewees, explaining informed consent, use and handling of data, the boundaries of anonymity and that participants could be identifiable if they divulged information that only they could know. Participants were informed that if they revealed information that could do harm to themselves or others, the team would be obliged to report it.

A key benefit of offering a safe and anonymous environment for participants to communicate their experiences is that they have the opportunity to speak freely about the workings of the system, without fear of it reflecting badly on them and damaging future prospects. Therefore, known bad security practices or potential for vulnerabilities are more likely to be revealed in the absence of the worry of reprisals. A further benefit is an understanding by all of the reasons for processes not being carried out as envisaged and the remedial actions required.

Aligning Understanding of Work-as-Done
Gap analysis between 'work-as-done' and 'work-as-imagined' reveals system weaknesses or potential vulnerabilities that could be exploited by an adversary. Both senior and security management may hold out-of-touch or over-idealised views of work in their organisation, not aligned with reality or work-as-done and they value feedback on behaviours that reveal gaps in processes. Highlighting these areas to management enables them to improve the security and efficiency of their processes.

4.3 Qualitative and Quantitative Methods

The importance and purpose of adopting individual quantitative or qualitative methods for analyses of different data is acknowledged in HF practice. Within cyber-security HF investigations, both qualitative and quantitative data can be utilised throughout the all phases of the process. This enables investigators to derive risk assessments and access contextual experience for further analyses. For example, exposure to the risk of social engineering was assessed using 'direct' questions, whereas expectations of blame for an incident was asked 'indirectly' with opportunities to comment.

Experience has shown there are significant benefits to be gained from utilising a mixed methods approach for some stages of the investigation process. For example, recording observations and behaviours, as well as self-reports of stated intention, e.g. visual cues of people looking to the locations of a password crib can be compared with their stated password practice.

Value of Quantitative Investigation Methods
The use of quantitative surveys and questionnaires has enabled the effective sampling of large populations, and provides the opportunity for statistical measurements of trends and cultural attitudes as well as validation to evidence findings. Quantitative methods are important for measuring the extent and risk of a human-centred problem and for comparison with other wider populations and overall security culture, where available.

Value of Qualitative Investigation Methods
In order to capture the socio-behavioural system in its entirety, qualitative methods, including interviews, discussion groups and observations, were also widely utilised.

These methods provided valuable insights into the unique experiences of groups and individuals within the system. For example, a participant who appeared visually frustrated during discussion, not speaking due to their seniors' presence in the room, proved to be a great source of information when interviewed alone. Comments made during discussions revealed a rich level of detail that often led to the revelation of significant vulnerabilities which may otherwise have remained undiscovered.

Use of Mixed Methods
The benefits of using mixed methods, that is collecting both quantitative and qualitative commentary responses for analysis, were significant for identifying, developing and quantifying areas for further investigation and potential vulnerabilities. Analyses were also enhanced by adopting alternative perspectives, from a cognitive approach focusing on the person purely as a rational information processing individual, to evaluating stimuli-response drivers of security behaviours. Interview texts were examined through the lens of discourse analysis [5], and primarily phenomenological approaches, using thematic analysis of first-person interviews to explore the lived experiences of individuals [6] within the socio-technical system. This was highly successful in facilitating deeper analysis, producing rich findings and a nuanced understanding of the investigation environment. Rather than asking questions that would only require quantitative, binary style 'yes' or 'no' responses, it was found that using open-ended questions, which were deliberately designed to elicit deeper responses, would provide personal insights that were invaluable to a holistic understanding of the socio-technical system.

A lesson learned was that utilising a survey covering a broad range of potential issues and vulnerabilities at the outset of an investigation, is effective in narrowing the lines of enquiry to those of most concern before physical engagements with users and stakeholders commence. By doing so, valuable interview time is maximized during initial interviews and discussion groups, resulting in greater efficiency and better evidence results being collected.

Stakeholder Workshop Feedback
Workshops held with the users and stakeholders can be a critical part of the investigation process. Once systems have been analysed, models constructed, and vulnerabilities identified, returning to the people operating within the system to validate the findings and gather end-user feedback on recommended courses of actions was important to moving forward. There would often be comments such as 'you should speak to [this person]' or 'you may want to look at [this information]' which would lead to further insight and data collection for review. It may also be that findings are disputed by a stakeholder, in which case further evidence would be collected to either bolster or alleviate the findings. Furthermore, the risks arising from some vulnerabilities discovered may be mitigated by other processes, so diminish in significance. Workshop feedback is an iterative process until all avenues have been explored within the boundaries of the system that were established at the outset.

5 Conclusion

Adopting a defined and systematic process from the start of any investigation, and ensuring that the system under investigation is well bound continues to be important for effectiveness. In addition, creating a robust HF data capture plan, before any investigations start is valuable to later success.

It remains important also that HF practitioners do not just utilise the existing technical process in place, but bring their knowledge from other domains to support and develop existing practices and enable full integration and knowledge sharing with the multi-disciplinary team.

Adopting a mixed methods approach and drawing from methodologies beyond a purely cognitive approach can add richness and insight from experience to the data collected from those who operate within the socio-technical system daily. This enables a wider data set and deeper analysis to be conducted, from which a more extensive range of vulnerabilities can be identified.

The most secure assessments of risk and resilience require evidenced analysis from both observations, and self-reports, in order to access the widest data set; and to generate, support and evidence the analysis argument for risks to resilience.

A significant take away, is ensuring the social element of the socio-technical system is investigated, by developing robust human-system models of interaction and by identifying the impact of organisational and security culture issues on vulnerabilities and risk. Risks can be mitigated, cyber-security resilience and security culture improved, once the impact of cultural issues in the organisation are identified.

Finally, it should be noted that whilst selective adoption of relevant approaches from the safety and cyber-security realms is effective, threat actors are actively seeking out vulnerabilities in order to manipulate and weave a path through them. Outcomes therefore shift from *unintended* failures to *intended* failures. This subtle difference changes the dynamic of the approach to evaluating resilience with an attacker mindset. Practitioners need to go beyond 'Murphy's law' to analyse how vulnerabilities, the 'holes in the cheese', could be exploited, and how humans could be manipulated to unwittingly align them, aiding attack path navigation.

References

1. IEA (2016). In: Shorrock, S., Williams, C.: Human Factors and Ergonomics in Practice, CRC Press, Boca Raton, p. 4 (2017)
2. Reason, J.: Managing the Risks of Organisational Accidents. Ashgate Publishing Limited, Aldershot (1997)
3. Hollnagel, E., Woods, D., Leveson, N.: Resilience Engineering: Concepts and Precepts. Ashgate, UK (2006)
4. Dekker, S.: The Field Guide to Understanding 'Human Error,' 3rd edn., p. 12. CRC Press, Boca Raton (2014)
5. Tileaga, C., Stokoe, E. (eds.): Discursive Psychology, Classic and Contemporary Issues. Routledge, Abingdon (2016)
6. Langdridge, D.: Phenomenological psychology, theory, research and method, Pearson Education Limited, Harlow (2007)

A Human Factor Approach
to Threat Modeling

Lauren S. Ferro[✉], Andrea Marrella, and Tiziana Catarci

Sapienza, University of Rome, Rome, Italy
{lsferro,marrella,catarci}@diag.uniroma1.it

Abstract. Cybersecurity has many challenges to address to ensure the protection of a system from an attacker. Consequently, strategies have been developed to address a system's weakness that an attacker may try to exploit. However, while these approaches may prevent an attacker from getting in from the outside, they do not consider the user's actions from the inside and how their behavior may inadvertently allow an attack to occur. This paper presents a human-centered approach to threat modeling titled STRIDE-HF, which extends the existing threat modeling framework STRIDE.

Keywords: Threat modeling · Human factors · Cybersecurity

1 Introduction

It is human nature to make mistakes. Mistakes can occur for many reasons such as feeling stressed, or from a lack of knowledge and understanding about something. One area where human error is becoming increasingly important to focus on is cybersecurity. With the increasing demand for technology and ubiquitous interaction, there has been a heavy burden to perform cybersecurity policies to protect systems from unwanted access. While there is a focus to prevent unwanted access from the outside (e.g., attackers), there has been a lack of approaches toward addressing vulnerabilities created from the inside due to human error (e.g., sharing passwords, downloading files from unknown senders, etc.). Such human errors could result in a user unknowingly allowing an attacker into a system. The impact could be more harmful if a user is unaware of the consequences of their actions. Thus, making it harder to trace the origin of the breach and consequently cause a delayed response and/or solution in addressing the breach.

Contemporary research is dedicated to understanding and categorizing human errors, and consequently human factors, across different contexts (e.g., medicine [7], aviation [38]). Unfortunately, these explorations have largely been specific to the circumstances that they were created for. Therefore, human factor research is limited in scope, consistency, and clarity.

From an outside-in approach, scholars and security practitioners have also examined how to identify weaknesses and errors, but within a system.

© Springer Nature Switzerland AG 2021
A. Moallem (Ed.): HCII 2021, LNCS 12788, pp. 139–157, 2021.
https://doi.org/10.1007/978-3-030-77392-2_10

These studies and approaches have all worked toward anticipating an attack via a concept known as *threat modeling*. Many studies present varied approaches to threat modeling [2,13,20,21,37,42]. Among the most popular there is the STRIDE approach (Spoofing, Tampering, Repudiation, Information Disclosure, Denial of Service, and Elevation of Privilege), which was introduced by Praerit Garg and Loren Kohnfelder at Microsoft [41] to classify vulnerabilities. However, despite the evident interest in threat modeling approaches, recent work by Xiong and Lagerström [46] found that "threat modeling is a diverse field lacking common ground, and definitions are numerous and used in many different ways". This is another issue related to how threat models are represented (e.g., graphical or formal).

Although particular aspects of human and system errors and weaknesses are explored in cybersecurity, a user-centered approach to threat modeling is an under-researched area. If human errors are of high concern in other areas and they are examined to address them, cybersecurity research should also adopt the same level of scientific rigor to understand how human error can be addressed as a threat to a system like system weaknesses are addressed via threat modeling.

To tackle this challenge, this paper proposes an approach to create a user-centered threat model, which complements traditional threat models to consider how human error could make it easier for an attack to occur.

Therefore, the following research questions were answered:

- RQ1: Which specific topics relating to human factors in cybersecurity are discussed within the literature?
- RQ2: What threat modeling techniques exist that work toward protecting a system from attacks?
- RQ3: How can we use the information to create a user-orientated threat model?

Based on this information, we theoretically developed a user-centered framework based on STRIDE, called STRIDE-HF. Considering that STRIDE has never been studied before along with human factors, this paper ventures into a new area of inquiry. Thus, a theoretical framework appears to be the most appropriate solution to address this research. The outcomes of this paper present a foundation to extend and iterate upon, which is user-focused. Therefore, we provide the following contribution:

- A novel (inside-out) approach toward user-centered threat modeling.
- Insight toward how threat modeling methods and human factors could be considered for developing more secured systems.
- Future research directions for user-centered threat modeling and future iterations of STRIDE-HF.

The rest of the paper is organized as follows. In Sect. 2 we present key concepts, relevant definitions, theories, and models and outline the key details of the STRIDE framework. In Sect. 3 we present our research model and the steps followed toward creating STRIDE-HF and its current implementations.

In Sect. 4 we discuss our observations and suggestions for future research. Finally, in Sect. 5, we present our conclusion.

2 Background and Related Work

Cybersecurity is a highly relevant area in today's society. In recent times, with the COVID-19 pandemic, our lives have unexpectedly and forcibly become online; resulting in an increase in online data sharing, privacy concerns, and changes to access protocols. With many users having to transition from traditional methods of working and interaction, even with the most simple of tasks (e.g., writing a document in a word processing software), they have inevitably been forced to learn and engage with several new online systems to work remotely. Consequently, there has also been an increase in cyberattacks [3].

Humans possess many flaws that make them vulnerable. Users argue for the privacy of their data while within the same breath they will post what they had for lunch, their relationship status, or what they think about the governments latest decision. All this information may seem trivial at first but it can provide an attacker with enough data to begin developing a plan of attack. Such behavior such as sharing information online or making trade-offs could relate to *Lack of Knowledge* regarding the sensitivity of certain types of information or how that information could be used in an attack. Our (heightened) sense of self also lets us down by allowing a user to be more vulnerable to the influence of attacks because they do not believe they could be the target of an attack or have worthwhile information. In other cases, users desire to reciprocate the seemingly "altruistic" actions of others or to help those who are seeking assistance allow them to fall victim to a cyber attack. However, the key concept here is that human behavior can put a user and their community in danger with seemingly little effort. Thus, we should find ways to protect users from being exploited and effectively from their own bad cybersecurity behavior.

2.1 Human Factors

Human errors can be the result of negligence, accident, or deliberate action [17]. Human factors have been the topic of study in many areas, namely within the context of aviation, which focuses behaviors leading up to human error. For example, the Dirty Dozen proposed by Dupont [15] describes twelve of the most common human factor-related errors, which may lead to aviation-related accidents or incidents.

- **Lack of Communication**: people not communicating with each other within a working and/or online environment.
- **Complacency**: a feeling of self-satisfaction that can lead to a lack of awareness of potential dangers.
- **Lack of Knowledge**: not having enough experience and specific knowledge that can lead to poor decisions.

- **Distraction**: when a user's attention has been taken away from the task that they must do.
- **Lack of Teamwork**: not providing enough support toward a group of people, coworkers, etc., reliant on your support.
- **Fatigue**: is a physiological reaction resulting from prolonged periods of work and stress.
- **Lack of Resources**: not having enough resources (e.g. time, tools, people, etc.) to complete a task.
- **Pressure**: pressure to meet a deadline interferes with our ability to complete tasks correctly, then it has become too much.
- **Lack of Assertiveness**: not being able or allowed to express concerns or ideas.
- **Stress**: acute and chronic stress from working for long periods of time or other demanding issues such as family or financial problems.
- **Lack of Awareness**: working in isolation and only considering one's own responsibilities, often leading to a disconnect from what others are doing.
- **Norms**: workplace practices that develop over time, which can then influence others behaviors.

While human factors is growing in many areas, one area that can greatly benefit from it is cybersecurity. This is because by understanding human factors we can begin gaining an improved understanding toward addressing human error and improving the security of systems and data.

2.2 Human Factors and Cybersecurity

Human factors in cybersecurity is becoming widely discussed (e.g., [1,4,25,32, 45,48]), which has led to several issues. The first is that there are many variations for often the same terms due to a lack of consistency or conventions to describe human factors. Furthermore, of the research that does exist, it often has a limited scope [48], ambiguous, or only acknowledges the concept of human factors rather than focuses on it [44].

If we could consider the broad definitions within other areas, we can begin finding commonalities such as the use of the same concepts or similar terms and work toward a more concise list. For example, if we consider *Norms* from Dupont's Dirty Dozen [15], there are similarities with other descriptions. For example, Da Veiga [10] describes pressures from norms that adopt common philosophy for completing tasks in certain ways because that is "the way things are done here" [26] or influential factors such as the personality of the organization [39]. Lastly, Henshel et al. [19] incorporates a user's culture as part of the human factors component within their holistic cybersecurity risk assessment framework. Considering these papers, they all relate to the broader concept of *Norms*. Similar examples also exist for a *Lack of Knowledge* and *Awareness* [23,49]. Therefore, it is likely that we could begin with one general human factor and continue to develop sub-factors that could relate to more specific circumstances.

Other current trends have also emerged that consider the human factors of users through two lenses: personal/user-centered and organizational/cultural such as those by Kraemer [25], Al-Darwish et al. [1], Badie and Lashkari [4], and Mortazavi-Alavi [32]. To this end, and like previous studies, human factors could be impacted by several aspects at once depending on a user's previous experiences and how a workplace impacts the user (e.g., both in a social and policy perspective). Therefore, we could consider the user as a node of a larger network that includes part of an (online) team, culture, and ultimately the system that they are interacting with [35].

There is an increase need by organizations to invest time to develop an information security culture [17] that should include all the personnel and leadership [18]. By building this culture, organizations can minimize the risk to the exposure of sensitive information [11].

Current research highlights that a positive information security culture can increase security policy compliance, strengthen the overall information security posture, and reduce the financial loss due to security breaches. For example, Chen and Zahedi [9] demonstrated that once users have perceive or experienced a cyber threat, they are more likely to take protective actions. From this study, we could consider this relating to a user's lack of knowledge or competency resulting from a lack of experience in such topics. For instance, Mashiane and Kritzinger [29] identified a large amount of constructs being proposed as the determinants of cybersecurity behavior. It makes it difficult to decide which constructs to focus on when designing cybersecurity behavior interventions. Moreover, it is also important to consider that an employee's attitude and involvement within a company can be influenced by their own experiences. Therefore, it may be key to ensure that employees are trained with scenarios that allow them to experience first-hand or in real-time threats that they may encounter to allow them to have this experience to internalize. This is also a consideration of Kraemer et al. [25] who identified nine thematic areas where key human and organizational factors were grouped into, which again, highlights the need for *Training*, thus declaring a fault in a users knowledge for cybersecurity issues. However, Kraemer's study appears to focus more on organizational related issues rather than the user. The study neglects to understand the overall connection between a user and their interaction and behavior within an environment.

2.3 Threat Modeling

To perform the threat modeling process, we must first understand what are the threats and attacks that we are trying to project ourselves again. Often, a cyber attack can be a highly effective n sophisticated attack, which can bypass even well thought out technological security structures. For a cyber attack to be successful, it typically follows a seven step approach known as the cyber kill chain. Generally, a cyber kill chain is a procedural path that an intruder takes to penetrate information systems over time to execute an attack on the target [47].

1. **Reconnaissance**: usually happens in anticipation before an actual attack. This is the initial phase where attackers select their targets, monitor a network system to try and develop a more informed understanding of the target.
2. **Weaponization**: uses the information from the reconnaissance stage to carefully develop an attack, which may include sending malware, launching a DoS attack, or hacking a system.
3. **Delivery**: is the transmission phase where the weaponization (e.g. malware, attack, etc.) is undertaken. The delivery of a payload or an attack can occur in many different ways (e.g. phishing email) depending on the objective of the attack.
4. **Exploitation**: is the first phase in the execution of a cyberattack where an attacker takes control of the targets environment by exploiting their weaknesses or taking advantage of their access to the system.
5. **Installation**: is where attackers may want to install malware (if they have entered a system) or deploy a payload if it has not been done by the user (e.g. downloading and installing software from a phishing email).
6. **Command and control**: is where the attackers take (remote) control of a system or device.
7. **Action on objective**: is where the attackers carry out their goals and objectives that have driven the attack in the first place.

The cyber kill chain highlights the steps involved if an attacker can gain enough useful information during the reconnaissance phase. For example, information about a person and/or the company that they work for can help the attacker to develop an angle to contact that user with to gain more information. From here, this information can be used to persuade and deceive victims because it helps to improve legitimacy of the attackers intentions. Consequently, victims are less likely to question the interaction. In some cases, other factors such as timeliness can be used to persuade and deceive victims because it helps improve legitimacy. For example, if there has been a large data breach, an attacker may use the fear and contact potential victims posing as a technician to improve security against the threat.

With an understanding of the process that an attacker can follow to access a system, we can begin to analyze how to protect it. One way that this is done is via threat modeling. Threat modeling as defined by Uzunov and Fernandez [43] as "a process that can be used to analyze potential attacks or threats, and can also be supported by threat libraries or attack taxonomies". However, while several other definitions exist that also define threat modeling [5,6,12,14,28,31,40] and as systematically assessed by Xiong and Lagerström [46]. Threat modeling allows security designers to accurately estimate and anticipate an attack and to prevent any unauthorized attacks that gains access to sensitive information, networks, and applications (e.g. Malware, Phishing, Denial of Service (DoS/DDoS)).

Beyond the definition, there are also many different types of threat modeling approaches, frameworks, techniques, models, and theories that all work toward identifying threats and approaches to address them [21,46]. Each of these have their own context in mind such as preventing attackers from breaching a system, finding weak points within a systems architecture, develop strategies to mitigate potential attacks, among others.

STRIDE. The STRIDE method is a mnemonic for six types of security threats [41]. It supplies the foundation of our theoretical model known as STRIDE-HF (Spoofing, Tampering, Repudiation, Information Disclosure, Denial of Service, and Elevation of privilege – Human Factor).

- **(S) Spoofing**: using someone else's credentials to gain access to otherwise inaccessible assets.
- **(T) Tampering**: changing data to mount an attack.
- **(R) Repudiation**: occurs when a user denies performing an action, but the target of the action has no way to prove otherwise.
- **(I) Information disclosure**: the disclosure of information to a user who does not have permission to see it.
- **(D) Denial of service**: reducing the ability of valid users to access resources.
- **(E) Elevation of privilege**: occurs when an unprivileged user gains privileged status.

STRIDE has also been used to address many concerns within cybersecurity (e.g., [8,24,28,36]) as well as variations such as STRIDE-per-element and STRIDE-per-interaction [41]. Moreover, Khan et al. [24] differentiate the two variations by describing STRIDE-per-element as a more complex method because it analyzes the behavior and operations of each system component; and STRIDE-per-interaction as a more simpler method to perform because it provides protection strategies sufficient enough to protect a system. However, the general version of STRIDE includes elements that are typical in many cybersecurity related situations.

When a system is developed, it is often driven by requirements that define interaction (i.e., what the user can and cannot do), and how the system is intended to work. Security requirements are driven by what should not occur (i.e., a user gaining access to areas/data that they should not be able to). However, it is extremely difficult to consider every kind of threat and/or behavior that a user can do with a system that can create security issues at a later stage. Yet, of those threats that have been defined after a thorough analysis and risk management, the security analyst must find ways to mitigate them. Risk management consists of risk assessment, risk reduction, and risk acceptance and from here the threats that are identified must be prioritized, often by damage and likelihood. For example, one way to approach managing a risk is presented by Myagmar et al. [33]:

- **Accept the risk**: the risk is very low and so costly to mitigate that it is worth accepting.
- **Transfer the risk**: transfer the risk to somebody else via insurance, warnings etc.

- **Remove the risk**: remove the system component or feature associated with the risk if the feature is not worth the risk.
- **Mitigate the risk**: reduce the risk with countermeasures.

By comparing risk assessment and the assessment of human errors, we can see that they too share similarities. For example, when we look at risks, we consider a potential incident, how it may occur and how we can either mitigate it or reduce its impact should a risk occur. For example, Mancuso et al. [27] propose a conceptual framework that aims to maintain interactions between the components of a cyber attack, which is described in terms of three dimensions: adversarial, methodological, and operational. Yet this approach does not consider the behavior of users like a threat model views the behavior of an attacker. Like human factors, considering the risks of a user sharing a password or downloading a potentially dangerous attachment could also be addressed as part of a user-centered approach with strategies in place.

If we consider threat modeling and risk management, these approaches are focused on preventing an attacker gaining entry into a system by assessing a system to identify areas of weaknesses that an attacker could exploit. Yet, even with the most well devise plan and risk management, all of these could be for nothing is a user unknowingly opens the proverbial door to an attack. Therefore, this study aims to consider and theoretically present all the aforementioned concepts and approaches but from a reversed engineered approach - that is to also view the user and their behaviors as risks and threats and to develop strategies along with traditional approaches.

3   STRIDE-HF

This section describes the theoretical and conceptual process [30] that we took to develop **STRIDE-HF**. This research adopted an inductive approach, that is starting with an observation of contemporary literature surrounding key areas, identified that there is a gap concerning user-centered threat models, and looked at how to address this gap by proposing a conceptual/theoretical framework.

The development of this work began by exploring the current literature surrounding human factors, threat modeling techniques, and discussions relating to these within cybersecurity. This was to understand how, if at all, current literature documents risks/security vulnerabilities from a user's perspective and not specifically from the attacker's perspective. Furthermore, this step explored how these vulnerabilities could be classified/related to human factors. We also chose for the time being to exclude aspects of decision making and attitude as they contain several aspects that also need further investigation and studies to determine their impact on human factors and cybersecurity.

After considering the discussion surrounding human factors models including those discussed within cybersecurity, we felt that the Dirty Dozen [15] provided an encompassing foundation to start with and to use and iterate upon in the future.

Next, similarly we look we looked for a threat model that could provide a general foundation to expand upon, therefore we chose STRIDE (Spoofing, Tampering, Repudiation, Information Disclosure, Denial of Service, and Elevation of privilege) [41]. The primary rationale behind the use of STRIDE was because it provided a neutral foundation that could be expanded upon (considering other elements beyond STRIDE) in future work and empirical validation.

The second step was considering the STRIDE model in the context of human factors and how it may relate to the STRIDE elements. After examining and discussing the relevant literature, we theorized that human factors could be threat modeled similarly to how attackers behavior is. In this way, we began considering different types of behaviors that were discussed within the literature and how they may align with STRIDE elements, as presented in Table 1 taken (and expanded upon) from Ferro and Sapio [16].

To use the STRIDE-HF model, security analysts and researchers will need to understand how users interact with each other and with the systems inside the workplace. This includes the type of environment (e.g. open-plan, cubicle-based, working from home, etc.), and culture (e.g. carefree and relaxed or strict and procedural). This may be achieved by qualitative (e.g. observations, questionnaires, and interviews with users) or quantitative (e.g. surveys) methods. From here, security analysts can begin to look at their threat models from an attacker's perspective and then consider how human factors could impact what has been modeled or managed.

3.1 Implementing STRIDE-HF into an Interactive Experience: Another Week at the Office

Since STRIDE-HF is still a developing model, it has been implemented within a serious game titled Another Week at the Office (AWATO) [16]. This game has provided a practical way to incorporate the STRIDE-HF framework to educate and assess users' behavior in a virtual office space. In AWATO, players take on the role of security analyst who must observe the characters within a typical workplace environment and identify erroneous behavior, such as leaving a computer unattended and unlocked or a post-it note on the ground with login information like in Figs. 1 and 2.

From here, the user must decide whether or not such behavior is bad and subsequently report it. Once an incident has been reported, the player must then classify the threat in accordance to STRIDE-HF as presented in Fig. 3.

Table 1. STRIDE - HF [16]

Threat	(Likely) Human Factor(s)	Behavior (*examples*)	Response (*examples*)
Spoofing	Lack of awareness, Lack of knowledge, Lack of resources	Downloading files online or via email attachments. Using a computer that is logged in by someone else to complete tasks (knowingly/unknowingly)	Educate users about what to look for when accessing links within emails. Make accounts automatically log out after a set amount of time. Implement two-factor confirmation for performing tasks (e.g. submitting files)
Tampering	Distraction, Lack of awareness, Stress, Pressure, Fatigue	Modifying files to backdate them to avoid punishment. Unblocking blocked ports to get access	Implement a platform where documents must be uploaded (logs date, time, user, etc.)
Repudiation	Stress, Norms Pressure	Accidentally deleting files. Not submitting files on time/to the right location	Change how files are managed, monitored, and time-stamped. Create a more friendly work atmosphere where employees can admit their mistakes or seek assistance when making errors so that they can be corrected as soon as they occur
Information disclosure	Complacency, Distraction, Norms, Stress, Pressure, Lack of assertiveness	Sharing passwords among colleagues for a time trade-off. Letting a friend borrow an access card	Enforce stronger punishments for password/access card sharing
Denial of service	Distraction, Lack of awareness, Stress, Pressure	Unplugging hardware for other purposes (e.g. additional charging space). Trying to resolve an issue (with little knowledge) without contacting support (e.g., IT technician)	Clearly label exposed cables to indicate their use. Make it easier for employees to get the assistance that they need
Elevation of privilege	Lack of Assertiveness Pressure Norms	Giving access to a file because someone with authority asked for it	Create a more accessible way to report the bad behavior of superiors
	* More likely to be responsible for the STRIDE element over other Human Factors		

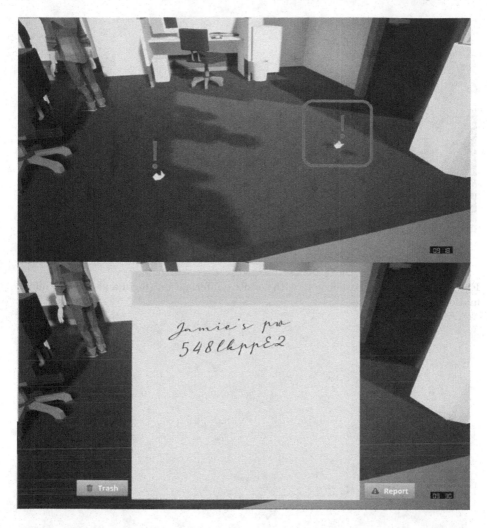

Fig. 1. Example of a post-it note with sensitive information (name and password)

We analyzed the use of STRIDE in terms of players observing generally bad cybersecurity practices and aligning them to the most relevant STRIDE-HF element. At this stage, the point was not to validate STRIDE-HF but to understand how a framework such as STRIDE-HF could be used practically. While the game did feature a short text-based primer to make the players familiar with the concepts of threat modeling, human factors, and STRIDE-HF, this study did offer insight on how we could address knowledge gaps observed through game-play in terms of more tailored training. A consideration that will be further elaborated as we begin to empirically validate STRIDE-HF.

Fig. 2. Example of a post-it note with sensitive information (login and account information)

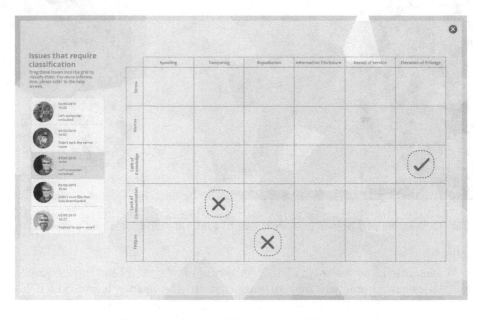

Fig. 3. Example of STRIDE-HF classification inside of AWATO

4   Discussion and Implications

For developing a user-centered threat model, a central issue has been to understand the discussions, definitions, and approaches for addressing human errors and threats to a system. On the one hand, human factor research is gaining momentum in cybersecurity, which has highlighted the role human factors play in cybersecurity. On the other hand, research and definitions are still very broad and context-specific. The purposes of this paper are (a) to explore contemporary research within human factors, including research within the context of cybersecurity, (b) explore contemporary research that describes approaches towards addressing threats to a system, and (c) how can this information be used to develop a more user-centered approach to threats where threats are defined as human errors. STRIDE-HF presents an approach that considers both human factors and threat modeling together to help understand what types of human errors could result in STRIDE elements.

4.1 Human Factors and Threat Modeling

Humans are prone to making mistakes, especially if our environment facilitates them. One area that has been the topic in the literature is workplace culture. Therefore, it could be an area to start with. There may be opportunities to assess the workplace environment by measuring employees' attitudes towards their employer, and workplace culture, to determine if more can be done to address negative issues. For example, if many employees are overworked, it is more likely that they will make trade-offs for time or disregard basic security protocols such as leaving a computer unlocked or sharing passwords. Therefore, by changing work practices or developing more strategic approaches to managing workloads, employees may feel more positive and be more prone to make fewer errors. Also, there may be ways to address and change workplace culture by encouraging employees to participate in activities that are orientated towards their commitment to the organization's security goals or to engage with like-minded colleagues [22]. In this way, addressing environmental and cultural factors could reduce the likelihood of human error resulting in a breach.

As demonstrated by Chen et al. [9], exposing users to threats in a controlled environment may also offer a way for them to understand the process leading up to a threat, the threat itself, and subsequent consequences of it being successful. However, it is also equally important to consider that more training is not always the solution. In these instances, training provides users with a personalized experience, that is meaningful because of the interaction that it affords. Ultimately, such experiences can also align with the level of access and/or responsibilities that they have within a workplace. This is also a contention that Öğütçü et al. [34] confirmed where users demonstrated more security-focused behavior when they could perceive threats and increase their awareness of the technology. Therefore, it may also come back to address a user's level of competency by actively exposing them to scenarios that allow them to experience these issues and develop personal and meaningful connections to security issues.

There is still a long way to go towards developing a consistent definition of human factors (and what they are) both at a general level and more specifically within a cybersecurity context. Similarly, there is also a lack of consistency when defining threat modeling.

Typically human factors and threat modeling has been considered two separate areas of study. However, threat modeling and risk assessment present similar approaches to human factors in ways to identify, understand, or anticipate weaknesses or likely errors. Thus, strategies and processes can be implemented to mitigate the effects of these weaknesses and errors. However, with this being said it is reassuring that while the terminology varies, there is some consistency with the errors or human factors that they are addressing. Therefore, it is likely as both fields mature so too will more concise definitions.

Another important consideration is understanding how to address human factors throughout a cyber kill chain or where certain factors are likely to be more damaging. For example, in a company that heavily uses social media, a user who is sharing work-related information online or even a photo on social networks, maybe enough to draw the attention of an attacker. However, it is not until the delivery or exploitation stage that human factors are more detrimental. Therefore, in such cases, more focus should be directed towards educating users about email security and social engineering. This may include training to identify persuasive techniques or how to validate the identity of callers or what to look for in emails from unknown senders.

4.2   STRIDE-HF as a User-Orientated Threat Modeling Approach

STRIDE-HF presents a novel direction to consider threat modeling from a human factor perspective. As discussed within this paper, research within human factors is gaining momentum within the field of cybersecurity. Yet, we are still far from a consistent discourse and terminology. To this end, this paper highlights the importance of working towards a more consistent definition standard and why we should begin to consider human factors as a type of threat towards systems security in a socio-technological world. In this way, we can begin to work towards the development of user-centered threat models. We aim for STRIDE-HF to become the beginning of a new paradigm that explores human error as a way to further protect the security of systems and the data within them.

The STRIDE-HF Framework functions by offering a way for security analysts to consider human factor-related behavior while assessing the types of breaches that could result from them. For example, if a user shares a password (because that is part of the workplace norms) it could result in an elevation of privilege where a user may disable certain settings unknowingly, thus creating a vulnerability. The procedure to use the framework requires that human factor elements are identified within a work environment, which can be done in several ways (e.g. observation or assessment). From here, the framework can help the user to identify the type of STRIDE element that aligns with the human factor that may influence it. Alternatively, the user can use STRIDE-HF in reverse where they identify the likely (STRIDE) issues and then the subsequent human factor(s). The fundamental difference that STRIDE-HF offers in comparison to traditional threat modeling methods is that it takes a "reversed engineered" approach towards classifying threats that may affect the security of a system from the perspective of users rather than an attacker.

4.3   Future Work

At present, STRIDE-HF is being iterated within the game Another Week at the Office [16]. However, we are striving towards developing this further to include training modules that can be used by security analysts to help them analyze current work practices and identify what human factors could weaken the security practices that are currently in place. Moreover, we would also like to include relevant material (e.g. approaches, activities, information) that could help even novice security analysts to understand the human factors within their work environment and how to address them. This material would also align with what users do within AWATO so that it can become a wholesome training and learning experience.

Future iterations of STRIDE-HF may include additional human factors that are relevant and extend beyond those defined within this paper as well as the incorporation/use of more psychological-based principles such as decision making, culture, and attitude. Since it is a requirement in any organization to make daily decisions. The types of decisions vary from habitual ones such as when to take a coffee break to download a document, all of which can lead to negative and positive outcomes. However, these decisions vary greatly depending on the needs of the user and the environmental/psychological factors that may be influencing them. Therefore, many approaches try to predict the way to predict a user or model their behavior. If we are to consider these aspects within the context of cybersecurity, the work environment, and the everyday user, there are several ways that a user could unknowingly/accidentally provide sensitive information to an attacker or leave sensitive information easily available for others to use and thus compromising cybersecurity. Consequently, future development may also explore such decision-making behaviors in a quantifiable way (i.e. through questionnaires) to develop a rubric for assessing the risk of a human factor(s) and/or STRIDE element.

5   Concluding Remarks

This paper presented an iterated version of the STRIDE threat modeling technique with STRIDE-HF, which is a user-centered threat model that is aligned with Dupont's Dirty Dozen [15].

As summarized in Sect. 2, the paper has drawn an informed insight to identify the gap that exists when discussing user-centered threat modeling as an additional technique to use along with traditional threat modeling and as part of the security design of a system. The paper, as discussed in Sect. 3 presented the development of a novel approach to threat modeling. Lastly, in Sect. 4, we discussed the implications of what this research has identified and how it could be continued and applied.

The field of human factors in cybersecurity is still maturing, and more work is needed to quantify the impact of implementing such strategies. This study contributes by providing initial insight into this developing field and a way to consider an approach to user-centered threat modeling. However, the authors want to stress that while STRIDE-HF does offer a starting point, much like traditional threat modeling, we do not suggest a "one size fits all" approach since the security of systems requires varied approaches. Therefore, further research should define human factors more concisely so that we can begin to identify those, which are more prevalent in specific security situations (e.g. local intranet versus protecting a server). To this end, we have provided a starting point to begin further research, which pushes the considerations of a more inside-approach to threat modeling.

Lastly, this paper also raised several interesting questions for future work. For instance, could more psychological elements be present that impact human factors and could these be quantitatively assessed to provide more insight toward high-risk human factors and the errors that they lead to? Such methods could also improve our understanding and highlight the level of impact that psychological aspects could have on human factors to better understand how it affects the security measures that are currently in place or how new ones should be designed and implemented. Therefore, empirical validation is the logical next step toward not only validating our theoretical model but also these additional considerations. The outcomes of such studies would not only lead to empirical improvements toward the understanding of user-specific aspects of threat modeling but also to further define what are human factors within the broader discourse of cybersecurity.

References

1. Al-Darwish, A.I., Choe, P.: A framework of information security integrated with human factors. In: Moallem, A. (ed.) HCII 2019. LNCS, vol. 11594, pp. 217–229. Springer, Cham (2019). https://doi.org/10.1007/978-3-030-22351-9_15
2. Alberts, C.J., Behrens, S.G., Pethia, R.D., Wilson, W.R.: Operationally critical threat, asset, and vulnerability evaluation (octave) framework, version 1.0. Technical report, Carnegie-Mellon Univ Pittsburgh Pa Software Engineering Inst (1999)
3. Andrade, R.O., Ortiz-Garcés, I., Cazares, M.: Cybersecurity attacks on smart home during covid-19 pandemic. In: 2020 Fourth World Conference on Smart Trends in Systems, Security and Sustainability (WorldS4), pp. 398–404. IEEE (2020)
4. Badie, N., Lashkari, A.H.: A new evaluation criteria for effective security awareness in computer risk management based on AHP. J. Basic Appl. Sci. Res. 2(9), 9331–9347 (2012)
5. Baquero, A.O., Kornecki, A.J., Janusz, Z.: Threat modeling for aviation computer security. crosstalk 21 (2015)
6. Bedi, P., Gandotra, V., Singhal, A., Narang, H., Sharma, S.: Threat-oriented security framework in risk management using multiagent system. Softw. Pract. Exp. 43(9), 1013–1038 (2013)
7. Bleetman, A., Sanusi, S., Dale, T., Brace, S.: Human factors and error prevention in emergency medicine. Emerg. Med. J. 29(5), 389–393 (2012)
8. Chen, X., Liu, Y., Yi, J.: A security evaluation framework based on stride model for software in networks. Int. J. Adv. Comput. Tech. (2012)
9. Chen, Y., Zahedi, F.M.: Individuals' internet security perceptions and behaviors: polycontextual contrasts between the United States and China. MIS Q. 40(1), 205–222 (2016)

10. Da Veiga, A.: A cybersecurity culture research philosophy and approach to develop a valid and reliable measuring instrument. In: 2016 SAI Computing Conference (SAI), pp. 1006–1015. IEEE (2016)
11. Da Veiga, A., Martins, N.: Information security culture and information protection culture: a validated assessment instrument. Comput. Law Secur. Rev. **31**(2), 243–256 (2015)
12. Dahbul, R., Lim, C., Purnama, J.: Enhancing honeypot deception capability through network service fingerprinting. J. Phys. Conf. Ser. **801**, 012057 (2017). IOP Publishing
13. Desolda, G., Di Nocera, F., Ferro, L., Lanzilotti, R., Maggi, P., Marrella, A.: Alerting users about phishing attacks. In: Moallem, A. (ed.) HCII 2019. LNCS, vol. 11594, pp. 134–148. Springer, Cham (2019). https://doi.org/10.1007/978-3-030-22351-9_9
14. Dhillon, D.: Developer-driven threat modeling: lessons learned in the trenches. IEEE Secur. Priv. **9**(4), 41–47 (2011)
15. Dupont, G.: The dirty dozen errors in maintenance. In: The 11th Symposium on Human Factors in Maintenance and Inspection: Human Error in Aviation Maintenance (1997)
16. Ferro, L.S., Sapio, F.: Another week at the office (AWATO) – an interactive serious game for threat modeling human factors. In: Moallem, A. (ed.) HCII 2020. LNCS, vol. 12210, pp. 123–142. Springer, Cham (2020). https://doi.org/10.1007/978-3-030-50309-3_9
17. Glaspie, H.W., Karwowski, W.: Human factors in information security culture: a literature review. In: Nicholson, D. (ed.) AHFE 2017. AISC, vol. 593, pp. 269–280. Springer, Cham (2018). https://doi.org/10.1007/978-3-319-60585-2_25
18. Guo, K.H.: Security-related behavior in using information systems in the workplace: a review and synthesis. Comput. Secur. **32**, 242–251 (2013)
19. Henshel, D., Sample, C., Cains, M., Hoffman, B.: Integrating cultural factors into human factors framework and ontology for cyber attackers. In: Nicholson, D. (ed.) Advances in Human Factors in Cybersecurity, vol. 501, pp. 123–137. Springer, Cham (2016). https://doi.org/10.1007/978-3-319-41932-9_11
20. Howard, M., LeBlanc, D.: Writing Secure Code. Pearson Education, London (2003)
21. Hussain, S., Kamal, A., Ahmad, S., Rasool, G., Iqbal, S.: Threat modelling methodologies: a survey. Sci. Int. (Lahore) **26**(4), 1607–1609 (2014)
22. Ifinedo, P.: Information systems security policy compliance: an empirical study of the effects of socialisation, influence, and cognition. Inf. Manag. **51**(1), 69–79 (2014)
23. Kemper, G.: Improving employees' cyber security awareness. Comput. Fraud Secur. **2019**(8), 11–14 (2019)
24. Khan, R., McLaughlin, K., Laverty, D., Sezer, S.: Stride-based threat modeling for cyber-physical systems. In: 2017 IEEE PES Innovative Smart Grid Technologies Conference Europe (ISGT-Europe), pp. 1–6. IEEE (2017)
25. Kraemer, S., Carayon, P., Clem, J.: Human and organizational factors in computer and information security: pathways to vulnerabilities. Comput. Secur. **28**(7), 509–520 (2009)
26. Lundy, O., Cowling, A.: Strategic human resource management. Cengage Learning EMEA (1996)
27. Mancuso, V.F., Strang, A.J., Funke, G.J., Finomore, V.S.: Human factors of cyber attacks: a framework for human-centered research. In: Proceedings of the Human Factors and Ergonomics Society Annual Meeting, vol. 58, pp. 437–441. SAGE Publications Sage CA, Los Angeles (2014)

28. Marback, A., Do, H., He, K., Kondamarri, S., Xu, D.: A threat model-based approach to security testing. Softw. Pract. Exp. **43**(2), 241–258 (2013)
29. Mashiane, T., Kritzinger, E.: Theoretical domain framework to identify cybersecurity behaviour constructs. In: Rønningsbakk, L., Wu, T.-T., Sandnes, F.E., Huang, Y.-M. (eds.) ICITL 2019. LNCS, vol. 11937, pp. 320–329. Springer, Cham (2019). https://doi.org/10.1007/978-3-030-35343-8_34
30. McGregor, S.L.: Understanding and Evaluating Research: A Critical Guide. Sage Publications, Thousand Oaks (2017)
31. Mitnick, K.D., Simon, W.L.: The Art of Deception: Controlling the Human Element of Security. John Wiley & Sons, Hoboken (2003)
32. Mortazavi-Alavi, R.: A risk-driven investment model for analysing human factors in information security. Ph.D. thesis, University of East London (2016)
33. Myagmar, S., Lee, A.J., Yurcik, W.: Threat modeling as a basis for security requirements. In: Symposium on Requirements Engineering for Information Security (SREIS), vol. 2005, pp. 1–8. Citeseer (2005)
34. Öğütçü, G., Testik, Ö.M., Chouseinoglou, O.: Analysis of personal information security behavior and awareness. Comput. Secur. **56**, 83–93 (2016)
35. Parsons, K., McCormac, A., Butavicius, M., Ferguson, L.: Human factors and information security: individual, culture and security environment. Technical report, Defence Science and Technology Organisation Edinburgh (Australia) Command (2010)
36. Ruffy, F., Hommel, W., von Eye, F.: A stride-based security architecture for software-defined networking. ICN **2016**, 107 (2016)
37. Saitta, P., Larcom, B., Eddington, M.: Trike v1 methodology document. Draft, work in progress (2005)
38. Salas, E., Maurino, D., Curtis, M.: Human factors in aviation: an overview. Hum. Fact. Aviat. 3–19 (2010)
39. Saunders, M., Lewis, P., Thornhill, A.: Research Methods for Business Students. Pearson Education, London (2009)
40. Scandariato, R., Wuyts, K., Joosen, W.: A descriptive study of Microsoft's threat modeling technique. Requirements Eng. **20**(2), 163–180 (2015)
41. Shostack, A.: Threat Modeling: Designing for Security. John Wiley & Sons, Hoboken (2014)
42. UcedaVelez, T., Morana, M.M.: Risk Centric Threat Modeling. Wiley Online Library, Hoboken (2015)
43. Uzunov, A.V., Fernandez, E.B.: An extensible pattern-based library and taxonomy of security threats for distributed systems. Comput. Stan. Interfaces **36**(4), 734–747 (2014)
44. Vieane, A., Funke, G., Gutzwiller, R., Mancuso, V., Sawyer, B., Wickens, C.: Addressing human factors gaps in cyber defense. In: Proceedings of the Human Factors and Ergonomics Society Annual Meeting, vol. 60, pp. 770–773. SAGE Publications Sage CA, Los Angeles (2016)
45. Widdowson, A.J., Goodliff, P.B.: CHEAT, an approach to incorporating human factors in cyber security assessments. In: 10th IET System Safety and Cyber-Security Conference 2015, pp. 1–5 (2015)
46. Xiong, W., Lagerström, R.: Threat modeling-a systematic literature review. Comput. Secur. **84**, 53–69 (2019)
47. Yadav, T., Rao, A.M.: Technical aspects of cyber kill chain. In: Abawajy, J.H., Mukherjea, S., Thampi, S.M., Ruiz-Martínez, A. (eds.) SSCC 2015. CCIS, vol. 536, pp. 438–452. Springer, Cham (2015). https://doi.org/10.1007/978-3-319-22915-7_40

48. Young, H., van Vliet, T., van de Ven, J., Jol, S., Broekman, C.: Understanding human factors in cyber security as a dynamic system. In: Nicholson, D. (ed.) AHFE 2017. AISC, vol. 593, pp. 244–254. Springer, Cham (2018). https://doi.org/10.1007/978-3-319-60585-2_23
49. Zwilling, M., Klien, G., Lesjak, D., Wiechetek, Ł., Cctin, F., Basim, II.N.: Cyber security awareness, knowledge and behavior: a comparative study. J. Comput. Inf. Syst. 1–16 (2020)

Smart Technologies and Internet of Things Designed for Aging in Place

Hélène Fournier[1]([✉]) [iD], Irina Kondratova[2] [iD], and Keiko Katsuragawa[3,4] [iD]

[1] Human Computer Interaction, Digital Technologies Research Centre,
National Research Council Canada, Moncton, NB, Canada
helene.fournier@nrc-cnrc.gc.ca
[2] Human Computer Interaction, Digital Technologies Research Centre,
National Research Council Canada, Fredericton, NB, Canada
irina.kondratova@nrc-cnrc.gc.ca
[3] Human Computer Interaction, Digital Technologies Research Centre,
National Research Council Canada, Waterloo, ON, Canada
keiko.katsuragawa@nrc-cnrc.gc.ca
[4] University of Waterloo, Waterloo, ON, Canada

Abstract. One of the challenges accompanying the global rise in aging populations is the increase in demand for care services. With an increase in age, the need for medical support also grows, which may lead to unplanned and frequent visits to the doctor. Recent developments in Smart technologies and the Internet of Things (IoT) will play an important role in designing suitable home healthcare support services for older adults and enable self-care for people as they age at home. The current COVID-19 pandemic has accelerated the push for telehealth technology solutions including remote patient monitoring for senior adults who are medically or socially vulnerable. Remote health services are being promoted as a means of preserving the patient-healthcare provider relationship at times when an in-person visit is not practical or feasible, especially during COVID-19 and beyond. Smart technologies and IoT could potentially improve health outcomes and save lives. This paper will explore issues and challenges in introducing smart technologies and IoT into the homes of older adults, as well as explore features of the technology and potential outcomes that could allow older adults to remain autonomous, independent, safe, and encourage aging in place. The paper also identifies technology gaps and areas for future research.

Keywords: Smart technologies · IoT · Remote healthcare · Seniors · Pandemic

1 Introduction

Internet of Things (IoT) has a broad range of definitions and authors across the research literature use inconsistent terms to address the devices present in the IoT environment [47]. Two popular definitions of IoT are:

© Her Majesty the Queen in Right of Canada 2021
A. Moallem (Ed.): HCII 2021, LNCS 12788, pp. 158–176, 2021.
https://doi.org/10.1007/978-3-030-77392-2_11

"A dynamic global network infrastructure with self-configuring capabilities based on standard and interoperable communication protocols where physical and virtual 'things' have identities, physical attributes, and virtual personalities and use intelligent interfaces, and are seamlessly integrated into the information network" [30].

"Things having identities and virtual personalities operating in smart spaces using intelligent interfaces to connect and communicate within social, environmental, and user contexts" [26].

The devices present in the IoT include mobile devices, smart devices, mobile technologies or mobile smart devices [47]. Interconnected objects play an active role in what might be called the "Future Internet" [26] with sensors as one of the key building blocks of IoT [4,33]. IoT technologies are also considered as enablers in future healthcare [33]. One of the challenges of an aging population is the increase in demand for care services [5,32]. As people age, their need for medical support grows, which may result in more frequent and unplanned visits to the doctor or trips to in-clinic healthcare services. Recent developments in smart technologies and IoT could play an important role in designing suitable home healthcare support services for older adults and enable self-care for people as they age [32]. There is a clear economic benefit in promoting aging in place, for example, for health policy makers in the 'aged care sector', assistive technologies to support older adults to age in place could provide less expensive (and preferable) alternatives to institutional care [10].

The current pandemic has created challenges for healthcare in both hospital and home care settings with an increased need for virtual care and online consultations for vulnerable populations. Seniors living alone, both in fair and poor health, are considered vulnerable and at-risk for health-related complications from COVID-19. Dr. Paul Hebert, Special Advisor tothe Canadian Red Cross [9] mentioned that "these are not new challenges for isolated older adults, especially those with chronic health concerns. The pandemic simply underscores them". The pandemic has also increased the proliferation of technological solutions for digital health, including IoT, wearables, and emerging smart home systems for daily living activities, health and wellness. Older adults are the primary users of technologies for aging in place and the main benefactors. However, the design and development of home healthcare technologies are often led by the requirements of social and caregiving environments, rather than by the needs and preferences of older adult users [12]. The mismatch between functionalities, intrinsic motivations and expected benefits can have a significant impact on technology acceptance [13] and can reduce the rate of technology adoption [10]. The next sections of the paper will explore research in the area of smart technologies and IoT, and the features and functionalities that could potentially enable older adults to remain autonomous, independent, safe, and to age in place at home.

2 Aging in Place with IoT and Health-Related Smart Home Technologies

IoT and health-related smart home technologies are being developed to meet the needs and requirements of a rapidly aging population. The literature identifies some challenges in the area of IoT and health-related smart home technologies for aging in place which will be examined in more detail in the next sections.

2.1 User Needs and Technology Requirements

Aging in place requires a more holistic view of user needs and requirements for autonomous and independent living at home [45] including: health, safety/security, peace of mind, independence, mobility, and social contact. Some smart technologies and IoT for monitoring and care have been found to target only certain aspects of older adult's requirements from a limited viewpoint (e.g., health monitoring, safety monitoring), without considering cognitive and sensory assistance. Requirements are not mutually exclusive, but often overlap instead. For example, it is possible for an application to offer improved mobility as well as reduce dependency on others, or provide independence and at the same time reinforce social interaction. Demiris [14] identified six categories of health-related smart home technologies that address needs and requirements that are important in supporting aging in place, including the following:

- Physiological monitoring: e.g., vital signals, temperature and blood pressure monitoring.
- Functional monitoring/Emergency detection and response: e.g., general activity level, gait and meal intake monitoring. Abnormal or critical situation is detected as emergency through the data collection.
- Safety monitoring and assistance: e.g., automated lighting, accident prevention, hazard detection, and warnings.
- Security monitoring and assistance: e.g., detecting intruders versus familiar people in one's social network, and reporting identified threats.
- Social interaction monitoring and assistance: e.g., facilitates social interaction by phone or video chat.
- Cognitive and sensory assistance: e.g., medication reminders, lost key locators, task reminders and water temperature indicator.

Smart living applications for older adults should be: (S)ensible, (M)odern, (A)daptable, (R)esponsive, and (T)angible in delivering value to users through careful design and HCI and human factors considerations [45]. IoT-based remote monitoring can help in the management of age-related diseases (both acute and chronic), impairments (e.g., visual, physical and speech), and decline (e.g., forgetfulness). Chronic conditions and diseases, if neglected, are major contributing factors in the decline of functioning and the ability to live independently, which leads to older adults being referred to nursing home facilities [5].

IoT technologies for 'Ambient Assisted Living' (AAL) include enhanced, intelligent ambient environments in the following areas of application: smart

Table 1. IoT and AAL for support key needs and motives for an aging population.

Activities	Supportive IoT or Ambient assisted living (AAL)
Daily activities and social connectedness	- Home care systems with integrated natural speech interaction - Robots or virtual assistants for socially isolated seniors - Applications for smartphones or tablets that offer social networks for communication and social networking (e.g., with caregivers or other old adults) as well as a number of public services such as medical assistance, shopping assistance, and Meals on Wheels - Reminders for daily activities (e.g., take medicine, diet and exercise reminders) - Applications that encourage social interaction: video-based communication to support mediated connections with family and virtual participation in activities etc.
Safety and security	- Applications for fall detection, (e.g., wearable sensors, context-aware visual systems and cameras) - Activity recognition/posture recognition using wearable sensors placed on the wrists, chest and ankle of the user for detecting unusual activities (e.g., decreased mobility, depression, etc.), personal emergency, and medication management systems - Safety monitoring: analysis of data that detect environmental hazards (e.g., gas leakage, stove on). Safety assistance includes functions such as automated lights for reducing trips and falls - Security monitoring: measurements that detect human threats such as intruder alarm systems and emergency response
Health monitoring	- Applications for managing chronic diseases, telehealth allowing remote interaction with the patient, and collecting continuous health records - Physiological assessment including pulse/respiration rates, temperature, blood pressure, blood sugar level, bowel and bladder outputs, etc. glucose, medication compliance, weight, and bio-sensors to track activities of daily living and health status, remote health monitoring using wireless medical devices (e.g., oxygen level tester, breathing, and blood sugar measurements) - Functional assessment: general activity level measurements, motion, gait identification, meal intake, etc. - Nutrition monitoring: food-related monitoring, physical activity monitoring and daily caloric expenditure for weight monitoring (by wireless scales), monitoring consumed meals and water - Cognitive monitoring: automatic reminders and other cognitive aids such as automated medication reminders, key locators, etc.; verbal task instruction technologies for appliances and sensor assisted technologies that help users with deficits such as sight, hearing, and touch

homes and smart environments, AAL and agent-based pervasive computing and decision-making methods, and IoT sensing technologies (wireless sensor networks, smart sensors, gateways, etc.) [2,5,33]. Current IoT solutions for AAL technology, home automation, and telehealth services include a combination of tools and devices to support aging in place. A consideration of key needs and motives in supporting activities of daily living, safety and security, as well as home health monitoring is required. Table 1 presents IoT solutions for AAL and key activities that are support from the literature [2,5,33].

The desire for autonomy is a primary driving factor for home monitoring sensor adoption [49]. Studies of smart home monitoring technologies show that older adults are willing to trade privacy (by accepting a monitoring technology), for autonomy [45,49]. As the information captured by the sensor becomes more intrusive and the infringement on privacy increases, sensors are accepted if the loss in privacy is traded for autonomy [25,45,49]. Even video cameras, the most intrusive sensor type, are accepted in exchange for greater autonomy and an option to age at home [49].

Al-Shaqi [2] conducted an extensive literature review to identify current practices and directions for future research in AAL and found that most studies and system designs were based on the belief that the behavior of end-users is consistent from day to day, or has a general pattern. The provision of 'support' for older adults often did not take into account irregular patterns and 'changes in daily routines' [2]. Besides health monitoring, one important aspect often ignored in system designs is the need for entertainment in the lives of older adults, which is equally important for their well-being. Entertainment and leisure activities can have a significant impact on the quality of life, and part of the challenge is to identify requirements for an entertainment support system from the perspective of older adults and their caregivers alike [2]. A comprehensive review on the state-of-the-art of smart homes for elderly healthcare has identified several research challenges. Table 2 presents key areas of concern that must be addressed in order to encourage technology adoption in the context of aging in place [32].

2.2   IoT Standards: Technical Challenges

There are major technical challenges related to standards in IoT and AAL (one author describe IoT and AAL standards as 'almost unavailable' [2]. Some of the issues around standards include the lack of adaptability of different system components (i.e., sensors, communication protocols and decision support) [2]. Standards are often linked to the 'developer initiative' and are not well maintained [2]. Issues around system integration and interoperability of devices could interfere with the ability of technology to meet the needs and requirements of users [2]. Although IoT applications and services may increase the quality of peoples' lives, especially those with age-related disabilities or specific needs, the lack of accessibility standards creates a huge barrier [2]. Some of the accessibility requirements for IoT applications and services include: 1) Ability to perceive all information and capabilities of an IoT application or service, 2) Ability to understand the information presented by an IoT application or service, and 3) Ability to perform the required operations of an IoT application or service. Accessibility issues create significant barriers for users, caregivers, and healthcare providers alike [2].

Table 2. Recent advances and research challenges for smart homes for elderly health-care and aging in place.

Categories	Research challenges
Privacy and security	- Identified as the most pressing concern for smart home technologies. Privacy and security of the transmitted health data; data that may contain sensitive, protected or confidential information that can endanger residents' privacy and safety, if breached. Educating older adults (and caregivers) in areas of privacy and security related to home health monitoring and digital health technologies is a priority
Performance: efficiency, optimization and cost	- There is a need to develop more robust and efficient algorithms for healthcare systems (and devices) along with effective data compression techniques - Portable and wearable physiological parameter measurement systems aimed at long-term monitoring need to be energy efficient. Energy harvesting techniques are being explored to fulfill the energy requirements of the devices - Current efforts to increase efficiency will drive down cost - Optimizing the performance of the smart home system for elderly healthcare will have an impact on cost which is a major factor in technology adoption (older adults are often on a fixed income)
Connecting complex systems and many discrete devices in one common platform	- Systems need to be designed to deal with integration issues among different devices, with an optimum number of sensors in order to avoid redundant data; infrastructure demands, maintenance cost, and energy consumption are key factors driving adoption - Reducing energy consumption and cost will impact technology adoption
Modularity, acceptance and adoption	- Modular, extensible structures, expanded capability and interoperability of systems and devices among different smart home platforms are vital for achieving flexibility and widespread adoption - Providing users with options to choose components from different manufacturers, or add (and remove) services will have an impact on cost and adoption rates

Standardization is key to providing needed functionality, interoperability, and security for smart home technologies. The IEEE Standards Association (IEEE-SA) has been working in a number of areas to help build consensus on the adoption of wearable devices, including standards that enable the communication between medical, healthcare and wellness devices, and with external computer systems (IEEE-P1912) [19]. This standard specifies approaches for end-user security through device discovery/recognition, simplification of user authentication, tracking (items/people) under user control/responsibility, as well as supporting alerts; privacy is maintained through user controlled sharing of information that is independent of the underlying wireless networking technology used by the devices [19]. Other standards address networking and communication layers that provide low-cost, low-speed ubiquitous communication between devices, including international standards for low power, short range, and extremely reliable wireless communication within the surrounding area (including wearables), and support a wide range of data rates (low-data-rate transmissions, energy-efficient wireless technology) for different applications [19].

3   Models to Inform IoT and Smart Technology Adoption

Various models have been applied in studies of technology adoption, specifically in the acceptance of technology by older adults. The next section will explore these models as well as important predictors for smart home healthcare technology adoption by older adults.

3.1   Technology Acceptance Model (TAM) and Unified Theory of Acceptance and Use of Technology (UTAUT)

The Technology Acceptance Model (TAM) has been widely used in a variety of contexts to understand an individual's intention to use a technology, including technology acceptance by older adults [31, 36, 44], and technology acceptance in the context of aging in place [40]. More recently, TAM has been applied to research on acceptance of IoT-based gerontechnology by older users [33]. The Unified Theory of Acceptance and Use of Technology (UTAUT) has been applied in studies looking at the intent to use technology in healthcare [39]. The key variables influencing the behavioral intent to use technology are Perceived Usefulness (PU) and Perceived Ease Of Use (PEOU) [40]. Older adults have been described as the main target population for IoT and healthcare solutions, however, they are also considered to be conservative users. This poses a serious challenge to the successful implementation of smart home healthcare systems and services [39]. Eight significant predictors related to acceptance behavior for smart home healthcare technologies were identified based on an online survey with 254 older adults aged 55 years and older [39]. Important predictors included:

- Performance Expectancy: *(user perceptions related to the degree to which using a technology will provide direct benefits in performing certain activities)* this was the most significant predictor of smart homes for healthcare acceptance among older adults.
- Effort Expectancy: *(the degree of ease associated with the use of any system)* this was also an important predictor of smart homes for healthcare acceptance among older adults.
- Expert Advice: *(the degree to which users rely on external experts' opinion like doctors, nurses, or pharmacists in taking decisions related to their health; if the experts' feel and believe that using smart home for healthcare will be*

beneficial) this factor also played a role (but was not significant) as a predictor of smart homes for healthcare acceptance among older adults. Perceived Trust: *(the feeling that their personal data will be safe, carefully protected, and anonymous)* was also a predictor (but was not significant) of smart homes for healthcare acceptance among older adults.
- Social influence: *(which includes the opinions or suggestions provided by a home care nurse, friends and/or relatives).* Other *facilitating conditions* included the degree to which an individual believes that an organizational and technical infrastructure exists to support the use of the system. *Technology anxiety* and *perceived cost* were also important predictors (although not significant) to consider in smart homes for healthcare acceptance among older adult.

TAM studies on the 'behavioral intention' to use technology have focused on attitudes and perceptions at the pre-implementation stage (i.e., survey responses to hypothetical scenarios for technology solutions that may not exist yet) and may have overlooked other important factors. A study of community-dwelling older adults found that coping strategies can also have an impact on perceptions and attitudes around technology acceptance [40]. For example, in a study of technology acceptance for aging in place, community-dwelling older adults reported not feeling the need for supportive technology [40]. Community-dwelling older adults in this study were found to employ coping strategies for dealing with decline, including *'trying to keep one's' mind from focusing on oneself and one's own vulnerability'* and *'focusing on the present'* [40].

IoT and smart home healthcare support and services are still evolving, therefore technology acceptance studies (e.g., TAM and UTAUT studies) should include comparative investigations for different demographics (i.e., age, gender, culture) for a better understanding of the differences in consumer resistance to IoT-based smart homes [39]. In addition, opinions from older adults who actually live in smart homes should be considered, as it will represent a more realistic scenario in taking into account the 'different types of resistance' to technology adoption. The identification of factors which contribute to passive, active, and very active resistance to smart homes and IoT warrants further investigation, especially from the perspective of older users [39]. For example, older adults might perceive current smart home technologies and IoT services to be immature and in an early developmental stage, and they may not trust technology to be mature enough to be useful for them. Further empirical studies from the perspective of HCI and human factors are required in this area.

3.2 Human/Activity/Space/Technology Model (HAST)

HAST is an established environmental gerontological theory that looks at relationships between smart home technologies, physical (built) environment and caregiving in the homes of older adults who are aging in place [10]. HAST considers the factors and risks specific to aging in place that have an impact on older adults' health and well-being, along with outcomes following the implementation of IoT-based smart home technologies [10]. The socio-technical context is also considered in the role IoT-based smart home technologies can play in aging in place, beyond technological and engineering problems; engaging the engineering community, scientists, policy makers and end-users in addressing risks and concerns should lead to a more significant social and technological impact [10]. For example, HAST uses a case study approach which has been applied to investigate how IoT-based smart home technologies can interact with the caregiving environment in the home, with the following considerations:

- Personal profile: includes the persons' situational/health/functional needs, along with current formal and informal care needs.
- Care profile: documents the care needs (formal and informal) prior to the technology being introduced.
- Functional limitations: examines the implications of a person's health status on their ability to be independent at home.
- Physical (built) environment: includes modifications received in the home, listing barriers the person has faced in their home environment that may be preventing them from undertaking tasks independently, along with descriptive information about the environments.
- Smart Home technology: introduces the technology into the picture and explains which activities in the home are supported, the context of use (who instigated it, for how long, and whether it has been successfully used); with a technology analysis limited to smart home technologies (devices for managing tasks in the home environment, not health technology devices).

The outcome of the HAST case study process results in a synthesis of collected data that documents the impact of the technology in terms of caregiving, health and well-being of the older person, as well as the impact on any caregivers. Limitations of the technology as experienced by the older person and family are also documented, and whether expectations and benefits of the technology have been met. Broader implications raised in case study approaches around the relationships between technology, physical (built) environments, care, health, and well-being warrant further research and discussion.

Despite technological advances in IoT-based smart homes, their adoption is still very low mainly due to their disruptive nature [39] and the inherent conservative nature of older adults in adopting any new technology [16, 48]. Older adults are described as having a different mindset compared to early adopters of new technology [39]. For example, for older adults, privacy and security concerns with health data that the smart homes can collect, and costs are important factors that influence technology acceptance or resistance; this includes IoT-based smart home solutions for healthcare management and for aging in place [39, 40]. It has also been suggested that to improve adoption, technical support and advice in real time could be provided by data centers and dedicated hotline numbers to assist older adults with customized help when needed [39], however, privacy and confidentiality laws around health data impose serious restrictions on the level of customized assistance available. Issues of privacy and security of smart home technologies and IoT will be examined in more detail in a subsequent section.

Other inhibiting factors may also have an impact on older adults' adoption of smart home technologies and IoT for aging in place, including an older person's unwillingness to learn new technology, lack of confidence with technology or the inability to maintain the technology [10]. An older adult may also dislike new smart home technology due to frustration, or fear of not being able to afford to continue to maintain or replace the technology [10]. Technical problems (e.g., power outages affecting connectivity of smart devices) and lack of proper training in the use of smart home technology could also affect technology adoption [10].

4   Designing Smart Technology and IoT for Aging in Place

Research in the field of IoT development and evaluation has recognized a number of challenges and limitations associated with past smart technology developments to support aging in place, calling for user centeredness and better integration with broader systems [3, 10, 39]. The factors that contribute to low technology adoption are complex and multifaceted, and are not limited to a person's chronological age or health status [10]. Poor interface design, issues of privacy and trust [54], as well as economic and educational barriers [51] also contribute to low rates of technology adoption by older adults. A number of studies have suggested that future IoT development will require a more user-centered and co-creative design approach [5, 20, 21, 24, 53] and age appropriate designs [41]. In addition to these considerations, more studies of IoT systems in the homes of older adults, in actual contexts of use, are required [40, 43].

The lack of adaptable designs for people with impairments has also been identified as a barrier to smart living and its application for aging in place, specifically in the use of wireless devices [45]. Research and development efforts are required in the area of mobility-based smart devices for the older adults, to deliver localized, context-dependent, and user adaptable designs that consider user characteristics and conditions, as well as emotional or affective aspects such as feel, value, sensitivity, and appeal [46]. The design of smart technologies and IoT should be human-centric and encourage older adults to be more self-reliant, enhance their self-efficacy, and confidence to live on their own with personal freedom and individuality, and provide support for practical necessities, but also be aesthetically pleasing [46]. Aesthetics is an important design consideration for older adults, along with safeguards that protect personal information and information about activities of daily living. These are necessary design considerations in autonomous living with smart home interfaces that need human-centric design to minimize their stress [46]. Continuous research efforts and formal usability studies are required for IoT-based smart homes and intelligent ambient environments, to achieve greater customization, automation, and more contextually-sensitive and responsive systems and devices, which require more efficient interfaces [46]. Ease of use, degree of satisfaction, and reduction of error rates by older users in operating interfaces and devices are areas requiring more empirical studies [46]. Identifying key attributes to measure satisfaction levels of older users and the types of errors made while operating interfaces should feed into improved designs, with HCI and human factors considerations to support better customization and optimization of IoT-based smart living environments for older adults [46].

5   IoT, Privacy and Security, Acceptance and Adoption

The issue of data privacy and overall trust in smart home services for healthcare is an important factor that needs further exploration. Key privacy threat factors should be identified with better threat/risk models that will enable the various smart home stakeholders to create better strategies and policies which can assure a greater success of their services. Moderating effects of gender and cultural background should also be investigated further.

The research literature points to a serious lack of a theoretical/conceptual approaches in user acceptance modelling as the current focus is on the underlying technologies and services, rather than on the end-user [40]. In addition to the technological aspects related to trust, privacy and security, educating the end-users on these issues is also important [17]. A good example of the multitude of issues related to privacy, security and trust are the concerns with the use of wearables by older adults.

User acceptance is critical for the technology to be integrated within daily living, especially in areas such as IoT and wearables. A wearable technology is used to collect and deliver information about health and fitness related activities. Wearable devices (e.g., smartwatch, smart ring, smart band, smart clothing, etc.) are used widely by the general population to track exercise and health [42]. Originally designed to support medical needs, some modern consumer wearables have sensors that monitor and record sensitive patient health information (such as heart rate, respiratory rate, oxygen saturation, blood pressure, temperature, ECG, etc.), and also record physical activity (e.g., steps taken, distance travelled, sleep patterns, exercise activity, falls, etc.) [42]. Despite the widespread proliferation of wearables, there are many privacy issues and risks associated with consumer wearables that have yet to be resolved by industry and lawmakers [6].

Researchers have identified a number of privacy risks for consumer wearables including user context privacy, bystander privacy during data collection, external data sharing privacy, with proposed technology solutions to mitigate the risks [6]. Along with privacy by design technology solutions for IoT and wearables, privacy laws and regulations need to provide clear notice and mechanism for consent to inform users on the nature of possible privacy and security issues related to the intended use. It has been noticed that wearable systems perceived as intrusive can impact user acceptance – a fact that many technology developers overlook [2]. Additionally, applications of technological wearable solutions frequently suffer from a socio-cultural misunderstanding of group differences, and, as a consequence, lead to poor acceptance of technology by older adults, caregivers, and clinicians [2,50].

While the research literature points to various barriers such as the concern for privacy, followed by lack of trust when adopting technologies for use by older adults [40], it has been observed that there is also a willingness to give up some privacy for the benefit of staying in ones home [27]. Older adults view personal data protection as one of several important dimensions of privacy concerning home healthcare technologies, and they also have other privacy concerns related to aspects of personal privacy, such as intrusiveness and a feeling of surveillance which also have an impact on technology acceptance [35,50]. To address privacy considerations and improve technology adoption, researchers emphasize that technology developers should include older adults in the design process, and gather privacy requirements for such technologies [34,54]. Privacy concerns should be considered when designing health technologies for in-home use, and include not only the privacy of personal user data; all levels of users should be consulted, including the end-user (older adults), secondary users (caregivers) and tertiary users (clinicians) [34]. An overarching theme that warrants further research exploration is the trade-off between privacy (data and information privacy), the sense of surveillance and the invasion of personal space, and the freedom of safely living independently at home [35,44]. Additionally, the end-user perspectives and the need for autonomy and control must be balanced with privacy, security and trust in systems and devices [44], including smart home technologies and IoT.

5.1   Technology Acceptance Interviews

We recently conducted an exploratory study with older adults that was focused on technology acceptance in the context of home health monitoring and tele-health management, and "lived experience" during the pandemic [29]. The study participants previously received a tablet and a smartwatch as part of the pilot study on home health monitoring and telehealth management in the province of New Brunswick (Canada) in 2019. After 6+ months of the pilot study, we have conducted interviews with older adults who chose to continue the study. The sample of older adults (N = 6, ages 66 to 92) included both females and males, all college or University educated, some with active lifestyles and no medical conditions, while others had medical conditions which required home health monitoring. All participants (but one) used computing devices on a regular basis, for work or leisure, with some owning several mobile devices and smartwatches. The major areas of concern and "lived experience" for this sample of knowledgeable older adults included:

- Issues with privacy: The use of virtual assistants in the home (e.g., Google Home), "Google picks up on private conversations", "total invasion of privacy", "Virtual Assistant picked up on words in our conversations and started recommending things based on words it has picked up", "suddenly my computer will start displaying ads and numbers for pizza". "That's the only drawback, it's like big brother is watching", when we're having a private chat, I unplug it." "I am concerned with privacy and security with the tablet for home health monitoring. I don't want to share my data". Another senior was a victim of a fraud so now "we (family) will only use the tablet for information coming one-way to us—and that's all we are going to allow."

- Security versus surveillance (fall detection): One older adult expressed a concern that if it's "For seniors being in their own home—if it means being hooked up to something for when I fall and can't get up, well ok, I'm good with that" but intrusiveness and surveillance were an issue, "I think having a camera would bother me".

- Technical issues: Some older adults reported "stress and aggregation of setting up the tablet" (for home health monitoring), "the tablet didn't synchronize with the watch very well" and there were several bugs, "it took them one year to work out all the bugs". There were also issues with technology reliability and stability, "every 3 or 4 months the system will go down", "had to reboot after a power outage, Bluetooth went out", and the older adult had "no idea how to turn it back on to get it working again"; getting immediate technical support was an issue. Some older adults expressed frustration in "not having control of the devices", from the software end of it, "no manual", and not being able to do something as simple as "resetting the time on my smartwatch".

Some older adults also reported experiencing "fear, anxiety and stress" during the ongoing pandemic and had not seen their physician since the beginning of the pandemic (e.g., routine follow ups and blood work for chronic conditions were not completed). They would "welcome virtual care" but were "not aware if their physician offered virtual care services".

Findings from our exploratory study of "lived experiences" during the ongoing pandemic demonstrate a profound need for more social and home technology support for vulnerable older adults. Care technologies in the home environment require different contextual considerations, where privacy issues are key. From a data privacy perspective, devices operating in the home are more exposed to unauthorized access than those in more controlled environments, such as nursing homes and hospitals [23]. Additionally, devices in the home also invade the personal space of the user, and their friends and family.

5.2 Privacy by Design, Usable Security for Home Healthcare Systems

Researchers have pointed out the potential benefits of smart technologies and IoT in providing home healthcare support to help older adults to age in place [10, 40, 52]. However, due to their novelty, complexity, and collection of vast amounts of sensitive personal health information, these technologies also pose serious privacy and security concerns for older adults. Further research is required to better understand the privacy and security attitudes and concerns of older users with respect to new emerging healthcare technologies in order to design usable and privacy preserving technologies [18]. Frik [18] has proposed a process for a usable security design which includes: a) capturing the privacy and security attitudes of older adults, b) building threat models, with surveys to empirically validate these models, c) participatory design sessions with older adults from the onset of the design process, to requirement gathering, model testing, and further threat model refinement, and d) making recommendations with regards to mitigation and control strategies. Better threat models and more usable security models are also required to empower older adults in the adoption and use of smart technologies and IoT for healthcare and for aging in place [1,18,40].

The importance of including older adults in co-design and in gathering privacy requirements for new emerging technologies for independent living has been emphasized in the research [2,54]. An overarching theme that warrants further exploration is the trade-off between privacy (data and information privacy), the sense of surveillance and the invasion of personal space, and the freedom of safely living independently at home [35,44]. User perspectives and the need for autonomy and control must be balanced with privacy, security and trust in systems and devices [44].

Smart technologies and IoT for home healthcare need to be built with cybersecurity in mind; with a consideration of user attitudes and perceptions around privacy and security in order to ensure successful use [15]. Research has shown that older adults are very aware of privacy issues [2,34] in the context of Ambient Assisted Living (AAL). Privacy seems to be more of an issue for technologies designed for aging in place, especially as older adults with health issues must learn to manage their personal health data [28]. Frequently, older adults are faced with challenges when navigating alone the complex relationship between loss of privacy and increased freedom for users and caregivers to collect data, as well as opening up the home environment to calls, checks, and home health monitoring [34,44,50].

Building usable security for older adults requires building privacy by design into the system [11] to improve security, and empower older adults to make informed decisions so that they have better control over their personal data. Further investigation is needed around privacy and security factors for various types of devices, types of data and how data is collected, choice of data recipients and context of use; how these factors affect older adults' privacy and security perceptions of emerging healthcare technologies, and, subsequently, widespread technology adoption, has yet to be explored in depth [18].

There is the potential for systems and devices to collect massive amounts of data and conduct non-stop surveillance which triggers privacy and security concerns among older adults, especially with respect to wearable devices, video recording and financial data, and a need to address inaccurate beliefs about the security of the technological systems in use [8]. Misconceptions about actual data collection and storage may cause security risks to be underestimated, and therefore lead to bad decisions regarding levels of protection for the user [8]. However, the World Health Organization (WHO) [38] argues that misconceptions about what data the system collects may raise false concerns that can be addressed when appropriate explanations are provided to the user.

Research has suggested that, in addition to the types of data collected, the recipients of data matter to older adults, i.e. it is important to know who accesses their data and how often, and to what level of detail [7]. A related concern is associated with the lack of feedback from the monitoring system about when it is in the recording mode. Older adults often rely on family members for support in "dealing with technology" [7]. Delegation of security (i.e., sharing login credentials with family members and caregivers) and issues with creating, remembering and entering passwords point to problematic security behaviors among older adults [7] and demonstrate that older adults' mental models of security and privacy may differ from those of younger populations [22]. All together, these findings underscore the complexity and diversity of privacy and security issues among older adults as a diverse group, and the need for further research [22].

6   Conclusion

One of the limitations in studies of smart technologies and IoT to support aging in place is that these services are relatively new and currently not available on a commercial scale. Therefore, the wide-scale introduction of services and technologies should be preceded by widespread technology usability studies, and followed up with further investigations into the actual technology acceptance as the step following the 'behavioral intention' to use. The issue of data privacy and overall trust in smart home healthcare services is an important factor that influences technology adoption by older adults. More detailed and careful analysis, with more threat factors identified and, subsequently, a threat/risk model created that will enable the various smart home stakeholders to create better strategies and policies will assure greater success of the services.

The moderating effects of age, gender, and cultural background on IoT and smart home technology acceptance have not been addressed sufficiently, and future studies should include a wider sampling of older adult users in various contexts of use, with co-design as a key factor in empowering older adults to take ownership of the health and well-being, and possibly influence technology adoption for aging in place as well. Future advances in research and development in these areas are anticipated under the National Research Council Canada, Aging in Place Program [37].

References

1. AL-mawee, W.: Privacy and Security Issues in IoT Healthcare Applications for the Disabled Users a Survey (2012)
2. Al-Shaqi, R., Mourshed, M., Rezgui, Y.: Progress in ambient assisted systems for independent living by the elderly. SpringerPlus 5(1) (2016). https://doi.org/10.1186/s40064-016-2272-8
3. Alraja, M.N., Farooque, M.M.J., Khashab, B.: The Effect of Security, Privacy, Familiarity, and Trust on Users' Attitudes Toward the Use of the IoT-Based Healthcare: The Mediation Role of Risk Perception. IEEE Access 7(May 2020), 111341–111354 (2019). https://doi.org/10.1109/access.2019.2904006

4. Ash, B.: Iot and wearable devices: How standardisation is helping to drive market adoption (Apr 2016), https://www.wearabletechnology-news.com/news/2016/apr/26/iot-and-wearable-devices-how-standardisation-helping-drive-market-adoption/
5. Azimi, I., Rahmani, A.M., Liljeberg, P., Tenhunen, H.: Internet of things for remote elderly monitoring: a study from user-centered perspective. Journal of Ambient Intelligence and Humanized Computing 8(2), 273–289 (2017). https://doi.org/10.1007/s12652-016-0387-y
6. Becker, M., Matt, C., Widjaja, T., Hess, T.: Understanding privacy risk perceptions of consumer health wearables-an empirical taxonomy. In: ICIS 2017: Transforming Society with Digital Innovation (2017)
7. Cahill, J., McLoughlin, S., O'Connor, M., Stolberg, M., Wetherall, S.: Addressing issues of need, adaptability, user acceptability and ethics in the participatory design of new technology enabling wellness, independence and dignity for seniors living in residential homes. In: International Conference on Human Aspects of IT for the Aged Population. pp. 90–109. Springer (2017)
8. Caine, K.E., O'Brien, M., Park, S., Rogers, W.A., Fisk, A.D., Van Ittersum, K., Capar, M., Parsons, L.J.: Understanding acceptance of high technology products: 50 years of research. In: Proceedings of the Human Factors and Ergonomics Society Annual Meeting. vol. 50, pp. 2148–2152. SAGE Publications Sage CA: Los Angeles, CA (2006)
9. Canadian Red Cross: Pandemic study reaffirms red cross concern for vulnerable seniors (May 2020), https://www.redcross.ca/about-us/media-news/news-releases/pandemic-study-reaffirms-red-cross-concern-for-vulnerable-seniors
10. Carnemolla, P.: Ageing in place and the internet of things - how smart home technologies, the built environment and caregiving intersect. Visualization in Engineering 6(1) (2018). https://doi.org/10.1186/s40327-018-0066-5
11. Cavoukian, A., Fisher, A., Killen, S., Hoffman, D.A.: Remote home health care technologies: How to ensure privacy? build it. In: Privacy by design. Identity in the Information Society 3(2), 363–378 (2010)
12. Cavoukian, A., Jonas, J.: Privacy by design in the age of big data (June 2012), https://jeffjonas.typepad.com/Privacy-by-Design-in-the-Era-of-Big-Data.pdf
13. Chen, K., Chan, A.H.: A review of technology acceptance by older adults. Gerontechnology (2011)
14. Demiris, G., Hensel, B.: Technologies for an aging society: A systematic review of "smart home" applications. Yearbook of medical informatics 3, 33–40 (08 2008). https://doi.org/10.1055/s-0038-1638580
15. Dodd, C., Athauda, R., Adam, M.: Designing user interfaces for the elderly: a systematic literature review (2017)
16. Ehrenhard, M., Kijl, B., Nieuwenhuis, L.: Market adoption barriers of multi-stakeholder technology: Smart homes for the aging population. Technological forecasting and social change 89, 306–315 (2014)
17. EPoSS: Internet of Things in 2020: A roadmap for the future (2008), https://docbox.etsi.org/erm/Open/CERP%2020080609-10/Internet-of-Things_in_2020_EC-EPoSS_Workshop_Report_2008_v1-1.pdf
18. Frik, A., Egelman, S.: Usable Security of Emerging Healthcare Technologies for Seniors. CHI Workshop "Designing Interactions for the Ageing Populations" (2018), https://networkedprivacy2018.files.wordpress.com/2018/04/frik.pdf
19. Gardašević, G., Katzis, K., Bajić, D., Berbakov, L.: Emerging wireless sensor networks and internet of things technologies–foundations of smart healthcare. Sensors 20(13), 3619 (2020)

20. Gkouskos, D., Burgos, J.: I'm in! towards participatory healthcare of elderly through iot. Procedia computer science **113**, 647–652 (2017)
21. Greenhalgh, T., Procter, R., Wherton, J., Sugarhood, P., Hinder, S., Rouncefield, M.: What is quality in assisted living technology? The ARCHIE framework for effective telehealth and telecare services. BMC medicine **13**(1), 1–15 (2015)
22. Gregor, P., Newell, A.F., Zajicek, M.: Designing for dynamic diversity: interfaces for older people. In: Proceedings of the fifth international ACM conference on Assistive technologies. pp. 151–156 (2002)
23. Henriksen, E., Burkow, T.M., Johnsen, E., Vognild, L.K.: Privacy and information security risks in a technology platform for home-based chronic disease rehabilitation and education. BMC medical informatics and decision making **13**(1), 1–13 (2013)
24. van Hoof, J., Kort, H.S., Rutten, P.G., Duijnstee, M.: Ageing-in-place with the use of ambient intelligence technology: Perspectives of older users. International journal of medical informatics **80**(5), 310–331 (2011)
25. Husebo, B.S., Heintz, H.L., Berge, L.I., Owoyemi, P., Rahman, A.T., Vahia, I.V.: Sensing technology to facilitate behavioral and psychological symptoms and to monitor treatment response in people with dementia: A systematic review. Frontiers in Pharmacology **10**(February), 1–13 (2020). https://doi.org/10.3389/fphar.2019.01699
26. INFSO D.4 Networked Enterprise & RFID INFSO G.2 Micro & Nanosystems (DG INFSO), in co-operation with the RFID Working Group of the European Technology Platform on Smart Systems Integration (EPOSS): Internet of things in 2020: A roadmap for the future (Sept 2008), https://docbox.etsi.org/erm/Open/CERP%2020080609-10/Internet-of-Things_in_2020_EC-EPoSS_Workshop_Report_2008_v1-1.pdf
27. Jaschinski, C., Allouch, S.B.: Listening to the ones who care: exploring the perceptions of informal caregivers towards ambient assisted living applications. Journal of ambient intelligence and humanized computing **10**(2), 761–778 (2019)
28. Kolkowska, E., Kajtazi, M.: Privacy dimensions in design of smart home systems for elderly people. In: Proceedings of the 10th AIS SIGSEC workshop on information security and privacy (2015)
29. Kondratova, I., Fournier, H., Katsuragawa, K.: Review of usability testing methods for aging in place technologies. In: Human-Computer Interaction - HCI International 2021 (2021)
30. van Kranenburg, R.: The Internet of Things: A critique of ambient technology and the all-seeing network of RFID. Institute of Network Cultures (2008)
31. Macedo, I.M.: Predicting the acceptance and use of information and communication technology by older adults: An empirical examination of the revised UTAUT2. Computers in Human Behavior **75**, 935–948 (2017). https://doi.org/10.1016/j.chb.2017.06.013
32. Majumder, S., Aghayi, E., Noferesti, M., Memarzadeh-Tehran, H., Mondal, T., Pang, Z., Deen, M.J.: Smart homes for elderly healthcare–recent advances and research challenges. Sensors **17**(11), 2496 (2017)
33. Maskeliunas, R., Damaševicius, R., Segal, S.: A review of internet of things technologies for ambient assisted living environments. Future Internet 11(12) (2019). https://doi.org/10.3390/FI11120259
34. McNeill, A.R., Coventry, L., Pywell, J., Briggs, P.: Privacy considerations when designing social network systems to support successful ageing. In: Proceedings of the 2017 CHI Conference on Human Factors in Computing Systems. pp. 6425–6437 (2017)

35. Mortenson, W.B., Sixsmith, A., Beringer, R.: No place like home? surveillance and what home means in old age. Canadian journal on aging= La revue canadienne du vieillissement 35(1), 103 (2016)
36. Mostaghel, R.: Innovation and technology for the elderly: Systematic literature review. Journal of Business Research **69**(11), 4896–4900 (2016). https://doi.org/10.1016/j.jbusres.2016.04.049
37. National Research Council Canada: Aging in place proposed program plan (Oct 2020), https://nrc.canada.ca/en/research-development/research-collaboration/programs/aging-place-proposed-program-plan
38. Organization W.H. World health statistics 2014: a wealth of information on global public health. World Health Organization, Technical report (2014)
39. Pal, D., Funilkul, S., Charoenkitkarn, N., Kanthamanon, P.: Internet-of-Things and Smart Homes for Elderly Healthcare: An End User Perspective. IEEE Access **6**, 10483–10496 (2018). https://doi.org/10.1109/ACCESS.2018.2808472
40. Peek, S.T., Wouters, E.J., van Hoof, J., Luijkx, K.G., Boeije, H.R., Vrijhoef, H.J.: Factors influencing acceptance of technology for aging in place: A systematic review. International Journal of Medical Informatics **83**(4), 235–248 (2014). https://doi.org/10.1016/j.ijmedinf.2014.01.004
41. Pietrzak, E., Cotea, C., Pullman, S.: Does smart home technology prevent falls in community-dwelling older adults: a literature review. Journal of Innovation in Health Informatics **21**(3), 105–112 (2014)
42. Radin, J.M., Wineinger, N.E., Topol, E.J., Steinhubl, S.R.: Harnessing wearable device data to improve state-level real-time surveillance of influenza-like illness in the usa: a population-based study. The Lancet Digital Health **2**(2), e85–e93 (2020)
43. Reeder, B., Meyer, E., Lazar, A., Chaudhuri, S., Thompson, H.J., Demiris, G.: Framing the evidence for health smart homes and home-based consumer health technologies as a public health intervention for independent aging: A systematic review. International journal of medical informatics **82**(7), 565–579 (2013)
44. Schomakers, E.M., Ziefle, M.: Privacy Concerns and the Acceptance of Technologies for Aging in Place. Lecture Notes in Computer Science (including subseries Lecture Notes in Artificial Intelligence and Lecture Notes in Bioinformatics) 11592 LNCS, 313–331 (2019)
45. Sharma, R., Nah, F.F.H., Sharma, K., Katta, T.S.S.S., Pang, N., Yong, A.: Smart living for elderly: design and human-computer interaction considerations. In: Human Aspects of IT for the Aged Population. Healthy and Active Aging. ITAP 2016. Lecture Notes in Computer Science. vol. 9755, pp. 112–122. Springer (2016)
46. Sharma, S., Wong, J.: Three-button gateway smart home interface (TrueSmartface) for elderly: Design, development and deployment. Measurement: Journal of the International Measurement Confederation 149, 106923 (2020). https://doi.org/10.1016/j.measurement.2019.106923
47. Silverio-Fernández, M., Renukappa, S., Suresh, S.: What is a smart device? - conceptualisation within the paradigm of the internet of things. Visualization in Engineering **6**(1), 1–10 (2018)
48. Sintonen, S., Immonen, M.: Telecare services for aging people: Assessment of critical factors influencing the adoption intention. Computers in Human Behavior **29**(4), 1307–1317 (2013)
49. Townsend, D., Knoefel, F., Goubran, R.: Privacy versus autonomy: A tradeoff model for smart home monitoring technologies. Proceedings of the Annual International Conference of the IEEE Engineering in Medicine and Biology Society, EMBS pp. 4749–4752 (2011). https://doi.org/10.1109/IEMBS.2011.6091176

50. Tsertsidis, A., Kolkowska, E., Hedström, K.: Factors influencing seniors' acceptance of technology for ageing in place in the post-implementation stage: A literature review. International journal of medical informatics **129**, 324–333 (2019)
51. Wang, J., Carroll, D., Peck, M., Myneni, S., Gong, Y.: Mobile and wearable technology needs for aging in place: Perspectives from older adults and their caregivers and providers. In: Nursing Informatics. pp. 486–490 (2016)
52. Wang, S., Bolling, K., Mao, W., Reichstadt, J., Jeste, D., Kim, H.C., Nebeker, C.: Technology to Support Aging in Place: Older Adults' Perspectives. Healthcare **7**(2), 60 (2019). https://doi.org/10.3390/healthcare7020060
53. Wherton, J., Sugarhood, P., Procter, R., Hinder, S., Greenhalgh, T.: Co-production in practice: how people with assisted living needs can help design and evolve technologies and services. Implementation Science **10**(1), 1–10 (2015)
54. Yusif, S., Soar, J., Hafeez-Baig, A.: Older people, assistive technologies, and the barriers to adoption: A systematic review. International Journal of Medical Informatics **94**, 112–116 (2016). https://doi.org/10.1016/j.ijmedinf.2016.07.004

Please Stop Listening While I Make a Private Call: Context-Aware In-Vehicle Mode of a Voice-Controlled Intelligent Personal Assistant with a Privacy Consideration

Jongkeon Kim and Jeongyun Heo[✉]

Kookmin University, Seoul, Republic of Korea
{jkeon72,yuniheo}@kookmin.ac.kr

Abstract. In recent years, research on Voice Assistant has been actively conducted in the areas of human interaction and lifestyle. The characteristic that only voice can interact with the device was noted for its usability in vehicles, and a number of studies were conducted to prove the effectiveness of an intelligent personal assistant (IPA) in Human-Vehicle interaction (HVI) studies. Vehicles not only enable movement but are also private spaces owned by individuals. In this paper, we examine how the user's car space is privacy-protected when using IPA with voice interaction and confirm that it provides a suitable function for the driving context, which is the original role of the car. The range of vehicles in this document includes not only private vehicles but also cultures, such as carpooling and car sharing. The experiment was conducted with Wizard of Oz prototyping designed on the basis of the current IPA level of functions and information, and participants were subjected to in-depth interviews after driving the simulator. Through in-depth interviews, the lack of IPA functions and the needs of voice interaction were confirmed, and the possibility of invasion of privacy of personal information was found in the overall function. The experimental results are intended to suggest not only functional and privacy suggestions for HVI when using IPA but also implications for the development of various vehicle services in the future.

Keywords: Intelligent personal assistant · Human–vehicle interaction

1 Introduction

Technologies that make voice interfaces useful and widely available have already been released in various contexts. Services that have already been released have made voice assistants usable in everyday life, and more features and platforms are constantly being added [1].

Users can perform a variety of tasks, from simple information requests to playing music, making phone calls, scheduling, or controlling the temperature or turning on lights through a smart home device [2, 3]. Services or products that communicate with users in natural language based on these voice interactions are called voice-activated

© Springer Nature Switzerland AG 2021
A. Moallem (Ed.): HCII 2021, LNCS 12788, pp. 177–193, 2021.
https://doi.org/10.1007/978-3-030-77392-2_12

personal assistants, conversational agents, virtual personal assistants, etc. [2, 4], and in this paper, they are called intelligent personal assistants (IPAs).

Several Surveys and studies have identified personal information security and privacy as among the most pressing concerns for people using new information technologies [5]. However, verbal speech and conversation are naturally audible to the public, and voice interactions with IPAs also have these characteristics. IPAs are being used more and more for support, and most of them are designed to operate with voice interaction. The main problem of those operating with voice interaction is that they are inconvenient to use in public places, and because the conversation with the IPA that interacts with voice is naturally audible to the public, accessibility of use is reduced [6].

However, vehicles that are considered to be personal spaces have diversified forms and are shared with others through carpooling and car sharing, and these services will also result in various autonomous vehicle services in the future [7]. Accordingly, the function supported by the IPA in the context of current level of vehicles guarantees the privacy of user personal information, and the necessity of the function in the context of driving and suitability as a personal space of the vehicle are examined.

In the study, a simulator experiment was conducted with a focus on verifying whether the information provided by the IPAs includes personal information and influences driving. Before the experiment, interviews of users with prior IPA experience were analyzed and analysis of several IPAs were carried out to divide the functions and information supported by the current level of IPAs into status and output information types. On the basis of classified information, various functional execution cases were identified, and an experiment scenario was created on the basis of these cases. We carried out a driving simulation experiment equipped with IPAs operating in the Wizard of Oz (WoZ) method.

After the driving simulation experiment, the evaluation of functions and information and in-depth interviews was conducted, focusing on three items to confirm the effectiveness and suitability of 15 drivers: contextual driving workload impact, usability of voice interaction in the vehicle, and privacy due to IPAs. Thus, the utility and suitability of current-level IPAs and the overall development insight of voice user interface (VUI) in vehicles are derived.

2   Background and Related Work

Most IPAs interact by voice and are referred to as voice user interfaces. VUI is the interaction between people and applications or devices through voice. VUI includes system prompts, grammar, and dialogue logic or flow. All voices played to the user during the conversation are recorded. Conversational logic usually responds by reading information from a database to respond to what the user has just said [8]. Speech recognition is the constant advancement of machine learning and statistical data mining technologies, which has provided many of the driving forces needed for machines to understand human speech. From a small vocabulary to continuous vocabulary, speech recognition has been developing continuously, enabling the establishment of the current IPA level [9].

However, voice interaction is more public than keyboard input or screen touch, which are interactions with general devices. Openly using IPAs has the potential for social embarrassment, which is a major concern for IPA users and is accepted as an obstacle to usability. There is a cultural component to this issue, and this type of embarrassment is framed by the cultural norms of phone use in public [4]. Owing to the embarrassment arising from unwanted public attention due to the interaction where the voice is publicly exposed, use in a personal space is preferred. Users are reluctant to use the voice function in a public space for the following four reasons [6]:

1. It draws public attention,
2. It disrupts the environment,
3. It intrudes the personal space of others, and
4. It verbalizes information of a private nature.

In several studies, when a user interacts with a voice in a public place environment with strangers, it can affect the attribute and usability, and users judge that the possibility that others can hear the user's voice commands can act as a problem in social situations. Thus, IPA users believe that during voice interactions, people around them can observe and evaluate their work [6, 10].

Moorthy and Vu [6] presented the findings of several case studies showing that IPAs are less frequently used in public spaces and users are reluctant to use them. Also, the acceptability of each IPA location is different; in particular, the degree of willingness to transmit private information is also dependent on where the user is located. In other experiments, according to participants' responses, users paid more attention to communicating personal information than non-personal information, with 55% of the participants reporting privacy concerns as the primary reason for avoiding IPA use. However, participants preferred to use IPAs over keyboard input in safe personal spaces.

The age of information is coming, and privacy is a problem in the present. Activities that were once private, shared with a minority now leave trails of data that expose our interests, traits, beliefs, and intentions [11]. Although it is true that sharing and collecting data on the Internet has benefited our society, it has had a significant impact on users' privacy. More and more personal information is being collected, processed, shared and disseminated. Privacy is a multi-faceted concept that can be interpreted differently depending on the direction of access such as users, data, and communication. So, the problem of user privacy cannot be conceived simply. Sensitive information about users must be kept private, the user's identity must be protected, and the user's actions must be untraceable [12]. Among the various approaches and interpretations of personal information, Eugene F. Stone et al. [13] focus on information privacy, denoted as the ability of the individual to control personal information about one's self. De Capitani Di Vimercati et al. [13] Was approached as a method to prevent the disclosure of the user's identity or attribute, and the functions provided by VUIs are publicly included in the scope of personal information defined in this way.

Love [14] used Hall's [15] interpersonal distance theory to define the extent of personal space in a study of the invasion of personal space due to incoming calls. Hall's [15] theory classified the types of space into four main categories (intimate, personal, social, and public), which humans can utilize considering the loudness of the voice, social situations, and sense of space. The theory categorized the social distance levels by giving the scope of each category as follows:

- intimate distance: less than 0.67 feet
- personal distance: less than 4 feet
- social distance: 12 feet or less
- public distance: greater than 12 feet

Among them, public distance is defined as enabling human-to-person conversation, and this conversation belongs to the category that others can hear and identify. Therefore, the range below the social distance can be referred to as the range of the space in which IPA users prefer to use voice interaction. Various personal spaces satisfy the conditions of social distance, and among them, vehicles are a space within a movable minor distance category. Hatuka, T., Toch, E. [16] described the portable private-personal territory (PPPT) in the relationship between information and communication technology and public space. The PPPT is a social personal territory, the locus of a complex web of relationships that includes both person-to-person connections and person-to-space connections. [17] PPPT separates privacy independently of public or private space, not limited to specific locations for various forms of exchange with social interaction. This experiment also defined the vehicle as a private space. In the vehicle space, IPA users can expect the security of personal information to be guaranteed when using voice interaction. However, before it is a personal space, the vehicle performs the main task of being driven and is given a changing situation, making prediction difficult, and thus, contextual information and functions are required [16].

The effectiveness of voice interaction in driving has been proven in numerous studies. Multitasking, such as using a smartphone while driving, reduces concentration on driving and is a major cause of car collisions. As an alternative to solving this problem, voice interaction is adopted, and IPA services using voice in vehicles are increasingly in use [18, 19]. Strayer et al. [20] demonstrated the effect of lowering the driver's driving workload in a driving test through an experiment focusing on Apple's Carplay and Google's Android Auto, which are vehicle IPA services. In high-workload scenarios, VUIs provide the lowest cognitive load and highest user satisfaction among different modalities [21]. Voice interaction through the use of GPS, vehicle systems, smartphones, etc. has been evaluated to be suitable in a car where situational disturbances can lead to accidents, as it reduces the use of hand and sight more than classical interactions do [4, 20]. Since IPA users expect complete hands-free interaction that minimizes the physical need to press a button in the interaction with the assistant, they have hands-free interaction with the vehicle as a common point [4].

Braun et al. [23] revealed positive effects of the use of in-vehicle interactive VUIs for issues such as cognitive needs or workloads, task-related exhaustion, trust, acceptance and environmental involvement. These are based on an analysis of the user's behavior and observed positive benefits and aims to have a safe, effective, engaging, and enjoyable interaction with in-vehicle agent interlocutors while meeting the user's expectations.

However, it is more difficult presently to prevent exposure of complete personal information owing to the natural verbal feature of VUIs. Vehicle modes of use are constantly evolving in various directions. Examples include carpooling, in which people ride together in a private vehicle, or car-sharing and ride-sharing, in which one vehicle is shared in turn. With the advent of models that use these vehicles in new forms, vehicles that are considered personal spaces are shared in various forms. Carpooling is a vehicle-sharing method that has a fairly long history as an activity recommended by governments in many countries [24]. Shared automated vehicles have the potential to revolutionize the choice of modes of transport in the future. Shared automated vehicles can be an innovative vehicle alternative, but it is very important to understand the factors that can influence usability concerns. [25] For mobility, new vehicle models such as car-sharing and carpooling are considered to be a development stage for the autonomous vehicle environment in the future, and autonomous vehicles actively utilize AI technology and voice interaction IPAs in the context of human–autonomous vehicle interaction. These new vehicle models present the direction of service centering on personification around a user's specific needs [1, 7]. Voice interaction IPA research in various vehicle models at the present stage results in the service of autonomous vehicles in the future.

Therefore, in this study, when the IPA operated by voice interaction is in a vehicle, the purpose of confirming the appropriateness of the driving context of the information provided by the functions and the ambiguous privacy standards is explored by studying real users. This study aims to improve IPA and future vehicle services from the perspective of human–vehicle interaction (HVI) by checking the vehicle environment not only in single-person vehicles but also in new mobility modes such as carpooling and car-sharing.

3   IPA Task

Various IPA services and products, such as Siri, Alexa, and Cortana, exist as assistants used in our daily lives and vehicles. They are developed by different companies, and accordingly, the particular support functions and response formats are different, which can confuse the user. Also, most of the IPA modes are not designed for vehicles or driving situations. Therefore, in this study, to achieve the goal of verifying the usefulness and suitability of IPAs, the experimental task is defined after collecting and arranging user interviews and IPA functions in services focusing on the issues of driving and personal information privacy.

3.1   IPA Functions Analysis in Vehicles

In order to classify the existing IPA functions, nine users (five males and three females in their 20s and one male in his 50s) with experience of using an IPA in vehicles were interviewed. The main content of the interview with IPA users was focused on the following questions:

1. Driving availability and experience: Can you drive? For how long have you been driving?
2. IPAs' functional recognition and existing perception: Did you know that an IPA is mounted on a GPS app or vehicle?
3. Frequency and experience of using IPAs: Have you ever used IPAs?
4. IPA's main purpose and function: What are the key usage features?
5. Primary IPA's service and reasons for them: Is there anything else IPAs need?

The functions of IPAs that are mainly used in vehicles are GPS, phone, music control, smartphone system control, and stopover guiding of GPS. The IPAs to be used for function research were selected by deploying the most frequently used IPA service mentioned by users in the interviews. The IPAs that were selected for the study were the following: Amazon's Alexa, the #1 global smart speaker according to overall market share; Google Assistant and Siri, which have been installed in software for driving and are respectively from Google and Apple, the two major makers of smartphone operating systems (OSs); and finally, Kakao's Kakao i and SK's NUGU, installed in an automotive navigation app.

Choi et al. [19] proposed to classify HVI system data into status information and output information. Status information is all information related with the driver's tasks, whereas output information is the information to be provided to the driver. Classified status information is shown in Table 1, and output information is shown in Table 2.

3.2 Personal Information of the IPAs

The actual user's verification of the information provided by the IPA function is to be carried out. In particular, it is necessary to assess whether the output information is

Table 1. Status information.

Function	Command example	IPA response example	Supported IPA
Music control	"Play the next song," "Volume down"	(Music playback actions), "Turned the volume down"	All IPAs
Texting	"Text Mom, I'm coming soon"	"Text to send to 'Mom' is… Do you want to send it?"	Google, Siri, Kakao, NUGU
Calling	"Call Mom"	"Calling Mom…"	
Unread notification	"Check out of unread notification"	Syncing	Siri

Table 2. Output information.

Function	Command example	IPA response example	Supported IPA
Weather	"Is it raining tomorrow?"/ "Is it cold outside?"	"It will be quite cold soon. A clear sky is expected tomorrow"	All IPAs
Music	"Play a song that suits the weather"	(Music playback actions)	Google, Kakao, NUGU
Stopover	"I need fuel"/"I want to go to the bathroom"	"Okay, I'll take you to the (stopover). Please check"	Google, Siri, Kakao, NUGU
GPS	"Please guide me to Seoul City Hall"	"Starting guiding to your destination"	All IPAs
Traffic	"Let me know the traffic is on (site e.g., highway)"	"There's a lot of traffic right now. It's 13 min from here to 5 km"	NUGU

suitable for the driving context and whether providing all information poses a risk of exposing personal information. In this paper, before creating an experiment scenario to check the user's actual opinion, we intend to create a scenario that can utilize each IPA function.

Driving context information was written as output information in Table 2; personal information identifies the user, and what constitutes personal information is based on the user's opinion [12, 26]. As a result, it was created focusing on three functions of calling, texting and GPS, which open up the possibility of information disclosure (Fig. 1).

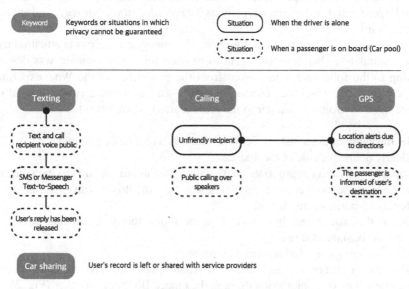

Fig. 1. Personal information case example

4   Method

On the basis of the hypothesis that the vehicle environment will offset the factors that determine the usability of voice interaction IPA, we have summarized cases in which IPA functions and the information provided are executed to evaluate the suitability of the IPA in the driving context and the degree of invasion of personal information. These cases are used as experimental scenarios focused on each IPA function. The hypothesis that we tried to check through experimentation is as follows:

6. In a vehicle that is determined to be suitable for IPA voice interaction, the current level of IPA would not have been able to accommodate all of the contextual functions.
7. The information provided by voice interaction in a space treated as a personal space will include the disclosure of personal information that is difficult for users to control.

The experiment was conducted with a virtual IPA designed with WoZ prototyping, and participants drove in a driving simulator and used a voice interaction assistant operated by WoZ. After the experiment, participants joined the in-depth interview.

4.1 WoZ-Prototype IPA

WoZ is a classic prototyping experiment wherein participants are unaware of the fact that they are interacting with a simulated system, rather than a real system, which simulates and interacts with the performance of an unimplemented or partially implemented system. Experimental participant interactions are recorded in various ways and analyzed for various purposes [27].

In this study, the WoZ experiment uses the IPA function in a driving situation using a vehicle simulator. Therefore, the agent to be used for the experiment was designed according to the following items, taken from the guidelines of the WoZ experiment of Large et al. [28], which was conducted with a simulator and a conversational user interface in an environment similar to the present study's experiment.

8. Set the name of the assistant. Set it up like it is a real name and make it work.
9. Clearly define the role of the assistant.
10. Begin by providing appropriate conversation and an introduction to the assistant.
11. Make it a functional conversation; do not distract the driver with small talk.
12. Replay responses consistently.
13. During the experiment, the conversation speed or response speed must be adjusted to be as constant as possible.
14. The assistant should follow social etiquette.
15. IPAs do not attract too much attention visually, but they have the same effect as experiencing voice interaction through the placed Bluetooth speaker (Fig. 2).

4.2 Participants and the Experiment Environment

The experiment and in-depth interviews were carried out by 15 ordinary people with driving licenses and experience.

- Gender: eight women and seven men
- Age group: ten participants in their 20s; three in their 30s; and two in their 40s
- Driving experience: three participants have less than 1 year; four have 1–3 years; and seven have years or more

In order to focus on driving situations rather than the function of IPA, the experiment explained to participants that they observed driving concentration due to the use of an IPA while driving. These experimental introductions prevent bias in recognizing IPA use and provisional information. After the experiment, the usability of the function was evaluated, the perception of each scenario was evaluated, and an in-depth interview was conducted.

In the virtual driving environment used by the participants, three monitors are placed on the front, the Logitech G29 steering wheel, gas pedal, brake pedal, gear shift lever, and car seat provide support, and the experimenter has a Bluetooth speaker placed on the right side of the seat of the participant. It plays back the audio designed to make it look like an IPA enabling voice interaction (Fig. 2).

Fig. 2. Driving simulator environment (left: bluetooth speaker used in the experiment/right: experiment participant running in a simulator)

4.3 Scenario

The main scenarios for participants to experiment with while driving in the simulator are three situations, and the functions and intentions to be performed in each situation are as shown in Table 3 (Scenario 1), Table 4 (Scenario 2), Table 5 (Scenario 3).

Table 3. Scenario 1. Personal vehicle driver only

Task/situations	Purpose	Confirmation
GPS	Is GPS function suitable for voice interaction in the driving context?	Contextual
Music recommend	Is music recommendation a suitable function for driving and vehicles?	Contextual
Weather guide	Is weather guidance suitable for driving and vehicles?	Contextual
Receive phone call	Is phone reception a suitable function for driving?	Contextual
Directions during a call	Is there any inconvenience in the possibility of exposing your location during a call with a less intimate partner?	Privacy

Table 4. Scenario 2. Personal vehicle with passenger

Task/situations	Purpose	Confirmation
Stopover	Is the disclosure of passengers' waypoints burdensome as information disclosure?	Privacy
Text received 1	Is text recipient disclosure to a passenger recognized as personal information disclosure?	Contextual/privacy
Text received 2	Is it recognized as the disclosure of personal information of the incoming text to the passenger?	Privacy
Send reply	Is it recognized as personal information that is sent by voice and disclosed reply by voice?	Contextual/privacy
Receive call	Is disclosure of incoming calls to passengers recognized as disclosure of personal information?	Contextual/privacy

Table 5. Scenario 3. Car-sharing

Task/situations	Purpose	Confirmation
Pairing with car-sharing	Can a Car-sharing be considered a private space? Can you link your information?	Privacy
Destination selection	Is the GPS function appropriate in the driving context of a Car-sharing? Is the destination function okay?	Contextual/privacy
Receive text	How is the transmission of incoming text messages, which are personal information, recognized on Car-sharing?	Privacy
Sync playlist	Is the ability to get an individual's playlist from a Car-sharing recognized as personal information?	Privacy

Before the start of the first scenario, participants had enough time to get used to driving the simulator. The first scenario (S1. Personal vehicle Driver only) where the driver alone got in was focused on the utility of functions and included scenarios in which information could be disclosed through telephone contact in a situation where personal space is perceived to take up. In the second scenario with a passenger (S2. Personal vehicle with Passenger), even when another person is present in a vehicle that is recognized as a personal space, information is disclosed by the IPA centering on the phone or text function, and the degree of awareness of privacy infringement at that time is confirmed. An assistant experimenter sat in the seat next to the passenger and the passenger's intimacy level was first stipulated, but after the experiment was completed, various levels of intimacy with the passenger were discussed to confirm the allowable range. The third scenario (S3. Car-sharing) induces an awareness of access to personal information centering on the linkage of user data and the IPA function installed in the car-sharing vehicle, a new type of vehicle, and later, the in-depth interview confirms the participants' perception of personal information when using the car-sharing vehicle.

4.4 Participants and the Experiment Environment

In this study, the experimental evaluation criteria and in-depth interview questions were reorganized following SART and a measure of voice assistant system research that Nasirian et al. [24] provided to confirm the hypothesis of the relationship between IPA information and system quality and trust, and the definition of privacy of personal information collected from literature studies [15, 18, 23] (Table 6).

Table 6. Experiment scenario measurement.

Construct	Description	Purpose	Sources
Instability	Likeness of situation to change suddenly	Driving overload	SART
Concentration	Degree that one's thoughts are brought to bear on the situation		
Division of attention	Amount of division of attention in the situation		
Trust	Participants' trust in using IPA with voice interaction	Voice interaction usability	Nasirian et al
Intention	Participants' intention in using IPA with Voice interaction		
Information privacy	Whether the information can identify participants or someone	Awareness of information disclosure	Stone, E. F. et al. and De Capitani Di Vimercati et al.

The experimental evaluation index can be classified into three major categories: the influence of the driver's workload, the usability of voice interaction in the vehicle, and the invasion of privacy due to IPA.

5   Evaluation

After the experiment was completed, functional evaluation and interviews were conducted according to the evaluation items, and the demographic information of the participants in this experiment is as follows:

- Gender: 7 males (46.7%) and 8 females (53.3%)
- Age group: 10 people in their 20s (66.7%), 3 people in their 30s (20%), and 2 people in their 40s (13.3%)
- Driving experience: 3 people (20%) with 1 year or less, 4 people with 1–3 years. (26.7%), 5 people (33.3%) with 3–7 years, and 3 people (20%) with over 7 years.
- Experiences using IPAs: 7 of the participants (46.7%) answered that they often use IPA and 8 (53.3%) did not.

5.1 Vehicle Contextual Function

The functions that provide contextual output information at the current in-vehicle IPA level are playing music, recommending music, providing weather updates, calling, texting, and giving directions and traffic information, mainly conducted in scenarios 1 and 2. Although the participants' evaluation of these functions was conducted differently for each function, opinions were in agreement. Functions relating to GPS, which is the most commonly used technology in vehicles, were evaluated as the most suitable vehicle context functions. Control functions such as music recommendation and music playback were also positively evaluated, but some participants said that control functions were not suitable for operation through voice interaction because control functions can be operated more easily with a controller attached to the handle. The weather guidance has already received the most negative evaluation in that users are located in a space inside the car and are not greatly affected by the outside.

It is said that people who ride in cars wear lighter clothes because cars are mostly moving from one inside to another. I don't feel that it is necessary to provide temperature guidance. (Participant B).

I don't trust the assistant, so I don't use it, but I think it's useful when stopping at a bathroom or coffee shop, or when I need to play music. (Participant C).

I never tried to use the voice assistant. Not only is the perception incorrect, but also there is no trust in the function. (Participant E).

5.2 Voice Interaction

During the experiment, one result was that the voice interaction with the function triggered a driving workload for some participants (four people, 26.7%), or the IPAs conversation could not be assessed by focusing on driving (six people, 40%). As mentioned earlier, some responded that the accessibility of the button attached to the existing handle is more convenient in the simple control (three people, 20%), and nine participants (60%) did not use the IPA even in actual driving situations, for reasons of awkward usage, a lack of trust in the technology, and inconvenient use of personal information.

The case of music control or an incoming call is executed just by moving a finger on the steering wheel, but I don't think I need to do it with voice. I didn't want to answer my assistant's question, but I just answered "Yes" because I was concentrating on driving. (Participant D).

I want to focus on driving as much as possible, but in thinking of voice commands, driving concentration diminishes. (Participant A).

5.3 Verbal Privacy

Of the 15 participants, fourteen (93.4%) said that their car is considered a private space, and nearly half of them, seven (46.7%), said that if a passenger is in the car, it is not a private space. In such a situation where personal space is perceived to take up and privacy is guaranteed, if the GPS function exposes the current location or destination to the called party or caller through the phone as a medium, all participants recognized it as infringing on their personal information but providing directions anyway. Opinions were that they wish it to be controlled (8 of 14, 57.1%). Also, some participants said that the driving workload could be sufficient depending on the content of the phone call.

Participants who recognize the vehicle as a personal space also responded that it was an uncomfortable feeling to disclose personal information about the situation in which the recipient of the contact is revealed or the person responds verbally and information is naturally disclosed.

It is difficult to recognize that the information was exposed to the other party by GPS function guidance, but I missed the content of the call that overlapped the phone and IPA guidance audio. (Participant B).

Most calls are short while driving, but I think the voice of the GPS function during this period is unnecessary. (Participant F).

5.4 Carpooling

In the experiment, participants presented various views on the exposure of personal information due to contact in the scenarios of car sharing and carpooling. It can be seen that the driver's destination is not considered personal information by responding that there is generally (12 people of 15, 80%) no issue on the disclosure of the destination and stopover to the passenger. However, at the current IPA functional level, the identity of the recipient (10 people of 15, 66.7%), the content of the text received (12 people of 14, 85.7%), the text message reply (8 people of 12, 66.6%), and the call information that were disclosed due to the contact (11 people of 15, 73.3%) were recognized as personal information. It is said that this difficulty varies greatly depending on the level of intimacy with the passenger and the relationship between the receiver and the passenger, and various opinions have emerged from participants who never allow passengers any personal information; it is possible from participants who never allow any personal information of the passenger to those who have seen it twice. Not only the intimacy with the passenger but also the relationship with the receiver and the relationship between the receiver and the passenger were important.

I think I can answer the phone if I think it's a close person. Also, the call can give real-time feedback that I am driving and who is next to me. (Participant D).

In a personal relationship with the passenger and the caller, the phone is very difficult to control, and I think it is included in the private area, but it is an area where you can control and send text messages…. (Participant I).

In a relationship where we have contact once a year, I think we can disclose text messages or calls from the vehicle. (Participant H).

Depending on the recipient, it will vary greatly from acceptance of the contact to recognition of personal information disclosure. It is more important who the recipient is, but I think that most of the time, if the passenger is a friend, it can be revealed. (Participant C).

It was more inconvenient to ride as a passenger than to use a Car-sharing vehicle. As well as contacting me, the disclosure of music playlists and music recommendations can be considered disclosure of my taste. (Participant G).

As in the interviews of some of the participants above, the degree of their perception of texts and telephones is different, and the range of disclosure for each individual varies significantly.

5.5 Car-Sharing

Among the scenarios, the function supported by car-sharing was perceived as the gravest form of invasion of personal information (14 people, 93.3%). However, this result was due to the lack of trust in the car-sharing vehicle itself rather than the IPA's voice interaction, and most of the participants recalled the device pairing itself to the IPA or OS mounted on the Car-sharing vehicle as the use of personal information.

For this reason, in an interview after the experiment, one participant said that when using a Car-sharing vehicle, participant did not pair or use a device mounted on the Car-sharing vehicle.

Seven people (46.7%) said that car-sharing vehicles were recognized as personal space during the rental period, and four people (28.5%) responded that the music play-back function linked to mobile phones is not considered personal information. Besides, when a passenger rides in a car-sharing vehicle, the exposure of personal information by an IPA in the second scenario can mean that it is difficult to guarantee privacy in the car-sharing vehicle. However, some participants were aware of this and actively utilized the collected information to provide quality services.

I think the car-sharing vehicle is my space during the rental period, but I feel uncomfortable when I think that my personal information is linked or collected in the car-sharing vehicle. (Participant B).

Even if the car-sharing vehicle is recognized as my space for a while, the pairing itself with the vehicle is considered the use of personal information. (Participant J).

6 Discussion and Future Research

In this study, the effectiveness of the information provided by the IPA function in the vehicle environment in terms of privacy of personal information due to the driving context and the characteristics of voice interaction was examined. In in-depth interviews after the simulator experiment, participants at the current level of IPA provided contextual information but did not feel that all currently available IPA functions were needed in the current environment and wanted to strengthen GPS. The possibility of privacy invasion was derived from the exposure of personal information due to phone calls and text message reception, especially, the range of intimacy of the user-acceptable other person (e.g. passenger, caller) is very different for each test participant. In Car-sharing vehicles, privacy arising from trust due to the collection or sharing of data felt very threatening to users.

This study conducted an experiment to confirm the VUIs-type IPA, which is expected to improve usability when defining a vehicle as a personal space in terms of driving context and personal information disclosure. Vehicles are moving spaces for driving beyond personal spaces, and future development of services within vehicles will lead to various services utilizing autonomous driving. Therefore, there is a variety of services centered on sharing, and at the current level, where many IPAs have been released in vehicles, we have confirmed the driving load and usability of users.

Based on the insights derived from the experiment, the range of functions desired by the user in terms of functions was sufficient, but improvement in speech recognition performance itself was found to lead to usability. In a carpool situation where the user is not alone but is boarded by someone else, it was desired to provide a private mode by allowing the vehicle to recognize the boarding of a passenger or allow the user to select. In particular, the scope of information provision varies depending on the degree of intimacy with the passenger and contact person, and the scope derived from the experiment and interview is shown in Fig. 3.

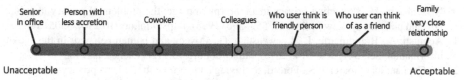

Fig. 3. Scope of information disclosure by intensity

The carpool culture and Car-sharing Services in which passengers are boarded are the stages of development up to the autonomous driving service. Therefore, research should be conducted to establish the basis for not only the Multi-mode support reflecting IPA privacy but also the lack of trust of car sharing service users before the full-scale autonomous driving service is commercialized.

Vehicles are emerging from the category of private vehicles and various models that fit the shared economy. At this time, most participants in the car will be passengers, not drivers. The results of the experiment also show that the vehicle IPA usability has been affected by being aware of the passenger. Therefore, it became more and more important to focus on passengers. The research will then focus on passenger research and improved confidence in car-sharing vehicle systems, which will serve as the cornerstone for self-driving shuttles or revitalizing the shared economy.

References

1. Porcheron, M., Fischer, J.E., Reeves, S., Sharples, S.: Voice interfaces in everyday life. In: Proceedings of the 2018 CHI Conference on Human Factors in Computing Systems, Montreal, QC, Canada, pp. 1–12. ACM (2018). https://doi.org/10.1145/3173574.3174214
2. Lopatovska, I., Oropeza, H.: User interactions with "Alexa" in public academic space. Proc. Assoc. Info. Sci. Tech. **55**, 309–318 (2018). https://doi.org/10.1002/pra2.2018.14505501034
3. Hoy, M.: Alexa, Siri, Cortana, and more: an introduction to voice assistants. Med. Ref. Serv. Q. **37**, 81–88 (2018). https://doi.org/10.1080/02763869.2018.1404391

4. Cowan, B.R., et al.: "What can i help you with?": infrequent users' experiences of intelligent personal assistants. In: Proceedings of the 19th International Conference on Human-Computer Interaction with Mobile Devices and Services, Vienna, Austria, pp. 1–12. ACM (2017). https://doi.org/10.1145/3098279.3098539
5. Acquisti, A., Grossklags, J.: Privacy attitudes and privacy behavior. In: Jean Camp, L., Lewis, S. (eds.) Economics of Information Security, pp. 165–178. Kluwer Academic Publishers, Boston (2004). https://doi.org/10.1007/1-4020-8090-5_13
6. Easwara Moorthy, A., Vu, K.-P.L.: Privacy concerns for use of voice activated personal assistant in the public space. Inter. J. Hum. Comput. Interact. 31, 307–335 (2015). https://doi.org/10.1080/10447318.2014.986642
7. Lugano, G.: Virtual assistants and self-driving cars. In: 2017 15th International Conference on ITS Telecommunications (ITST), pp. 1–5 (2017). https://doi.org/10.1109/ITST.2017.7972192
8. Cohen, M.H., Giangola, J.P., Balogh, J.: Voice User Interface Design. Addison-Wesley Professional (2004)
9. Johar, S.: Where speech recognition is going: conclusion and future scope. In: Johar, S. (ed.) Emotion, Affect and Personality in Speech, pp. 43–49. Springer , Cham (2016). https://doi.org/10.1007/978-3-319-28047-9_6
10. Nissenbaum, H.: Protecting privacy in an information age: the problem of privacy in public law and philosophy. Law Philos. 17, 559–596 (1998). https://doi.org/10.2307/3505189
11. Acquisti, A., Brandimarte, L., Loewenstein, G.: Privacy and human behavior in the age of information. Sci. 347, 509–514 (2015). https://doi.org/10.1126/science.aaa1465
12. De Capitani Di Vimercati, S., Foresti, S., Livraga, G., Samarati, P.: Data privacy: definitions and techniques. Int. J. Unc. Fuzz. Knowl. Based Syst. 20, 793–817 (2012). https://doi.org/10.1142/S0218488512400247
13. Stone, E.F., Gueutal, H.G., Gardner, D.G., McClure, S.: A field experiment comparing information-privacy values, beliefs, and attitudes across several types of organizations. J. Appl. Psychol. 68, 459–468 (1983). https://doi.org/10.1037/0021-9010.68.3.459
14. Love, S., Kewley, J.: Does personality affect peoples' attitude towards mobile phone use in public places? In: Mobile Communications: Re-negotiation of the Social Sphere, pp. 273–284. Springer, London (2005). https://doi.org/10.1007/1-84628-248-9_18
15. Hall, E.T.: The Hidden Dimension. Anchor Books, New York (1990)
16. Hatuka, T., Toch, E.: The emergence of portable private-personal territory: smartphones, social conduct and public spaces. Urban Stud. 53, 2192–2208 (2016)
17. Lofland, L.H.: The Public Realm: Exploring the City's Quintessential Social Territory (1998)
18. Saifuzzaman, M., Haque, M., Zheng, Z., Washington, S.: Impact of mobile phone use on car-following behaviour of young drivers. Accid. Anal. Prev. 82, 10–19 (2015). https://doi.org/10.1016/j.aap.2015.05.001
19. Choi, J., Park, H.S., Hwang, Y., Kim, K.-H.: Exhibition speaker: driver-oriented intelligent human-vehicle interaction system. In: 2012 3rd International Conference on Intelligent Systems Modelling and Simulation, Kota Kinabalu, Malaysia, pp. 14–16. IEEE (2012). https://doi.org/10.1109/ISMS.2012.149
20. Strayer, D.L., et al.: Visual and cognitive demands of carplay, android auto, and five native infotainment systems. Hum. Factors 61, 1371–1386 (2019). https://doi.org/10.1177/0018720819836575
21. Alvarez, I., Alnizami, H., Dunbar, J., Johnson, A., Jackson, F., Gilbert, J.: Designing driver-centric natural voice user interfaces (2011)
22. Reimer, B., Mehler, B.: The effects of a production level "voice-command" interface on driver behavior: summary findings on reported workload, physiology, visual attention, and driving performance, p. 19 (2013)

23. Braun, M., Mainz, A., Chadowitz, R., Pfleging, B., Alt, F.: At your service: designing voice assistant personalities to improve automotive user interfaces. In: Proceedings of the 2019 CHI Conference on Human Factors in Computing Systems, Glasgow Scotland UK, pp. 1–11. ACM (2019). https://doi.org/10.1145/3290605.3300270
24. Bresciani, C., Colorni, A., Costa, F., Lue, A., Studer, L.: Carpooling: facts and new trends. In: 2018 International Conference of Electrical and Electronic Technologies for Automotive, Milan, pp. 1–4. IEEE (2018). https://doi.org/10.23919/EETA.2018.8493206
25. Barbour, N.: Shared automated vehicles: a statistical analysis of consumer use likelihoods and concerns. Transp. Policy **80**, 86–93 (2019)
26. Nasirian, F., Ahmadian, M., Lee, O.-K. (Daniel): AI-based voice assistant systems: evaluating from the interaction and trust perspectives. In: AMCIS 2017 Proceedings (2017)
27. Dahlbäck, N., Jönsson, A., Ahrenberg, L.: Wizard of Oz studies—why and how. Knowl. Based Syst. **6**, 258–266 (1993). https://doi.org/10.1016/0950-7051(93)90017-N
28. Large, D.R., Burnett, G., Clark, L.: Lessons from Oz: design guidelines for automotive conversational user interfaces. In: Proceedings of the 11th International Conference on Automotive User Interfaces and Interactive Vehicular Applications: Adjunct Proceedings, Utrecht, Netherlands, pp. 335–340. ACM (2019). https://doi.org/10.1145/3349263.3351314

Enterprise Data Sharing Requirements: Rich Policy Languages and Intuitive User Interfaces

Karsten Martiny[1], Mark St. John[2], Grit Denker[1][✉], Christopher Korkos[2], and Linda Briesemeister[1]

[1] SRI International, Menlo Park, CA, USA
{karsten.martiny,grit.denker,linda.briesemeister}@sri.com
[2] Pacific Science and Engineering, San Diego, CA, USA
{markst.john,christopherkorkos}@pacific-science.com

Abstract. Enterprises, from medical to financial, commercial, and military commonly share many types of data with many partner enterprises to accomplish their goals. Enterprise data sharing comes with three challenges: First, it needs to be tailored and selective so that not all of an enterprise's data is shared with everyone, or even that whichever data an enterprise decides to share is shared with all. Rather enterprises want to share only on a need-to-know basis. Second, data sharing policies need to be represented in a machine-readable format so that requests for data can be handled in an automated way to ensure fast, reliable, and consistent sharing. Third, an intuitive and easy to use data sharing language is essential to facilitate effective creation and management of data sharing policies by end users. To overcome these challenges, we have developed 1) a rich policy language that allows the expression of data sharing intentions through a small number of concise policy definitions that can adapt to a wide variety of different scenarios, and 2) highly usable interfaces for creating and reviewing policies without requiring intensive training. We previously described aspects of a system that works towards these goals (Briesemeister et al. 2019; Martiny et al. 2018). Here, we describe system improvements that bring us closer to highly expressive yet highly usable tailored data sharing capabilities for enterprises.

Keywords: Data privacy · Data sharing · Data access control

1 Introduction

Enterprises, from medical to financial, commercial, and military commonly share many types of data with many partner enterprises to accomplish their goals. Enterprise-level data sharing deserves attention as a distinct domain due to the complexity and scale of data sharing. Enterprises typically have many types of data that might be quite sensitive and damaging if exploited maliciously, and enterprises typically have many different partners with whom they share different data sets and whom they may or not trust to varying degrees. Enterprise data sharing is also typically dynamic, with both data types and data sharing partners changing over time.

© Springer Nature Switzerland AG 2021
A. Moallem (Ed.): HCII 2021, LNCS 12788, pp. 194–211, 2021.
https://doi.org/10.1007/978-3-030-77392-2_13

The following examples illustrate this need for tailored and adaptive enterprise data sharing. In the medical domain, a physical therapist only needs to know about the physician encounter that led to the diagnosis and call for treatment. They do not need to know every aspect of a patient's record, such as psychiatric examinations. In the humanitarian assistance and disaster relief (HADR) domain, nations collaborate to bring relief to affected populations, yet not every nation or organization wants to share information about all of their capabilities and supplies with everyone, nor does the host nation want all relief organizations to know everything about their infrastructure and security. For example, as part of a civilian evacuation, a host nation might share information about their civilians' medical status with medical organizations and share information about local security issues with security organizations, but not vice versa. In fisheries enforcement, nations collaborate to enforce international fishing agreements and police against illegal poaching. For example, a nation might share ship location information drawn from sensitive sources, but only about specific ships or within specific regions, rather than sharing all ship tracking worldwide. Finally, these data sharing policies often change over time, as new therapists are added, new organizations volunteer to support HADR operations, and new suspect fishing vessels enter enforcement zones. These considerations argue that the ability to tailor and modify data sharing for different partners and changing circumstances is an essential challenge for an enterprise data sharing system.

A second challenge is that the scope and complexity of enterprise data sharing suggests the need for automated sharing. As requests for data from partners arrive, they can be evaluated automatically against data sharing policies to decide whether and how to oblige the request. Automating these decisions ensures speed, correctness, and consistency. However, automating data sharing decisions requires that data sharing policies be specified in machine-readable formats that may require expertise to specify and may require very many specific policies to cover a rich data sharing objective. Such policies can be problematic to write, maintain, and understand, and require expertise in technical languages and systems.

The machine-readability challenge therefore leads to a third challenge. This expertise may be untenable for many enterprises because of its potential costs, delays, and error due to the difficulty of oversight into an opaque process. Instead, policy specification should be easy and intuitive for lay users to create, maintain, and understand.

A number of machine-readable privacy policy languages exist to protect access to sensitive information. Most notable are Ponder (Damianou et al. 2001) EPAL (Ashley et al. 2003), Rei (Kagal et al. 2003), KAoS (Uszok et al. 2004) AIR (Kagal et al. 2008), SecPAL (Becker et al. 2010), and XACML (OASIS XACML Standard 2013). A common feature of all of these languages is that they provide some means of privacy protection through role-based access control policies. Based on their specification of affected data, these contributions can be categorized into different approaches: In XACML, SecPAL, and Ponder, the unique resources targeted by policies need to be explicitly specified, and requested objects need to exactly match a specified policy object in order to trigger a policy decision. If several related resources are to be shared in these systems, dedicated policies have to be specified for each resource, leading to a large number of very similar policies. Other approaches such as EPAL specify policies based on category labels (such as "location data"). This approach significantly reduces the number of required policies to share a set of similar records. However, it only provides very coarse ways of characterizing data, and thus does not allow for fine-grained tailoring of access policies. KAoS, Rei, and AIR on the other hand are expressive enough to represent rich relationships between targeted resources. They achieve their power by essentially exposing a complete logic language to the policy author, who is left to define the precise semantics of each policy from scratch. Neither type of approach lends itself to building systems with a focus on usability: In the first type of approach the sheer number of required rule specifications makes the task of managing policies tedious and error prone. In the second type of approach, the user is required to learn syntax and semantics of a complex, formal policy language, which makes the systems inaccessible for most users.

We have been developing a system to address these challenges that is composed of two major threads, a rich policy language and decision engine that can be used to specify data sharing policies at a convenient high level of description (Martiny et al. 2018), and intuitive interfaces that make this policy language available to lay users (Briesemeister et al. 2019). A "policy authority" for an enterprise creates data sharing policies to share specific data types with specific enterprise partners. Policy authorities can also create policies to deny sharing. Through the interaction of allow and deny sharing policies, complex specifications can be created. "Data requesters" from these partner enterprises request data, and those requests are evaluated against the policies by a decision engine. The engine may approve a request, approve it with certain constraints, or disapprove it entirely. The decision engine operates on a data model that specifies the semantic relationships among data types, and the rich policy language and sharing decisions are specified by a shareability theory that specifies the sharing implications of policies. The user interface needs to span the process of creating policies, including which data to share, with whom to share it, and whether any constraints or limitations will be applied, reviewing the policies' effects to ensure correctness, and modifying policies as circumstances change.

Here, we describe improvements to three components of the system that bring us closer to highly expressive yet highly usable tailored data sharing capabilities for enterprises: 1) a new, more intuitive and expressive interface for specifying partner enterprises based on combinations of requester attributes, 2) an extension of shareability theory to class hierarchies, and 3) a visualization of data sharing decisions.

2 Data Requester Specification

The first system component that was improved was the specification of data requesters to increase both its expressivity and ease of use of this step in the data sharing policy creation process (shown in Fig. 1). The data sharing policy creation process is broken into four steps, collecting basic information, such as the policy name, specifying the data requesters, specifying the data and any constraints on the data, and specifying a precedence level among policies.

The first improvement made to the data requester specification step was to develop the ability to define sets of data requesters. Each data requester is referred to as a group, such as Canada, General Motors, or the Red Cross. This new ability allows policy authorities to define groups of groups, called super-groups. These super-groups can then

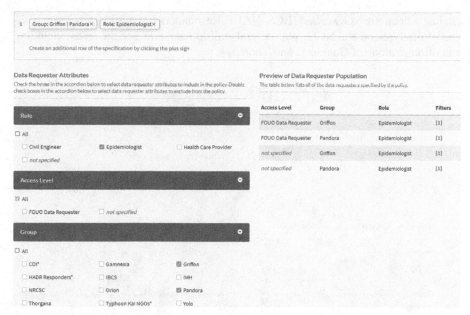

Fig. 1. The general layout of data requester specification user interface. The functionality of the filter section at the top, the accordion, and the table are described below.

be combined with other groups or super-groups to create larger super-groups. Using this capability, policy authorities can create arbitrary hierarchies of super-groups to suit their needs.

This super-group definition capability allows policy authorities to quickly reference a super-group in multiple policies rather than enumerate each of the member groups each time. Aside from the shortcut in naming groups, the ability to create and user super-groups has the important benefit of generalization. If a new nation were added to the HADR Responders super-group, data sharing policies that reference that super-group would automatically apply to the new member.

For example, consider a fictional group of nations on an island archipelago called the Coaster Islands: Griffon, Orion, Pandora, and Yolo. They have been damaged by a recent typhoon named Kai, and various nations and international organizations are responding to the HADR crisis. A policy authority could define a super-group for the Coaster Islands nations and then reference the super-group rather than the individual nations. A policy authority could also create a super-group of the responding nations and organizations called HADR Responders and even a super-group that combines those two super-groups.

Figure 2 shows a portion of the group manager user interface. Base-groups, including the individual Coaster Islands nations, are shown along with several super-groups. COI is the Coaster Islands super-group. Typhoon Kai NGOs is a second super-group composed of several international nongovernmental organizations responding to the crisis, including a fictitious NGO called IBCS. HADR Responders is a third super-group composed of the Typhoon Kai NGOs plus several nations responding to the crisis, including the fictitious nations of Gamnesia and Thoranga.

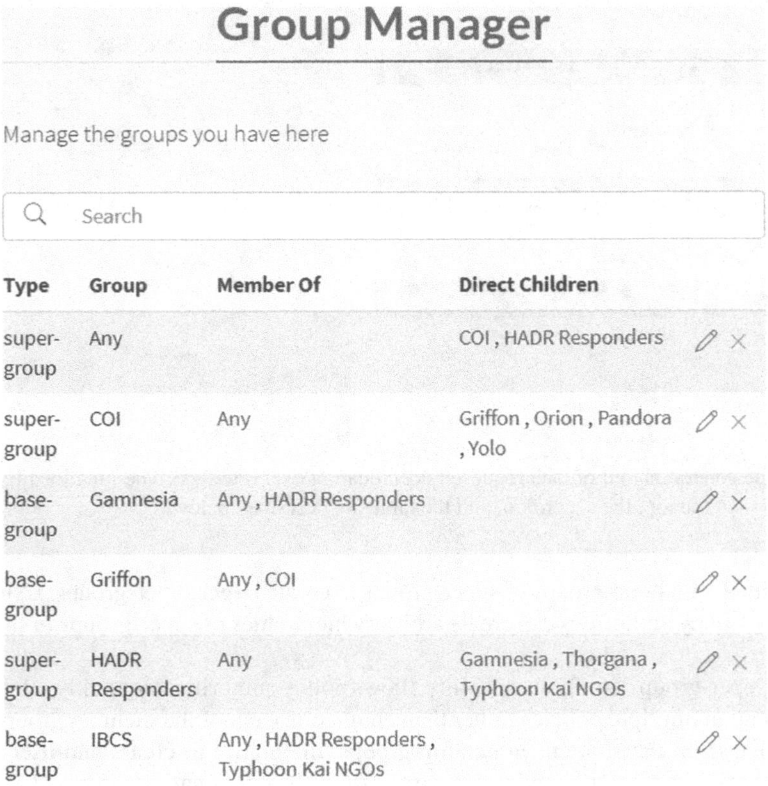

Group Manager

Manage the groups you have here

Q Search

Type	Group	Member Of	Direct Children	
super-group	Any		COI , HADR Responders	✎ ✕
super-group	COI	Any	Griffon , Orion , Pandora , Yolo	✎ ✕
base-group	Gamnesia	Any , HADR Responders		✎ ✕
base-group	Griffon	Any , COI		✎ ✕
super-group	HADR Responders	Any	Gamnesia , Thorgana , Typhoon Kai NGOs	✎ ✕
base-group	IBCS	Any , HADR Responders , Typhoon Kai NGOs		✎ ✕

Fig. 2. The group manager user interface showing a selection of base-groups and super-groups. The group and super-group concepts allow the policy authority to define general-purpose groupings of requesters that might be used in multiple different policy specifications.

A second improvement to the data requester specification step of policy creation was to allow policy authorities to reference groups by their attributes as well as their names. The system provides the ability to define different attributes for each use case so that it can be tailored to the specific requirements of any use case.

The three attributes developed for our example use case were group and super-group membership, role, and permissions, though other attributes could be developed, as well. Group membership could include nations, organizations, companies, and super-groups of those groups. Roles would depend on the use case. For example, for multi-national humanitarian assistance and disaster relief (HADR), roles would include health care providers, epidemiologists, civil engineers, logistics, and security. Permissions could include permission to view only public information or for official use only information

(FOUO), proprietary information, or personal health information (PHI). Policy authorities could then, for example, specify sharing data with health care providers from the Red Cross and epidemiologists from the Centers for Disease Control who have permission to see PHI.

Our goal was to create a capability that allows policy authorities to define sets of data requesters that could be expressed using arbitrary propositional logic formulas over attributes. While the super-group capability is geared toward reuse across policies, the requester attribute specification is geared toward creating sophisticated specifications of sets of data requesters for a specific policy. The list below shows examples of increasingly complex specifications of sets of data requesters.

1. Pandora (reference to a group)
2. Pandora and Griffon epidemiologists (reference to groups and roles)
3. All COI epidemiologists except Orion epidemiologists (reference to a super-group plus exclusion of a super-group member)
4. Pandora civil engineers and Griffon health care providers (but not Pandora health care providers or Griffon civil engineers; that is, two alternative sets)

Unfortunately, lay users are well known to misunderstand logical expressions and find them even more difficult to create (e.g., Essens et al. 1991; Greene et al. 1990). Consequently, rather than ask policy authorities to write logical expressions in a formal language, such as (Group = Pandora OR Group = Griffon) AND Role = Epidemiologist for example 2, e-commerce sites were taken as inspiration for a filter metaphor that is commonly used to create complex specifications of product attributes.

Figure 3 shows a common "accordion" design for specifying complex sets of filters. The blue bars represent categories, and the items within bars represent choices within a category. Choices within categories are treated as ORs, while choices between categories are treated as ANDs. Selecting the Epidemiologist role and the Pandora and Griffon groups creates the desired logical expression, but in a more intuitive way.

Example 3, shown in Fig. 4 shows the selection of the COI super-group along with the exclusion of the member group Orion. A three-way checkbox was used to show no selection (empty box), an inclusion selection (green check), and an exclusion selection (red x).

Finally, the ability to specify multiple alternative sets was added, as required by example 4. This specification requires working through the accordion twice, once for the Pandora civil engineers and then again for Griffon health care providers. Each pass through the accordion creates a row of filters represented as "pills" to specify a portion of a data requester specification. Rows are combined using an OR function. Figure 5 shows the two rows of pills created to specify example 4. Passing through once and selecting all four pills on a single row would include Pandora health care providers and Griffon civil engineers, but those inclusions are not desired in example 4.

Speaking formally, the accordion and pill design provides features for atomic negation (via the three-way checkbox), conjunction of literals (via the combination of different attributes), and disjunction of conjunctive formulas (via multiple rows of pills), and thereby allows the specification of any arbitrary propositional logic formula in Disjunctive Normal Form (DNF). Moreover, the DNF notion is extended with an additional inner

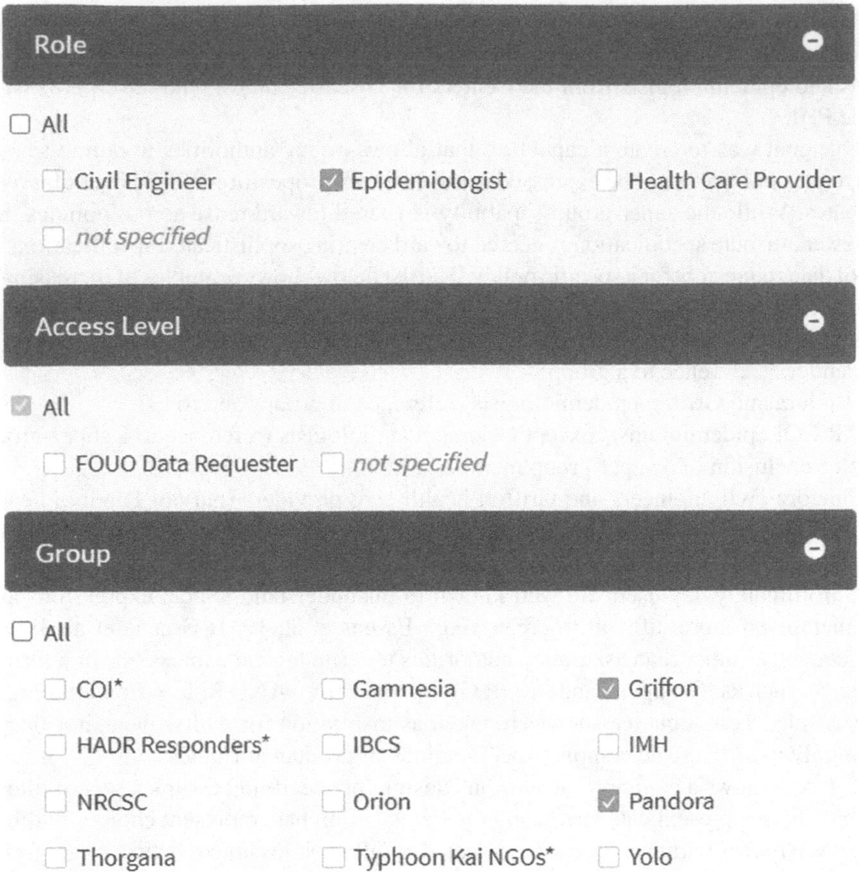

Fig. 3. The accordion design for specifying combinations of data requesters. The accordion is showing the selections for example 2.

OR (to connect multiple choices within an attribute), which does not increase expressivity of the approach, but may reduce the size of specifications significantly, which in turn increases usability.

A third improvement to the data requester specification step was to provide a preview table located next to the accordion that displays a list of the data requesters specified by the rows of pills. Policy authorities can review this table to ensure their specification is correct. Policy authorities can also select a row of pills, and the requesters specified by that row become highlighted in the table. For example, selecting the second row of pills, as shown in Fig. 5, highlights the data requesters in the table specified by that row, as shown in Fig. 6. That is, the second row of pills specifies the combination of group = Griffon AND role = Health Care Provider. The highlighted rows in the table list two data requesters that match this combination of filters: a Griffon health care provider who has no access level specified (described below) and a Griffon health care provider who has access level = FOUO Data Requester. The rightmost column of the table points back

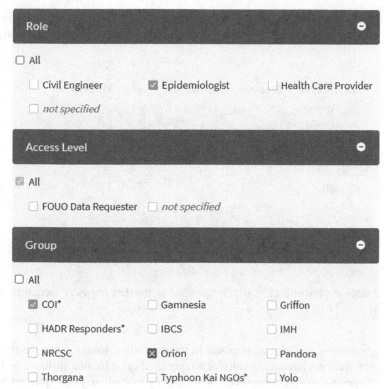

Fig. 4. Accordion selections for example 3. The red X indicates an exclusion. The asterisks indicate super-groups. (Color figure online)

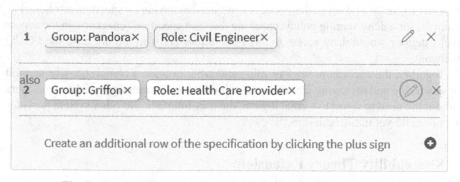

Fig. 5. The "pill" representation of alternative sets of data requesters.

to the second row of pills. Using this table, policy authorities can easily check each row of the specification to determine whether the desired requesters appear in the table.

This connection between the rows of pills and the preview table provides the policy authority with instant feedback about the requester specification by providing bidirectional analysis capabilities: Inspecting the results corresponding to a particular pill row shows whether the specification had the intended effect, and vice versa, inspecting any particular row in the preview table shows which pill row(s) were responsible for this requester.

Access Level	Group	Role	Filters
FOUO Data Requester	Griffon	Health Care Provider	[2]
FOUO Data Requester	Pandora	Civil Engineer	[1]
not specified	Griffon	Health Care Provider	[2]
not specified	Pandora	Civil Engineer	[1]

Fig. 6. The table display of data requesters specified in the data requester accordion and pill specification.

Finally, selecting "all" for an attribute in the accordion would cause the policy to apply to data requesters having any value or no specified value for that attribute. Selecting one or more specific attributes would cause the policy to apply to just requesters having those attribute values. Selecting "not specified" would cause the policy to apply only to requesters who have no attribute specified for that category. This "not specified" role is especially important and intuitive for policies that deny data sharing. It allows a policy authority to create a policy to deny access to requesters having no specified attribute. For example, for a deny sharing policy, checking the "not specified" checkbox in the access level category would deny access to any data requesters who did not have the FOUO attribute.

Together, the accordion, rows of pills, and table provide a comprehensive method for specifying and reviewing arbitrary propositional logic expressions of data requesters without the need to resort to formal logic in the user interface. No other system provides this powerful yet intuitive design.

3   Shareability Theory Extension

The second system component that was improved was to extend our shareability theory that governs data sharing decisions to address class hierarchies. In this section, we provide an informal characterization of our shareability theory by summarizing key concepts from our earlier publication (Martiny 2018), followed by a discussion of the extension to class hierarchies.

For most privacy policies, it is not only of interest to control which values are allowed to be shared, but also—and in most cases more importantly—to control *how* different values are allowed to be joined. A well-known study (Sweeney 2000) shows that more than 85% of the population of the United States can be uniquely identified by the combination of their gender, zip code, and birth date; i.e., if a data set (such as voter registration lists or patient data from hospitals) contains triples of these attributes, it is possible to identify most persons in the data set. This identification is only possible if the attributes in question are given as triples. On the other hand, three individual sets of genders, zip codes, and birth dates will usually not enable the identification of any individuals, although in both cases exactly the same values are given. The difference is that in the former scenario, connected information between individual values is given, while this information is lacking in the latter scenario. Thus, an effective privacy policy framework clearly requires a specification of possible combinations of individual attributes.

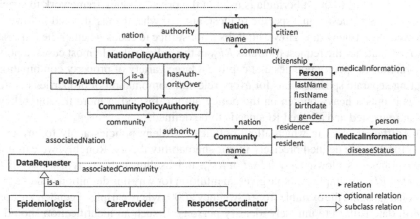

Fig. 7. A section of the Common Data Model used in several related use cases. Class names are represented in boldface and start with capital letters; class property names are represented in regular face and start with lowercase letters. Data in this section of the model is centered around nations, their communities, and persons. Persons are citizens of a country, residents of a community, and have medical information. Policy authorities (PAs) are categorized into nation and community PAs, and each nation and each community has a corresponding PA. Nation PAs have authority over their subordinate community PAs. Data requesters are associated either with a nation or with a community and are categorized into epidemiologists, care providers, and response coordinators.

As an example, consider the data model depicted in Fig. 7 and assume we want to request a list of last names of nations' residents. Note that the data model does not contain a direct connection between nations and their residents, but instead resident information is provided per community, and communities in turn are associated with nations. Thus, to express the concept "nations' residents", we need to specify a path from the class Nation via its property community. This property points to the class Community, which in turn has a property resident pointing to the class Person, thus identifying communities' residents, and, by transitivity, the corresponding nations' residents. To associate these persons with their corresponding nations, a second path points to nation's name property. Thus, the concept "nations' residents" is specified as a set of paths informally represented as {Nation.name, Nation.community.resident.lastName}. In our policy framework, such sets of paths through the data model form the specifications of policy data, so-called Request Formulas (RF).

This small example illustrates some important features of the RF representation. First, note that the data model excerpt from Fig. 7 allows for two different ways of joining nation data with person data to identify (i) a nation's residents (through the intermediate class community), and (ii) a nation's citizens. These two associations represent different concepts and will usually result in different data sets. Thus, it does not suffice to simply specify that names of nations should be joined with persons' last names, but it needs to be explicitly specified *how* (i.e., on which properties) the data types are to be joined. Second, even though the above RF specification traverses through the class Community, it does not reveal the association between persons and specific communities, since no data type from the class Community is contained in the RF.

The concept of Request Formula is used in the privacy policy framework to specify (i) what data is requested in a specific request, and (ii) what data is affected (allowed or disallowed) by a policy rule. However, it does not suffice to check whether the requested RF *exactly* matches the request formulas RF_p in the policy rules. In most cases, a policy author intends to specify policies that capture a large variety of property combinations. Expecting separate specifications for every relevant combination of properties is infeasible, as it puts a heavy burden on the policy author. Instead, a more flexible relation between requested and allowed RFs needs to be defined.

The different ways in which allow policies and deny policies apply to any given request for data are defined precisely in our shareability theory. Roughly, we can think of allow policies as allowing any *subset* of RF_p, and disallow policies as disallowing any *superset* of RF_p. A simple example gives an intuition for why this definition makes sense: Let's consider again the example from (Sweeney 2000) where a triple of gender, zip code, and birth date is used to uniquely identify persons. If such an identification should be prevented, we need a disallow policy for such triples. Any singletons or pairs in this set usually don't contain enough information to identify individual persons, and thus can be shared without compromising the policy's intent. On the other hand, any supersets (i.e., sets containing this triple and additional data types) clearly contain (more than) enough information to identify individual persons and thus should be denied. Technically, this decision is realized by checking allow policies for whether the policy data implies sharing of the requested data. For deny policies, the direction of this implication check is simply reversed, i.e., it is checked whether the policy data is implied by the requested data.

The policy engine is not only able to return plain allow or deny decisions, but it can also refine decisions by optionally attaching constraints to specific data items. For instance, a policy authority might be willing to share personal information of residents over the age of 18 years, while retaining the more sensitive data of children. The ability to attach constraints to decisions is an important feature that we will use below to handle class hierarchies correctly.

With these preliminaries, we are now able to discuss how our framework can be extended to handle decisions across class hierarchies. To illustrate the effects of policies on different levels of a class hierarchy, consider the simplified data model excerpt shown in Fig. 8: Ships have names and locations, and they can be classified into commercial ships and military ships. These classes can in turn be further classified into cargo ships and ferries, and submarines and frigates, respectively.

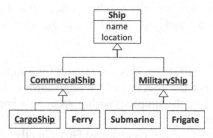

Fig. 8. A class hierarchy for ships.

To illustrate how the policy framework should handle policies and requests for differing class hierarchy levels, we start with discussing an application of the existing policy semantics together with a naïve rule to capture hierarchical relationships. Based on the undesired results achieved by this naïve approach, we outline requirements for a suitable hierarchy semantics and discuss how this revised approach leads to intended sharing decisions for both allow and deny policies across different hierarchy levels.

As a first approximation, we can use a simple rule to specify that a policy implies sharing of a requested class if it implies sharing of a superclass of the requested class. To illustrate the effects of this rule, consider first a simple policy P1, informally specified as *"P1: allow sharing of commercial ships' names and locations"*, and requests for the names and locations of different classes of ships:

1. Request for information about ships: This is a request for a superclass of what is being allowed by a policy. No rule applies to this situation, and thus no sharing decision is returned.
2. Request for information about commercial ships: This directly matches the class level specified in the policy rule and thus this request is allowed.
3. Request for information about cargo ships: As shown in Fig. 8, Cargo ships are a subclass of commercial ships. Thus, the simple rule for class hierarchies applies, and the request is allowed.

So far, this behavior largely complies with the intended policy specifications: if information about commercial ships is allowed to be shared, corresponding requests for this class and any of its subclasses are allowed. Requests for superclasses do not yield any decision (which usually corresponds to not sharing any data). A request for information about the general ship class would also include military ships, and since no policy specifies any sharing decisions for military ships, no decision is returned. While this is a policy-safe result, it is too restrictive and therefore not ideal. Even though military ship data should be denied, the system could respond to the request for all ship data by sharing just the (allowed) commercial ship data.

However, combining this simple rule about class hierarchies with deny policies uncovers significant problems. As described above, the direction of checking implied sharing decisions is reversed for deny policies, i.e., whereas allow policies apply to all requests for *subsets* of the policy data, deny policies apply to all *supersets* of the policy data. A side effect of this semantics is that this definition also reverses the direction of class hierarchies. To illustrate, consider another policy *"P2: deny sharing of military ships' names and locations,"* and requests for names and locations of different classes of ships:

1. Request for information of ships: This is a request for a superclass of what is being denied by a policy. Since the direction of the implication check is reversed for deny policies (deny supersets), the simple class hierarchy rule applies and consequently yields a deny decision.
2. Request for information of military ships: This directly matches the class level specified in the policy rule and thus this request is denied.
3. Request for information of submarines: As shown in Fig. 8, submarines are a subclass of military ships. However, since the direction of hierarchies is reversed for deny policies, this situation is analogous to the superclass case for P1, i.e., the policy does not apply and no decision is issued.

Again, the first case is safe with respect to policies but overly restrictive: requests for all ship data are denied, even though the deny decision really only applies to the subset of military ships. However, the serious problem lies within the third case: The policy states that no information about military ships must be shared, but this policy does not apply to requests for submarines' information, even though submarines are a subclass of military ships. If combined with other allow policies, this might lead to unintended sharing of protected information and thus undermine the policy's intent. This illustrates the need for a more refined approach to addressing class hierarchies. From the discussed examples, we can extract the following requirements for reasoning about class hierarchies:

1. *Subclasses*: Both allow and deny policies should also apply to subclasses of the specified data. As a result, sharing implication rules that handle sub*classes* of requested data should *not* reverse the direction of the implication check for deny policies, opposed to the handling of sub*sets* where this reversion captures the intended semantics.
2. *Superclasses for deny policies:* For deny policies it is mandatory that decisions also extend to superclasses of specified data. As illustrated in the above example, if information about military ships is denied, this decision must somehow extent to requests for information about the general class ships.
3. *Superclasses for allow policies:* For allow policies decisions must not completely extend to superclasses, as this could lead to oversharing. If the decision about sharing information of commercial ships was extended to requests for the general class ship, this would also apply to military ships and thus could incorrectly allow sharing of data.

To address all of these requirements, we add two separate shareability rules for subclass and superclass sharing, and explicitly consider the hierarchy direction based on the type of policy (allow or deny policy):

Subclass Sharing Rule: This rule specifies under which circumstances data specified in the "premise" applies to the "goal." When reasoning about allow policies, the premise corresponds to the policy data and the goal corresponds to the requested data, while those roles are reversed for deny policies. This rule now takes the type of policy (allow or deny) into account and defines that (i) for allow policies, a class in the premise also applies to all of its *subclasses* in the conclusion, and (ii) for deny policies, a class in the premise also applies to all of its *superclasses* in the goal.

The effect is best illustrated by returning to our previous example: For our allow policy P1, the premise would contain specifications about commercial ships, and a subclass goal could for example be for cargo ships, consequently resulting in successfully handling the request for a subclass of an allow policy.

For our disallow policy P2, inputs are reversed such that the premise contains specifications about, say, a submarine, and the goal contains specifications for military ships. Since our sharing implication check still checks whether the premise implies the goal, we now need to switch the hierarchical relation from subclass to superclass relations in line 5. Effectively, this leads to a double reversion of the hierarchical relation (we switch the role of premise and goal *and* we switch from sub- to superclass relations). As a result, this rule now ensures that requests for subclasses of data specified in policies are now treated uniformly regardless of the type of policy. This satisfies our first requirement about subclass semantics, but at the same time makes this rule inapplicable for any situations in which superclasses of specified policy data are requested.

Superclass Sharing Rule: The main idea to satisfy the requirements for superclass relations of both allow and deny policies is to extend decisions to superclasses but automatically attach constraints to these decisions such that they only apply to instances of the corresponding classes.

The first part of the rule works accordingly to the subclass sharing rule with opposite hierarchical relations to check whether there exist policies that yield sharing decisions for a subclass of the requested data class. To make sure that these decisions do not incorrectly extend to instances of other subclasses, the decisions need to be constrained accordingly. To support these constraints, the case distinction for reversed implication order additionally determines how class membership needs to be constrained: For allow policies the subclass of the requested data that is actually allowed to be shared by some policy corresponds to the class specified in the premise. Conversely, for deny policies the requested data is constrained to the class specified in the goal. We use this information to automatically create an *InstanceOf* constraint, requiring that all returned instances must be instances of the respective class, and add this constraint to the result. To illustrate this solution again with specific examples, consider our policies P1 and P2 to allow commercial ship data and deny military ship data, respectively and assume that information about the superclass Ship is requested. In the case of P1 the class in the premise is Commercial-Ship, and thus a result of the form *"allow requests for instances of class Ship, but restrict the decision to instances of the subclass CommercialShip"* is created. Accordingly, for P2 we have MilitaryShip as the class specification of the goal, which then results in a decision *"deny requests for instances of class Ship, but restrict the decision to instances of the subclass MilitaryShip"*. Note that both P1 and P2 can be defined simultaneously. In this case, a request for information about ships would result in two complementary decisions simultaneously, allowing access to commercial ship information and denying access to military ship information, exactly as the policies intended, without being more restrictive than necessary nor revealing more information than intended. This extension to class hierarchies makes our policy language very expressive, but without the requirement to laboriously specify every hierarchical implication.

4   Policy Review Matrix

The third system component that was improved was the visualization of the data sharing decisions. A new display was developed to support reviewing data sharing decisions within a single view. This view can be scanned quickly to review the effects of all policies interactions on sharing and identify any errors. The visualization takes the form of a matrix in which the rows of the matrix are the data requesters, and the columns are different types of data. The cells of the matrix display the decision whether to share that data type with that data requester.

Figure 9 shows a policy review matrix from the perspective of Griffon. In this example, there are only seven types of data, representing different topics, such as infrastructure, security, and medical private health information (PHI). Checkmarks with solid blue circles indicate full sharing. Checkmarks with open blue circles indicate partial or constrained sharing.

The matrix shows the combined results of three Griffon data sharing policies. First, Griffon has set a policy to share all data topics with its own data requesters. Second, based on the policy for example 2 from the data requester specification, Griffon is sharing medical PHI with Griffon and Pandora epidemiologists. The matrix defaults to showing the role subclasses where there is sharing. That is why it does not show other roles or even the epidemiologist roles for other groups.

The third policy is more complex. Griffon is sharing security information with the Coaster Islands super-group, but excluding Orion. Additionally, the policy limits sharing to only the Oyster Bay region of Griffon. Security information from other regions of Griffon is not shared. This constrained sharing is indicated in the matrix by the checkmark with the open blue circle. Note that both Pandora and Yolo have checkmarks with open circles, but that Orion has no checkmark due to its exclusion.

In the figure, the Pandora-Security cell has been selected which causes the decision explanation to appear to the right of the matrix. The column describes the constrained sharing decision and lists the policy responsible for the decision. In some cases, a decision may be based on the interaction of multiple policies.

This third policy illustrates the ability to specify logical tests to constrain data sharing. These tests could refer to geographic regions, timeframes, or, in the case of more complex data models, types of data, data with instances having values greater than a test value, or even individual instances. For example, a policy could share data about commercial ships, cargo ships having a capacity over 50,000 tons, or data about an individual ship.

The decision matrix is an effective display for reviewing policies because it is easy to scan and interrogate. However, it does have a few limitations. First, it can only display a small number of topics and data requesters before the matrix becomes overly large and

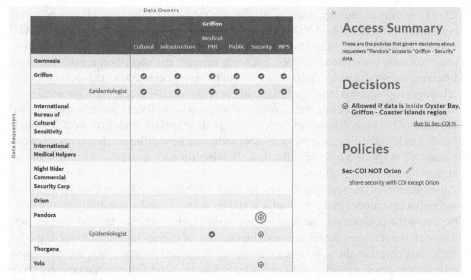

Fig. 9. The decision matrix for Griffon. The cell for sharing Griffon's security information with Pandora is selected, and the explanation for the decision is shown on the right.

difficult to navigate. This limitation could be overcome partially by allowing the policy authority to choose which data types and data requesters to review at a single time.

A more important limitation is that the decision matrix works best for very simple data models with few data types, such as the seven topics in the example. More complex data models have an exponentially large possible set of combinations of data types that could be specified to share with data requesters. However, in most use cases policies refer to only a few specific data sets, such as gender, zip code, and birth date, or the names and locations of fishing vessels within a specific region. Each of these commonly used date sets could be assigned a column in the matrix. Users could then review which data requesters were allowed access to which of these specific data sets. Such visualization tools offer an important contribution to monitoring enterprise data sharing.

5 Summary

Enterprise-level data sharing is commonplace, complex, and at scale. What is needed are effective tools for creating sophisticated data sharing policies that are machine-readable yet easy to specify by non-expert users. Here, we have built on earlier work to create a system that comes closer to realizing this challenging objective.

- A new, more intuitive and expressive interface for specifying partner enterprises (data requesters) based on combinations of requester attributes. For example, a requester may be a member of an organization or nation, have a profession or role, and have a clearance to see restricted information. Rather than requiring users to write complex logical expressions of ANDs, ORs, and NOTs, the interface draws inspiration from e-commerce websites by using an accordion and checkboxes to create a filter metaphor.

Checks within a category, such as nation, are treated as ORs, and checks between categories are treated as ANDs. Three-way checkboxes are used to create a NOT option. Moreover, the accordion can be used multiple times to specify alternative combinations, also treated as ORs. Each trip through the accordion creates a row of filters represented as pills. The combination of these concepts allows the user to express arbitrary propositional logic formulas without requiring the user to have knowledge of formal logic. A table beside the accordion displays a list of data requesters specified by the filters. Users can review this table to ensure their specification is correct. Through labels and highlighting, this preview table indicates how different data requesters are connected to specific rows of pills, thus allowing for easy analysis and review of the current specification's effects.

- An extension of shareability theory to class hierarchies. Shared data is specified through a data model in the form of a semantic network, and shareability theory governs how the decision engine reasons over data sharing policies and the data model. This extension allows the inclusion of hierarchies of classes in a data model (e.g., the data class *Ship* has the subclasses *CommercialShip* and *MilitaryShip*, which in turn have subclasses *CargoShip* and *Ferry*, and *Submarine* and *Frigate*, respectively). We describe how the semantics of our shareability theory can be extended to correctly capture sharing decisions across different hierarchy levels. For example, if a policy allows access to data about commercial ships, then requests for data about the subclass cargo ships will be honoured. Requests for data about the superclass all ships, however, would be addressed by restricting sharing to just data about commercial ships. Meanwhile, requests for data about military ships would be restricted entirely. With this extension, a single policy specification about specific classes in the data model can be applied correctly to a variety of different requests based on the hierarchical class structure in the data model.

- A visualization of data sharing decisions. A matrix view of data sharing decisions allows users to quickly scan to understand who is allowed to access which data and easily identify errors. Each row of the matrix specifies a data requester, and each column specifies a data type. In very simple data models that only specify topics, such as medical, security, and infrastructure, each column could be a topic. In more complex data models, each column could be a frequently shared combination of data types, such as ship names, owners, and their lat/long locations. The cells of the matrix are the decisions whether to share that data with that requester and any constraints on sharing. Interrogating a cell displays an explanation for the decision including which policies were involved.

The interplay of an expressive shareability theory together with intuitive interfaces gives users the ability to define and review complex data sharing policies across data and requesters without requiring intensive training or deep technical knowledge.

Acknowledgment. Approved for Public Release, Distribution Unlimited. This research was developed with funding from the Defense Advanced Research Projects Agency (DARPA) and the Navy under Contract No. N660001-15-C-4069. The U.S. Government is authorized to reproduce and distribute reprints for Government purposes not withstanding any copyright notation thereon. The views, opinions, and/or findings expressed are those of the authors and should not be interpreted as representing the official views or policies of the Department of Defense or the U.S. Government.

References

Ashley, P., Hafa, S., Karjoth, G., Powers, C., Schunter, M.: Enterprise Policy Authorization Language (2003). https://www.w3.org/Submission/2003/SUBM-EPAL-20031110/. Accessed 15 Jun 2020

Becker, M., Fournet, C., Gordon, A.: SecPAL: design and semantics of a decentralized authorization language. J. Comput. Sec. **18**(4), 619–665 (2010)

Briesemeister, L., et al.: Policy creation for enterprise-level data sharing. In: Moallem, A. (ed.) HCII 2019. LNCS, vol. 11594, pp. 249–265. Springer, Cham (2019). https://doi.org/10.1007/978-3-030-22351-9_17

Damianou, N., Dulay, N., Lupu, E., Sloman, M.: The ponder policy specification language. In: Sloman, M., Lupu, E.C., Lobo, J. (eds.) POLICY 2001. LNCS, vol. 1995, pp. 18–38. Springer, Heidelberg (2001). https://doi.org/10.1007/3-540-44569-2_2

Essens, P.J., McCann, C.A., Hartevelt, M.A.: An experimental study of the interpretation of logical operators in database querying. Acta Psychologica **78**(1–3), 201–225 (1991)

Greene, S.L., Devlin, S.J., Cannata, P.E., Gomez, L.M.: No IFs, ANDs, or ORs: a study of database querying. Int. J. Man Mach. Stud. **32**(3), 303–326 (1990)

Kagal, L., Finin, T., Joshi, A.: A policy language for a pervasive computing environment. In: Policy 03: 4th International Workshop on Policies for Distributed Systems and Networks (2003)

Kagal, L., Hanson, C., Weitzner, D.: Using dependency tracking to provide explanations for policy management. In: 2008 IEEE Workshop on Policies for Distributed Systems and Networks, pp. 54–61 (2008)

Martiny, K., Elenius, D., Denker, G.: Protecting privacy with a declarative policy framework. In: 12th IEEE International Conference on Semantic Computing (ICSC), Laguna Hills, California, USA (2018)

OASIS XACML Standard, Version 3.0 (2013). https://docs.oasis-open.org/xacml/3.0/xacml-3.0-core-spec-os-en.html. Accessed 12 Jun 2020

Sweeney, L.: Simple demographics often identify people uniquely. Health (San Francisco) **671**(2000), 1–34 (2000)

Uszok, A., Bradshaw, J.M., Jeffers, R.: KAoS: a policy and domain services framework for grid computing and semantic web services. In: Jensen, C., Poslad, S., Dimitrakos, T. (eds.) iTrust 2004. LNCS, vol. 2995, pp. 16–26. Springer, Heidelberg (2004). https://doi.org/10.1007/978-3-540-24747-0_2

Heuristic Evaluation of Vulnerability Risk Management Leaders' Presentations of Cyber Threat and Cyber Risk

Chris Nichols, Geoff Stoker[✉], and Ulku Clark

University of North Carolina Wilmington, Wilmington, NC 28403, USA
{cmn9093,stokerg,clarku}@uncw.edu

Abstract. This work is an initial investigation into the way cybersecurity companies convey the concept of cyber-related threat and/or cyber-related risk to their clients. We survey the current cybersecurity business landscape and examine product outputs from a select group of companies identified by the analyst firm Forrester [24] as leading providers of vulnerability risk management services. Of specific interest are those tools/products that reflect a cybersecurity company's efforts to combine data related to vulnerability information, threat intelligence, asset criticality, and/or network exposure in order to distill and quantify the complex ideas of cyber threat and cyber risk into relatively simple outputs like a single value or chart. We conduct a heuristic evaluation [9, 11] of static views of the vendors' offerings and introduce the concept of the mythical average, reasonable IT professional (MARIP) to inspect the product outputs with respect to the key HCI principles of familiarity and consistency as they pertain to use of colors, numbers, and charts.

Keywords: Cybersecurity · HCI · Heuristic evaluation

1 Introduction

Aggregating and then distilling complex data into a single number, a few words, a simple chart or image, etc., to convey meaning effectively and efficiently presents a continual challenge in almost every field of endeavor. In the education field, the academic grade point average (GPA) is probably one of the best-known of such efforts. But there are also very commonly used and less well-understood examples in other fields such as the FICO® Score 5 (Equifax) for mortgage applicants. Walk into any hospital emergency room and you are likely to see numbers and graphs used in concert to convey vital information to medical professionals regarding the current state of a patient's heart and lungs via the output of an electrocardiograph, plethysmograph, pulse oximeter, and respiratory monitor. Gathering, quantifying, and reducing data into a recognizable and commonly understood form is one indication in a field that the understanding of key aspects of that field are maturing; however, it remains a difficult undertaking and one quite likely to improve slowly and incrementally.

© Springer Nature Switzerland AG 2021
A. Moallem (Ed.): HCII 2021, LNCS 12788, pp. 212–225, 2021.
https://doi.org/10.1007/978-3-030-77392-2_14

While a few groups of people have fully understood the importance of cybersecurity for over half a century, it is only relatively recently that the importance of cybersecurity has become more commonly apparent among many members of organizations of all sizes across the public and private sectors. Along with this common awareness has come the need to convey complex concepts related to cyber threat and cyber risk to people with a broad range and varying depth of cybersecurity knowledge and skills. Finding ways to effectively quantify the degree of cyber threat/risk posed by some aspect of the cyber landscape and to helpfully communicate that information to non-experts has become paramount.

Many groups and organizations have worked to usefully quantify and express cyber-security concepts of threat or risk as easy to understand numeric values or with color coding. A fundamental example is the Common Vulnerability Scoring System (CVSS) that assigns scores of 0–10 to publicly disclosed common vulnerabilities and exposures (CVE) [2]. The CVEs are further assigned to a severity group which has an associated color as well. The CVSS has been through two revisions since its introduction in 2005 with the latest adjustments reflected in Table 1.

Table 1. Numeric ranges, categories, and colors for Common Vulnerability Scoring System (CVSS) versions 2 and 3.

CVSS score	CVSSv2	CVSSv3
9.0 – 10.0	High	Critical
7.0 – 8.9	High	High
4.0 – 6.9	Medium	Medium
0.1 – 3.9	Low	Low
0.0	Low	None

The following sections provide background on some of the efforts to convey threat/risk in the cybersecurity area, the method followed to collect relevant data for this investigation, the results of data examination, some analysis, and conclusions and ideas for future work based on the results.

2 Background

The National Institute of Standards and Technology (NIST) defines a vulnerability as "a weakness in an information system, system security procedures, internal controls, or implementation that could be exploited by a threat source [15]." Within the context of the Common Vulnerabilities and Exposures (CVE) list maintained in the National Vulnerability Database (NVD) coordinated between NIST and the MITRE Corporation, the definition is refined further to "a weakness in the computational logic found in software and hardware components that, when exploited, results in a negative impact to confidentiality, integrity, or availability [13]."

Prior to 1999, organizations interested in maintaining awareness of cybersecurity vulnerabilities independently managed their own lists using disparate naming and numbering schemes. In a white paper [8] presented in January 1999, Mann and Christey outlined a concept for a centralized mechanism for Common Vulnerability Enumeration (CVE) which directly led to the creation of the original CVE list of 321 entries.

Consensus can take a long time and remain a work-in-progress for many years. While adoption was quick for some organizations, others joined the CVE effort more slowly. For example, it was not until 2017 that Microsoft stopped publishing their Security Bulletins with their own numbering scheme and opted into the CVE system. Today, the centralized CVE-enumeration mechanism is widely adopted and the de facto standard for identifying vulnerabilities by cybersecurity companies building tools and products that help organizations manage their cybersecurity posture.

Shortly after the CVE list was established, it became clear that a mechanism was needed to provide standard severity ratings for the CVEs. This led, in 2005, to the creation of the Common Vulnerability Scoring System (CVSS) [2] by the National Infrastructure Advisory Council (NIAC). In releasing CVSSv1, NIAC declared, "There is a critical need to help organizations appropriately prioritize security vulnerabilities across their constituency. The lack of a common scoring system has security teams worldwide solving the same problems with little or no coordination."

The initial version was reportedly not sufficiently peer-reviewed before release and suffered from many issues when used in production, which led to CVSSv2 being released just two years later, in 2007. Further refinements were made to the scoring system culminating in the release of CVSSv3 in 2015.

As CVSS became an accepted standard and the CVSS score provided cybersecurity practitioners a way to consistently judge the severity of CVEs, many IT departments began to make use of CVSS scores to prioritize which vulnerabilities to patch first. When faced with a small number of vulnerabilities in a small network, this might be a workable approach. However, prioritizing vulnerability mitigation strictly by CVSS in large enterprise networks has become less and less workable for several reasons.

For one thing, the number of disclosed vulnerabilities has significantly changed over time. Since 2017, we have seen a very rapid rise in the annual number of disclosed vulnerabilities (Fig. 1). The current disclosure rate would require a $7 \times 24 \times 365$ operation to read, process, evaluate, and action (or not) ~2 vulnerabilities every *hour*.

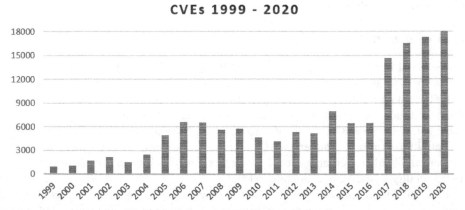

Fig. 1. Number of CVEs disclosed annually.

Secondly, since the release of CVSSv3 in 2015, the CVSS score distribution has skewed more heavily into the High and Critical severity categories (Fig. 2). This leads to the common problem that when more things are designated a high priority, the less anything is really a high priority.

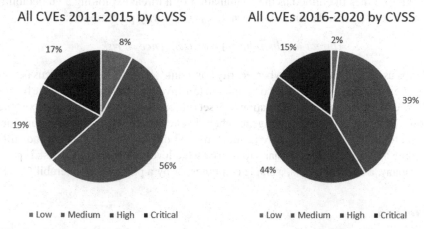

Fig. 2. Five-year distributions of CVSS scores by severity for 2011–2015 and 2016–2020.

The CVSS score is an objective evaluation of a vulnerability's severity outside of any operational context. It does not consider any notion of a vulnerability's subjective appeal to the hacker community, the business criticality of an asset that has the vulnerability, or the network exposure of that asset. Despite some NIST guidance [14] that CVSS data "can be used by itself to aid in prioritizing vulnerability remediation efforts," some research [1] has found that the efficacy of prioritizing patching by CVSS is no better than patching by random when considering which vulnerabilities are actually exploited. Other research [6] has found prioritization by CVSS to be a bit better than random in some cases (i.e. CVSS $>= 9$) due to the non-uniform distribution of CVSS scores of those vulnerabilities exploited-in-the-wild; however, a significant drawback is that it is still quite work intensive, inefficient, and only narrowly useful.

It turns out that the number of vulnerabilities actually exploited in the wild is relatively low. Studies of these numbers have resulted in values ranging from 1.3% [22] to 15% [10] with a mean of around 3%. Regardless of the exact value, the results indicate that a large majority of vulnerabilities (85% – 98.7%) appear to never be exploited.

Because the number of exploited vulnerabilities is low and the number of publicly disclosed vulnerabilities is so high – to say nothing of the multiple instances of each disclosed vulnerability found in networks – methods beyond CVSS are needed to assist with prioritization of mitigation efforts. These efforts have primarily shifted focus to considerations of cyber threat and risk.

NIST has defined risk as "a measure of the extent to which an entity is threatened by a potential circumstance or event, and is typically a function of: (i) the adverse impacts that would arise if the circumstance or event occurs; and (ii) the likelihood of occurrence [15]." This definition implies the following:

$$impacts * likelihood = risk$$

If we reorder the terms, substitute the word consequences for impacts, and further understand NIST defines likelihood as the combination of a threat exploiting a vulnerability, we can arrive at a formulation well-known to cybersecurity practitioners:

$$(threat * vulnerability) * consequence = risk$$

This helps us understand where cybersecurity companies have shifted their focus beyond CVSS when creating tools. All the companies in this investigation try to add value beyond CVSS by considering some combination of asset criticality, network exposure, existence of known exploits, and threat intelligence about hacker interest in select vulnerabilities. They create tools that try to capture as much related data as possible and then distill it into simple numbers, words, or charts to convey what level of cybersecurity risk is posed to a company, a class of assets, a single computer, or by a particular vulnerability.

3 Method

This study is designed to narrowly consider how the complex ideas of cyber threat and cyber risk are presently being conveyed by cybersecurity companies that provide tools for purposes related to vulnerability risk management. Of particular interest are outputs from tools that calculate the threat posed by vulnerabilities and that determine levels of risk for organizations and/or assets. The authors conducted a heuristic evaluation of a subset of the outputs produced by selected companies' tools. During the evaluation, we were not concerned with how users might interact with and manipulate the tools, but rather were only interested in the display of the threat/risk data and how easily they might be understood by an "average" IT worker.

3.1 Participants

The three authors conducted the heuristic evaluation. None have a degree of training, education, or experience in HCI/visualization that would constitute an expert level, but all are familiar with the general principles and spent time understanding the narrow set of principles of interest for this evaluation. All three have extensive IT cybersecurity domain knowledge from education and/or work experience that ranges from 10–20+ years. Using three evaluators falls in line with recommendations [12] for conducting a heuristic evaluation.

To evaluate each company's threat/risk presentation techniques, we introduce the concept of the mythical average, reasonable IT professional (MARIP). The MARIP was a useful convention for thinking about the concepts of familiarity and consistency [4] since we were interested in the degree to which a MARIP's experience and knowledge could be drawn upon for insight versus the "average" person on the street. We understand the potential risk and likely concern of some readers in our adopting this approach, but we lean on the long-established reasonable person standard in law [5] in deciding that using this mechanism is worth the risk. As well, contextual reasonableness has its place, for example it seems reasonable to believe that someone from northern Mexico is likely to be familiar with the Spanish greeting "Hola" and unfamiliar with the Basque greeting "Kaixo," whereas someone from northern Spain is likely to be familiar with both. Given this working and "reasonable" description of MARIP, we conducted our evaluations.

3.2 Dataset

There are many ways to choose which and how many cybersecurity companies' offerings to evaluate. Given the prominence of tech industry analysts, Gartner, Forrester, and International Data Corporation (IDC), we first looked to see what they had to say about leaders in the vulnerability risk management space. We decided to make use of a Q4 2019 report [24] from Forrester that had identified 13 companies as being leaders in the vulnerability risk management area. There are many popular cybersecurity companies not included in this particular report (e.g. FireEye, Symantec, ThreatConnect, etc.), but the scope of this investigation is such that it is not likely to be greatly disadvantaged by their exclusion.

Finding the 13 companies' interfaces of interest required web searches of company web sites, YouTube, and the internet at large for data sheets, user guides, demo videos, promotional videos, and screenshots/images. For 11 of the 13 companies we were able to find meaningful and useful product outputs. One company, Expanse, interestingly has a white paper titled "Security Ratings Are a Dangerous Fantasy" [3] and takes the stance that, "Security professionals don't like security ratings, also known as cybersecurity risk scores." Thus, they do not readily provide any. The other company from the 13 not evaluated was RiskIQ which appears to be more of a tool helping customers discover infrastructure they did not know existed, rather than a threat/risk evaluation provider. Regardless of where we found images/videos, we took screenshots of the relevant portions of the tool outputs and placed them in a PowerPoint slide deck, one slide per company. This slide deck is available upon email request but is not included for space reasons. A sampling of the outputs from parts of 4 tools randomly selected from the 11 is provided in Fig. 3 to give a sense of what we were evaluating.

3.3 Procedure

Each company's slide was evaluated independently by each of the authors from the MARIP perspective while considering three specific categories: color use, number scheme, and visual chart.

There are many HCI principles with which we were not concerned and which we leave for future investigation. We focus in this study exclusively on how these cybersecurity companies' presentations of cybersecurity threat/risk relate to the principles of familiarity and consistency. Drawing from Hinze-Hoare's 2007 review of HCI Principles [4], our working definitions for these two principles as they apply to the MARIP engaged in cybersecurity tasks are:

- Familiarity – the degree to which the average IT practitioner can draw on real-world experience and knowledge to most easily understand the way data are presented. The more intuitive the numbers, graphs, colors, etc., the less cognitive load and the more likely the user will be able to quickly extract meaning. For example, red means stop, threat, or that something is wrong.

• Consistency – similarity of appearance of the way data is presented as the average IT practitioner moves from one context to another within a given tool and amongst different tools. For example, number lines that increase in value from left to right, regardless of the context being used, would be expected in all tools.

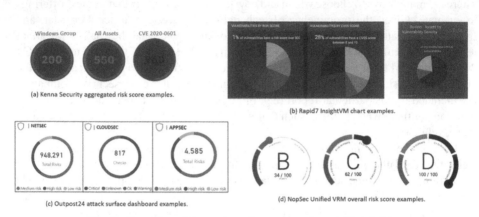

(a) Kenna Security aggregated risk score examples.

(b) Rapid7 InsightVM chart examples.

(c) Outpost24 attack surface dashboard examples.

(d) NopSec Unified VRM overall risk score examples.

Fig. 3. Sampling of the static tool outputs evaluated. [7, 16–21]

To score the tool outputs, we settled on a severity scale from 0 to 3 with the following parameters:

• 0 – no usability issue noticed
• 1 – minor usability issue; causes user some hesitation ($<$ ~1 s, but no "reasoning" required); minor irritation
• 2 – moderate usability issue; causes user delay ($>$ ~1 s and $<$ ~30 s, reasoning/recall needed); moderate irritation
• 3 – major usability issue; causes user failure or significant delay ($>$ ~30 s, requires hard reasoning effort); extreme irritation

For each of the 11 companies evaluated, we recorded 3 scores per evaluator – one each for color use, number scheme, and visual chart. The lowest score in any area could be 0 – no usability issue noticed, while the highest score would be unbounded and depend on the number of issues noted and the severity of those issues. For example, if when considering color use an evaluator noted two minor issues and one major issue, the color use score for that evaluator would be $(2 * 1) + (1 * 3) = 5$.

The evaluators' scores in each of the three categories were then averaged and the averages then summed to create a total score. Lower scores represent a combination of fewer issues noted and/or lower severity of the issues noticed.

4 Results

In this section, results from the heuristic evaluation of the static images of selected cyber-security companies' tool outputs are presented and discussed. As well, some data and observations are provided on the three usability categories: color use, number scheme, and visual chart.

4.1 Relationship of Scores to Tool Outputs

Total scores computed from the heuristic evaluation are displayed in Table 2. The rows alphabetically list all 13 companies identified in the Forrester Wave™ report [24] as leading vulnerability risk management providers (Expanse and RiskIQ had no meaningful tool outputs to evaluate.). The lowest possible theoretical total score is 0 while total scores on the high end are unbounded. Scores ranged from 1.7 to 6.3 with Skybox Security receiving the lowest score and Qualys receiving the highest.

Table 2. Evaluation scores by the three authors, noted as columns e1, e2, and e3, for each of the three categories of interest. Total is found by averaging the author/evaluator scores in each category and then summing.

	Color Use			Number Scheme			Visual Chart			Total
	e1	e2	e3	e1	e2	e3	e1	e2	e3	
Brinqa	3	5	4	1	1	1	1	1	1	6.0
Digital Defense	2	2	1	2	5	5	0	0	0	5.7
Expanse										
Kenna Security	1	1	1	1	1	0	1	1	1	2.7
NopSec	1	1	0	1	2	1	1	2	1	3.3
Outpost24	0	1	0	3	2	3	3	3	3	6.0
Qualys	2	2	3	1	1	2	3	2	3	6.3
Rapid7	1	1	1	2	2	2	1	2	2	4.7
RedSeal	1	2	2	2	2	2	1	1	1	4.7
RiskIQ										
RiskSense	1	0	1	2	2	2	1	2	2	4.3
Skybox Security	0	0	1	1	2	1	0	0	0	1.7
Tenable	1	2	1	0	0	2	0	0	0	2.0

While the total scores have the look of a precise calculation, they are more useful as a relative comparison among tool outputs than as a "grade" with well-defined meaning. Higher numbers indicate that more and/or more severe usability issues were noticed by the evaluators. What is not captured in the evaluation is the difference in what was found during web searches and the quantity/quality of tool outputs readily available for evaluation. For example, Skybox Security has the lowest score indicating a mix of the fewest/least severe issues found. This is in part because the images/videos available for review were more limited compared with other companies. This is a limitation of this investigation that could be overcome in future work by scheduling demos and talking with actual users of these systems.

4.2 Color Use

In addition to the heuristic evaluation scores, we provide in this subsection and the next two some additional details regarding the three specific categories considered. In Table 3, we present color use information for each company as it maps to severity categories. The different shades of color presented in the table reflect the sampling of actual outputs and is meant to match as closely as possible to what companies are using.

Table 3. Distribution of color usage by the companies as mapped to severity categories. Companies with an asterisk (*) after their name did not use Low-Medium-High-Critical category naming; where the different category naming is known, it is provided in the chart.

	Other	Low	Medium	High	Critical
Brinqa*	n/a				
Digital Defense	Trivial				
Expanse					
Kenna Security*	n/a				n/a
NopSec	n/a				
Outpost24	n/a				n/a
Qualys*	Sev 1	Sev 2	Sev 3	Sev 4	Sev 5
Rapid7*	n/a				
RedSeal*	OK	Model	Config	Vulns	n/a
RiskIQ					
RiskSense	Info				
Skybox Security	n/a				
Tenable	n/a				n/a

All 11 companies use colors to augment representation of the degree of risk or threat posed by a vulnerability or to an asset or group of assets. Shades of orange and red are used by all 11 companies to indicate some level of threat/risk. Five companies use shades of yellow-orange-red – colors normally associated with risk/threat, while six companies use colors to represent threat/risk at the low level that are not traditionally associated with risk/threat/danger (green/blue). One company, Digital Defense, uses a non-traditional danger color, purple, at the high end to indicate critical.

Perhaps modeled after CVSS categories, six of the companies explicitly use categories of low-medium-high and/or critical. For Brinqa, Kenna Security, and Rapid7, category naming is not explicit. Qualys uses its own category naming of "Severity 1" through "Severity 5." RedSeal uses different categorization entirely and colors groups of issues:

model problems, configuration problems, and vulnerabilities, without differentiation of severity within those category groups.

4.3 Number Scheme

In Table 4, we indicate which companies use which different scales for assigning threat or risk scores with their tools. While all 11 of the companies make some kind of numeric calculation to determine levels of threat/risk, 9 of the companies explicitly display those values when conveying the threat/risk information to users and 2 do not. Of the 9 displaying numeric values, 8 of them use some kind of base-10 scale while 1, RedSeal, uses an 850-point scale similar to what is used for many U.S. credit score models. Two companies, Digital Defense and NopSec, augment these scores with a GPA conversion and/or letter grade assignment. Kenna Security uses two scales: a 100-point scale for scoring vulnerabilities and a 1000-point scale for scoring assets.

Table 4. Categorizing the companies' use of various scoring schemes.

	Point scales					Letter
	10	100	1000	850	GPA	Grade
Brinqa	x					
Digital Defense		x			x	x
Expanse						
Kenna Security		x	x			
NopSec		x				x
Outpost24						
Qualys						
Rapid7			x			
RedSeal				x		
RiskIQ						
RiskSense	x					
Skybox Security		x				
Tenable			x			

4.4 Visual Chart

All 11 companies use some kind of chart to help convey risk/threat information. Five of the companies use dials or semi-circular gauges (e.g. Fig. 3, a & d) combined with numbers and colors when presenting threat or risk scores. Eight companies use donut or pie charts (e.g. Fig. 3, b & c) to present information about the proportional relationship of severity categories of vulnerabilities or other risks.

5 Analysis

This initial investigation into several leading companies' cyber threat/risk score presentations has revealed that there is not currently a lot of convergence towards what might be considered a useful standard. Considering that it took Microsoft 17 years to agree to participate in the CVE list as the centralized, industry-standard vulnerability enumeration mechanism, it is not surprising at this point that leaders in vulnerability risk management services do not share more in common when presenting scores for cyber threat and cyber risk. It is perhaps especially telling that one of the Forrester-identified leaders (Expanse) seems highly critical of the industry efforts to date. Adding to the general difficulties of finding convergence among any large group is the seeming disincentive created by the fact that these companies are all trying to make a living selling their cybersecurity tools and likely prefer differentiation. We are still early in the arc of cybersecurity industry history, so perhaps in time, companies will glean lessons from older industries (e.g. automobiles) which struck a balance in conveying information to users (think speedometer, tachometer, gas gauge, etc.) while still remaining attractive to different groups of consumers.

It seems unfortunate that 5 of the 11 companies' tool outputs evaluated are using green to indicate low levels of threat/risk. Given green's traditional use in traffic lights internationally, it is confusing to expect users of cybersecurity tools to switch to thinking that green means low threat/risk. Color should be relatively easy to standardize. Shades of the colors yellow, orange, and red have long been used to indicate warning or danger (no one receives a green card in football/soccer). Green could reasonably be used to indicate "no risk" when appropriate or track when tasks, like vulnerability remediation, are complete.

It is unsurprising that all but one company are using a base-10 scoring system. Nor is it surprising that efforts are pretty evenly spread across the various orders of magnitude scales: 10-point, 100-point, and 1000-point. Standardizing to one particular scale could probably be accomplished; however, because the individual calculations of threat/risk are likely considered "secret sauce" by each company, comparing a score of 771 from one company with a score of 771 at another company would presumably be much more difficult.

Chart convergence is currently a mixed bag. The use of circular/semi-circular dials/gauges by 5 of the 11 companies to augment the use of numbers and colors to convey the magnitude of a threat/risk score is helpful. All dials/gauges fill logically clockwise from lower left (low) to lower right (high). This is even one area where standardization is probably less important as far as the exact look of dials/gauges is concerned. The use of donut or pie charts by eight companies is less helpful and seems to buck the adage to "communicate do not decorate." It has, unfortunately, become very easy to generate donut/pie chart widgets, so they are used a lot and often with data that would be better conveyed with a different presentation [23]. Common problems seen with pie chart use include: adjacent pie charts of the same size showing proportions of populations that differed by one or two orders of magnitude, ordering pie pieces by severity in different directions in different charts, and presenting a donut or pie with more than 5 parts (often 8–13) making it difficult to reason about the data.

6 Conclusions and Future Work

This article examined the current state of cybersecurity companies' attempts to distill complex concepts of cyber threat and cyber risk into easy-to-understand depictions. In the three specific areas of color use, number scheme, and visual chart considered during this evaluation, there appears to be some convergence on:

- the use of shades of orange/red to indicate various medium/high levels of threat/risk
- the use of base-10 scales for threat/risk scores
- the use of circular/semi-circular gauges to reinforce the idea of threat/risk levels

However, there is also a fair amount of divergence or inappropriate use across the three specific areas of consideration that would make switching from one tool to another a non-trivial cognitive load task for a MARIP. This includes:

- companies labeling risk categories with colors (e.g. green) not traditionally associated with threat/risk/danger
- companies using different base-10 orders of magnitude scales, as well as one-off uses of an 850-point credit-score-like scale, letter grades, and a GPA
- companies too often using pie charts which makes differentiation among many categories difficult and hides differences in orders of magnitude

There is likely not much incentive for independent companies to synchronize how ideas of cyber threat and cyber risk are conveyed to users, but convergence in this area would provide a definite benefit to the cybersecurity community at large.

While conducting this initial investigation using heuristic inspection of static views of a select group of cybersecurity companies' tool outputs with three evaluators generated interesting insights, there are clear ways to pursue a deeper understanding of this important topic. These ways include expanding the number of companies evaluated, inspecting tools while in operation, and surveying IT practitioners using the tools.

It would be interesting to first extend this examination beyond the 13 companies selected from the Forrester Wave™ report [24] to include other well-known cybersecurity companies like FireEye, Symantec, ThreatConnect, etc. as well as well-known IT companies that have significant cybersecurity divisions like Microsoft and AT&T. Observing demos or IT practitioners using tools would permit more comprehensive evaluations across a greater number of HCI principles. Subsequently broadening this study to gather feedback from IT professionals who use the tools examined (or a subset of them) on a regular basis would provide both richer data and a way to judge the validity of the idea of MARIP as a "reasonable" means of an initial heuristic evaluation context.

References

1. Allodi, L., Massacci, F., Comparing vulnerability severity and exploits using case-control studies. In: ACM Transactions on Information and System Security (2014). https://dl.acm.org/doi/pdf/10.1145/2630069. Accessed 2 Feb 2021
2. Common Vulnerability Scoring System SIG. https://www.first.org/cvss/. Accessed 2 Feb 2021

3. Expanse White Paper. Security Ratings Are a Dangerous Fantasy (2020). https://go.exp anse.co/rs/221-SBF-942/images/WP_Expanse_Security_Ratings_101_EN.pdf. Accessed 2 Feb 2021
4. Hinze-Hoare, V.: Review and Analysis of Human Computer Interaction (HCI) Principles (2007). arXiv preprint. https://arxiv.org/ftp/arxiv/papers/0707/0707.3638.pdf. Accessed 2 Feb 2021
5. Holmes, O.W.: The Common Law. Little, Brown, and Company, Boston, MA (1909). https://www.google.com/books/edition/The_Common_Law/xXouAAAAIAAJ?hl= en&gbpv=1&bsq=reasonable. Accessed 2 Feb 2021
6. Jacobs, J., Romanosky, S., Adjerid, I., Baker, W.: Improving vulnerability remediation through better exploit prediction. J. Cybersecurity **6**, 1 (2020) https://academic.oup.com/cybersecu rity/article/6/1/tyaa015/5905457. Accessed 2 Feb 2021
7. Kenna Security. Getting Started w/ Kenna.VM. https://www.youtube.com/watch?v=CvnEp7 MJZSk. Accessed 2 Feb 2021
8. Mann, D.E., Christey, S.M.: Towards a common enumeration of vulnerabilities. In: 2nd Workshop of Research with Security Vulnerability Databases (1999). https://cve.mitre.org/docs/ docs-2000/cerias.html. Accessed 2 Feb 2021
9. Molich, R., Nielsen, J.: Improving a human-computer dialogue. Commun. ACM **33**(3), 338–348 (1990). https://dl.acm.org/doi/pdf/10.1145/77481.77486. Accessed 2 Feb 2021
10. Nayak, K., Marino, D., Efstathopoulos, P., Dumitras, T.: Some vulnerabilities are different than others. In: International Workshop on Recent Advances in Intrusion Detection, pp. 426–446 (2014). https://ssltest.cs.umd.edu/~kartik/papers/1_vuln.pdf. Accessed 2 Feb 2021
11. Nielsen, J., Molich, R.: Heuristic evaluation of user interfaces. In: Proceedings of the SIGCHI Conference on Human Factors in Computing Systems, pp. 249–256 (1990). https://dl.acm. org/doi/pdf/10.1145/97243.97281. Accessed 2 Feb 2021
12. Nielsen, J.: How to conduct a heuristic evaluation. Nielsen Norman Group 1, pp. 1–8 (1995). https://www.ingenieriasimple.com/usabilidad/HeuristicEvaluation.pdf. Accessed 2 Feb 2021
13. NIST National Vulnerability Database, Vulnerabilities. https://nvd.nist.gov/vuln. Accessed 2 Feb 2021
14. NIST Special Publication 800–126, Revision 3. The Technical Specification for the Security Content Automation Protocol (SCAP) (2018). https://nvlpubs.nist.gov/nistpubs/SpecialPubli cations/NIST.SP.800-126r3.pdf. Accessed 2 Feb 2021
15. NIST Special Publication 800–30, Revision 1. Guide for Conducting Risk Assessments (2012). https://nvlpubs.nist.gov/nistpubs/Legacy/SP/nistspecialpublication800-30r1. pdf. Accessed 2 Feb 2021
16. NopSec Datasheet, New Unified VRM. https://www.nopsec.com/wp-content/uploads/Unifie dVRM-datasheet.pdf. Accessed 2 Feb 2021
17. NopSec Image C. https://www.nopsec.com/wp-content/uploads/Home-page.png. Accessed 2 Feb 2021
18. NopSec Image D. https://www.nopsec.com/tag/unified-vrm/page/2/. Accessed 2 Feb 2021
19. Outpost24 Risk Overview Snapshot. https://outpost24.com/sites/default/files/glazed_bui lder_images/Outpost24%20full%20stack_3.png. Accessed 2 Feb 2021
20. Rapid7 InsightVM Dashboard image. https://www.rapid7.com/globalassets/_images/pro duct/insightvm/insightvm-key-features-dashboard.jpg. Accessed 2 Feb 2021
21. Rapid7 Solution Brief, Quantifying Risk with InsightVM. (2020). https://www.rapid7.com/ globalassets/_pdfs/product-and-service-briefs/rapid7-solution-brief-quantifying-risk-insigh tvm.pdf. Accessed 2 Feb 2021
22. Sabottke, C., Suciu, O., Dumitras, T.: Vulnerability disclosure in the age of social media: exploiting twitter for predicting real-world exploits. In: 24th (USENIX) Security Symposium, pp. 1041–1056 (2015). https://www.usenix.org/system/files/conference/usenixsecuri ty15/sec15-paper-sabottke.pdf. Accessed 2 Feb 2021

23. Siirtola, H.: The cost of pie charts. In: 23rd International Conference Information Visualisation (IV), pp. 151–156 (2019). https://core.ac.uk/download/pdf/250169498.pdf. Accessed 2 Feb 2021
24. Zelonis, J., Lyness, T., The Forrester Wave™: Vulnerability Risk Management, Q4 2019 (2019). https://www.rapid7.com/info/vrm-wave/. Accessed 2 Feb 2021

Human Individual Difference Predictors in Cyber-Security: Exploring an Alternative Scale Method and Data Resolution to Modelling Cyber Secure Behavior

George Raywood-Burke[1,2(✉)], Laura M. Bishop[1,2(✉)], Phoebe M. Asquith[1,2(✉)], and Phillip L. Morgan[1,2(✉)]

[1] Human Factors Excellence Research Group, School of Psychology, Cardiff University, Tower Building, 70 Park Place, Cardiff CF10 3AT, UK
{raywood-burkeg,bishoplm2,asquithpm,morganphil}@cardiff.ac.uk
[2] Airbus Central R&T, The Quadrant, Celtic Springs Business Park, Newport NP10 8FZ, UK
{george.raywood-burke.external,laura.l.bishop.external,
phoebe.p.asquith.external,phillip.morgan.external}@airbus.com

Abstract. With the increase in reliance upon technology in our everyday lives, users are more vulnerable than ever to cybercrime and data security breaches. Whilst it is important, and valued, to develop technology-based interventions to mitigate this risk, it is also important to consider the impact of human error on cyber safety, and how this can be measured. Data collected from a diverse sample of 189 participants using an alternative measurement scale to more traditional Likert scales, the Visual Analogue Scales (VAS), was adopted for previously researched measures of individual differences (age, gender, education level, personality, decision-making style, risk-taking preferences, acceptance of the internet, and related Theory of Planned Behavior and Protection-Motivation Theory concepts) to expand understanding of the relationships between individual differences and user-end cybersecurity behaviors, and explore the significance of this alternative measure in the field of Cyber Psychology. Findings demonstrate the use of VAS can be a reliable and valid method capable of identifying a variety of potential human vulnerabilities and strengths on an individual level. These findings highlight the importance of considering a human-centered approach to cyber-security, and future research should consider then importance of these individual differences in tailoring practical interventions.

Keywords: Cyber-security behavior · Individual differences · Visual Analogue Scale

1 Introduction

Within the field of Cyber Psychology, some significant of research has focused upon technological interventions to reduce to the risk of cyber-attack [1]. Whilst technological interventions can be useful, given the advance in technology over recent years [2, 3],

© Springer Nature Switzerland AG 2021
A. Moallem (Ed.): HCII 2021, LNCS 12788, pp. 226–240, 2021.
https://doi.org/10.1007/978-3-030-77392-2_15

it is also important to consider the role of the human user in preventing cyber-attacks. A recent report by CybSafe, for example, found that 90% of cyber incidents in 2019 within businesses had human error as a contributing factor [4]. Human error can arise through system misconfiguration, poor patch management, use of default usernames and passwords/easy-to-guess passwords, lost hardware, and disclosure of regulated information via the use of incorrect email addresses [5]. Multiple cognitive elements are thought to be relevant to these behaviors and outputs, including user perception of security risk [6], company security culture and user awareness [7], intentional and unintentional maladaptive behavior [8], individual vulnerabilities and strengths [9], and contextual pressures [10].

Although research has begun to characterize the psychological aspects influencing cyber safe and cyber-risky behaviors in Human-Computer Interaction (HCI) and Human-Machine Interaction (HMI), research in this field is in its infancy. A traditional subjective measurement technique, Likert scales, appears to be the dominant scale for these forms of research – for example Bishop et al. [9] has utilized 5- and 7-point Likert scales self-report measures to understand individual differences and user behavior which have provided useful insight. The aims of this present study are two-fold; first to build on knowledge regarding possible relationships between human individual differences and cyber-security behaviors. To do this, we used a self-report scale not previously used in this area - the Visual Analogue Scale (VAS). Our second aim was to evaluate reliability and validity of the VAS, compared to more widely used 5- and 7-point Likert scales. Using an alternative scale across the same measures used in Bishop et al. [9], we can further our knowledge of these relationships, as well as gaining a better understanding of the extent to which different scales and measurement vectors within scales may impact findings. Using the findings from this work and drawing upon those from some other studies – such as Bishop et al. [9] - we will be better able to provide recommendations to how tailored interventions could be created for practical use to aid the mitigation of human susceptibility to cyber-attacks.

2 Background

Technologically driven interventions in the field of cyber-security tend to assume a "one size fits all" solution. For example, system monitoring is a common risk mitigation driven by system anomalies, used across all users within a business. This is useful but used by in isolation does not fully address and mitigate user-centered vulnerabilities. More work research is needed on human-focused approaches – specifically to develop more targeted interventions to adapt to the ever-changing cyber-security landscape. In particular, understanding which psychological aspects of individual users may increase vulnerability to cyber-security risk is critical to further develop targeted and effective interventions.

2.1 Individual Differences in Cyber-Security

A number of studies have examined how various individual differences may relate to online cyber-security behaviors to estimate human cyber-security strengths and vulnerabilities, for example the SeBIS Online Security Behaviors Questionnaire [11]. This framework, and others, are based upon well-researched psychological models of predicting behavior, attitudes, and intentions including the Protection Motivation Theory [12] and the Theory of Planned Behavior [13]. Using these methods gender has been found to be a significant predictor of some cyber secure behaviors - whereby men may be more likely to form stronger passwords, engage in updating software more regularly, and search for cyber risk cues proactively [14]. Some aspects of personality such as conscientiousness may also predict select cyber secure behaviors [14–16]; and risk-taking attitude, decision making strategies and impulsivity have also been found to be significantly related to cyber secure behaviors [11].

More recently, attempts have been made to refine individual difference models of cyber secure behavior, as some measures are highly correlated across frameworks [11, 17, 18]. The present study work aims to calculate the significance of a range of independent individual difference measures in predicting cyber secure behavior. However, there are noted differences in findings that need to be addressed. For example - Gratian et al. [14] found gender predicted cyber secure behavior, and higher impulsivity has been found to be significantly negatively correlated to cyber secure behaviors [11]. However, these significant findings were not found in Bishop et al. [9].

2.2 Measurement Techniques and Data Resolution

Whilst there is a possibility that discrepancies in findings on gender and impulsivity could be due to co-variance of predictors or indeed low power, it is also important to critique the method of self-report and the potential influencing role on findings. In Egelman and Peer [11] and Bishop et al. [9], participants rated items on either 5- or 7-point Likert scales (ordinal data). In these instances, each point is essentially a 'landmark' on a scale – e.g. an extreme value at each end of the scale, a neutral value in the middle, and equally distanced points / gradations leaning to one extreme or another (see Fig. 1, left). Whilst Likert scales like these have the benefit of demonstrating the direction an individual may agree or disagree with presented statements (unless a neutral rating is selected), the degree of rating extremity comparison in variability between participants is less clear as there are only a few points to choose from on the scale – e.g., '1', '2', '4,' or '5' on a five-point scale. Furthermore, these points are fixed in equal points away from each other; thus, individuals could be more likely to form a central tendency (e.g. gravitate towards a neutral rating) or be polarized in the direction of one 'landmark' or the other. Having a number of differing points for different Likert scale predictors for individual differences in the same model also serves as a problem - data for those with more points can be viewed to a greater resolution, impacting the significance (or not) of analyses used.

A solution that potentially addresses all of these issues is proposed and presented in the current paper. The proposed method is to use scales collecting data closer to interval rather than ordinal properties, to increase the freedom of choice in selecting *an area*, rather than fixed data-point on the scale. Whilst Wu and Lueng [19] conclude data distribution is easier to interpret when there is an increase to 11-points on Likert scales as data is closer to that of interval data (e.g., '1' similar to 10% agree, '10' similar to 100% agree) there could still be the issue of fixed 'landmark' points polarizing ratings. This problem, however, is arguably mitigated in Visual Analogue Scales (VAS) – whereby the only fixed ratings on a scale are those at the polar ends (0 and 100), with a continuous line between them (See Fig. 1, right). Participants simply mark a point on the continuous line without being polarized by landmarks and resulting data would approximate an interval-scale level [20] through measurement of points marked – e.g., on a scale of 0–100 or even at a finer grained level – e.g., with decimal places.

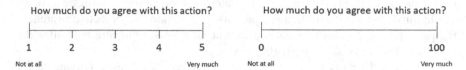

Fig. 1. Example of a 5-point Likert scale (left) and a Visual Analogue Scale (right).

With these things in mind, this paper explores whether the use of VAS in human cyber-security strength and vulnerability measures is suitable to form models investigating relationships between individual differences (gender, age, education, personality, risk-taking, decision-making, impulsivity, acceptance of the internet, and relevant Theory of Planned Behavior and Protection-Motivation Theory concepts) and cyber secure behaviors (device securement, updating, password generation, and proactive awareness), how this compares to findings collected using more commonly used Likert scales, predicting similar findings to those found in Bishop et al. [9], and to note what could be gained from adopting these measures.

3   Method

3.1   Participants

189 participants (109 Male, 79 Female, 1 Non-Binary) with a good level of the English Language and normal/corrected-to-normal vision were recruited voluntarily via Prolific online marketing tool [21]. Participants were aged between 18 and 56 years old (M = 24.53, SD = 6.40), and were well educated (all educated at least up to UK GCSE), with 90% holding at least UK A level or equivalent qualifications, and 58.3% holding at least an undergraduate degree. Informed consent was obtained from all participants and upon completion all were fully debriefed and were compensated £7.50 for participation. This study was approved by Cardiff University School of Psychology Research Ethics Committee (CU-SREC).

3.2   Study Design, Materials and Procedure

Using a between-subjects design, this study investigated how individual differences (gender, age, education, personality, risk-taking, decision-making, impulsivity, acceptance of the internet) and component factors within both Protection-Motivation Theory (PMT) and the Theory of Planned Behavior (TPB) related to cyber-security behaviors (See Table 1 for summary of subscale measures).

Participants signed up to the study on Prolific [21] and accessed the survey tool via a link from their laptop or desktop PCs. The survey was created on Qualtrics©, an online survey platform. Upon reading a brief introduction sheet and consenting to take part in the study, participants were first asked to provide their demographic information including age, education level, and gender, before completing measures for individual differences and cyber secure behavior. The first measure was the SeBIS online security behavior questionnaire [11] consisting of 16 statements containing items made up of four subscales (updating, device securement, password generation, and proactive awareness). Participants provided ratings for each statement on a VAS, reflecting how often they exhibit these behaviors (0 = Never, 100 = Always).

Personality IPIP traits [15] consisted of 50 statements (10 each relating to subscales including Extraversion, Openness, Conscientiousness, Neuroticism, and Agreeableness). Participants were asked to rate the extent to which each statement applied to themselves on a VAS (0 = Completely disagree, 100 = Completely agree). For the Decision-making GDMS questionnaire [22] participants were asked to rate the extent to which they agree/disagree with 25 statements, representing five decision-making styles (five each for intuitive, dependent, avoidant, rational, spontaneous style) on a VAS (0 = Completely disagree, 100 = Completely agree).

Participants were asked to rate how likely they were to engage in 30 risky behaviors from the DOSPERT Risk-taking preferences [23] on a VAS (0 = Never, 100 = Definitely). These 30 items were subdivided into subscales each containing six questions per subscale (social, recreational, financial, health/safety, ethical).

For impulsivity, participants gave ratings on the Barrett Impulsiveness Scale (BIS-11) [24] to indicate how regularly they had experienced a list of 30 statements, on a VAS ranging from 0 (Completely disagree) to 100 (Completely agree). Next, the UTAUT2 was used to assess the acceptance of the internet [25]. This questionnaire consists of 30 statements with nine subscales (performance expectancy, effort expectancy, social influence, trust, facilitating conditions, hedonic motivation, price value, habit, and behavioral intention), rating the extent to which the participant agrees with each statement on a VAS (0 = Completely disagree, 100 = Completely agree).

Finally, a combined list of 43 statements relating to cyber behaviors and the PMT and TPB [17] was presented. This formed nine subscales (Information security awareness, information security organization policy, information security experience and involvement, attitude, subjective norms, perceived behavioral control, threat appraisal, information security self-efficacy, information security conscious care behavior), each with a VAS to rate the extent to which they agree with statements presented (0 = Completely disagree, 100 = Completely agree). Before exiting the survey platform, participants were then provided with debrief information and provided with a Prolific code for participation payment.

Attention check items (e.g. To ensure you are paying attention please rate this as 0) were randomly placed across all measures to test whether attention to items was maintained throughout, and all checks were met for all participants. All items within each measure were randomized in order to reduce inattentive ratings for similar items.

Table 1. Summary of subscales for individual differences and cyber secure behavior measures.

Measurement	Subscales
Demographics	Age Group (18–24, 25–34, 35–44, 45–54, 55–64) Gender Education level (GCSEs or Equivalent, A-levels or Equivalent, Undergraduate degree, Masters degree, PhD/Doctorate, Other specified)
IPIP Personality [15]	Extraversion Openness Conscientiousness Neuroticism Agreeableness
GDMS Decision-making style [22]	Intuitive Dependent Avoidant Rational Spontaneous
DOSPERT Risk-taking preferences [23] (Likelihood of engaging in risky behaviours scales only)	Social behavior Recreational behavior Financial behavior Health/Safety behavior Ethical behavior
Barratt Impulsiveness Scale [24]	BIS-11 Total
UTAUT2 Acceptance of the Internet [25]	Performance expectancy Effort expectancy Social influence Trust Facilitating conditions Hedonic motivation Price value Habit Behavioral intention
Combined PMT and TPB Questionnaire [17]	Information security awareness Information security organisation policy Information security experience and involvement Attitude Subjective norms Perceived behavioral control Threat appraisal Information security self-efficacy Information security conscious care behavior

(continued)

Table 1. (continued)

Measurement	Subscales
SeBIS online security behaviour [11]	Updating Device securement Password generation Proactive awareness

4 Results

We are interested in exploring relationships between demographic categories (age, gender, and education level) and individual differences (personality, risk-taking, decision-making, impulsivity, acceptance of the internet, and relevant Theory of Planned Behavior and Protection-Motivation Theory concepts), with a variety of cyber security behaviors (Updating, device securement, Password generation, and Proactive awareness). Results are grouped according to the 4 subscales from the SeBIS online behaviors questionnaire [11]: device securement (Sect. 4.1) proactive awareness (Sect. 4.2), updating (Sect. 4.3) and password generation (Sect. 4.4). VAS scale ratings were classified as ordinal and therefore non-parametric statistical tests were used. Table 2 provides an overall summary of findings and how they compare to Bishop et al. [9].

Independent-samples Kruskal-Wallis (K-W) tests compared responses from each of 4 SeBIS subscales across demographic groups age, gender, and education levels. Spearman's rank 2-tailed correlations compared responses from each of the 4 SeBIS subscales with subscales from individual differences questionnaires. These were self-reported personality traits [15], Decision-making styles [22], Risk-taking preferences [23], Impulsivity [24], Acceptance of the Internet [25], and other cyber behavior statements developed in accordance with PMT and TPB [17].

Mean substitution imputation was used in cases where data was missing for individual item measures to reduce bias. Cronbach's Alpha test was used to test internal consistency between subscale items for all questionnaire measures. Internal consistency at $\alpha > 0.5$ was found for all subscales except for Introversion component of the IPIP Extraversion subscale ($\alpha = .425$) and Facilitating conditions subscale of the UTAUAT2 ($\alpha = .164$).

4.1 SeBIS Device Securement

An independent-samples K-W test revealed no significant differences between age groups, gender or education levels on the SeBIS device securement subscale. Neuroticism was found to a significant weak negative correlation with the SeBIS Device Securement subscale ($r = -.161$, n = 189, p = .027) but no significant relationships were found for other personality subscales.

Ethical and Avoidant decision-making styles both had significant but weak negative correlations with Device Securement ($r = -.162$, n = 189, p = .026 and r = -.147, n = 189, p = .044 respectively). Rational decision-making style had a significant weak positive correlation with Device Securement ($r = .159$, n = 189, p = .029). There were no significant relationships found for Intuitive and Spontaneous GDMS subscales and

Device Securement. No significant relationships were found between any DOSPERT subscales and Device Securement.

A significant weak negative relationship was found between Impulsivity and Device Securement (r = −.144, n = 189, p = .048). No significant correlations were found for any UTAUT2 subscales and Device Securement.

Analysis found there were significant positive correlations between Device Securement and Information Security Awareness (r = .293, n = 189, p < .001), Information Security Organization Policy (r = .170, n = 189, p = .019), Information Security Experience and Involvement (r = .259, n = 189, p < .001), Attitude (r = .264, n = 189, p < .001), Perceived Behavioral Control (r = .202, n = 189, p = .005), Threat Appraisal (r = .213, n = 189, p = .003), and Information Security Conscious Care Behavior (r = .270, n = 189, p < .001). No significant correlations were found between Device Securement and Subjective Norms or Information Security Self-Efficacy subscales from the combined PMT/TPB questionnaire.

4.2 SeBIS Proactive Awareness

Using a K-W test, no significant differences were found between age, gender, or education levels with the SeBIS Proactive Awareness subscale. For the IPIP personality subscales, significant positive correlations were found between Proactive Awareness and Agreeableness (r = .196, n = 189, p = .007), Conscientiousness (r = .221, n = 189, p = .002), and Openness (r = .258, n = 189, p < .001). No other significant findings were found for other personality subscales and Proactive Awareness. For the GDMS decision-making subscales, Proactive Awareness ratings were found to have significant negative correlations with Intuitive (r = −.181, n = 189, p = .013), Avoidant (r = −.156, n = 189, p = .032), and Spontaneous subscales (r = −.218, n = 189, p = .003). A significant positive correlation as found between Proactive Awareness and the Rational GDMS subscale (r = .282, n = 189, p < .001), however no significant correlation was found between Proactive Awareness and the Ethical GDMS subscale. For Proactive Awareness ratings and DOSPERT risk-taking subscales, Proactive Awareness was found to significantly correlated in a negative relationship with only the Recreational Behavior subscale (r = −.198, n = 189, p = .006) and Ethical Behavior (r = −.272, n = 189, p < .001).

Impulsivity was found to be significantly negatively correlated with Proactive Awareness (r = −.352, n = 189, p < .001). For Acceptance of the Internet subscales and Proactive Awareness, Performance Expectancy (r = .168, n = 189, p = .021) and Effort Expectancy (r = .163, n = 189, p = .025) scales positive correlated with Proactive Awareness but negatively for Trust (r = −.150, n = 189, p = .039).

Analysis of the subscales from the combined PMT and TPB questionnaire found there were significant positive correlations between Proactive Awareness and Information Security Awareness (r = .316, n = 189, p < .001), Information Security Organization Policy (r = .288, n = 189, p = .001), Information Security Experience and Involvement (r = .278, n = 189, p < .001), Attitude (r = .311, n = 189, p < .001), Perceived Behavioral Control (r = .172, n = 189, p = .018), Threat Appraisal (r = .299, n = 189, p < .001), Information Security Self-Efficacy (r = .219, n = 189, p = .002), and Information Security Conscious Care Behavior (r = .309, n = 189, p < .001). No significant correlations were found between Proactive Awareness and the Subjective Norms subscale from the combined PMT/TPB questionnaire.

4.3 SeBIS Updating

No significant differences were found between age, gender, or education levels and Updating SeBIS subscale ratings using a K-W test. For Personality, a significant finding was only found for the Openness subscale and Updating showing a positive correlation (r = .211, n = 189, p = .004). For GDMS decision-making subscales, Avoidant style ratings were significantly negatively correlated to Updating (r = −.151, n = 189, p = .038) and Rational style ratings were significantly positively correlated to Updating ratings (r = .238, n = 189, p < .001). No other GDMS subscales significantly correlated with Updating. Regarding the DOSPERT questionnaire, only the Ethical Behavior subscale was significantly correlated with Updating demonstrating a weak negative relationship (r = −.193, n = 189, p = .008).

Impulsivity was found to have a significant negative relationship with Updating (r = −.250, n = 189, p = .001). Of the Acceptance of the Internet subscales, only Performance Expectancy and Hedonic Motivation demonstrating significant findings revealing weak positive correlations with Updating (r = .151, n = 189, p = .038 and r = .161, n = 189, p = .027 respectively).

Analysis of the subscales from the combined PMT and TPB questionnaire found there were significant positive correlations between Updating and Information Security Awareness (r = .324, n = 189, p < .001), Information Security Organization Policy (r = .317, n = 189, p < .001), Information Security Experience and Involvement (r = .249, n = 189, p = .001), Attitude (r = .228, n = 189, p = .002), Perceived Behavioral Control (r = .174, n = 189, p = .016), Threat Appraisal (r = .216, n = 189, p = .003), Information Security Self-Efficacy (r = .179, n = 189, p = .014), and Information Security Conscious Care Behavior (r = .296, n = 189, p < .001). No significant correlations were found between Updating and the Subjective Norms subscale from the combined PMT/TPB questionnaire.

4.4 SeBIS Password Generation

From the use of an independent-sample K-W test, it was found there was no significant difference found between gender, age groups, or education levels for the SeBIS Password Generation subscale. For personality, Password Generation was found to significantly positively correlated with Conscientiousness (r = .229, n = 189, p = .002) and Openness (r = .147, n = 189, p = .043) subscales only. Regarding decision-making, Password Generation was significantly negatively correlated with Avoidant decision-making style ratings (r = −206, n = 189, p = .005) and significantly positively correlated with Rational style ratings (r = .167, n = 189, p = .021), but other subscales yielded non-significant results. No significant relationships were found between Risk-taking preference subscales and Password Generation.

Impulsivity was found to have a significant negative correlation with Password Generation (r = −.219, n = 189, p = .002). Only Trust (r = −.153, n = 189, p = .036) and

Habit ($r = -.192$, $n = 189$, $p = .008$) subscales of the Acceptance of the Internet measures were found to significantly correlate with Password Generation, demonstrating a negative relationship.

Analysis of the subscales from the combined PMT and TPB questionnaire found there were significant positive correlations between Updating and Information Security Awareness ($r = .302$, $n = 189$, $p < .001$), Information Security Organization Policy

Table 2. Findings from correlational analyses of individual difference subscales and the SeBIS online security behavior subscales. *Note. 1 = Positive relationship, 2 = Negative relationship, - represents no significant relationship, a = Significant finding consistent with Bishop et al.* [9]

Individual difference	Device securement	Proactive awareness	Updating	Password generation
Demographics	-	-	-	-
Personality	Neuroticism^2	Agreeableness^1 Conscientiousness^1 Openness^1	Openness^1	Conscientiousness^1 Openness^1
Decision-making	Ethical^2 Avoidant^2 Rational^1	Intuitive^2 Avoidant^2 Rational^1 Spontaneous^2	Avoidant^2 Rational^1	Avoidant^{2} [a] Rational^1
Risk-taking	-	Recreational behavior^2 Ethical behavior^2	Ethical behavior^2	-
Impulsivity	BIS-11 Total^2	BIS-11 Total^2	BIS-11 Total^2	BIS-11 Total^2
Acceptance of the Internet	-	Performance expectancy^1 Effort expectancy^{1} [a] Trust^{2} [a]	Performance expectancy^1 Hedonic motivation^{1} [a]	Trust^2 Habit^2
PMT & TPB	ISA^1 ISOP^{1} [a] ISEI^1 Attitude^{1} [a] PBC^1 Threat appraisal^{1} [a] ISCCB^1	ISA^{1} [a] ISOP^{1} [a] ISEI^{1} [a] Attitude^{1} [a] PBC^{1} [a] Threat appraisal^{1} [a] ISSe^{1} [a] ISCCB^1	ISA^{1} [a] ISOP^{1} [a] ISEI^{1} [a] Attitude^{1} [a] PBC^1 Threat appraisal^{1} [a] ISSe^{1} [a] ISCCB^1	ISA^{1} [a] ISOP^1 ISEI^1 Attitude^{1} [a] PBC^{1} [a] Threat appraisal^{1} [a] ISSe^1 ISCCB^1

Note. ISA = Information Security Awareness, ISOP = Information Security Organization policy, ISEI = Information Security Experience and Involvement, PBC = Perceived Behavioral Control, ISSe = Information Security Self-efficacy, ISCCB = Information Security Conscious Care Behavior.

(r = .240, n = 189, p = .001), Information Security Experience and Involvement (r = .266, n = 189, p < .001), Attitude (r = .276, n = 189, p < .001), Perceived Behavioral Control (r = .188, n = 189, p = .010), Threat Appraisal (r = .236, n = 189, p = .001), Information Security Self-Efficacy (r = .191, n = 189, p = .008), and Information Security Conscious Care Behavior (r = .277, n = 189, p < .001). No significant correlations were found between Updating and the Subjective Norms subscale from the combined PMT/TPB questionnaire.

5 Discussion

This study set out to investigate how various individual difference (gender, age, education, personality, risk-taking, decision-making, impulsivity, acceptance of the internet, and relevant Theory of Planned Behavior and Protection-Motivation Theory concepts) measures may impact a variety of cybersecurity behaviors (updating, device securement, password generation, and proactive awareness). Findings found a number of significant findings, primarily combined TPB and PMT concepts (See Table 2), that support Bishop et al. [9]. Significant, and consistent, findings were also found notably for measures of personality, decision-making style, risk-taking preferences, impulsivity, and select measures of Acceptance of the Internet. However, a some of these results from using Visual Analogue Scales show deviance from previous research and are discussed below. The findings from this study not only convey the importance of considering end-user strengths and vulnerabilities to mitigate the risks of cyber-attacks, but also suggest the use of Visual Analogue Scales for these measures are reliable and valid.

The first dimensions of individual differences investigated in the present study were age, gender, and level of education to examine whether demographically participants differed in engagement with various online security behaviors. Whilst Gratian et al. [14] had found that men were significantly more likely to engage in a range of good cyber secure behaviors compared to women, like Bishop et al. [9], we found no significant differences between groups for gender – despite having a balanced sample. Similarly, we also found no differences between age groups or levels of education. However, Gratian et al. [14] employed a larger sample and their results show the significant gender differences are very weak relationships, thus findings could differ due to this sample difference.

Regarding personality, unlike Bishop et al. [9] which found no significant relationships for any subscales, we found conscientiousness to have a significant positive relationship with Proactive Awareness – a consistent finding with Gratian et al. [14] to a similar degree of effect size. However, in the present study we found no significant relationship between extraversion and device securement – differing from some previous research on perceived security risks [14, 26]. Although, significant findings were also found for conscientious and password generation, and higher openness being related to higher password generation and proactive awareness. This significant finding across more than one form of cyber secure behavior could signify how select individual differences may be more significant to reducing cyber-security risks from an end-user perspective compared to others. This remains true when examining decision-making styles and observing consistent positive relationships for rational styles across all cyber secure behaviors measured, and how avoidant styles of decision-making should be (ironically) avoided due to their negative relationship across all SeBIS behaviors – although further analysis is needed to further understand the nature of these relationships.

Furthermore, findings found less ethical, riskier, behavior was significantly negatively related to updating and proactive awareness could indicate the need for libertarian paternalism, or 'nudges' [27, 28]. However, as no significant relationship was found for password generation or device securement it is not clear whether these forms of nudges would be effective for these cyber secure behaviors. However, it is of interest to understand how these forms of interventions could be adapted to reduce impulsivity – as ratings for this measure found to be a significantly related to all measured forms of cyber secure behaviors. Regarding participants' acceptance of the internet, the degree of trust individuals has in relation to password generation and likelihood of engaging in proactive awareness appears to be of interest as this could highlight a particular significant vulnerability which cyber offenders could take advantage of using targeted persuasion techniques.

For a large number of subscale measures from the combined PMT/TPB questionnaire [17] it is encouraging to see consistent findings with previous research [9] as this could suggests not only that these individual differences be reliably measured, but that VAS are capable of detected similar findings. A potential reason for these findings being found to be significant in both Bishop et al. [9] and the present study, but not measures in personality, decision-making styles, or impulsivity, could be in part due to the differences in participant sizes and the strength of relationships found. On average, significant correlations found from the PMT/TPB questionnaire appear to be stronger than a number of other relationships found – suggesting the variance of behavior accounted for could be greater in relation to motivation and planned behavior. However, this needs further analysis to determine precisely. The present study also furthers Bishop et al. [9] due to the greater diversity in the sample data is collected. By collecting data from participants from a mixture of mainly European and American countries, we can be more confident findings being applicable to the general population and across cultures. To further validate this, further investigations should adopt the VAS in subjective measurements to evaluate replicability in diverse samples.

6 Limitations

As with these forms of online survey studies, not all responses may truly represent participants' ratings for individual difference and cyber secure behavior measures – therefore the true extent to which these ratings represent individuals may be open to responder biases. However, attention checks and data quality checks were carried out to reduce the likelihood of attention significantly influencing overall data analyses, and all items were randomized within each measure to reduce the likelihood of inattentive responses.

As correlational analyses were mainly used between variables, it cannot be concluded at this stage the nature of these variables and the extent to which individual differences variance may account for cyber secure behaviors. Although further analysis to form regression models with other potential individual difference predictors will be explored to evaluate how interventions for cyber risk could be best targeted in varying contexts. Whilst the present study does indicate the use of Visual Analogue Scales could be a valid alternative for exploring relationships between variables, it cannot at this stage be determined whether this form of scale may be more beneficial than traditional Likert scales. A comparison between the use of VAS and Likert scales for variables using data from similarly derived sources whilst controlling for sample size should be a future direction in this field to determine how measurement of the same data in different forms may influence the distributions and significance of data.

It was noted from the use of Cronbach's Alpha tests a few scales appeared to have questionable or weak internal consistency. Facilitating conditions subscale of the UTAUAT2 ($\alpha = .164$) and the IPIP introversion sub-component of the Extraversion subscale ($\alpha = .425$) in particular had very low consistency, which in turn may limit the extent to which these specific findings in relation to cyber secure behavior measurements may be debatable and need further exploration to examine whether specific items may limit these analyses. It was also noted internal consistency for the disagreeable sub-component of the IPIP Agreeableness subscale ($\alpha = .55$) and Performance Expectancy subscale of the Acceptance of the Internet questionnaire were close to the moderate internal consistency threshold, suggesting the degree these specific measures are measuring their overarching concept needs to be explored further. Finally, as only moderate internal consistency was found for Updating and Device Securement subscales from the SeBIS questionnaire ($\alpha = .524$ and $\alpha = .523$ respectively), with Proactive Awareness and Password Generation SeBIS subscales close to the upper end of the moderate threshold ($\alpha = .598$ and $\alpha = 601$ respectively), there is a necessity to explore whether specific items may influence significance of relationships.

7 Conclusions and Future Directions

Considering currently how increasingly reliant people are on technology for both work and leisure, it is also of paramount importance to consider how valued users are to mitigate the rising threat of cyber-security breaches and incidents. As highlighted from the results from this study, both vulnerabilities and strengths of individuals need to be truly understood with the aim for these to be utilized in the tailoring of interventions at both individual and organizational levels. Understanding the extent to which user variables relate to security behaviors is the next logical step to determine how humans can become the strongest defense to online risks. The findings from this study not only convey the importance of considering end-user strengths and vulnerabilities to mitigate the risks of cyber-attacks, but also suggest the use of Visual Analogue Scales for these measures are reliable and valid. Future research using more direct comparisons of Likert and VAS data should be carried out to evaluate the extent to which these measurement scales alter data resolution and distribution. From an increase in data resolution, this could allow for finer adjustment to Human-Computer Interaction (HCI) and Human-Machine Interaction (HMI) measurements and interventions - For example, accurately understanding how different people are likely to secure personal and work devices, how perceptions of cyber-security policy influence likelihood in ensuring software is updated, how actively individuals may seek to keep up-to-date with ever-changing cyber-security risks, and trust of equipment used can we fine-tune efficient interventions. There is a need to consider the interactions between individuals and the environment in which they sit to fully comprehend which behaviours can be, and should be, encouraged or avoided; and when hard constraints built into HMI and HCI designs may be more appropriate in a way which does not hinder productivity or increase harm.

Acknowledgements. This research was supported through an Endeavr Wales funded PhD studentship awarded to the first author (George Raywood-Burke) from the School of Psychology at Cardiff University. Other support was provided by Airbus where the PhD student is a member of the Airbus Accelerator in Human-Centric Cyber Security team, under the Technical Leadership of the fourth author (Professor Phillip Morgan) who is also George Raywood-Burke's PhD Lead Supervisor.

References

1. Singh, S., Silakari, S.: A survey of cyber attack detection systems. Int. J. Comput. Sci. Network Secur. **9**(5), 1–10 (2009)
2. Gupta, M., Abdelsalam, M., Khorsandroo, S., Mittal, S.: Security and privacy in smart farming: challenges and opportunities. IEEE Access **8**, 34564–34584 (2020). https://doi.org/10.1109/ACCESS.2020.2975142
3. Okamoto, T.: SecondDEP: resilient computing that prevents shellcode execution in cyberattacks. Procedia Comput. Sci. **60**, 691–699 (2015)
4. CybSafe. Human error to blame for 9 in 10 UK cyber data breaches in 2019 (2020). https://www.cybsafe.com/press-releases/human-error-to-blame-for-9-in-10-uk-cyber-data-breaches-in-2019/. Accessed 12 Mar 2021
5. IBM Security Services. Cyber Security Intelligence Index (2014). https://media.scmagazine.com/documents/82/ibm_cyber_security_intelligenc_20450.pdf. Accessed 30 Oct 2019
6. Van Schaik, P., Jeske, D., Onibokun, J., Coventry, L., Jansen, J., Kusev, P.: Risk perceptions of cyber-security and precautionary behaviour. Comput. Hum. Behav. **75**, 547–559 (2017)
7. Parsons, K.M., Young, E., Butavicius, M.A., McCormac, A., Pattinson, M.R., Jerram, C.: The influence of organizational information security culture on information security decision making. J. Cogn. Eng. Decis. Making **9**(2), 117–129 (2015). https://doi.org/10.1177/1555343415575152
8. Chowdhury, A., Skinner : The impact of time pressure on cybersecurity behaviour: a systematic review. Behav. Info. Technol. (2019). https://doi.org/10.1080/0144929X.2019.1583769
9. Bishop, L.M., Morgan, P.L., Asquith, P.M., Raywood-Burke, G., Wedgbury, A., Jones, K.: Examining human individual differences in cyber security and possible implications for human-machine interface design. In: Moallem, A. (ed.) HCII 2020. LNCS, vol. 12210, pp. 51–66. Springer, Cham (2020). https://doi.org/10.1007/978-3-030-50309-3_4
10. Dykstra, J., Paul, C.L.: Cyber Operations Stress Survey (COSS): Studying fatigue, frustration, and cognitive workload in cybersecurity operations. In: 11th USENIX Workshop on Cyber Security Experimentation and Test (CSET 2018) (2018)
11. Egelman, S., Peer, E.: Scaling the security wall: developing a security behavior intentions scale (sebis). In Proceedings of the 33rd Annual ACM Conference on Human Factors in Computing Systems, pp. 2873–2882. ACM (2015)
12. Van Bavel, R., Rodriguez-Priego, N., Vila, J., Briggs, P.: Using protection motivation theory in the design of nudges to improve online security behaviours. Inter. J. Hum. Comput. Stud. **123**, 29–39 (2019)

13. Ajzen, I.: The theory of planned behaviour: reactions and reflections. Psychol. Health **26**(9), 1103–1127 (2011)
14. Gratian, M., Bandi, S., Cukier, M., Dykstra, J., Ginther, A.: Correlating human traits and cybersecurity behaviour intentions. Comput. Secur. **73**, 345–358 (2017)
15. Shappie, A.T., Dawson, C.A., Debb, S.M.: Personality as a predictor of cybersecurity behavior. Psychol. Popular Media **9**(4), 475–480 (2020). https://doi.org/10.1037/ppm0000247
16. Posey, C., Roberts, T.L., Lowry, P.B.: The impact of organizational commitment on insiders' motivation to protect organizational information assets. J. Manag. Info. Syst. **32**(4), 179–214 (2015)
17. Safa, N.S., Sookhak, M., Von Solms, R., Furnell, S., Ghani, N.A., Herawan, T.: Information security conscious care behaviour formation in organisations. Comput. Secur. **53**, 65–78 (2015)
18. Sommestad, T., Karlzen, H., Hallberg, J.: The sufficiency of theory of planned behaviour for explaining information security policy compliance. Secur. Cult. info. Technol. **23**(2), 200–217 (2015)
19. Wu, H., Leung, S.-O.: Can likert scales be treated as interval scales? — a simulation study. J. Soc. Serv. Res. **43**(4), 527–532 (2017). https://doi.org/10.1080/01488376.2017.1329775
20. Reips, U.D., Funke, F.: Interval-level measurement with visual analogue scales in Internet-based research: VAS Generator. Behav. Res. Methods **40**, 699–704 (2008). https://doi.org/10.3758/BRM.40.3.699
21. Prolific Academic Ltd., Oxford, UK. www.prolific.co
22. Scott, S.G., Bruce, R.A.: Decision-making style: the development and assessment of a new measure. Educ. Psychol. Meas. **55**(5), 818–831 (2006)
23. Blais, A.R., Weber, E.U.: A domain-specific risk-taking (DOSPERT) scale for adult populations. Judgement Decis. Making **1**(1), 33–47 (2006)
24. Patton, J.H., Stanford, M.S., Barratt, E.S.: Factor structure of the Barratt impulsiveness scale. J. Clin. Psychol. **51**(6), 768–774 (1995)
25. Venkatesh, V., Thong, J.Y., Xu, X.: Consumer acceptance and use of information technology: extending the unified theory of acceptance and use of technology. MIS Q. 157–178 (2012)
26. P. Riquelme, I., Román, S.: Is the influence of privacy and security on online trust the same for all type of consumers? Electron. Markets **24**(2), 135–149 (2014). https://doi.org/10.1007/s12525-013-0145-3
27. Thaler, R., Sunstein, C.: Libertarian Paternalism. Am. Econ. Rev. **93**, 175–79 (2003)
28. Thaler, R., Sunstein, C.: Nudge: Improving Decision about Health, Wealth, and Happiness. Yale University Press , New Haven (2008)

Privacy Design Strategies and the GDPR: A Systematic Literature Review

Marco Saltarella[1,2], Giuseppe Desolda[1(✉)], and Rosa Lanzilotti[1]

[1] Department of Computer Science, University of Bari Aldo Moro, Bari, Italy
{marco.saltarella,giuseppe.desolda,rosa.lanzilotti}@uniba.it
[2] FINCONS SpA, Bari, Italy

Abstract. Article 25 of the GDPR states that data collection, processing and management measures should be implemented following tnhe privacy by design and privacy by default paradigms. This paper presents a systematic literature review to identify useful guidelines to support the development of GDPR-compliant software. Selected papers are categorized under 8 different data-oriented and process-oriented strategies and their contributions are reported. Future activities will highlight the HCI community's attitude towards these new technical and organizational approaches in order to bridge the identified gaps and shortcomings.

Keywords: GDPR · Privacy by design · Usable privacy

1 Introduction

In a world that is always online, with billions of connected devices, producing, exchanging and processing data, the cybersecurity risk has never been as threating. The University of Maryland estimated that a cyber-attack occurs every 39 s on average [90] representing a huge risk for our digital data-space. According to a report by IBM [91], the average cost of a data breach for a company is $3.86M with an average time to identify and contain the breach of 280 days. In this context, introducing effective security measures is fundamental not only to protect our digital assets but also to comply with the current normative.

In this regard, in May 2018 the European Union (EU) General Data Protection Regulation (GDPR) came into effectiveness, setting a new milestone in the data protection field, as the most advanced regulation related to the collection, management and processing of personal data. The GDPR demands that clear organizational and technical measures need to be implemented to guarantee specific principles and rights to data subjects. Specifically, as stated in Article 25, such measures must also be implemented following the by design (security and privacy should be considered from the earliest design phase of a system) and by default (the system should be configured to be as secure and privacy-preserving as possible) paradigms.

The term privacy by design was first defined by Ann Cavoukian whom in one of her most relevant studies defines the 7 foundational principles of privacy by design [92]: 1) Proactive not Reactive; Preventative not Remedial, 2) Privacy as the Default Setting, 3)

© Springer Nature Switzerland AG 2021
A. Moallem (Ed.): HCII 2021, LNCS 12788, pp. 241–257, 2021.
https://doi.org/10.1007/978-3-030-77392-2_16

Privacy Embedded into Design, 4) Fully Functionality – Positive-Sum, not Zero-Sum, 5) End-to-End Security – Full Lifecycle Protection, 6) Visibility and Transparency – Keep it Open, 7) Respect for User Privacy – Keep it User Centric.

These seven principles influenced and inspired the GDPR. If we focus the attention on the last principle, we can see how important is for Cavoukian that privacy is built around the user from the ground-up. Indeed, also the GDPR is seen as a step forward towards the user-centric approach [93]; however, due to the new technical challenges introduced by the regulation, the lack of usability for security and privacy features remains one of the most concerning issues. In the security field, the user has always been recognized as the weakest link of the chain [94]. Many studies have been carried out to understand how to address this problem on different levels [95, 96] and methodologies have been proposed [97]. Accordingly, it is necessary to consider advanced methodologies that support the design and development of GDPR compliant software to ensure the safe-guarding of users' privacy while still maximizing the level of usability. By integrating the user-centric approach across all the development processes it is possible to implement innovative solutions that are secure and usable to satisfy, at the same time, both users' and businesses' objectives.

With the introduction of the GDPR, software engineers are now facing a new challenge: how to effectively translate the GDPR obligations into software requirements. Indeed, implementing these new requirements can be a daunting task [98], especially for developers that lack a baseline understating of both the legal and security concepts expressed in the regulation [99].

For these reasons, this paper presents a systematic literature review to frame the current best practices of GDPR-compliant software design and development implementing the privacy-by-design and privacy-by-default paradigms. After defining a rigorous research protocol in line with the guidelines proposed by Kitchenham et al. [101], more than 900 articles were collected from the major scientific digital libraries. Each article was assessed through specific inclusion and exclusion criteria in an iterative process to identify those that answer the defined research question. From the final selection of papers, the main results and lesson-learned were extracted and categorized under 8 different data-oriented and process-oriented, privacy design strategies [100]. The long-term goal of this work is to understand the impact that the new technical and organizational solutions implemented after the GDPR had on both users and developers, in order to address how to successfully satisfy both regulation constraints and users' privacy expectations. The knowledge acquired during this review will be useful to critically evaluate current solutions both from a security and a usability point of view and to identify what issues are still open to fill the gaps with future activities.

The paper is organized as follows: Sect. 2 describes the methodology followed for this systematic literature review. Section 3 presents and discusses the results of the review. Section 4 presents the conclusions and future work.

2 Methodology

To conduct this systematic literature review (SLR), a research protocol has been first defined following the guidelines proposed by Kitchenham et al. [101]. In line with this protocol, the following phases were carried out:

- *Planning*: including the definition of the research question, identification of relevant keywords and definition of the inclusion and exclusion criteria;
- *Execution*: retrieval of papers from the main research engines and iterative selection of the studies according to the defined inclusion and exclusion criteria;
- *Analysis*: extraction and discussion of relevant results to address the research questions.
- In the next sections, we report on the details of each phase.

2.1 Planning

Formulation of the Research Question

The first phase starts with the definition of the research question, which aim to address the main goal of this SLR, i.e., to systematize the current best practices of GDPR-compliant software design and development implementing privacy-by-design and privacy-by-default paradigms. In Article 25, the GDPR explicitly states that the data controller shall implement state-of-the-art technical and organizational measures to ensure data protection-by-design and default. Thus, the research question is:

RQ) *How to make effective the Privacy-By-Design and Privacy-By-Default paradigms during the design and development of GDPR compliant software?*

Definition of the Query String

In order to define the search string a set of keywords were identified: the main keywords (GDPR, privacy by design and privacy by default) were combined with related concepts (e.g., guidelines, patterns) in Boolean formula to discover relevant studies trying to answer the research question.

Thus, the following search query was defined:

```
(GDPR OR "General Data Protection Regulation") AND (pri-
vacy OR "privacy by design" OR "privacy by default" OR
security OR software) AND (engineering OR guidelines OR
"informed consent" OR patterns)
```

Selection of Data Sources

The query string was used to query 4 major digital libraries: ACM DL, IEEE Xplore, Scopus, Google Scholar.

Inclusion and Exclusion Criteria

To select articles that fit the research question, the following inclusion and exclusion criteria were defined:

Inclusion criteria:

- The article focuses on privacy-by-design and/or privacy-by-default for GDPR
- The article is published in a relevant journal or conference
- The article has been peer-reviewed

Exclusion criteria:

- The article is not focused on the GDPR
- The article is not related to ICT or HCI fields

2.2 Execution

The execution of the search string on all the scientific digital libraries resulted in 653 articles (ACM DL = 36, IEEE Xplore = 103, Scopus = 258, Google Scholar = 256). From these articles, 133 resulted duplicated and thus removed, obtaining a total of 520 paper to be analyzed. From this point on, an iterative selection process was conducted applying inclusion and exclusion criteria. First, articles were analyzed based on their title and abstract only. The application of the criteria allowed us to exclude 238 papers. After that, a more detailed analysis has been conducted by reading the whole manuscripts, leading to the selection of 91 papers.

3 Results Analysis

Data Extraction Strategy

The analysis of the 91 papers selected for the research question was based on "Privacy Design Strategies" [100], in which 8 different strategies are defined, with the aim of helping system designers translating in privacy-friendly way legal requirements into system requirements. These 8 strategies are divided in two sub-categories:

Category 1) Data-oriented strategies focused on the data processing itself:

1. Minimize: reduce the amount of data collected and processed to the minimum;
2. Separate: distribute data processing and storage;
3. Abstract: Limit the detail level of data processing as much as possible;
4. Hide: personal data should be hidden from unauthorized third-parties.

Category 2) Process-oriented strategies focused on the process handling the personal data lifecycle:

1. Inform: duly inform the users about the whole data processing lifecycle;
2. Control: empower the users with full control over their personal data;
3. Enforce: enforce a privacy-friendly data processing;
4. Demonstrate: demonstrate the enforcement of the privacy-friendly data processing.

Based on these eight categories, we extracted relevant results, best-practices, and guidelines from the selected papers. A table reporting the distribution of the papers inside each strategy, with a brief explanation of their contribution, is reported in Appendix ().

Table 1. Distribution of the RQ1 papers inside the 8 strategies, with a brief explanation of their contribution.

1. Minimize	
In order to avoid unnecessary disclosure, only data that is strictly needed should be displayed to users	4,9
Data to be processed should be carefully selected	9,70
Collection of data should be limited to only data required for the proper functionality of the application	14,40
Minimize data storage retention to reduce the risks associated with data breaches	40
2. Separate	
Adopt a MVC architecture	4
Process data in a distributed fashion through isolation and virtualization	9,29,70
Interconnect systems via overlay networks or message brokers	12,36
Separate users' data into sub-profile, in order to avoid account wide data breaches	12,44
Ensure cross-domain unlikability through context separation (physical and digital)	1,44
Opt for a Decentralized storage	40,84
3. Abstract	
Homomorphic encryption	5,40,37
k-anonymity	5,8,18,19,40,70,71
l-diversity	18,19,40
t-closeness	19,40
Derivation: replace detailed information with equivalent but more general ones (example: substitute Data of Birth with age)	18
Approximation: replace information with less specific one	18
Differential Privacy	5,8,19,70,71
Use Privacy aware data-analysis algorithms	8
Aggregate data over time	21,40,70
4. Hide	
Use Encryption both for storage and transfer	1,14,17,18,19,21,37,40,53,70,89
Use Anonymization at different layers and pseudonymization	1,3,4,11,15,16,19 ,20,21,28,37,44,52,63,69,70,78,89
Use Attribute Based Encryption and/or Attribute-Based Access Control	5,36,40,44,64

(continued)

Table 1. (*continued*)

Always use application layer protocols over TLS	5,11,14
Use Tor network	5,63,78
Never log sensitive information	17
Masking: delete or mask certain part of personal data (e.g.. Credit card number: 1234 **** **** 6789)	18
Mixing: if the only purpose of data is to derive descriptive statistics (mean, variance, etc.) the values can be mixed across the records to avoid detectability of individuals	18
Tokenization: replace data with a unique identifier that is used to retrieve the original value	18
5. Inform	
Privacy policy as a new ISO/IEC 29110 product. It should report how the data will be managed by the involved parties and regulate the process of requesting, storing, processing and disposing data	4
Explain the process of personal data processing in detailed, but concise and understandable way	9,24,42,48,53,73,75,84,88
Users must be explicitly informed about any data collection, sharing and processing taking place	14,21,22,23,48
Asking for a user's consent for processing his/her personal data must be separated from asking consent for other aspects of services offered by developers	9,14
Users must be informed about which data is collected for which duration and eventually how data from different sources is combined. Also the must be informed on how to request data removal and withdrawal of consent	21,23,42,48
At the level of policy, a list of third parties to which personal data may be forwarded should be maintained, together with the territories under the jurisdiction of which the third parties operate and associated legal justifications	48,23
Inform users about what data is necessary for the offered service and what data can be instead voluntarily shared	24
Cookie Consent is preferrable in the lower left corner (on desktop) or the bottom of the screen (on mobile)	31
Notify users of a policy update	42
Employ Transparency Enhancing Tools	27,58,60
Explain consequence of not providing data	48,73
Inform about data breach	48,72
Use Visual reminders	48,51,53,75,84

(*continued*)

Table 1. (*continued*)

6. Control	
Specify policies in a machine-readable format and automate the informed-consent process (e.g., by using P3P, PPL or LPL)	5,59,66,74,78,81
Users should be given a chance to learn and practice their rights (access, rectification, erasure, giving and withdrawing consent, and portability) through system UI	14,48,52,73,89
Service providers must enable users to withdraw their consent at any time	14,21,48,52,87,88,89
Service provider should offer the possibility to determine how long data can be stored for and who can access them	21
Consider client-side encryption	21
Consent should be provided in forms and at times that minimize users fatigue and maximize the likelihood that they make appropriate decisions	22,48,87
Provide options to access and update collected data and to opt-out from collection	48
Provide a Privacy dashboard to empower users full control on their data at any time	41,70
Move away from a take it or leave it and empower the user in choosing a balance between functionality and privacy	84,47
For IoT devices Disconnect options should be considered	88
7. Enforce	
Include privacy and data protection functions in general purpose engineering tools	2
Model driven design: Use Model Based Testing for verification of correct application of mechanisms for access control to personal data	2
Perform code Static Analysis	3,67
Define a Sensitive Data Dictionary to keep track of sensible data processed by the service	4
Use Role-Based Access Control / Functionality	4,16
Use Sticky policies	47,70,78,84
Use PkI or eIDAS supported Unique Identifier	12

(*continued*)

Table 1. (*continued*)

Personal data can be collected only if the current consent given by the data subject (external entity) covers the purpose of this collection Personal data can be collected only if this collection is logged At any moment, a data subject can request to change their current consent for what concerns the purpose of collection of their personal data	13,14
Recording, Usage, Disclosure and Retrieval of personal data can be performed only if mentioned in the current consent. Any of these operations must be logged. Personal data can be retained as recorded only if the current retention time given by the data subject has not expired. At any moment, a data subject can request to change their current consent	13,89
Enforce Strong password policy	14
By default, least privacy invasive choices should be selected for the users	16
Use models to support GDPR compliance and verification	25,33,34,35,43
During data portability requests: Users must be authenticated thought the service access control mechanism. Users must be notified of the event. Requested data should be available only for a limited time to avoid possible leakage	30,45
Awareness and education for the whole development team	39,48,65,76,90
Ontologies to model information related to personal data to improve interpretation, visualization and compliance checking against privacy policies	50,56,79,86
Execute a process to regularly assess test and evaluate the effectiveness of the technical and organizational measure concerned with the data processing	7,25,38,52,89
Constantly update anti-virus	53
Access by third parties is requested from user and agreed prior to disclosure	53
Support users' privacy expectation and ease the requirement elicitation process	54,83
Educate users	75,84
Employ HCI patterns to ease information access	77
Operationalize GDPR principles into relevant privacy requirements and use automated tests to continuously verify these requirements	85

(*continued*)

Table 1. (*continued*)

8. Demonstrate	
Performa a Data Protection Impact Assessment	1,6,10,16,23,24,32,88
Adopt a privacy threat modelling and management strategy (e.g. LINDDUN)	2,6,46,55,57,68,80,91
Log when sensitive information is being accessed and processed	3,4,9,11
Maintain database of cryptographically signed records of relevant information to "decide the accountability of any decision made"	12,23,26
Service Providers have to keep a record of users' consent decision and make it available on request	14,23,52,89
Data Controller to store the consents obtained from DS so they can demonstrate GDPR compliance	22,23
Enforce the Global Privacy Standard principles	61
Adopt a personal data-centric lifecycle model also to support the identification of critical activities and associated privacy risks	49,61,62,82

4   Discussion

As Table 1 in appendix shows, most of guidelines focus on process-oriented strategies. Specifically, solutions that propose models that help in complying with various GDPR directives are well discussed: in [2] the authors highlight how developers are not prepared to deal with privacy requirements and lack tools (and methods) to translate those requirements into the software. Thus, they suggest adopting a model-driven design to support engineers with GDPR compliant software development. In this sense, [56] proposes a data management model to make consent, specific and unambiguous enabling a GDPR compliant data processing (in line with the *enforce* strategy). Moreover, in [62] a UML-based data lifecycle model is proposed; in [33] the authors present a privacy-aware system design model to mitigate possible regulation violations during the design process; in [79] an ontology-based business process methodology to address GDPR requirements is presented.

The adoption of such methods also supports the *demonstrate* strategy enabling the compliance verification and transparency as directly requested by the GDPR. Among *demonstrate* guidelines, most authors seem to agree that performing a Data Protection Impact Assessment (DPIA), even in that cases are not mandatory by the regulation, can help in complying with the GDPR as the DPIA is considered a powerful self-assessment tool. Along those lines, logging should be always performed when the user consents to processing and when accessing, processing, updating and deleting personal data [3]. To this end, indeed, users should always be given the opportunity to express their rights (*control* strategy). This, should also be implemented in a way that minimize fatigue while maximizing the likelihood for the user to make the appropriate decision

[22] and can be enabled, for example, by a privacy dashboard [70] or by supporting users' decision by using machine-readable policy formats [5, 78]. In any case, users should be able to always access and update collected data and to opt-out from collection [48]. Eventually, users could be provided the option to specify how long data can be stored and used for [21].

A relevant user-oriented solution worth mentioning is defined as "Sticky Policies", where users can define a set of rules that specifies how the data they are sharing shall be handled by service providers. However, this solution presents a few shortcomings that are addressed in [47].

On the other hand, service providers should move away from a take it or leave it approach [47] and leave users the choice of their preferred balance between functionality and privacy [84]. All of this should be provided in an agile fashion [88]. Nevertheless, service providers should distinguish between data necessary for using the service and data that can be, instead, voluntarily shared [24] (although as [14] and [40] suggest, only data exclusively required for the proper functionality of the service should be collected according to the *minimize* strategy) and consequences of not providing data should be explained [48, 73]. This falls under the *inform* strategy: users should always be explained the whole personal data process in a detailed but understandable and concise way [97]. Many authors agree that this could be supported by visual reminders [48]. To this end, [51] proposes a methodology to generate visual representations. However [88] argues that icons might not always be the best tool for communication.

Any policy update must be notified to users [42]. Users must be informed on what data is being collected and for what and for how long data will be stored [21]. However, the process of asking users consent must be separated from the choice of enabling other service-related features [9, 14].

Considering data-oriented strategies and specifically the *minimize* strategy, the amount of data collected and processed should be reduced to the minimum possible, and this should be decided on case by case basis [9, 70]. According to this strategy irrelevant information should be removed from the user's representation [4, 9]. Minimizing storage retention also reduces the risk associated with data breaches [40]. To this end, account wide data breaches can be avoided by adopting a *separate* strategy in which users' data is divided into sub-profiles [12, 44]. In any case, cross-domain unlinkability should be ensured by physical and digital separation [1, 44]. Decentralized storage [40, 84], isolation and virtualization [9, 70] and system interconnection via overlay networks or message brokers are also suggested [12, 36].

Many solutions are discussed under the *abstract* and *hide* strategies, including homomorphic encryption, k-anonymity, l-diversity, t-closeness and differential privacy. Data aggregation over time is also well suggested.

Anonymization and pseudonymization are the most common implementation of the *hide* strategy and encryption is always recommended both for storage and transfer. Attributed-Based Encryption is suggested as a method to easily provide both confidentiality and access control in a scalable way, without the need of a complex security infrastructure. Masking (hide part of the data), Mixing (mix data from multiple records) and Tokenization (replace data with unique ids) are also suggested as ways to implement this strategy [18].

In any case, it is worth to highlight how educating the development team [48] as well the end-users [84] is considered crucial to make these eight strategies effective. Indeed, education has always been a pillar of usable security and privacy [102]. However, educating, especially the end user, is a really ambitious and challenging task to achieve.

5 Conclusions and Future Work

This paper has presented a literature review that systematized current best-practices in designing and developing GDPR-compliant software following the by-design and by default paradigms. Selected studies were analyzed under different dimensions and categorized under Hoepman's design strategies. The analysis showed that from a technological point of view many different solutions exist to effectively support GDPR requirements implementation on different levels. However, there is still a lot to be done to make these tools and methods more user centered. As a result, since the development of security features has often overlooked the principles of usability and human-computer interaction in general, a future goal of this work is to propose a technical and methodological framework to support the user-centric design of GDPR-compliant software.

References

1. Mougiakou, E., Virvou, M.: Based on GDPR privacy in UML: case of e-learning program. In: 2017 8th International Conference on Information, Intelligence, Systems Applications (IISA), pp. 1–8 (2017). https://doi.org/10.1109/IISA.2017.8316456
2. Martin, Y., Kung, A.: Methods and tools for GDPR compliance through privacy and data protection engineering. In: 2018 IEEE European Symposium on Security and Privacy Workshops (EuroS PW), pp. 108–111 (2018). https://doi.org/10.1109/EuroSPW.2018.00021
3. Hjerppe, K., Ruohonen, J., Leppänen, V.: The general data protection regulation: requirements, architectures, and constraints. In: 2019 IEEE 27th International Requirements Engineering Conference (RE), pp. 265–275 (2019). https://doi.org/10.1109/RE.2019.00036
4. Morales-Trujillo, M.E., Garcia-Mireles, G.A.: Extending ISO/IEC 29110 basic profile with privacy-by-design approach: a case study in the health care sector. In: 2018 11th International Conference on the Quality of Information and Communications Technology (QUATIC), pp. 56–64 (2018). https://doi.org/10.1109/QUATIC.2018.00018
5. Li, C., Palanisamy, B.: Privacy in internet of things: from principles to technologies. IEEE Internet Things J. **6**, 488–505 (2019). https://doi.org/10.1109/JIOT.2018.2864168
6. Sion, L., et al.: An architectural view for data protection by design. In: 2019 IEEE International Conference on Software Architecture (ICSA), pp. 11–20 (2019). https://doi.org/10.1109/ICSA.2019.00010
7. Ayala-Rivera, V., Pasquale, L.: The grace period has ended: an approach to operationalize GDPR requirements. In: 2018 IEEE 26th International Requirements Engineering Conference (RE), pp. 136–146 (2018). https://doi.org/10.1109/RE.2018.00023
8. Sokolovska, A., Kocarev, L.: Integrating technical and legal concepts of privacy. IEEE Access. **6**, 26543–26557 (2018). https://doi.org/10.1109/ACCESS.2018.2836184
9. Colesky, M., Ghanavati, S.: Privacy shielding by design—a strategies case for near-compliance. In: 2016 IEEE 24th International Requirements Engineering Conference Workshops (REW), pp. 271–275. IEEE (2016)

10. Coles, J., Faily, S., Ki-Aries, D.: Tool-supporting data protection impact assessments with CAIRIS. In: 2018 IEEE 5th International Workshop on Evolving Security Privacy Requirements Engineering (ESPRE), pp. 21–27 (2018). https://doi.org/10.1109/ESPRE.2018.00010

11. Badii, C., Bellini, P., Difino, A., Nesi, P.: Smart city IoT platform respecting GDPR privacy and security aspects. IEEE Access. **8**, 23601–23623 (2020). https://doi.org/10.1109/ACCESS.2020.2968741

12. Pedrosa, M., Costa, C., Dorado, J.: GDPR impacts and opportunities for computer-aided diagnosis guidelines and legal perspectives. In: 2019 IEEE 32nd International Symposium on Computer-Based Medical Systems (CBMS), pp. 616–621 (2019)

13. Antignac, T., Scandariato, R., Schneider, G.: Privacy compliance via model transformations. In: 2018 IEEE European Symposium on Security and Privacy Workshops (EuroS PW), pp. 120–126 (2018). https://doi.org/10.1109/EuroSPW.2018.00024

14. Hatamian, M.: Engineering privacy in smartphone apps: a technical guideline catalog for app developers. IEEE Access. **8**, 35429–35445 (2020). https://doi.org/10.1109/ACCESS.2020.2974911

15. Groen, E.C., Ochs, M.: CrowdRE, user Feedback and GDPR: towards tackling GDPR implications with adequate technical and organizational measures in an effort-minimal way. In: 2019 IEEE 27th International Requirements Engineering Conference Workshops (REW), pp. 180–185 (2019). https://doi.org/10.1109/REW.2019.00038

16. Mustafa, U., Pflugel, E., Philip, N.: A novel privacy framework for secure M-Health applications: the case of the GDPR. In: 2019 IEEE 12th International Conference on Global Security, Safety and Sustainability (ICGS3), pp. 1–9 (2019). https://doi.org/10.1109/ICGS3.2019.8688019

17. Papageorgiou, A., Strigkos, M., Politou, E., Alepis, E., Solanas, A., Patsakis, C.: Security and privacy analysis of mobile health applications: the alarming state of practice. IEEE Access. **6**, 9390–9403 (2018). https://doi.org/10.1109/ACCESS.2018.2799522

18. Saatci, C., Gunal, E.S.: Preserving privacy in personal data processing. In: 2019 1st International Informatics and Software Engineering Conference (UBMYK), pp. 1–4 (2019). https://doi.org/10.1109/UBMYK48245.2019.8965432

19. Gruschka, N., Mavroeidis, V., Vishi, K., Jensen, M.: Privacy issues and data protection in big data: a case study analysis under GDPR. In: 2018 IEEE International Conference on Big Data (Big Data), pp. 5027–5033 (2018). https://doi.org/10.1109/BigData.2018.8622621

20. Hiller, J., Schuldes, M., Eckstein, L.: Recognition and pseudonymization of data privacy relevant areas in videos for compliance with GDPR. In: 2019 IEEE Intelligent Transportation Systems Conference (ITSC), pp. 2387–2393 (2019). https://doi.org/10.1109/ITSC.2019.8917267

21. Mannhardt, F., Petersen, S.A., Oliveira, M.F.: Privacy challenges for process mining in human-centered industrial environments. In: 2018 14th International Conference on Intelligent Environments (IE), pp. 64–71 (2018). https://doi.org/10.1109/IE.2018.00017

22. Morel, V., Cunche, M., Métayer, D.L.: A generic information and consent framework for the IoT. In: 2019 18th IEEE International Conference On Trust, Security And Privacy In Computing And Communications/13th IEEE International Conference On Big Data Science And Engineering (TrustCom/BigDataSE), pp. 366–373 (2019)

23. Butin, D., Métayer, D.L.: A guide to end-to-end privacy accountability. In: 2015 IEEE/ACM 1st International Workshop on Technical and Legal aspects of data Privacy and Security, pp. 20–25 (2015). https://doi.org/10.1109/TELERISE.2015.12

24. Wachter, S.: Ethical and normative challenges of identification in the internet of things. In: Living in the Internet of Things: Cybersecurity of the IoT – 2018, pp. 1–10 (2018). https://doi.org/10.1049/cp.2018.0013

25. Torre, D., Soltana, G., Sabetzadeh, M., Briand, L.C., Auffinger, Y., Goes, P.: Using models to enable compliance checking against the GDPR: an experience report. In: 2019 ACM/IEEE 22nd International Conference on Model Driven Engineering Languages and Systems (MODELS), pp. 1–11 (2019). https://doi.org/10.1109/MODELS.2019.00-20

26. Masmoudi, F., Sellami, M., Loulou, M., Kacem, A.H.: Optimal evidence collection for accountability in the cloud. In: 2018 IEEE 15th International Conference on e-Business Engineering (ICEBE), pp. 78–85 (2018). https://doi.org/10.1109/ICEBE.2018.00022

27. Tapsell, J., Akram, R.N., Markantonakis, K.: Consumer centric data control, tracking and transparency – a position paper. In: 2018 17th IEEE International Conference On Trust, Security And Privacy In Computing And Communications/12th IEEE International Conference On Big Data Science And Engineering (TrustCom/BigDataSE), pp. 1380–1385 (2018)

28. Damjanovic-Behrendt, V.: A Digital twin-based privacy enhancement mechanism for the automotive industry. In: 2018 International Conference on Intelligent Systems (IS), pp. 272–279 (2018). https://doi.org/10.1109/IS.2018.8710526

29. Ladjel, R., Anciaux, N., Pucheral, P., Scerri, G.: Trustworthy distributed computations on personal data using trusted execution environments. In: 2019 18th IEEE International Conference On Trust, Security And Privacy In Computing And Communications/13th IEEE International Conference On Big Data Science And Engineering (TrustCom/BigDataSE), pp. 381–388 (2019). https://doi.org/10.1109/TrustCom/BigDataSE.2019.00058

30. Singh, J., Cobbe, J.: The security implications of data subject rights. IEEE Secur. Priv. **17**, 21–30 (2019). https://doi.org/10.1109/MSEC.2019.2914614

31. Utz, C., Degeling, M., Fahl, S., Schaub, F., Holz, T.: (Un) Informed consent: studying GDPR consent notices in the field. In: Proceedings of the 2019 ACM SIGSAC Conference on Computer and Communications Security, pp. 973–990. Association for Computing Machinery, New York (2019). https://doi.org/10.1145/3319535.3354212

32. Ahmadian, A.S., Strüber, D., Riediger, V., Jürjens, J.: Supporting privacy impact assessment by model-based privacy analysis. In: Proceedings of the 33rd Annual ACM Symposium on Applied Computing, pp. 1467–1474. Association for Computing Machinery, New York, NY, USA (2018). https://doi.org/10.1145/3167132.3167288

33. Ahmadian, A.S., Strüber, D., Jürjens, J.: Privacy-enhanced system design modeling based on privacy features. In: Proceedings of the 34th ACM/SIGAPP Symposium on Applied Computing, pp. 1492–1499. Association for Computing Machinery, New York (2019). https://doi.org/10.1145/3297280.3297431

34. Ahmadian, A.S., Jürjens, J., Strüber, D.: Extending model-based privacy analysis for the industrial data space by exploiting privacy level agreements. In: Proceedings of the 33rd Annual ACM Symposium on Applied Computing, pp. 1142–1149. Association for Computing Machinery, New York (2018). https://doi.org/10.1145/3167132.3167256

35. Kupfersberger, V., Schaberreiter, T., Quirchmayr, G.: Security-driven information flow modelling for component integration in complex environments. In: Proceedings of the 10th International Conference on Advances in Information Technology. Association for Computing Machinery, New York (2018). https://doi.org/10.1145/3291280.3291797

36. Coroller, S., Chabridon, S., Laurent, M., Conan, D., Leneutre, J.: Position paper: towards end-to-end privacy for publish/subscribe architectures in the internet of things. In: Proceedings of the 5th Workshop on Middleware and Applications for the Internet of Things. pp. 35–40. Association for Computing Machinery, New York (2018). https://doi.org/10.1145/3286719.3286727

37. Notario, N., Ciceri, E., Crespo, A., Real, E.G., Catallo, I., Vicini, S.: Orchestrating privacy enhancing technologies and services with BPM tools: the WITDOM data protection orchestrator. In: Proceedings of the 12th International Conference on Availability, Reliability and Security. Association for Computing Machinery, New York (2017). https://doi.org/10.1145/3098954.3104057

38. Diamantopoulou, V., Mouratidis, H.: Practical evaluation of a reference architecture for the management of privacy level agreements. Inf. Comput. Secur. **26**, 711–730 (2019). https://doi.org/10.1108/ICS-04-2019-0052

39. Lodge, T., Crabtree, A.: Privacy engineering for domestic IoT: enabling due diligence. Sensors (Switzerland) **19**, 4380 (2019). https://doi.org/10.3390/s19204380

40. Abdulghani, H.A., Nijdam, N.A., Collen, A., Konstantas, D.: A study on security and privacy guidelines, countermeasures, threats: IoT data at rest perspective. Symmetry **11**, 774 (2019). https://doi.org/10.3390/sym11060774

41. Piras, L., et al.: DEFeND architecture: a privacy by design platform for GDPR compliance. In: Gritzalis, S., Weippl, E. R., Katsikas, S. K., Anderst-Kotsis, G., Tjoa, A. M., Khalil, I. (eds.) TrustBus 2019. LNCS, vol. 11711, pp. 78–93. Springer, Cham (2019). https://doi.org/10.1007/978-3-030-27813-7_6

42. Mohan, J., Wasserman, M., Chidambaram, V.: Analyzing GDPR compliance through the lens of privacy policy. In: Gadepally, V., et al. (eds.) DMAH/Poly -2019. LNCS, vol. 11721, pp. 82–95. Springer, Cham (2019). https://doi.org/10.1007/978-3-030-33752-0_6

43. Agostinelli, S., Maggi, F. M., Marrella, A., Sapio, F.: Achieving GDPR compliance of BPMN process models. In: Cappiello, C., Ruiz, M. (eds.) Information Systems Engineering in Responsible Information Systems: CAiSE Forum 2019, Rome, Italy, June 3–7, 2019, Proceedings, pp. 10–22. Springer, Cham (2019). https://doi.org/10.1007/978-3-030-212 97-1_2

44. Gabel, A., Schiering, I.: Privacy patterns for pseudonymity. IFIP Adv. Inf. Commun. Technol. **547**, 155–172 (2019). https://doi.org/10.1007/978-3-030-16744-8_11

45. Martino, M.D., Robyns, P., Weyts, W., Quax, P., Lamotte, W., Andries, K.: Personal information leakage by abusing the GDPR right of access. In: Proceedings of the 15th Symposium on Usable Privacy and Security, SOUPS 2019, pp. 371–386 (2019)

46. Muntes-Mulero, V., Dominiaky, J., Gonzalezz, E., Sanchez-Charles, D.: Model-driven evidence-based privacy risk control in trustworthy smart IoT systems. In: CEUR Workshop Proceedings, pp. 23–30 (2019)

47. Gol Mohammadi, N., Leicht, J., Ulfat-Bunyadi, N., Heisel, M.: Privacy policy specification framework for addressing end-users' privacy requirements. In: Gritzalis, S., Weippl, E. R., Katsikas, S. K., Anderst-Kotsis, G., Tjoa, A. M., Khalil, I. (eds.) TrustBus 2019. LNCS, vol. 11711, pp. 46–62. Springer, Cham (2019). https://doi.org/10.1007/978-3-030-27813-7_4

48. Ataei, M., Degbelo, A., Kray, C., Santos, V.: Complying with privacy legislation: From legal text to implementation of privacy-aware location-based services. ISPRS Int. J. Geo-Inf. **7**, (2018). https://doi.org/10.3390/ijgi7110442

49. Ujcich, B., Bates, A., Sanders, W.: A Provenance model for the European union general data protection regulation. In: Belhajjame, K., Gehani, A., Alper, P. (eds.) IPAW 2018. LNCS, vol. 11017, pp. 45–57. Springer, Cham (2018). https://doi.org/10.1007/978-3-319-98379-0_4

50. Pandit, H.J., O'Sullivan, D., Lewis, D.: An ontology design pattern for describing personal data in privacy policies. In: CEUR Workshop Proceedings, pp. 29–39 (2018)

51. Palmirani, M., Rossi, A., Martoni, M., Hagan, M.: A methodological framework to design a machine-readable privacy icon set. In: Jusletter IT (2018)

52. Fernandes, M., Da Silva, A.R., Gonçalves, A.: specification of personal data protection requirements: analysis of legal requirements from the GDPR regulation. In: ICEIS 2018 - Proceedings of the 20th International Conference on Enterprise Information Systems, pp. 398–405 (2018)

53. O'Connor, Y., Rowan, W., Lynch, L., Heavin, C.: Privacy by design: informed consent and internet of things for smart health. In: Procedia Computer Science, pp. 653–658 (2017). https://doi.org/10.1016/j.procs.2017.08.329

54. Diamantopoulou, V., Angelopoulos, K., Pavlidis, M., Mouratidis, H.: A metamodel for GDPR-based privacy level agreements. In: CEUR Workshop Proceedings, pp. 299–305 (2017)
55. Martín, Y.-S., Del Álamo, J.M.: A meta model for privacy engineering methods. In: CEUR Workshop Proceedings, pp. 41–48 (2017)
56. Fatema, K., Hadziselimovic, E., Pandit, H., Debruyne, C., Lewis, D., O'Sullivan, D.: Compliance through informed consent: Semantic based consent permission and data management model. In: CEUR Workshop Proceedings (2017)
57. Meis, R., Heisel, M.: Towards systematic privacy and operability (PRIOP) studies. In: De Capitani di Vimercati, S., Martinelli, F. (eds.) SEC 2017. IAICT, vol. 502, pp. 427–441. Springer, Cham (2017). https://doi.org/10.1007/978-3-319-58469-0_29
58. Spagnuelo, D., Bartolini, C., Lenzini, G.: Modelling metrics for transparency in medical systems. In: Lopez, J., Fischer-Hübner, S., Lambrinoudakis, C. (eds.) TrustBus 2017. LNCS, vol. 10442, pp. 81–95. Springer, Cham (2017). https://doi.org/10.1007/978-3-319-64483-7_6
59. Pardo, R., Le Métayer, D.: Analysis of privacy policies to enhance informed consent. In: Foley, S. (eds.) Data and Applications Security and Privacy XXXIII. DBSec 2019. Lecture Notes in Computer Science, vol. 11559, pp. 177–198, Springer, Cham https://doi.org/10.1007/978-3-030-22479-0_10
60. Spagnuelo, D., Ferreira, A., Lenzini, G.: Accomplishing transparency within the general data protection regulation. In: 5th International Conference on Information Systems Security and Privacy. To appear (2018)
61. Alshammari, M., Simpson, A.: Towards a principled approach for engineering privacy by design. In: Schweighofer, E., Leitold, H., Mitrakas, A., Rannenberg, K. (eds.) Privacy Technologies and Policy, APF 2017. Lecture Notes in Computer Science, vol. 10518, pp. 161–177. Springer, Cham https://doi.org/10.1007/978-3-319-67280-9_9
62. Alshammari, M., Simpson, A.: A UML profile for privacy-aware data lifecycle models. In: Katsikas, S. et al. (eds.) Computer Security, SECPRE 2017, CyberICPS 2017, Lecture Notes in Computer Science, vol. 10683, pp. 189–209 Springer, Cham. https://doi.org/10.1007/978-3-319-72817-9_13
63. Diamantopoulou, V., Argyropoulos, N., Kalloniatis, C., Gritzalis, S.: Supporting the design of privacy-aware business processes via privacy process patterns. In: 2017 11th International Conference on Research Challenges in Information Science (RCIS), pp. 187–198. IEEE (2017)
64. Michael, J., Koschmider, A., Mannhardt, F., Baracaldo, N., Rumpe, B.: User-centered and privacy-driven process mining system design for IoT. In: Cappiello, C., Ruiz, M. (eds.) Information Systems Engineering in Responsible Information Systems: CAiSE Forum 2019, Rome, Italy, June 3–7, 2019, Proceedings, pp. 194–206. Springer, Cham (2019). https://doi.org/10.1007/978-3-030-21297-1_17
65. Hadar, I., et al.: Privacy by designers: software developers' privacy mindset. Empirical Softw. Eng. 23(1), 259–289 (2017). https://doi.org/10.1007/s10664-017-9517-1
66. Gerl, A., Bennani, N., Kosch, H., Brunie, L.: LPL, towards a GDPR-compliant privacy language: formal definition and usage. In: Hameurlain, A., Wagner, R. (eds.) Transactions on Large-Scale Data- and Knowledge-Centered Systems XXXVII, pp. 41–80. Springer, Berlin (2018). https://doi.org/10.1007/978-3-662-57932-9_2
67. Ferrara, P., Spoto, F.: Static analysis for GDPR compliance. In: ITASEC (2018)
68. Sion, L., Van Landuyt, D., Wuyts, K., Joosen, W.: Privacy risk assessment for data subject-aware threat modeling. In: 2019 IEEE Security and Privacy Workshops (SPW), pp. 64–71. IEEE (2019)
69. Hillen, C.: The pseudonym broker privacy pattern in medical data collection. In: 2015 IEEE Trustcom/BigDataSE/ISPA, pp. 999–1005. IEEE (2015)

70. Kung, A., et al.: A privacy engineering framework for the internet of things. In: Kung, A., et al.: A privacy engineering framework for the internet of things. In: Data Protection and Privacy: (In) visibilities and Infrastructures, pp. 163–202. Springer, Cham (2017)
71. Roig, A.: Safeguards for the right not to be subject to a decision based solely on automated processing (Article 22 GDPR). Eur. J. Law Technol. **8**, (2018)
72. Roubtsova, E., Roubtsov, S., Alpár, G.: Presence patterns and privacy analysis. In: Shishkov, B. (ed) Business Modeling and Software Design, BMSD 2018, Lecture Notes in Business Information Processing, vol. 319, pp. 298–307. Springer, Cham (2018). https://doi.org/10.1007/978-3-319-94214-8_21
73. Betzing, J.H., Tietz, M., vom Brocke, J., Becker, J.: The impact of transparency on mobile privacy decision making. Electron. Markets 1–19 (2019)
74. Su, X., et al.: Privacy as a service: protecting the individual in healthcare data processing. Computer **49**, 49–59 (2016)
75. G Karácsony, G.: Managing Personal Data in a Digital Environment-Did GDPR's Concept of Informed Consent Really Give Us Control? In: International Conference on Computer Law, AI, Data Protection & The Biggest Tech Trends. (2019).
76. Li, Z.S., Werner, C., Ernst, N., Damian, D.: GDPR Compliance in the Context of Continuous Integration. arXiv preprint arXiv:2002.06830. (2020)
77. Loruenser, T., Pöhls, H.C., Sell, L., Laenger, T.: CryptSDLC: Embedding cryptographic engineering into secure software development lifecycle. In: Proceedings of the 13th International Conference on Availability, Reliability and Security, pp. 1–9 (2018)
78. Martucci, L. A., Fischer-Hübner, S., Hartswood, M., Jirotka, M.: Privacy and social values in smart cities. In: Angelakis, Vangelis, Tragos, Elias, Pöhls, Henrich C., Kapovits, Adam, Bassi, Alessandro (eds.) Designing, Developing, and Facilitating Smart Cities, pp. 89–107. Springer, Cham (2017). https://doi.org/10.1007/978-3-319-44924-1_6
79. Bartolini, C., Muthuri, R., Santos, C.: Using ontologies to model data protection requirements in workflows. In: Otake, M., Kurahashi, S., Ota, Y., Satoh, K., Bekki, D. (eds.) New Frontiers in Artificial Intelligence, pp. 233–248. Springer, Cham (2017). https://doi.org/10.1007/978-3-319-50953-2_17
80. Sion, L., Yskout, K., Van Landuyt, D., Joosen, W.: Solution-aware data flow diagrams for security threat modeling. In: Proceedings of the 33rd Annual ACM Symposium on Applied Computing. pp. 1425–1432 (2018)
81. Neisse, R., Baldini, G., Steri, G., Mahieu, V.: Informed consent in internet of things: the case study of cooperative intelligent transport systems. In: 2016 23rd International Conference on Telecommunications (ICT). pp. 1–5. IEEE (2016)
82. Alshammari, M., Simpson, A.: Personal Data Management for Privacy Engineering: An Abstract Personal Data Lifecycle Model. Oxford, UK, CS-RR-17–02 (2017)
83. Stach, C., Steimle, F.: Recommender-based privacy requirements elicitation-EPICUREAN: an approach to simplify privacy settings in IoT applications with respect to the GDPR. In: Proceedings of the 34th ACM/SIGAPP Symposium on Applied Computing, pp. 1500–1507 (2019)
84. Custers, B., Dechesne, F., Pieters, W., Schermer, B.W., van der Hof, S.: Consent and privacy. In: Müller A., Schaber, P. (eds.) The Routledge Handbook of the Ethics of Consent. Routledge, London, pp. 247–258 (2018)
85. Agarwal, S., Steyskal, S., Antunovic, F., Kirrane, S.: Legislative compliance assessment: framework, model and GDPR instantiation. In: Medina, M., Mitrakas, A., Rannenberg, K., Schweighofer, E., Tsouroulas, N. (eds.) Privacy Technologies and Policy, APF 2018, Lecture Notes in Computer Science, vol. 11079, pp. 131–149. Springer, Cham (2018)
86. Besik, S., Freytag, J.-C.: A formal approach to build privacy-awareness into clinical workflows. SICS Softw-Intensive Cyber-Phys. Syst. **35**(1–2), 141–152 (2019). https://doi.org/10.1007/s00450-019-00418-5

87. Hyysalo, J., Hirvonsalo, H., Sauvola, J., Tuoriniemi, S.: Consent management architecture for secure data transactions. In: ICSOFT 2016 - Proceedings of the 11th International Joint Conference on Software Technologies, pp. 125–132 (2016). https://doi.org/10.5220/000594 1301250132

88. Wachter, S.: GDPR and the Internet of Things: Guidelines to Protect Users' Identity and Privacy. SSRN (2018)

89. Al-Momani, A., Kargl, F., Schmidt, R., Kung, A., Bösch, C.: A privacy-aware v-model for software development. In: 2019 IEEE Security and Privacy Workshops (SPW), pp. 100–104 (2019). https://doi.org/10.1109/SPW.2019.00028

90. University of Maryland Study: Hackers Attack Every 39 Seconds. https://eng.umd.edu/news/story/study-hackers-attack-every-39-seconds. Accessed 02 Nov 2021

91. IBM Security Cost of a Data Breach Report 2020 https://www.ibm.com/security/data-breach. Accessed 02 Nov 2021

92. Cavoukian, A.: Privacy by design: The 7 foundational principles. Inf. Priv. Commissioner **5**, 12 (2009)

93. Sobolewski, M., Mazur, J., Paliński, M.: Gdpr: a step towards a user-centric internet? Intereconomics **52**(4), 207–213 (2017)

94. Leach, J.: Improving user security behaviour. Comput. Secur. **22**(8), 685–692 (2003)

95. Schultz, E.E., Proctor, R.W., Lien, M.C., Salvendy, G.: Usability and security an appraisal of usability issues in information security methods. Comput. Secur. **20**(7), 620–634 (2001)

96. Sunshine, J., Egelman, S., Almuhimedi, H., Atri, N., Cranor, L.F.: Crying wolf: an empirical study of SSL warning effectiveness. In: USENIX security symposium (SSYM 2009), pp. 399–416 (2009)

97. Muñoz-Arteaga, J., González, R.M., Martin, M.V., Vanderdonckt, J., Álvarez-Rodríguez, F.: A methodology for designing information security feedback based on user interface patterns. Adv. Eng. Softw. **40**(12), 1231–1241 (2009)

98. Urquhart, L., Rodden, T: A Legal Turn in Human Computer Interaction? Towards "Regulation by Design" for the Internet of Things. Available at SSRN: https://ssrn.com/abstract=2746467 (2016)

99. Martin, Y.S., Kung, A.: Methods and tools for GDPR compliance through privacy and data protection engineering. In: 2018 IEEE European Symposium on Security and Privacy Workshops (EuroS&PW), pp. 108–111 (2018)

100. Hoepman, J.-H.: Privacy design strategies. In: Cuppens-Boulahia, N., Cuppens, F., Jajodia, S., Abou El Kalam, A., Sans, T. (eds.) SEC 2014. IAICT, vol. 428, pp. 446–459. Springer, Heidelberg (2014). https://doi.org/10.1007/978-3-642-55415-5_38

101. Kitchenham, B.: Procedures for performing systematic reviews. Keele UK Keele Univ. **33**, 1–26 (2004)

102. Sasse, M.A., Flechais, I.: Usable security: why do we need it? how do we get it? In: Cranor, L.F., Garfinkel, S. (eds.) Security and Usability: Designing secure systems that people can use, pp. 13–30. O'Reilly, Sebastopol (2005)

User Behavior Analysis in Cybersecurity

'Just-in-Time' Parenting: A Two-Month Examination of the Bi-directional Influences Between Parental Mediation and Adolescent Online Risk Exposure

Zainab Agha[1]([envelope]), Reza Ghaiumy Anaraky[2], Karla Badillo-Urquiola[1], Bridget McHugh[3], and Pamela Wisniewski[1]

[1] University of Central Florida, Orlando, FL, USA
{zainab.agha,kcurquiola10}@knights.ucf.edu, pamwis@ucf.edu
[2] Clemson University, Clemson, SC, USA
rghaium@clemson.edu
[3] Ohio State University, Columbus, OH, USA
mchugh.159@osu.edu

Abstract. Parental mediation is a key factor that influences adolescents' exposure to online risk. Yet, research on this topic has mostly been cross-sectional and correlative, not exploring whether the relationship between parental mediation and adolescent online risk exposure could be bi-directional, where teens' risk exposure influences parenting practices. To address this gap, we conducted an eight week, repeated measures web-based diary study with 68 adolescents (aged 13–17) and their parents to examine the relationships between three parental mediation strategies (active mediation, monitoring, and restriction) and three adolescent online risk types (explicit content, sexual solicitations, and online harassment) teens reported encountering online. Overall, parents and teens had significantly different perceptions regarding parental mediation, which yielded some consistent and conflicting results. Parents and teens agreed that *parental restriction* significantly increased the week in which the teen encountered all three risk types, and *active mediation* increased during the week in which the teen encountered online harassment. Parents and teens also consistently reported that *restriction* significantly decreased the week after an online harassment incident. Overall, we found that parental mediation and teen online risk exposure were most often significantly correlated in the same week, suggesting parenting occurred 'just-in-time,' rather than parents and teens' behaviors bi-directionally influencing one another significantly from week-to-week. Our findings provide new insights into parent-teen perspectives on parental mediation and highlight the bi-directional relationship of parental mediation and online risk. We offer recommendations to facilitate 'just in time' parenting and provide teens with the necessary support to help keep them safe online.

Keywords: Adolescent online safety · Parental mediation · Online risks · Online harassment · Sexual solicitations · Explicit content

© Springer Nature Switzerland AG 2021
A. Moallem (Ed.): HCII 2021, LNCS 12788, pp. 261–280, 2021.
https://doi.org/10.1007/978-3-030-77392-2_17

1 Introduction

Despite the numerous benefits the internet and social networking sites (SNS) provide to teens, evidence shows teens are still susceptible to online risks [1]. For instance, a recent study by Pew Research Center found online harassment to be a serious issue for 90% of the teens in the US, and almost 59% of these teens previously experienced some form of online risk [2]. Consequently, adolescent online safety has been an increasingly important topic in the HCI community, studying teens' online wellbeing from different perspectives [3, 4]. Meanwhile, parental mediation is considered within the literature to be an effective strategy to ensuring teens' online safety [5, 6]. As a result, the influence of parental mediation on teens' online activity has been studied extensively; with respect to different parenting styles [7, 8], parental digital literacy [9, 10], and cross-national differences [11]. However, this existing literature provides conflicting results. For example, Lwin et al. found parental mediation increases teens' risk-seeking behaviors [12]; yet, Sorbring and Lundin found parental mediation to have no significant effects on teens' exposure to online risks [13]. Given these conflicting results, Wisniewski et al. emphasized the importance of moving beyond cross-sectional studies to conduct research that examines both parent and teen behaviors, to get a better understanding of parental mediation in relation to teens' online risk experiences [14].

To address this gap, we conducted an eight-week repeated measures web-based diary study with adolescents (aged 13–17) and their parents to understand the dynamics of parent-teen influences with respect to online risk experiences. We took a family systems approach, which posits that the influences within the parent-teen relationship can be bi-directional [15], implying that parents and teens can influence one another in regards to parental mediation strategies and teens' online risk experiences. This approach is unique as it steps away from the traditional mode of studying teen online risks exposure as a unidirectional outcome of parental mediation. The over-arching research questions for this study were:

- **RQ1:** *How do parental mediation strategies influence teens' exposure to online risks in the subsequent week?*
- **RQ2:** *How does teens' online risk exposure influence parental mediation strategies in the subsequent week?*
- **RQ3**: *In the same week, how do teens' online risk exposure and parental mediation influence one another?*

To answer these questions, we asked teens to report weekly on their online risks, specifically these three types: exposure to explicit content, sexual solicitations and online harassment, [14]. We also asked teens and parents to report on parental mediation strategies each week. We focused on three parental mediation types defined by Valkenburg; including *active mediation* – involving conversation and discussion between the parent and teen regarding online activity, *restrictive mediation* - involving rules and limits on the teens' online activity, and *monitoring* – involving surveillance and checking of the teen's online activity [16]. To analyze participants' responses, we used cross-lagged panel modeling and conducted the analysis based on teen responses only, and the joint responses of parents (regarding their mediation each week) and teens (regarding their weekly exposure to online risks). Our work makes important contributions to adolescent online safety literature by applying the theoretical framework of family systems to identify bi-directional influences between parents and teens with respect to teens' online risk exposure. We move beyond cross-sectional and individual level analyses by conducting repeated measures analysis on dyadic data. Based on the joint perspective of parents and teens, we found that teens' risk exposure significantly influences parental mediation (parents tend to support teens after online risk exposure by reducing restrictions). Our paper introduces important comparisons between parent-teen perceptions on parental mediation and provides recommendations for researchers that can facilitate parents' timely response to teens' risk exposure in the same week.

2 Background

In the sections below, we synthesize the literature related to adolescent online safety and risks, along with research on parental mediation in relation to teens' online risks.

2.1 Adolescent Online Safety and Risks

To maximize the benefits and mitigate the risks associated with teens use of technology use and online engagement, adolescents' online safety has become an important area of interest within the HCI community. Adolescent online safety researchers have studied different perspectives of teens online behaviors and safety; ranging from teens use of mobile devices [1] and social media [3] to the involvement of parental controls [17] and mediation of teens' online activity [9]. More recent approaches to online safety have focused on empirical methods that can empower youth and develop effective adolescent online safety, such as involving teens in design-based activities [18], interviews [19], participatory design [4], and co-mediation with parents [20].

In studying adolescent online safety, the types of risks faced by teens have been operationalized in several ways. For example, Livingstone et al. conducted a survey study on the online safety of European children which divided online risks into three broad groups of content, contact, and conduct related risks [11]. A different study by Wisniewski et al. extended this approach by categorizing online risks based on risk events, including harassment, solicitations, exposure, informational, and ethical risks [14]. These categories were later refined into four major types of risks; online harassment, sexual solicitations, exposure to explicit content, and information breaches [21]. We build upon these risk types to get an authentic understanding of the risks encountered by teens. The next section synthesizes the literature on parent-teen influences regarding online safety and identifies the gaps in existing research.

2.2 Parental Mediation Influence on Adolescent Online Risk Exposure

Adolescents' use of technology has been widely studied in relation to parental me issues between parents and teens regarding technology mediation in the home [22, 23]. A commonality among these works is that they largely studied the effects of parental mediation strategies, considering parental mediation as a predictor for adolescent online risks. For example, Yardi et al. [24] found that parents struggled with mediating their teen's social media use and identified tensions between balancing parental authority and teen autonomy. Similarly, Blackwell et al. found that parents underestimate teens' online activity, while teens often felt that parental mediation invaded their privacy [25]. Wisniewski et al. found that direct interventions may reduce teens' exposure to online risks but could be most beneficial for teens when combined with active mediation [26]. Subsequent research by Hiniker et al. [27] found that restrictive mediation is more impactful when the rules limit certain technologies completely (e.g., no Snapchat), than restricting technology use in context-specific situations (e.g., no phone at the dinner table). Yet, effects in the opposite direction remain under-studied, as the influence of teens' online risk exposure on parental mediation has rarely been investigated.

Moreover, the current literature on the impact of parental mediation on teens online well-being and safety [8, 22, 26] provides inconsistent results and no decisive findings regarding causality. For example, Lwin et al. conducted a quasi-experimental study to see the effects of parental mediation strategies and found active mediation to be effective in reducing teens online information disclosure behaviors, whereas restrictive mediation was shown to be associated with more risk-seeking behaviors [22]. Alternatively, a survey study reported that active mediation and conversational strategies have no effect on teens online behaviors [26]. Similarly, conflicting findings can be observed for monitoring where Berson et al. reported monitoring to be associated with a decrease in teens exposure to online harassment [28], whereas Ghosh et al. found monitoring to be associated with increased risk exposure [29]. These conflicting results may be related to the cross-sectional nature of these studies, forming mostly correlational findings instead of causations. Alternatively, the inconsistencies may be a result of reliance on either parents or teens as the informants reporting on parental mediation and teens' risk exposure. In the next section, we explain the family systems theory and its relevance to studying parental mediation in relation to teens' online safety.

3 A Family Systems Approach

The family systems theory [15] provides a comprehensive framework for overcoming the limitations of cross-sectional data and one-sided reports, which has rarely been employed in the study of adolescent online safety. Family systems theory builds upon the model of "transactional family theory," introduced by Schermerhon et al. [30], which describes the familial influences process between the parent and child to be bi-directional and multi-dimensional. Where previously a child's behavior was studied as a function of parenting, the transactional family theory brought the inverse effect into light, in which a child can equally influence a parent [30]. Family systems theory consists of three main principles including: 1) a focus on transactional and bi-directional influences, 2) longitudinal effects, and 3) multi-level analysis [15]. While family systems approach has been employed in youth research including youth obesity [31], or cognitive disorders [32], it has seldom been used in adolescent online safety research. Wisniewski et al. emphasizes the need to utilize the family systems approach in studying teens' online risks and safety to get a full picture of the parent-teen influences and perspectives regarding online safety [14]. Proposed methods to study transactional theory in family systems research include longitudinal studies [15], which can help better understand the family dynamics and consequences [14].

Researchers have begun using longitudinal approaches and dyadic data to examine unexplored bi-directional influences between parents and adolescents. For instance, Koning et al. [33] conducted a two-wave study and found bi-directional effects between parental mediation and adolescents' symptoms of internet gaming disorder and social media disorder. We derived motivation from these related works and the family systems theory, extending beyond the existing literature by incorporating both parents and teens reports of parental mediation in establishing bi-directional influences between parental mediation and teens' online risk exposure. In the next section, we elaborate on our study design and methodology.

4 Methods

In this section, we provide an overview of our diary study design and methodological details regarding study measures, recruitment, and data analysis.

4.1 Diary Study Overview

To get an authentic understanding of the effects of teens' risk exposure and parental mediation, we chose diary studies as the most suitable method for this study due to their "in-situ" nature, providing participants with the ability to report in real-time. The diary study was conducted online for 8 weeks, through a web-based application developed using PHP and MySQL, along with surveys linked to the Qualtrics API. All participants were given access to a custom dashboard with a personal log-in to enter their responses each week over the course of eight weeks. Parents and teens were provided with separate logins to protect the privacy of both parties. To collect responses for the diary study, participants could use the custom dashboard to enter new responses each week, as well as view their old entries. Each participant had one week to complete a weekly diary entry and were able to edit their responses till the end of the week. Surveys utilized an in-situ approach, with participants providing a qualitative description of each event along with responses to structured, standardized scales. The next section describes the measures utilized in these surveys.

4.2 Diary Study Measures

Teens' Online Risk Exposure. To measure risk exposure on a week to week basis, teen participants were asked if they had encountered risks within each category over the last week on a 5-point Likert Scale (1 = never, 5 = almost every day), The following risk categories were measured: online harassment, sexual solicitations and exposure to explicit content. However, in the survey questions, these risk types were relabeled to be less severe and more relatable for teens. Online harassment was referred to as "online interactions" and was defined as bullying and other negative online interactions that may be considered threatening or harassing. Sexual solicitations were labeled as "online flirtations" and described as sexual requests from people that the teens may or may not have known, with examples such as "cybering" or "sexting." Explicit content exposure was labeled as "online content" and included pornographic, violent or upsetting content online. The responses for each risk type were averaged and used as a measure for the weekly risk exposure. Cronbach's alpha was calculated and indicated acceptable reliability with values above .70 on average.

Parental Mediation Strategies. To measure weekly parental mediation strategies, we utilized items from Livingstone et al. [11] that included questions on three different mediation types; active mediation, restrictive mediation and monitoring. Parents and teens responded to these questions on a 5-point Likert frequency scale. Scale point labels were the same for active mediation, restrictions and monitoring (1 = None of the time, 5 = All of the time), to assess the level of mediation employed by the parent. Cronbach's alpha indicated excellent reliability across weeks and in the pre-study survey (above .80 on average).

4.3 Data Analysis Approach

To study both parents' and teens' reports of parental mediation with teens' online risk exposure, we ran two separate models for each of the risk types: 1) a **teen model**, solely based on teens' reports of online risk exposure and parental mediation, and 2) a **parent-teen model** which included teens report of online risk exposure and parental reports of mediation behaviors. Our goal was to see how parental mediations influence teens' future risk exposures and how teens' risk exposures influence future parental mediation behaviors. Therefore, we conducted a cross-lagged panel model [34] with R language to analyze this data. Cross-lagged panel models are used to analyze reciprocal relationship or directional influences of one variable to another over time [35]. This approach is common in studies that use diary or longitudinal data since it helps researchers estimate the effects of a variable at time t on another variable at time t+1 [36–38].

Since we collected data from both parents and teens, we ran two separate models for parent and teen reports in our analysis. Using recommendations from the literature, we compared the change in deviance between a full model (with independent variables) and an intercept only model (the "null" model) to assess model fit [39]. In addition, we used the sum score of each construct for the analysis. To study the effects of parental mediation on teens risk exposure (RQ1), we regressed each risk type (dependent variables) on parental mediation behaviors of the week before (independent variables). We conducted a separate analysis for each of the mediation strategies (active mediation, restrictive mediation, and monitoring). To address RQ2, we studied the effect of teens' online exposure on parental mediation. Therefore, we regressed parental mediation behaviors (dependent variables) on each of the four risk types of the week before (independent variables). Likewise, we carried out separate analysis for each parental mediation strategy. Lastly, to address RQ3, we studied the correlations between teens' risk exposure and parental mediation in the same weeks.

4.4 Participant Recruitment

Participants were recruited through two channels. Firstly, recruitment was conducted through a database of local parents provided by the psychology department of the university. We also contacted youth serving organizations, such as YMCAs, non-profit organizations, family-based community centers, churches, clinics, and after school programs. We reached out to participants in these organizations via phone calls and emails. After completion of the pre-survey, a collective gift card of $25 was sent to the parent and teen. After that, participants earned their incentive based on the number of weekly diary entries completed. The maximum reward was a $75 Amazon or Walmart gift card, which was given in case of all diary entries being completed. Recruitment and participation in this study occurred over the course of eight months in 2014.

5 Results

In this section, we present the descriptive statistics of our participants, followed by the key findings for each risk type based on the teen and parent-teen models to answer each of our research questions.

5.1 Descriptive Statistics

Data was collected from 68 teens and their parents living in the US, with participants identifying as White/Caucasian (73%); African American (13%), Hispanic (5%), Asian (3%), and other (5%). Teen participants were between the ages of 13–17 with more female (63%) than male participants. The age distribution of teens was as follows: 13 (15%), 14 (31%), 15 (24%), 16 (19%), and 17 (12%). The parent or legal guardian of our teen participants included 60 mothers, 7 fathers, and 1 grandmother. 85% of these parents or legal guardians were between the ages of 35 and 54 with 9% being younger and 6% older. Most of the parent-teen dyads (87%) completed all parts of the study, including all eight weekly diary surveys. An additional 10% of participants completed at least half of the weekly diary surveys. A power analysis was conducted which confirmed that the number of observations (434) were enough to detect effects with a small effect size ($\beta = .04$) and .80 power. A total of 176 online risk events were reported during the study, where most of the teens (80%) reported at least one risk event. Explicit content exposure ($N = 119$) was observed to be the most experienced risk type, followed by sexual solicitations ($N = 29$) and online harassment ($N = 28$). We report the mean and standard deviation of the frequency of teens' risk exposure (per risk type) and parental mediation strategies based on parent and teen reports in Table 1. The responses to each item are coded as (1- not at all, 2- once, 3- two to three times, 4- four to five times, 5- six or more). In the following sections, we answer our research questions by presenting results from the teen model and the parent-teen model for each risk type.

Table 1. Risk exposures' and mediations' descriptive statistics

Construct	Mean (SD)		Cronbach's alpha		Mean Difference
Parental Mediation	P	T	P	T	t-value
Active Mediation	2.08 (0.91)	1.73 (0.94)	0.90	0.92	8.41***
Restriction	3.61 (1.19)	3.90 (1.08)	0.91	0.88	6.87***
Monitoring	1.72 (1.09)	2.13 (1.10)	0.92	0.92	9.05***
Risk Exposure	T		T		
Online Harassment	1.05 (0.21)		0.860		N/A
Sexual Solicitations	1.04 (0.21)		0.692		N/A
Explicit Content	1.24 (0.53)		0.829		N/A

P=Parent, T=Teen; *** indicates p <.001, ** indicates p <.01, * indicates p <.05, † indicates p <.10.

5.2 Exposure to Explicit Content

We found significant effects of parental mediation on teen's exposure to explicit content in the next week (**RQ1**). The teen model presented unusual results where active ($\beta = 0.034, p < .05$) and restrictive mediation ($\beta = 0.020, p < .05$) lead to an *increase* in teens' exposure to explicit content in the following week. In contrast, the parent-teen model–relying on parental reports of mediation and teen reports of risk exposure–showed active mediation ($\beta = -0.024, p < .05$) to significantly *decrease* exposure to explicit content in the next weeks (see Fig. 1).

Our analysis in the opposite direction showed teens' explicit content exposure to also influence parental mediation significantly in the next week (**RQ2**). According to the teen model, we found that teens' exposure to explicit content had a positive relationship with restrictive mediation in the next week ($\beta = 0.085, p < .05$), indicating that parents increase restrictions on teens in the week after they are exposed to explicit content. The parent-teen model contradicted with this result, suggesting that exposure to explicit content would lead to significantly lower levels of restrictive mediation in the week after ($\beta = -0.207, p < .05$).

Lastly, we found bi-directional influences between parental mediation and teen's exposure to explicit content in the same week (**RQ3**). The teen model showed adolescent exposure to explicit content to be significantly correlated with restrictive mediation in the same week ($\beta = 3.401, p < .01$). Similar effects were observed with the parent-teen model which showed a positive correlation between parents increased active mediation ($\beta = 2.330, p < .01$) and restrictions ($\beta = 3.485, p < .01$) with teen's exposure to explicit content in the same week. In summary, we found the effects from the teen and parent-teen models to contradict with each other, except for consistent bi-directional effects between parental mediation and teen exposure to explicit content in the same week.

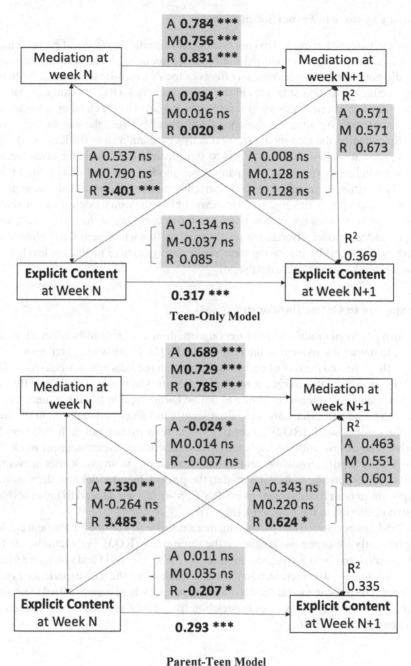

A 0.784 ***
M0.756 ***
R 0.831 ***

Mediation at week N

Mediation at week N+1

A 0.034 *
M0.016 ns
R 0.020 *

R^2
A 0.571
M 0.571
R 0.673

A 0.537 ns
M0.790 ns
R 3.401 ***

A 0.008 ns
M0.128 ns
R 0.128 ns

A -0.134 ns
M-0.037 ns
R 0.085

R^2
0.369

Explicit Content at Week N

Explicit Content at Week N+1

0.317 ***

Teen-Only Model

A 0.689 ***
M0.729 ***
R 0.785 ***

Mediation at week N

Mediation at week N+1

A -0.024 *
M0.014 ns
R -0.007 ns

R^2
A 0.463
M 0.551
R 0.601

A 2.330 **
M-0.264 ns
R 3.485 **

A -0.343 ns
M0.220 ns
R 0.624 *

A 0.011 ns
M0.035 ns
R -0.207 *

R^2
0.335

Explicit Content at Week N

Explicit Content at Week N+1

0.293 ***

Parent-Teen Model

*** indicates $p < .001$, ** indicates $p < .01$, * indicates $p < .05$, † indicates $p < .10$.

Fig. 1. Bi-directional influences between parental mediation and explicit content

5.3 Risk Exposure to Sexual Solicitations

The teen and parent-teen models did not present any significant effects of parental mediation on teen's exposure to sexual risks in the subsequent week (**RQ1**). Similarly, both
models did not establish any significant effects of teen's exposure to sexual solicitations
on any parental mediation strategies in the following week (**RQ2**). Although parental
mediation and adolescent exposure to sexual risks did not affect each other in subsequent
weeks, we observed significant bi-directional influences between them in the same week
(**RQ3**). Specifically, the teen model showed active mediation ($\beta = 0.832, p < .01$) and
restrictive mediation ($\beta = 1.108, p < .01$) to significantly increase in the same week as
an online sexual risk experience. The parent-teen model supported this finding, where
we found a positive correlation between restrictive mediation and sexual risk exposure
in the same week ($\beta = 0.793, p < .01$). However, unlike the teen model, active mediation
did not have a significant correlation with sexual risk exposure in the same week, based
on the parent-teen model. Overall, our results indicate that when teens face online sexual
risks, parents respond by increasing their active and restrictive mediation levels in the
same week, as shown in Fig. 2 (next page).

5.4 Exposure to Online Harassment

Results from the **teen model** showed parental mediation to significantly affect adolescent
exposure to online harassment in the next week (**RQ1**). In particular, active mediation
significantly increased the risk of online harassment in the subsequent week ($\beta = 0.011$,
$p < .001$). However, the **parent-teen** model did not show any significant effects of
mediation strategies on teens' exposure to online harassment in the subsequent week.

We also found online harassment to significantly influence parental mediation strategies in the coming week (**RQ2**). According to the **teen model**, online harassment had
a negative relationship with parental restrictive mediation in the subsequent week ($\beta = -0.769, p < .05$), indicating that parents reduce restrictions in the week after harassment
incidents. Corresponding to the teen model, the **parent-teen model** also demonstrated
that exposure to online harassment ($\beta = -0.807, p < .05$) would lead to lower levels of
restrictive mediation in the next week (Fig. 3).

Our findings confirmed that parental mediation and teen's online harassment encounters significantly influence one another in the same week (**RQ3**). For example, the **teen
model** revealed that both active mediation ($\beta = 1.085, p < .001$) and restrictive mediation ($\beta = 0.844, p < .01$) increased in the same week when the teen experienced online
harassment. The **parent-model** showed identical results where parents raised their active
mediation ($\beta = 1.084, p < .001$) and restriction ($\beta = 1.109, p < .01$) levels in the same
week as online harassment.

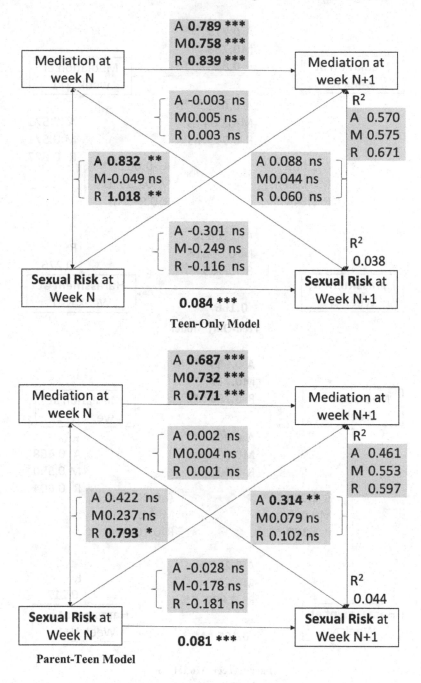

Fig. 2. Bi-directional influences between parental mediation and sexual solicitations

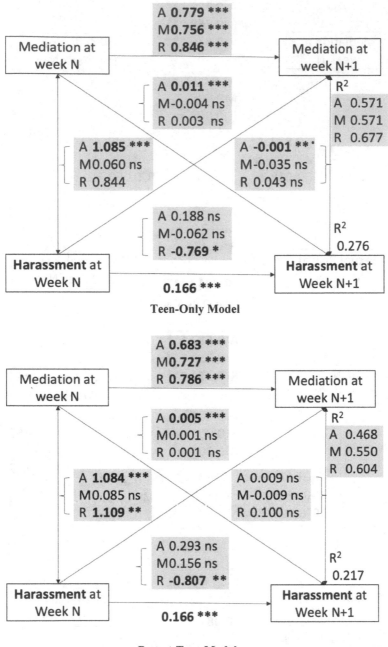

Fig. 3. Bi-directional influences between parental mediation and online harassment

6 Discussion

In this section, we compare the results from the teen-only and parent-teen models to discuss the implications of our findings and opportunities for future research. Table 2 summarizes the high-level results from each model.

Table 2. Summary of results between parental mediation and teen's risk exposure

Risk / Mediation Type	Teen Model		Parent-Teen Model	
Risk Type	Same Week	Subsequent Week	Same Week	Subsequent Week
Explicit Content	+*Restriction*	+Restriction	+Active Mediation +*Restriction*	**-Restriction**
Sexual Solicitations	+Active Mediation +*Restriction*	*ns*	+*Restriction*	*ns*
Online Harassment	+*Active Mediation* +*Restriction*	-Restriction	+*Active Mediation* +*Restriction*	-Restriction
Mediation Type	Same Week	Subsequent Week	Same Week	Subsequent Week
Active Mediation	+Sexual Solicitations +*Online Harassment*	+**Explicit Content** +Online Harassment	+Explicit Content +*Online Harassment*	**-Explicit Content**
Monitoring	ns	ns	ns	ns
Restriction	+ *Explicit Content* +*Sexual Solicitations* +*Online Harassment*	+Explicit Content	+*Explicit Content* +*Sexual Solicitations* +*Online Harassment*	ns

Note: **Bold Italic** font denotes parent-teen agreement across models, and **Red Bold** font denotes conflicting results. Normal font indicates significant and non-significant effects identified in one model but not the other.

6.1 Parent vs. Teen Perceptions of Mediation and Risk Exposure

Like past studies [22, 27], we uncovered some conflicting results based on the self-reported accounts of parents and teens. For instance, parents reported significantly higher levels of active mediation and monitoring, while teens reported significantly higher levels of parental restriction overall (Table 1). As shown in Table 2, teens reported increased levels of parental restriction the week after they were exposed to explicit online content, while parents reported decreased levels of restriction. The teen model suggested that active mediation increased subsequent exposure to explicit content, while the parent-teen model implied that active mediation decreased such exposure. A theme across these conflicting findings is that teens tend to report more negative outcomes associated with parental mediation (e.g., increased restriction and exposure to risk), while parents' reports tend to suggest more positive outcomes (e.g., decreased restriction and reduced exposure to risk).

An important implication of these conflicting findings is that both teens and parents seem to exhibit social desirability biases [40], which surface the unique developmental tensions within the parent-teen relationship. These tensions arise due to the boundary negotiation process between asserting teen autonomy versus parental control regarding online safety and risks that has been highlighted in past research [19]. For instance, differences in parent-teen perspectives regarding teens' online risk exposure have been brought up by researchers previously, where Blackwell et al. [25] found that parents underestimate teens' online experiences and think they actively mediate, but teens are more likely to view this mediation as restriction. Another possible explanation for these conflicting findings may be that parents are often unaware of the risks their teens are exposed to online; therefore, it is difficult to mediate these situations [21]. Therefore, it is important in future research that studies continue to incorporate and triangulate the perceptions of teens and their parents when examining the relationships between online risk exposure and parental mediation strategies. Not including both perspectives would likely lead to knowledge gaps and biases that could negatively impact recommended parenting interventions, policy changes, and design implications.

Inversely, a strength of our research is that we uncovered several consistent results across the teen and parent-teen models. For instance, all parental mediation types (active mediation, restrictive mediation, and monitoring) significantly predicted their respective mediation for the subsequent week for both teen and parent-teen models (see Fig. 1, Fig. 2, Fig. 3). This implies that parents tend to mediate in the same way through consecutive weeks and overall, parental mediation levels remain consistent over time. The same applies to risk exposure. A main predictor of each of the risk exposures, was the level of exposure to that risk in the previous week (Fig. 1, Fig. 2, Fig. 3). Further, our results showed significant agreement between the teen model and the parent-teen model results in the same week, both of which showed bi-directional influences between parental mediation and adolescent online risk exposure (see Table 2). Given these convergent results between teen and parent-teen reports in Table 2, we can say with a good amount of confidence that these relationships hold and give unique insights into the cross-sectional and bi-directional influences between teen risk exposure and parental mediation strategies. Moving beyond cross-sectional data and individual reports, our study confirms that parents and teens have similarities in their perceptions of mediation in the same week that teen is exposed to online risks, but differences arise in the influence of parental mediation in subsequent weeks.

6.2   Risk Exposure Affects Parental Mediation

While earlier research on the topic studied teens' risk exposure as a function of parental mediation [24, 26], our study is the first to bring the inverse effect of risk exposure on parenting into light. Findings from both models demonstrated a lower level of restrictive mediation by parents in response to teens experiencing online harassment or explicit context exposure. This leniency may be due to parents offering support in the form of reduced restrictions to help their teens cope with an unpleasant experience. Our results provide a contrast to the established understanding that parents always seek to protect through limiting teens' online interactions [17]. Instead, we demonstrate how parents can prefer protecting the wellbeing of their teens by allowing them to self-regulate their online experiences and overcome the negative effects of an online risk. Therefore, designers and practitioners working on mediative technologies should provide features that offer parents flexibility to adjust restrictions on teens' online activity.

Additionally, researchers should consider ways for parents to assess effective ways to support their teen struggling with online risks. For example, creating peer support platforms for parents [41] where they can engage with others on best practices to help teens after a risky encounter will improve the support provided to teens along with fostering a sense of community for parents. An alternative explanation for reduced restrictions after the risk exposure is parents' lack of awareness on the online risks their teens may be experiencing. We encourage researchers to extend our work by incorporating parental perceptions of online risks to form more conclusive findings on the effects of adolescent risk exposure on parental restrictions and other strategies.

6.3 'Just-in-Time' Parenting

Our findings from both the teen and the parent-teen reports strongly suggested active and/or restrictive mediation significantly increases in the same week as teens exposure to online harassment, explicit content, or sexual solicitations. However, no significant effects were seen for monitoring, which may be due to the passive nature of technical monitoring leaving it unaffected by risk exposure. Moreover, for sexual solicitations, parenting did not have much effect on risk exposure (low r-square). This may be because teens do not have control over when they are solicited and sexual interactions (such as flirting) are often concealed from parents. Overall, we presented consistent bi-directional effects between parental mediation and teens' risk exposure in the same week across both models. Therefore, we encourage researchers to move beyond studying online risk exposure as an outcome of parental mediation and to equally consider the influence of parents and teens on each other in shaping the online safety of a child.

Additionally, an essential implication of increased active and restrictive mediation in the same week as online risks is that parents respond just-in-time to their teens' risk exposure by adjusting their mediation levels. Designers of online safety features or collaborative mediation apps should consider this immediate parental concern and create tools that provide teens with the option to ask for parental support or notify parents about online risks in a timely manner. One way to keep parents well-informed about online risks is to design real-time interventions or "nudges" [42] that can ensure timely parental support for the teen. However, implementing nudging interventions for online safety without compromising on teen's privacy and autonomy is a challenging task. As recently found by Badillo-Urquiola et al., teens often wish to keep their online activity and risks confidential from parents [43].

One approach that can negotiate differences or value conflicts between different stakeholders is Value Sensitive Design (VSD) [44], which aims to incorporate important human values into the design process. Previously, adolescent online safety researchers have employed VSD to identify and balance tensions between teen autonomy and parental control [45]. For instance, Badillo-Urquiola et al. [18] used VSD to design features for parental control apps that improve parent-teen communication and promoted values such as trust and support. To accommodate both parents and teens perspectives regarding parental mediation [46], we encourage future researchers to utilize collaborative approaches such as value sensitive design that integrate similar parent-teen values and resolve differences of parents and teens regarding mediation, leading to online safety strategies that can cater to all.

6.4 Limitations and Future Research

A limitation of our work is that we conducted this study with a relatively small sample size over a relatively short (two-month) period. Future work should recruit a larger and more diverse sample and extend the length of the study to span multiple years for more conclusive findings. Additionally, we used cross-lagged panel modeling which relies on a few assumptions, such as synchronicity [47], which assumes that all participants reported at the same time points. However, since we used rolling recruitment, participants did not report at the same times. This method also assumes stationarity - that the relationship between the independent and dependent variables is completely uniform across time points [47], which might not have been the case. Lastly, it assumes that there are no stable between group differences throughout the course of the study, leading to a higher rate of Type I errors [48]. Moreover, some of the patterns we uncovered may vary based on demographic information, such as the age and gender of the teen. Future work may overcome these limitations by using alternative methods, such as hierarchical linear modeling, that address between group differences and invariance when controlling such these factors. We also encourage adolescent online safety researchers to extend our work and take a socio-ecological perspective in studying bi-directional influences regarding online safety, by involving other support figures in the teens' life, including other family members, teachers, and peers.

7 Conclusion

We established the importance of bi-directional influences of parental mediation and teen's online risk exposure and identified gaps between parents' and teens' perception on parental mediation. We also introduced new narratives regarding the impact of teens' online experiences on parental mediation, such as parents reducing restrictions to support teens after negative online experiences. Our research sets the foundation for identifying significant bi-directional parent-teen influences in the same week which indicated quick parenting in response to online risks.

Acknowledgements. This research was partially supported by the William T. Grant Foundation (#187941, #190017) and National Science Foundation under grants CHS-1844881. Any opinion, findings, and conclusions or recommendations expressed in this material are those of the authors and do not necessarily reflect the views of our sponsor.

References

1. Livingstone, S., Smith, P.K.: Annual research review: harms experienced by child users of online and mobile technologies: the nature, prevalence and management of sexual and aggressive risks in the digital age. J. Child Psychol. Psychiatry **55**, 635–654 (2014). https://doi.org/10.1111/jcpp.12197
2. Anderson, M.: A Majority of Teens Have Experienced Some Form of Cyberbullying. https://www.pewinternet.org/2018/09/27/a-majority-of-teens-have-experienced-some-form-of-cyberbullying/. Accessed 03 Oct 2019
3. Yardi, S.A.: Social Media at the Boundaries: Supporting Parents in Managing Youth's Social Media Use. ProQuest LLC (2012)
4. Ashktorab, Z., Vitak, J.: Designing cyberbullying mitigation and prevention solutions through participatory design with teenagers. In: Proceedings of the 2016 CHI Conference on Human Factors in Computing Systems. pp. 3895–3905. Association for Computing Machinery, San Jose, California, USA (2016). https://doi.org/10.1145/2858036.2858548
5. Lee, S.-J.: Parental restrictive mediation of children's internet use: effective for what and for whom? New Media Soc. **15**, 466–481 (2013). https://doi.org/10.1177/1461444812452412
6. Livingstone, S., Helsper, E.J.: Parental mediation of children's internet use. J. Broadcast. Electron. Media. **52**, 581–599 (2008). https://doi.org/10.1080/08838150802437396
7. Eastin, M.S., Greenberg, B.S., Hofschire, L.: Parenting the internet. J. Commun. **56**, 486–504 (2006). https://doi.org/10.1111/j.1460-2466.2006.00297.x
8. Valcke, M., Bonte, S., De Wever, B., Rots, I.: Internet parenting styles and the impact on internet use of primary school children. Comput. Educ. **55**, 454–464 (2010). https://doi.org/10.1016/j.compedu.2010.02.009
9. Lee, S.-J., Chae, Y.-G.: Balancing participation and risks in children's internet use: the role of internet literacy and parental mediation. Cyberpsychology Behav. Soc. Networking. **15**, 257–262 (2012). https://doi.org/10.1089/cyber.2011.0552
10. Mendoza, K.: Surveying parental mediation: connections, challenges and questions for media literacy. J. Media Literacy Educ. **1**, 3 (2013)
11. Livingstone, S., Haddon, L., Görzig, A., Ólafsson, K.: The perspective of European children. 171 (2011)
12. Lwin, M., Stanaland, A., Miyazaki, A.: Protecting children's privacy online: how parental mediation strategies affect website safeguard effectiveness. J. Retail. **84**, 205–217 (2008). https://doi.org/10.1016/j.jretai.2008.04.004
13. Sorbring, E., Lundin, L.: Mothers' and fathers' insights into teenagers' use of the internet. New Media Soc. **14**, 1181–1197 (2012). https://doi.org/10.1177/1461444812440160
14. Wisniewski, P., Xu, H., Carroll, J., Rosson, M.B.: Grand challenges of researching adolescent online safety: a family systems approach. In: AMCIS 2013 Proceedings (2013)
15. Cummings, E.M., Bergman, K.N., Kuznicki, K.A.: Emerging methods for studying families as systems. In: McHale, S.M., Amato, P., Booth, A. (eds.) Emerging Methods in Family Research. pp. 95–108. Springer International Publishing, Cham (2014). https://doi.org/10.1007/978-3-319-01562-0_6.
16. Valkenburg, P.M., Krcmar, M., Peeters, A.L., Marseille, N.M.: Developing a scale to assess three styles of television mediation: Instructive mediation, restrictive mediation, and social coviewing. J Broadcast. Electron. Media. **43**, 52–66 (1999). https://doi.org/10.1080/08838159909364474
17. Ghosh, A.K., Badillo-Urquiola, K., Rosson, M.B., Xu, H., Carroll, J.M., Wisniewski, P.J.: A matter of control or safety?: Examining parental use of technical monitoring apps on teens' mobile devices. In: Proceedings of the 2018 CHI Conference on Human Factors in Computing Systems, CHI 2018, pp. 1–14. ACM Press, Montreal QC, Canada (2018). https://doi.org/10.1145/3173574.3173768

18. Badillo-Urquiola, K., Chouhan, C., Chancellor, S., De Choudhary, M., Wisniewski, P.: Beyond parental control: designing adolescent online safety apps using value sensitive design. J. Adolesc. Res. **35**, 147–175 (2020). https://doi.org/10.1177/0743558419884692

19. Erickson, L.B., Wisniewski, P., Xu, H., Carroll, J.M., Rosson, M.B., Perkins, D.F.: The boundaries between: parental involvement in a teen's online world. J. Assoc. Inf. Sci. Technol. **67**, 1384–1403 (2016). https://doi.org/10.1002/asi.23450

20. Ghosh, A.K., Hughes, C.E., Wisniewski, P.J.: Circle of trust: a new approach to mobile online safety for families. In: Proceedings of the 2020 CHI Conference on Human Factors in Computing Systems, pp. 1–14. Association for Computing Machinery, Honolulu, HI, USA (2020). https://doi.org/10.1145/3313831.3376747

21. Wisniewski, P., Xu, H., Rosson, M.B., Carroll, J.M.: Parents just don't understand: why teens don't talk to parents about their online risk experiences. In: Proceedings of the 2017 ACM Conference on Computer Supported Cooperative Work and Social Computing, CSCW 2017, pp. 523–540. ACM Press, Portland, Oregon, USA (2017). https://doi.org/10.1145/2998181.2998236

22. Cranor, L.F., Durity, A.L., Marsh, A., Ur, B.: Parents' and teens' perspectives on privacy in a technology-filled world. In: Presented at the 10th Symposium On Usable Privacy and Security ({SOUPS} 2014) (2014)

23. Livingstone, S., Haddon, L., Görzig, A., Ólafsson, K.: Risks and safety on the internet: the perspective of European children: full findings and policy implications from the EU Kids Online survey of 9–16 year olds and their parents in 25 countries. https://www.eukidsonline.net/. Accessed 02 Feb 2021

24. Yardi, S., Bruckman, A.: Social and technical challenges in parenting teens' social media use. In: Proceedings of the SIGCHI Conference on Human Factors in Computing Systems. pp. 3237–3246. Association for Computing Machinery, Vancouver, BC, Canada (2011). https://doi.org/10.1145/1978942.1979422

25. Blackwell, L., Gardiner, E., Schoenebeck, S.: Managing expectations: technology tensions among parents and teens. In: Proceedings of the 19th ACM Conference on Computer-Supported Cooperative Work & Social Computing, CSCW 2016, pp. 1388–1399. ACM Press, San Francisco, California, USA (2016). https://doi.org/10.1145/2818048.2819928

26. Wisniewski, P., Jia, H., Xu, H., Rosson, M.B., Carroll, J.M.: Preventative vs. Reactive: how parental mediation influences teens' social media privacy behaviors. In: Proceedings of the 18th ACM Conference on Computer Supported Cooperative Work & Social Computing. pp. 302–316. Association for Computing Machinery, Vancouver, BC, Canada (2015). https://doi.org/10.1145/2675133.2675293

27. Hiniker, A., Schoenebeck, S.Y., Kientz, J.A.: Not at the dinner table: parents' and children's perspectives on family technology rules. In: Proceedings of the 19th ACM Conference on Computer-Supported Cooperative Work & Social Computing. pp. 1376–1389. Association for Computing Machinery, New York (2016). https://doi.org/10.1145/2818048.2819940

28. Berson, I.R., Berson, M.J.: challenging online behaviors of youth: findings from a comparative analysis of young people in the United States and New Zealand. Soc. Sci. Comput. Rev. (2016). https://doi.org/10.1177/0894439304271532

29. Ghosh, A.K., Badillo-Urquiola, K., Guha, S., LaViola Jr, J.J., Wisniewski, P.J.: Safety vs. Surveillance: what children have to say about mobile apps for parental control. In: Proceedings of the 2018 CHI Conference on Human Factors in Computing Systems. CHI 2018, pp. 1–14. ACM Press, Montreal QC, Canada (2018). https://doi.org/10.1145/3173574.3173698

30. Schermerhorn, A.C., Cummings, E.M., Davies, P.T.: Children's representations of multiple family relationships: organizational structure and development in early childhood. J. Family Psychol. **22**, 89–101 (2008). https://doi.org/10.1037/0893-3200.22.1.89

31. Kitzman-Ulrich, H., Wilson, D.K., St. George, S.M., Lawman, H., Segal, M., Fairchild, A.: The integration of a family systems approach for understanding youth obesity, physical activity, and dietary programs. Clin. Child Fam. Psychol. Rev. **13**, 231–253 (2010). https://doi.org/ 10.1007/s10567-010-0073-0

32. Day, I.: A family systems approach to the understanding and treatment of internet gaming disorder. Family J. **25**, 264–270 (2017). https://doi.org/10.1177/1066480717711108

33. Koning, I.M., Peeters, M., Finkenauer, C., van den Eijnden, R.J.J.M.: Bidirectional effects of Internet-specific parenting practices and compulsive social media and Internet game use. J. Behav. Addict. **7**, 624–632 (2018). https://doi.org/10.1556/2006.7.2018.68

34. Kenny, D.A., Harackiewicz, J.M.: Cross-lagged panel correlation: practice and promise. J. Appl. Psychol. **64**(4), 372–379 (1979)

35. Kenny, D.: Cross-lagged panel correlation: a test for spuriousness. Psychol. Bull. **82**, 887–903 (1975). https://doi.org/10.1037/0033-2909.82.6.887

36. Volonte, M., Anaraky, R.G., Knijnenburg, B., Duchowski, A.T., Babu, S.V.: Empirical evaluation of the interplay of emotion and visual attention in human-virtual human interaction. In: ACM Symposium on Applied Perception 2019. pp. 1–9. Association for Computing Machinery, New York (2019). https://doi.org/10.1145/3343036.3343118

37. Yao, M.Z., Zhong, Z.: Loneliness, social contacts and Internet addiction: a cross-lagged panel study. Comput. Hum. Behav. **30**, 164–170 (2014). https://doi.org/10.1016/j.chb.2013.08.007

38. Quartana, P.J., Wickwire, E.M., Klick, B., Grace, E., Smith, M.T.: Naturalistic changes in insomnia symptoms and pain in temporomandibular joint disorder: a cross-lagged panel analysis. PAIN®. **149**, 325–331 (2010). https://doi.org/10.1016/j.pain.2010.02.029

39. Aguinis, H., Boik, R.J., Pierce, C.A.: A generalized solution for approximating the power to detect effects of categorical moderator variables using multiple regression. Organ. Res. Methods **4**, 291–323 (2001). https://doi.org/10.1177/109442810144001

40. Fisher, R.J.: Social desirability bias and the validity of indirect questioning. J. Consum. Res. **20**, 303–315 (1993). https://doi.org/10.1086/209351

41. Bray, L., Carter, B., Sanders, C., Blake, L., Keegan, K.: Parent-to-parent peer support for parents of children with a disability: a mixed method study. Patient Educ. Couns. **100**, 1537–1543 (2017). https://doi.org/10.1016/j.pec.2017.03.004

42. Masaki, H., Shibata, K., Hoshino, S., Ishihama, T., Saito, N., Yatani, K.: Exploring nudge designs to help adolescent SNS users avoid privacy and safety threats. In: Proceedings of the 2020 CHI Conference on Human Factors in Computing Systems, pp. 1–11. Association for Computing Machinery, Honolulu, HI, USA (2020). https://doi.org/10.1145/3313831.337 6666

43. Badillo-Urquiola, K., Shea, Z., Agha, Z., Lediaeva, I., Wisniewski, P.: Conducting risky research with teens: co-designing for the ethical treatment and protection of adolescents. Proc. ACM Hum.-Comput. Interact. **4**, 231:1–231:46 (2021). https://doi.org/10.1145/3432930

44. Friedman, B., Kahn, P.H., Borning, A.: Value sensitive design and information systems. In: Human-Computer Interaction and Management Information Systems: Foundations. M.E. Sharpe, pp. 348–372 (2006)

45. Czeskis, A., et al.: Parenting from the pocket: value tensions and technical directions for secure and private parent-teen mobile safety. In: Proceedings of the Sixth Symposium on Usable Privacy and Security. pp. 1–15. Association for Computing Machinery, New York (2010). https://doi.org/10.1145/1837110.1837130

46. Agha, Z., Chatlani, N., Razi, A., Wisniewski, P.: Towards conducting responsible research with teens and parents regarding online risks. In: Extended Abstracts of the 2020 CHI Conference on Human Factors in Computing Systems. pp. 1–8. Association for Computing Machinery, Honolulu, HI, USA (2020). https://doi.org/10.1145/3334480.3383073

47. Kearney, M.: Cross-Lagged Panel Analysis. Presented at the January 1 (2017)
48. Mund, M., Nestler, S.: Beyond the cross-lagged panel model: next-generation statistical tools for analyzing interdependencies across the life course. Adv. Life Course Res. **41**, 100249 (2019). https://doi.org/10.1016/j.alcr.2018.10.002

Understanding User Behavior, Information Exposure, and Privacy Risks in Managing Old Devices

Mahdi Nasrullah Al-Ameen[1]([⊠]), Tanjina Tamanna[2], Swapnil Nandy[3], and Huzeyfe Kocabas[1]

[1] Utah State University, Logan, USA
mahdi.al-ameen@usu.edu, huzeyfe.kocabas@aggiemail.usu.edu
[2] University of Dhaka, Dhaka, Bangladesh
[3] Jadavpur University, Kolkata, India

Abstract. The goal of this study is to understand the behavior of users from developing countries in managing an old device (e.g., computer, mobile phone), which has been replaced by a new device, or suffers from technical issues providing a notion that it may stop working soon. The prior work explored the ecology and challenges of repairing old devices in developing regions. However, it is still understudied how the strategies of people from developing countries in managing their personal information on old devices could impact their digital privacy. To address this gap in existing literature, we conducted semi-structured interview with 52 participants, including 37 participants living in two developing countries (e.g., Bangladesh, Turkey) and 15 first-generation immigrants from developing regions living in the USA. We found that users leave sensitive information, and online accounts logged in while they give away or sell their old devices. All of our immigrant participants in the USA keep backup of their personal data from an old device, however, some of them store that information in an unprotected medium. Instead of keeping backup, the participants living in Bangladesh and Turkey often keep the old device as a digital storage, or give away to someone where their right to access their information would be preserved. Based on our findings, we unpacked the relation between trust and privacy in managing old devices.

Keywords: Old device · Privacy risks · Qualitative study

1 Introduction

People use a wide-range of digital devices for communication, information storage, entertainment, and utility in everyday life. In this paper, the term: *'device'* refers to a mobile phone or computer/laptop, unless otherwise specified. In general, users purchase a new device once their current device stops working, or they identify any technical issue realizing that their device may stop working in the

A. Moallem (Ed.): HCII 2021, LNCS 12788, pp. 281–296, 2021.
https://doi.org/10.1007/978-3-030-77392-2_18

near future. They also purchase a new device to avail the state-of-art amenities. Here, we do not consider how long a device has been used by a user to denote it as an *old device*, rather for simplicity, any device that a user has replaced by a new device, or a device that suffers from technical issue showing a notion that it may stop working in the near future, is noted as an old device.

The study on sustainability [10] highlighted the importance of rethinking design to encourage the choice of supporting maintenance of old devices over decisions to discard and replace them. The prior study [22] showed that people in developing countries reuse their old devices through availing the repair services, where Jackson et al. [24] studied the importance and challenges of repairing an old device in the context of Bangladesh, a country in South Asia. The study of Ahmed et al. [2] unfolded the privacy risks of users in the Global South when they leave their mobile phones with repairers to fix the technical issues. In another work, Jang et al. [25] explored the privacy implications of user's trust on the repairers in a remote area at rural Philippines.

While prior studies examined the ecology and challenges of repairing old devices in developing countries, there is a dearth in existing literature to understand the privacy implications of users' behavior with managing their information in old devices. We addressed this gap in our work through investigating the following research questions: i) How do users manage their information once they identify that an old device may stop working in the near future? ii) How do users manage an old device and the information stored in it once they get a new device? iii) What are the privacy and security implications of users' strategies of managing their old devices and the information stored in those devices?

According to the recent studies [7,20,41], privacy is contextual that demands a situated understanding of users' perceptions and behavior in order to explore the design and policy practices. In this paper, we focused on the participants who currently live in a developing country (e.g., Bangladesh, Turkey) or are the immigrants from developing regions living in a developed country (e.g., USA). In particular, we interviewed 52 participants; 29 of them (denoted by *BP*) live in Bangladesh, eight of them (denoted by *TP*) live in Turkey, and 15 participants (denoted by *IP*) are first-generation immigrants in the USA who are originally from the developing countries located in different continents, including Bangladesh (located in South Asia), Turkey (a country straddling Eastern Europe and Western Asia), Bolivia (located in central South America), Nigeria (located in West Africa), and Pakistan (located in South Asia).

Our results unfold the strategies of participants in managing their information in an old device. All of our immigrant participants in the USA keep backup of their personal data from an old device, however, they often fail to understand the requirements and strategies for secure backup, and thus, end up with storing information and credentials in an unprotected medium. On the other hand, the participants living in Bangladesh and Turkey often keep the old device as a digital storage, or give away to someone where their right to access their information would be preserved. We identified the rationals behind users' choice of mediums to keep backup of information from their old devices, and discussed how these strategies could expose them to privacy risks due to their misconceptions, lack of technical efficacy, and dependency on caregivers.

We reported the unexpected incidents of information loss and exposure in the process of managing old devices. We found that users leave sensitive information (e.g., bank account number), and important online accounts logged in while they give away or sell their old device; in these contexts, our analysis unpacked how user's behavior is related to their situated trust on peers, risk perceptions, and the awareness of existing controls offered by a device. Taken together, our findings have important implications to advance the HCI and Privacy community's understanding of user behavior and corresponding privacy risks in managing old devices.

2 Related Work

In this section, we briefly describe the findings from notable prior studies on user's security and privacy behavior, followed by a discussion on existing literature in the context of situated privacy and security.

The study of Wash [43] identified eight 'folk models' of threat in the context of hackers and computer viruses – used by people in deciding which security software to use on their home computer. The findings from this study [43] shed light on how the users exploit these models to justify their insecure behavior in computing environment. In another study [23], Ion et al. compared the online security practices of expert and non-expert users, where they found differences in their security behavior. For instances, expert users generally install updates, use password manager, and leverage two-factor authentication, where the non-expert users prefer to use antivirus application, change their passwords, and visit only the known websites [23].

The study of Ruoti et al. [35] found that users' security behavior depend upon their understanding of a threat, evaluation of risks, and the estimation of impact, where they select coping strategies based on their evaluation of the trade-offs between potential harms and the costs to take protective measures. As reported by Habib et al. [19], users' motivations behind using private browsing mode could extend beyond the privacy reasons, e.g., to address their practical and security needs. People have certain misconceptions about private browsing mode, where they are found to overestimate the protection guarantee offered by private browsing mode, especially from online tracking and targeted advertising [19].

The study of Nthala et al. [32] identified a wide-range of security practices that exist when people ask for help from their social circles to address the security issues on their digital devices, where the survival or outcome bias, and availability and quality of security support impact people's security decisions in a home environment. Zou et al. [44] focused on Equifax data breach, where the findings revealed users' perceived risks of data leakage. The authors [44] identified the factors that could influence users towards not taking a protective measure, which include but not limited to the optimism bias, procrastination until harms occur, and the costs of taking a security-preserving action. In a separate study [18], Frik et al. found uncertainty among older adults about the information flow, and data persistence, which lead them to rely on ineffective security protection techniques.

The authors [18] also revealed the privacy and security misconceptions of older adults, for example, they tend to think that a user who has nothing to hide, does not need to protect her digital privacy.

2.1 Situated Privacy and Security

Privacy is contextual that demands a situated understanding of users' perceptions and behavior in order to explore the design and policy practices [15,30,33]. The findings from recent usable privacy studies [3,7,13] support this argument that local values often contrast with the liberal notions of privacy embedded in current computing systems. However, the digital privacy research beyond Western contexts and a liberal framing is still at its very early stage [14,42]. Below, we briefly discuss the notable usable privacy studies conducted outside the Western contexts.

Although online threats are global, perceptions of threat are very localized [7,13,20,26]. The study of Al-Ameen et al. [7] explored how the privacy perceptions of people relate to their effort to deal with the issues of urbanization and the opportunities that come with digitization in the Global South. The authors [7] examined how users balance their needs, conveniences, and privacy in the context of data collection and sharing by apps, and unveiled how privacy leakage incidents affect app usage behavior. The study of Haque et al. [20] presented how clientelization, reputation, and situated morality influence the privacy behavior of people in the digital service centers at Bangladesh. In another study [13], Chen et al. investigated the security and privacy practices of the people in urban Ghana while browsing Internet. The study [13] shows that participants judge the trustworthiness of a website based on the appearance, lack of popups, and loading speed, where they reported confidence of being able to defend against cyberattacks despite passwords often being their only line of defense.

The religious views and cultural norms of people have impacts on their sense of confidentiality and privacy. The study of Alghamdi et al. [8] investigated the privacy and security practices for households bank customers in Saudi Arabia, showing that trust, driving restrictions, and the esteem placed in family motivate female participants to share their banking information with male family members, including their father, and husband. The study of Abokhodair et al. [1] examined how the youth in the middle east conceptualize values such as privacy, intimacy, and freedom of expression in the context of social media. The authors [1] found that the interpretation of privacy among participants goes beyond the concerns for security, safety, and having a control to separate oneself from a larger group, where they observed adherence to Islamic teachings, maintenance of reputation, and the careful navigation of activity in social media to preserve respect and modesty.

Digital harassment is a growing concern in many developing countries, wherein the majority of cases, female users are the victims of such incidents [6,31]. The study of Nova et al. [31] reveals the online harassment that women in Bangladesh encounter while using anonymous social media (ASM).

Participants reported receiving sexually offensive messages and dating inquiries from the people in ASM. While public discussion on sex or any topic containing sexual content are considered taboo and frowned upon in Bangladesh [29,34], the curtain of anonymity in ASM provides a safer way to break these invisible norms of society without being judged or scrutinized. In another study, Sambasivan et al. [38] identified that the risks and fear of harassment refrained the women in urban India to provide their phone number for accessing public Wi-Fi services.

Digital devices, such as mobile phones that are designed for developing regions often fail to satisfy their local needs. In a study conducted with low-literate Berber women in Morocco [16], the authors examined the gap between high rates of mobile phone ownership and low use of productive features - noted as 'mobile utility gap'. The study identified that lack of functional literacy and non-standard mobile phone interface including a complex language environment with both Arabic and Berber dialects presented significant barriers to using mobile phones, which contributed to the mobile utility gap in that community. The studies conducted by Ahmed et al. [4] and Sambasivan et al. [37] demonstrate that the mobile phones often do not have one-to-one mapping with a user in the resource-constrained settings of developing countries, while the social fabric in these societies is based on the notions of trust and collectivism. Thus, the strict privacy requirements in using digital technology could disrupt the relationships with friends and family members [4,37]. In a separate study with women in Global South [36], the authors explored the privacy negotiation of female users from their family members while using a mobile phone.

Our Study. The overall findings from these studies indicate that the misconceptions about local culture by developers or designers may result in inappropriate threat modeling, where there is a dearth in existing literature to understand the behavior of users from developing countries in managing old devices. We addressed this gap in our work through investigating how users manage their old device and the information stored in it once they identify that their device may stop working in the near future or once they get a new device, where we identified the privacy implications of users' strategies in managing their old devices.

3   Methodology

We conducted semi-structured interview (audio-recorded) with 52 participants. We recruited participants through sharing the study information via email and online social media, posting flyers on public places, snowball sampling, and leveraging authors' personal connections. We interviewed the participants over telephone, via Skype, or in person. The study was approved by the Institutional Review Board at our university.

During interview, we asked participants about how they manage their information when they identify that an old device may stop working in the near future, and how they manage an old device and the information stored in it once

Table 1. The highlight of participants' demographic traits [*Either completed or currently studying at the noted education level]. **Note:** *IP*: Immigrant participants living in the USA; *BP*: Participants living in Bangladesh; *TP*: Participants living in Turkey

Gender	Participants
Male	BP1-BP3, BP6-BP9, BP11, BP15, BP17-BP29, IP1-IP4, IP7, IP8, IP9-IP11, IP13, IP14, IP15, TP1, TP3, TP4, TP6, TP8
Female	BP4, BP5, BP10, BP12-BP14, BP16, IP5, IP6, IP12, TP2, TP5, TP7
Age-range	
18–24	BP4, BP7, BP8, IP5, IP6, IP15
25–29	BP2, BP3, BP5, BP6, BP9, BP19, BP20, BP25, IP2, IP7-IP14, TP1-TP3
30–34	BP1, BP17, BP18, BP21, BP24, BP28, IP1, IP3
35–39	BP23, TP6
40–44	BP16, BP22, BP26, BP27, BP29, IP4
45–49	BP14, TP4, TP7
50–54	BP15, TP5, TP8
55+	BP10, BP11, BP12, BP13
Literacy level*	
Fifth Grade	BP19, BP27, BP29, TP6, TP7
Between eighth and Tenth grade	BP17, BP20, BP22, BP24, BP25, BP26, BP28, TP4
Twelfth grade	BP12, BP18, BP21, BP23, IP15, TP2, TP5, TP8
Undergraduate and above	BP1-BP11, BP13-BP16, IP1-IP14, TP1, TP3
Profession	
Student	BP4, BP5, BP7, BP9, IP1-IP3, IP6-IP13, IP15
Employee at Industry	BP1-BP3, BP6, BP8, BP11, BP17-BP19, BP21-BP29, IP5, TP3, TP4, TP6
Employee at Educational	BP10, BP15, IP4, IP14
Or non-profit org	TP1
Car driver	BP20
Housewife	BP12-BP14, TP2, TP5, TP7
Physician	BP16
Retired	TP8

they get a new one. Then they were asked about their experiences of dealing with old devices that they had purchased or received as gifts, and the past incidents of information loss and privacy breach in the process of managing old devices.

At the end, participants answered a set of demographic questionnaire. On average, each session took between 20 and 30 min.

The interview was audio recorded. We transcribed the audio recordings at the end of data collection. We conducted the interview in English with the immigrant participants living in the USA. For the participants living in Bangladesh and Turkey, the authors of this paper who are originally from these countries conducted the interview in their local language (e.g., Bengali, Turkish), and translated the transcriptions into English.

We performed thematic analysis on our transcriptions [11,12]. Two researchers independently read through the transcripts of half of the interviews, developed codes, compared them, and then iterated again with more interviews until we had developed a consistent codebook. Once the codebook was finalized, two researchers divided up the remaining interviews and coded them. After all interviews had been coded, both researchers spot-checked the other's coded transcripts and did not find any inconsistencies. Finally, we organized and taxonomized our codes into higher-level categories.

Participants. Among our 52 participants, 13 of them are women, and 39 are men. Table 1 presents their demographic information. Most of our participants were in the age range of 18 to 55, where four participants were above 55 years old. 60% of our participants were either undergraduate students or had already earned the degree, where the literacy level of other participants were between fifth and twelfth grade. 31% of our participants were students, where others were from diverse professions, including physician, car driver, housewife, and the employee at industry, educational institution, or non-profit organization.

4 Results

In this section, we report the findings from our study. We used following terms to represent the frequency of comments in participants' responses: *a few* (0–10%), *several* (10–25%), *some* (25–40%), *about half* (40–60%), *most* (60–80%), and *almost all* (80–100%).

4.1 Managing Accessibility to Information

All of our immigrant participants living in the USA have reported that when they identify any technical issue in an old device giving a notion that it may stop working in the near future, they keep backup of at least some of their information. On the other hand, most of the participants living in Bangladesh and Turkey do not keep backup from their old devices.

Participants Who Keep Backup. Among participants who keep backup of their information, most of them use the external hard drive, USB flash drive, or online cloud storage. The participants who prefer local storage (e.g., hard drive/USB flash drive) to cloud service to keep backup from an old device, emphasized on two reasons behind their preference. First, local storage gives them a sense of security that no one would be able to gain their personal documents without having a physical access to their storage devices. The less-understood security threats (e.g., how an online hacking works [17]) make some participants less comfortable with storing their sensitive information in a cloud storage. Second, several participants reported concern about the internet speed and delays involved in uploading documents to the cloud storage.

A few participants email their important documents to themselves, or use social networking accounts to store photos and information from their old devices. IP19 stores the username and password of her online accounts in a file on her computer. When she identifies any technical issue in her device realizing that it may stop working in the near future, she writes down her authentication secrets on a paper, so that she could later restore that once a new device is purchased.

Participants Who Do Not Keep Backup. Participants who do not keep back up of their information, try to ensure their access to that after purchasing a new device in one of three different ways: i) They keep the old device as a digital storage of their personal documents and information; ii) They give away an old device to someone for use, where their right to access documents (as a previous owner) will be preserved; iii) They directly transfer their documents to the new device.

Our participant, BP11 used to directly transfer his information to a new device from the old one. According to him, *"I am not a technical person and don't know much about transferring documents...While transferring I lost many of my data before. When I was transferring data to my new device somehow these information were missed out and eventually got deleted."* Thus, he now keeps his old device with him (a new one is purchased, too) along with his documents and information stored in it. Several participants, who live in Bangladesh, take help from their family members to directly transfer the documents and photos from the old device to a new one. For instance, BP13 requests her daughter to complete the transfer process for her. Participants also reported taking help from their friends and colleagues (whom they mentioned as 'tech-savvy') to transfer their documents to the new device.

4.2 Privacy Protection Strategies

Our participants reported to handle the old device (once they get a new one) in one of three different ways: they keep the device, give it to a family member or friend as a gift, or sell it. In this section, we present our findings on users' strategies to protect their privacy as they adopt one of these three approaches to manage their old devices.

Keeping Old Devices. As discussed in Sect. 4.1, keeping the old device is considered as a potential way to preserve personal information and documents. IP3 commented, *"I have all of my old devices with me. I didn't throw them out because I'm worried about what will happen with my information, my apps that are in that cell phone."* Several participants living in Bangladesh and Turkey keep the old device as a backup one, so that they could use it in case their current device gets broken or lost, where BP5 said, *"If the device can still be used then I keep that as a backup device as long it survives, and if the device is dead then I dump it."* Most of the participants in these two groups who keep the old device as a backup one, or use it to keep their information stored, do not sign out of their online accounts, nor delete any of their information from the device. They keep their old devices in a container, drawer, or under the cabinet at their home with no apparent physical security (e.g., using a physical lock).

A few participants, who live in Bangladesh, mentioned keeping the old device so that their family members could use it for entertainment, where they do not take any steps to protect their privacy while sharing the device. For instance, BP12 said, *"Old devices remain in the house, used by my youngest grandson for playing games. All information remain intact in there. All applications and accounts are logged in."* On the other hand, IP5 worried about the security and privacy risks of giving away or selling an old device. She reported concern that the adversary might find a backdoor to access her information even if she deletes that from her device; she added, *"Right now I just keep all the old devices with me just for security, because I don't know what [else] to do with [an old device]."*

Giving Away Old Devices. Around one-third of our participants reported that they give their old device as a present to their family member or friend. Among them, several participants keep their personal information stored, and the online accounts logged in while giving a device to the recipient. IP14 gives his old laptop to his family member whom he trusts. He is not willing to sell the device as he worried that the information in his device could be exposed to a stranger in that case. Several participants referred to trust as the reason why they did not delete any information from their old smartphone while giving it to their friend or family member. Here, we identified situated trust among participants while giving away their old devices. For instance, IP2 was comfortable with keeping his online accounts logged in while giving his old smartphone as a present to his girlfriend, who, however, would prefer to factory-reset the device if he would give it to any of his other friends.

Several participants living in Bangladesh and Turkey prefer to give the old device to their friend or family member instead of selling it to a stranger, so that they could preserve their right to access their personal information residing in that device, and could retrieve any photos or documents as per their need in the future. The participants in this group did not delete any information from the old device while giving it away for their friend or family member to use. In this context, a few participants intend to keep a balance between having the information stored in their old device while giving it away and protecting that from being exposed to the recipient. Here, TP8 chose to hid his personal information inside his old computer while giving it away, and expressed his belief that the recipient's technical efficacy would not suffice to retrieve that information from a secret folder in the device.

Several participants reported taking steps to protect their information while giving away their computer or mobile phone for someone else to use. We found instances where participants factory-reset the old device before giving it away, where several other participants mentioned, they had deleted some of their information and documents from the old device depending upon their relationship with the recipient. The perceptions of relations, and so on, the protection strategies varied among participants. For instance, IP12 trusts her siblings with the photos and documents in her smartphone. So, she only signed out of her online accounts and kept other information stored in the phone as she gave it to her sibling.

Selling Old Devices. About one-fifth of our participants reported selling the old device to a previously unknown person (no participant reported selling an old device to someone they already knew, e.g., a friend or family member), where above half of them reported that they had factory-reset their device before handing it over to the buyer. Among other participants who sold their old devices, some of them signed out of their online accounts, but did not delete any of their information, documents, or photos from their devices, where other participants deleted those information only, that they considered would put their privacy into risks if exposed to a stranger. We found that several participants were not aware of the factory-reset option available in their phones.

4.3 Information Loss and Exposure

Participants' Information. Several participants reported unpleasant experiences of information loss and privacy breach from their old devices. A few of our participants who used an old computer to store files and information instead of keeping a backup in an external storage, lost access to their documents when their device stopped working. IP12 lost access to personal documents stored in her old phone that she used to use before she purchased a new phone, as she could no longer recall the password to unlock her old phone.

IP2 did not keep backup of his personal documents stored in his smartphone, when he sent it to the manufacturer for fixing a technical issue. He expected that the device would be returned after a repair, however, instead he received a new device as a replacement. As a result, IP2 lost access to all of his information in that old phone. A few participants living in Bangladesh reported the privacy risks when they avail cost-savvy third-party services to repair their old devices. BP5 reported an incident, where she found that her personal information from her mobile phone was accessed by the repairer without taking her permission.

Others' Information. Above one-third of our participants reported receiving a used device through purchase or as a present from someone they know, where about half of them found personal information of the previous owner residing in that old computer or mobile phone.

Several participants living in Bangladesh have reported that they are trusted with the information in a device when they receive it as a gift from their family member. BP12 received a smartphone from her husband, where she said, *"Every information of my husband is still in there [smartphone]. He just gave me the device, and all his apps, photos, videos, contact numbers, and messages were in there."* In the case of BP20, participant's family member who gave away her mobile phone, explicitly requested the recipient (BP20) not to delete her personal information residing in that device, so that those information could be accessed by that family member in the future. In some instances, the previous owner puts trust on the recipient to delete their personal information from the device and sign out of their online accounts. BP25 who received a used smartphone from his elder brother, said, *"He [elder brother] showed me the way of resetting the device and following his way, I reset the device and started using it. Before resetting everything was intact in his device which I used for one or two days."*

Our findings indicate that personal information of users may remain in the used mobile phones and computers when those devices are sold. IP2 purchased a smartphone where he found the financial information (e.g., bank account number) of the previous owner. A few participants noticed that the previous owner did not sign out of social networking and communication apps. BP3 said, *"I am using a second-hand laptop, and the laptop contained all the information of the previous owner."* In such instances, participants reported deleting the stored information and signing out of online accounts of the previous owner of the device.

5   Discussion

Security Perceptions and Behavior. The participants living in the USA use different mediums to keep backup of their information from an old device, where a local storage device (e.g., external hard drive, USB flash drive), although not protected by passwords, provides them with a higher sense of security than a password-protected cloud storage service. The physical possession of a local storage device, coupled with participants' uncertainty about the attacker's strategies to steal information from an online server, contributed to their higher comfort level with keeping backup in an external hard drive or USB flash drive. We found instances where participants perceive that if the adversaries get physical access to their old devices, they would manage to find a backdoor to access all of their information including the deleted ones. So, they see no security benefits in deleting personal documents from an old device although it is no longer in use, and prefer to keep the device instead of selling or giving it away, to protect their personal information.

Trust and Privacy. Participants' approach towards information management while giving away an old device depends upon their situated trust on the recipient. In some instances, participants simply believe that the recipient would not access their information, while in other cases, they explicitly ask to delete their information and trust the recipient with doing so. We found that several participants living in Bangladesh and Turkey want to preserve their right to access information in the old device while giving it away to a friend of family member. Their personal information remains stored in that device, and in most cases, they trust the recipient with protecting their information. While prior studies [21,28] revealed the risks of privacy violation and digital abuse when there occurs a change in trust and relationship, we suggest that the future research should further investigate the privacy implications for the previous owner of an old device as their relationship with the recipient of that device changes over time.

Technical (In)Efficacy and Privacy Risks. Due to the lack of technical efficacy, several participants living in Bangladesh take help from others to transfer documents from the old device to a new one. To avail such help, participants need to share their devices with caregivers, which may pose privacy risks to them as shown in prior studies on mobile phone sharing in Bangladesh [5,36]. Our results reveal that users leave sensitive personal information in their old devices while selling, or giving those away. One reason behind such behavior is the unawareness of available features (e.g., factory-reset option in mobile phone) to protect user privacy.

Limitations. In this study, we followed the widely-used method for qualitative research [9,11,12], where we focused in depth on a small number of participants and continued the interviews until no new themes emerged (saturation). We acknowledge the limitations of such study that a different set of samples might yield varying results. Our sample size is not uniformly distributed across geographic regions, or demographic traits. For instance, the age of most of our participants were below 55, where three-fourth of our participants identified as male. Thus, we do not draw any quantitative, generalizable conclusion from this study. In addition, self-reported data might have limitations, like recall and observer bias.

Our study is based in urban areas. We note that users' privacy perceptions might be different in rural areas. Since users' security and privacy perceptions are positively influenced by their knowledge and technical efficacy [23,27,39], and the literacy rate is generally higher in urban areas as compared to that in rural areas [40], we speculate that the privacy perceptions and behavior of users reported in this paper represent an upper bound in the context of managing old devices.

6   Conclusion

Our study unpacked users' strategies of managing information in their old devices, and revealed the underlying privacy risks. Based on our findings, we shed light on users' security and privacy perceptions of storage mediums to keep backup of information from an old device, identified the relation between trust and privacy, and discussed how the lack of technical efficacy and awareness of available tools and features could expose users' private information in the context of managing old devices. In our future work, we would extend the findings from this study through a large-scale online survey with the participants from diverse demographic traits, backgrounds, and technical efficacy.

References

1. Abokhodair, N., Vieweg, S.: Privacy & social media in the context of the arab gulf. In: Proceedings of the 2016 ACM Conference on Designing Interactive Systems, DIS 2016, pp. 672–683. Association for Computing Machinery, New York (2016). https://doi.org/10.1145/2901790.2901873
2. Ahmed, S.I., Guha, S., Rifat, M.R., Shezan, F.H., Dell, N.: Privacy in repair: an analysis of the privacy challenges surrounding broken digital artifacts in Bangladesh. In: Proceedings of the Eighth International Conference on Information and Communication Technologies and Development, pp. 1–10 (2016)
3. Ahmed, S.I., Guha, S., Rifat, M.R., Shezan, F.H., Dell, N.: Privacy in repair: an analysis of the privacy challenges surrounding broken digital artifacts in Bangladesh. In: Proceedings of the Eighth International Conference on Information and Communication Technologies and Development, ICTD 2016, pp. 11:1–11:10. ACM, New York (2016). https://doi.org/10.1145/2909609.2909661
4. Ahmed, S.I., Haque, M.R., Chen, J., Dell, N.: Digital privacy challenges with shared mobile phone use in Bangladesh. In Proceedings of the ACM on Human-Computer Interaction, (CSCW), vol. 1, pp. 17:1–17:20 (December 2017). https://doi.org/10.1145/3134652
5. Ahmed, S.I., Haque, M.R., Chen, J., Dell, N.: Digital privacy challenges with shared mobile phone use in Bangladesh. In: Proceedings of the ACM on Human-Computer Interaction, (CSCW), vol. 1, p. 17 (2017)
6. Ahmed, S.I., et al.: Protibadi: a platform for fighting sexual harassment in urban bangladesh. In: Proceedings of the SIGCHI Conference on Human Factors in Computing Systems, CHI 2014, pp. 2695–2704. Association for Computing Machinery, New York (2014). https://doi.org/10.1145/2556288.2557376
7. Al-Ameen, M.N., Tamanna, T., Nandy, S., Ahsan, M.A.M., Chandra, P., Ahmed, S.I.: We don't give a second thought before providing our information: understanding users' perceptions of information collection by apps in urban Bangladesh. In: Proceedings of the 3rd ACM SIGCAS Conference on Computing and Sustainable Societies (COMPASS 2020), pp. 32–43. Association for Computing Machinery, New York (2020). https://doi.org/10.1145/3378393.3402244
8. Alghamdi, D., Flechais, I., Jirotka, M.: Security practices for households bank customers in the kingdom of Saudi Arabia. In: Proceedings of the Eleventh USENIX Conference on Usable Privacy and Security, SOUPS 2015, pp. 297–308. USENIX Association, USA (2015)

9. Baxter, K., Courage, C., Caine, K.: Understanding Your Users: A Practical Guide to User Research Methods, 2nd edn. Morgan Kaufmann Publishers Inc., San Francisco (2015)
10. Blevis, E.: Sustainable interaction design: invention & disposal, renewal & reuse. In: Proceedings of the SIGCHI Conference on Human Factors in Computing Systems, pp. 503–512 (2007)
11. Boyatzis, R.E.: Transforming Qualitative Information: Thematic Analysis and Code Development. Sage, Thousand Oaks (1998)
12. Braun, V., Clarke, V.: Using thematic analysis in psychology. Qual. Res. Psychol. **3**(2), 77–101 (2006)
13. Chen, J., Paik, M., McCabe, K.: Exploring internet security perceptions and practices in urban Ghana. In: Proceedings of the Tenth USENIX Conference on Usable Privacy and Security, SOUPS 2014, pp. 129–142. USENIX Association, USA (2014)
14. Cobb, C., Sudar, S., Reiter, N., Anderson, R., Roesner, F., Kohno, T.: Computer security for data collection technologies. Dev. Eng. **3**, 1–11 (2018)
15. Crabtree, A., Tolmie, P., Knight, W.: Repacking 'privacy' for a networked world. Comput. Supported Coop. Work **26**(4-6), 453–488 (2017). https://doi.org/10.1007/s10606-017-9276-y
16. Dodson, L.L., Sterling, S.R., Bennett, J.K.: Minding the gaps: cultural, technical and gender-based barriers to mobile use in oral-language Berber communities in morocco. In: Proceedings of the Sixth International Conference on Information and Communication Technologies and Development, ICTD 2013, vol. 1, pp. 79–88. Association for Computing Machinery, New York (2013). https://doi.org/10.1145/2516604.2516626
17. Florêncio, D., Herley, C., Van Oorschot, P.C.: An administrator's guide to internet password research. In: 28th Large Installation System Administration Conference (LISA 2014), pp. 44–61 (2014)
18. Frik, A., Nurgalieva, L., Bernd, J., Lee, J., Schaub, F., Egelman, S.: Privacy and security threat models and mitigation strategies of older adults. In: Fifteenth Symposium on Usable Privacy and Security (SOUPS 2019) (2019)
19. Habib, H., et al.: Away from prying eyes: analyzing usage and understanding of private browsing. In: Fourteenth Symposium on Usable Privacy and Security (SOUPS 2018), pp. 159–175 (2018)
20. Haque, S.M.T., et al.: Privacy vulnerabilities in public digital service centers in Dhaka, Bangladesh. In: Proceedings of the 2020 International Conference on Information and Communication Technologies and Development, ICTD 2020, Association for Computing Machinery, New York (2020). https://doi.org/10.1145/3392561.3394642
21. Havron, S., Freed, D., Chatterjee, R., McCoy, D., Dell, N., Ristenpart, T.: Clinical computer security for victims of intimate partner violence. In: 28th USENIX Security Symposium, pp. 105–122 (2019)
22. Houston, L., Jackson, S.J., Rosner, D.K., Ahmed, S.I., Young, M., Kang, L.: Values in repair. In: Proceedings of the 2016 CHI Conference on Human Factors in Computing Systems, pp. 1403–1414 (2016)
23. Ion, I., Reeder, R., Consolvo, S.: ...no one can hack my mind: Comparing expert and non-expert security practices. In: Proceedings of the Eleventh USENIX Conference on Usable Privacy and Security, SOUPS 2015, pp. 327–346. USENIX Association, USA (2015)
24. Jackson, S.J., Ahmed, S.I., Rifat, M.R.: Learning, innovation, and sustainability among mobile phone repairers in Dhaka, Bangladesh. In: Proceedings of the 2014 Conference on Designing Interactive Systems, pp. 905–914 (2014)

25. Jang, E.H.B., et al.: Trust and technology repair infrastructures in the remote rural Philippines: Navigating urban-rural seams. In: Proceedings of the ACM on Human-Computer Interaction (CSCW), vol. 3, pp. 1–25 (2019)
26. Kumaraguru, P., Cranor, L.: Privacy in India: attitudes and awareness. Priv. Enhancing Technol. **3856**, 243–258 (2006)
27. Mazurek, M.L., et al.: Measuring password guess ability for an entire university. In: Proceedings of the 2013 ACM SIGSAC Conference on Computer & Communications Security, CCS 2013, pp. 173–186. Association for Computing Machinery, New York (2013). https://doi.org/10.1145/2508859.2516726
28. McCormick, L.: The internet and social media sites: A shift in privacy norms resulting in the exploitation and abuse of adolescents and teens in dating relationships. Alb. Gov't L. Rev. **7**, 591 (2014)
29. Nahar, P., Van Reeuwijk, M., Reis, R.: Contextualising sexual harassment of adolescent girls in Bangladesh. Reprod. Health matters **21**(41), 78–86 (2013)
30. Nissenbaum, H.: Privacy as contextual integrity. Wash L. Rev **79**, 119 (2004)
31. Nova, F.F., Rifat, M.R., Saha, P., Ahmed, S.I., Guha, S.: Online sexual harassment over anonymous social media in Bangladesh. In: Proceedings of the Tenth International Conference on Information and Communication Technologies and Development, ICTD 2019, pp. 1:1–1:12. ACM, New York (2019). https://doi.org/10.1145/3287098.3287107
32. Nthala, N., Flechais, I.: Informal support networks: an investigation into home data security practices. In: Fourteenth Symposium on Usable Privacy and Security (SOUPS 2018), pp. 63–82 (2018)
33. Patrick, A.S., Kenny, S.: From privacy legislation to interface design: implementing information privacy in human-computer interactions. In: Dingledine, R. (ed.) PET 2003. LNCS, vol. 2760, pp. 107–124. Springer, Heidelberg (2003). https://doi.org/10.1007/978-3-540-40956-4_8
34. Rashid, S.F., Standing, H., Mohiuddin, M., Ahmed, F.M.: Creating a public space and dialogue on sexuality and rights: a case study from Bangladesh. Health Res. Policy Syst. **9**(1), S12 (2011)
35. Ruoti, S., Monson, T., Wu, J., Zappala, D., Seamons, K.: Weighing context and trade-offs: How suburban adults selected their online security posture. In: Thirteenth Symposium on Usable Privacy and Security (SOUPS 2017), pp. 211–228 (2017)
36. Sambasivan, N., et al.: Privacy is not for me, it's for those rich women: performative privacy practices on mobile phones by women in south Asia. In: Fourteenth Symposium on Usable Privacy and Security (SOUPS 2018), pp. 127–142. USENIX Association, Baltimore (August 2018). https://www.usenix.org/conference/soups2018/presentation/sambasivan
37. Sambasivan, N., Rangaswamy, N., Cutrell, E., Nardi, B.: Ubicomp4d: infrastructure and interaction for international development-the case of urban Indian slums. In: Proceedings of the 11th International Conference on Ubiquitous Computing, UbiComp 2009, pp. 155–164. Association for Computing Machinery, New York (2009). https://doi.org/10.1145/1620545.1620570
38. Sambasivan, N., Weber, J., Cutrell, E.: Designing a phone broadcasting system for urban sex workers in India. In: Proceedings of the SIGCHI Conference on Human Factors in Computing Systems, CHI 2011, pp. 267–276. Association for Computing Machinery, New York (2011). https://doi.org/10.1145/1978942.1978980

39. Seng, S., Kocabas, H., Al-Ameen, M.N., Wright, M.: Poster: Understanding user's decision to interact with potential phishing posts on Facebook using a vignette study. In: Proceedings of the 2019 ACM SIGSAC Conference on Computer and Communications Security, CCS 2019, pp. 2617–2619. Association for Computing Machinery, New York (2019). https://doi.org/10.1145/3319535.3363270
40. of Statistics, B.B.: Literacy assessment survey 2008 (November 2008). http://www.un-bd.org/Docs/Publication/Bangladesh_Literacy_Assessment_Survey_2008.pdf
41. Sultana, S., et al.: Understanding the sensibility of social media use and privacy with Bangladeshi Facebook group users. In: Proceedings of the 3rd ACM SIGCAS Conference on Computing and Sustainable Societies (COMPASS 2020), pp. 317–318. Association for Computing Machinery, New York (2020). https://doi.org/10.1145/3378393.3402235
42. Vashistha, A., Anderson, R., Mare, S.: Examining security and privacy research in developing regions. In: Proceedings of the 1st ACM SIGCAS Conference on Computing and Sustainable Societies (COMPASS 2018), COMPASS-18, Association for Computing Machinery, New York (2018). https://doi.org/10.1145/3209811.3209818
43. Wash, R.: Folk models of home computer security. In: Proceedings of the Sixth Symposium on Usable Privacy and Security, pp. 1–16 (2010)
44. Zou, Y., Mhaidli, A.H., McCall, A., Schaub, F.: I've got nothing to lose: Consumers' risk perceptions and protective actions after the Equifax data breach. In: Fourteenth Symposium on Usable Privacy and Security (SOUPS 2018), pp. 197–216 (2018)

Perceptions of Security and Privacy in mHealth

Ana Ferreira[1]([⊠]) [iD], Joana Muchagata[3] [iD], Pedro Vieira-Marques[1] [iD],
Diogo Abrantes[4] [iD], and Soraia Teles[2] [iD]

[1] CINTESIS – Center for Health Technologies and Services Research, Faculty of Medicine,
University of Porto, Rua Plácido Costa, 4200-450 Porto, Portugal
`{amlaf,pmarques}@med.up.pt`

[2] CINTESIS – Center for Health Technologies and Services Research, ICBAS, University of
Porto, Rua Jorge de Viterbo Ferreira 228, 4050-313 Porto, Portugal

[3] Independent Researcher, Porto, Portugal

[4] Faculty of Science, University of Porto, Rua do Campo Alegre s/n, 4169-007 Porto, Portugal

Abstract. Mobile health applications have a great potential in improving patient's
monitoring and adherence to therapeutics, anytime/anywhere. However, security
is often overlooked in the design of those applications, and their low adoption
is partially explained by end-users' security and privacy concerns. A change of
the current "one-app-fits-all" paradigm to a more customized view of mHealth
security features, for different user groups, skills, concerns or contexts, is required.
This study aims to explore if content, context and users' characteristics, influence
the perception of security and privacy in mHealth apps. An anonymous online
survey was administered to social network users (n = 69). Statistically significant
associations were found between age and security variables such as: i) type of
requested data, ii) type of connection used and iii) access to sensitive health data
comprising a child's records. Other statistically significant associations were found
between the access to specific health sensitive data and the type of connection and
device used. Pursuing this line of research has the potential to help mapping
users' privacy and security perceptions to mHealth data. This can promote a better
understanding of how ensuing apps should be visually, technically and security-
wise.

Keywords: MHealth · Privacy and security · Users' perceptions and
interaction · Users' acceptance and awareness

1 Introduction

Mobile health applications (mHealth apps) have great potential in increasing healthcare
quality and adherence to therapeutics, anytime/anywhere, as well as expanding access to
services, reducing services' costs, and improving personal wellness and public health [1,
2]. However, mHealth also raises significant privacy and security challenges [3]. *Ethics,
Privacy and Security* was categorized as one of the seven great challenges in Human
Computer Interaction (HCI) [4]. In fact, low adoption of mHealth solutions has been
reported and is also explained by users' security and privacy concerns [5]. Moreover, the

© Springer Nature Switzerland AG 2021
A. Moallem (Ed.): HCII 2021, LNCS 12788, pp. 297–309, 2021.
https://doi.org/10.1007/978-3-030-77392-2_19

perceived risk of information sharing can be one of the most important determinants of privacy behaviour [6]. For example, individuals who have stronger privacy preferences should perceive the risk of information sharing to be higher.

When interactions with healthcare technology are devised having in mind users' privacy and security, in a transparent and usable way, the sense of trust in that technology increases and so does the probability to a continuous patient's adherence to that technology [7].

In order to disrupt the way mHealth security has been tackled until now, we need a change from the current "one-app-fits-all" paradigm to a more customized view of mHealth security features for different user groups, skills, concerns or contexts [8].

Although future developments of mHealth technology need to integrate patients' perceptions of risk, trust, ease of use and usefulness of mHealth technology, little attention has been paid to understanding technology acceptance in mHealth with a particular focus on privacy and security [9].

This study aims to explore if content, context and users' characteristics, influence the perception of security and privacy in mHealth apps. Only by truly understanding how patients perceive and trust their interactions with those apps, can these be adapted to their real needs and requirements. This is even more urgent in current pandemic times: on one hand, chronically ill or emergency patients may need to improve their autonomy to closely monitor their health outcomes; one the other hand, the general population facing the lockdown may benefit from similar services.

Next section provides more validation on the explored topic while Sect. 3 indicates the methods used to study the perceptions of security and privacy of mHealth users. Section 4 presents the results of the study; Sect. 5 discusses the results and Sect. 6 concludes the paper.

2   Background

2.1   Privacy, Security and Trust

Privacy is a fundamental human right of individuals to maintain their personal data private [10], while security is composed of the actual measures to assure that such rights are guaranteed in practice. These two concepts can influence the way technology is used and how and if it complies with mandatory legislation (Fig. 1). This means that interactional, technical and legal aspects need to converge to provide a more comprehensive privacy protection when patients interact with mHealth technology. By guaranteeing privacy and trust, safer and better health results can be achieved, with patients getting more empowered and more in control of their personal health data protection.

Once users are confident that their personal and sensitive data are kept private within certain technological solutions, they can be more willing to trust and use them. The continued use of technology in healthcare can lead to an increased adherence to therapeutics, which may have a serious impact on patients' health. Thus, increased privacy and trust can help promoting patients' wellbeing and safety.

But this is not all. When security is integrated into the technology, it needs to support the regulations and legislation that are mandatory to comply with. Moreover, this integration directly affects how users interact with the technology and this is bidirectional:

i) the way users interact with technology can affect security and privacy of their data, and ii) how security measures are built into the technology can also influence how the users will react and use the available functionalities. All this affects and dynamically builds the perceptions that end users have during such interactions.

Figure 1 illustrates how privacy, security and trust are related and how these can affect interactions with technology.

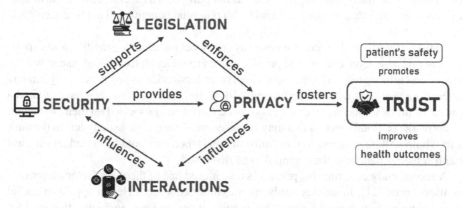

Fig. 1. Privacy, security, trust and their relation (based on [11]).

2.2 mHealth – Drawbacks and Breakthroughs

Current mHealth solutions have several drawbacks such as: i) limited connection between patients and professionals; ii) technical issues; iii) lack of awareness; iv) different skills and adoption rates according to age groups; v) low levels of patients' and professionals' satisfaction [12]; and vi) privacy and security concerns [12, 13]. These issues need to be taken into consideration when exploring the full potential of mHealth solutions. Due to the uncertainty and lack of validation of mHealth content [14, 15], health professionals themselves are also wary of recommending mHealth apps to their patients [14], but their support can be crucial to a successful implementation of such solutions [13].

There is a need to disrupt the way mHealth is being developed and made available because this technology has the potential to improve and enhance health outcomes. This was evidenced in some areas, where mHealth enables early detection of problems which can lead to: swift therapeutic response or remote reassurance [16, 17], improve medication adherence [18, 19] or perform digital diagnostic for low-income patients or where expert clinical advice is difficult to access [20].

However, since there is not a significant and continued use of mHealth, it is difficult to study and generate high-quality evidence of mHealth impact on patients' health outcomes. One of the main challenges still is privacy and security so systems need to integrate both social and technical measures to address this problem [13]. Researchers and practitioners in the mHealth field would benefit from better understanding how users perceive and experience privacy and security and how this can be effectively translated into the mHealth practice.

2.3   mHealth – End-Users' Perceptions

Although mHealth apps, as an innovative technology, can transform the way healthcare is performed, the continued use of those apps depends on the extent to which patients trust in their safety and security. One work in the literature discusses that trust in this field may only be achieved with the application of traditional regulatory mechanisms, which will certainly limit the potential that this technology can have [15]. If patients are not willing to use the technology because it is not perceived as useful, easy to use or they have concerns over data security, then mHealth potential benefits will not be concretized [9].

This is why we need to propose new ways to foster better understanding and experiences in mHealth. Concerns around privacy related to mHealth technology use as well as privacy and information sharing, remain poorly understood, and this most likely hinders patients' engagement with that technology [9]. Mobile devices and apps have created a new set of privacy concerns because data can be stored and processed on them, or shared via networks or cloud services that may be unsecure. Patients are usually left in the dark as to whom will have access to their information, where it would be stored and if their health sensitive data have the potential to be disclosed.

A recent study confirms that privacy is considered one of the main factors determining users' trust [21]. In another study, although patients see mHealth apps as a useful complementary tool, some problems relate to their optimal use, including the need for more personalized designs, the cost that some of these apps incur, the validity of the information delivered, and, again, security and privacy issues [22].

On the way to understand the attributes of mHealth apps that would make them trustworthy to their users, a study [21] derived 5 main categories:

1. *Informational content* - users expect mHealth content to be informed by robust research, be clearly explained and provide transparency on how their data are processed;
2. *Organizational attributes* – well-known branding and reputation (mainly from non-profit organisations);
3. *Societal influence* - recommended by family, friends or acquaintances were viewed as highly trustworthy (even without proper checks);
4. *Technology-related features* – **usability** and **privacy**;
5. *User control factors* – autonomy, empowerment, digital literacy and indifference;

In this context, one should look to answer the question: how can we offer a better understanding of users' perceptions about privacy and security in mHealth? One study suggests that enhancing technological literacy can be one relevant option to increase trust in mHealth, as otherwise, there is the risk of making mHealth applications seem less safe than other protected mobile activities, such as banking [23]. However, improving digital literacy is not enough to provide the best and most secure experience to each individual user according to how they perceive risk and trust in different mHealth apps, or even inside each app, for all the interactions and features it may comprise.

Not much similar work was encountered on this subject which strongly justifies the objective of this study: exploring end-user's perceptions of privacy and security in relation to mHealth and the factors that contribute to form such perceptions.

3 Methods

A cross-sectional study was conducted. Digitally literate Portuguese users were recruited by advertising an anonymous online survey on social and professional networks (e.g., Facebook, LinkedIn). No additional inclusion or exclusion criteria were defined, besides providing consent to participate, as the aim was to reach diverse user profiles. The questionnaire was programmed in a fill-in form by using an open source survey tool (*Lime Survey*). The survey was open for two weeks and the data were collected in September 2019. All the information gathered during that period was hosted in the secure servers of the University of Porto, Portugal.

The first page of the online survey included the study information and asked for the consent of potential participants. This page described the purpose of the survey, provided information about the research project and conditions to participate (e.g. anonymity, voluntary participation, no compensation).

In web-based questionnaires a unique identifier is implemented by default to block multiple participation and ballot-box filling. However, this feature is not used to track the participant back in any other way.

The second part of the survey comprised questions regarding participants' demographics as well as smartphone and mHealth use data (Table 1).

Table 1. Variables, type of questions and answer options in the second part of the survey.

Variables	Question type	Answer options
Demographics		
Age	Open	Number
Gender	Single-choice; radio (list)	Male; Female; Other
Schooling	Single-choice; radio (list)	Basic; High School; Degree; Other
Profession	Open	n/a
Smartphone use		
Frequency	5-point Likert scale	Always; Many times; Sometimes; Rarely; Never
mHealth use		
Frequency	5-point Likert scale	Always; Many times; Sometimes; Rarely; Never
Number*	Single-choice; radio (list)	> 40; 21–40; 11–20; 6–10; < 5; None
App type*	Multiple choice	Consultation; Historic; Prescriptions; Disease monitoring; Chronical diseases monitoring; Nutrition & Healthy living; Fitness & Wellbeing; Manage mental health, anxiety & depression; Pregnancy; Manage therapeutics; News and advances on health research; First-aid; Other; None
Keeping data private	5-point Likert scale	Totally agree; Agree; Neutral; Disagree; Totally disagree

*Over the previous year

The third part of the survey integrated questions related with the analysis of a fictitious scenario of accessing an mHealth app in a public space. Within the survey, Fig. 2 was presented to the participants with the following associated scenario:

Maria is on her way home after work in a busy underground. Maria connects to a "myHealth" app on her smartphone using the publicly available wi-fi network. Her medical information recorded on the app comprise appointments, prescriptions, exams, etc. She notices a new message alert with expected results from a genetic exam.

Fig. 2. Image inside the survey associated to the scenario description.

Table 2. Variables, type of questions and answer options in the third part of the survey.

Variables	Question type	Answer options
On Maria's situation, I would access:		
Genetic data	5-point Likert scale	Totally agree; Agree; Neutral; Disagree; Totally disagree
Medication prescriptions	5-point Likert scale	Totally agree; Agree; Neutral; Disagree; Totally disagree
A child's medical records	5-point Likert scale	Totally agree; Agree; Neutral; Disagree; Totally disagree
Additional remarks	Open	n/a
I would like the app to show:	Single-choice; radio (list)	All available data; All available data except personal data; All available data except health sensitive data; All available data except personal & health sensitive data; No data; Other
I would like the app to hide/show data according to:	Multiple choice	Current location; Type of requested data; Need-to-know at that moment; Type of connection; Type of device; Other

The types of questions related to the presented scenario are shown in Table 2.
Data analysis was performed using IBM SPSS Statistics 26.

To explore statistically significant associations, the chi-square test for independence was used to determine the relationships between categorical variables. The Fisher's Exact Test values are reported when appropriate. All p values are two-sided with a significance level of 0.05.

4 Results

Sixty-nine participants were registered but only 47 surveys were fully completed and included in the analysis. This represents a dropout of 31.9%, which is in accordance to the average dropout rate reported for online surveys [24]. Most participants are female (79%, n = 37), 19% (n = 9) are between 18 and 30 years old, 68% (n = 32) between 31 and 50, and 13% (n = 6) are more than 50 years old. The majority has a degree (83%, n = 39) (Fig. 3).

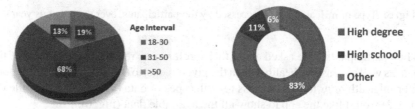

Fig. 3. Sample's age (left) and education (right).

The sample is very diverse in terms of professional activities, including: researchers (n = 6), informatics specialists (n = 6), students (n = 3), professors (n = 3), lawyers (n = 3), nurses (n = 2), and many others (n = 24).

For smartphone and mHealth use trends, 91% (n = 43) of participants reported to always or frequently use smartphones, while only 23% (n = 11) always or frequently use mHealth apps (Fig. 4). Ninety six percent (**96%, n = 45) of respondents fully agree or agree that privacy and security is very important in mHealth.**

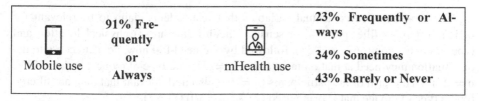

Fig. 4. Participants' smartphone (left) and mHealth (right) use.

The most frequently reported use of mHealth concerns accessing and managing medical appointments and exams (45%, n = 21), as well as monitoring health and fitness data (40%, n = 19). A quarter of participants (n = 12) uses mHealth to access prescription information and only 8% (n = 4) use such solutions to monitor chronic diseases, get information/manage mental health or pregnancy (Fig. 5).

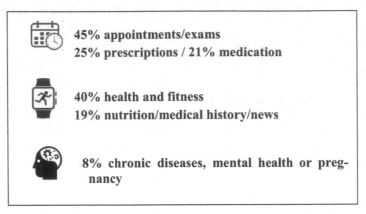

Fig. 5. Type of mHealth content accessed by the participants, over the previous year.

When participants were asked about their preferences regarding the control of their personal as well as sensitive health data in the given scenario (Fig. 2), almost half reported to prefer mHealth *apps* to block access to both types of data (49%, n = 23), while only 4% (n = 2) would like the app to show all the available data (Fig. 6).

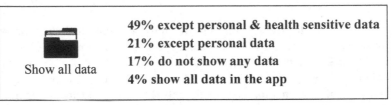

Fig. 6. Type of data participants would like the mHealth app to show/hide, taking into consideration the presented scenario (Fig. 2).

The most selected contextual variables that respondents claim to be relevant for mHealth *apps* to filter personal or sensitive health data are: i) physical location and type of connection (66%, n = 31), followed by the need-to-know, i.e. get access to the information they need at that moment (57%, n = 27) and type of requested data (49%, n = 23). One fourth of the participants (n = 12) also find relevant that data are filtered by the type of device that is being used (21%, n = 10) (Fig. 7).

In terms of the type of sensitive health data participants would access if they were on the introduced scenario (Fig. 2), 28% (n = 13) would access genetic data, 55% (n = 26) medication information and 32% (n = 15) child health-related data (Fig. 8).

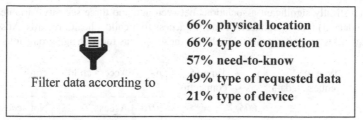

	66% physical location
	66% type of connection
	57% need-to-know
Filter data according to	49% type of requested data
	21% type of device

Fig. 7. Type of variables participants would like the mHealth app to filter available data, taking into consideration the presented scenario (Fig. 2).

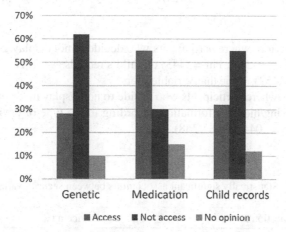

Fig. 8. Percentage of participants that would (blue) or would not (orange) access Genetic, Medication or child health-related data, or have no opinion (grey) on these matters. (Color figure online)

Statistically significant associations between analysed variables are displayed in Tables 1 and 2. In terms of users' demographic characteristics, only the variable age shows a significant association (Table 1) with the following security variables (Table 3):

1. **type of requested data**, with younger participants giving more relevance to information display according to data sensitiveness ($\chi^2(2, N = 47) = 10.029$, p = .006, Cramer's v = .450);
2. **type of connection**, also with younger participants valuing more this security criteria ($\chi^2(2, N = 47) = 7.550$, p = .018, Cramer's v = .420);
3. **child's medical records**, with the 31–50 age group (commonly a childbearing age group) showing more reluctance in accessing such information in a public place, with a wi-fi connection ($\chi^2(2, N = 47) = 6.512$, p = .031, Cramer's v = .413).

In terms of security and privacy perceptions, the decision of **displaying/not displaying sensitive data in a public place** is statistically associated (Table 2) with the following two variables (Table 4):

Table 3. Statistically significant associations between age and three security variables: i) type of requested data, ii) type of connection and iii) access to a child's health records. Absolute and relative frequencies for participants that selected those options for each age group are shown.

n (%)	Type of requested data	p	Type of connection	p	Access child's records		p
Age Groups:		.006		.018	Access	Not access	.031
< 30	6 (66.7)		8 (88.9)		3 (37.5)	5 (62.5)	
31–50	17 (56.7)		21 (70)		7 (25.9)	20 (74.1)	
> 50	0 (0)		2 (25)		5 (83.3)	1 (16.7)	

1) **type of connection,** where participants who decide to not display genetic ($\chi^2(1, N = 42) = 6.299$, p = .009, Phi = .443) or child's records ($\chi^2(1, N = 41) = 6.805$, p = .005, Phi = .462), value that variable more;
2) **type of device,** where participants who decide to not display medication data, value more the showing/hiding information according to the type of device ($\chi^2(1, N = 40) = 3.480$, p = .044, Phi = .358).

Table 4. Statistically significant associations between security variables.

Type of:	Connection n (%)		p	Device n (%)		p
Access to:	Access	Not access		Access	Not access	
Genetic	5 (17.2)	24 (82.8)	.009	–	–	–
Child	6 (21.4)	22 (78.6)	.005	–	–	–
Medication	–	–	–	3 (33.3)	6 (66.7)	.044

5 Discussion

This exploratory study aims to understand what factors can influence mHealth users' perceptions of security and privacy regarding their personal and health sensitive data.

Although the study does not comprise a large and more heterogeneous sample, which is skewed by gender and education, the latter was expected as we were aiming for digitally skilled participants that would have no impediment in using such type of technology. Education is a well-known determinant of internet use, thus a more educated sample was expected [25]. However, though small, the sample included participants with a wide range of professional activities, which can certainly have a large spectrum of perspectives and experiences.

Interestingly, for a highly educated sample participating in this study, with almost 100% of frequent smartphone users, there is a very low usage of mHealth apps. The reasons underlying this trend need to be further analyzed. A possible explanation is the fact that the sample includes most participants with less than 50 years old, so younger people that may present less health-related issues and still do not need to closely monitor their health status. In fact, most participants use mHealth for managing their health agenda (e.g. appointments, exams) and documentation, and to monitor nutrition and fitness, and less to support chronic, or other diseases or conditions (8%).

In terms of security and privacy perceptions, half the sample would like the app to, by default, automatically block or filter personal and health sensitive data to appear in such public scenarios (Fig. 2). So, they equally consider both types of data private, although, when alone, personal data is the favored one to keep private (Fig. 6). The 4% of participants that would not see the need for the app to block any type of data are respondents of the extreme age groups, e.g., less than 30 and more than 50 years old, while participants (17%) that indicate that no data should be shown by the mHealth app, are between 31 and 50 years old. These results suggest that age can be an important factor influencing users' perceptions of security and privacy in mHealth.

The participants' perceptions regarding contextual variables and how these can influence their decisions to keep their data private focus mostly on the physical location and type of connection available, although the need-to-know and the type of data that is requested, are given with less relevance. The type of device is less considered as having an influence in the security perceptions of our sample. Still, this is statistically significantly associated with access to medication, the type of health data considered by the sample as the least confidential/private. The perception of the content of medication may not be associated with security, but with how the content of data are being displayed on a specific physical device. However, this needs further analysis since users' privacy perceptions may not be directly linked to medication content but the association with medication and types of diseases can be very strong and an indicative of highly sensitive data content that must, as well, be kept private. Can this be raising the need for more education and awareness on the dangers of the types of health data and how these can be affected by privacy breaches?

Indeed, the sample in this study considers that different types of health data can have different levels of security/privacy associated: considered more sensitive are genetics, followed by a child's medical record while, as already mentioned, medication are considered the least sensitive. Genetic and child's medical records have statistically significant associations with the type of connection used. This indicates that the sample perceives the type of communication channel where the data travels to be the "physical space" that needs to be protected, as opposed to the user's physical location. This may also occur because of the specific public physical location that has been analyzed by the participants (Fig. 2). This issue must be further clarified in future studies.

Finally, for the statistically significant associations found between age groups and the type of connection, younger participants value more the type of connection but also the type of requested data they want to visualize at a certain moment. If these participants perceive they are accessing less private data, their interactions with the mHealth app in such public scenarios would change according to that. It is also interesting to notice that the 31–50 age group shows more reluctance in accessing a child's medical records in a public place, with a public wi-fi connection. This may be explained by the fact that this is commonly a childbearing age group that are probably more aware of the dangers of sharing private data regarding their child, and therefore be more protective of them. This shows that, not only age and other users' characteristics can influence perceptions of security and privacy in mHealth, but also factors such as previous experiences, or even the life and social contexts.

Future work includes extending this study by applying the survey to a larger and more heterogeneous sample, including different scenarios/contexts. This would help mapping users' privacy and security perceptions, and their unique characteristics, to mHealth data to foster a better understanding of how ensuing apps should be visually, technically and security prepared.

6 Conclusions

In what concerns perceptions of security and privacy in mHealth, many factors come into play. The complexity of such interactional ecosystem explains why privacy and security is one of the great challenges in human computer interactions [4]. Although this is an exploratory study with a small sample, it already raised many questions and even shows some statistically significant associations between several factors. Examples of these are: i) demographics, such as age; ii) contextual variables, such as type of connection, type of device and type of requested data, which related to the various levels of sensitiveness that are perceived by the users regarding their health data.

These results corroborate the need for a change of the current "one-app-fits-all" paradigm to a more customized view of mHealth security features, for different user and contextual factors. In order for mHealth to fulfil their true potential a better understanding of how the mHealth apps must be devised in terms of privacy and security is essential.

Acknowledgements. This work has been supported by TagUBig - Taming Your Big Data (IF/00693/2015) from Researcher FCT Program funded by National Funds through FCT.

References

1. Anglada-Martinez, H., Riu-Viladoms, G., Martin-Conde, M., Rovira-Illamola, M., Sotoca-Momblona, J.M., Codina-Jane, C.: Does mHealth increase adherence to medication? Results of a systematic review. Int. J. Clin. Pract. **69**, 9–32 (2015)
2. Sulkowski, M., Luetkemeyer, A.F., Wyles, D.L., et al.: Impact of a digital medicine programme on hepatitis C treatment adherence and efficacy in adults at high risk for non-adherence. Aliment. Pharmacol. Ther. **51**, 1384–1396 (2020)
3. Kotz, D., Gunter, A., Kumar, S., Weiner, J.: Privacy and security in mobile health: a research agenda. Computer **49**(6), 22–30 (2016)
4. Stephanidis, C., Salvendy, G., et al.: Seven HCI grand challenges. International Journal of Human-Computer Interaction **35**(14), 1229–1269 (2019)
5. Zhou, L., Bao, J., Watzlaf, V., Parmanto, B.: Barriers to and facilitators of the use of mobile health apps from a security perspective: mixed-methods study. JMIR Mhealth Uhealth, **7**(4), e11223 (2019)
6. Vaibhav, G., Kevin, B., Camp, L.: The privacy paradox: a Facebook case study. SSRN Electron. J. (2014)

7. Lynch, J.K., Fisk, M.: mHealth, Trust and the security of personal data. In: Marston, H., Freeman, S., Musselwhite C. (eds.) Mobile e-Health. Human–Computer Interaction Series. pp. 237–249. Springer, Cham (2017). https://doi.org/10.1007/978-3-319-60672-9_11
8. Audie, A., et al.: Consumer attitudes and perceptions on mHealth privacy and security: findings from a mixed-methods study. J. Health Commun. **20**(6), 673–679 (2015)
9. Schnall, R., Higgins, T., Brown, W., Carballo-Dieguez, A., Bakken, S.: Trust, perceived risk, perceived ease of use and perceived usefulness as factors related to mHealth technology use. Stud. Health Technol. Inf. **216**, 467–471 (2015)
10. UN General Assembly, Universal Declaration of Human Rights, 10 December 1948, 217 A (III), Article 12. https://www.refworld.org/docid/3ae6b3712c.html. Accessed 28 Dec 2020
11. Ferreira, A., Almeida, R., Almeida, R., Jácome, C., Fonseca, J., Vieira-Marques, P.: mHealth to Securely Coach Chronic Patients. In: Jarm, T., Cvetkoska, A., Mahnič-Kalamiza, S., Miklavcic, D. (eds.) EMBEC 2020. IP, vol. 80, pp. 805–813. Springer, Cham (2021). https://doi.org/10.1007/978-3-030-64610-3_90
12. Alwashmi, M.F., Fitzpatrick, B., Davis, E., Gamble, J.M., Farrell, J., Hawboldt, J.: Perceptions of Health Care Providers Regarding a Mobile Health Intervention to Manage Chronic Obstructive Pulmonary Disease: Qualitative Study. JMIR mHealth uHealth, **7**, e13950 (2019)
13. Rowland, S.P., Fitzgerald, J.E., Holme, T., et al.: What is the clinical value of mHealth for patients? Digit. Med. **3**, 4 (2020)
14. Larson, R. S.: A path to better-quality mHealth apps. JMIR mHealth uHealth **6**(7), e10414 (2018)
15. Sheppard, M.K.: mHealth apps: disruptive innovation, regulation, and trust—a need for balance. Med. Law Rev. **28**(3), 549–572 (2020)
16. Dirkjan, K., et al.: Advantages of mobile health in the management of adult patients with congenital heart disease. Int. J. Med. Inf. **132**, 104011 (2019) ISSN 1386–5056
17. Denis, F., et al.: Randomized trial comparing a web-mediated follow-up with routine surveillance in lung cancer patients. J. Natl. Cancer Inst. **109**, (2017)
18. Ni, Z., Liu, C., Wu, B., Yang, Q., Douglas, C., Shaw, R.J.: An mHealth intervention to improve medication adherence among patients with coronary heart disease in China: development of an intervention. Int. J. Nurs. Sci. **5**(4), 322–330 (2018)
19. Dumais, K., et al.: Preferences for use and design of electronic patient-reported outcomes in patients with chronic obstructive pulmonary disease. Patient Patient-Centered Outcomes Res. **12**(6), 621–629 (2019)
20. Rowe, A.K., Rowe, S.Y., Peters, D.H., Holloway, K.A., Chalker, J., Ross-Degnan, D.: Effectiveness of strategies to improve health-care provider practices in low-income and middle-income countries: a systematic review. Lancet Glob. Health **6**(11), e1163–e1175 (2018)
21. van Haasteren, A., Gille, F., Fadda, M., Vayena, E.: Development of the mHealth App Trustworthiness checklist. Dig. Health **5**, 2055207619886463 (2019)
22. Vo, V., Auroy, L., Sarradon-Eck, A.: Patients' perceptions of mHealth apps: meta-ethnographic review of qualitative studies. JMIR Mhealth Uhealth **7**(7), e13817 (2019)
23. Arora, S., Yttri, J., Nilse, W.: Privacy and security in mobile health (mHealth) research. Alcohol Res. **36**(1), 143–151 (2014)
24. Galesic, M.: Dropouts on the web: effects of interest and burden experienced during an online survey. J. Off. Stat. **22**, 313–28 (2006)
25. Goldfarb, A., Prince, J.: Internet adoption and usage patterns are different: Implications for the digital divide. Inf. Econ. Policy **20**, 2–15 (2008). https://doi.org/10.1016/j.infoecopol.2007.05.001

Understanding User's Behavior and Protection Strategy upon Losing, or Identifying Unauthorized Access to Online Account

Huzeyfe Kocabas[1(✉)], Swapnil Nandy[2], Tanjina Tamanna[3],
and Mahdi Nasrullah Al-Ameen[1]

[1] Utah State University, Logan, USA
huzeyfe.kocabas@aggiemail.usu.edu, mahdi.al-ameen@usu.edu
[2] Jadavpur University, Kolkata, India
[3] University of Dhaka, Dhaka, Bangladesh

Abstract. A wide-range of personal and sensitive information are stored in users' online accounts. Losing access, or an unauthorized access to one of those accounts could put them into the risks of privacy breach, cause financial loss, and compromise their accessibility to important information and documents. A large body of prior work focused on developing new schemes and strategies to protect users' online security. However, there is a dearth in existing literature to understand users' strategies and contingency plans to protect their online accounts once they lose access, or identify an unauthorized access to one of their accounts. We addressed this gap in our work, where we conducted semi-structured interview with 59 participants from three different countries: Bangladesh, Turkey, and USA. Our findings reveal the unawareness, misconceptions, and privacy and accessibility concerns of users, which refrain them from taking security-preserving steps to protect their online accounts. We also identified users' prevention strategies that could put their online security into further risks.

Keywords: User behavior · Qualitative study · Protection strategy · Contingency plan · Online accounts · Cross-cultural study

1 Introduction

The authentication secrets of 620 million user accounts are stolen by adversaries from 16 different websites [39], where many users are unsure of how they could recover access to their accounts [26]. Users are found to understand the risks of data breaches [20], however, their security behavior is influenced by costs associated with protective measures, where they have a general tendency towards delaying action until harm has occurred [41]. The study of Marques et al. [24] investigated users' perceptions of unauthorized physical access to smartphones,

A. Moallem (Ed.): HCII 2021, LNCS 12788, pp. 310–325, 2021.
https://doi.org/10.1007/978-3-030-77392-2_20

where they analyzed the relation between social trust, personal relationship, and security vulnerabilities.

To prevent unauthorized access to users' accounts, the prior studies focused on studying users' password management strategies [22,25,34], improving the security and usability of authentication schemes [3,5,8], developing automated techniques to detect unauthorized access to an account [21], and designing educational tools and warning system to prevent social engineering attacks [6,23,33]. However, a little study is conducted to date, to understand users' behavior once they lose access or identify an unauthorized access to their online account. To address this gap, we focused on the following research questions in our work: i) How do users respond to a situation when they lose access, or identify an unauthorized access to their online account? ii) What are the strategies and contingency plans of users to protect their online accounts in the future? iii) How do users' strategies and contingency plans to protect their online accounts vary across geographic regions?

The study of Haque et al. [17] divided online accounts into four categories (e.g., financial, identity, content, and sketchy), where they emphasized on the protection of financial, and identity accounts (e.g., email, social networking). Thus, our study focused on user's protection behavior for financial and identity accounts, considering the sensitivity of user information stored, or shared through these accounts. Security and Privacy, being contextual, demand a situated understanding of user's perceptions and behavior in order to explore the design and policy practices [13,27,28]. Thus, it is important to investigate the security perceptions and behavior of users beyond Western contexts. In our study, we conducted semi-structured interview with 59 participants from three different countries, including Bangladesh (a developing country located in South Asia), Turkey (a developing country straddling Eastern Europe and Western Asia), and USA (a developed country in North America).

Contributions. Our findings reveal the unawareness and uncertainty of participants in taking appropriate steps once they lose access or identify an unauthorized access to their online account. In this context, we unpack the misconceptions of participants, which refrain them from taking security-preserving actions, or lead them to adopt prevention strategy that could put their online security into further risks. Our results shed light on the relation between users' security behavior to protect their online accounts, privacy concern with sharing personal information for secondary authentication (used to recover access to an account, like when password is forgotten [38]), and their perceptions of accessibility related to two-factor authentication. Taken together, our study contributes to advance the understanding of Security and HCI community on users' security vulnerabilities and usability challenges in protecting their online accounts.

2 Related Work

In this section, we first report the findings from prior studies on user's security perceptions and behavior, followed by a discussion on notable usable security and privacy studies conducted outside the Western regions.

The study of Ion et al. [18] compared the online security practices of expert and non-expert users, where they found differences in their security behavior. For instances, expert users generally install updates, use password manager, and leverage two-factor authentication, where the non-expert users prefer to use antivirus application, change their passwords, and visit only the known websites [18]. Karunakaran et al. [20] investigated users' expectations of how companies should respond to data breaches. The authors [20] found that users understand the risk of data leakage, and have certain expectations from the organizations in case of a data breach, which include sending users an immediate notification, enabling two-factor authentication, and resetting their passwords.

The study of Zou et al. [41] focused on Equifax data breach, where the findings revealed users' perceived risks of data leakage. The authors [41] identified the factors that could influence users towards not taking a protective measure, which include but not limited to the optimism bias, procrastination until harms occur, and the costs of taking a security-preserving action. In a separate study [30], Ruoti et al. found that users' security behavior depend upon their understanding of a threat, evaluation of risks, and the estimation of impact, where they select coping strategies based on their evaluation of the trade-offs between potential harms and the costs to take protective measures.

Although local values often contrast with the liberal notions of privacy and security embedded in current computing systems [1,4,11], the digital privacy and security research beyond Western contexts is still at its very early stage [12,37]. In a recent study [29], the author recruited participants from both within and outside of Western countries. The findings from this study [29] show that the user's behavioral response to a suspicious login attempt to their Facebook account depends upon their awareness, and mental model of the incident, where cultural background and past experiences could also influence their security decision.

Although online threats are global, perceptions of threat are very localized [4,11,16,36]. The study of Al-Ameen et al. [4] explored how users balance their needs, conveniences, and privacy in the context of data collection and sharing by smartphone apps, and unveiled how privacy leakage incidents affect app usage behavior in the Global South. The study of Haque et al. [16] shed light on how situated morality influence the privacy behavior of people in the digital service centers at Bangladesh. In a study conducted in urban Ghana [11], the participants reported confidence of being able to defend against cyberattacks despite passwords often being their only line of defense.

Digital devices, such as mobile phones that are designed for developing regions often fail to satisfy their local needs. In a study conducted with low-literate Berber women in Morocco [14], the authors identified that the lack of functional literacy presented significant barriers to using mobile phones. The studies conducted by Ahmed et al. [2] and Sambasivan et al. [32] demonstrate that the mobile phones often do not have one-to-one mapping with a user in the resource-constrained settings of developing countries, where a recent study with the women in Global South [31] examined the privacy negotiation of female users from their family members while using a mobile phone.

Our Study. The findings from these studies indicate that there is a dearth in existing literature to understand users' strategies and contingency plans to protect their online accounts once they lose access, or identify an unauthorized access to one of their accounts. We addressed this gap in our work.

3   Methodology

We conducted semi-structured interview with 59 participants. We recruited participants through sharing the study information via email and online social media, posting flyers on public places, snowball sampling, and leveraging authors' personal connections. We interviewed the participant over telephone, via Skype, or in person. Our study was approved by the Institutional Review Board (IRB) at our university.

3.1   Procedure

The interviews were conducted in the country's official language. That is, the interviews with the participants living in the USA, Bangladesh, and Turkey were conducted in English, Bengali, and Turkish, respectively. During the interview, we asked them a set of questions on online accounts, in particular, financial and identity accounts (e.g., email, social networking). Participants were asked about their past experience of losing access to their financial and identity accounts, identifying an unauthorized access to any of these accounts, and what protection steps they had taken in such instances. At the end, participants responded to a set of demographic questionnaire. The interviews were audio recorded. On average, each session took between 20 and 30 min.

3.2   Analysis

We transcribed the audio recordings. For the interviews with the participants from Bangladesh and Turkey, the researchers who are the native speaker of Bengali and Turkish translated the transcriptions into English. We then performed thematic analysis on our transcriptions [9,10]. Two researchers independently read through the transcripts of half of the interviews, developed codes, compared them, and then iterated again with more interviews until we had developed a consistent codebook. Once the codebook was finalized, two researchers divided up the remaining interviews and coded them. After all interviews had been coded, both researchers spot-checked the other's coded transcripts and did not find any inconsistencies. Finally, we organized and taxonomized our codes into higher-level categories.

Table 1. The Highlight of Participants' Demographic Traits [*Either completed or currently studying at the noted education level] **Note:** *UP*: Participants living in the USA; *BP*: Participants living in Bangladesh; *TP*: Participants living in Turkey

Gender	Participants
Male	BP1-BP3, BP6-BP9, BP11, BP15, BP17-BP29, UP1-UP4, UP7, UP8, UP10-UP12, UP14-UP16, UP18, UP20-UP22, TP1, TP3, TP4, TP6, TP8
Female	BP4, BP5, BP10, BP12-BP14, BP16, UP5, UP6, UP9, UP13, UP17, UP19, TP2, TP5, TP7
Age-range	
18–24	BP4, BP7, BP8, UP5, UP6, UP19, UP21, UP22
25–29	BP2, BP3, BP5, BP6, BP9, BP19, BP20, BP25, UP2, UP7-UP15, UP18, UP20, TP1-TP3
30–34	BP1, BP17, BP18, BP21, BP24, BP28, UP1, UP3, UP16, UP17
35–39	BP23, TP6
40–44	BP16, BP22, BP26, BP27, BP29, UP4
45–49	BP14, TP4, TP7
50–54	BP15, TP5, TP8
55+	BP10, BP11, BP12, BP13
Literacy Level*	
Fifth Grade	BP19, BP27, BP29, TP6, TP7
Between Eighth	BP17, BP20, BP22, BP24, BP25, BP26,
and Tenth Grade	BP28, TP4
Twelfth Grade	BP12, BP18, BP21, BP23, UP19, UP21, UP22, TP2, TP5, TP8
Undergraduate and above	BP1-BP11, BP13-BP16, UP1-UP18, UP20, TP1, TP3
Profession	
Student	BP4, BP5, BP7, BP9, UP1-UP3, UP6-UP14, UP18, UP19, UP22
Employee at Industry	BP1-BP3, BP6, BP8, BP11, BP17-BP19, BP21-BP29, UP5, TP3, TP4, TP6
Employee at Educational or Non-profit Org	BP10, BP15, UP4, UP15-UP17, UP20, UP21, TP1
Car Driver	BP20
Housewife	BP12-BP14, TP2, TP5, TP7
Physician	BP16
Retired	TP8

3.3   Participants

Table 1 presents the demographic information of our 59 participants, where 16 of them are women, and 43 are men. Almost all of our participants were in the age range of 18 to 55, where four participants were above 55 years old.

The literacy level of 39% of our participants was between fifth and twelfth grade, where others were either undergraduate students or had already earned the degree. Thirty-two percent of our participants were students, where others were from diverse professions, including physician, car driver, housewife, and the employee at industry, educational institution, or non-profit organization. Among our participants, twenty two of them live in the USA, eight participants live in Turkey, and 29 participants live in Bangladesh. In this paper, the participants living in the USA, Bangladesh, and Turkey are denoted by *UP*, *BP*, and *TP*, respectively.

4 Results

Twenty-six (USA: 17, Bangladesh and Turkey: 9) out of 59 participants reported losing access, or identifying unauthorized access to their financial, or identity account, where we unpacked their strategies to regain access and protect their accounts. For other participants, we reported their contingency plan in case of losing access or identifying an unauthorized access in the future (see Sect. 4.3).

4.1 Losing Access to Online Account

Nineteen participants (USA: 12, Bangladesh and Turkey: 7) reported losing access to at least one of their financial, or identity (e.g., email, or social networking) accounts, where most of them could not recover the access. Below, we report our findings revealing why participants lost access to their accounts.

Lack or Failure of Secondary Authentication. Among the participants who lost access to their financial or identity accounts, about half of them including from all three countries reported that they could not recover the access upon forgetting their primary authentication code, e.g., password. Among them, some participants failed to recover their access as they forgot their secondary authentication code. For instance, UP19 could not recall the answer to her security question for secondary authentication: *"There were some other special questions that asked like, what was your third grade teacher or some special question, and I just didn't remember them. So I had to create another email [account]."* UP15 reported losing access to his online bank account as he could not recall his email ID connected to that account for secondary authentication. Several participants lost access to their account as they had not set a secondary authentication code during account creation, where UP3 commented, *"I think that if I designed some security question at the beginning of creating account, now I would not lose that access and recover my account."*

BP20 could not recover access to one of his online accounts upon forgetting the primary authentication code where he also forgot the password of his email account that was registered for secondary authentication. UP1 commented, *"I lost like many times, I mean my email accounts"*. Including UP1, a few participants lost access to their online accounts multiple times due to forgetting their authentication codes. TP8 has reported, several online accounts require him to change his password once every three months, which makes it difficult for him to remember the new password.

Geographic Relocation. Several U.S. participants reported geographic relocation as the reason behind losing access to their online accounts. Many service providers block suspicious login attempts from an unusual location to protect their users' online accounts from unauthorized access. In such cases, a user might be asked to prove her identity by entering a one-time-code delivered to her phone number, registered with the system [15]. We found that such security measures could pose accessibility challenges to users, causing them to lose access to their online accounts. For instance, one of our participants (UP17) who moved to the USA from a country in Asia, could no longer authenticate to her social networking account after geographic relocation. Her login attempt from the USA was considered suspicious by the system, where she could not prove her identity through her phone number in the USA as it was not registered with her account.

UP15 mentioned that he was blocked from accessing his email account: *"There was one email account that I lost completely because I had not connected my phone number with it, and I tried using it from a different country using a wrong password and it blocked me out."* He then contacted the customer service to recover his account: *"I tried calling them. For some reason that did not work and you know what happened after that [could no longer access this account]."* Due to the risks of information leakage, he reported concern about registering his phone number with an online account.

Adversary's Action. Among those participants who lost access to online accounts, several of them reported that their account was hacked followed by changing the authentication code by adversaries. BP5 reported an incident of losing access to multiple online accounts, where a social networking account, hacked by the adversary was linked to other accounts through a single sign-on feature. Most participants are not sure whether they were the victim of a targeted attack by someone they know, or their passwords were leaked to unknown attackers. UP4, who lost access to his social networking account, perceives that the leakage of his password could be prevented if the service provider would have taken appropriate measures to protect users' credentials.

BP10 reported an incident of robbery, where the attacker forcefully gained access to victim's bank account from his smartphone. In another instance, the attacker demanded ransom from BP20 over phone threatening our participant to ruin his reputation through posting inappropriate contents on the hacked social networking account.

4.2   Unauthorized Access to Online Account

Thirteen participants (USA: 7, Bangladesh and Turkey: 6) reported that they had identified unauthorized access to at least one of their financial or identity

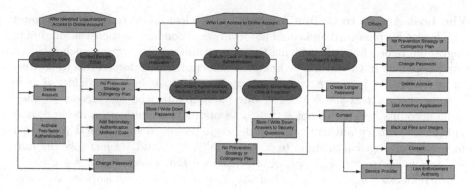

Fig. 1. Prevention strategies and contingency plan of our participants

accounts, where they did not lose access to that account. Among them, a few participants identified unauthorized access to their social networking account through checking the activity log, where most of others reported, they got aware of unauthorized access through email notification from the service provider. For instance, UP1 mentioned an email delivered to him, which provided him with the location information of an adversary logging into his social networking account. This participant perceives that the service providers of different online accounts work together to protect their users' online security, which assures him that he does not need to worry about unauthorized access to his online accounts.

UP2 reported an incident where he received an email asking him to change his password for a bank account, because *"someone else was using my information, hacked the account or something."* The similar incidents were reported by BP5 and UP18, where they received an email asking to change their authentication secret for a social networking account. UP12 mentioned, *"Once I got an email from Gmail that someone is trying to access my account and gave me a link [to change password]...I went to the link and changed my password."*

TP8 reported that his bank account was accessed from a foreign country, incurring him financial loss. He suspects, he was a victim of phishing attack, where his bank account was accessed after he had provided his account information in a website that tricked him to believe that he had won a lottery.

4.3   Prevention Strategy and Contingency Plan

Twenty-six participants reported that they had lost access, or identified unauthorized access (but did not lose access) to one of their financial or identity accounts. A few participants encountered both instances. In this section, we report our findings on the steps taken by our participants upon losing access or identifying unauthorized access to their accounts (Fig. 1 illustrates the prevention strategy and contingency plan of our participants).

Who Lost Access to Online Account. UP15 lost access to his email account as he forgot his password and could not leverage secondary authentication due to geographic relocation (e.g., moving to a new country). To prevent such incident from happening in the future, he now stores his authentication secrets to address the memorability issue: *"I try to save my password somewhere whether it is in browser or in a text file."* Most of our participants who lost access to their online accounts because of not setting a secondary authentication method, now store their primary authentication code, e.g., password in a digital (e.g., text file, email) or physical medium (e.g., notebook). UP1 said, *"I just take the note like, you know, to my notebook. And I just use that one to reach my account, just to remember my password...And the steps I took like are working very well for now."*

Participants who store their password in a physical medium reported confidence in securing that from unwanted entities. For instance, UP9 commented, *"I am more aware [now] and so like I write them [passwords] down. But no one will see it but myself."* Participants who could not recover their accounts due to forgetting secondary authentication code (e.g., answer to a security question), consider it as a safer option to write down the answers to their security questions for secondary authentication, instead of storing their primary authentication code (e.g., password). Our participants store their password, or answer to a security question in plaintext.

Among those participants whose online accounts were compromised by the adversary, UP4 mentioned creating a stronger password for his new account to prevent such incident from happening in the future: *"I chose a longer password."* The other participants did not report taking any security-preserving steps to protect their online accounts from an unauthorized access. Some of them, including from all three countries feel helpless in face of adversary's action, and are unsure of how they could protect their online security. For example, when we asked about their steps, taken to prevent unauthorized access to their accounts in the future, UP2 said, *"I cannot do anything."* Similarly, TP8 perceives that it is not possible to recover an online account if it is compromised by an adversary, in which case, the victim would need to create a new account. In this context, a few U.S. participants reported a contingency plan that they would meet the customer service personnel in person, if their online accounts are further compromised by an adversary.

Who Identified Unauthorized Access. Among the participants from all three countries who identified unauthorized access to their online account, most of them did not take any preventive steps. We found that participants place trust on the service provider to protect their online security. For instances, a few participants believe that the service providers take required steps whenever an adversary attempts to compromise their account, and notify them through email when such unauthorized attempts to access their account fail due to organization's security protection in place.

Some participants do not have a clear idea about what steps they should take once an unauthorized access is identified, where UP18 said, *"I don't know what to do...what i am going to do. I don't know."* TP8 experienced unauthorized access to his bank account. Including him, a few other participants mentioned the importance of being more careful about security issues, however, they were unsure of the strategy or plan that could protect their online accounts from unauthorized access in the future.

A few participants from Bangladesh and USA reported to change their password of email and social networking account using the link provided in the email that had informed them about an unauthorized access to their account. In this context, UP13 did not change her password for the account where an unauthorized access was identified, rather she set up security questions and added a recovery email ID for secondary authentication, so that she could recover her access to that account if the primary authentication code is changed by the adversary. She preferred not to add her mobile phone number for two-factor authentication as she was concerned that she might not be able to access her account when she would be out of her phone's network coverage.

Once UP21 identified an unauthorized access to his social networking account through checking the activity log, he considered that deleting that account would be the best line of defense to protect his personal information. Then, he took a series of steps to prevent unauthorized access in the future. He created a new social networking account, and divided his online accounts into two categories: 'important' and 'non-important'. For his 'important' accounts, he created new passwords that are different from each other, as this participant was afraid that the adversary accessing his social networking account might be able to guess his password for other accounts. He then activated two-factor authentication for his 'important' accounts by adding his phone number.

Others. Among those participants who did not lose access or identify any unauthorized access to their online accounts, a few of them were confident that they would not encounter any such incidents in the future, where UP6 commented, *"They [adversaries] cannot get my password."* We identified uncertainty among participants from all three countries when we asked them about their contingency plan in case they lose access to an online account. Several U.S. participants mentioned, they would contact the tech support of the service provider, however, were not sure how to reach out to them. Here, UP22 mentioned that he would contact the upper management in Google if his access to email account is compromised.

If an unauthorized access to the online account is identified, several participants mentioned that they would change the password of that account. However, UP7 and TP6 also reported uncertainty if this step would be sufficient to protect their account from the adversary. In this context, UP10 and UP11 believe that the only way to protect an account is to delete it upon identifying an unauthorized access. UP10 would also reach out to the law enforcement agency to identify the adversary in order to protect his online accounts; he added, *"[It is] always difficult to track who is trying to hack your account. But I think this day with technology, I've heard police is able to track or know who is sending what from where.*" Similarly, several participants from Bangladesh and Turkey who did not lose access, or identify an unauthorized access to their online account, mentioned that they would ask help from the law enforcement authority if they identify an unauthorized access to their online account in the future.

UP22 reported using an antivirus software in his computer, where he perceives that the antivirus application would protect his computer and online accounts from adversaries. A few participants keep local backup of their personal documents and photos that are shared or stored online, so that they do not lose access to those files in case their email or social networking accounts are compromised.

5   Discussion

5.1   Prevention Strategies, Risks, and Concerns

Our findings indicate that the prevention strategies taken by users upon losing access to an online account could increase their exposure to cyber attacks, and in turn, weaken their security protection. Forgetting passwords, coupled with geographic relocation or the failure/lack of secondary authentication caused our participants losing access to their online account. As a prevention strategy, they started to write down their password (in plaintext) on paper, or store that in a digital medium, e.g., textfile or email. Participants who could not leverage secondary authentication to recover their account due to forgetting answers to security questions, now write down those answers to address the memorability issue. However, writing down or storing password in an unprotected medium could lead to password leakage [40], increasing the risks of unauthorized access to their online accounts. The future research should further investigate how users protect the medium that they use to write down their passwords.

Our participants mentioned the email notification that asked to change their password for an online account. It was out of the scope of this study to verify the legitimacy of the reported emails, however, we note that the dependency of participants on email notifications to identify an unauthorized access could be exploited by adversaries to conduct phishing attacks [6]. The future research should explore the relation between users' strategies to protect their online accounts and underlying susceptibility to social engineering attacks, e.g., phishing.

Our results show that the uncertainty about accessibility could refrain users from taking security-preserving steps to protect their online accounts. While one-time password based two-factor authentication using mobile phones contribute to enhance online security [15], participants reported concern that they might loose access to their online account if they are out of their cellphone's network coverage, e.g., due to geographic relocation. Also, participants worried about privacy leakage in sharing their mobile phone number with the service providers.

5.2   Security (Mis)conceptions

In this section, we discuss about the misconceptions of participants, which give them a false sense of security in protecting their online accounts. We emphasize that future research should focus on identifying appropriate measures to alleviate user's misconceptions, so that they could make an informed security decision.

Writing down a secondary authentication code in an unprotected medium could be as vulnerable as writing down a primary authentication secret (e.g., password); if adversaries gain access to the answer of a security question, they could exploit the secondary authentication method to compromise a user's account [19,40]. However, the participants who write down their secondary authentication code (e.g., answer to a security question), perceive it as a more secure approach than writing down their password.

Some service providers (e.g., Google[1]) inform their customers through email about login from a new device or location, to help them with identifying unauthorized access and taking appropriate actions. However, the purpose of such email notifications is misunderstood by several participants. As they perceive, receiving such email indicates that adequate security measures are taken by the service provider, requiring no further action at user's end. Our findings indicate the need of redesigning email-based security alerts, to help users with better understanding of security risks and protective measures.

Participants place over-reliance on security software as they lack understanding of how that system works. Antivirus application, in general, is designed to protect a computer from malicious software [35], where a few participants perceive that the antivirus application also protects their online accounts from the adversaries. Such reliance provides them with a false sense of security, which in turn, refrains them from taking security measures to protect their online account.

5.3   Similarities and Differences Across Geographic Locations

Our findings show that more U.S. participants, in comparison to the participants in Bangladesh and Turkey reported losing access or identifying unauthorized access to their financial, or identity account. Participants' responses on how they had identified an unauthorized access were similar across all three countries. While the lack or failure of secondary authentication, and adversary's action are reported by the participants from all three countries why they had lost access to their online accounts, only U.S. participants mentioned geographic relocation as the reason behind losing access to their account. It is possible, although we cannot confirm from our study, that the participants from Bangladesh and Turkey did not travel outside their country, and thus, did not experience losing access to an online account due to geographic relocation.

Overall, we found similarities in protection strategies across the participants from USA, Bangladesh, and Turkey. However, none of our participants from Bangladesh and Turkey reported activating two-factor authentication when an

---

[1] https://support.google.com/accounts/answer/2590353?hl=en.

unauthorized access to their online account was identified, or contacting service provider in case of losing access to their account. We believe, further investigations are required in the contexts of developing countries, including Bangladesh and Turkey to understand the availability and usability of two-factor authentication, and the scopes and challenges involved in getting help from the service provider when a user loses access to her online account.

6   Limitations and Conclusion

We interviewed 59 participants in our study, where we followed the widely-used methods for qualitative research [7,9,10], focusing in depth on a small number of participants and continuing the interviews until no new themes emerged (saturation). We acknowledge the limitations of such study that a different set of samples might yield varying results. Thus, we do not draw any quantitative, generalizable conclusion from this study. In addition, self-reported data might have limitations, like recall and observer bias.

Despite these limitations, our study unpacks the strategies of users to protect their online account, where we identified the unawareness, misconceptions, and accessibility and privacy concerns of users that refrain them from taking security-preserving steps. In our future work, we would conduct a large-scale survey with the participants from diverse age-groups and literacy levels to attain quantitative and more generalizable results.

References

1. Ahmed, S.I., Guha, S., Rifat, M.R., Shezan, F.H., Dell, N.: Privacy in repair: an analysis of the privacy challenges surrounding broken digital artifacts in Bangladesh. In: Proceedings of the Eighth International Conference on Information and Communication Technologies and Development, ICTD 2016, pp. 11:1–11:10. ACM, New York (2016). https://doi.org/10.1145/2909609.2909661
2. Ahmed, S.I., Haque, M.R., Chen, J., Dell, N.: Digital privacy challenges with shared mobile phone use in Bangladesh. In: Proceedings of the ACM Human-Computer Interaction 1(CSCW), 17:1–17:20, December 2017. https://doi.org/10.1145/3134652
3. Al-Ameen, M.N., Fatema, K., Wright, M., Scielzo, S.: The impact of cues and user interaction on the memorability of system-assigned recognition-based graphical passwords. In: Eleventh Symposium on Usable Privacy and Security (SOUPS 2015), pp. 185–196 (2015)
4. Al-Ameen, M.N., Tamanna, T., Nandy, S., Ahsan, M.A.M., Chandra, P., Ahmed, S.I.: We don't give a second thought before providing our information: Understanding users' perceptions of information collection by apps in urban Bangladesh. In: Proceedings of the 3rd ACM SIGCAS Conference on Computing and Sustainable Societies (COMPASS 2020), pp. 32–43. Association for Computing Machinery, New York (2020). https://doi.org/10.1145/3378393.3402244
5. Al-Ameen, M.N., Wright, M.: Exploring the potential of Geopass: a geographic location-password scheme. Interacting Computs. **29**(4), 605–627 (2017)

6. Alsharnouby, M., Alaca, F., Chiasson, S.: Why phishing still works: user strategies for combating phishing attacks. Int. J. Hum.-Comput. Stud. **82**, 69–82 (2015)

7. Baxter, K., Courage, C., Caine, K.: Understanding Your Users: A Practical Guide to User Research Methods, 2nd edn. Morgan Kaufmann Publishers Inc., San Francisco (2015)

8. Biddle, R., Chiasson, S., Van Oorschot, P.C.: Graphical passwords: learning from the first twelve years. ACM Comput. Surv. (CSUR) **44**(4), 1–41 (2012)

9. Boyatzis, R.E.: Transforming Qualitative Information: Thematic Analysis and Code Development. Sage, Thousand Oaks (1998)

10. Braun, V., Clarke, V.: Using thematic analysis in psychology. Qual. Res. Psychol. **3**(2), 77–101 (2006)

11. Chen, J., Paik, M., McCabe, K.: Exploring internet security perceptions and practices in urban ghana. In: Proceedings of the Tenth USENIX Conference on Usable Privacy and Security, SOUPS 2014, pp. 129–142. USENIX Association, USA (2014)

12. Cobb, C., Sudar, S., Reiter, N., Anderson, R., Roesner, F., Kohno, T.: Computer security for data collection technologies. Dev. Eng. **3**, 1–11 (2018)

13. Crabtree, A., Tolmie, P., Knight, W.: Repacking 'privacy' for a networked world. Comput. Supported Coop. Work **26**(4–6), 453–488 (2017). https://doi.org/10.1007/s10606-017-9276-y

14. Dodson, L.L., Sterling, S.R., Bennett, J.K.: Minding the gaps: Cultural, technical and gender-based barriers to mobile use in oral-language berber communities in morocco. In: Proceedings of the Sixth International Conference on Information and Communication Technologies and Development: Full Papers - Volume 1, ICTD 2013, pp. 79–88. Association for Computing Machinery, New York (2013). https://doi.org/10.1145/2516604.2516626

15. Eldefrawy, M.H., Alghathbar, K., Khan, M.K.: OTP-based two-factor authentication using mobile phones. In: Proceedings of the 2011 Eighth International Conference on Information Technology: New Generations, ITNG 2011, pp. 327–331. IEEE Computer Society, USA (2011). https://doi.org/10.1109/ITNG.2011.64

16. Haque, S.M.T., et al.: Privacy vulnerabilities in public digital service centers in Dhaka, Bangladesh. In: Proceedings of the 2020 International Conference on Information and Communication Technologies and Development, ICTD 2020. Association for Computing Machinery, New York (2020). https://doi.org/10.1145/3392561.3394642

17. Haque, S.T., Wright, M., Scielzo, S.: A study of user password strategy for multiple accounts. In: Proceedings of the Third ACM Conference on Data and Application Security and Privacy, CODASPY 2013, pp. 173–176. Association for Computing Machinery, New York (2013). https://doi.org/10.1145/2435349.2435373

18. Ion, I., Reeder, R., Consolvo, S.: "...no one can hack my mind": Comparing expert and non-expert security practices. In: Proceedings of the Eleventh USENIX Conference on Usable Privacy and Security, SOUPS 2015, pp. 327–346. USENIX Association, USA (2015)

19. Just, M., Aspinall, D.: Personal choice and challenge questions: a security and usability assessment. In: Proceedings of the 5th Symposium on Usable Privacy and Security pp. 1–11 (2009)

20. Karunakaran, S., Thomas, K., Bursztein, E., Comanescu, O.: Data breaches: user comprehension, expectations, and concerns with handling exposed data. In: Symposium on Usable Privacy and Security, pp. 217–234 (2018)

21. King, M., Alhadidi, D., Cook, P.: Text-based detection of unauthorized users of social media accounts. In: Bagheri, E., Cheung, J.C.K. (eds.) Canadian AI 2018. LNCS (LNAI), vol. 10832, pp. 292–297. Springer, Cham (2018). https://doi.org/10.1007/978-3-319-89656-4_29

22. Kothari, V., Koppel, R., Blythe, J., Smith, S.: Password logbooks and what their amazon reviews reveal about their users' motivations, beliefs, and behaviors. In: European Workshop on Usable Security (2017)

23. Lastdrager, E., Gallardo, I.C., Hartel, P., Junger, M.: How effective is anti-phishing training for children? In: Symposium on Usable Privacy and Security, pp. 229–239 (2017)

24. Marques, D., Guerreiro, T., Carriço, L., Beschastnikh, I., Beznosov, K.: Vulnerability & blame: making sense of unauthorized access to smartphones. In: Proceedings of the 2019 CHI Conference on Human Factors in Computing Systems, pp. 1–13 (2019)

25. Mayer, P., Volkamer, M.: Addressing misconceptions about password security effectively. In: Workshop on Socio-Technical Aspects in Security and Trust, pp. 16–27 (2018)

26. Miller, R.: That time i got locked out of my google account for a month, 22 December 2017. https://techcrunch.com/2017/12/22/that-time-i-got-locked-out-of-my-google-account-for-a-month/

27. Nissenbaum, H.: Privacy as contextual integrity. Wash L. Rev. **79**, 119 (2004)

28. Patrick, A.S., Kenny, S.: From privacy legislation to interface design: implementing information privacy in human-computer interactions. In: Dingledine, R. (ed.) PET 2003. LNCS, vol. 2760, pp. 107–124. Springer, Heidelberg (2003). https://doi.org/10.1007/978-3-540-40956-4_8

29. Redmiles, E.M.: "Should i worry?" a cross-cultural examination of account security incident response. In: 2019 IEEE Symposium on Security and Privacy (SP), pp. 920–934. IEEE (2019)

30. Ruoti, S., Monson, T., Wu, J., Zappala, D., Seamons, K.: Weighing context and trade-offs: how suburban adults selected their online security posture. In: Thirteenth Symposium on Usable Privacy and Security (SOUPS 2017), pp. 211–228 (2017)

31. Sambasivan, N., et al.: "Privacy is not for me, it's for those rich women": performative privacy practices on mobile phones by women in south Asia. In: Fourteenth Symposium on Usable Privacy and Security (SOUPS 2018), pp. 127–142. USENIX Association, Baltimore, August 2018. https://www.usenix.org/conference/soups2018/presentation/sambasivan

32. Sambasivan, N., Rangaswamy, N., Cutrell, E., Nardi, B.: Ubicomp4d: Infrastructure and interaction for international development-the case of urban Indian slums. In: Proceedings of the 11th International Conference on Ubiquitous Computing, UbiComp 2009, pp. 155–164. Association for Computing Machinery, New York (2009). https://doi.org/10.1145/1620545.1620570

33. Seng, S., Kocabas, H., Al-Ameen, M.N., Wright, M.: Poster: Understanding user's decision to interact with potential phishing posts on facebook using a vignette study. In: Proceedings of the 2019 ACM SIGSAC Conference on Computer and Communications Security, CCS 2019, pp. 2617–2619. Association for Computing Machinery, New York (2019). https://doi.org/10.1145/3319535.3363270

34. Stobert, E., Biddle, R.: The password life cycle. ACM Trans. Privacy Secur. **21**(3), 1–32 (2018)

35. Sukwong, O., Kim, H., Hoe, J.: Commercial antivirus software effectiveness: an empirical study. Computer **3**, 63–70 (2010)

36. Sultana, S., et al.: Understanding the sensibility of social media use and privacy with Bangladeshi facebook group users. In: Proceedings of the 3rd ACM SIGCAS Conference on Computing and Sustainable Societies (COMPASS 2020), pp. 317–318. Association for Computing Machinery, New York (2020). https://doi.org/10.1145/3378393.3402235

37. Vashistha, A., Anderson, R., Mare, S.: Examining security and privacy research in developing regions. In: Proceedings of the 1st ACM SIGCAS Conference on Computing and Sustainable Societies, COMPASS 2018 (COMPASS 2018). Association for Computing Machinery, New York (2018). https://doi.org/10.1145/3209811.3209818

38. Weiner, A.J., Ne'man, R.: Fallback identity authentication techniques, 3 October 2017, US Patent 9,781,105

39. Williams, C.: 620 million accounts stolen from 16 hacked websites now for sale on dark web, seller boasts, 11 February 2019. https://www.theregister.co.uk/2019/02/11/620_million_hacked_accounts_dark_web/

40. Zhang-Kennedy, L., Chiasson, S., van Oorschot, P.: Revisiting password rules: facilitating human management of passwords. In: 2016 APWG Symposium on Electronic Crime Research (eCrime) pp. 81–90. IEEE, Toronto (2016)

41. Zou, Y., Mhaidli, A.H., McCall, A., Schaub, F.: "I've got nothing to lose": consumers' risk perceptions and protective actions after the equifax data breach. In: Fourteenth Symposium on Usable Privacy and Security (SOUPS 2018), pp. 197–216 (2018)

CyberPin - Challenges on Recognizing Youngest Cyber Talents

Birgy Lorenz[1]([⊠]) [iD], Kaido Kikkas[1], Aleksei Talisainen[1], and Taavi Eomäe[2]

[1] Tallinn University of Technology, Tallinn, Estonia
{Birgy.lorenz,Kaido.Kikkas,Aleksei.Talisainen}@taltech.ee
[2] University of Tartu, Tartu, Estonia
Taavi.Eomae@eesti.ee

Abstract. Various countries run campaigns that aim to spot gifted students early on, be it about PISA tests, talented musicians and singers, or winners of other contests and competitions. The same applies to cybersecurity and digital safety. While there are several competitions for upper grades such as European Cyber Security Challenge (EU), CyberPatriot (USA), CyberSpike and CyberCracker (Estonia), recent initiatives like Safer Internet aim to target younger children as well. This paper introduces a successful initiative in Estonia called CyberPin that was launched in Spring 2020 by Tallinn University of Technology (together with participants from upper-level cybersecurity contests), aiming to help schools spot gifted students from grades 1 to 6. The one-month competition in February 2020 had 7568 Estonian-speaking and 1305 Russian-speaking participants. The results show differences by mother tongue, but also by gender. We also had a critical look at the pilot test in order to improve the oncoming 2021 event.

Keywords: Cyber challenge · Digital competences · K-12 programs · Gifted students · Talents

1 Introduction

Until recently, the common point of view was that IT-inclined youth should be discovered during their secondary education to guide them towards suitable curricula at universities. By today, this has shifted earlier, and the process starts in Grades 4.-9. But even regarding this, several studies (as well as our practical experience) have pointed out that girls have already decided their future career choices by then - and even if they show interest towards IT, they have fallen behind boys in their IT experience and will thus easily give up the perspective [1]. It has therefore been suggested that IT talent scouting should start even earlier, in Grade 3. the latest - there are initiatives targeting the younger age group (e.g. InSafe/Safer Internet - Better Internet for Kids or Hour of Code). The goal is to promote the natural curiosity and 'hacker' mindset before they are forced to retreat by the 'one fits all' education as well as puberty kicking in. Developing creativity - one of the five qualities often outlined by employers - is also emphasized.

© Springer Nature Switzerland AG 2021
A. Moallem (Ed.): HCII 2021, LNCS 12788, pp. 326–336, 2021.
https://doi.org/10.1007/978-3-030-77392-2_21

1.1 The Concepts

We based our understanding of talent on the model by Renzull (1978) and Mönks (1990) [4] that explain influences on creativity, motivation and scholastic aptitude from different sides (school, family, and friends) (see Fig. 1).

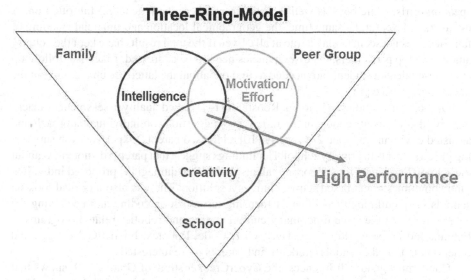

Fig. 1. Renzull (1978) and Mönks (1990) talents model [4].

Being a talent means being gifted in a given field. Giftedness is usually defined as being recognized for performance that is superior to that of one's peers [17] but we feel that this is sometimes too narrow understanding. The model above links one's natural abilities to one's efforts as well as a wider, context-based success factor (creativity). We strived to achieve similar results via choosing the types of exercises (puzzles, logic, functional reading, spotting and solving problems) - as the target group is young and lacks experience in cybersecurity, we considered these types of exercises more adequate to actual cybersecurity tasks, while still building skills vital for future specialists. We also note that a gifted child needs support, but currently this is often found rather outside the mainstream education.

The Estonian experience shows that in IT and cybersecurity, talents tend to be discovered via clubs and competitions. At the same time, these places may involve others who can even be not that interested in the area - this may happen when parents decide that their child absolutely must receive complementary training in that field, or it is introduced as a compulsory subject at school. Similar challenges have been identified elsewhere, but they are often reduced to just solving mathematical problems [5, 12, 12, 16]. In some cases, tests have been used to help faster identification of talented students [6].

Yet another issue that has been raised in times is fair testing regardless of the student's gender [3]. Also, the PISA periodical studies (in every three years) analyze numbers of students on different levels and various characteristics of studies (including the impact of financial standing and gender balance) [11].

1.2 The Estonian Experience

The PISA test results of Estonian students over the years show top results from Estonian-speaking girls, while boys as well as Russian speakers (both genders) fall often under the average level (at the same time, the geographical location and financial standing of families does not seem to play a role at all). Even if the total results have kept the country among the top performers, the discrepancies need to be addressed. Likewise, follow-up studies on talented students are needed to find out about the latter-life chances to put the talent into practice [13].

Of the related studies in Estonia, Roosfeldt [14] studied quality assessment of teaching gifted students at schools in 2016, making suggestions on individual approach and adjusted environments. The 2019 study [10] addressed parents' experiences in supporting gifted students in primary school. Her findings suggest that parents do not know about the schools' measures for supporting talents. In 2019, Pajumägi [9] proposed individual (and sometimes home-based) curriculum as a solution. There is also a critical look on schools [15], outlining the danger of focusing too much on coding and neglecting the 'big picture'. At the same time, many current coding and robotics related programs in Estonia and in the world (ProgreTiger, Girls Code, Robotex, FirstLEGO League and others) help to make schools, students and parents more interested.

Concerning gender differences, the CyberCracker study of Grades 4.-9. shows that girls excel at less complex tasks involving rapid reaction and social skills (e.g. "How to counter cyberbullying?") while boys are better in tasks involving technical skills and more complex thinking (e.g. "How to discover malware on a website?") [7]. Overall, the results of girls and boys are comparable – yet starting from Grade 7, the number of girls participating keeps falling. Therefore, in the CyberPin study, we try to find out the situation in Grades 1–6 regarding gender, also addressing the language background (as 80% of the participating were Estonian- and 20% Russian-speaking) that is usually not addressed in any of the studies so far.

2 Methods

The CyberPin is a school-based competition for Grades 1–6 that aims to introduce various topics about digital safety and cybersecurity. The tasks are divided into four areas and four difficulty levels. The competition in February 2020 coincided with the Safer Internet campaign to promote safe Internet use. The test was taken by 7568 Estonian-speaking (representing 35% of schools) and 1305 Russian-speaking (15% of schools) students all over Estonia. We note that the language difference is personal rather than institutional – some schools accommodate both languages, and some Russian-speaking students go to Estonian-language schools (see Fig. 2).

The topical areas were called "Pay Attention!" (simple mathematical statements), "Messed-Up Technology" (technical tasks), "Puzzles" and "What's This?" (simple cryptography). The tasks were created by both security experts and participants of previous

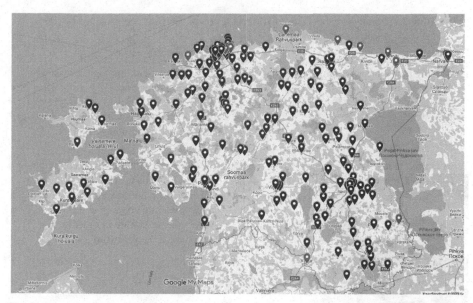

Fig. 2. The map of schools (Estonian-speaking ones in blue, Russian-speaking ones in green) [8].

cybersecurity competitions - the goal was to offer exercises promoting skills that are needed at Capture The Flag (CTF) competitions and would also be generally helpful in later life (noticing small details, thinking outside the box, making use of limited tools, math/crypto). The exercises also included some directly IT-related questions, to spot students with existing IT knowledge. More picture-based questions were given to the youngest age group (see Tables 1 and 2).

Table 1. Distribution for different age groups.

	Grades 1–2	Grades 3–4	Grades 5–6
Picture recognition, simpler functional reading	3 easy 2 intermediate	3 easy 3 intermediate 1 hard 1 very hard	3 easy 4 intermediate 1 hard 2 very hard
Logic - math, conversion text puzzle	1 easy	1 easy 1 intermediate	1 easy 1 intermediate 3 hard 1 very hard
	6 questions/10 points	10 questions/18 points	16 questions/40 points

All the tasks were available both in Estonian and Russian. The students were allowed just pen and paper, outside help (both on- and offline) was not permitted. The answers were e-mailed to teachers, and the results/feedback were provided after completing the test.

Table 2. Examples of exercises in different levels of difficulty are provided below.

Example	Level	Explanation
How many non-Windows computers are here? (Multiple choice answer)	Easy	Picture recognition, logical reasoning, functional reading The hardest exercises of this type had up to 20 pictures with complex boolean equations using many different qualifiers
What is this? (Free-form answer)	Intermediate	Picture recognition (text recognition, using IT skills to solve the challenge) The hardest level exercise required the participant to zoom in to the low-quality picture in order to recognize the password
What is in your pocket? 3v3rY 5tUDN3t H43 5M4rtPh0n3 1n TH31R p0Ck3T	Hard	Logic. Text puzzle, contextual solving, functional reading. Easy level exercise changed the word "informatics" over and hardest used a simple 1-letter Caesar cipher. (where every letter is shifted one position in the alphabet (A-> B, B-> C and so on)

We outlined a number of limitations at the 2020 test. One was the testing environment itself which was pioneered for the first time – there was no certainty that the tasks are appropriate and understandable for students (command of language, functional reading skill).

Another one was the delivery of tasks and right answers to teachers. The teachers were instructed not to guide their students, yet there were five schools (2% overall answers) which allowed repeated submissions to improve the results. Still, the results suggest that the large majority did not cheat as the overall success factor was low – most students got about 1/3 of answers right and very few reached the talent levels. It is interesting to note that despite the modest results, most teachers were happy with the test – in their feedback, they mention 'discovering' students who had not been notable earlier; many of them also used the test to discuss the results and possible solutions with their students later.

3   Results and Discussion

The results show that for the Grades 1–3, the easiest was the picture puzzle (water flowing in pipes) and for the Grades 4–6, the math puzzle where pictures had to be converted to numbers. For Grade 1, the hardest was the intermediate-level propositional calculus task – while it was presented in pictures, it nevertheless demanded some functional reading skills. For Grade 2, the most difficult was the "ports and plugs" task which was also difficult for older students. From Grade 3 upwards, harder tasks did not get solved – one of the reasons was not knowing proper terminology (the student might recognize the object but not know how it is called). It should also be noted that there was no difference in the two language groups (see Figs. 3 and 4).

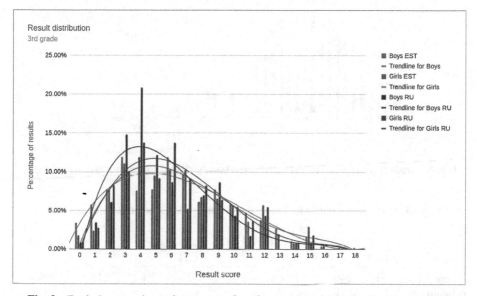

Fig. 3. Grade 3 comparison of test scores from boys/girls and Estonian/Russian student.

Up to Grade 3, there seem to be no real differences neither in gender nor language/ethnicity (the results seem to slightly favor girls). However, the differences appear by Grade 6 – among Estonian-speakers, girls pull ahead, among Russian-speakers they lag increasingly behind while Russian-speaking boys are not far from Estonian-speaking girls. On the other hand (as already mentioned at the CyberCracker study), the strong side of Estonian-speaking boys (compared to other groups) lies in more technical and/or more sophisticated questions. Also, Estonian-speaking schools displayed more coherent results all over the spectrum while there was more variation among Russian speakers.

Moreover, the difference by language showed in questions where functional reading was important (the 'tricky' questions) – in these, Estonian-speakers did remarkably better. It is possible that this kind of skill is not stressed in Russian-language schools – Russian-speakers seemed to excel at clearly-worded questions needing logic/math skills (see Table 3).

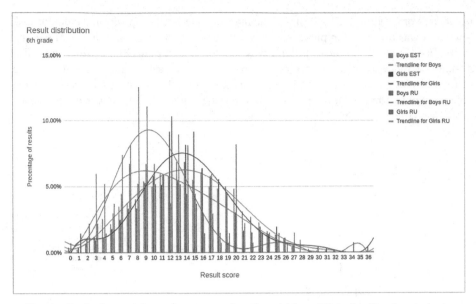

Fig. 4. Grade 6 comparison of test scores from boys/girls and Estonian/Russian students.

Table 3. Comparison of Grade 3 and 6 female/male and Estonian/Russian answers.

	3 M EST	3 F EST	3 M RU	3 F RU	6 M EST	6 F EST	6 M RU	6 F RU
Picture recognition, functional reading (easy)	63%	64%	77%	73%	72%	78%	84%	78%
Picture recognition, functional reading (intermediate)	38%	41%	27%	42%	59%	69%	49%	51%
Picture recognition, functional reading (very hard)	22%	21%	32%	35%	34%	29%	32%	26%
Picture recognition, content skills/IT (hard)	37%	38%	33%	26%	34%	29%	32%	26%

(continued)

Table 3. (*continued*)

	3 M EST	3 F EST	3 M RU	3 F RU	6 M EST	6 F EST	6 M RU	6 F RU
Math, conversion	58%	58%	73%	71%	83%	88%	90%	88%
Logic puzzle, sequence (easy)	66%	68%	77%	80%	65%	68%	77%	77%
Picture recognition (text recognition, using IT skills to solve the challenge) (hardest)	5%	4%	6%	10%	21%	17%	25%	21%
Text puzzle, contextual solving, functional reading (easy)	52%	61%	70%	72%	73%	82%	81%	79%
Text puzzle, contextual solving, functional reading (intermediate)	36%	46%	27%	26%	57%	71%	32%	38%
Picture recognition, content skills/IT (intermediate)	23%	17%	66%	64%	32%	28%	75%	56%

4 Critical Remarks

Most questions of the 2020 tests seemed to address either attention-paying or spatial IQ. The test should be based more on psychological factors (to include other abilities than purely technical knowledge). Also, while adding more specifically cybersecurity-oriented questions would be difficult for at least younger age groups (due to their lack of technical knowledge), the questions can be tuned to further stress the qualities that are beneficial for a career in cybersecurity (creative mindset, ability to find or create suitable tools etc.).

Some more specific points on different types of questions:

- other types of questions might be preferred to free-form, verbal questions as they rely on language skills and functional reading, and in many cases, need to be verified manually (problematic with more than 7000 participants). For instance, many Estonian-speaking students recognized the hard disk from the picture, but did not know the proper term (at the same time, in Russian there are less variants for the word, so there were more correct answers);
- subjective reasoning and estimates should be avoided (e.g. "Fake or not") if detailed explanation is not provided. If it is used, the participant should be able to comment on it. Language-specific wording should be avoided. For instance, some questions used negation (ct English "Isn't it?") which can be interpreted differently in different languages;
- textual exercises are problematic for first graders, as the reading and arithmetic skills may not suffice yet. Even if the choices provided are textual/numeric, the task should be presented as graphically/visually as possible. Another consideration would be using a sound clip to present the task.

More background information could be collected – to find out other factors the students face in their lives and their possible impact.

5   Future Steps

An important question is the follow-up – what is done after spotting the talents. If this will be the school's responsibility, then teachers should be supported in order to give them time and skills for working with these students. Due to their young age, local activities near their homes (clubs, after-school events etc.) should be preferred to national-level programs.

Another question is whether (or how much) this kind of talent can be developed. There is a definite role for families and homes, but further studies on this are possibly needed. In Estonia, the study showed that the talented students were dispersed quite even all over the country – at the same time, abilities need to be developed and the conditions can considerably vary by school.

Finally, the positive note is that, according to PISA, the results of Estonian schools do not depend on location, parents' education or financial standing. Also, the results of Russian-speaking students in Estonia exceed their language peers in Russia and elsewhere.

The question about lack of girls in IT remains, even if there is a multitude of various support programs both in Estonia and elsewhere. As seen above, the lack of related skills is rather not the reason, at least among Estonian speakers who do well at the primary and middle school level but then fail to convert their good results into future IT careers. At the same time, girls from Russian-speaking schools lag behind boys in IT at early stages already.

6 Conclusion

Spotting gifted students early helps the young person to see the potential avenues in his/her life and helps to conserve school resources. While most cybersecurity initiatives tend to define talent through 'hacking' skills, spotting in early stages should rather be done in terms of more generic creative thinking and problem-solving. Our test shows that the differences start to develop already in primary school – even if it did not assess typical school activities, the results fall in line with the PISA results in Grade 9. While it is often assumed that the lack of girls in IT comes from their worse results, our results point out the contrary (in the middle school stage, Estonian-speaking girls beat boys in most types of exercises that were used).

The test of 2020 should be refined and re-used in the coming years to see if the spotted students display similar performance later as well. The next studies could look also at extracurricular activities (robotics, IT) and their impact on students' cybersecurity and digital safety skills. Also, there is an ongoing need to set the course for those students whom the schools identify as talents – schools need guidance and support for this.

Acknowledgments. This study is supported by the Estonian Ministry of Defense program Cyber Olympic and program Safer Internet Centre in Estonia that is funded from the European Commission Connecting European Facility Programme.

References

1. Antropoloogia. Tuleviku tegija teekond startup ökosüsteemi (2018). https://media.voog.com/0000/0037/5345/files/Raport%2015.11.18.pdf
2. Baltaci, S.: Examination of gifted students' probability problem solving process in terms of mathematical thinking. Malaysian Online J. Educ. Technolo. 4(4), 18–35 (2016)
3. Dori, Y.J., Zohar, A., Fischer-Shachor, D., Kohan-Mass, J., Carmi, M.: Gender-fair assessment of young gifted students' scientific thinking skills. Int. J. Sci. Educ. **40**(6), 595–620 (2018)
4. Giftedness vs. High performance. Renzull (1978) and Mönks (1990) Model. https://www.xn--knnen-macht-spass-zzb.de/en/news-reader/giftedness-vs-high-performance/ Accessed 14 July 2020
5. Gremalschi, A.: Pedagogical models for preparing gifted and extra-gifted students for national and international competitions in informatics. Acta et commentationes (Ştiinţe ale Educaţiei) **18**(4), 26–36 (2019)
6. Kashani-Vahid, L., Afrooz, G., Shokoohi-Yekta, M., Kharrazi, K., Ghobari, B.: Can a creative interpersonal problem solving program improve creative thinking in gifted elementary students? Thinking Skills Creativity **24**, 175–185 (2017)
7. Lorenz, B., et al.: KüberPähkel 2019 tulemused. shorturl.at/rzIRX. Accessed 14 July 2020
8. Lorenz, B.: Mapf of CyberPin 2020. shorturl.at/huEKZ. Accessed 14 July 2020
9. Pajumägi, H.: Andekuse mõiste ja andekat õpilast toetavate tugimeetmete käsitlus Eesti õiguses ning Harjumaa koolides. Master Thesis. University of Tartu (2019). https://dspace.ut.ee/handle/10062/65343
10. Pedaste, M.: Lapsevanemate kogemused lapse annete arengu toetamisel I kooliastmes ja ootused annete arengu toetamise suhtes. Master thesis. University of Tartu (2019). https://dspace.ut.ee/handle/10062/65338

11. PISA 2018 Results (Volume II) Girls' and boys' performance in PISA. https://www.oecd-ili brary.org/education/pisa-2018-results-volume-ii_f56f8c26-en. Accessed 14 July 2020
12. Poulos, A., Mamona-Downs, J.: Gifted students approaches when solving challenging mathematical problems. In: Singer, Florence Mihaela (ed.) Mathematical creativity and mathematical giftedness. IM, pp. 309–341. Springer, Cham (2018). https://doi.org/10.1007/978-3-319-73156-8_12
13. Pärismaa, S.: Kas poisse tuleks tukast sugeda? Õpetajate Leht (2014). https://opleht.ee/2014/04/kas-poisse-tuleks-tukast-sugeda/. Accessed 14 July 2020
14. Roostfeldt, T.: Koolipõhised andekate õppe kvaliteedi indikaatorid. Master thesis. University of Tartu (2016). https://dspace.ut.ee/handle/10062/52897
15. Stepanova, J. Koostöine õpetamine robootikaga rikastatud tunnis 3. klassi matemaatika näitel. Master Thesis. Tallinn University (2020). https://www.etis.ee/Portal/Mentorships/Display/83cd1237-e8a8-4101-a96b-a3c4d31f8187. Accessed 14 July 2020
16. Uçar, F.M., Uçar, M.B., Çalişkan, M.: Investigation of gifted students' problem-solving skills. J. Educ. Gifted Young Sci. 5(3), 1–14 (2017)
17. Worrell, F.C., Subotnik, R.F., Olszewski-Kubilius, P., Dixson, D.D.: Gifted students. Ann. Rev. Psychol. 70, 551–576 (2019). https://www.annualreviews.org/doi/abs/10.1146/annurev-psych-010418-102846

It's Not My Problem: How Healthcare Models Relate to SME Cybersecurity Awareness

Brian Pickering[1]([envelope]) [iD], Costas Boletsis[2] [iD], Ragnhild Halvorsrud[2] [iD],
Stephen Phillips[1] [iD], and Mike Surridge[1] [iD]

[1] Electronics and Computer Science, IT Innovation, University of Southampton,
Gamma House, Enterprise Road, Southampton SO16 7NS, UK
{j.b.pickering,s.c.phillips,ms8}@soton.ac.uk
[2] SINTEF Digital, Forskningsveien 1, 0373 Oslo, Norway
{konstantinos.boletsis,ragnhild.halvorsrud}@sintef.no

Abstract. Small and medium enterprises (SMEs) make up a significant part of European economies. Despite their economic importance, they are often described as poorly placed to deal with cyber risks because of resource constraints or commercial interests. Providing appropriate tooling would facilitate a greater appreciation of the risks and provide mitigation strategies. In a series of workshops demonstrating visualization tools for cybersecurity, constructs from healthcare models such as awareness, self-efficacy, and a willingness to engage were investigated to throw light on the likelihood that the technologies would be adopted. Although most constructs were validated, it turns out that self-efficacy could more appropriately be interpreted as a desire to understand a broader company narrative rather than empowering any individual to identify and manage cyber risk. As part of an ongoing examination of technology acceptance, this work provides further evidence that technology must be contextualised to make sense for the individual as part of the SME rather than as individual employee.

Keywords: Cybersecurity awareness · SME · Small-story narrative · Qualitative methods · Technology adoption · Health Belief Model · Normalisation Process Theory

1 Introduction

The increasing sophistication of cyber-attacks may have particularly negative consequences for organizations such as small and medium enterprises (SMEs). They are focused on their main business and may not therefore have the resource or expertise to identify and handle such risks. In this study, we investigate the use of constructs from healthcare models specifically conceived in relation to risk awareness and behavioural change in an attempt to understand the willingness of this type of enterprise to engage with cybersecurity tooling.

© Springer Nature Switzerland AG 2021
A. Moallem (Ed.): HCII 2021, LNCS 12788, pp. 337–352, 2021.
https://doi.org/10.1007/978-3-030-77392-2_22

1.1   The SME Landscape

The risk of cyber-attacks for SMEs is well established. Sharma et al. [26] list the types of attack that have been reported, while Bell [3] suggests that SMEs may not have the resource to deal with them. Lewis and his colleagues [15] maintain that while individual threats are significant, an SME as part of a supply-chain presents additional cybersecurity concerns since any vulnerability they display can affect others across the chain. They attempt, therefore, to identify the perceived sensitivity of individual threats in relation to SME willingness to share information about cybersecurity readiness. In his report, Bell [3] focuses primarily on technology vulnerabilities, while Sharma et al. [26] and more recently Vakakis et al. [29] recognise vulnerability associated with individual employee behaviour, making them targets themselves [31]. Not surprisingly, Lewis et al. [15] identify training and awareness as important and shareable aspects of cybersecurity status. Further, individuals are not necessarily attuned to cyber risks [14]. So, if people are not aware of appropriate behaviours, we need to understand how to encourage them to change how they act [4]. This is true in all aspects of our lives [32]. However, as the WannaCry attack illustrates, for those vulnerable to it, such as the NHS in the UK, individual actions and a lack of organizational procedures exacerbate the risk [16].

Understanding personal risk, it has been suggested, is a key motivator to engage with a whole range of preventative behaviours, including models such as the Health Belief Model (HBM) [7,8,27]. As well as this perception of risk, however, for an intervention to be sustained, patients or users in other domains need to believe the specific intervention will help them to manage the risk. Thus, self-efficacy was introduced in later iterations of the HBM. Taking health interventions as a metaphor for the well-being of the SME, demonstrating the constructs of the HBM are relevant might throw some light on the likelihood of cybersecurity tool adoption. Specifically, if the model reveals SME awareness of risk, introducing appropriate tools might encourage responsibility-taking and behavioural change [4]. This exploratory study seeks to investigate first the levels of cybersecurity threat awareness and then how decision-support technologies might encourage self-efficacy as a precursor of protective behavioural change.

2   Background

Evaluation of new or enhanced technologies is often underpinned implicitly with one of several causal behavioural models. Typically, they seek to predict the intention to adopt based on some situational context, which may include the demographics of the target users, and some other decision criteria. An early broader formulation derives from the Theory of Reasoned Action (TRA) and thence of Planned Behaviour (TPB) [2,12,20]. Significantly, as TRA developed into TPB, the notion of self-efficacy was introduced: those who might be motivated to act in a given way – adopt a technology or change behaviour – would believe that adoption would improve their self-belief in achieving a goal.

Focusing specifically on technology at the decision point, Davis [10,11] and then Venkatesh [30] tended to focus on characteristics of the technology itself at the decision point and on moderating factors like the context for technology use and the experience of adopters. Quantitative instruments were developed to capture constructs such as the perceived ease-of-use of the technology and the dependent perceived usefulness of the technology. Together or independently, these are assumed to predict the intention to adopt a given technology. Similar models have also been applied to the adoption of healthcare interventions [9]. Here the focus is on patient awareness and response to risk (Health Belief Model) or to fear (Protection Motivation Theory).

One of the inherent issues with TPB and similar models, however, is that the decision point leads to an intention to behave in a given way, or an intention to adopt the technology. The bridge between this intention and the actual behaviour is often overlooked. So, conceptual frameworks such as diffusion of innovations (DoI) focus on factors including but not confined to the technology which might predict up-scaling and spread of technology (innovation) beyond the decision point itself [24].

In our own recent work, we have questioned whether quantifying usability and usefulness can really predict the willingness to adopt technology [21,22]. From our exploratory work, we concluded that potential adopters need to develop an understanding of how the technology can help them or their colleagues specifically with their individual responsibilities. In other words, we found some evidence for the importance of self-efficacy as a construct for technology adoption. Further, in creating narratives around the use of technology, we argued that individuals internalise the potential with the technology to make sense of it in their own context. We report below a specific empirical investigation into the use of visualization tools for cybersecurity. We aimed to explore both the decision point and potential influences for longer term adoption and use.

2.1 Health Belief Model (HBM)

With parallels to TPB, HBM contextualised the decision to adopt a suggested intervention based on constructs related to the context for the intervention, including how it might improve self-efficacy, and perceived individual control [1,7,8]. A patient for a given intervention would thereby consider their risk regarding a specific condition, such as obesity or contracting an illness, and its likely impact. In addition, the model suggests, they would consider how the proposed intervention might help them address the risks and impacts, and the latitude they have to take action [7,8]. This echoes, we maintain, cyber risk awareness and the adoption of technologies like firewalls and anti-virus software [25]. Protection Motivation Theory (PMT), which shares structural similarities with HBM, was part of the development of a research model intending to predict the adoption of cybersecurity enhancing behaviours in SMEs [6] where the focus is on coping strategies (or self-efficacy). Warkentin and his colleagues went further to explore long-term cybersecurity aware behaviours based on a contextualised and empirically validated version of PMT [33]. It is such contextualization, they conclude, which is key to longer term adoption of appropriate behaviours.

In a similar vein, we explore the operational context within which SME employees need to identify and implement appropriate actions regarding cybersecurity. We use constructs from HBM because this focuses on the more general awareness rather than specific and individual fear as with PMT. It was felt that awareness might encourage responsibility taking as an employee of the SME.

2.2   Normalisation Process Theory (NPT)

As stated above, even if the intention to adopt technology were to predict its actual adoption, continuing the behaviour is a different issue. In addition to constructs of the HBM as they relate to risk and impact awareness around cybersecurity, a supplementary question arises. If SME employees show some appreciation of the risks and potential impact when exploring cybersecurity visualization tools would they also show appreciation that the tools could help them take action to protect against cyber-attacks? Indeed, Warkentin et al. [33] specifically target the continuation of appropriate behaviours in response to the fear, in PMT terms, surrounding a potential attack. Looking at the propagation of innovation in the first instance, perhaps the DoI might throw some light on how technology use may persist. However, and specifically for healthcare again, frameworks have been developed which look at the actual adoption and adherence to an intervention. One such framework is the NPT [18,19,23].

Based on extensive empirical investigation, it predicts four main thematic areas which need to be explored, including the user community's buy in to the concept behind an intervention (its coherence), its willingness to engage (cognitive participation) and to act towards implementation (collective action) [17]. Crucially, the fourth involves continuous reflexive monitoring. The other constructs are consistent with the intention to adopt and the initial stages of adoption. The fourth, however, introduces the notion that users should continue to engage and explore technology or intervention benefits and affordances. In NPT terms, would they demonstrate cognitive participation and a willingness to take collective action? Cognitive participation would derive from the awareness signalled with the constructs from HBM. A willingness to take collective action extends HBM self-efficacy and the perceived benefit of the tools into the awareness of personal responsibility for cybersecurity risk mitigation. As May and his colleagues state, these four phases do not necessarily occur sequentially [19]. We might expect users, therefore, to begin to develop a narrative involving the technology from the early stages of exposure to it as part of cognitive participation which would then lead to collective action: they appreciate where the technology fits and what value it brings, but then see a broader context for its usefulness.

3   Method

This study uses mixed methods to explore SME awareness and attitudes to cybersecurity risk. Constructs from HBM and NPT were used to explore SME employees' awareness of cybersecurity risks and their willingness to adopt appropriate tooling to mitigate such risks. These were validated initially against issues from an independently developed quantitative instrument aimed at a sample of SME employees. The constructs were then explored during ethnographic observation followed by a more detailed thematic analysis of a series of workshops within the context of a European project looking at providing technical support for cybersecurity[1].

Table 1. Coding scheme for thematic analysis of the workshops.

Code	Model	Description
Risk awareness	HBM	Awareness that there is a risk from cyber attacks
Impact awareness	HBM	Awareness of the potential impact of such attacks
Self-efficacy	HBM	Perceived ability to deal with cyber risks
Benefits of tool use	HBM, NPT	Perceived benefit of using tools
Tool cohesion	NPT	Perception that tools provide a coherent view of risks
Adoption willingness	NPT	Willingness to adopt and explore the tools
Increase in understanding	NPT	Expression of increased awareness

3.1   Design

An anonymous online survey had been developed in a separate study based on input from cybersecurity experts when they were asked to consider what important issues might affect SME risk. It allowed one of the researchers (CB) to collect SME attitudes and practices regarding cybersecurity through the employee lens. As such, it provides a useful comparison with analyses effected in the present study.

For the qualitative analyses reported here, we had previously investigated the use of qualitative methods in understanding how potential adopters react to technology [21,22]. A coding scheme was defined in advance based on the main constructs from the HBM and on the phases of the NPT as described above by one of the researchers (BP). The scheme was intended as the basis for analysis of direct engagement with representative SMEs via a series of workshops and was not shared with the other researchers until after the online survey and workshops. It should be remembered that the goal of the workshops was to understand SME business operations not explicitly participant awareness about cybersecurity risk.

---

[1] The work reported here was approved by the Faculty of Engineering and Physical Science Research Ethics Committee (Ref ERGO/FEPS/62067).

The coding scheme is summarised in Table 1, including a brief description of each construct. These initial constructs are more typical, of course, for exploring health interventions, including technology. Although we argue that risk awareness regarding cybersecurity commercially might be seen as analogous with health and well-being awareness individually, some level of validation of these constructs seemed appropriate and was carried out against the results from an independent, anonymous, 24-item online survey and as part of ethnographic observation during the workshops described below.

3.2 Participants

The online survey attracted 164 self-selecting participants recruited via internal networks (an opportunity sample of 23) and a 3rd party (141 from a purposive sample). For the workshops, eight participants from four SMEs already engaged with the project took part in the workshops as well as the researchers themselves. Typically, only one researcher moderated the sessions whilst the others attended solely to ask questions or respond to specific points when asked. Participants were not cybersecurity experts, nor did they have any such specific responsibility within their respective organizations.

3.3 Data Collection

The online survey had been launched via an external platform and ran for approximately 3 weeks. The workshops were run over several months, with participants from SMEs across four domains: finance, healthcare, utilities and automotive manufacturing. Participants from a given SME engaged separately; a given workshop, therefore, was attended mainly by employees from one SME only. The workshops were organised as an introduction to issues of cyber security and the use of tools to help individuals or the enterprise as a whole understand and manage any such threats [5]. Thirteen workshops lasting over 27 h in total were recorded across the four domains individually. The objective of the workshops was to understand the operational context for each of the SMEs and were not explicitly intended to explore participant understanding or awareness of cyber risks and mitigation. The second and third workshops involved a focused discussion of cybersecurity, including a demonstration of tools which visualise threats associated with the infrastructure [28] on the one hand, and typical business processes on the other [13]. In the third interview, participants were encouraged to work with the researchers to develop visualisations of their business infrastructure using the tools. Transcripts of the initial workshop for each SME were pseudonymised and checked with participants to ensure accuracy. Transcripts of the remaining workshops were automatically generated, a process which did not pre-serve identifiers of the original participants. Some ten and a half hours have been analysed thus far.

3.4   Analysis

The online survey had been independently developed on the basis of specific questions felt by cybersecurity experts was compared by one the researchers (CB) against the constructs in Table 1 with the intention of identifying a correspondence between the cybersecurity experts' views and the coding schema. We do not cover all responses to those questions here. In addition, one of the re-searchers (RH) made field notes during the workshops. These were then compared against the constructs in the coding schema as an initial indication that the issues of awareness, impact and willingness to adopt technology were felt salient.

Finally, after each workshop was recorded and transcribed verbatim, a third researcher (BP) used the coding scheme to carry out a thematic analysis of what participants discussed. This included all constructs from Table 1 and not just those validated in the previous two phases (comparison with the online survey and ethnographic observation).

4   Results

The following sections summarise first the validation of the model constructs from the quantitative survey (Sect. 4.1), followed by the qualitative analysis of the workshops described previously (Sect. 4.2 for the ethnographic observations; and Sect. 4.3 for the thematic analysis of the workshop transcripts).

4.1   Cybersecurity Coverage (Anonymous Survey)

The survey indirectly captures SME employee awareness of cybersecurity risks through examining their knowledge of the cybersecurity-related practices in the SMEs they work for. For example, and without detailing all responses, 70% of the responses to *Does your company offer courses or training material for employees to raise awareness about cybersecurity?* said no such education and training was available; while in reply to *Does your company have positions dedicated to cybersecurity at any level?* 60% said no and 7% don't know; and so forth.

For the rest, Table 2 simply lists the questions compared with a given construct without summary statistics of responses. So, it turns out the survey based on cybersecurity experts' perceptions of what is important for SMEs coincides with the first four constructs of Table 1, namely from the HBM. These are summarised in Table 2.

Apart from seeking to address the individual HBM constructs, the survey provided an additional motivation to explore SME employee willingness to adopt appropriate tooling as represented by the NPT-based constructs which had not been possible via the survey.

Table 2. Construct correspondence in the online survey.

Code	Description
Risk awareness	- Does your company offer courses or training material for employees to raise awareness about cybersecurity?
	- Does your company have positions dedicated to cyber-security at any level?
	- Do you discuss cybersecurity issues on your company meetings or presentations or, in general, internally in your company?
Impact awareness	- To what degree do you fear for a cybersecurity attack towards your company?
	- How long do you think your critical applications and systems can be shut down before significant disruption is caused to the company?
Self-efficacy	- How would you characterise your own knowledge about cybersecurity?
Benefits of tool use	- What security measures is your company taking to avoid cybersecurity attacks?
	- Does your company use specific processes or tools to assess risk to its IT assets?
	- Does your company use specific processes or tools for identifying cybersecurity vulnerabilities?
	- Does your company use specific processes or tools for identifying cybersecurity attacks?

4.2 Ethnographic Observations

Remembering that the intention of the workshops was to gain an understanding of the operational and business environment of the SMEs, observational notes from one of the researchers (RH) were reviewed in regard to the constructs proposed in Table 1. This analysis is summarised in Table 3 here.

As with the coverage of the questions in the anonymous survey, without directing discussion, separate ethnographic observation readily supports some of the constructs to be used for the proposed thematic analysis. From both the independent anonymous survey and ethnographic observations during the workshops themselves, the constructs selected look well-motivated regarding cybersecurity awareness even though the underlying models (HBM, NPT) were originally conceived in a different domain.

4.3 Exploring Model Constructs Specifically

The interviews were analysed qualitatively, using the constructs of Perceived Susceptibility, Perceived Impact and Self-efficacy from the HBM to code participant comments. Other constructs were not used systematically. Preliminary findings

Table 3. Summary of ethnographic observations.

Construct	Observations
Risk/Impact awareness	- Some were aware only of the potential for technical risks
	- Some were less aware, if at all, of risk associated with employees, such as social engineering attacks or an evil insider
	- Notwithstanding who might be responsible for security, many saw regulatory or similar compliance as sufficient to guarantee cybersecurity risk
Self-efficacy	- Some SMEs outsource their infrastructure and so lack the awareness and ability to take responsibility for cybersecurity
	- Some reported a lack of communication from the ICT infrastructure provider
	- Some participants reported frustration that ICT colleagues would not always share knowledge or know-how
Willingness to adopt	- Having seen the tooling demonstrated, some expressed enthusiasm for using the kind of tooling demonstrated to enhance their awareness of risk

reveal high levels of threat awareness: participants confirmed their awareness that cyberattacks could and do occur; further, they described potential impact to their clients, and to their own products and services. This would predict an intention to engage with and deal with the cyber risks. Offering the tools demonstrated during the sessions to help understand and manage such risks would be predicted to increase Self-efficacy, not least as applied directly to each SME's own business environment as part of the demonstrations. Although they acknowledge the potential benefit of the tools in the context of cybersecurity, participants appear to avoid personal responsibility: they identified other parts of their organization or third-party providers who should handle such matters instead.

Participants evidenced risk awareness associated with cyber-attacks, as predicted by the first construct of the model. They were very specific about the types of risks which could impact their business. For instance, maintaining patch levels is important not least to overcome known vulnerabilities. However, managing patch deployment would need attention:

"... there's always a trade-off between waiting until [a] patch has been tested in a non-production environment, and the problem that you leave the vulnerable system in the operational environment for longer" (P4) and careful consideration of associated risks:

"But if you apply the patch as soon as you get it, especially if you are the first in the world to do that, if you're really, really fast, then you can crash your system, right?" (P4)

The implications or impact awareness is also well-understood. Failure to provide access to data, would have serious consequences, for example:

"Without this real time data, they would be like blind . . . being cut off completely from the market data" (P3)

as would issues with data sharing:

"It's mostly data protection . . . Always the fear that the [personal] data goes to the wrong person, either unintentionally or someone steals it" (P4)

or even in regard to tampering with software:

"And this is very, very dangerous because somebody can hack it in a way where instead of detecting a pedestrian your model detects free space. So, this means that the car can drive on that area, which would be very, very bad" (P1)

Given this level of awareness both in terms of risk and impact, participants were positive about exploring the specific tooling being developed. They identified benefits to individual employees:

"from [this] project, [we would like] not only a checklist but something we are able to run on. . . err. . . on a permanent way to get and to have a monitoring of all the potential security threats" (P2)

as well as for the SME as a whole:

"but also... to the auditor. Maybe to show that we are aware" (P3)

Participants are unsurprisingly aware that the tools being developed would be useful to support them dealing with the risks and potential impacts they had identified, therefore. But they also appreciate that to be cohesive, the tooling must handle complex perspectives and requirements:

"We have to comply to cybersecurity threats also according to the requirements that we get from our customers . . . So, there are quite a number of security checks that you have to comply with in order to gain the trust of the customer in order to work with them" (P1)

To be of real benefit, therefore, the visualizations the tooling offers must present a coherent view:

"The relations are really complex, but as you just presented it, it looks relatively simple" (P3)

Participants do show, however, that their own understanding of cybersecurity issues is shifting. For example, they are beginning to think not only in terms of their own responsibilities – in this case software development – but of the overall implications for enterprise security:

"We usually use the term safe or functional safety as opposed to security and cybersecurity" (P1)

even to the extent of prompting the demonstrators:

"As long as you have everything . . . thought about everything, do not forget any assets" (P3)

showing increased understanding of the complexities of cybersecurity:

"As you mentioned before... Yeah, it's... I think there are a few things you need to watch out for as well" (P3)

So, moving forward, there is a willingness to adopt the tooling and adapt to their own needs:

"we would like to be able to see a potential cyberattack risk, maybe not in real time, but at least to be alerted and to react on to act" (P2)

And explore how the technology would benefit them specifically.

"So, one of the things we're hoping to do in [the project] is model the jobs that people do and figure out if [there] are any more risk[s]" (P3)

But the prospect seems attractive:

"...I'm absolutely excited about this and impressed" (P3)

The benefits afforded by technology in terms of self-efficacy were ambiguous. When shown the specific tooling being developed, there was an appreciation that tooling could benefit the individuals:

"This looks really, really useful for ourselves" (P3)

But the issue is more complex. Understanding regulatory requirements might not be easy in specific areas. For a non-lawyer, for example, it's not clear that the tools might meet all the needs of individuals to extend and improve awareness:

"Our lawyer... of course he's not [a] technical person, so he tries to translate these regulations to us but in the end I'm ...I'm really not sure" (P3)

Some of the SMEs outsourced their infrastructure. This creates a dependency on a third party. And they may not provide all the information that the SME directly involved in the business might need:

"[In] the end this I found this a little bit unsatisfying that afterwards they also did not communicate that much" (P3)

So, awareness both of potential risks and their impact may lead to a willingness to engage with tooling. However, this does not automatically relate to complete confidence in individual ability to act (self-efficacy). The context for SMEs is complicated by outsourcing, for example, and the range of issues which need to be considered. These are not just technical, such as monitoring and mitigating against cyber-attacks, but also regulatory in maintaining and proving compliance with industry standards and (data protection) law.

With the exception of self-efficacy, therefore, the constructs from HBM and NPT are largely supported in the context of exploring operational concerns and requirements for cybersecurity tooling amongst SMEs. Given the motivation for the models used here, this would suggest that participants were aware of cyber-attack risk and impacts. On that basis, they were willing to engage with the technology since they appreciate that tooling would help address the risks identified. Further, and thinking specifically around continued adoption, support for the constructs from NPT suggest a willingness to engage further with the technology in the context of their own SME business.

5   Discussion

We interpret these preliminary results as confirmation in the first instance for the constructs of health-related models and frameworks in the context of cyber-security technology adoption. The applicability of such models to cybersecurity and SMEs is not new [33]. Nor is the need to think not just about the causal behavioral model behind adoption, but the longer-term contextualization of the technology or behaviors. That being said, what we have found in this study specifically is twofold. First, that individuals need to see the utility of a given technology as it suits their own context. So, as participants describe their awareness of cyber risks and the potential benefit of the tools they were shown, they begin to engage with the technology via cognitive participation, as NPT formalises it, seeing an opportunity for collective action to adopt and explore the tools they have been shown in their specific environment. Both the awareness indicated by the constructs of the HBM and the ongoing adoption processes from the NPT [17–19,23] are necessary, of course. This confirms our previous findings [21,22]. Their willingness to incorporate their knowledge and understanding together with the tools they were shown into the company narrative suggests the technology is being operationalised to suit their existing SME processes rather than changing their own behaviour necessarily.

Secondly, however, there is an appreciation that their operational context in regard to cybersecurity, risk assessment and mitigation is more complex than individual responsibility taking. Researchers such as Bell [3] and Lewis and his colleagues [15] identify cyber risks for SMEs to be resource dependent and to relate to an unwillingness to share information with potential co-competitors. The findings here suggest a different view. Individuals reported risk awareness and an appreciation of the consequences, but they also described frustration that cyber-security involves multiple actors, whom they did not necessarily understand or who did not share all the relevant information, and factors in mitigating those risks, which prevented a level of general oversight. Self-efficacy, therefore, emerges as something beyond individual enablement. The tools demonstrated would benefit the SME as a whole, they reported, though not necessarily in their own individual job role. Risk mitigation is the responsibility of someone else after all such as an IT manager. But there was also a suggestion that they wanted to understand on an individual level what those responsible were doing and why they were doing it. Self-efficacy here does not therefore imply taking action individually but being able to appreciate the actions which are taken by others.

If, as we have suggested elsewhere, technology acceptance involves situating the technology into the company narrative, this might explain individual vulnerability [26,29,31]. Many refuse to click on a link in a personal email received at home outside office hours, and yet, might respond to a phishing attack at work if the phishing email looks to be part of their daily tasks. So, individuals do not behave inappropriately through ignorance. Instead, they behave this way because they do not understand how their own actions fit into the overall company narrative respecting cybersecurity. Visualization tools like those demonstrated in the workshops here need to emphasise chains of events across the socio-technical network and encourage a shared understanding of the consequences of those events.

6   Limitations and Future Work

The participants in this study were motivated to engage with the technologies being demonstrated, since all were funded through a single European project. It might be expected, therefore, that they would want to respond positively to what they were being shown and would be more attuned to identify possible benefit of those technologies. However, if – as we conclude – the discussions are consistent with other studies where even limitations in technology can be overlooked so long as what the technology offers aligns with the broader needs of the company, then other studies might provide evidence of the importance of the 'company narrative' as part of a willingness to engage with technology irrespective of any other ties between participant and researcher. s Indeed, the research direction which has emerged here was not known in advance to those who took part. In the short term, we will continue to analyse this and other workshops to understand how potential adopters react to technology.

7   Conclusion

A mixed-methods approach to understand the cybersecurity imperatives for SMEs has partly confirmed findings from other studies in terms of risk and impact awareness. However, the qualitative analysis of discussion around cybersecurity visualization tools, using a coding scheme derived from well-motivated behavioural models, suggest a complex interaction between awareness, self-efficacy and situating cybersecurity into a broader company narrative. The discussions were nominally about demonstrating technology. But as SME participants engaged, they began to consider a broader narrative and not only the potential usefulness to others within their organization. Contextualizing causal behavioural models should therefore include an overall appreciation for how individuals make sense of their environment.

Acknowledgements. This work was supported by the EU H2020 project CyberKit4SME (Grant agreement: 883188).

References

1. Abraham, C., Sheeran, P.: The health belief model. Predict. Health Behav. **2**, 28–80 (2005)
2. Ajzen, I.: The theory of planned behavior. Organ. Behav. Hum. Decis. Process. **50**(2), 179–211 (1991)
3. Bell, S., et al.: Cybersecurity is not just a 'big business' issue. Gov. Dir. **69**(9), 536 (2017)
4. Blythe, J.: Cyber security in the workplace: understanding and promoting behaviour change. In: Proceedings of CHI taly 2013 Doctoral Consortium, vol. 1065, pp. 92–101. CEUR Workshop Proceedings (2013)
5. Boletsis, C., Halvorsrud, R., Pickering, B., Phillips, S., Surridge, M.: Cybersecurity for SMEs: introducing the human element into socio-technical cybersecurity risk assessment. In: Proceedings of the IVAPP 2021 Conference, vol. to appear. Scitepress (2021)
6. Browne, S., Lang, M., Golden, W.: Linking threat avoidance and security adoption: A theoretical model for SMEs (2015)
7. Carpenter, C.J.: A meta-analysis of the effectiveness of health belief model variables in predicting behavior. Health Commun. **25**(8), 661–669 (2010)
8. Champion, V.L., Skinner, C.S.: The health belief model. In: Glanz, K., Rimer, B.K., Viswanath, K. (eds.) Health Behavior and Health Education: Theory, Research, and Practice, pp. 45–65. John Wiley & Sons, 4th edn. (2008)
9. Conner, M., Norman, P.: Predicting Health Behaviour, 2nd edn. Open University Press, Maidenhead (2005)
10. Davis, F.D.: A technology acceptance model for empirically testing new end-user information systems: Theory and results. Ph.D. thesis, Massachusetts Institute of Technology (1985)
11. Davis, F.D., Bagozzi, R.P., Warshaw, P.R.: User acceptance of computer technology: a comparison of two theoretical models. Manag. Sci. **35**(8), 982–1003 (1989)
12. Fishbein, M., Ajzen, I.: Belief, attitude, intention, and behavior: an introduction to theory and research. J. Bus. Ventur. **5**, 177–189 (1977)

13. Halvorsrud, R., Haugstveit, I.M., Pultier, A.: Evaluation of a modelling language for customer journeys. In: Proceedings of IEEE Symposium on Visual Languages and Human-Centric Computing (VL/HCC), pp. 40–48. IEEE (2016)
14. Jackson, J., Allum, N., Gaskell, G.: Perceptions of risk in cyberspace. Technical report, London School of Economics and Politics (2004). Cyber trust & crime prevention project (04/1157)
15. Lewis, R., Louvieris, P., Abbott, P., Clewley, N., Jones, K.: Cybersecurity information sharing: a framework for information security management in UK SME supply chains. In: Proceedings of the 22nd European Conference on Information Systems, pp. 1–15 (2014)
16. Martin, G., Ghafur, S., Kinross, J., Hankin, C., Darzi, A.: WannaCry - a year on. BMJ **361**, k2381 (2018)
17. May, C., et al.: Normalization Process Theory On-line Users' Manual, Toolkit and NoMAD instrument (2015). http://www.normalizationprocess.org. Accessed 11 Feb 2021
18. May, C., Finch, T.: Implementing, embedding, and integrating practices: an outline of normalization process theory. Sociology **43**(3), 535–554 (2009)
19. May, C.R., et al.: Development of a theory of implementation and integration: normalization process theory. Implement. Sci. 4, 29:1–29:9 (2009)
20. Montaño, D.E., Kasprzyk, D.: Theory of reasoned action, theory of planned behavior, and the integrated behavioral model. Health Behav. Theor. Res. Pract. **70**(4), 231 (2015)
21. Pickering, B., Bartholomew, R., Nouri Janian, M., López Moreno, B., Surridge, M.: *Ask me no questions*: increasing empirical evidence for a qualitative approach to technology acceptance. In: Kurosu, M. (ed.) HCII 2020, Part I. LNCS, vol. 12181, pp. 125–136. Springer, Cham (2020). https://doi.org/10.1007/978-3-030-49059-1_9
22. Pickering, B., Janian, M.N., López Moreno, B., Micheletti, A., Sanno, A., Surridge, M.: Seeing potential is more important than usability: revisiting technology acceptance. In: Marcus, A., Wang, W. (eds.) HCII 2019, Part IV. LNCS, vol. 11586, pp. 238–249. Springer, Cham (2019). https://doi.org/10.1007/978-3-030-23535-2_18
23. Pope, C., Halford, S., Turnbull, J., Prichard, J., Calestani, M., May, C.: Using computer decision support systems in NHS emergency and urgent care: ethnographic study using normalisation process theory. BMC Health Serv. Res. **13**, 111:1–111:13 (2013)
24. Rogers, E.M.: Diffusion of Innovations, 5th edn. Free Press, New York (2010)
25. Rokkas, T., Neokosmidis, I.: Factors affecting the market adoption of cyber-security products in energy and electrical systems: the case of spear. In: Proceedings of the 15th International Conference on Availability, Reliability and Security, pp. 1–8 (2020)
26. Sharma, K., Singh, A., Sharma, V.P.: SMEs and cybersecurity threats in e-commerce. EDPACS EDP Audit Control Secur. Newsl. **39**(5–6), 1–49 (2009)
27. Simon, J.: Attitudes of Hungarian asthmatic and COPD patients affecting disease control: empirical research based on health belief model. Front. Pharmacol. **4**, 135 (2013)
28. Surridge, M., et al.: Modelling compliance threats and security analysis of cross border health data exchange. In: Attiogbé, C., Ferrarotti, F., Maabout, S. (eds.) MEDI 2019. CCIS, vol. 1085, pp. 180–189. Springer, Cham (2019). https://doi.org/10.1007/978-3-030-32213-7_14

29. Vakakis, N., Nikolis, O., Ioannidis, D., Votis, K., Tzovaras, D.: Cybersecurity in SMEs: the smart-home/office use case. In: 2019 IEEE 24th International Workshop on Computer Aided Modeling and Design of Communication Links and Networks (CAMAD), pp. 1–7. IEEE (2019)
30. Venkatesh, V., Morris, M.G., Davis, G.B., Davis, F.D.: User acceptance of information technology: toward a unified view. MIS Q. **27**(3), 425–478 (2003)
31. Von Solms, R., Van Niekerk, J.: From information security to cyber security. Comput. Secur. **38**, 97–102 (2013)
32. Ward, K.: Social networks, the 2016 US presidential election, and Kantian ethics: applying the categorical imperative to Cambridge analytica's behavioral microtargeting. J. Media Ethics **33**(3), 133–148 (2018)
33. Warkentin, M., Johnston, A.C., Shropshire, J., Barnett, W.D.: Continuance of protective security behavior: a longitudinal study. Decis. Support Syst. **92**, 25–35 (2016)

Understanding the Last Line of Defense: Human Response to Cybersecurity Events

Summer Rebensky(iD), Meredith Carroll$^{(\boxtimes)}$ (iD), Andrew Nakushian(iD),
Maria Chaparro(iD), and Tricia Prior(iD)

Florida Institute of Technology, Melbourne, FL 32901, USA
mcarroll@fit.edu

Abstract. Cybersecurity in consumer, corporate, and military settings, continues to be a growing concern in the modern and technologically driven world. As Wiederhold (2014) puts it, "the human factor remains the security's weakest link in cyberspace." A literature review related to human response to cybersecurity events reveals three phases involved in the cybersecurity response process, including: (1) Susceptibility, the phase preceding an event, which primarily encompasses behaviors that impact vulnerability to a cybersecurity event; (2) Detection of the event when it occurs; and (3) Response to the event after it occurs. In order for an individual to effectively protect themselves and their organizations from cybersecurity breaches, they must understand and be sensitive to the susceptibility of their devices, and when a potential breach occurs, must exhibit rapid and effective response. The goal of this effort was to examine the human factors surrounding non-expert response to a cybersecurity vulnerability or event and create a framework based on the literature. Recommendations for what steps can be taken to better prepare individuals to respond to cyber events is provided.

Keywords: Cybersecurity · Internet of Things (IoT) · Human factors · Information security · Decision making

1 Introduction

Cybersecurity is increasingly becoming a threat across a range of different industries. In a report by the United States Government Accountability Office (GAO), 23 of the 24 major federal agencies noted information security as a major problem that needed more management, with 19 of those agencies noting their weakness in information security procedures. The number of cybersecurity incidents for federal agencies has increased from 5,503 in 2006 to 77,183 in 2015 [1]. In 2016, the U.S. Navy experienced a breach of 134,386 sailor names and social security numbers from the compromise of only one laptop [2]. These threats are not limited to the government and military, as three billion users were affected by the Yahoo! Inc. hack in 2016 and 143 million by the Equifax Inc. hack in 2017 [3].

Prevention of breaches in cybersecurity has typically focused on providing technical solutions such as hardening networks and improving computer systems that detect

© Springer Nature Switzerland AG 2021
A. Moallem (Ed.): HCII 2021, LNCS 12788, pp. 353–366, 2021.
https://doi.org/10.1007/978-3-030-77392-2_23

intrusions and enhance safe information sharing, with little focus on the device user [1]. However, the device user is often the last line of defense. In fact, in 2017 the U.S. GAO highlighted the lack of properly trained personnel as one of the needed areas of improvement for cybersecurity effectiveness and noted a lack of sufficiently trained staff and procedures for cybersecurity response [1]. Although it is the last line of defense, "the human factor remains the security's weakest link in cyberspace" (p. 131, [4]). This highlights some critical questions. Are device users equipped with the training and tools necessary to recognize cybersecurity vulnerabilities and detect when a system is being compromised? Do device users know how to respond once a cybersecurity event is detected?

These questions are of particular interest to the Internet of Things (IoT) device industry as everyday electronic devices are becoming more connected to the outside world. Suresh et al. (2014) defines the Internet of Things as "a connection between humans – computers – things (p. 2, [5])." From doorbells to refrigerators to smart phones, more devices are being connected to the internet than ever before. Consumers are adding these devices into their homes and connecting them with the internet creating "Smart Homes" [6]. These smart home devices are now ubiquitous in homes and workplaces of many people. While these smart devices may seem benign in terms of cybersecurity risks, they are connected to the internet and as such they pose a risk to private personal information leaks. Despite the widespread usage of IoT devices, there is a significant lack of knowledge in IoT security. Many smart home owner's do not recognize risks associated with the IoT devices and trust device manufactures to protect their privacy [7]. Further, individuals who are knowledgeable about the risks of IoT devices do not use the recommended safety best practices [8]. For example, many users understand two-factor authentication can better protect their devices and accounts but still fail to utilize this technique as they find the cost of doing so to outweigh the associated risks [9]. As such, it is important to understand if consumers can effectively recognize and respond to potential cybersecurity threats to applications such as these.

The goal of this effort was to examine the human factors surrounding detection of, and response to, a cybersecurity event by a device user, who is not a cybersecurity expert. Specifically, how do device users, whose focus is not cybersecurity, make decisions regarding potential privacy vulnerabilities or events, and what steps can be taken to better prepare them to respond to such events? To achieve this, we reviewed the literature to determine what research has found regarding the human factors of cybersecurity decision making. The effort examined research conducted to date in various domains including IoT. The methods and findings, along with recommendations for promoting effective cybersecurity decision making in IoT and beyond, are described in the following sections.

2   Method

A literature review was conducted to identify what research exists regarding consumer preparation for, and decision making associated with, cybersecurity vulnerabilities and cybersecurity events across several domains, including IoT.

Using a compiled list of keywords targeting user decision-making associated with cybersecurity events, we performed an extensive keyword search of databases including: Sage Journals, ScienceDirect, Wiley Online, IEEE Xplore, Proquest, SpringerLink,

Defense Technical Information Center, Taylor and Francis Online, and Florida Institute of Technology library holdings. The following keyword phrases were utilized: trust and cyber-attack, human factors and cyber-attack, cyber event and trust, system hack and trust/aviation, human detection of cyber events, human behavior cyber-attack, human cyber detection, cyber situational awareness, human cyber malicious attack, human cognitive cyber information hacking, prospect theory behavioral cyber threat, information security, IoT Cybersecurity, Smart Home, user trust of IoT devices, and framing theory. Throughout the duration of the literature review, we reviewed approximately 450 abstracts to determine if the articles focused on human factors of cybersecurity events. Abstracts were reviewed to ensure the focus of the article was on the device user and the decision process, detection of cybersecurity events, influencing factors, or the human response to cybersecurity events. Of the initially reviewed abstracts, we selected 72 of the publications for full review to determine if they were relevant to a device user's cybersecurity decision process. Based on a full review of these publications, we selected a total of 44 publications for analysis. We examined literature from several domains that explored how individuals make decisions related to cybersecurity events and associated human factors concerns. The domains included: Personal Computing (e.g., individual home computer use), Corporate Information Security (e.g., system security, encrypting files, updating software), Network Security (e.g., observing network activity on a server), IoT (e.g., smart home devices, artificial intelligence assistants), and General Cybersecurity (e.g., articles that addressed cybersecurity as a whole or across multiple domains). Twenty-two empirical studies, nineteen theoretical publications, and three online media sources were reviewed in detail and analyzed. See the summary of the literature review process is presented in Fig. 1.

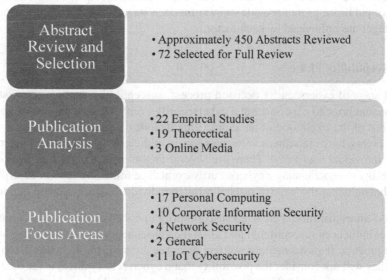

Fig. 1. Literature review process

Each article was analyzed and data related to human interaction with the cybersecurity event was extracted, including: (a) the type of event, (b) factors that influenced the decision process during the event, (c) the factors that influenced user response to the event, (d) how the event influenced a user's performance on, and future trust in, a system, and (e) mitigations, or steps that can be taken to improve human response to similar events. The research team then analyzed the data for trends and extracted two types of categorical themes: (a) stages of human response to cybersecurity events and (b) factors that influence human response to cybersecurity events. From this, a framework of factors which impact the three stages of human response to cybersecurity events was developed.

3   Results: Framework of Human Response to Cyber Security Event

Three stages of cybersecurity decision making were evident from the literature reviewed, including: (1) Susceptibility, the stage preceding the event which primarily encompasses behaviors that impact vulnerability to a cybersecurity event, (2) Detection of the event when it occurs, and (3) Response to the event after it occurs. Second, nine factors were identified from that literature that influenced a user's cybersecurity decision making process across these three stages, including: (a) perceived susceptibility, (b) safeguard cost and effectiveness, (c) privacy fatigue, (d) system trust, (e) system reliability, (f) system knowledge, (g) cybersecurity knowledge and experience, (h) saliency of the cybersecurity event, and (i) system transparency. Table 1 presents a mapping of the three stages of the cybersecurity decision making process to the nine factors which influence these stages. Also included in the table are descriptions and examples of the three stages, number of publications that provide support for each stage, and indication (via an X) of which stages are influenced by each factor.

3.1   Susceptibility Phase

The first stage of cybersecurity decision process, susceptibility, is the a priori state of the individual prior to experiencing a cybersecurity event. This stage focuses on one's perceptions of the likelihood of an attack. This includes awareness of potential cybersecurity events, how individuals view the security of their systems, and the preventative steps an individual user takes. There are several factors which impact an individual's susceptibility to experiencing a cybersecurity event. The following section describes the factors that influence the stage of susceptibility in individuals across a range of domains.

Perceived Susceptibility. Perceived susceptibility to cybersecurity events is a critical factor that influences susceptibility and all of the subsequent stages of the cybersecurity decision process. If someone does not feel that they are susceptible, when an anomaly occurs, they will not consider the possibility that a cybersecurity threat is the cause, and in turn, may not respond effectively [10]. Further, if individuals understand that they are susceptible and that there is a threat, they are more likely to exhibit safe security behaviors [11]. Research across multiple domains has shown that many individuals exhibit optimism bias, the belief that they are not at risk and do not need to take steps to prevent cybersecurity events [12, 13].

For example, research has shown that executives often see their companies as less likely to be targeted and believe that they better protect themselves from a cybersecurity threat than their competitors [14]. Research has also shown that, with respect to IoT devices, younger generations, regardless of gender, expressed more concern towards the

Table 1. Cybersecurity decision response framework

		Phase		
		Susceptibility	Detection	Response
Hypothetical Examples		Checking the last time an application was updated to gauge current risk Feeling hesitant to open a link in an email with poor spelling	Noticing changes in device displays that were not initiated by the user or frequent and inexplicable program crashes	Checking security information to determine website safety; subsequent use/disuse of website after cybersecurity event
# of Supporting Studies		15	14	5
Factors influencing decision process	Perceived Susceptibility	X	X	X
	Perceived Safeguard Cost & Effectiveness	X		X
	Privacy Fatigue	X		X
	System Trust	X		
	System Reliability	X		
	System Knowledge	X	X	
	Cybersecurity Knowledge & Experience	X	X	X
	Saliency of Cybersecurity Event		X	
	System Transparency		X	

risk of susceptibility to cyberattacks, when compared to older generations, and these concerns were more likely to influence purchasing decisions [15].

Safeguard Cost & Effectiveness and Privacy Fatigue. Individuals will not engage in security compliance or assurance behaviors, such as frequently changing passwords, if they do not perceive safeguards as effective (i.e., do not understand how their behaviors improve cybersecurity), or feel that it is not their job or that the safeguard is too costly [16]. This can lead to negative attitudes towards security, and psychological distancing from security responsibility [17]. The resulting lack of effective security behaviors can leave systems more vulnerable to attacks. Choi et al. (2018) explain that as data breaches increase in frequency individuals may feel tired of taking actions to prevent data loss and will stop devoting energy to safeguarding information [9]. This is because the "fatigued" individuals believe the safeguard cost is greater than the safeguard effectiveness. This phenomenon is called privacy fatigue. For example, Breitinger et al. (2020) explain that while most individuals will use passwords on their smartphones, they do not take part in other recommended safe practices such as using a VPN while connected to public WiFi and turning off unused features, resulting in mobile devices being less secure than desktop computers [8].

Trust and Reliability. Trust in the system plays a key role in the susceptibility stage and is highly dependent on another factor, system reliability. Trust in a system is dynamic and contingent on system reliability and performance, and can be comprised of attitudes, expectations, attributes, feelings, intention, and traits [18]. If a system is highly reliable, individuals are likely to form habitual trust, which can decrease perception of risk, and as a result, decrease awareness and detection of a cybersecurity event [10]. Similar to findings from the trust-in-automation literature [19], consistent shutdowns or false alerts from a system can degrade a user's trust in that system's performance, this could eventually lead to disregard of a cybersecurity alert during a cybersecurity event that shares similar characteristics [20]. Therefore, system reliability is critical to ensure trust is properly calibrated. Research has also shown that ease of use, perceived usefulness, community interest, as well as an individual user's social network can also influence trust [21]. For example, smart home owners trust the device manufactures to protect their private data, and the user's perception of how useful and convenient the IoT device is influences their privacy behaviors and trust [7].

System Knowledge and Cybersecurity Knowledge and Experience. System knowledge impacts susceptibility to a cybersecurity event. Users who have system knowledge and understand associated cybersecurity vulnerabilities are more likely to trust a system's ability to protect information confidentiality, integrity, and availability, whereas individuals who lack system knowledge tend to exhibit misplaced trust in a system [22]. For example, IoT device use is ubiquitous in the modern world and these devices are used in places where many people may not consider cyber-vulnerabilities (e.g., utilizing a QR code in a grocery store [23]. If a device is connected to the internet in any way then it is not 100% secure from cybersecurity threats. Therefore, the question arises: do users have the knowledge of the system to protect themselves, as devices that were not originally connected become connected?

Knowledge of, and experience with, cybersecurity events also influence susceptibility. A study in 2010 found that the perceived damage after a cybersecurity attack affects an individual's likelihood to continue to use that system [24]. If there are comparable alternatives, individuals are more likely to move to comparable systems, even if the affected system has a higher perceived usefulness. Further, individuals who do not have a full mental model of how cybersecurity threats occur can develop ineffective coping mechanisms, which could include avoiding the use of a susceptible system altogether [25].

3.2 Detection Phase

The second stage of the cybersecurity decision process is detection of the cybersecurity event. This includes the ability of a user to detect and correctly identify a cybersecurity event, or distinguish a cybersecurity attack from a system anomaly due to a potential system error. Several of the factors that influence susceptibility also influence how likely an individual is to detect a cybersecurity event. The following section describes the factors that influence the stage of detection.

Cybersecurity Knowledge and Experience. A user's knowledge of, and experience with cybersecurity events can also affect their ability to detect such events. A study conducted by Ben-Asher and Gonzalez (2015), which examined participants' response to malicious network attacks, found that cybersecurity experts, or those with extensive cybersecurity experience and knowledge, were more effective at detecting malicious attacks, and had significantly fewer false alarms than their novice counterparts [26]. The authors suggest this may be due to the experts' ability to detect relevant cues and meaningful patterns indicative of a cybersecurity attack. IoT device users are often unaware of security setting or security mitigations for the device [6] and as such, users are vulnerable to IoT manufacturers pulling personal data from the IoT device. Many users do not perceive the risk associated with IoT devices or regard them as convenient enough to be worth the risk [7].

System Knowledge and System Transparency. A user's system knowledge can influence their ability to detect a cybersecurity event. Multiple studies have shown that users must have sufficient knowledge about how the system operates to determine whether system behavior is abnormal, and potentially indicative of a cybersecurity attack [27], as cited in [25, 26, 28–30]. System transparency also impacts detection of a cybersecurity event. A user must use information that the system provides to determine if a threat is occurring. If the system does not provide information related to current system processes (e.g., confirmation that the most up-to-date security patches are installed), new software installed, or system status (e.g., system resources currently being overloaded), individuals cannot determine if the abnormal system behavior is due to a cybersecurity event [31]. Furthermore, manufacturers are often not transparent with device security and frequently users cannot change the security settings [6]. This practice leads to a lack of awareness of the risks the device poses and means by which to instill protections.

Saliency of Cybersecurity Event. Saliency of a cybersecurity event can also influence detection. For example, a conspicuous attack is one that results in obvious cues, such as a computer crashing or control of the computer being taken over, versus a less salient attack which may only result in slowed system response. A study conducted by Hirshfield et al. (2015) found that users are more likely to detect salient cybersecurity attacks than less salient attacks that appear to be due to a user or system error [30].

3.3 Response Phase

The third stage of the cybersecurity event response is user execution of a response to the cybersecurity event. The literature suggests that multiple factors impact how an individual responds to cybersecurity events. The following section describes the factors that influence the response stage.

Perceived Susceptibility, Safeguard Cost Effectiveness, and Privacy Fatigue. In a study examining computer user response to spyware, Huigang and Yaijong (2010) found that individual response to potential cybersecurity threats was influenced by a chain reaction of inter-related factors [32]. Individuals must (1) believe the threat exists (perceive susceptibility), (2) believe that the threat is avoidable (perceive safeguard effectiveness), and be willing to burden safeguard cost (e.g., financial, time-related, or resources costs with implementing safeguards such as frequently changing passwords), and (3) detect the threat. If the threat is perceived as low risk or safeguards costs are perceived as either too high cost or ineffective at combating the threat, individuals may not take the steps necessary for cybersecurity protection. Interestingly, the attitudes individuals have towards cybersecurity and their behaviors tend to differ, a phenomenon referred to as the privacy paradox [33]; while many individuals may state that they care about protecting the security of their devices, due to a perception of high safeguard costs, safeguards necessary to ensure security are not implemented. The concern and worry expressed towards cybersecurity events also depends on the type of information being held by the device [34]. For example, users tend to be more concerned about the privacy of bank account information compared to height and weight information.

Cybersecurity Knowledge and Experience. A user's cybersecurity knowledge and experience can impact detection as presented above but can also influence how they respond to a cybersecurity event. In a study examining participant response to secure and insecure websites, Kelly and Betenthal (2016) found that participants with high levels of cybersecurity knowledge collected more information before proceeding with a login (as indicated by mouse trajectories), than individuals with low levels of cybersecurity knowledge [35]. As a result, those with high levels of cybersecurity knowledge were also more likely to proceed in logging into secure websites whereas those with low levels of cybersecurity knowledge failed to recognize the right cues and logged into unsecure websites. In a study conducted by Rosoff, Cui, and John (2013), computer users were asked how they would respond to a cybersecurity dilemma encountered while downloading online music or buying from an online store [36]. Results indicated that recall of prior cybersecurity experiences influenced how the users would respond: recall of negative cybersecurity experiences (e.g., experienced a loss of data due to a virus) led to less-risky responses; recall of positive cybersecurity experiences (e.g., remained unaffected during a security breach) led to higher-risk responses.

4 Strategies for Improving Response

The three stages presented in the framework of a device user's cybersecurity decision process provide opportunities to better support the user in making the right decision. The literature review uncovered numerous mitigation strategies that can be utilized to achieve this. Below we present mitigation strategies, including system design, training, and procedure recommendations that can be utilized to target each of the three stages of the cybersecurity decision process across numerous domains, whether an individual is using an IoT device at the office or using their personal computer at home.

4.1 Mitigations for the Susceptibility Stage

Increase Awareness of Cybersecurity Vulnerabilities. Users need to be aware of cybersecurity vulnerabilities and how these can affect their systems. Employees who do not manage security as their main job, often do not understand how their behaviors affect security [16]. Removing the bias that they are not susceptible is the first step. SETA (Security Education, Training, and Awareness) programs, or programs focusing on improving attitudes, effort, and one's responsibilities to improve cybersecurity, have shown to decrease unsafe behaviors and improve precaution taking [17]. Increased awareness training could provide users insight into the vulnerabilities in their IoT devices. For example, users could be made aware of their own current exposure to cybersecurity threats such as the sharing of their private information with third party vendors. Since many users do not perceive themselves at risk, demonstrating their actual exposure could influence them to change their behaviors and take more precautions. Similarly, awareness could be increased by a company's own IT department explaining actual events that have happened at the company.

Develop Procedures and Training for Cybersecurity Safeguards. Users should be trained on procedures that can help protect their systems from potential cybersecurity vulnerabilities. Given that steps to ensure security may cost users much needed time to perform their primary task, safeguards must be quick, logical, and easy to complete. Individuals are likely to avoid effective security behaviors if a) they believe they are unlikely to be targeted, b) risks are low, c) they find safeguards ineffective, d) they find safeguards too costly, or e) they lack the skills to implement safeguards [37]. An example, of a procedure to help maintain user compliance with cybersecurity safeguards would be to provide a "security status update" which would highlight current vulnerabilities and ways to protect oneself in a brief and easy to understand format. This status update could be sent to users on a weekly basis the same way some smartphones send a weekly activity log. These updates would convey best practices, and over time, train users to have better cybersecurity habits.

Utilize Positive Framing in Training. Too much fear instilling during training can cause users to not exhibit safe security behaviors. Framing training in a positive frame (i.e., what you will gain from protection), versus loss (i.e., what will happen if you do not protect your systems) has been shown to be a more effective method for security training [11, 36, 38]. For example, a company could create a cybersecurity training course that highlights the benefits of following these recommended best practices. Instead of telling users, "if you do not take precautions you will get hacked", the training could convey "taking precautions will keep you safe and save you precious time and energy in the long run."

4.2 Mitigations for the Detection Phase

Increase System Transparency. It is important that the information systems provide users with information regarding data source, validation, and update feeds. This includes detail regarding activity, changes, inconsistencies, and potential compromises that are relevant to the cybersecurity of their system information. If the display does not give enough detail on information sources and the status of these sources, it will be very difficult for an individual to correctly determine if an event is a cybersecurity attack [31]. Many IoT systems such as a smart watch and fitness tracking applications collect personal information and track user behavior [39]. These devices should make it evident to individual users what information is being collected, where it is being stored, and how it is being used. Applications should also inform users about the integrity of the storage location, whether it is being stored locally on the device or remotely on a server, and what parties have access to this information.

Provide System Feedback. Information systems should provide feedback when false alarms, errors, or failures occur, allowing users to have a better understanding of "normal" system behavior [18]. Users need to understand what unreliable system behavior looks like (e.g., from error alerts), in order to have a baseline with which to compare a cybersecurity event.

Provide Security Alerts and Status. Information systems should incorporate automated detection and alert of cybersecurity vulnerabilities and compromises, where possible. Given that most users are not cybersecurity experts, they will need support in detecting and diagnosing these events. Further, during normal operations, information systems should provide symbols or notifications that connections are secure, safe, and up-to-date [20, 35]. For example, providing security messages, when users' private information is requested, that prompt users to decide what information to share and whether to accept or deny a request to access specific information [40]. Providing alerts such as these allows devices to be more transparent to users.

Train System Knowledge. Users need to have an understanding of where both incoming information comes from and where outgoing information goes. This allows a user to discern between system behavior and cybersecurity threat behavior. System knowledge has shown to improve a user's correct detection of a cybersecurity attack across information security, networking, and personal computing domains [22, 25, 26, 35]. Increasing system knowledge in less reliable systems will assist users in understanding what is causing behavior in the system, and whether or not it should raise concern [10, 18, 22]. For example, IoT devices should inform users about different aspects of the system and implications for cybersecurity and privacy, including disclosing the type of sensors, what data is collected, when the next security update will be, what physical actuations the device has, purpose of data collection, and where data is being stored [41]. Providing this information will allow a user to be aware of what the device is doing with their information and detect any suspicious activity.

4.3 Mitigations for the Response Phase

Develop Procedures and Training for Cybersecurity Response. Users should be provided procedures for how to respond to a potential cybersecurity threat. Providing individuals with procedures to determine if a cybersecurity attack has occurred can improve the rate of correctly identifying cybersecurity events [20, 25, 42]. An example of a system that helps one determine whether a cybersecurity event has occurred would be an antivirus software on a PC. These software packages give step by step instructions for handling the event. Implementing software packages like this on all IoT devices would have users better identify and respond to cybersecurity events.

Provide Opportunity to Report Potential Cybersecurity Events. Users should be given access to a reporting system that allows reporting of any system behavior that they suspect might be due to a cybersecurity vulnerability. Such a system provides the opportunity to improve the system security and inform procedures and training [43]. For example, many banking applications will show users how to identify and report unauthorized account activity. In the case of IoT devices this could be a form on the manufacturer's website or within the controlling application.

Train Basic Cybersecurity Knowledge. While training all users as cybersecurity experts is infeasible, training users on basic cybersecurity knowledge, relevant to their systems, will increase their ability to detect the onset of cybersecurity events and to effectively respond. It is inevitable that as information systems, whether they be smart home IoT systems or smartphones become more automated and digitized, future users will need to exhibit more computer aptitude to support more effective performance [44].

5 Conclusion

This research effort sought to explore the human factors associated with the cybersecurity decision process for device users who are not cybersecurity experts. A review of literature in this domain revealed three key stages in this process that are influenced by nine separate factors. Based on the literature review findings, this paper puts forward recommended mitigations for influencing these nine factors and improving cybersecurity response in a range of domains. Such mitigations have shown great promise. For instance, in federal agency network systems, there has been a 50% drop in incident reports from 2015 to 2016, due to the implementation of mitigation strategies such as adding cybersecurity infrastructure for reporting and managing cybersecurity events [1]. By taking the necessary actions, the human factors associated with cybersecurity and privacy can be more effectively managed. Developers can use this framework to design features that allow users to make more educated decisions about managing their data.

If one understands how the apparent safeguard costs affect decision making regarding user settings, developers could develop better applications and companies could educate their employees on making good privacy decisions in order to protect company data.

Future steps in this effort involved validating the framework. Currently we are administering an online survey to college students and military personnel examining their cybersecurity perceptions, knowledge and behaviors associated with IoT device use. The results of this ongoing study will provide information to help develop guidance for the development of applications to address all three stages. Future studies should empirically examine user response to simulated cybersecurity or privacy events to more thoroughly examine the proposed influencing factors and to explore the effectiveness of the recommended mitigations.

References

1. GAO, Cybersecurity: Actions needed to strengthen U.S. Capabilities, GAO-17-440T, Washington, D.C., 14 February 2017
2. Chief of Naval Personnel Public Affairs: Security Breach Notification of Sailors' PII FAQ (2016). https://www.public.navy.mil/bupers-npc/Documents/PII_Data_Breach_FAQ.pdf
3. Morgan, S.: 2017 cybercrime report. Cybersecurity Ventures (2017)
4. Wiederhold, B.K.: The role of psychology in enhancing cybersecurity. Cyberpsychology Behav. Soc. Netw. **17**, 131–132 (2014)
5. Suresh, P., Daniel, J.V., Parthasarathy, V., Aswathy, R.H.: A state of the art review on the Internet of Things (IoT) history, technology and fields of deployment. In: 2014 International Conference on Science Engineering and Management Research (ICSEMR), pp. 1–8 (2014). https://doi.org/10.1109/ICSEMR.2014.7043637
6. Covington, H.: Smart homes: IoT security and ethical concerns. In: Proceedings for the Northeast Region Decision Sciences Institute (NEDSI), pp. 531–547 (2019)
7. Zheng, S., Apthorpe, N., Chetty, M., Feamster, N.: User perceptions of smart home IoT privacy. In: Proceedings of the ACM on Human-Computer Interaction (2018). https://doi.org/10.1145/3274469
8. Breitinger, F., Tully-Doyle, R., Hassenfeldt, C.: A survey on smartphone user's security choices, awareness and education. Comput. Secur. **88** (2020). https://doi-org.portal.lib.fit.edu. https://doi.org/10.1016/j.cose.2019.101647
9. Choi, H., Park, J., Jung, Y.: The role of privacy fatigue in online privacy behavior. Comput. Hum. Behav. **81**, 42–51 (2018). https://doi.org/10.1016/j.chb.2017.12.001
10. Pienta, D., Sun, H., Thatcher, J.: Habitual and misplaced trust: the role of the dark side of trust between individual users and cybersecurity systems. In: 2016 International Conference on Information Systems (2016)
11. Mittal, S.: Understanding the human dimension of cyber security. Indian J. Criminol. Criminalistics **34**(1), 141–152 (2017)
12. Rhee, H., Ryu, Y., Kim, C.: Unrealistic optimism on information security management. Comput. Secur. **31**(2), 221–232 (2012)
13. Pfleeger, S.L., Caputo, D.D.: Leveraging behavioral science to mitigate cybersecurity risk. Comput. Secur. **31**(4), 597–611 (2012)
14. Coovert, M.D., Dreibelbis, R., Borum, R.: Factors influencing the human-technology interface for effective cyber security performance. In: Zaccaro, S.J., Dalal, R.S., Tetrick, L.E., Steinke, J.A. (eds.) Psychosocial Dynamics of Cyber Security, pp. 267–290. Routledge (2016)

15. Albert, L.J., Rodan, S., Aggarwal, N., Hill, T.R.: Gender and generational differences in consumers' perceptions of internet of things (IoT) devices. E-J. Soc. Behav. Res. Bus. **10**(3), 41–53 (2019)
16. Zaccaro, S.J., Dalal, R.S., Tetrick, L.E., Steinke, J.A. (eds.): Psychosocial Dynamics of Cyber Security. Routledge, Milton Park (2016)
17. Burns, A., Roberts, T., Posey, C., Bennett, R., Courtney, J.: Assessing the role of security education, training, and awareness on 'insiders' security-related behavior: an expectancy theory approach. In: 2015 48th Hawaii International Conference on System Sciences (2015)
18. Hoffman, R.R., Lee, J.D., Woods, D.D., Shadbolt, N., Miller, J., Bradshaw, J.M.: The dynamics of trust in cyberdomains. IEEE Intell. Syst. **24**(6), 5–11 (2009)
19. Lee, J.D., See, K.A.: Trust in automation: designing for appropriate reliance. Hum. Factors **46**(1), 50–80 (2004). https://doi.org/10.1518/hfes.46.1.50_30392
20. Conti, G., Ahamad, M., Stasko, J.: Attacking information visualization system usability overloading and deceiving the human. In: Proceedings SOUPS' 2005 (2005)
21. AlHogail, A.: Improving IoT technology adoption through improving consumer trust. Technologies **6**(3), 64 (2018). https://doi.org/10.3390/technologies6030064
22. Jang, Y., Chang, S., Tsai, Y.: Smartphone security: understanding smartphone 'users' trust in information security management. Secur. Commun. Netw. **7**, 1313–1321 (2014)
23. Daubert, J., Wiesmaier, A., Kikiras, P.: A view on privacy & trust in IoT. In: 2015 IEEE International Conference on Communication Workshop, ICCW 2015, pp. 2665–2670 (2015). https://doi.org/10.1109/ICCW.2015.7247581
24. Lee, M., Lee, J.: The impact of information security failure on customer behaviors: a study on a large-scale hacking incident on internet. Inf. Syst. Front. **14**(2), 375–393 (2010)
25. Furman, S., Theofanos, M., Choong, Y., Stanton, B.: Basing cybersecurity training on user perceptions. IEEE Secur. Priv. **10**(2), 40–49 (2012)
26. Ben-Asher, N., Gonzalez, C.: Effects of cyber security knowledge on attack detection. Comput. Hum. Behav. **48**, 51–61 (2015). https://doi.org/10.1016/j.chb.2015.01.039
27. Grazioli, S.: Where did they go wrong? An analysis of the failure of knowledgeable Internet consumers to detect deception over the Internet. Group Decis. Negot. **13**, 149–172 (2004)
28. Proctor, R.W., Chen, J.: The role of human factors/ergonomics in the science of security: decision making and action selection in cyberspace. Hum. Factors **57**(5), 721–727 (2015)
29. Legg, P.A.: Enhancing cyber situation awareness for Non-Expert Users using visual analytics. In: 2016 International Conference on Cyber Situational Awareness, Data Analytics and Assessment (CyberSA) (2016)
30. Hirshfield, L., et al.: The role of the device users' suspicion in the detection of cyber attacks. Int. J. Cyber Warfare Terrorism **5**(3), 28–44 (2015)
31. Mahoney, S., Rothe, E., Steinke, K., Pfautz, J., Wu, C., Farry, M.: A cognitive task analysis for cyber situational awareness. In: Proceedings of the Human Factors and Ergonomics Society Annual Meeting, vol. 54, no. 4 (2010)
32. Huigang, L., Yaijong, X.: Understanding security behaviors in personal computer usage: a threat avoidance perspective. J. Assoc. Inf. Syst. **11**(7), 394–413 (2010)
33. Acquisti, A., Brandimarte, L., Loewenstein, G.: Privacy and human behavior in the age of information. Science **347**(6221), 509–514 (2015)
34. Brough, A.R., Martin, K.D.: Critical roles of knowledge and motivation in privacy research. Curr. Opinion Psychol. **31**, 11–15 (2020). https://doi-org.portal.lib.fit.edu. https://doi.org/10.1016/j.copsyc.2019.06.021
35. Kelley, T., Bertenthal, B.: Real-world decision making: logging into vs. insecure website. In: USEC 2016 (2016)
36. Rosoff, H., Cui, J., John, R.: Heuristics and biases in cyber security dilemmas. Environ. Syst. Decis. **33**(4), 517–529 (2013)

37. Liang, H., Xue, Y.: Understanding security behaviors in personal computer usage: a threat avoidance perspective. J. Assoc. Inf. Syst. **11**(7), 394 (2010)
38. Sharma, K.: Impact of framing and priming on 'users' behavior in cybersecurity. Masters thesis (2017)
39. Lee, H., Kobsa, A.: Understanding user privacy in Internet of Things environments. In: 2016 IEEE 3rd World Forum on Internet of Things (WF-IoT), pp. 407–412 (2016). https://doi.org/10.1109/wf-iot.2016.7845392
40. Jia, Y.J., et al.: ContexloT: towards providing contextual integrity to appified IoT platforms. In: NDSS, vol. 2, no. 2, p. 2 (2017)
41. Emami-Naeini, P., Agarwal, Y., Faith Cranor, L., Hibshi, H.: Ask the experts: what should be on an IoT privacy and security label? In: 2020 IEEE Symposium on Security and Privacy (SP), pp. 447–464 (2020). https://doi-org.portal.lib.fit.edu. https://doi.org/10.1109/SP40000.2020.00043
42. Bowen, B.M., Devarajan, R., Stolfo, S.: Measuring the human factor of cyber security. In: 2011 IEEE International Conference Technologies for Homeland Security (HST), pp. 230–235. IEEE (2011)
43. Fagan, M., Fagan, M., Megas, K.N., Scarfone, K., Smith, M.: Foundational cybersecurity activities for IOT device manufacturers. US Department of Commerce, National Institute of Standards and Technology (2020)
44. Meneghello, F., Calore, M., Zucchetto, D., Polese, M., Zanella, A.: IoT: Internet of Threats? A survey of practical security vulnerabilities in real IoT devices. IEEE Internet Things J. **6**(5), 8182–8201 (2019). https://doi-org.portal.lib.fit.edu. https://doi.org/10.1109/JIOT.2019.2935189

Security and Privacy Awareness

The Effectiveness of Video Messaging Campaigns to Use 2FA

Elham Al Qahtani(✉), Lipsarani Sahoo(✉), and Mohamed Shehab(✉)

University of North Carolina, Charlotte, USA
{ealqahta,lsahoo1,mshehab}@uncc.edu

Abstract. For exploring messaging campaigns that motivate users to adopt a new security behavior and affect their security decisions, we designed different informational videos asking users to adopt Duo Two-Factor Authentication (2FA) on their university account. These videos used five different communication techniques: Authoritarian, Logic, Benefit, Personal Risk, and Enterprise Risk. During the two weeks of the messaging campaigns, our preliminary results showed that no significant differences were found between the treatment groups and the control group regarding adoption rate of Duo. However, we found that Authoritarian (20% of university employees enabled Duo 2FA on their university accounts) and Benefit (17%) had the highest percentages in enabling Duo 2FA compared to other groups. All groups stated that Duo 2FA is annoying but not difficult to use. In addition, we identified a preliminary list of improvements in the messaging design. Our findings suggest that including the improvements in the messaging will increase users' willingness to adopt new security features.

Keywords: Messaging campaigns · Video messaging · Two-Factor Authentication · Duo · Risk communication · User's behaviour · Usability and security of 2FA

1 Introduction

Numerous organizations have experienced data breaches, such as compromised personal information, database password leaks, or phishing attacks [25,26,33] that have motivated them to apply Two-Factor Authentication (2FA) [19]. Adding 2FA as an extra layer of protection reduces security risks in the organization and prevents unauthorized access to technology. This additional factor can be something users obtain (e.g., a one-time use code provided through text), or something users have, such as a biometric (e.g., a fingerprint). Governments and large enterprises have been utilizing 2FA for the long term, and recently the majority of social media, e-commerce, mobile banking, and online services have been offering 2FA free to home end-users [8]. However, the adoption rate of 2FA remains low despite the prevalence of acceptance of 2FA among security communities. Petsas et al. [28] showed the low rate of adoption for 2FA; based on the results, 6.4% of users enabled the 2FA on their Google accounts.

© Springer Nature Switzerland AG 2021
A. Moallem (Ed.): HCII 2021, LNCS 12788, pp. 369–390, 2021.
https://doi.org/10.1007/978-3-030-77392-2_24

Universities have large amounts of sensitive information, such as the personal data of users (e.g., faculty, staff, graduate assistants, and students), emails, payroll details, and university online services, all of which may be targeted by remote attacks. Recently, many universities [1, 2, 4–6] have been requiring their full-time, part-time, adjunct faculty, and students who are in the payroll system to enable Duo 2FA on their university accounts. Duo 2FA [3] is a two-factor authentication service provided by universities to help protect university accounts. In addition, Duo 2FA provides a second layer of verification when accessing university accounts by requiring the user to verify their identity through another channel, such as receiving a PIN code or a push notification through the Duo Mobile app as shown in Fig. 1.

Due to the universities that require their employees to enable Duo 2FA on their university accounts, we contributed in exploring the effectiveness of different types of video messages from Information Technology Services (ITS). At our university, beginning on November 26, 2018 for two weeks, they are encouraging adoption of Duo 2FA in a more naturalistic setting. The video messages are: Authoritarian (employees followed the authority suggestion for enabling Duo 2FA on their accounts), Logic (a logical statement about how enabling Duo 2FA makes sense), Benefit (the benefit of changing the password will be once a year instead of every 90 days), Personal Risk (employees risk consequences if their account is compromised by accessing the inbox or their personal email), and Enterprise Risk (employees risk consequences if their account is compromised by exposing and misusing sensitive information).

More specifically, in our study, we investigate the following research questions:

- **RQ1**: Do the video messages motivate university employees and staff to enable Duo 2FA on their university accounts?
- **RQ2**: How do university employees and staff perceive Duo's usability and security after enabling it?
- **RQ3**: How could the video or messaging be improved for more effective message design?

Our findings showed that no significant differences were found between the treatment groups and the control group regarding adoption rate of Duo. We found that the adoption rate of Duo 2FA in the Authoritarian group from the messaging campaigns in the first two weeks was 20%. Over the same duration, the adoption rates among the other groups were 17% for university employees in the Benefit group, 16% in both the Enterprise and the Control groups, 15.71% in the Personal group, and 13.89% in the Logic group.

All groups stated that Duo 2FA is annoying but not difficult to use, except the Control group (38.4%). Based on the recommendations we obtained, we identified a preliminary list of messaging improvements to enhance the message design.

This paper is organized as follows. Section 2 discusses the relevant literature. Section 3 describes the methodology of the present study. The study results are presented in Sect. 4. Section 5 presents a discussion of the results. Section 6 notes the limitations of the present study and offers suggestions for future work. Section 7 concludes our paper.

2   Related Work

Two main research topics are relevant to our study: dealing with security communications and two factor authentication in terms of usability and security.

Fig. 1. A push notification send to the Duo Mobile

2.1   Security Communications

Designing security cues in security communication plays an important role in motivating users' behavior. Even for risk communication methods (e.g., online training materials, embedded training, videos, and texts), user references have stated that the combined security delivery methods which increased individual security awareness were text-based, game-based, and video-based delivery methods [7]. The essential stages for changing security behavior do not concentrate on risk information or security behavior. These stages focused on comprehending the risk, applying the security advice, motivating users to cope with security methods, and changing intentions and attitudes [14].

The following study provided insights into improving risk communication (e.g., risk perception, security behavior, or attention) by using computer security dialogues. Pattinson et al. [27] conducted two pilot studies that discussed how to improve users' risk perceptions through risk communication by using graphics in the information security messages. In the first study, the authors found no significant difference when they sent phishing emails without any symbols or graphics. In the second study, they embedded graphics inside the phishing emails and found no significant difference based on the users' responses on the semantic differential grid. In this second study, they concentrated on the method of communicating the risk related to the users' decisions and their risk perceptions. Regarding the security notification messages, they found no significant improvement in the risk communication applying this method.

One issue that can address these differences in risk perceptions is conducting effective risk communication using threats and copying appraisals with fear appeals via videos, which alter the risk-cost-benefit perspective of users who do not follow the security advice [10,12]. Also, Harbach et al. [22] investigated motivation cues of presenting a user's personal information to alter users' risk perceptions of the possible risks to their data when they are authorizing Android permissions. They found that including these cues altered users' risk perceptions, encouraging them to make the right security decision. Based on the factors of perceived costs, benefits, and risks, which affect users' security decisions, we created the motivation cues for each video message in our study.

Two studies [8,11] addressed the challenge of a low rate of adopting 2FA using video messages as a powerful motivation to affect users' security decisions. Preston [8] explored the impact of a fear appeal video on undergraduate students to adopt 2FA. This video message includes cybercrime statistics, a recommendation to use 2FA, and the implementation of 2FA for Google accounts. Participants, after a week, reported if they enabled 2FA on their account or not. They found that 31% of participants enabled 2FA within a week after watching this fear appeal video. Another study was conducted on Amazon's MTurk by Albayram et al. [11]. They investigated the effectiveness of video tutorials with three themes (Risk: presenting security incidents and threat examples of not using 2FA, Self-efficacy: demonstration on setting up 2FA, and Contingency: discussion on negative consequences of using 2FA and their solutions) that impact participants' behavior toward 2FA perceptions and adoption. Their findings showed that willingness and intentions to try 2FA were found to be higher for participants who were exposed to both the Risk and Self-efficacy themes. Also, they found in the follow-up study that 27% of participants mentioned that they had enabled 2FA. Therefore, we contribute to this literature by exploring the impact of different messaging approaches on 2FA adoption in a more naturalistic setting and measuring its effect on users' actual behavior.

2.2 Usability and Security of 2FA

Several studies investigated the usability and security of 2FA adoption as follows. Reese et al. [30], conducted a usability study of five common 2FA methods (SMS, TOTP, pre-generated codes, push notifications, and U2F security keys) as well as a laboratory study to assess the general usability of the setup procedure. Their findings showed that participants found these methods easy to use to set-up 2FA, whereas the other two studies [18,31] showed how participants struggled with the setup instructions of Yubico Security Key. In the following studies [13,35], they investigated to understand the security and usability of 2FA for e-banking customers who agreed that 2FA provides high-level security and usability.

Moreover, for understanding the perceptions of 2FA adoption, Colnago et al. [17] conducted an exploratory study to understand users' perception and adoption of Duo 2FA. Their results show that 2FA adopters found it annoying but easy to use as well as the negative perceptions that were perceived by users who were required to adopt 2FA compared to those who adopted voluntarily. Also, Dutson et al. [20] measured the sentiment around Duo 2FA from students, faculty, and staff at their university after they adopted it one year. The results showed that students and faculty generally had more negative perceptions of Duo 2FA compared to staff, and all of them stated that Duo 2FA protects their account, and it was easy to use. We wanted to understand how different messaging approaches impact users' security decision after enabling Duo 2FA and their perception of Duo's usability and security.

3   Methodology

Our university required all university employees to use Duo 2FA service [3] to access their university accounts by the end of January 2019. The university started to use Duo's service in 2015, and the adoption rate of Duo 2FA for faculty/staff (60%) is shown in Fig. 2 before our study began. Therefore, for the first phase of our study, we investigated the effectiveness of the video messages in motivating the remaining part (N = 1955) of university employees and staff (who had not yet adopted Duo 2FA) to enable Duo 2FA on their university accounts, beginning on November 26, 2018, for two weeks. In the second phase of the study, we ran a follow-up study to ask university employees to fill out an online survey. The first part of the survey was assigned to all groups (treatment and control groups) and asked them to answer a set of questions about the impact of this security decision after enabling Duo 2FA and their perception of Duo's usability and security. In the second part of the online survey, which was assigned to the treatment groups, we asked them to provide their feedback on the assigned video so that we can make future improvements in the messaging.

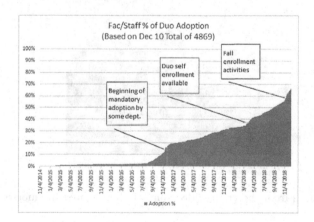

Fig. 2. The enrollment into Duo 2FA of all faculty/staff when our study began

3.1   Video Design

The video messages, specifically the motivating cues, were created by using different themes (e.g., Authoritarian, Risks, benefit) that associated with the university employees' and staff's access to different university systems such as Canvas or Gmail.

(a) A frame from the logic video content

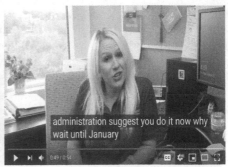

(b) A frame from the authoritarian video content

(c) A frame from the benefit video content

(d) A frame from the personal risk video content

(e) A frame from the enterprise risk video content

Fig. 3. Frames from the group video contents highlighted the motivated cues

The themes of the video messages were inspired by prior works. For example, several researchers [15,16,34] found that authoritarian leadership in organizations can be conducive to employee performance and a positive correlation found between authoritarian leadership and employee outcomes. Our university administration required all university employees to use Duo 2FA service to access their university accounts by the end of January 2019. Based on these prior works, we created the motivating cue for the Authoritarian message: "The university administration suggests you do it now and not wait until January."

Human beings use a rational model in their decision making as Herley [23] mentioned that the leading cause of following the recommended security behavior is weighing the costs against the benefits for security actions, which impacts a user's security decisions (e.g., when a user rejects the security action due to deciding the cost is too high and/or the benefit is too low). Two studies showed the rational reasons why users follow security practices such as considering the benefit of using 2FA on online accounts [21] and a screen lock on smartphones [9]. In our study, the benefit of enabling Duo 2FA allows university employees and staff to change their passwords once a year instead of every 90 days. So, the motivating cue created for the Benefit message was: "The benefit of using Duo is that you will only have to change your password once a year instead of every 90 days .... Do not wait till January to enjoy the benefits of improving your security."

Moreover, human behavior depends on the differences of their perceptions and the level of perceived intelligence [32]. Huang et al. [24] investigated what factors influence people perceptions on common security threats. They found that people's perceptions of information security based on these factors: knowledge about threats, threat impact on people, ability to perceive the severity of the threat, ability to control the threat, possibility that the threat happens and awareness of threats. So, perceiving the personal or enterprise risks play a vital role in university employees' and staff's security decisions. Therefore, we designed the motivating cue for Personal risk message: "If your account is compromised this may provide access to your inbox, and embarrassing emails could be sent to your contacts.... Do not wait till January to protect your information," whereas the Enterprise risk message: "If your account is compromised, then this sensitive information may be exposed and misused in many different ways. This may affect not only your reputation but also other employees, students, and the university.... Do not wait till January to improve the security of your accounts."

The last motivating cue was created for the Logic message: "Why wait? It makes sense to do it now" and considered as a baseline compared to other cues.

The six groups below were included in our study designed to investigate the effectiveness of the messaging campaigns. Examples of the video messages are shown in Fig. 3, highlighting the motivated cues for each group. The video transcripts are in the Appendix. The email templates as shown in Fig. 4(a) for the treatment groups include video and text (not link) such as, "sign up today - we can help!," the deadline for using it (January 31, 2019), and helpful three FAQs links (e.g., how do I sign up for Duo, how do I use Duo, and search all other Duo FAQS). Whereas the email template for the control group as shown in Fig. 4(b), they received an image showing text such as, "sign up for Duo," the deadline for using it (January 31, 2019), and links to three FAQS. Also, the length of the videos ranges from 54 s to 1 min.

- **Authoritarian video**: watched a video that included the definition of Duo, the purpose of using Duo, the deadline for using it, and a motivating cue.[1]
- **Benefit video**: watched a video that included the definition of Duo, purpose of using Duo, the deadline for using it, and a motivating cue.[2]
- **Personal risk video**: watched a video that included the definition of Duo, the purpose of using Duo, the deadline for using it, and a motivating cue.[3]
- **Enterprise risk video**: watched a video that included the definition of Duo, the purpose of using Duo, the deadline for using it, and a motivating cue.[4]
- **Logic video**: watched a video that included the definition of Duo, the purpose of using Duo, the deadline for using it, and a motivating cue.[5]
- **Control group** was not shown any video.

(a) The email template including the video that was sent to the treatment groups

(b) The email template that was sent to the Control group

Fig. 4. Transcript of email templates

3.2   Hypotheses

In the present study, we propose the following hypothesis:

- **Hypothesis 1 (H1)**: There will be differences among groups regarding the number of university employees and staff who enabled Duo on their university account.
- **Hypothesis 2 (H2)**: There will be differences among all the groups in terms of their responses about the usability and security of adopting Duo.

---

[1] https://www.youtube.com/watch?v=cIM9WnChGU0.
[2] https://www.youtube.com/watch?v=zD2H1dn1gxM.
[3] https://www.youtube.com/watch?v=ps-oykvSPUw.
[4] https://www.youtube.com/watch?v=nMIygQFJzFU.
[5] https://www.youtube.com/watch?v=Qk8YO3BMbbY.

3.3 Study Design

The first phase of the study aimed to analyze the effectiveness of the video message campaigns in getting users to adopt the Duo Two-Factor Authentication (2FA) in real-time scenarios before university employees had enabled it. The follow-up study aimed to measure users' perception of Duo Two-Factor Authentication (2FA) adoption after they had activated it on their university accounts, as well as to obtain feedback on the video messages (for the treatment groups).

The first phase ran from November 26, 2018, for two weeks. Thus, Information Technology Services (ITS) sent email messaging campaigns randomly (including videos for treatment groups) at the beginning of this period to each group of university employees who had not installed Duo on their accounts. ITS used the Duo portal, which gives data on who had not enabled Duo 2FA on their university account. The recruitment was provided by ITS via email. They recruited 1955 university employees who had not installed Duo 2FA previously. ITS randomly assigned 319 of university employees to the Authoritarian group, 324 to the Logic group, 328 to the Benefit group, 312 to the Personal risk group, 353 to the Enterprise risk group, and 319 to the Control group. In this phase, university employees were automatically enrolled in the study by ITS.

In the follow-up study, ITS collaborated with the research announcements team to send an online survey to university employees from the same groups that had been studied in the first phase of the study and had installed Duo 2FA. ITS sent emails including the online survey to the same groups. The consent was emailed to the same groups to help them decide whether or not to participate in our study before filling out the survey. The criteria for the recruitment handled through ITS were employees who were age 18 or older and had enabled the Duo Two Factor Authentication. The first 30 respondents to participate in this study received a $5 Starbucks gift card by email after they filled out the online survey.

The online survey consisted of two sets of questions:

- The first part included a set of questions about the adoption of Duo that was distributed to all groups.
- The second part comprised video evaluation questions that were sent to the treatment groups.

All questions are discussed in more depth in the Evaluation section.

Our study was approved by our university Institutional Review Board (Study #18-0465).

4 Evaluation

Our quantitative data is not normally distributed. Therefore, we used the Kruskal-Wallis test (H) (non-parametric test) for the analysis comparing all the groups independently by SPSS.

4.1   First Phase

We wanted to understand the effectiveness of the video messages in motivating university employees and staff to enable Duo 2FA on their university accounts. To answer the first research question, we assumed (H1) that there would be differences among groups regarding the number of university employees and staff who enabled Duo on their university accounts once the messaging campaigns started. Using Kruskal-Wallis test to compare the number of university employees and staff who enabled Duo of all six groups, we found no significant differences among treatment and control groups at $p = 0.45$. The test statistic for each group is shown in Table 1. The findings from the first phase of our study were handled by ITS and taken from the Duo 2FA portal. We found that the adoption rate of Duo 2FA in the Authoritarian group from the messaging campaigns during two weeks was 20%. Over the same duration, the adoption rates among the other groups were 17% for university employees in the Benefit group, 16% in both the Enterprise and the Control groups, 15.71% in the Personal group, and 13.89% in the Logic group as shown in Table 1.

Table 1. The percentages of adoption rate of Duo 2FA of total number in each group and the value of Kruskal Wallis test for all groups

Groups	Adoption rate (Adopters' number)	Test statistic
Authoritarian	20% of 319 (64)	$H(5) = 318$
Benefit	17% of 328 (56)	$H(5) = 327$
Enterprise	16% of 353 (57)	$H(5) = 352$
Logic	13.89% of 324 (52)	$H(5) = 323$
Personal	15.71% of 312 (49)	$H(5) = 311$
Control	16% of 319 (51)	$H(5) = 318$

Regarding the number of employees who watched video messages during the messaging campaigns, we found that 64 and 65 participants watched the Authoritarian and the Benefit videos, respectively. In addition, 46 participants watched the Personal Risk as well as the Logic video messages, and 55 watched the Enterprise Risk video. However, the university employees were not tracked while they were watching all the content in the videos through ITS account.

Regarding the device type for Duo authentication, we found that 86.8% of university employees chose mobile devices to authenticate their university accounts, 7.1% chose fob, and 6.1% chose a landline phone.

4.2   Second Phase

We wanted to understand the impact of this security decision after enabling Duo 2FA and the perception of Duo's usability and security. In the follow-up study of after the messaging campaigns period, the university employees were asked to fill out the online survey. The first part of the survey was assigned to all groups, asking them to answer a set of questions about the impact of this security decision after enabling Duo 2FA and their perceptions of Duo's usability and security. In the second part of the survey, the treatment groups were asked to provide their evaluation of the video that was assigned to their treatment group. We found that 25 participants filled out the online survey in the Authoritarian group, 22 in the Benefit group, 23 in the Enterprise risk group, 21 in the Logic group, 18 in the Personal risk group, and 26 in the Control group. In total, there were 135 participants in the follow-up study. At the end of the study, the first 30 participants who submitted the survey early were received a $5 Starbucks gift card.

To answer the second research question, we assumed that there would be differences among all the groups in terms of their responses about the usability and security of adopting Duo. To test the hypothesis (H2), we asked participants in all six of the groups four questions related to the usability and security of Duo, as follows.

- The first question was, "Has enabling Duo Two-Factor Authentication (2FA) on your university accounts affected your decision to activate 2FA on other accounts (e.g., email or financial accounts)?" The possible answers for this question were, "Yes," "No," or "Maybe"
- The second question was, "Is using Duo 2FA difficult?" which was measured on a scale ranging from (1) "Not at all difficult" to (5) "Very difficult."
- The third question was, "Is using Duo 2FA annoying?" which was measured on a scale ranging from (1) "Strongly Disagree" to (5) "Strongly Agree."
- The fourth question was, "Using Duo 2FA helps protect my university account," which was measured on a scale ranging from (1) "Strongly Disagree" to (5) "Strongly Agree."

Regarding the first question, participants were asked after they had enabled Duo 2FA on their university account if their security decisions were affected to activate 2FA on their other email or financial accounts. No significant difference was found among all the groups at $p = .171$, with $H(5) = 7.736$. We noted that 28% and 31.8% of participants in the Authoritarian and Benefit, respectively enabled 2FA on their other online accounts, as compared to the other groups as follows: 17.4% of participants from the Enterprise group, 9.5% of the Logic group, 11.1% of the Personal group, and 26.9% of the Control group.

For the second question, participants were asked if using Duo 2FA was difficult. No significant difference was found among all the groups at $p = .914$, with $H(5) = 1.496$. Table 2 shows the descriptive statistics, as follows: mean, median (Med), and SD for each group. Participants in the Control group (38.4%) found using Duo 2FA difficult, whereas in the other groups, the rates were as follows: Authoritarian, 16%; Benefit, 22.7%; Enterprise, 8.6%; Logic, 9.6%; and Personal, 16.7%.

Participants were also asked if using Duo 2FA was annoying. No significant difference was found among any of the groups at $p = .806$, with $H(5) = 2.301$.

Table 2. Descriptive statistics for this question: "Is using Duo 2FA difficult?"

Groups	Mean	Med	SD
Authoritarian	2.1	2	1.3
Benefit	2.4	2	1.4
Enterprise	1.9	2	1
Logic	1.9	2	1.1
Personal	2.1	2	1.2
Control	2.12	2	1.1

Table 3 shows the descriptive statistics, as follows: mean, median (Med), and SD for each group. Above half of the participants in all groups agreed that Duo 2FA was annoying; the rates for each group were as follows: Authoritarian, 56%; Benefit, 68.2%; Enterprise, 51.7%; Logic, 52.3%; Personal, 66.6%; and Control, 61.6%.

Table 3. Descriptive statistics for this question: "Is using Duo 2FA annoying?"

Groups	Mean	Med	SD
Authoritarian	3.6	4	1.4
Benefit	3.8	4	1.3
Enterprise	3.6	4	1.1
Logic	3.5	4	1.4
Personal	3.9	4	1.2
Control	3.5	4	1.4

Regarding their perception of the security of using Duo, participants were asked if using Duo 2FA helped protect their university account. No significant difference was found among any of the groups at p = .714 with H(5) = 2.911. Table 4 shows the descriptive statistics, as follows: mean, median (Med), and

Table 4. Descriptive statistics for this question: "Using Duo 2FA helps protect my university account"

Groups	Mean	Med	SD
Authoritarian	3.3	3	1.4
Benefit	3.3	3	1.4
Enterprise	3.5	4	1.3
Logic	3.7	4	1.4
Personal	3.5	4	1.5
Control	3.8	4	.9

SD for each group. Participants in most groups agreed that Duo 2FA helped to protect their accounts: Authoritarian (48% of participants), Benefit (45.5%), Enterprise (52.1%), Logic (57.2%), Personal (55.6%), and Control (57.7%).

Following this statement, participants were asked to indicate the type of information on their university accounts that Duo 2FA would help protect. The options were as follows: Employee accounts, Student information, University data, My personal data, and None. The highest percentages were reported for each group as follows: 72% of participants chose "Employee account" and "University data" as information that would be protected by Duo 2FA in the Authoritarian group, and 76% and 63% of participants chose "My personal data" in the Logic and Benefit groups, respectively. Moreover, 73% and 77% of participants chose "Employee account" in the Enterprise Risk and Personal Risk groups, respectively, and 84% chose "Student information" from the Control group.

Improvements of Messaging. We are interested in targeting improvements of the video aspects to design effective video messages for adopting new security features. To answer the third research question, we asked the treatment groups the open-ended question, "How can the video or messaging be improved?" and five questions to evaluate the different aspects of each video as follows:

- "How useful was the explanation of Duo's purpose in the video?"
- "How informative was the video in explaining the benefits of Duo?"
- "How persuasive was the video in highlighting the need to install Duo?"
- "What aspects of the video did you like?"
- "What aspects of the video did you not like?"

First, participants answered the five questions following the open-ended question at the end of a follow-up study. For the first aspect of the video, participants were asked this question, "How useful was the explanation of Duo's purpose in the video?" The answer to this question was measured on a scale ranging from (1) "Not at all useful" to (5) "Very useful." We found no significant difference among treatment groups at p = .59, with $H(4) = 2.766$. Table 5 shows the descriptive statistics, as follows: mean, median (Med), and SD for each group. Percentages of participants who rated the video as either "Useful" or "Very useful" for

Table 5. Descriptive statistics for this question: "How useful was the explanation of Duo's purpose in the video?"

Groups	Mean	Med	SD
Authoritarian	3.2	3	1.2
Benefit	3.2	3.5	1.4
Enterprise	3.6	4	1.3
Logic	3.5	4	1.3
Personal	3.6	4	.9

each group were as follows: Authoritarian, 44% (where 32% of participants were neutral, median = 3); Benefit, 50% (where the median = 3.5); Enterprise, 66.7% (where the median = 4); Logic, 52% (where the median = 4); and Personal, 55.6% (where the median = 4).

In addition, we asked participants this question: "How informative was the video in explaining the benefits of Duo?" The answer to this question was measured on a scale ranging from (1) "Not at all informative" to (5) "Very informative." We found no significant differences among treatment groups at p = .287, with H(4) = 5.007. Table 6 shows the descriptive statistics, as follows: mean, median (Med), and SD for each group. Percentages of participants who rated the video as either "Informative" or "Very informative" for each group were as follows: Authoritarian, 44% (where 32% of participants were neutral, median = 3); Benefit, 40% (where 40.9% of participants were neutral, median = 3); Enterprise, 66.6% (where the median = 4); Logic, 47.6% (where median = 3); and Personal, 61.1% (where the median = 4).

Table 6. Descriptive statistics for this question: "How informative was the video in explaining the benefits of Duo?"

Groups	Mean	Med	SD
Authoritarian	3.2	3	1.3
Benefit	3.3	3	1.1
Enterprise	3.8	4	1.2
Logic	3.3	3	1.2
Personal	3.7	4	.8

Participants were asked, "How persuasive was the video in highlighting the need to install Duo?" The answer to this question was measured on a scale ranging from (1) "Not at all persuasive" to (5) "Very persuasive." We found no significant differences among the treatment groups at p = .581, with H(4) = 2.865. Table 7 shows the descriptive statistics, as follows: mean, median (Med), and SD for each group. Percentages of participants who rated as either "Persuasive" or "Very persuasive" for each group were as follows: Authoritarian, 32% (where the

Table 7. Descriptive statistics for this question: "How persuasive was the video in highlighting the need to install Duo?"

Groups	Mean	Med	SD
Authoritarian	3	3	1.3
Benefit	2.6	3	1.2
Enterprise	3	3	1.3
Logic	3.2	3	1.3
Personal	2.9	2.8	1.6

median = 3); Benefit, 22.7% (where the median = 3); Enterprise, 42.8% (where the median = 3); Logic, 47.6% (where the median = 3); and Personal, 27.8% (where the median = 2.8).

In addition, we asked participants in the treatment groups two questions: "What aspects of the video did you like?" and "What aspects of the video did you not like?" Participants identified the aspect they preferred for the assigned video. We found that 88% of the Authoritarian group and 63% of the Benefit group liked the simplicity of video presentation and the video length, whereas 71% and 50% of participants liked the length of the Logic and Personal Risk videos, respectively. Additionally, 43% of participants chose "enough information" as the preferred aspect for the Enterprise video. The majority of participants chose "None" as an aspect that they did not like in the video messages for all groups (percentages ranged from 61% to 72%).

Results showed that all groups agreed about the usefulness of the videos' explanation of Duo's purpose, the informativeness of the videos' explanation of the benefits of Duo, and the persuasiveness of the videos' highlighting the need to install Duo.

For analyzing this qualitative data (the open-ended question), the inductive approach was utilized. Two researchers coded the data independently, discussed the codes, and updated these codes to resolve any disagreements. We used Cohen's Kappa (k) to test the reliability. We found almost perfect agreement (k = .93) at p <.001.

At the end of the follow-up study, a research question was asked of all participants in the treatment groups: "How can the video or messaging be improved?" Among participants, 16% (17 responses) commented that including the installation or log-in process in the video would improve it, 13% (14 responses) said that the video was good as is, 9% (9 responses) stated that a visual explanation would improve the video, 6% (6 responses) commented that it would be better if we included more risk and motivation examples, 5% (5 responses) reported that it would be better if we included written instructions (e.g., bullets), 4% (4 responses) mentioned shortening the video length, and 3% (3 responses) stated that including location-tracking information, an off-campus usage explanation, or out-of-US Duo code generation information would improve the video messages. Participants also submitted other comments that were not related to the question of improving the video message. They complained about using Duo on their university account as follows: Duo should be optional, not mandatory (9%), Duo is annoying (4%), Duo is difficult to use when outside the US (1%), Duo is a mental burden (no access if a user forgets the phone) (1%), and Duo is a problem when using devices during exam time (1%).

Several participants' complaints for improving the messaging are as follows. One participant stated that the invasive tracking could be explained in the video as, "The duo is an invasion of privacy. You cannot turn off Location in-app permissions. Even if my location is off it still reports my location. None of this invasive tracking was included in the video. I was told you could delete the app and it would still work. That was not true. IT had me reinstall the app again to make it work. Duo also creates a problem in class for students. They need their phone to login. I don't want them to have phones during tests. So they have to get up and down disturbing the class. A less invasive approach is to send a text message with a code. Good enough for banks should be good enough for [the university]." Another comment about the backup access was, "Include how to get back up access when a cell phone is lost or dead." Also, no cost for the authentication option was mentioned by one participant: "Message doesn't address that the university wants you to use your own phone (that the university does not pay for) for this requirement."

5   Discussion

Once the messaging campaigns started, our finding in the first stage of this study showed that no significant differences were found among groups. However, when it come to the descriptive statistics, both Authoritarian(20% of university employees enabled Duo 2FA on their university accounts) and Benefit (17%) had the highest percentages in enabling Duo 2FA when compared to the other groups. This could be that the video messages included the same video aspects, such as Duo's definition, the purpose of using Duo, and the deadline for using it (January 31, 2019), which might have impacted our results by encouraging university employees to enable Duo 2FA. Even though our study started on November 26, 2018, for two weeks and we still had more than two months until the deadline for Duo 2FA adoption (January 31, 2019).

In the Authoritarian group, we think that the university employees may follow the authority's (the university administration's) suggestion for enabling Duo 2FA on their accounts, and the motivating cue included in this video was, "The university administration suggests you do it now and not wait until January." Regarding the Benefit group, university employees may value using Duo 2FA on their accounts because of the benefit, which was that changing the password would be required only once a year instead of every 90 days. As Herely [23] mentioned that the leading cause of following the recommended security behavior is weighing the costs against the benefits for security actions, which impacts a user's security decisions. Based on the messages, the results showed that all the treatment groups similarly agreed about the usefulness of the video explanation of Duo's purpose, the informativeness of videos' explanations of the benefits of Duo, and the persuasiveness of the videos' highlighting the need to install Duo, even though the motivating cues differed for each video message.

Regarding usability and security from participants' viewpoints, they were highly motivated to enable 2FA on their different online accounts in the Authoritarian and Benefit groups compared to other groups. We also found that all groups stated that using Duo 2FA was annoying but not difficult to use, except for the Control group, in which 38.4% of participants agreed that using Duo 2FA is difficult. This could be interpreted as occurring because the Control did not watch a video about the importance of Duo 2FA adaption or receive guidelines for installing Duo 2FA during the messaging campaigns.

All groups were aware of the importance of enabling Duo 2FA to protect their university accounts. We noted that the majority of participants chose the type of information on their university accounts that Duo 2FA would help protect related to the motivating cues in each video message. The findings showed that 72% of participants chose their employee account and university data in the Authoritarian group, whose video mainly focused on the administration's suggestions as a motivating cue, whereas 76% and 63% of participants chose personal data in the Logic and Benefit groups, respectively. Additionally, 73% and 77% of participants chose their employee account in the Enterprise Risk and Personal Risk groups, respectively, and the videos for those groups centered on the possible consequences if their university accounts were compromised. In contrast, 84% of the Control group participants, which did not watch a video, valued the student information that they needed to protect instead of considering other types of information, Duo 2FA would protect that.

Regarding improvements to the video messages, we present a preliminary list of improvements of the messaging below to enhance the design of the video messages that will be displayed to those who take voluntary action to adopt 2FA on their accounts.

- **Include the Duo installation process in the video**. The majority of participants suggested that if the installation of the Duo or log-in process were included in the video as bullet points, it would improve the messaging quality. Our results were supported by Redmiles et al. study [29], which mainly focused on how participants designed the motivating messages. They used bullet points for setting up 2FA in their design, even though, at the end of each video, the speaker mentioned that if they need more information about the Duo installation, they could click on the links below the video which directed them to Duo related web pages (e.g., installation, frequent question, etc.). In other words, participants preferred to see the installation process explained in the same video, which increased their willingness to follow the new security features more easily.
- **Include visual explanation in the video**. The majority of participants stated that it would be better if we included visual explanation step-by-step with screenshots to the installation Duo or logging-in process, how Duo works with a cell phone, the Duo app, or office phone, and a more detailed explanation of the reasoning behind the Duo platform. Providing visual explanations of the Duo installation process and simulating the risks of not being protected by Duo 2FA in the video could greatly improve the messaging quality.
- **Include more risk scenarios in the video**. Representing more risk scenarios and possible consequences of real situations that have happened to the university would explain the rationale that could motivate university employees or staff if they have not enabled Duo 2FA. Adding more risk scenarios could convincingly enhance messaging's effectiveness and motivate users to change their behavior, especially for those who have the voluntary option to use Duo 2FA. Perceiving the security threats of not activating 2FA and the benefits of 2FA showed the university employees' willingness to enable Duo

2FA on their university accounts and their desire to learn more about the risk consequences of not enabling 2FA the university.

- **Include location-tracking and code generation usage and backup access information in the video**. These concerns were raised by participants as issues that need to be addressed in the video messages. Regarding the location-tracking information that invades their privacy by reporting their current location, they turned off the app's location permissions. Similar issues included providing solutions in the messaging for privacy concerns, Duo code generation when participants are out of the country (e.g., there could be network issues with phone and internet service providers), and backup access if their smartphones are lost or not charged (e.g., authenticating an enrolled second device using Duo's self-service feature), all of which would strength the video content. This suggests that possible solutions should be included in the messaging for such inconvenient situations, which may affect users' adoption decisions.

6   Limitations and Future Work

Our study is not without limitations. We worked with ITS for both phases of the study. Everything was handled through ITS, and we did not ask university employees and staff their educational backgrounds or demographic information. Our focus mainly centers on investigating the effectiveness of different types of ITS messages in videos and how these messages could be improved to be used with new security features.

The confounding factors in our study that impact the generalizability of the results are that there were university employees who had already enabled Duo 2FA when our study began (see Fig. 2). We only considered the remaining number of university employees that had not yet adopted Duo 2FA on their university accounts. The deadline to adopt 2FA by January 31, 2019, was included in emails for treatment and control groups and the videos (treatment groups) and might have impacted our results by encouraging university employees to enable Duo 2FA. A further study is needed to address these factors.

Moreover, the sample size of those who participated in both phases of our study was small; a larger sample size could improve the validity of the findings. In addition, the university employees were not tracked to confirm if they were watching the whole video. The results from the online survey for this part were limited by their self-reported nature. This can be addressed by conducting controlled lab studies that measure users' eye movements and their facial expressions while watching the assigned video. It would also be better if users could comment on the video directly (e.g., using the Video Collaboratory tool, the VoiceThread tool, etc.) and determine which part of the video should be highlighted for marking up, analyzing, and providing further discussion. A future study is also needed to investigate if users are willing to watch a lengthy video that addressed the main improvements of the content of the videos.

For future work, we will conduct a controlled lab study and design video messages that address the comments about improving the messaging by simulating different themes of threats among university students, since they are not required to enable Duo 2FA on their university accounts. Based on that, we will see how such video messaging affects students' security decisions and behavior, as well as addressing other factors that can be measured by different tools.

7 Conclusion

For testing the effectiveness of different types of ITS messages in videos, we designed different types of video messages (authoritarian, logic, benefit, personal risk, and enterprise risk) to motivate university employees to enable Duo 2FA on their university accounts. Results showed that, during the two weeks after the messaging campaigns started, that no significant differences were found among groups regarding the adoption rate for Duo 2FA. In the follow-up study, groups reported that Duo 2FA was annoying but not difficult to use. In addition, based on the design suggestions that we obtained, we addressed improvements in the messaging design that will support designers in designing effective messages for adopting new security features. Furthermore, these suggestions will provide a way for changing users' decisions toward following security recommendations.

A   Video Transcripts

Note: (between parentheses are repetitive parts in each video)

– **Logic Message**

(**Introduction**) Hi, my name is Jessica, I am an employee at UNC Charlotte. I am here to talk to you about Duo.

(**Duo Definition**) What is Duo? well, it is a two-factor authentication service provided by the university to help protect your online accounts. All university employees are required to use Duo before the end of January 2019.

(**Duo Purpose**) Duo provides a second layer of verification when accessing your university accounts, by requiring you to verify your identity through another channel, such as receiving a pin code or a push notification through the Duo mobile app. These second factors of authentication will make it much harder for someone to access your account if it has been compromised.

(**Deadline**) All university employees are required to use Duo by January 31, 2019.

Why wait it makes sense to do it now. Click the links below to get more information about Duo.

– **Benefit Message**

(**Introduction**), (**Duo Definition**), (**Duo Purpose**) In addition to extra security, another benefit of using Duo is that you will only have to change your password once a year instead of every 90 d reducing password reset hassels, (**Deadline**), Don't wait till January to enjoy the benefits of improving your security; do it now. Click the links below to get more information about Duo.

– **Authoritarian Message**

(**Introduction**), (**Duo Definition**), (**Duo Purpose**), (**Deadline**), The university administration suggests you do it now and not wait until January. Click the links below to get more information about Duo.

– **Personal Risk**

(**Introduction**), (**Duo Definition**), As you know your university accounts provide access to sensitive personal information such as your email, social security number and, financial information. If your account is compromised this may provide access to your inbox and embarrassing emails could be sent to your contacts. In an effort to further enhance the security of your online accounts the university is providing Duo, (**Duo Purpose**), (**Deadline**), Don't wait till January to protect your information; do it now. Click the links below to get more information about Duo.

– **Enterprise Risk**

(**Introduction**), (**Duo Definition**), As you know your university accounts provide access to sensitive university information such as student records, and financial data. If your account is compromised, then this sensitive information may be exposed and misused in many different ways. This may affect not only your reputation but also other employees, students and the university. In an effort to further enhance the security of your online accounts the university is providing Duo, (**Duo Purpose**), (**Deadline**), Don't wait till January to improve the security of your accounts; do it now. Click the links below to get more information about Duo.

References

1. Miami University: Two-factor authentication is a must for all employees (2015). http://www.shorturl.at/qB479. Accessed 26 Dec 2019
2. Carnegie Mellon University: Two-factor authentication (2fa) (2016). http://www.shorturl.at/AE149. Accessed 26 Dec 2019
3. Duo (2019). https://duo.com/. Accessed 26 Dec 2019
4. Fort Hays State University: duo security (2019). http://www.shorturl.at/CJQ02. Accessed 26 Dec 2019
5. Students, faculty reflect on duo security six months after introduction (2019). http://www.shorturl.at/opyA8. Accessed 26 Dec 2019

6. UNC Charlotte: Duo two factor authentication (2019). http://www.shorturl.at/eFP13. Accessed 26 Dec 2019
7. Abawajy, J.: User preference of cyber security awareness delivery methods. Behav. Inf. Technol. **33**(3), 237–248 (2014)
8. Ackerman, P.: Impediments to adoption of two-factor authentication by home end-users. SANS Institute InfoSec Reading Room (2014)
9. Al Qahtani, E., Javed, Y., Lipford, H., Shehab, M.: Do women in conservative societies (not) follow smartphone security advice? A case study of Saudi Arabia and Pakistan (2020)
10. Al Qahtani, E., Shehab, M., Aljohani, A.: The effectiveness of fear appeals in increasing smartphone locking behavior among Saudi Arabians. In: Fourteenth Symposium on Usable Privacy and Security ({SOUPS} 2018), pp. 31–46 (2018)
11. Albayram, Y., Khan, M.M.H., Fagan, M.: A study on designing video tutorials for promoting security features: a case study in the context of two-factor authentication (2fa). Int. J. Hum.-Comput. Interact. **33**(11), 927–942 (2017)
12. Albayram, Y., Khan, M.M.H., Jensen, T., Nguyen, N.: "... better to use a lock screen than to worry about saving a few seconds of time": effect of fear appeal in the context of smartphone locking behavior. In: Thirteenth Symposium on Usable Privacy and Security ({SOUPS} 2017), pp. 49–63 (2017)
13. Althobaiti, M., Mayhew, P.: Security and usability of authenticating process of online banking: user experience study, vol. 2014, pp. 1–6, October 2014. https://doi.org/10.1109/CCST.2014.6986978
14. Bada, M., Sasse, A.M., Nurse, J.R.: Cyber security awareness campaigns: why do they fail to change behaviour? arXiv preprint arXiv:1901.02672 (2019)
15. Cheng, B.S., Chou, L.F., Wu, T.Y., Huang, M.P., Farh, J.L.: Paternalistic leadership and subordinate responses: establishing a leadership model in Chinese organizations. Asian J. Soc. Psychol. **7**(1), 89–117 (2004)
16. Cheng, B., Chou, L., Huang, M., Farh, L.J., Peng, S.: A triad model of paternalistic leadership: evidence from business organizations in Mainland China. Indigenous Psychol. Res. Chin. Soc. **20**, 209 (2003)
17. Colnago, J., et al.: "It's not actually that horrible": exploring adoption of two-factor authentication at a university. In: Proceedings of the 2018 CHI Conference on Human Factors in Computing Systems. CHI 2018. Association for Computing Machinery, New York (2018). https://doi.org/10.1145/3173574.3174030
18. Das, S., Russo, G., Dingman, A., Dev, J., Kenny, O., Camp, L.: A qualitative study on usability and acceptability of Yubico security key, December 2017
19. Davis, J.: List of websites and whether or not they support 2fa. twofactorauth.org (2018). https://twofactorauth.org/. Accessed May 2019
20. Dutson, J., Allen, D., Eggett, D., Seamons, K.: Don't punish all of us: measuring user attitudes about two-factor authentication. In: 2019 IEEE European Symposium on Security and Privacy Workshops (EuroS&PW), pp. 119–128. IEEE (2019)
21. Fagan, M., Khan, M.M.H.: Why do they do what they do?: a study of what motivates users to (not) follow computer security advice. In: Twelfth Symposium on Usable Privacy and Security ({SOUPS} 2016), pp. 59–75 (2016)
22. Harbach, M., Hettig, M., Weber, S., Smith, M.: Using personal examples to improve risk communication for security & privacy decisions. In: Proceedings of the SIGCHI Conference on Human Factors in Computing Systems, pp. 2647–2656. ACM (2014)
23. Herley, C.: So long, and no thanks for the externalities: the rational rejection of security advice by users. In: Proceedings of the 2009 Workshop on New Security Paradigms Workshop, pp. 133–144. ACM (2009)

24. Huang, D.-L., Rau, P.-L.P., Salvendy, G.: A survey of factors influencing people's perception of information security. In: Jacko, J.A. (ed.) HCI 2007. LNCS, vol. 4553, pp. 906–915. Springer, Heidelberg (2007). https://doi.org/10.1007/978-3-540-73111-5_100

25. Kitten, T.: Linkedin: Hashed passwords breached. inforisktoday.com, June 2012. https://tinyurl.com/y2oqkxyx. Accessed May 2019

26. McCandless, D.: World's biggest data breaches & hacks. informationisbeautiful.net, April 2019. https://tinyurl.com/ycho2xx4. Accessed May 2019

27. Pattinson, M.R., Anderson, G.: How well are information risks being communicated to your computer end-users? Inf. Manag. Comput. Secur. 15(5), 362–371 (2007)

28. Petsas, T., Tsirantonakis, G., Athanasopoulos, E., Ioannidis, S.: Two-factor authentication: is the world ready?: quantifying 2fa adoption. In: Proceedings of the Eighth European Workshop on System Security, p. 4. ACM (2015)

29. Redmiles, E.M., Liu, E., Mazurek, M.L.: You want me to do what? A design study of two-factor authentication messages. In: SOUPS (2017)

30. Reese, K., Smith, T., Dutson, J., Armknecht, J., Cameron, J., Seamons, K.: A usability study of five two-factor authentication methods. In: Fifteenth Symposium on Usable Privacy and Security (SOUPS 2019). USENIX Association, Santa Clara, August 2019. https://www.usenix.org/conference/soups2019/presentation/reese

31. Reynolds, J., Smith, T., Reese, K., Dickinson, L., Ruoti, S., Seamons, K.: A tale of two studies: the best and worst of Yubikey usability. In: 2018 IEEE Symposium on Security and Privacy (SP), pp. 872–888. IEEE (2018)

32. Salvendy, G.: Human factors and Ergonomics. Lawrence Erlbaum Associates (1999)

33. Ur, B., et al.: "I added '!' at the end to make it secure": observing password creation in the lab. In: Eleventh Symposium On Usable Privacy and Security ({SOUPS} 2015), pp. 123–140 (2015)

34. Wang, H., Guan, B.: The positive effect of authoritarian leadership on employee performance: the moderating role of power distance. Front. Psychol. 9, 357 (2018)

35. Weir, C.S., Douglas, G., Richardson, T., Jack, M.: Usable security: user preferences for authentication methods in ebanking and the effects of experience. Interact. Comput. 22(3), 153–164 (2010)

A Study on Online Businesses' Commitment to Consumer Privacy

May Almousa[1,2], Yang Liu[2], Tianyang Zhang[3], and Mohd Anwar[2(✉)]

[1] Information Technology Department, College of Computer and Information Sciences, Princess Nourah Bint Abdulrahman University, Riyadh, Saudi Arabia
[2] Computer Science Department, College of Engineering, North Carolina A&T State University, Greensboro, NC 27401, USA
manwar@ncat.edu
[3] Electrical and Computer Engineering Department, College of Engineering, University of Massachusetts Amherst, Amherst, MA 01003, USA

Abstract. In today's digital economy, consumers are heavily dependent on online businesses. As consumers browse and purchase products and services online, a trove of data about them is collected by businesses. Consumers need protection from the collection and misuse of their personal information. However, not all businesses are sincere about ensuring consumer privacy online or responsibly handling consumer information. In this paper, we study privacy policies and information practices of a sample of 27 well-known and lesser-known online businesses to understand and explore whether well-known sites have stronger privacy commitment than the lesser-known ones. Our study adaptively reuses the methodology from a similar study done by the Federal Trade Commission (FTC) in 1999. Since then, the online businesses have grown manifold; consumer behaviors have changed significantly; and technologies for information capture and data analyses have become so much powerful that consumer privacy is at huge risks, needing this study. This study reveals weak privacy postures and practices of online businesses.

Keywords: Consumer privacy · Online businesses · Data protection regulations · Privacy assessment

1 Introduction

Globally, consumers spent a whopping $2.93 trillion online in 2018, and the Digital commerce 360, an e-commerce news outlet, predicts that global consumers

The work of May M. Almousa was supported by the Deanship of Scientific Research at Princess Nourah bint Abdulrahman University through the Fast-track Research Funding Program.
M. Almousa, Y. Liu, T. Zhang—Contributed equally to this work.

A. Moallem (Ed.): HCII 2021, LNCS 12788, pp. 391–402, 2021.
https://doi.org/10.1007/978-3-030-77392-2_25

will spend nearly \$3.46 trillion online in 2019[1]. The Census Bureau of the Department of Commerce reported that retail sales are expected to total \$1.38 trillion in the third quarter of 2019, up 1.4% (±0.2%) from the second quarter of 2019. E-commerce is projected to grow 16.9% (±1.4%) in the third quarter of 2019 over the third quarter of 2018, while total retail sales are projected to grow 4.0% (±0.4%) over the same period [20]. E-retail revenue is expected to grow to \$6.54 trillion by 2022[2]. According to a report by Grand View Research Inc., the global business-to-consumer (b2c) e-commerce market will approach \$8 trillion by 2025[3].

The success of online business depends on understanding the consumers, which has led to the collection and analyses of any data that they can gather about consumers. Although consumers enjoy the convenience and personalized services from utilizing the gathered data, they face increased risk of erosion of privacy.

It is natural for people to desire privacy. The need for privacy is relative, and the majority of consumers seek a balance between privacy and societal exposure. It is the duty of the data gathering business to accommodate the privacy needs of their consumers. Privacy protects consumers from surveillance and protects their data from being misused.

For consumers, one of the privacy management steps is to read the privacy policy or statement of the practice of the business website they visit [15]. Therefore, it is important to understand how committed or how informative the businesses are about their privacy practices. In 1999, the Federal Trade Commission (FTC) conducted a study on privacy policies of online businesses [3]. However, in today's growing digital economy and the deployment of powerful data science technologies, that study is out of date. Our study seeks to fill that gap.

Online businesses supposedly showcase their privacy posture through the privacy policy/statement of practice. The goal of this study is to look into policy statements in order to investigate to what extent the online business sites are responsive to concerns of consumer privacy – specifically about *security*, *access*, *choice* and *notice* principles of privacy protection. We extracted the evaluation rubrics from the survey in federal trade commission (FTC) [3] and added some new questions which are more fitting for today's e-commerce. We also compared the privacy postures of well-known sites with lesser-known sites. Three surfers, who are cyber security researchers holding master's degrees, participated in this study to rate the questions for each rubric based on what they found in the policy statement. We evaluated the results of three surfers and compared the well-known and lesser-known sites on each principle. Inter-rater reliability has been calculated to evaluate the agreement of three surfers.

We make a two-fold contribution by exploring: (i) how informatively or transparently the businesses communicate their privacy postures through their policies/statements, (ii) how different the privacy postures are between well-known

---

[1] https://www.digitalcommerce360.com/article/global-ecommerce-sales.

[2] https://www.statista.com/statistics/379046/worldwide-retail-e-commerce-sales.

[3] https://www.grandviewresearch.com/press-release/global-b2c-e-commerce-market.

and lesser-known businesses. To the best of our knowledge, there is no other recent studies that have contributed in a similar way as stated above. We study privacy policy and information practice statements along with four assessment principles: *security, access, choice,* and *notice.*

This paper is organized as follows. Section 2 contains a discussion of related work, and in Sect. 3 we describe our study methods. In Sect. 4, we present our study results, and we discuss our findings in Sect. 5. Lastly, in Sect. 6 we conclude with the proposal for future work.

2   Related Work

Privacy is traditionally defined as "the ability for people to determine for themselves when, how, and to what extent information about them is communicated to others" [21]. A number of studies and consumer surveys [1,10,17] have shown that the websites users are concerned about their privacy while surfing websites.

Recently, some works focus on the concerns of protecting user contents from the site operators [2,6]. The authors of [16] focus on privacy controls on social media sites, providing the user with the ability to manage access to their content by other users. Their work comprehensively considers privacy among the site operators and customers on technical levels.

The survey conducted by Milne and Culnan [14] stated that, since 1998 the Federal Trade Commission has conducted three investigations of websites to assess whether websites have published online privacy disclosures. This study compares equivalent subsets of website data from the 1998, 1999, 2000, and 2001 web surveys. The significance of using such research to inform public policy is discussed.

Nyshadham [18] aimed to understand the privacy policies of online vendors of airline tickets that are related to the privacy concerns of consumers and regulators. The author analyzed the privacy policies of some US air travel agencies that were posted on their respective websites.

Wu et al. [22] explored the trust and privacy issues related to individuals' willingness to provide personal information on the Internet under the influence across culture. This study explores the relationship between the content of online privacy statements, privacy concerns, and consumer trust, and explores the moderating effects of different cultural backgrounds on respondents.

Several studies have examined the reasons why consumers show inaction on data breaches. Mikhed and Vogan [13] found clear evidence of being affected by a breach encouraged consumers to sign up for fraud protection services. In addition, Kude et al. [11], studying Target's data breach, found that whether compensation is perceived adequate was largely shaped by consumers' personality traits.

Reference [9] analyzed 64 privacy policies, including their accessibility, writing, content, and evolution over time. The researchers examined how well these policies met user needs and how to improve them. Peterson et al. [19] compared the effectiveness of third-party seals with self-reported privacy policy statements regarding potential e-commerce customers' willingness to provide various types of personal information to websites. This study explores users' needs and satisfaction with privacy policies and concerns about providing various types of personal information to websites.

Online businesses need to make their privacy policies more accessible and representative of the services they describe. It is also important that privacy policies provide users the option to opt-out of certain collections and uses of their personal data. All these information needs to be stated clearly in privacy policies and can be easily understood by regular users. To help users understand the privacy policy better, Kumar et al. [12] introduce Opt-Out Easy, a web browser extension. Their method is used to automatically detect the opt-out choices in privacy policy text and their presentation to users through a web browser extension. A study conducted by [7] to explore the usefulness and usability of privacy choices offered by websites. The authors asked the participants of the study to find and use choices related to email marketing, targeted advertising, or data deletion on a set of different websites. They found that privacy choices that were tested by the participants are difficult for consumers to exercise in practice. As a result, the authors provide design and policy recommendations for making those website opt-outs and deletion choices more useful and usable for consumers.

According to FTC [3], the privacy policy is a comprehensive description of information practices of a website that can be found in one place, whereas the information practice statement is a discrete statement that explains about a specific information practice. In this paper, we study how committed the online business websites are to protect consumer privacy and their personal information as specified in their privacy policies or information practice statements.

3   Methods

3.1   Study Sample: Websites of 9 Categories

The study samples 27 websites from 9 categories of online business sites: General Marketplace, Auction Marketplace, Social Media, Handmade and Crafts Marketplace, On-Demand Production Marketplace, Unique Items Marketplace, Classified Listings Website, Comparison Shopping Engines, and Daily Deals Sites (shown in Table 1). Under each category, we randomly selected some popular global online business sites, namely well-known websites. On the other hand, the lesser-known websites are selected based on their low ranks in familiarity on SimilarWeb[4] statistics, as of December 2019.

3.2   Sample Selection: 27 Websites

In our study sample, we combine both well-known and lesser-known online business sites under each category of web sites.

---

[4] https://www.similarweb.com.

Table 1. A sample of 27 websites

Category	URL	Website type	Category rank
General Marketplace	1. https://www.amazon.com	Well-known	1
	2. https://www.tesco.com/zones/gm	Well-known	1
	3. https://www.jet.com	Lesser-known	487
Auction Marketplace	4. https://www.ebid.net	well-known	163
	5. https://www.proxibid.com	Well-known	40
	6. http://www.ubid.com	Lesser-known	993
Social Media	7. https://www.pinterest.com	Well-known	8
	8. https://www.instagram.com	Well-known	3
	9. https://www.dingtalk.com	Lesser-known	254
Handmade and Crafts Marketplace	10. https://www.zibbet.com	Well-known	122
	11. https://www.mybluprint.com	Well-known	4
	12. https://greenheartshop.org	Lesser-known	4437
On-Demand Production Marketplace	13. https://www.zazzle.com	Well-known	155
	14. https://www.redbubble.com	Well-known	40
	15. https://cdbaby.com	Lesser-known	734
Unique Items Marketplace	16. https://www.bonanza.com	Well-known	243
	17. https://www.storenvy.com	Well-known	343
	18. https://www.sweetgrasstradingco.com	Lesser-known	N/A
Classified Listings Website	19. https://www.gumtree.com	Well-known	12
	20. https://craigslist.org	Well-known	1
	21. https://www.oodle.com	Lesser-known	652
Comparison Shopping Engines	22. http://www.shopzilla.com	Well-known	93
	23. http://www.bing.com/shop	Well-known	5
	24. https://community.channeladvisor.com	Lesser-known	368
Daily Deals Sites	25. https://www.livingsocial.com	Well-known	144
	26. https://www.woot.com	Well-known	12
	27. https://www.1sale.com	Lesser-known	731

3.3 Assessment of Websites

To assess these websites, we use the evaluation rubrics from the earlier survey by FTC [3] and added some new questions which are more fitting for today's e-commerce. A questionnaire with 19 items is used to assess the privacy commitments of businesses along following categories: *security, access, notice, choice,* and *visibility of policy.*

Three surfers (masters-level cybersecurity experts) assessed the websites by answering the questionnaire. Two surfers piloted the assessment tasks on a website to validate the questionnaire. Opinions and subjective satisfaction of surfers are gathered through a survey on a 5-point Likert scale.

3.4   Study Piloting

Two out of three surfers piloted the tasks on a website. From the screen recording, we measured difficulty in locating privacy policy or information practice statement on a website. The pilot study also helped us validate our questionnaire.

3.5   Inter-rater Reliability (IRR)

We calculated inter-rater reliability (IRR) to demonstrate consistency among observational scores provided by three surfers. The surfers made independent ratings about the privacy policy/statement of practice by answering 19 questions on a set of rubrics/privacy principles: *security, access, choice,* and *notice.*

4   Results

4.1   Sample Statistics

Three surfers evaluated 27 websites (shown in Table 1) using total 19 questions (shown in Table 2) on five principles. Each surfer worked independently to rate each website, we simply map 'Yes' or 'No' answers to each question as 1 and 0 respectively for security, access, notice, choice principles. For the visibility principle, we measured finding time in seconds. We present the evaluations from three surfers with box and whisker plots.

4.2   Comparing of Well-Known vs. Lesser-Known Websites

We compared the privacy postures of well-known and lesser-known websites along four privacy protection principles as shown in Fig. 1.

Under *security* category, the median values of mean scores for both well-known and lesser-known sites were 1.5. However, the interquartile ranges were 1.75 and 1 for well-known and lesser-known sites respectively. Therefore, the scores of well-known sites have higher variance than lesser-known sites.

Under *access* category, the median value of well-known sites' mean scores was 3.25 which is 7% lower than the median score of lesser-known sites. The inter-quartile ranges for well-known and lesser-known sites were 1.6 and 1.5, respectively. Therefore, the consumers found it slightly easier to access personal information or opt-in/opt-out of marketing communications on the lesser-known websites than well-known websites.

Under *choice* category, the median value (3.5) of mean scores of well-known sites beats that of lesser-known sites (3.0); the inter-quartile range of well-known sites was 0.62 which is 50% lower than that of lesser-known sites. The well-known websites tend to give more choices regarding the disclosure and use of personal information of consumers than lesser-known websites.

Under *notice* category, the two groups of websites have similar performance. The median values of mean scores of both well-known and lesser-known sites were 4. The inter-quartile ranges for well-known sites and lesser-known sites were also both 0.5, though the mean value of 3.8 for well-known sites was higher than the 3.6 mean for lesser-known sites.

Table 2. Rubrics of each topic.

Principles	Rubric
Security	1. Does the Privacy Policy or Information Practice Statement say that the domain takes any steps to provide security? 2. Does the Privacy Policy or Information Practice Statement say that the domain takes steps to provide security, for personal information the domain collects, during transmission of the information from the consumer to the domain? 3. Does the Privacy Policy or Information Practice Statement say that the domain takes steps to provide security, for personal information the domain has collected, after the domain has received the information (i.e., not during transmission, but after collection)? 4. Does the Privacy Policy or Information Practice Statement say that there will be some compensation to customers for any privacy breach? (specify of any compensation for privacy leakage)? 5. Does the Privacy Policy or Information Practice Statement say that if they will notify customers about a privacy breach?
Access	1. Does the Privacy Policy or Information Practice Statement say that the domain allows consumers to review at least some personal information about them? 2. Does the Privacy Policy or Information Practice Statement say that the domain allows consumers to have inaccuracies corrected in at least some personal information about them? 3. Does the Privacy Policy or Information Practice Statement say that it allows consumers to have at least some personal information about them deleted from the domain's records? 4. Does the Privacy Policy or Information Practice Statement say that consumers have the right to unsubscribe/opt-out of marketing communications? (such as postal marketing or telemarketing). 5. Does the Privacy Policy or Information Practice Statement say that the domain allows only authorized individuals to obtain personal information through an access request?
Choice	1. Does the Privacy Policy or Information Practice Statement say anything about Whether or not the domain offers consumers a choice regarding the disclosure of their personal information to third parties? 2. Does the Privacy Policy or Information Practice Statement say anything about how the domain may use personal information it collects for internal purposes? 3. Does the Privacy Policy or Information Practice Statement say anything about whether the domain uses personal information it collects to send communications to the consumer? 4. Does the policy or statement of practice say anything about using personal information for commercial solicitation?
Notice	1. Does the website specify what information try to collect? 2. Does the Privacy Policy or Information Practice Statement say anything about whether the domain discloses personal information it collects to third parties? 3. Does the Privacy Policy or Information Practice Statement say anything about whether the DOMAIN places cookies? 4. Does the Privacy Policy or Information Practice Statement say anything about whether third parties may place cookies and/or collect personal information on the domain?
Visibility of Policy	1. How many seconds did consumer spend to find the Privacy Policy or Information Practice Statement in the website?

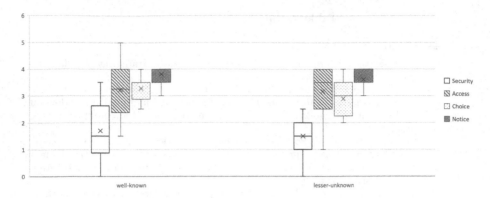

Fig. 1. Comparison between well-known and lesser-known websites through box and whisker plots on security, access, notice, choice principles (the mean score labeled with x, the median score labeled with bar).

4.3   Comparing Well-Known vs. Lesser-Known Websites on Visibility of Policies

The median value of privacy policy look-up time on well-known websites was 15.3 s and the median value for lesser-known websites was 15.1 s, the inter-quartile ranges for well-known sites were 5.9, which were 34 % higher than lesser-known sites. The surfers' search time varied more for the well-known websites, and they spent more time to find the policy (Fig. 2).

4.4   Inter-rater Reliability

Three web surfers independently rated a set of websites. We seek to evaluate the level of agreement among the surfers. Each surfer answered with a 'YES' or 'NO'

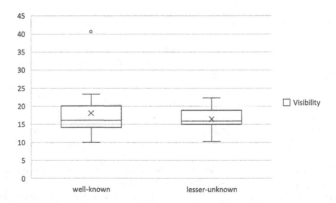

Fig. 2. Comparison between well-known and lesser-known websites through box-whisker plots on visibility of policies (The mean score labeled with x, the median score labeled with bar, the outlier labeled with o).

for 486 questions in total for 27 websites, 18 questions per website (excluding the visibility question). We evaluated an overall agreement as well as the pair-level agreement among the surfers using, as appropriate, the methods of Cohen's kappa and Fleiss' kappa.

To measure the inter-rater reliability of two raters who have judged categorical variables, the statistic of Cohen's kappa can be used [5,8]. A complete agreement between the two raters yields a kappa value of 1. When judges' agreement is identical to what is expected by random chance, the kappa statistic is 0. In the case of worse than the random agreement between judges, the kappa values can become negative.

To measure inter-rater agreement between any fixed number of raters requires a generalization such as Fleiss' kappa [4]. Using the Fleiss' kappa, we found the overall agreement to be 0.559. This represents a moderate level of overall agreement for the three surfers on all items. Because this is an overall number, it does not identify which of the surfers agree more or less or which of the questions or websites are more agreed upon.

We compared the pair-wise agreement of surfers by Cohen's kappa. The highest level of agreement was 0.806 between surfer1 and surfer3. This represents a strong level of agreement. Neither of the other two surfer-to-surfer comparisons showed similarly high levels of the agreement; both values were of only weak to the moderate agreement (0.4-0.5 kappa). This implies that it is surfer2 who provided the most different rating overall on all items as compared to the other two surfers.

4.5 Surfers' Opinions and Comments

Because we see some disagreement on surfers' evaluations, we conducted a survey to gather their opinions and comments. Three surfers answered seven questions (shown in Table 3). All questions are Likert items on a scale of 1 to 5–1 is the worst, 5 is the best. We calculated the average (Avg) and standard deviation (STD) on each Likert item.

Based on these comments, surfers are generally dissatisfied with the privacy policy or how online businesses plan to handle consumer privacy. Surfers generally believe that online businesses give more attention and provide more information for "Notice", while they do not give adequate consideration and provide less information in terms of "Security" and "Choice". Surfers expect more information provided for "Security" and "Access", but they do not seem to pay as much attention to "Notice".

To seek surfer's opinion, we asked the following question: what is the most important observation do you have about the privacy policy/ information practice statement of the online business websites you surfed? For all of the surfers, we noticed that finding the privacy policy was fairly easy for both well-known and lesser-known websites. However, the privacy policy for well-known websites are more organized and covered almost all the required information to answer the questions. Whereas, some lesser-known websites do not cover important aspects

Table 3. Comments of surfers

Survey questions	Avg	STD
1. How easy was it for you to find the privacy policy or information practice statement?	4	0
2. Based on this research, how much do you think online businesses are concerned about consumer privacy?	3	0.82
3. When you visit online business websites, how concerned do you get about your privacy ?	4	0.82
4. How similar are these websites to the websites you visit for your daily online activities?	4.33	0.82
5. Based on your assessment activities, rank and score how the online businesses are concerned in terms of access, choice, notice, and security		
Access:	3.67	0.82
Choice:	3	0.82
Notice:	4.33	1.63
Security:	3	0.82
6. Rank and score how you as a customer are concerned in terms of access, choice, notice and security		
Access:	4.67	0.82
Choice:	4.33	0.82
Notice:	4.33	0.82
Security:	5	0
7. How satisfied are you with the privacy policies of these websites?	4	0.82

of what security mechanisms do they apply and how do they secure the consumers' data after saving them in their databases.

5   Discussion

During the analysis of business websites provided by surfers, we noticed that on the security principle, the scores of well-known sites have higher variance than lesser-known sites. We found that there is a lot of variation in terms of security disclosures. Both types of businesses performed poorly, and the mean scores are all below 2. Some well-known sites (e.g., pinterest) and lesser-known sites (e.g., cdbaby) got 0 scores in the security principle. In the visibility principle, the outlier is the well-known site *Amazon*, for which the average time the surfers took to locate privacy policy is 41 s due to the location of the privacy policy in an inconspicuous place. Some well-known sites have the complex layout and abundant buttons, making it hard to find the privacy policy.

6   Conclusion

E-commerce sites and their desire for collecting consumer data are expected to increase in the coming years. Thus, the data about consumers, like their personal information, credit card numbers, and their purchase behaviors, will be increasingly available to companies. It is very important to understand how consumers' data are being transmitted, stored, handled, or shared by online businesses. The privacy and security risks of consumers' data are amplified with the increase in the number of data breach attacks and data analytics techniques in recent years.

Privacy policies are commonplace and can provide important information about what data privacy responsibilities companies assume and what rights are afforded to consumers. In this paper, we study the privacy postures of online businesses as manifested through websites' privacy policies and information practice statements of a sample of 27 different well-known and lesser-known websites. We reused some questions from the survey conducted by the Federal Trade Commission in 1999 and added some questions. We study how good and clear are self-reported privacy practices of online businesses as stated in their privacy policy and how informative the privacy policies are to the users. Three surfers answered all questions along with four principles, and the overall agreement was good. To our surprise, even a well-known website lacks security principle on their policy. For example, there was no clear policy about notification of privacy breach to consumers or some compensation to consumers in the event of a privacy breach. On some sites (e.g., Amazon), three surfers answered the questions with high consistency. That was because such a company provides adequate information in the privacy policy/information practice statement. However, the privacy policies of other lesser-known companies lack some important information about security, access, choice, and notice. Some issues also were discovered related to the clarity of the polices. Such information should not be buried deeply between lines where users have to spend a long time or have to have advanced skills to discover them.

This study has a limited number of surfers and a smaller set of websites. In the future, we want to increase the size of the sample of websites, such as E-Banking, and have more expert surfers to examine these websites.

References

1. Acquisti, A., Brandimarte, L., Loewenstein, G.: Privacy and human behavior in the age of information. Science **347**(6221), 509–514 (2015)
2. Baden, R., Bender, A., Spring, N., Bhattacharjee, B., Starin, D.: Persona: an online social network with user-defined privacy. ACM SIGCOMM Comput. Commun. Rev. **39**, 135–146 (2009)
3. Federal Trade Commission, et al.: Privacy online: fair information practices in the electronic marketplace: a report to congress. Federal Trade Commission, Washington, DC (2000)

4. Fleiss, J.L.: Measuring nominal scale agreement among many raters. Psychol. Bull. **76**(5), 378 (1971)
5. Fleiss, J.L., Cohen, J., Everitt, B.S.: Large sample standard errors of kappa and weighted kappa. Psychol. Bull. **72**(5), 323 (1969)
6. Guha, S., Tang, K., Francis, P.: NOYB: privacy in online social networks. In: Proceedings of the First Workshop on Online Social Networks, pp. 49–54. ACM (2008)
7. Habib, H., et al.: "It's a scavenger hunt": usability of websites' opt-out and data deletion choices. In: Proceedings of the 2020 CHI Conference on Human Factors in Computing Systems, pp. 1–12 (2020)
8. Hallgren, K.A.: Computing inter-rater reliability for observational data: an overview and tutorial. Tutor. Quant. Methods Psychol. **8**(1), 23 (2012)
9. Jensen, C., Potts, C.: Privacy policies as decision-making tools: an evaluation of online privacy notices. In: Proceedings of the SIGCHI Conference on Human Factors in Computing Systems, pp. 471–478 (2004)
10. Jensen, C., Potts, C., Jensen, C.: Privacy practices of internet users: self-reports versus observed behavior. Int. J. Hum. Comput. Stud. **63**(1–2), 203–227 (2005)
11. Kude, T., Hoehle, H., Sykes, T.A.: Big data breaches and customer compensation strategies: personality traits and social influence as antecedents of perceived compensation. Int. J. Oper. Prod. Manag. IJOPM **37**(1), 56–74 (2017)
12. Kumar, V.B., et al.: Finding a choice in a haystack: automatic extraction of opt-out statements from privacy policy text. In: The Web Conference (the Web Conference) (2020)
13. Mikhed, V., Vogan, M.: Out of sight, out of mind: consumer reaction to news on data breaches and identity theft (2015)
14. Milne, G.R., Culnan, M.J.: Using the content of online privacy notices to inform public policy: a longitudinal analysis of the 1998–2001 us web surveys. Inf. Soc. **18**(5), 345–359 (2002)
15. Milne, G.R., Culnan, M.J.: Strategies for reducing online privacy risks: Why consumers read (or don't read) online privacy notices. J. Interact. Mark. **18**(3), 15–29 (2004)
16. Mondal, M., Druschel, P., Gummadi, K.P., Mislove, A.: Beyond access control: managing online privacy via exposure. In: Proceedings of the Workshop on Useable Security, pp. 1–6 (2014)
17. Norberg, P.A., Horne, D.R., Horne, D.A.: The privacy paradox: personal information disclosure intentions versus behaviors. J. Consum. Aff. **41**(1), 100–126 (2007)
18. Nyshadham, E.A.: Privacy policies of air travel web sites: a survey and analysis. J. Air Transp. Manag. **6**(3), 143–152 (2000)
19. Peterson, D., Meinert, D., Criswell, J., Crossland, M.: Consumer trust: privacy policies and third-party seals. J. Small Bus. Enterp. Dev. **14**, 654–669 (2007)
20. U.S. Census Bureau: Quarterly retail e-commerce sales 3rd quarter 2019. U.S. Department of Commerce (2019)
21. Westin, A.F.: Privacy and freedom London. The Bodley Head (1970)
22. Wu, K.W., Huang, S.Y., Yen, D.C., Popova, I.: The effect of online privacy policy on consumer privacy concern and trust. Comput. Hum. Behav. **28**(3), 889–897 (2012)

Help the User Recognize a Phishing Scam: Design of Explanation Messages in Warning Interfaces for Phishing Attacks

Joseph Aneke[1] , Carmelo Ardito[2] , and Giuseppe Desolda[1]([✉])

[1] Dipartimento di Informatica, Università degli Studi di Bari Aldo Moro, Bari, Italy
{joseph.aneke,giuseppe.desolda}@uniba.it
[2] Dipartimento di Ingegneria Elettrica e dell'Informazione, Politecnico di Bari, Bari, Italy
carmelo.ardito@poliba.it

Abstract. Remote work due to the COVID-19 pandemic is expected to be the new normal, suggesting a situation where people use their personal computers at home for several activities like reading emails, surfing the web, chatting with friends. While doing this, users are not focused on securing their systems and they often do not have the skills and knowledge to defend against cybercrime. In this paper, we present the design and the evaluation of a novel interface that warns users against phishing attacks. This interface looks like the ones shown by browsers like Chrome and Firefox when opening a suspicious phishing website, but it includes information that explains the reasons why the website might be a scam. Such explanations are based on website features commonly used by AI-based systems to classify a website as phishing or not and aim to help users detecting phishing websites. To ensure a high understandability and effectiveness of the explanations, the C-HIP model was adopted to design such messages, which have been iteratively refined performing a static analysis of their comprehension, sentiment, and readability.

Keywords: Polymorphic warning messages · Usable security · Cybersecurity

1 Introduction

Remote work due to the COVID-19 pandemic is expected to be the new normal [1], suggesting a situation where people use even more their computers, smartphones, and tablets at home for several activities. These devices often lack professional antivirus protection programs, or firewalls [2]. In some cases, software in use may have simply reached the end of its life cycle, implying no relevant security updates, as seen in Microsoft Windows 7 lately [3], obviously exposing users to attacks. Although the new normal would facilitate user protection since they can comfortably work in their homes, this situation resulted in the upsurge of cybercrime and further exploitation of user vulnerabilities increased by 600% in March 2020 [4, 5]. These vulnerabilities are often also due to certain human factors and poor designs of security warnings messages [5–7].

© Springer Nature Switzerland AG 2021
A. Moallem (Ed.): HCII 2021, LNCS 12788, pp. 403–416, 2021.
https://doi.org/10.1007/978-3-030-77392-2_26

In most cases, the last barrier between victims and attackers are the warning messages. It is typical of phishing attacks: when browsers detect fraudulent phishing websites they show warning messages that ask users to open or not the target website. Therefore, users need the right information presented in a manner that they can understand easily, and at the time they need to make the decision [8]. There is a need for warnings to appear with specific features in a simple language, which are polymorphic [7] and that is not generalized in terms of look and feel [9, 10]. Understanding of the warning becomes an important factor since human decisions are involved. Current warning designs focus on describing the potentially dangerous outcome if the warning is not heeded. Existing literature on improving comprehension recommends using simple plain language avoiding technical jargon [5, 6], and to describe the specific risks clearly and being as brief [5].

This paper aims to improve the effectiveness of warning messages defending users from phishing attacks. In the last years, we worked on the design of a warning message that not only informs users of an ongoing attack but that also explains the reasons why the target website could be fraudulent [10]. The design of our solution is based on lessons drawn from warning literature on best practices [11–13]. This paper advances our previous research [10] focusing on the understandability of the explanations provided by the warning messages. For each type of explanation provided by the message, three variants have been designed following the C-HIP model. Then, an evaluation of resulting variants has been conducted performing a static analysis of the messages' comprehension, sentiment, and readability.

In the next section, an overview of related work of phishing attacks is provided. In Sect. 3 we present the design of warning messages and evaluation metrics. Finally, Sect. 4, discusses our findings with conclusions and future work.

2 Background and Related Work

2.1 Human Factors in Cybersecurity

There has been an upsurge in scams and malware attacks recently with phishing attacks, which increased by 600% in March 2020 [4]. Google also blocked 18 million malware and phishing emails related to the COVID19 virus daily in April 2020 [14]. According to [15], cybercrime will cost the world $6 trillion annually by 2021, up from $3 trillion in 2015, with 95% cases due to human errors attributed, in some cases, non-compliance to warning messages that alert users on cyberattacks. This has made research in warning messages grow considerably over the past decades [16–18]. During this time researchers have continued to investigate a wide variety of variables, e.g., user behavior, environmental stimuli, text evaluation. Again, the concepts of uncertainty and risks are difficult for people to evaluate when faced with issues that require critical decisions [19]. For designers of security systems, it is essential to understand how users would evaluate and take decisions regarding security [19, 20]. Authors in [21] showed that the central problem of human interaction with IT security systems is that users should be able to make informed decisions without further help. They illustrated this by designing and implementing two applications that make visible the visualization of network events and the integration of action and configuration of available security mechanisms.

Felt et al. in [22] evaluated whether Android users pay attention to, understand, and act on permission information during installation. Their study participants (Internet survey and laboratory) displayed low attention and comprehension rates. About 17% paid attention to permissions during installation, and only 3% of Internet survey respondents could correctly answer all three permission comprehension questions. These results suggest that current Android permission warnings do not help most users make correct security decisions.

In the study reported in [23], the authors observed a disparity between actual changes made by Windows 7 updates and the changes the participants thought were being made. A multi-method approach was used (interview, survey, and computer log data); data were collected from 37 Windows 7 users to investigate what the users thought was happening on their computers (interview and survey data), what users want to happen on their computer (interview and survey data), and what was going on (log data). Results showed that 75% of participants had a misunderstanding about what was happening on their computer and that over 50% of the participants could not execute their intentions for computer management.

Bravo-Lillo et al. in [24] examined the behavior novice users exhibit when confronted with situations in which they should make security decisions. They demonstrate that these categories of users are not aware of the sensitivity of their data and mostly started to worry after deciding to allow access.

Fagan et al. in [25] investigated user motivations on why some users follow advice on security aspects and others do not. They conducted a survey study with 290 partici- pants using a rational decision model as well as current thoughts on human motivation where they asked participants about their motivations regarding (not) updating, using a password manager, using two-factor authentication, and changing passwords frequently. The authors determined that following security advice was mainly a trade-off decision between convenience and security, where users actively considered features such as set- up time and weighed that against the potential security benefits. They concluded that the value of convenience may be used to help motivate the use of security tools and techniques

Almuhimed et al. in [26] investigated factors that may contribute to why people ignore warnings. Through an online survey-based experiment they did to gain more insight into the effects of reputation on warning adherence. Participants said that they trusted high-reputation websites more than the warnings; however, their responses sug- gest that a notable minority of people could be swayed by providing more information. Gainsbury et al. in [27] conducted a field experiment to examine the impact of warn- ing message content on gambling behavior, found that warning messages focused on self-appraisal (positively) framed messages were more frequently recalled than infor- mative (negatively) framed messages, but that negatively framed messages were more influential.

In [28] the authors examined the impact of negative message framing on security tech- nology adoption. Based on previous studies, they hypothesized that negatively framed messages would have a greater effect on the adoption of security technologies that detect system abuse than on technologies for prevention and that internet security managers should become more sensitive to how new security technologies are introduced and to the factors that help shape adoption intentions. Authors in [29] suggest that people may pay attention to warnings but are most likely to ignore those that do not map well onto a clear and understandable course of action. Experimental studies in [30, 31] indicate that a large percentage of users do not read computer warnings, rarely understand them, and are most likely not to heed them, even when there are obvious risks. Qualitative insight into warning assessment by users of different skill levels, age, and exposure is presented in [24] they conclude that all aspects of warning design need to be considered holistically to improve warnings. Stating that the process of reading a warning is central to warning message reception and understanding.

2.2 Design Warning Messages: The C-HIP Model

Warning messages play a fundamental role in defending users against cyberattacks since they often are the last barrier between the attacker and the victim. However, as we discussed above, warning messages shown by the browsers in case of phishing attacks often fail in helping users understand if the target website is fraudulent or not. Besides the guidelines proposed to design warning messages for phishing attacks [16], the design of these messages can also benefit from the use of models for the design of generic warnings. One of the most adopted models in the literature and that we used to design our warning messages is the Communication-Human Information Processing (C-HIP) model, which defines the critical route and sets the foundation for structuring warning messages (see Fig. 1) [17].

The model summarizes the most important activity and entity involved in the communication of a warning. The model starts with a source delivering a warning through a channel to a receiver, who then takes it along with other stimuli (environmental or internal) that subject the message to a lot of distractions or distortions. It then identifies a set of steps between the delivery of a warning and the user's final behavior or response which is usually based on the resultant effect of the various processes such warnings had undergone. An essential part of a warning message is defined by [18] as there must be a signal word that should be noticeable (salient) e.g., Danger, Warning, Caution and Notice. This signal word helps increase the effectiveness of the warning. In 2011, Bravo-Lillo et al. [32] compiled a set of design guidelines and presented rules for descriptive text, which includes:

- Briefly describe the risk and consequences of not complying with advice;
- Illustrate clearly how to avoid the risk;
- Be transparent and avoid technical jargon were possible;
- Be brief as possible.

2.3 Evaluating Warning Messages Comprehension

After a warning message captures a user's attention, the next step is message comprehension. Most warning designers assume that users understand the hazard been described and subsequently adhere to prescribed advice. This has proven not to be so, as reported in [25, 33, 34]. Users exhibit different levels of comprehension and interpretations of given

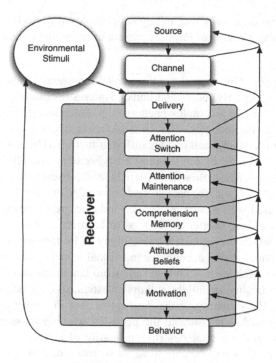

Fig. 1. C-HIP model [17].

texts, which subsequently influences their actions or inaction. Due to technical complexity, novice users may not fully understand what URL mimicking warning means (a situation where an attacker mimics a genuine URL, thus re-directing unsuspecting users to a similar webpage to steal their sensitive credentials). Therefore, warning message text should be targeted at least skilled users stripping off complex technical terms as much as possible. To this aim, the design of warning messages for phishing attacks might benefit from the use of static evaluations of the readability and sentiment. In the following sections, we briefly report on some of the most adopted metrics for text readability and sentiment, which were also used to design the warning messages proposed in this paper.

Sentiment Analysis. Sentiment Analysis involves determining the evaluative nature of a piece of text. These texts convey emotions which are key components in communication to effectively communicate messages and to understand reactions to messages [35, 36]. These messages could be classified as positive, negative, or neutral [37]. This analysis is common in customer reviews, newspaper headlines [38], novels and emails [36, 38–42], blogs and tweets [41, 42] and negative messages were found to appeal to certain behavioral anticipated responses. Surveys by [42, 43] give a summary where, using Natural Language Processing (NLP) techniques (e.g., IBM Watson [44]), automated agents can gain the ability to process and analyze text at different levels of abstraction, exploiting the speed and computational power of modern systems. Within the computer security software vendor community, the use of negatively framed messages to influence the adoption of their products is not novel. A growing trend among purveyors of information assurance and computer security technology is to employ negatively framed messages to provoke a favorable behavioral response among existing and potential clientele [45, 46].

Readability Measures. Given a piece of text, readability metrics measure the degree to which a person can read, easily understand, and find interesting that text [47–49]. Reading sometimes may appear like a complex phenomenon dependent on several factors e.g., cognitive, behavioral, and social [50–52]. To measure readability, several formulas have been established in literature, each one for different metrics. The most popular are the Flesch-Kincaid Grade Level, Flesch Reading Ease Formula, and SMOG formula [53–55]. A combination of word length, sentence length, and conversancy with word has been used to predict readability, with the background knowledge that longer words/sentences, which are usually used with a complex syntax, indicate greater reading difficulty and recall [56, 57]. Also, since shorter words tend to be more common than longer ones in English, longer words are considered less likely to be familiar to the reader [58]. While these assumptions do not account for individual readers' vocabulary and reading experience, simple metrics such as sentence and word length can provide a useful initial step in assessing readability. In [59] the authors investigate the application of readability measures to assess the difficulty of the descriptive text in warning messages. They agree that adapting such a measure to the needs of warning message design allows objective feedback on the textual description quality of a warning. They concluded that an automated process will be able to assist software developers and designers in creating more readable and hence more understandable security warning messages. In the following sections, we provide a brief description of these widely adopted formulas and their results over the evaluation of our warning messages.

Flesch – Kincaid Grade Level and Flesch Reading Scores. The Flesch–Kincaid readability tests are designed to indicate how difficult a provided text, usually in English, can be understood [60]. They involve primarily two groups of tests, the Flesch Reading Ease Test, and the Flesch–Kincaid Grade Level Test [54, 60]. Although they utilize the same metrics (word length and sentence length), they have different weighting ratios that are used to approximate the reading grade level and scores of a text. Flesch Reading Ease score is graded between 1 and 100, while the Flesch Kincaid Grade Level reflects the US education system needed to understand a text [49, 54]. They are both calculated with the same units, but they return two different readability scores. The authors of [53] explained that the higher the Reading score, the easier for a particular text to be read by the majority of people (Table 1).

SMOG Index. SMOG is an acronym for Simple Measure of Gobbledygook. It is widely recognized to be provide a valid support to Robert Gunning's Fog Index Credited to G Harry McLaughlin [55], the SMOG Index estimates the years of education a person needs to be able to comprehend a passage, it was developed as an improvement of other readability measures [61]. It involves estimation of two statistics: the number of sentences of the selected article and the number of words with three or more syllables [62].

Table 1. Description and predicted reading grade for Flesch Reading Ease Scores [53].

Reading ease score	Description	Predicted reading grade	Estimated % of US reading adults
0–30	Very difficult	College	4.5%
30–50	Difficult	College	33%
50–60	Fairly difficult	10th–12th	54%
*60–70	**Standard**	**8th–9th**	**83%**
70–80	Fairly easy	7th	88%
80–90	Easy	6th	91%
90–100	Very easy	5th	93%

3 Toward Explanations Inside Warning Interfaces for Phishing Attacks

3.1 A Polymorphic Warning Message to Prevent Phishing Attacks

The goal of our research is to improve the effectiveness of warning messages against phishing attacks. To this aim, we already proposed an interface similar to the ones shown by browsers like Chrome and Firefox when opening a suspicious phishing website, but that also includes information clarifying the reasons why the website might be a scam [9, 10]. Such explanations are based on website features commonly used by AI-based systems to classify a website as a scam or not (e.g., by Google Safe Browsing [23]). We considered those features that can be explained to and understood by non-technical users, i.e.:

- server location;
- website time life;
- presence in the Wayback Machine;
- rank in a search engine;
- fake HTTPS certificates;
- mimicked URLs;
- domain name.

To this aim, when a suspect website is detected, our system first computes the website features (e.g., HTTPS certificate = self-signed, time life = 2 days) and then it ranks all the feature values according to a metric we elaborated and that is based on the feature entropy. In the end, the warning message selects and shows the most informative features.

According to the example in Fig. 2, the proposed warning interface explains that the bank website going to be visited by the user is detected as phishing for two reasons: it uses a fake HTTPS certificate and it has been created just 2 days ago. Such information, properly structured and adequately shown to the users, help them to make informed decisions and avoid opening scam websites.

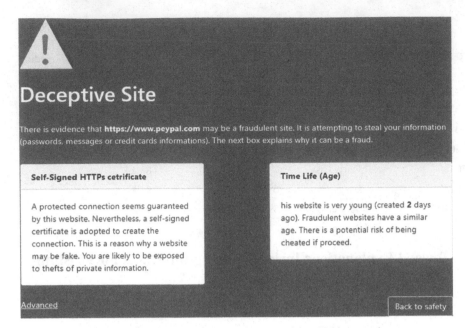

Fig. 2. Polymorphic warning message against phishing attacks

It is worth noticing the polymorphic behavior of the interface: the three panels show different information according to the suspect website, thus different reasons would be reported with different phishing websites. Thanks to this warning message, its polymorphic behavior and the explanations it provides, we address three important goals, i.e.:

1. *Prevent user habituation*: a polymorphic message decreases the clickthrough effect caused by the user habituation [22];
2. *Provide an explanation about the attack*: useful information about the causes of the phishing attacks support the users in deciding if the website is (or not) a phishing attack [23];
3. *Educate the users on cyberattacks and related risks*: a long-term training of the users on phishing attacks is performed since they understand the reasons for this attack [16, 24].

In the next section, we briefly describe how the C-HIP model has been used to design the feature explanations (Table 2).

3.2 Warning Text Design

Based on best practices from warning literature [59], we designed our warning message texts aimed at warning users against attacks. In this paper, we report the design of two out of the seven indicators: Website time life (Age) and Hypertext transfer protocols (HTTPS). The design and the evaluation of the other 5 messages is an ongoing activity.

The generation of the explanations is based on a generic pattern we purposely defined to instantiate each message, i.e.:

Feature value + illustrated example of feature [optional] + Hazard Identification + Effects of a successful attack

For example, a warning message text mimicking a URL indicator reads as follows:

"A protected connection seems guaranteed by this website. Nevertheless, a self-signed certificate is adopted to create the connection. This is a reason why a web-site may be fake. You are likely to be exposed to thefts of private information".

Table 2. Schema elucidation.

Feature	A protected connection seems guaranteed by this website
Illustrated example of feature [optional]	None
Hazard identification	Nevertheless, a self-signed certificate is adopted to create the connection. This is a reason why a website may be fake
Effects of a successful attack	You are likely to be exposed to thefts of private information

As the next steps, we produced three variants of messages (see Table 3) in line with warning guidelines indicated in [32, 52, 63], for each indicator which had the same objective but in different ways.

We then subjected these messages to sentiment analysis and readability measures evaluations as discussed above. We also used online text Inspector tools listed in [63, 64] to measure the lexical diversity of text in the warning messages. Table 4 summarizes the results of the static analysis of the texts.

All the warning texts had negative values for the sentiment analysis with ranges between –0.39 and –0.95. The readability scores, which include the word count (total number of words in a sentence), returned an average of 30 counts ranging between 22 and 40. Reach, which is a measure of the proportion of your target audience that can read your content easily, calibrated against the literate general public (so a reach of 100% indicates your content is readable by about 85% of the public), all returned an average of 100%. All readability measures metrics are in line with the recommendation proposed in [12, 58, 65].

Table 3. Warning message variants for URL and HTTPS.

Features (Indicators)	Message variants
Website time life (Age)	1. This website was created recently (n days ago). This is typical of fraudulent websites. It likely aims to steal your private information 2. This website is very young (created n days ago). Fraudulent websites have a similar age. There is a potential risk of being cheated if you proceed 3. The target website was created n days ago. Young websites are famous for criminal activities. There is a potential risk if you proceed
Self-signed HTTPS certificate	4. This website seems to have a protected connection. However, its connection uses a self-issued certificate. This indicates it may be a fraud. You will most likely be exposed to thefts of private information 5. A protected connection seems guaranteed by this website. Nevertheless, a self-signed certificate is adopted to create the connection. This is a reason why a website may be fake. You are likely to be exposed to thefts of private information 6. This website seems to offer a safe connection. This is not safe since it is a self-validated certificate. Attackers self-validate their websites to cheat and defraud users. Your private information is at risk

Table 4. Warning message statistics using online tools.

Warning message variant	Flesch reading ease score	Flesch-kin grade level	SMOG index	Sentiment analysis	Word count	Sentence count
Age (V1)	57.1	7.1	6.8	−0.90	22	3
Age (V2)	67.9	5.9	6	−0.95	26	3
Age (V3)	63	6.4	6	−0.39	23	3
HTTPs (V1)	61.4	6.8	7.8	−0.83	34	4
HTTPs (V2)	62.3	7.1	8.3	−0.59	40	4
HTTPs (V3)	62.6	6.7	7.2	−0.71	35	4

4   Conclusion and Future Work

We set out to design warning messages that provided explanations to users, who do not have expertise in IT or security, why they should not oblige to attacker's request on phishing websites. In this paper we have reported results on two indicators (Website time life (Age) and HTTPS), three variants for each. During our investigations, we found several aspects of warning message texts that could improve user's comprehension and adherence. First, the architectural CHIP Model, which we adopted in building our schema (Feature value + Hazard identification + effects of a successful attack), supported the design of our explanations. Then, an iterative process subjected the negatively framed text messages to sentiment analysis and finally evaluated them for readability compliance. The three message variants for each selected indicator showed to be compliant with our set out objectives - comprehension and adherence - as evident in results from the online tools used. Some researchers still have reservations about the use of online tools for the evaluation of messages claiming that textual statistics alone cannot address certain emotions and complexities required in a message. We were able to address this concern by tailoring our warning messages to return negative values during the sentiment analysis. As described in the previous sections, and in line with our objectives, it is common among computer security technology to employ negatively framed messages to provoke a favorable behavioral response among existing and potential clientele [45, 46].

As the next steps, we will design more indicators which include: Server location, Domain name, Mimicked URLs, Rank in a search engine, and presence in the Wayback machine, and subsequently evaluate our polymorphic warning messages with those found in popular browsers (Chrome and Firefox) involving real users. We agree that, as illustrated in [48, 65], while readability formulas may not measure the context, prior knowledge, interest level, difficulty of concept, or coherence of text of users, it however has the potential to provide designers and developers with an automatic tool that can estimate how readable and understandable a warning will be for their target audience, thus suffixing for those developers that cannot afford specialist help.

References

1. Brynjolfsson, E., Horton, J.J., Ozimek, A., Rock, D., Sharma, G., TuYe, H.-Y.: COVID-19 and remote work: an early look at US data, pp. 0898–2937. National Bureau of Economic Research (2020)
2. Wiggen, J.: The impact of COVID-19 on cyber crime and state-sponsored cyber activities (2020)
3. Bott, E.: How many people still run windows 7. https://www.zdnet.com/article/as-support-ends-windows-7-users-head-for-the-exits/. Accessed 28 Oct 2020
4. Gallagher, S., Brandt, A.: Facing down the myriad threats tied to COVID19 (2020). https://news.sophos.com/enus/2020/04/14/covidmalware. Accessed 28 Oct 2020
5. Dhamija, R., Tygar, J.D., Hearst, M.: Why phishing works. In: Proceedings of the SIGCHI Conference on Human Factors in Computing Systems, pp. 581–590 (2006)
6. Friedman, B., Hurley, D., Howe, D.C., Felten, E., Nissenbaum, H.: Users' conceptions of web security: a comparative study. In: CHI 2002 Extended Abstracts On Human Factors in Computing Systems, pp. 746–747 (2002)
7. Bravo-Lillo, C., Cranor, L., Komanduri, S., Schechter, S., Sleeper, M.: Harder to ignore? Revisiting pop-up fatigue and approaches to prevent it. In: 10th Symposium On Usable Privacy and Security (SOUPS 2014), pp. 105–111 (2014)
8. Jackson, C., Simon, D.R., Tan, D.S., Barth, A.: An Evaluation of Extended Validation and Picture-in-Picture Phishing Attacks. In: Financial Cryptography and Data Security, Berlin, Heidelberg, pp. 281–293 (2007)

9. Desolda, G., Di Nocera, F., Ferro, L., Lanzilotti, R., Maggi, P., Marrella, A.: Alerting users about phishing attacks. In: Moallem, Abbas (ed.) HCII 2019. LNCS, vol. 11594, pp. 134–148. Springer, Cham (2019). https://doi.org/10.1007/978-3-030-22351-9_9

10. Aneke, J., Ardito, C., Desolda, G.: Designing an intelligent user interface for preventing phishing attacks. In: IFIP Conference on Human-Computer Interaction, pp. 97–106 (2019)

11. Alsharnouby, M., Alaca, F., Chiasson, S.: Why phishing still works: user strategies for combating phishing attacks. Int. J. Human-Comput. Stud. **82**, 69–82 (2015)

12. Harbach, M., Fahl, S., Yakovleva, P., Smith, M.: Sorry, i don't get it: an analysis of warning message texts. In: International Conference on Financial Cryptography and Data Security, pp. 94–111 (2013)

13. Greenwald, S.J., Olthoff, K.G., Raskin, V., Ruch, W.: The user non-acceptance paradigm: INFOSEC's dirty little secret. In: Proceedings of the 2004 Workshop on New Security Paradigms, pp. 35–43 (2004)

14. Kumaran, N., Lugani, S.: Protecting businesses against cyber threats during COVID-19 and beyond. Google Cloud, vol. 16 (2020)

15. Williams, C.M., Chaturvedi, R., Chakravarthy, K.: Cybersecurity risks in a pandemic. J. Med. Internet Res. **22**, e23692 (2020)

16. Wogalter, M.S.: Handbook of Warnings. CRC Press, Boca Raton (2006)

17. Laughery, K., DeJoy, D., Wogalter, M.: Warnings and Risk Communication. Taylor and Francis, Philadelphia (1999)

18. Wogalter, M.S., Conzola, V.C., Smith-Jackson, T.L.: Research-based guidelines for warning design and evaluation. Appl. Ergon. **33**, 219–230 (2002)

19. West, R.: The psychology of security. Commun. ACM **51**, 34–40 (2008)

20. Kumaraguru, P., et al.: Getting users to pay attention to anti-phishing education: evaluation of retention and transfer. In: Proceedings of the Anti-Phishing Working Groups 2nd Annual eCrime Researchers Summit, pp. 70–81 (2007)

21. De Paula, R., et al.: Two experiences designing for effective security. In: Proceedings of the 2005 Symposium on Usable Privacy and Security, pp. 25–34 (2005)

22. Felt, A.P., Ha, E., Egelman, S., Haney, A., Chin, E., Wagner, D.: Android permissions: User attention, comprehension, and behavior. In: Proceedings of the Eighth Symposium on Usable Privacy and Security, pp. 1–14 (2012)

23. Wash, R., Rader, E., Vaniea, K., Rizor, M.: Out of the loop: how automated software updates cause unintended security consequences. In: 10th Symposium On Usable Privacy and Security ({SOUPS} 2014), pp. 89–104 (2014)

24. Bravo-Lillo, C., Cranor, L.F., Downs, J., Komanduri, S.: Bridging the gap in computer security warnings: a mental model approach. IEEE Secur. Priv. **9**, 18–26 (2011)

25. Fagan, M., Khan, M.M.H.: Why do they do what they do? A study of what motivates users to (not) follow computer security advice. In: Twelfth Symposium on Usable Privacy and Security (SOUPS 2016), pp. 59–75 (2016)

26. Almuhimedi, H., Felt, A.P., Reeder, R.W., Consolvo, S.: Your reputation precedes you: History, reputation, and the chrome malware warning. In: 10th Symposium on Usable Privacy and Security (SOUPS 2014), pp. 113–128 (2014)

27. Gainsbury, S.M., Russell, A., Gainsbury, S., Aro, D., Ball, D., Tobar, C.: Optimal content for warning messages to enhance consumer decision making and reduce problem gambling. Knowl. Educ. Law Manage. **11**(3), 64–80 (2015)

28. Shropshire, J.D., Warkentin, M., Johnston, A.C.: Impact of negative message framing on security adoption. J. Comput. Inf. Syst. **51**, 41–51 (2010)

29. Witte, K.: Putting the fear back into fear appeals: the extended parallel process model. Commun. Monogr. **59**, 329–349 (1992)

30. Egelman, S., Cranor, L.F., Hong, J.: You've been warned: an empirical study of the effectiveness of web browser phishing warnings (2008)

31. Sunshine, J., Egelman, S., Almuhimedi, H., Atri, N., Cranor, L.F.: Crying wolf: an empirical study of SSL warning effectiveness. In: USENIX Security Symposium, pp. 399–416 (2009)
32. Bravo-Lillo, C., Cranor, L.F., Downs, J., Komanduri, S., Sleeper, M.: Improving computer security dialogs. In: IFIP Conference on Human-Computer Interaction, pp. 18–35 (2011)
33. Furnell, S.: Why users cannot use security. Comput. Secur. **24**, 274–279 (2005)
34. Herzberg, A.: Why Johnny can't surf (safely)? Attacks and defenses for web users. Comput. Secur. **28**, 63–71 (2009)
35. Thelwall, M.: The heart and soul of the web? Sentiment strength detection in the social web with sentistrength. In: Hołyst, J.A. (ed.) Cyberemotions. UCS, pp. 119–134. Springer, Cham (2017). https://doi.org/10.1007/978-3-319-43639-5_7
36. Mohammad, S.M.: Challenges in sentiment analysis. In: Cambria, E., Das, D., Bandyopadhyay, S., Feraco, A. (eds.) A Practical Guide to Sentiment Analysis, pp. 61–83. Springer, New York (2017). https://doi.org/10.1007/978-3-319-55394-8_4
37. Kiritchenko, S., Zhu, X., Mohammad, S.M.: Sentiment analysis of short informal texts. J. Artif. Intell. Res. **50**, 723–762 (2014)
38. Bellegarda, J.R.: Emotion analysis using latent affective folding and embedding. In: Proceedings of the NAACL HLT 2010 Workshop on Computational Approaches to Analysis and Generation of Emotion in Text, pp. 1–9 (2010)
39. Boucouvalas, A.C.: Real time text-to-emotion engine for expressive internet communications. In: Proceedings of International Symposium on Communication Systems, Networks and Digital Signal Processing (CSNDSP-2002) (2002)
40. Francisco, V., Gervás, P.: Automated mark up of affective information in english texts. In: International Conference on Text, Speech and Dialogue, pp. 375–382 (2006)
41. Mohammad, S.M.: Sentiment analysis: Detecting valence, emotions, and other affectual states from text. In: Meiselman, H.L. (ed.) Emotion measurement, pp. 201–237. Elsevier, Duxford (2016)
42. Liu, B., Zhang, L.: A survey of opinion mining and sentiment analysis. In: Aggarwal, C., Zhai, C. (eds.) Mining Text Data, pp. 415–463. Springer, Boston (2017). https://doi.org/10.1007/978-1-4614-3223-4_13
43. Pang, B., Lee, L.: Opinion mining and sentiment analysis. In: Foundations and Trends® in Information Retrieval, vol. 2, pp. 1–135 (2008)
44. Biondi, G., Franzoni, V., Poggioni, V.: A deep learning semantic approach to emotion recognition using the IBM watson bluemix alchemy language. In: International Conference on Computational Science and Its Applications, pp. 718–729 (2017)
45. Whaley, C.: Security companies might be messing with IT managers' minds. Comput. Can. **31**, 17 (2005)
46. Johnston, A.C.: Fear appeals and information security behaviours: an empirical study. MIS Q. **34**, 549–566 (2010)
47. Richards, J.C., Platt, J., Platt, H.: Longman Dictionary of Language Teaching Applied Linguistics, vol. 288 (1992)
48. Zamanian, M., Heydari, P.: Readability of Texts: State of the Art. Theor. Pract. Lang. Stud. **2**, 43–53 (2012)
49. Dale, E., Chall, J.S.: The concept of readability. Elementary Engl. **26**, 19–26 (1949)
50. Gee, J.P.: Three paradigms in reading (really literacy) research and digital media. In: Reading at a Crossroads? Disjunctures and Continuities in Current Conceptions and Practices, vol. 35 (2015)
51. Paris, S.G., Stahl, S.A.: Children's reading comprehension and assessment. Routledge (2005)
52. Cranor, L.F.: A framework for reasoning about the human in the loop (2008)
53. DuBay, W.H.: The Principles of Readability. In: Online Submission (2004)
54. Flesch, R.: A new readability yardstick. J. Appl. Psychol. **32**, 221 (1948)

55. Mc Laughlin, G.H.: SMOG grading-a new readability formula. J. Read. **12**, 639–646 (1969)
56. Feng, L., Elhadad, N., Huenerfauth, M.: Cognitively motivated features for readability assessment. In: Proceedings of the 12th Conference of the European Chapter of the ACL (EACL 2009), pp. 229–237 (2009)
57. Redmiles, E.M., et al.: First steps toward measuring the readability of security advice, ed (2018)
58. Harbach, M., Fahl, S., Muders, T., Smith, M.:Towards measuring warning readability. In: Proceedings of the 2012 ACM Conference on Computer and Communications Security, pp. 989–991 (2012)
59. Felt, A.P., et al.: Improving SSL warnings: comprehension and adherence. In: ACM Conference on Human Factors in Computing Systems, Seoul, Republic of Korea (2015)
60. Flesch, R.: Flesch-Kincaid readability test. Retrieved October, vol. 26, p. 3 (2007)
61. Scranton, M.A.: SMOG grading: a readability formula by G. Harry McLaughlin. Kansas State University (1970)
62. Zhou, S., Jeong, H., Green, P.A.: How consistent are the best-known readability equations in estimating the readability of design standards? IEEE Trans. Prof. Commun. **60**, 97–111 (2017)
63. Webex. https://www.webfx.com/tools/read-able/check.php. Accessed 28 Dec 2020
64. Hidayatillah, N., Zainil, Y.: The readability of students' textbook used in semantic and pragmatic course in english language education program of UNP. J. Engl. Lang. Teach. **9**, 144–159 (2020)
65. Heydari, P., Riazi, A.M.: Readability of texts: human evaluation versus computer index. Mediterr. J. Soc. Sci. **3**, 177–190 (2012)

Social Engineering Attacks: Recent Advances and Challenges

Nikol Mashtalyar$^{(\boxtimes)}$, Uwera Nina Ntaganzwa$^{(\boxtimes)}$, Thales Santos$^{(\boxtimes)}$,
Saqib Hakak$^{(\boxtimes)}$, and Suprio Ray$^{(\boxtimes)}$

Faculty of Computer Science, University of New Brunswick, Fredericton, Canada
{nmashtal,untaganz,tsantos,saqib.hakak,sray}@unb.ca

Abstract. The world's technological landscape is continuously evolving with new possibilities, yet also evolving in parallel with the emergence of new threats. Social engineering is of predominant concern for industries, governments and institutions due to the exploitation of their most valuable resource, their people. Social engineers prey on the psychological weaknesses of humans with sophisticated attacks, which pose serious cybersecurity threats to digital infrastructure. Social engineers use deception and manipulation by means of human computer interaction to exploit privacy and cybersecurity concerns. Numerous forms of attacks have been observed, which can target a range of resources such as intellectual property, confidential data and financial resources. Therefore, institutions must be prepared for any kind of attack that may be deployed and demonstrate willingness to implement new defense strategies. In this article, we present the state-of-the-art social engineering attacks, their classification and various mitigation strategies.

Keywords: Social engineering attacks · Phishing · Spam · Email fraud

1 Introduction

In the domain of cybersecurity, social engineering is an attack strategy that relies on the exploitation of human vulnerabilities through social manipulation to infiltrate security. [1] The attackers use persuasive tactics to make the victim do what the attacker intends. Social engineers sell sensitive information acquired from victims to underground economies and on the dark web, in order to capitalize on valuable data [2]. Social engineers can also use manipulation and deceit to trick victims into sending them money that cannot be traced (usually by wire) or be destructive for the sake of being destructive.

User susceptibility contributes largely to the success of social engineering attacks. Many users rely on social networking service providers for their security and privacy [3], and are very likely to click on links or provide information to people they trust, people with authority, and people with urgent requests [4].

Social engineering attacks involve a number of steps as shown in Fig. 1 [5]. There are four common phases through which attackers acquire information that

© Springer Nature Switzerland AG 2021
A. Moallem (Ed.): HCII 2021, LNCS 12788, pp. 417–431, 2021.
https://doi.org/10.1007/978-3-030-77392-2_27

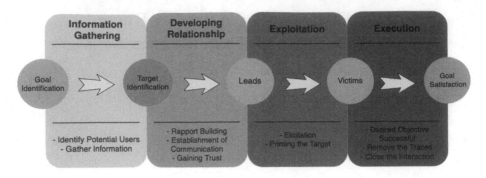

Fig. 1. Social engineering process

would otherwise be inaccessible to them. These phases, also known as the *social engineering attack cycle*, involve "information gathering, developing relationships, exploitation, and execution" [6]. In these four phases, investigation begins by identifying the victims, gathering information, and setting attack methods. Next, attackers engage the victims, obtain information from them over a period of time, and then exit without leaving any trace of their existence.

Social engineering attacks are an urgent security threat, with the number of detected attacks rising each year. In 2011, a global survey of 853 information technology professionals revealed that 48% of large companies have experienced 25 or more social engineering attacks in the past two years [1]. In 2018, the annual average cost of organizations that were targets of social engineering attacks surpassed 1.4 million dollars [1]. The ISACA's State of Cybersecurity report 2018 deemed social engineering as a top cyberthreat for organizations [1]. Over the past decade, research has demonstrated that social engineering threats and expenses are increasing; now it is up to industry to follow appropriate countermeasures in order to avoid such attacks.

During times of crises, social engineering attacks may rise due to the vulnerability of the people. The current COVID-19 pandemic is also no exception with a significant surge in cyber-attacks [7], including social engineering attacks, as shown in Fig. 2. Attackers sent unsolicited emails and telephone calls, claiming to be from a medical office, insurance company, or COVID-19 vaccine center requesting personal and medical information in order to determine eligibility for clinical vaccine trials [8]. Furthermore, the number of COVID-19 spear phishing attempts has increased by 667% [9]. In April 2020, Google reported that it blocked 18 million daily malware and phishing emails related to COVID-19, in addition to 240 million COVID-19 daily spam messages [10]. Palo Alto Networks found that from January to March 2020, there were 116,357 newly registered domains using COVID-19 related keywords. The organisation determined that 34% of those domains posed a high risk rate [11].

The objective of this study is to explore the most recent social engineering strategies and current mitigation trends. The organisation of the rest of this article is as follows: literature review is presented in Sect. 2. Section 3 presents

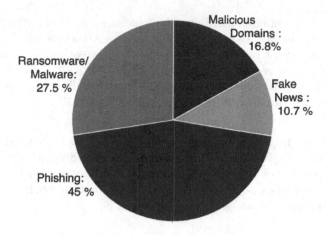

Fig. 2. Social engineering attacks during COVID-19

potential mitigation strategies. Research challenges are highlighted in Sect. 4. Future research directions are explored in Sect. 5. Section 6 concludes the article.

2   Literature Review

In this section, popular social engineering attacks are highlighted and a brief overview of the most recent works is provided. We have categorised the existing approaches into two categories of technical studies and non-technical studies. Both technical and non-technical studies are further sub-categorised into Human-based social engineering attacks and Computer-based social engineering attacks. Figure 3 presents the classification of both these attacks. The social engineering attacks under the technical studies classification, were proposed or created by their respective authors in the forms of code, algorithms, design framework and experiments [12–19]. The attacks are mostly phishing attacks carried out by artificial intelligence (AI) enabled bots [14,15], and by use of persuasion [19]. The attacks under the non-technical studies section of the diagram are defined and elaborately discussed by their respective authors; however, no experiments were conducted to observe their nature. Lastly, suggested solutions for social engineering attacks and countermeasures are summarized in the 'solutions' section of the diagram.

The main approaches used for human-based and computer-based attacks are briefly discussed below.

2.1   Human-Based Social Engineering Attacks

Human-based social engineering requires direct interaction with humans to gain the desired information [9]. Human based methods include impersonation, posing as an important user, posing as a relevant third party, and posing as desktop support, as shown in Fig. 3. An overview of these approaches are provided next.

Persuasion. A unanimous attribute of all social engineering attacks, persuasion, is arguably the key to any profitable attack. Attackers will influence the victims in a positive or negative manner in order to reach their intended goal. For example, a positive influence of persuasion includes the deceit of reward if a certain action is completed. Whereas, a negative influence of persuasion is completed through threat or authoritative intimidation [19].

Impersonation. Impersonation involves pretending to be a valid user, such as an employee, to gain physical access to a system. Similarly, posing as an important user involves impersonating a high-level manager with authority to use computer systems or files while third parties pretend to have permission from authorized users to access systems and files [6].

Tailgating or Piggybacking. During a tailgating or piggybacking social engineering attack, the attackers trick authorised employees to get access into restricted areas (such as company premises) [20]. The attackers use various strategies to fool authorised employees, such as following behind them to gain access, wearing fake identification badges, entering in parking lot doors and other impersonation approaches as mentioned above [21].

Shoulder Surfing. This method of social engineering involves obtaining sensitive information from a victim by means of observation. Attackers watch from a distance, or within proximity, while victims type passwords, identification information and other valuable personal details [2]. Attackers will also observe and listen to conversations between members of companies or institutions, whilst the victims discuss amongst themselves and present information [20].

Dumpster Diving. In this social engineering attack, the attackers attempt to obtain victims' information through physical means. The attackers try to get the personal information such as IP address, bank account details by collecting pieces of trash from the organisation's trash bins [20]. The retrieval of information is not confined to the trash bins alone; the attackers also try to access organisational charts and phone-lists, which might assist them to carry out successful attacks [2].

2.2 Computer-Based Social Engineering Attacks

Computer-based social engineering uses computer software to gain the information from the victims [9]. Computer based methods include phishing, social phishing, spear phishing, baiting, online scams such as brand theft and typosquatting, and email fraud to mention a few. An overview of these approaches is presented next.

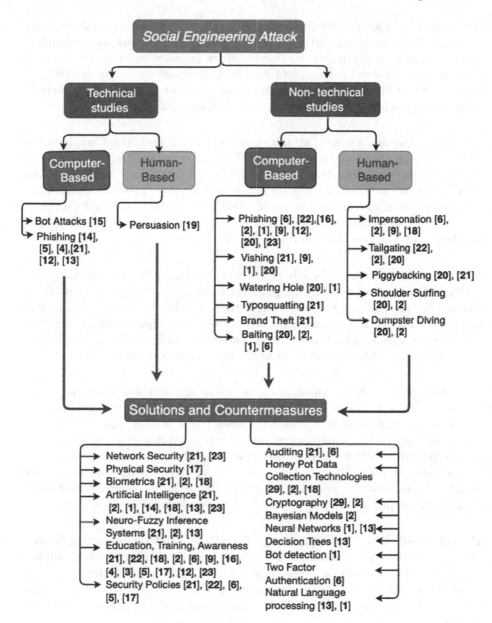

Fig. 3. Taxonomy of existing studies

Phishing. Phishing is the act of gaining access to victim's credentials and then using this data as a way to infect an organization's database or information system with malicious viruses or malware [22,23]. Similarly, social phishing uses techniques involving social media accounts of employees in order to gain access to organizational networks [21]. Spear phishing is conducted in a similar manner to social phishing, as this attack creates a point of entry into an information system; some of which may even contain other malware, such as Trojan, with the intent of industrial spying and committing financial frauds [6]. Baiting is a similar form of attack whereby attackers lure victims by manipulating them to open links, email attachments or download malware [12].

Vishing. Through Vishing, attackers pretend to be authorised employees of a private/government organisation, which provides essential services (such as healthcare-support, tax-related services and other third-party services) [7,20]. As most of the users heavily rely on phone and Internet, cyber criminals often use this approach to abuse voice over IP (VoIP) services and scam individuals by taking their personal information such as bank account details, social security numbers and other relevant information [7,9].

Watering Hole. Attackers will find a suitable target by stalking the cyber activity of an organization to determine which websites or domains are regularly visited. Social engineers will then infect these specific websites with malware or viruses. The victims unknowingly access the now compromised websites and their devices will download malicious scripts in the background, which have the potential to spread to other devices in the organization [1,20].

Bot Attacks. With the surge of online users and increase in use of social-media platforms, attackers have started exploiting social-bots for malicious activities [15]. A social bot is an automated software that mimics human-behaviour. Numerous organisations implement social bots for different purposes such as interacting with customers. Attackers have started exploiting these social-bots in combination with other strategies such as vishing, whereby an automated social-bot interacts with and targets victims. This strategy saves attackers a lot of time due to the automated nature of setting up bots [15].

Brand Theft and Typosquatting. Brand theft and typosquatting hackers automate exploits such as brand theft to lure staff [21]. In brand theft, employees are tricked into believing that they are interacting with legitimate services or websites [21]. Additionally, typosquatting can lead to trademark infringement and loss of trust in the original organizations, according to Aldawood and Skinner.

2.3   Recent Advances

For the many social engineering attacks that exist today, countermeasures have been established. Depending on the nature of the attack, the countermeasures range from non-technical actions such as training and awareness, to more technical actions like endpoint security measures, which include two-factor authentication, use of antiviruses, and host-based intrusion detection systems.

A recurring theme in the discussion of challenges in dealing with social engineering attacks is what Parthy and Rajendran refer to as the carelessness of the human mind [20]. Humans always find a way to circumvent security measures especially when they interfere with the performance of the software artifacts in question. As a result, procedures and policies need to be in place to ensure that security measures are observed. Table 1 presents a snapshot of recent advances in the area of social engineering attacks.

Lansley et al. [13] designed an automated system (referred to as SEADer++ v2) in order to detect social engineering attacks in online chat environments. The proposed system examined the dialogue using natural language processing and uses an artificial neural network multi-layer perceptron classifier to classify possible attacks. In order to determine which dialogues contained a social engineering attack, the study categorized the criteria as features; this ranged from malicious links to the history of the attacker. The classification techniques used to detect and extract the various features included decision trees, random forest, fuzzy logic prediction, topic blacklists and neural networks. The authors evaluated their proposed method using real and semi-synthetic data sets and the system was able to detect social engineering attacks with very high accuracy.

Table 1. A snapshot of social engineering technical studies

Study	Attack experiments			Detection/Defense experiments			Proposed model solution		
	Spear phishing	Socio-technical attacks	Drive-by-downloads	Artificial intelligence	Natural language processing	Anomaly detection (DAS)	User-centric framework	Susceptibility model	Awareness, training and policy
E. J. Williams et al. [4]	✓	✗	✗	✗	✗	✗	✗	✗	✓
F. Breda et al. [5]	✗	✓	✗	✗	✗	✗	✗	✗	✓
R. Heartfield et al. [24]	✓	✗	✓	✗	✗	✗	✗	✓	✓
S. M. Albladi and G. R. Weir [3]	✗	✗	✗	✗	✗	✗	✓	✓	✓
F. Salahdine and N. Kaabouch [2]	✓	✓	✓	✓	✗	✓	✓	✓	✓
M. Lansley et al. [13]	✗	✗	✗	✓	✓	✗	✗	✗	✗
S. M. Albladi and G. R. Weir [12]	✗	✗	✗	✗	✗	✗	✗	✓	✓
A. Basit et al. [14]	✓	✓	✗	✓	✗	✗	✗	✗	✓

In [12], the authors developed a novel conceptual model to predict user vulnerability to social engineering victimisation. The study conducted a scenario-based experiment whereby the model tested the weakest points of detection behaviour in users and predicted vulnerable individuals. The model used several perspectives of user characteristics such as motivation, level of involvement, and competence regarding network threats. The most significant behaviour predictor was perceived trust, and the conceptual model supports the finding that vulnerable users can be identified by their characteristics. The following should be taken into consideration for the design of comprehensive awareness and training programs. The metrics used to evaluate the results included reliability and convergent validity tests, assessment of collinearity and path coefficients, hypothesis testing, bootstrap re-sampling procedure and regression analysis. The main limitation of the study was the restriction of conducting a scenario-based experiment rather than a live attack study, however it was considered unavoidable due to ethical considerations.

Heartfield et al. [24] conducted two experiments, which consisted of a survey and exhibit-based test, to explore user susceptibility of deception based attacks. Participants were exposed to spear-phishing, obfuscated URLs, drive-by downloads, spoofed websites and scareware. In both experiments, participants were asked to categorize examples as attacks or non-attacks. The authors identified a set of features and produced logistic regression and random forest models for predicting susceptibility to attacks, with accuracy rates of .68 and .71. The authors observed that a general aptitude in security awareness creates a significant difference in users' ability to distinguish deception attempts, specifically if the user has strong computer literacy, familiarity and high frequency of use.

Basit et al. [14] explored four Artificial Intelligence (AI) techniques: deep learning, machine learning, hybrid learning, and scenario based techniques to detect social engineering attacks. For each AI technique, the authors examined and compared different studies conducted in the detection of phishing attacks. The deep learning technique described used data sets with two main threshold frequencies and rules strength. Similarly, machine learning techniques used testing and training data sets to develop algorithms and evaluation techniques. For deep learning techniques, the products of the data set evaluation techniques lead to the development of models that detect phishing attacks. The proposed scenario-based detection techniques are different, however. Topical and game-based techniques were employed to understand social engineering attack scenarios. Based on the outcome of the games, users gained better understanding of phishing attacks and so, allowed them to take "preventive" activities against phishing attacks. Suggested hybrid learning techniques coupled machine learning with approaches such as Search and Heuristic Rule and Logistic Regression (SHLR) to distinguish legitimate web information from that intended to carry out phishing attacks.

3 Potential Mitigation Strategies

Based on the discussion from the above-mentioned related studies, the following mitigation strategies will prove helpful in mitigating social engineering attacks.

3.1 Awareness Programs

Protection measures such as awareness programs and training of staff are a non-technical approach to addressing social engineering attacks. Since one of the factors that leads to social engineering is the deficiency of ongoing education [18,23], security awareness measures equip users with the knowledge and tools to identify and report social engineering attacks. Awareness programs include conferences, awareness campaigns, and theme-based training. Training methods include virtual labs, simulations, games, and use of modern applications. Both awareness programs and training methods can be offered through workshops, lectures, and other virtual learning tools [22]. Enhanced information security awareness programs on password protection, non-sharing of any work-related information on social media and other gaming websites can all be included in an organisation's counterattack strategy [21].

3.2   Endpoint Security

Endpoint security is a significant method of mitigating social engineering attacks done by securing the entry points, or endpoints, of end-user devices such as phones and computers. Endpoint security includes the use of updated anti-viruses, anti-malware, and host-based intrusion detection systems (HIDS) [22]. Biometric and two-factor authentication, safe web browsing, and application of artificial intelligence techniques to detect threats are also components of endpoint security and these methods are crucial because they warrant access control.

3.3   Blockage of Phishing Attacks

A new generation of malicious email blockers can be applied by each email service provider in order to prevent malicious emails from reaching their clients. For example, Google blocks 100 million malicious emails, in the form of spam, phishing attempts and malware, every day [10]. The company's techniques can block 99.9% of threats from reaching Gmail inboxes [25]. Google implements a Tensor Flow deep-learning model trained with TFX. These document analyzers are responsible for parsing the document, identifying common attack patterns, extracting macros, de-obfuscating content, and performing feature extraction.

3.4   Validate Information

As discussed earlier, a lack of knowledge on the part of the victim can lead to social engineering attacks. In order to help combat this, governments and organizations are attempting to validate information. For example, on the World Hearth Organization's website, users may report misinformation about various social media platforms [26], as well as read which information is currently valid or invalid [27]. The FBI has released a list of fraud schemes that are currently active in relation to COVID-19 vaccines [8]. The Government of the United Kingdom and the University of Cambridge have created a game called, "Go Viral", which users can play to learn more about accurate information related to COVID-19 [28]. Various valid sources can also run joint campaigns in order to stop the spread of misinformation. The World Health Organization and the UK government have run a joint campaign to stop the spread of misinformation related to COVID-19 [29].

4   Research Challenges

In this section, we highlight emerging research challenges within the domain of cybersecurity (Table 2).

Table 2. Research challenges and possible solutions

	Challenges	Possible solutions
5G technology	High-data rate, low latency, more bandwidth, assisted botnet networks create and increase attack surfaces for attackers. Denial of service attacks are accelerated	Use AI enabled bot detectors, endpoint security measures and educate people on network security threats and defense mechanisms
Cyborgs	Automated, follow no fixed pattern, and can sometimes be controlled by humans which makes them difficult to detect	Use machine learning and neuro-fuzzy and inference systems to learn about and predict cyborg behaviour
Edge computing	Low bandwidth costs and cast amounts of data processed attract attackers	Use two-factor authentication and endpoint security measures such as anti-viruses and anti-malware.
Blockchain and cryptocurrency	Use of cryptocurrency is a new and attractive way to capitalize on data.	Encourage individuals to educate themselves on personal security and practice it

4.1   Attack Surfaces Using 5G Technology

5G or fifth generation cellular technology is designed to provide high-data speed compared to existing 4G networks with reduced latency. 5G networks are expected to provide data rates of up to 10 Gbps and thousands of devices can maintain reliable connection at the same time [30]. Although high-data rate, low latency, and more bandwidth has its own advantages for users, ultimately it will also create more attack surfaces for the attackers. The attackers will be able to create more computational bots to carry out social engineering attacks. This malicious network can be further accelerated using 5G assisted botnet networks. Attackers can also accelerate denial of service attacks by disrupting the services of the users and simultaneously launch vishing attacks to manipulate the victims.

4.2   Detection of Cyborgs

There are a variety of tools available for attackers to implement social engineering attacks such as spam bots for phishing activities, wardialing for vishing activities and so on. Bots are the automated computational programs that are created for repetitive tasks. Numerous research studies have focused on bot detection such as [31–35]. However, with the emergence of cyborgs, detection has become more difficult. Cyborgs are also automated programs, yet to evade detection, the human behind the program can take control. Compared to social bots, cyborgs follow no specific or fixed pattern which makes detection one of the key challenges. Therefore, combating attackers that use cyborgs to carry out social engineering on social media platforms needs immediate countermeasures.

4.3 Edge Computing Security Risks

Edge computing allows for data to be analyzed and processed at the edge of the network and within a terminal device [36]. This technology was developed as a result of the increasing number of IoT (Internet of Things) devices, which use the Internet to deliver and receive information and data to and from the cloud. One of the main goals for advancing edge computing was to reduce bandwidth costs for IoT devices and other devices that require extensive data processing, in addition to improving reliability and reducing response times [36]. While edge computing was developed to better handle the increasing volume of data from IoT devices, edge computing is also very susceptible to security threats such as social engineering. Therefore, it is of utmost importance to prevent attackers from obtaining these vast quantities of data for illegal purposes, and organisations must ensure that their edge environments are meticulously protected [36].

4.4 Blockchain and Cryptocurrency Cautions

In 2008, blockchain was created to act as a decentralized ledger for Bitcoin [37]. Today, this technology is being used by many established and aspiring cryptocurrencies. As with regular social engineering attacks, scammers are able to use social engineering techniques to exploits users, instead of the technical aspects surrounding blockchain and cyrptocurrency. Attackers created a fake twitter account with a name similar to that of Elon Musk, and proceeded to manipulate victims to send 0.5–1 ether (the cryptocurrency of the Ethereum) in order to receive 5–10 ether as a reward [38]. Moreover, there have been COVID-19 cryptocurrency scams detected, whereby attackers pretend to be health-related organizations and deceive victims to send them cryptocurrency. Such attacks will continue as blockchain technology and the adoption of cryptocurrency becomes ubuiqitious.

5   Future Directions and Recommendations

With the rapid increase of cyber-crime, and its impact on the global market, organizations are beginning to recognize the importance of strategies to mitigate social engineering [22]. Cyber-attacks are continuously evolving each day and social engineers are using new and sophisticated strategies for deception.

Consequently, there is a great need for robust detection and countermeasure techniques to rectify these attacks [2].

As previously stated, awareness for the general population is a key component in defense against social engineering. Many modern employees are not aware of the basic protection measures to ensure they remain safe and vigilant in the digital workplace and at home. Therefore, training programs must begin at an early age, even in schools for K-12 students. Training students at a younger age can decrease the number of victims in the future while unloading the need for further training later in life [2].

One of the main reasons for lack of security training is due to budget constraints [2]. Wherever possible, management must realize that security is of top concern, and that organizations could lose profit and reputation if their staff members are victims of social engineering. One study found that the length of time since the last security training is significant; accordingly, institutions must recognize the importance of conducting regular training [24].

We would also stress that further research is required to delve deeper into the aforementioned problems. While we recognize that awareness is the key component in battling social engineering, there are still cases where employees can fall prey to these techniques. Thus, we recommend further study into methods of training, as well as exploring other emerging technologies such as edge-computing [36,39], artificial intelligence based approaches (such as machine learning, federated learning) [40] and blockchain-technology [40,41] to mitigate social engineering attacks.

Lastly, cybersecurity is an immense field with a growing demand. Currently, there are only a handful of universities in North America that provide quality programs in cybersecurity. Thus, this leads to numerous jobs in the cybersecurity field that are not filled due to the lack of graduates [2]. Governments and organizations need to fund and stress the importance of these programs and employment opportunities in order to acquire a greater number of qualified specialists in the field.

6   Conclusion

In conclusion, with the increasing rate of cybercrime, awareness and prevention methods are more important than ever for individuals and organizations. This paper familiarized the reader with the main types of social engineering attacks, explained the common techniques to mitigate or possibly eliminate the risks caused by those same attacks, and finally discussed the areas which can be improved by businesses and users. Recommendations were then made in order to provide the reader with a sense of how to keep alert, prepared and safe in this ever-changing era of cyberspace.

References

1. Wang, Z., Sun, L., Zhu, H.: Defining social engineering in cybersecurity. IEEE Access **8**, 85094–85115 (2020)

2. Salahdine, F., Kaabouch, N.: Social engineering attacks: a survey. Future Internet **11**(4), 89 (2019)

3. Albladi, S.M., Weir, G.R.S.: User characteristics that influence judgment of social engineering attacks in social networks. Hum.-Cent. Comput. Inf. Sci. **8**(1), 1–24 (2018). https://doi.org/10.1186/s13673-018-0128-7

4. Williams, E.J., Hinds, J., Joinson, A.N.: Exploring susceptibility to phishing in the workplace. Int. J. Hum. Comput. Stud. **120**, 1–13 (2018)

5. Breda, F., Barbosa, H., Morais, T.: Social engineering and cyber security. In: Proceedings of International Technology, Education and Development Conference (2017)

6. Kumar, A., Chaudhary, M., Kumar, N.: Social engineering threats and awareness: a survey. Eur. J. Adv. Eng. Tech. **2**(11), 15–19 (2015)

7. Hakak, S., Khan, W.Z., Imran, M., Choo, K.-K.R., Shoaib, M.: Have you been a victim of COVID-19-related cyber incidents? Survey, taxonomy, and mitigation strategies. IEEE Access **8**, 124134–124144 (2020)

8. FBI. Federal agencies warn of emerging fraud schemes related to COVID-19 vaccines. [Online]. Available: https://www.fbi.gov/news/pressrel/press-releases/federal-agencies-warn-of-emerging-fraud-schemes-related-to-covid-19-vaccines

9. Alzahrani, A.: Coronavirus social engineering attacks: issues and recommendations. Int. J. Adv. Comput. Sci. Appl. **11**(5), 9 (2020). https://doi.org/10.14569/IJACSA.2020.0110523

10. Google. Protecting businesses against cyber threats during COVID-19 and beyond. [Online]. Available: https://cloud.google.com/blog/products/identity-security/protecting-against-cyber-threats-during-covid-19-and-beyond

11. Szurdi, J., Starov, O., McCabe, A., Chen, Z., Duan, R.: Studying how cyber-criminals prey on the COVID-19 pandemic. [Online]. Available: https://unit42.paloaltonetworks.com/how-cybercriminals-prey-on-the-covid-19-pandemic/

12. Albladi, S.M., Weir, G.R.: Predicting individuals' vulnerability to social engineering in social networks. Cybersecur. **3**(1), 1–19 (2020)

13. Lansley, M., Kapetanakis, S., Polatidis, N.: SEADer++ v2: detecting social engineering attacks using natural language processing and machine learning. In: 2020 International Conference on Innovations in Intelligent Systems and Applications (INISTA), pp. 1–6. IEEE (2020)

14. Basit, A., Zafar, M., Liu, X., Javed, A.R., Jalil, Z., Kifayat, K.: A comprehensive survey of AI-enabled phishing attacks detection techniques. Telecommun. Syst. **76**(1), 139–154 (2020). https://doi.org/10.1007/s11235-020-00733-2

15. Abreu, J.V.F., Fernandes, J.H.C., Gondim, J.J.C., Ralha, C.G.: Bot development for social engineering attacks on Twitter. arXiv preprint arXiv:2007.11778 (2020)

16. Smith, A., Papadaki, M., Furnell, S.M.: Improving awareness of social engineering attacks. In: Dodge, R.C., Futcher, L. (eds.) WISE 2009/2011/2013. IAICT, vol. 406, pp. 249–256. Springer, Heidelberg (2013). https://doi.org/10.1007/978-3-642-39377-8_29

17. Saleem, J., Hammoudeh, M.: Defense methods against social engineering attacks. In: Daimi, K. (ed.) Computer and Network Security Essentials, pp. 603–618. Springer, Cham (2018). https://doi.org/10.1007/978-3-319-58424-9_35

18. Zulkurnain, A.U., Hamidy, A., Husain, A.B., Chizari, H.: Social engineering attack mitigation. Int. J. Math. Comput. Sci. **1**(4), 188–198 (2015)

19. Bullée, J.-W., Montoya, L., Pieters, W., Junger, M., Hartel, P.H.: The persuasion and security awareness experiment: reducing the success of social engineering attacks. J. Exp. Criminol. **11**, 97–115 (2015)

20. Parthy, P.P., Rajendran, G.: Identification and prevention of social engineering attacks on an enterprise. In: 2019 International Carnahan Conference on Security Technology (ICCST), pp. 1–5. IEEE (2019)
21. Aldawood, H.A., Skinner, G.: A critical appraisal of contemporary cyber security social engineering solutions: measures, policies, tools and applications. In: 2018 26th International Conference on Systems Engineering (ICSEng), pp. 1–6. IEEE (2018)
22. Aldawood, H., Skinner, G.: An academic review of current industrial and commercial cyber security social engineering solutions. In: Proceedings of the 3rd International Conference on Cryptography, Security and Privacy, pp. 110–115 (2019)
23. Campbell, C.C.: Solutions for counteracting human deception in social engineering attacks. Inf. Technol. People **32**(5), 1130–1152 (2019)
24. Heartfield, R., Loukas, G., Gan, D.: You are probably not the weakest link: towards practical prediction of susceptibility to semantic social engineering attacks. IEEE Access **4**, 6910–6928 (2016)
25. Google. Improving malicious document detection in gmail with deeplearning (2020). [Online]. Available: https://security.googleblog.com/2020/02/improving-malicious-document-detection.html. Accessed 16 January 2021
26. World Health Organisation. How to report misinformation online (2020). [Online]. Available: https://www.who.int/campaigns/connecting-the-world-to-combat-coronavirus/how-to-report-misinformation-online. Accessed 16 January 2021
27. W.H.O. Coronavirus disease (COVID-19) advice for the public: mythbusters (2020). [Online]. Available: https://www.who.int/emergencies/diseases/novel-coronavirus-2019/advice-for-public/myth-busters. Accessed 16 January 2021
28. U.Gov. (2020) Go viral! a 5 minute game that helps protect you against COVID-19 misinformation. [Online]. Available: https://www.goviralgame.com/en?utm_source=EO&utm_medium=SocialMedia&utm_campaign=goviral&utm_content=Eng. Accessed 16 January 2021
29. WHO. Countering misinformation with the government of the United Kingdom (2020). [Online]. Available: https://www.who.int/news-room/feature-stories/detail/countering-misinformation-about-covid-19. Accessed 16 January 2021
30. Shafi, M., et al.: 5g: a tutorial overview of standards, trials, challenges, deployment, and practice. IEEE J Sel. Areas Commun. **35**(6), 1201–1221 (2017)
31. Cresci, S.: A decade of social bot detection. Commun. ACM **63**(10), 72–83 (2020)
32. Heidari, M., Jones, J.H.: Using bert to extract topic-independent sentiment features for social media bot detection. In: 11th IEEE Annual Ubiquitous Computing, Electronics and Mobile Communication Conference (UEMCON), vol. 2020, pp. 0542–0547. IEEE (2020)
33. Kudugunta, S., Ferrara, E.: Deep neural networks for bot detection. Inf. Sci. **467**, 312–322 (2018)
34. Wu, W., Alvarez, J., Liu, C., Sun, H.-M.: Bot detection using unsupervised machine learning. Microsyst. Technol. **24**(1), 209–217 (2018)
35. Abou Daya, A., Salahuddin, M.A., Limam, N., Boutaba, R.: A graph-based machine learning approach for bot detection. In: IFIP/IEEE Symposium on Integrated Network and Service Management (IM), vol. 2019, pp. 144–152. IEEE (2019)
36. Huh, J.-H., Seo, Y.-S.: Understanding edge computing: engineering evolution with artificial intelligence. IEEE Access **7**, 164229–164245 (2019)
37. Xia, P., et al.: Don't fish in troubled waters! characterizing coronavirus-themed cryptocurrency scams (2020)

38. Weber, K., Schütz, A., Fertig, T., Müller, N.: Exploiting the human factor: social engineering attacks on cryptocurrency users **07**, 650–668 (2020)
39. Khan, W.Z., Ahmed, E., Hakak, S., Yaqoob, I., Ahmed, A.: Edge computing: a survey. Future Gener. Comput. Syst. **97**, 219–235 (2019)
40. Hakak, S., Ray, S., Khan, W.Z., Scheme, E.: A framework for edge-assisted healthcare data analytics using federated learning. In: IEEE International Workshop on Data Analytics for Smart Health (DASH) 2020. IEEE BigData (2020)
41. Hakak, S., Khan, W.Z., Gilkar, G.A., Haider, N., Imran, M., Alkatheiri, M.S.: Industrial wastewater management using blockchain technology: architecture, requirements, and future directions. IEEE Internet of Things Mag. **3**(2), 38–43 (2020)

Brand Validation: Security Indicator to Better Indicate Website Identity

Tetsuya Okuda[1]([envelope])[ORCID], Naoko Chiba[1], Mitsuaki Akiyama[1],
Toshinori Fukunaga[1], Ryohei Suzuki[1], and Masayuki Kanda[2]

[1] NTT Secure Platform Laboratories, Tokyo, Japan
tetsuya.okuda.uy@hco.ntt.co.jp
[2] Information-technology Promotion Agency, Tokyo, Japan

Abstract. Extended validation (EV) certificates provide web users with information about the identity of the visited websites, and the security indicators of EV certificates provide information on how to distinguish whether a visited website is legitimate. Although EV certificates have been used for over ten years, general web users still do not sufficiently understand the mechanism of EV certification or what the indicators mean. Through preliminary interviews, we extracted the relationship between three key factors in security conception on the basis of users' cognitive processes: attention, comprehension, and trust. Specifically, indicators should draw users' attention and have clear meanings for increasing their comprehension; thus, indicators can assure users of the trustworthiness of websites on the basis of users' correct attention and comprehension. We designed brand validation (BV) indicators, which are new website identity indicators that display brand or service names on the URL bar and certification processes in the detailed dialogue. According to results of an online survey to evaluate identity indicators, our BV indicators were more trusted by participants than the ordinary EV ones. Besides, because most opinions on domain validation (DV) indicators being trustworthy were based on misunderstandings or habituation, by excluding these incorrect opinions, our BV indicators were far more trusted by participants than the DV ones. Our BV indicators could better educate participants to comprehend the meaning of website identity more correctly than the ordinary EV and DV ones.

Keywords: Brand validation · Extended validation · Website identity

1 Introduction

As HTTPS-enabled phishing sites have dramatically increased [7], traditional security behavior, i.e., *paying attention to the padlock icon on a web browser*, has become less effective to guard against phishing sites. HTTPS allows websites to indicate the identity verified by certificate authorities (CAs) by using X.509 certificates [5]. Among three levels of validation (domain validation (DV), organization validation (OV), and extended validation (EV)), EV is the strictest

© Springer Nature Switzerland AG 2021
A. Moallem (Ed.): HCII 2021, LNCS 12788, pp. 432–447, 2021.
https://doi.org/10.1007/978-3-030-77392-2_28

as it requires the website owners to prove their legal identity and provide much more information about themselves [9]. Although EV certificates have been used for over ten years, general web users still do not sufficiently understand the mechanism of EV certification and the differences in the different validation levels. Users' low attention to and comprehension of EV indicators were revealed by Thompson et al. [21]. This resulted in some browser vendors recently changing EV indicators by moving the certificate information from the address bar, a.k.a. the primary user interface (UI), to only the detailed dialogue, a.k.a. the secondary UI [24]. However, Thompson et al. [21] mentioned that the browser indicators could offer an opportunity to educate users by explaining the website's identity and that more work is needed to understand the effectiveness of browser indicators. Our study goal is to re-design website identity indicators to provide users with an opportunity to improve their comprehension and to better support them in making decisions about website identity. First, to collect users' opinions about phishing websites and the countermeasures, we conducted preliminary interviews with security-conscious users regarding their countermeasures against phishing attacks and use of EV certificate indicators. Through these interviews, we extracted the relationship between the three key factors of their security behavior on the basis of their cognitive processes: attention, comprehension, and trust. In other words, the indicators should draw the attention of users and have clear meanings, thus assuring users in the trustworthiness of websites (Fig. 1). We designed new website identity indicators suitable for users' cognitive processes. Specifically, our proposed brand validation (BV) indicators display brand or service names on the URL bar and certification processes in the secondary UI. To evaluate our indicators, we conducted an online survey including non-tech-savvy users. We asked the participants to select the indicators (DV, EV, or BV) they comprehended the most and trusted the most, and to explain why. From the online survey results, our BV indicators were more trusted than the ordinary EV ones. Besides, because most opinions about DV indicators being trustworthy were based on misunderstandings or habituation, by excluding these incorrect opinions, our BV indicators were far more trusted than the DV ones. As a result, our BV indicators could educate participants to comprehend website identity better than the ordinary EV and DV ones, because the BV indicators clearly explain the relationship of the stakeholders around the websites and enable users to verify this information by themselves. If the BV indicators become pervasive, it can be expected that the misunderstandings will decrease and users will correctly understand website identity and become better at resisting phishing attacks.

2   Background and Related Work

2.1   Phishing Attacks on Human Vulnerabilities

The amount of damage by phishing attacks is increasing dramatically and was reported to be about US\$48.2 million in 2018 [3]. As technical countermeasures, various methods have been developed such as detection methods based on URLs [1]. In addition, phishing attacks target human vulnerabilities; therefore, the research on countermeasures also focuses on human's understanding and behavior. In chronological order, in 2006, Dhamija et al. conducted the first experiment on phishing attacks based on human vulnerabilities and reported that most participants did not focus on websites' URLs or other indicators [6]. Participants in a 2007 experiment with WindowsXP / IE6-7 tended to ignore HTTPS indicators, e.g., padlock icons, and carelessly sent their information to websites with no HTTPS indicators [19]. In another experiment in 2016, Felt et al. conducted a user study on designing better icons and strings to improve user comprehension of HTTPS connection security on Google Chrome [8].

2.2 Security Indicators

Security indicators are used for summarizing the security status of objects (e.g., websites), and major web browsers display padlock icons or shields as security indicators [8]. Users can confirm the security status of visited websites by checking the indicators on the web browsers. W3C published UI guidelines to provide users with web security context information [16]. These guidelines define two important UIs: (i) *Primary UI*: the display for a user visiting a website, which is to increase user attention, and (ii) *Secondary UI*: the display for a user clicking on the primary UI to solicit further information, which is to improve user comprehension [16]. According to these definitions, in the context of HTTPS-enabled websites, a padlock icon is displayed as the primary UI and certificate information is displayed as the secondary UI.

2.3 Website Identity and X.509 Certificate

URLs and X.509 certificates can inform users of websites' identities [9,11].

A URL is the most common indicator of website identity; however, several attacks causing visual confusion, such as homograph attacks and combosquatting attacks, are pervasive [15], and users cannot accurately judge website identity by using only URL information [14].

X.509 certificates are used for HTTPS-enabled websites to indicate website identity. They are generally proved by CAs; however, users should not trust HTTPS-enabled websites unconditionally because there are different levels of validation for certificates: DV, OV, and EV. DV proves the domain owner usually by exchanging confirmation emails with the administrative contact of the domain. OV proves business registration information as well as the domain ownership on the basis of the baseline-requirement guidelines [10].

EV is the strictest as it requires the website owners to prove their legal identity on the basis of the EV certificate guidelines [9]. Due to the strict EV certification process, far fewer phishing websites have valid EV certificates than have valid DV and OV certificates [7]. In addition, websites can provide users with more information about the owners based on their legal identity. However, possible attacks against EV indicators have been reported (e.g., picture-in-picture attack [12] and cross-jurisdiction collision attack [21]), and the more realistic problem with EV indicators is that they do not sufficiently draw users' attention or increase users' comprehension about the meaning of EV certificates. In chronological order, experiments were conducted on increasing users' attention on Firefox 3.0 in 2008 [20] and improving their comprehension regarding the distinction between connection security and website identity on IE7 in 2009 [2]. In a recent study on Google Chrome in 2019, users' attention to and the comprehension of EV indicators on recent web browsers were found to still be low [21]. However, Thompson et al. [21] previously mentioned that the browser indicators could be an opportunity to educate users by explaining website identity and that more work is needed to understand the indicators' effectiveness. Our study aimed to re-design website identity indicators, especially the secondary UI, to improve users' comprehension of website identity and evaluated the re-designed indicators.

As related specifications, there are "Logotypes" published by IETF [17]. Logotypes display the brand logos of websites next to the address bar on the web browser for users to feel familiar with and correctly judge the website identity [17]. However, Logotypes convert logo images in different sizes into the pre-defined small and fixed squarespace next to the address bar. In contrast, our proposed BV indicators display only brand names in an address bar and brand logos are moved into a detailed dialogue.

3   Study Design

To achieve our study goal of re-designing website identity indicators, our study contains preliminary interviews, the design of new website identity indicators for both primary and secondary UIs, and the evaluation of the proposed indicators by using an online survey. The detailed procedure is as follows.

- Step-1-1: Conduct preliminary interviews to extract participants' opinions and behaviors for browser indicators, including EV indicators
- Step-1-2: Explain EV certificates and certification processes and conduct additional preliminary interviews to extract users' concerns about EV indicators
- Step-2: Design new website identity indicators for both primary and secondary UIs
- Step-3: Conduct an online survey to evaluate these indicators

We interviewed the same participants in Step-1-1 and Step-1-2 and surveyed different participants in Step-3. Step-1-1, Step-1-2, and Step-2 were conducted from January to March in 2019, and Step-3 was conducted from January to March in 2020.

4   Opinions and Behaviors for Browser Indicators

In preliminary interviews for Step-1-1 and Step-1-2, first, we asked participants about their opinions about and behaviors toward browser indicators, including

EV indicators. Then, we explained EV certificates and certification processes to participants. Finally, we additionally asked participants about their concerns about EV indicators.

4.1 Recruiting

We recruited Japanese participants[1] from a recruiting agency who had relatively high IT literacy and were aware of information security risks to collect their opinions about security behavior and strategy (N=35, ages 20–60, male/female ratio=1.05). For details of the recruiting, see Appendix A. We paid participants about US$70 (including travel expenses) for 2-h interviews.

4.2 Preliminary Interview Method

We conducted semi-structured interviews (Step-1-1) to collect the participants' opinions on the EV indicators after showing examples of browser indicators, including EV indicators, on a web browser. We coded the collected opinions on the basis of the thematic analysis [13] in accordance with the related work [23]. One coder developed the code-book, and an other validated it, and both coded the interview results. The Cohen's Kappa, which is the coefficient indicating the consistency between two coders' coding, was 0.958, which is high enough to assure the consistency of the coding processes. The details of the interview process are listed in Appendix B (Table 1).

Table 1. Demography of participants. Participants were divided into six groups for group interviews as below.

ID	Age	Gender
A-1–A-6	40–49	Female
B-1–B-6	60–69	Female
C-1–C-6	60–69	Male
D-1–D-5	20–29	Female
E-1–E-6	20–29	Male
F-1–F-6	40–49	Male

4.3 Preliminary Interview Results

In this section, we describe the participants' opinions about and behaviors toward the EV indicators. As a result of the interview analysis, we obtained three representative opinions: (i) Attention: to pay attention to the security indicators on primary UI, (ii) Comprehension: to comprehend the meaning of the security indicators on primary and secondary UIs, and (iii) Trust: to have trust in using a website.

---

[1] Interviews were conducted in Japanese, and the responses are translated into English in this paper.

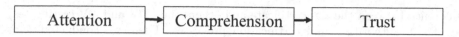

Fig. 1. Relationship of attention, comprehension, and trust

Attention. There were opinions revealing correct and incorrect attention. Regarding correct attention, many participants mentioned the companies that adopted EV certificates: (C-2)*"Most bank websites are green."* and (C-5)*"Most (of the examples) were financial companies."* Regarding incorrect attention, some participants mentioned that they paid attention to items not originally from the EV indicators: A-5, B-5, D-2, and E-4 mentioned that they had checked the padlock icons, A-1 and A-4 mentioned that they had seen the letter 's' of https.

Comprehension. There were opinions revealing the adequate and the inadequate comprehension of EV indicators. Regarding adequate comprehension, a few participants mentioned the meaning and the scope of EV certificates: B-1 and F-1 mentioned that the padlock icons mean only that the connection is encrypted and the website's credibility is a different matter. Regarding inadequate comprehension (i.e., lack of understanding), most participants mentioned the difficulty for them to understand who the CAs are and how the certification processes work: C-2 and F-4 mentioned that they could not understand whether the 'certificate authority' was a government office, public institution, or some other organization. A-5 and A-6 mentioned that they could not understand the details of the certification processes.

Trust. There were opinions on the trustworthiness of EV indicators: (F-2)*"EV indicators are displayed commonly on the credible websites such as bank websites."* On the other hand, there were opinions that the participants considered certificate authorities as untrustworthy: (F-6)*"It seems unsafe if the name of the certificate authority is not well-known."*, (D-2)*"I wonder if I should trust or suspect the 'certificate authority'."*, and there were opinions that the participants considered certification processes as untrustworthy: (E-2)*"Since there is an enormous number of websites, I feel a little anxious to what extent websites are certified."*, and (E-6)*"I'm concerned whether the certificate authority does this automatically because the workload of certification seems to be huge."* These opinions reveal that the lack of comprehension about certificate authorities and certification processes prevent participants from trusting EV indicators.

In general, the indicators should draw users' attention and have clear meanings for helping users' comprehension, assuring users in the trustworthiness of websites (Fig. 1). Through the interview analysis, however, we found that many participants failed to trust websites because of their lack of correct attention to and comprehension of EV indicators.

4.4   Additional Preliminary Interview Method

After the preliminary interviews, we educated all participants by explaining the details of EV certificates and the certification processes, for example, the difference between the EV certificate and others (i.e., DV and OV certificates), certificate authorities, and certification processes. Then, we conducted semi-structured interviews to collect the problems of EV indicators.

4.5 Additional Preliminary Interview Results

We obtained two representative opinions: the problem of displaying for "attention" and the problem of education for "comprehension". These opinions were taken into consideration in designing our proposed BV indicators described in the next section.

The Problem of Displaying for "Attention". One participant doubted the effectiveness of displaying company names: (D-4) *"Displaying company names is sometimes confusing because they are different from service names."* This opinion indicated that service or brand names, which are more familiar to participants, are required for the URL bar on a web browser, and it was taken into consideration for our indicator (primary UI) in the next chapter.

The Problem of User Education for "Comprehension". There were many opinions about the problem of user education such as the following.

After the explanation of EV indicators, the lack of user education was pointed out by many participants. For example (A-3) *"All of us should know about these things."*, (A-4) *"Why don't most of us know about them (EV certification processes)?"*, (A-5) *"It'd be good for TV to teach people."*, and (A-1) *"There are no news programs about this, so no one knows."* Educating users is expected to help them correctly judge websites' trustworthiness by using EV indicators. These opinions were taken into consideration for our indicator (secondary UI) in the next chapter.

In addition, many participants said they were willing to trust EV indicators after learning their meaning. For example, (F-1) *"The certification process is not completed online but validated in the real world. It leads to higher security."*, (F-3) *"When I see the EV indicator, I'll think the company seems highly reliable."*, (D-5) *"With EV indicators, we would be less likely to be deceived by phishing websites."*, (D-2) *"I was impressed to know such companies work properly even while I didn't know."*, and (F-3) *"I came to think that the Internet works more properly than I had thought."* In the end, these opinions also suggest that the education about EV certification has been insufficient for not only the security-conscious participants but also the general public.

4.6 Summary of Opinions for Re-designing EV Indicators

We summarize the additional preliminary interview results for re-designing EV indicators. Since the problem of "attention" can be solved by displaying noticeable phrases, we take these opinions into consideration in re-designing our primary UI. Since the problem of "comprehension" can be solved by clearly explaining the details of certification processes (i.e., user education), we take these opinions into consideration in re-designing our secondary UI.

5   Brand Validation: Proposed Website Identity Indicators

Our new website identity indicators, called brand validation (BV) indicators, are extensions of the original EV indicators. BV indicators were designed in accordance with the requirements raised in the preliminary interviews to help users assess the *trustworthiness* of websites by improving user *attention* and *comprehension*. We developed prototype images of BV indicators on a web browser. In designing these images, we considered the primary and secondary UIs in accordance with the existing web security UI guidelines [16].

5.1   Our Indicator for Primary UI (URL Bar)

Our indicator for the primary UI was designed to increase user attention. To this end, the service or brand name is displayed as the indicator of website identity instead of the owner name on the left of the URL bar (Fig. 2). The service or brand names are more noticeable for users because the companies usually use them rather than company names in advertising to increase consumer awareness. When users click on the primary UI, the dialogue (i.e., the secondary UI) is displayed giving details of the certification information.

Fig. 2. Our BV indicator (primary UI)

5.2   Our Indicator for Secondary UI (Detailed Dialogue)

Our indicator for the secondary UI was designed to improve user comprehension, assuring trust. Since HTTPS-enabled websites are common, the information of website identity has become more important than that of connection security (i.e., whether HTTPS or not). Therefore, our indicator for the secondary UI enriches the information of website identity. To this end, the following components were added to the page of certificate information as the secondary UI (Fig. 3).

- The service or brand logo is displayed because the visual component is effective in associating it with the corresponding organization (e.g., a company as website owner).

– The certification process to confirm website identity is displayed. In this prototype, we adopted the confirmation source, such as the name of the government office with jurisdiction or its official document name. Qualified Website Authentication Certificates, a type of certificate with certificate chains verified by government agencies [18], can be used for displaying such information in our BV indicators.

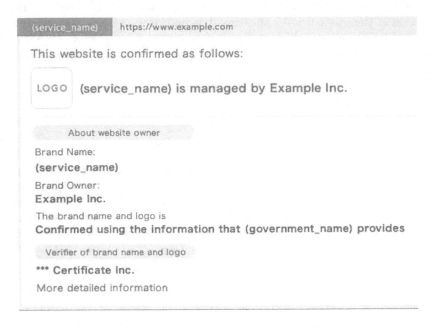

Fig. 3. Our BV indicator (secondary UI)

6   Evaluation of Proposed Indicators

6.1   Evaluation Method and Recruiting

To evaluate the effectiveness of BV indicators, we conducted an online survey. We recruited 595 participants in the U.S. from Amazon MTurk who had all used browsers on PCs. We paid participants about US$7.5. We made sample images for DV, EV, and BV (Fig. 4) and displayed them in random order for each participant. We asked participants to select which indicator they comprehended the most and which one they trusted the most. We did not conduct an evaluation in terms of attention through our online survey, because it is difficult to directly observe how participants pay attention to indicators and it would have been necessary to conduct an experience sampling method in participants' daily lives [22]. Therefore, we focused on the evaluation of comprehension and trust. The phrases in our questionnaire was referred to the previous work [21]. The questionnaire is fully shown in Appendix C and partly shown below.

- Take a look at the 3 images ((A), (B), (C)) given below and answer the following questions.[2]
  - Q. Which one can you "understand" the most?
    Select one of the following: ((A) / (B) / (C)) and Why?
  - Q. Which one can you "trust" the most ?
    Select one of the following: ((A) / (B) / (C)) and Why?

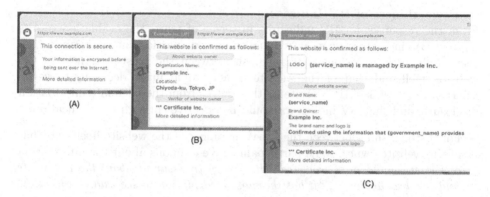

Fig. 4. DV(A), EV(B), and BV(C) images used for our online survey

6.2 Evaluation Results

We obtained responses from 595 participants in total. The number of all answers are shown in Table 2. Since users usually encountered DV indicators on a web browser in their daily lives, DV indicators scored highly in terms of comprehension. However, DV indicators scored less in terms of trust than comprehension. In addition, the opinions to trust DV indicators were mainly based on misunderstandings or habituation as detailed later. On the other hand, since users had never encountered our proposed BV indicators on a web browser in their daily lives, BV indicators scored less than DV indicators in terms of comprehension. However, BV indicators scored higher in terms of trust than comprehension. We analyzed the collected opinions: One coder coded the qualitative responses, and an other validated it. The Cohen's Kappa was 0.982, which is high enough to assure the consistency of the coding processes.

---

[2] Three images ((A), (B), (C)) like in Fig. 4 were displayed in random order for each participant.

Table 2. The number of answers

	DV	EV	BV
Comprehension	340	135	120
Trust (all answers)	258	138	199
Trust (excluding misunderstandings or habituation)	129	132	198

Trustworthiness of BV Indicators

From the responses for BV indicators in terms of trust, the evaluation results for our BV indicators were as we had expected: participants opinioned that they could make decisions to distinguish between the trustworthiness of the website itself and that of the website owner, could make decisions to verify the trustworthiness of the website by themselves from the adequate information disclosure, and that BV indicators would be effective through user education.

– For distinguishing between the trustworthiness of the website itself and that of the website owner, some participants gave opinions about the information of the stakeholders of websites: *"It is very transparent about the certificate and involved holders."*, *"It has the most information to see who is behind the website."*. Others gave opinions about using company or brand information in an actual situation: *"Information about a company or brand is a more common concept that extends beyond the internet, so I can apply that information to it."*

– For verifying the trustworthiness of the website from the adequate information disclosure, some participants gave opinions about verifying websites by themselves: *"Good information to verify it for myself. More than just 'is secure'."*, *"It would be nice if there was a way to verify that info provided is legitimate, besides 'because the browser says so'."*. Others gave opinions about the control of browsing by themselves: *"It has all the info I need to make an informed choice."*, *"I feel more in control of my browsing"*, *"It would be easy to fact check this information."*,

These opinions were assumed to be the main factors for the participants to trust BV indicators the most. Other responses were as follows.

– There were opinions that BV indicators were understandable even for non-tech-savvy participants. One participant who thought of her/himself as generally IT literate selected the BV indicators because *"It's easy for me to understand, as a normal computer user."*

– One participant who most trusted DV indicators thought that the BV indicators can be understandable and trustable in the future through user education: *"I think (BV) would become trust-able with time."*

The Misunderstanding and the Habituation for Participants to Trust DV Indicators

From the responses of participants who trusted DV indicators, the main obstacles for the ordinary EV indicators not to become widely used seem to be misunderstanding and habituation for ordinary browser indicators. 50% (129 out of 258) of participants, who most trusted DV indicators, did so on the basis of these misunderstandings or habituation.

- Regarding misunderstanding, 41 participants said that they trusted the DV indicators because it said information was "encrypted" and 78 participants did so because it said the connection was "secure". However, displaying words like "encrypted" and "secure" does not mean the site is genuine since HTTPS-enabled phishing websites are pervasive. Thus, these opinions are no longer correct [8]. These users need to learn the right countermeasures against phishing attacks, such as judging website identity, and browser indicators are applicable for this education [21]. Through this education, users should be taught to comprehend that the DV indicators focusing on the connection security become less valuable and the BV and EV indicators focusing on the website identity become more valuable as countermeasures against phishing attacks in the HTTPS-enabled world. The responses belonging to this category were as follows: *"Encryption makes sure the data doesn't fall into wrong hands."*, and *"This explains, essentially, that the site is secure."*
- Regarding habituation, 53 participants said that they trusted the DV indicators because they were "familiar with", "used to", or "seen" it. For these users, habituation can be an obstacle to new precise indicators, so a transition period is needed for them to become accustomed to new precise indicators, which would increase correct comprehension and trust. The responses were as follows: *"Image (DV) is very familiar, therefore I would prefer and trust it more."*, and *"I trust this one the most because it's the one I am most used to seeing."*

50% (129 out of 258) of participants, who most trusted DV indicators, did so on the basis of these misunderstandings or habituation. By excluding these answers, only 129 participants most trusted DV indicators, far fewer than the 198 participants who most trusted BV indicators, as shown in Table 2. The chi-squared test result is $p < 0.005$, suggesting that there is significant difference.

As a result, BV indicators are assumed to be the most trusted indicators among DV, EV, and BV indicators.

7 Discussion

7.1 Effectiveness Against Cross-Jurisdiction Collision Attack

The ordinary EV indicators have been criticized because they are vulnerable to the cross-jurisdiction collision attack, which involves the same company name being registered in an another country or state by an another party [21]. However, the proposed BV indicators are tolerant against this attack because brand names are usually registered globally, which makes it difficult for other parties to register the same brand names in other countries or states.

7.2   Evaluation of Attention to BV Indicators

Although we also proposed the primary UI of BV indicators to improve attention, we could not evaluated attention, because we could not conduct an in-situ study like an experience sampling method [22]. For future work, we should conduct an in-situ study to evaluate the attention to BV indicators by implementing the indicators on users' everyday browsers.

7.3   Research Ethics

The interview study in this work was approved by the Privacy Information Assessment (PIA) committee in our organization. All the data, including the answers and the record of the interviews, were anonymized so as not to identify specific people. No proper nouns were included.

We carefully designed our interview and online survey process, including questions and image materials, not to harm the reputation of actual third parties; they did not include any specific company, service, and brand names. In the same way, the browser's UI design is our original one, so no specific company, service, brand name, or logo was included in the explanation.

8   Conclusion and Future Work

We designed new website identity indicators called brand validation (BV) indicators. We conducted preliminary interviews regarding user understanding of extended validation (EV) indicators and found that users' attention and comprehension are important to ensure the trustworthiness of websites.

We evaluated the BV indicators through an online survey and found that they increased trust in websites more than the ordinary EV indicators. Besides, because most opinions about domain validation (DV) indicators being trustworthy were based on misunderstandings or habituation, by excluding these incorrect opinions, more participants trusted the BV indicators than the DV indicators. The BV indicators, especially the secondary UI, could improve the users' comprehension of website identity and were the most trusted among DV, EV, and BV indicators. BV indicators will contribute to the current design of browser indicators by other browser vendors.

Appendices

A. Recruiting Detail of the Preliminary Interview

We recruited participants as following conditions:

- using PC and browser
- security-conscious to have installed anti-virus software
- high IT-literacy to spent much time and money on websites and to know about words like "URL", "browser", "domain name" and "address bar"

B. Interview Flow Detail

The group interview flow was as follows:

- interviewed participants about their everyday internet use
- interviewed participants about internet security risks they recognized
- interviewed participants about their countermeasures against security risks when using e-mail, what they took care to do, and why
  Follow-up:
  - what e-mails they conceived as suspicious, and why
  - whether they trusted URLs or links in e-mails, why they thought URLs or links were safe or suspicious
  - what countermeasures they used such as provider services, security vendor software, or other manual approaches
  - what actions they took when they received spam e-mails
  - whether they felt secure by taking these countermeasures only, and why
  - if they took no countermeasures, why not
- interviewed participants about their countermeasures against security risks when using web browsers, what they took care to do, and why
  Follow-up:
  - whether they trusted URLs or links in search engine results, why they thought URLs or links were safe or suspicious
  - why they trusted websites, what they saw as important, and why
  - what countermeasures they used such as provider services, security vendor software, or other manual approaches
  - whether they felt secure by taking these countermeasures only, and why
  - if they took no countermeasures, why not
- explained websites' vulnerabilities because of URLs, and explained EV certificates as a countermeasure
- interviewed participants about recognition of EV certificate & indicator and their problems as follows:
  - whether they looked at URL bar with company or organization names in green, on what websites they saw it
    Follow-up:
    * their first impression of the indicator

- whether they had known about the EV certificate, certificate authorities, and certification processes before this interview
  Follow-up:
    * why they had known or noticed
    * whether they clicked on the indicator or searched for the meaning, and why
- how they felt or thought about the EV certificate after the explanation
  Follow-up:
    * why they felt trust
    * why they felt EV certificate was difficult to understand, how it could be easier to understand
    * whether they could differentiate EV certificate from the others
    * why they had not noticed
    * what current EV certificate & indicator seemed to lack
- what they thought about the strict certification processes for EV certificate & indicator
  Follow-up:
    * how differently they felt about websites with EV certificate after learning about these certification processes conducted by third parties, and why
    * whether they had known about indicators displaying company or organization names, and how they felt about them, how they would be better for user recognition than company or organization names

C. The details of the online survey

Q1. Time to spend on the internet for private use (on a weekday).
Q2. Time to spend on the internet for private use (on a holiday).
Q3. Your OS.
Q4. Your Web Browser.
(Q5 - Q7). Take a look at the 3 images ((A), (B), (C)) given below and answer the following questions.
Q5. Which one can you "recognize" the most?
Select One of the following: ((A) / (B) / (C)) and Why?
Q6. Which one can you "understand" the most?
Select One of the following: ((A) / (B) / (C)) and Why?
Q7. Which one can you "trust" the most?
Select One of the following: ((A) / (B) / (C)) and Why?

References

1. Althobaiti, K., Rummani, G., Vaniea, K.: A review of human- and computer-facing URL phishing features. In: EuroUSEC (2019)

2. Biddle, R., Oorschot, P.C., Patrick, A.S., Sobey, J., Whalen, T.: Browser interfaces and extended validation SSL certificates: an empirical study. In: CCSW (2009)
3. Internet Crime Complaint Center. 2018 Internet crime report (2018)
4. Close, T.: Petname tool: enabling web site recognition using the existing SSL infrastructure. In: W3C (2005)
5. Cooper, S.D., Santesson, S., Farrell, S., Boeyen, R., Polk Housley, W.: RFC5280: Internet X.509 public key infrastructure certificate and certificate revocation list (CRL) Profile (2007)
6. Dhamija, R., Tygar, J.D., Hearst, M.: Why phishing works. In: CHI (2006)
7. Drury, V., Meyer, U.: Certified phishing: taking a look at public key certificates of phishing websites. In: SOUPS (2019)
8. Felt, A.P., et al.: Rethinking connection security indicators. In: SOUPS (2016)
9. CA/Browser Forum. Guidelines for the issuance and management of extended validation certificates (2007)
10. CA/Browser Forum. Baseline requirements for the issuance and management of publicly-trusted certificates (2011)
11. Jackson, C., Simon, D.R., Tan, D.S., Barth, A.: An evaluation of extended validation and picture-in-picture attacks. In: USEC (2007)
12. Jakobsson, M., Tsow, A., Shah, A., Blevis, E., Lim, Y.K.: What instills trust? A qualitative study of phishing. In: USEC (2007)
13. Lazar, J., Feng, J.H., Hochheiser, H.: Research Methods in Human-Computer Interaction, 2nd edn. Elsevier Inc, Amsterdam (2017)
14. Lin, E., Greenberg, S., Trotter, E., Ma, D., Aycock, J.: Does domain highlighting help people identify phishing sites. In: CHI (2011)
15. Luo, M., Starov, O., Honarmand, N., Nikiforakis, N.: Hindsight: understanding the evolution of UI vulnerabilities in mobile browsers. In: CCS (2017)
16. Roessler, T., Sladhana, A.: Web security context: user interface guidelines. In: W3C (2010)
17. Santesson, S., Housley, R., Freeman, T.: RFC3709: internet x.509 public key infrastructure: logotypes in X.509 certificates. In: IETF (2004)
18. ENISA. Qualified Website Authentication Certificates (2016)
19. Schechter, S.E., Dhamija, R., Ozment, A., Fischer, I.: The emperor's new security indicators. In: S&P (2007)
20. Sobey, J., Biddle, R., Oorschot, P.C., Patrick, A.S.: Exploring user reactions to new browser cues for extended validation certificates. In: ESORICS (2008)
21. Thompson, C., Shelton, M., Stark, E., Walker, M., Schechter, E., Felt, A.P.: The web's identity crisis: understanding the effectiveness of website identity indicators. In: USENIX Security (2019)
22. Reeder, R.W., Felt, A.P., Consolvo, S., Malkin, N., Thompson, C., Egelman, S.: An experience sampling study of user reactions to browser warnings in the field. In: ACM CHI (2018)
23. Cranor, L.F.: A framework for reasoning about the human in the loop. In: USENIX (2008)
24. Chromium. EV UI moving to page info (2019)

Study on the Impact of Learning About Information Security Measures on Mental Models: Applying Cybersecurity Frameworks to Self-learning Materials

Satoshi Ozaki[(✉)] and Hiroshi Furukawa

University of Tsukuba, 1-1-1 Tennodai, Tsukuba, Ibaraki, Japan
s1730150@s.tsukuba.ac.jp, furukawa@risk.tsukuba.ac.jp

Abstract. The shortage of information-security workers is a problem. Appropriate mental models are considered important to encourage learners to appropriately plan, understand, and act on security measures. We aim to create materials to help security staff members acquire the right mental model in their learning and improve the learning effect. To create such materials, it is important to investigate the current mental model of the staff, how the model changes through learning, and its impact on the learning efficiency.

A preliminary experiment was conducted on individuals who had not received such education and individuals who had participated in security-related work for a few to several years. The participants self-studied both standard and revised materials on information security measures, and we conducted tests and semi-structured interviews to examine the changes in their performance and confidence as well as the changes to their mental models before and after self-learning.

Four mental models were identified during the experiment: role-based, timeline/phase-based, framework-based, and unstructured models. After learning, for those with security-related work experience, we identified examples of changing to a framework-based model, and for groups with no security education, we identified examples of acquiring a role-based model. Instances when the model did not change were also noted. The test scores and degree of confidence of both groups improved after the self-learning, and a significant difference was shown for questions regarding which security measures contribute to which security function based on a small sample size

Keywords: Mental model · Cybersecurity framework · Ecological interface design · Self-learning

1 Introduction

The shortage of human resources related to information security has been a problem in Japan since the last decade, and an improvement in learning effectiveness is needed. According to the "Fundamental Research for Education of Information Security Human Resources" published by the Information-technology Promotion Agency, Japan (IPA) in

© Springer Nature Switzerland AG 2021
A. Moallem (Ed.): HCII 2021, LNCS 12788, pp. 448–474, 2021.
https://doi.org/10.1007/978-3-030-77392-2_29

2012 and its continued research published in 2014 [1], the shortage of human resources in the cybersecurity field is estimated to be approximately 81,000, and 61,000 people are working for companies that do not have a human resource department in this area. In addition, the Institute of Information Security stated in its "Report on Questionnaire Survey on Information Security Incident" [2] that approximately 25% of small and medium-sized enterprises (SMEs) in Japan do not have human resources in the field of cybersecurity, and that approximately 41% have only one cybersecurity information staff member holding a concurrent post. Therefore, approximately 67% of SMEs have limited or no human resources in this field. Moreover, there have been some reports on advanced persistent threats in which malicious players have attempted to attack related groups or companies that are less secure to an initial attack. One such example was reported by the IPA, Japan [3]. It is therefore important to improve their cybersecurity in less secure communities, such as SMEs.

To improve this situation, a working group for the development of human resources for cybersecurity was organized in the Cyber Security Center in Japan, which published its "Measures for Developing Cybersecurity Human Resources Inter-Group Working Report" [4] in 2018. In this report, it was indicated that not only are specialists required to work in the domain of cybersecurity or general IT operations, experts who have a good understanding of both security and business activities are also needed. The idea of an expert is also mentioned in the "Report of Cyber Security Human Resource Development Study Group" [5] published by the Cyber Risk Intelligence Center, in which it is stated that experts supervise the security activities in a company.

SMEs need to train experts who can make comprehensive proposals on security measures, considering their company profile. To this end, we believe that self-learning methods are important for enabling security staff members to acquire a comprehensive and appropriate mental model of security measures.

We created improved self-learning materials and conducted a control experiment to check what occurs to the learner's mental model during learning and how the efficiency is changed. Self-learning materials are based on published standard learning materials for SMEs. In self-learning materials, the sections are mapped to the categories of the framework core of the Cybersecurity Framework 1.1 [6], which we suppose can be the foundation of a comprehensive and appropriate mental model.

In this study, as a preliminary experiment for actual security staff members, we interviewed, tested, and surveyed five members of a group who had not received any security education, four members of a group who had been involved in security-related work for 1 year, and four members of an actual security staff working for several years. Two types of teaching materials were used to confirm the effectiveness of the revised learning materials, i.e., a user interface explicitly expressing the relationship between each category of the cybersecurity framework core, and the published standard learning materials.

As the main contributions of this paper, we confirmed that there are four mental models applicable to an overview of the security measures: role-based, time-based, framework-based, and unstructured (partial) mental models. We observed an attempt to transform the mental model by presenting a framework to a group of people with security-related work experience and to a group of people without security education who had also acquired a structured mental model after self-learning. We were also able to confirm that, despite the small sample size, a statistically significant difference could be found for questions regarding the function of the framework core to which the security measures contribute.

As a future study, a survey with a statistically sufficient sample size and interviews of security staff members will be conducted to detect the effects of the revised self-learning materials and the changes in the mental model of the information security staff.

2 Methodology

In Sect. 2.1, we describe the revised learning materials intended to improve the learning effectiveness. First, however, the recruitment and demographers are described in Sect. 2.2, the experiment design is detailed in Sect. 2.3, and the data analysis procedure is provided in Sect. 2.4.

2.1 Improved Learning Materials for the Experimental Group

The creation of teaching materials is based on the theory of an ecological interface design (EID), particularly the abstraction hierarchy (AH). EID provides a method for designing an interface that externalizes the mental model the users should have about the system, including its limitations. This EID-based interface helps the user obtain the correct mental model that users should have and optimize the cognitive load of the users [7]–9]. One of the important diagrams of EID is the AH, which is a hierarchical expression of the mental model in which each component is connected hierarchically with a means-end relationship, which can provide a comprehensive and appropriate understanding of the system. Normally, the top of the hierarchy refers to the functional purpose of the whole system, and lower levels are sub-functions used to achieve the upper-level function.

The cybersecurity framework core has the same structure as the AH. Categories are a means to achieve the functions, and sub-categories are a means to achieving categories. The framework core is a model that integrates several security guidelines and security measures. The framework core has a layered structure, where each element is called a function, category, or sub-category. Functions are the highest-level cybersecurity activities and include identification, protection, detection, response, and recover. A category is a group summarizing several close security measures to achieve a function (Table 1). We decided to revise the published standard learning materials of the Guideline of Information Security for SMEs 3rd edition [10] based on the framework core of Cybersecurity Framework 1.1.

By applying this framework, which has the same structure as the AH of the materials, we suppose that a comprehensive and systematic mental model can be instilled into learners, and its learning efficiency can be improved.

We partially took a text-mining approach, which uses tf-idf, and checked the similarity to the framework core of Cybersecurity Framework 1.1. Applying it to each chapter and section of the standard material, we clarified the correspondence between each chapter and section in the document as well as the framework core of Cybersecurity Framework 1.1 [11].

We changed the standard materials in which the sections are mapped to the categories of the framework core based on the results of the text mining and template coding. The correspondence between each section and category is shown in Appendix Table 7.

Table 1. Function and Category of Unique Identifiers (quoted from Cybersecurity Framework 1.1 [6])

Function ID	Function	Category ID	Category
ID	Identify	ID.AM	Asset Management
		ID.BE	Business Environment
		ID.GV	Governance
		ID.RA	Risk Assessment
		ID.RM	Risk Management Strategy
		ID.SC	Supply Chain Risk Management
PR	Protect	PR.AC	Identity Management and Access Control
		PR.AT	Awareness and Training
		PR.DS	Data Security
		PR.IP	Information Protection Processes and Procedures
		PR.MA	Maintenance
		PR.PT	Protective Technology
DE	Detect	DE.AE	Anomalies and Events
		DE.CM	Security Continuous Monitoring
		DE.DP	Detection Processes
RS	Respond	RS.RP	Response Planning
		RS.CO	Communications
		RS.AN	Analysis
		RS.MI	Mitigation
		RS.IM	Improvements
RC	Recover	RC.RP	Recovery Planning
		RC.IM	Improvements
		RC.CO	Communications

The user interface of the created materials is shown in Fig. 1. On the left side of the screen, the categories of the cyber security framework cores are listed (B), and next to them, the table of contents of the Guideline of Information Security for SMEs is listed (C), with the text displayed on the right side of the screen (D). When hovering a mouse over an item in the table of contents, a line will show which category the item is related to (A). A strong association is indicated by a solid line, and a weaker association is indicated by a dashed line. By clicking on the table of contents, the page transitions to

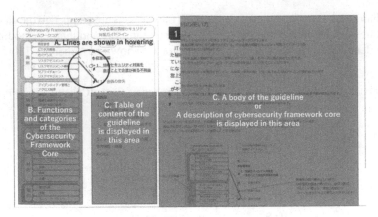

Fig. 1. User interface of the revised materials

a more detailed table of contents. Clicking on each item of a category or function will display a detailed description of each item. The category and feature descriptions are based on Cybersecurity Framework 1.1.

2.2 Recruitment and Demographics

Five employees or students of the author's acquaintance who were not related to information technology, four employees of the security product company to which the author

Table 2. Demographics and experiment conditions

ID	Security experience	Age	Phase	Company size	Experimental or control group
1	1 year	20s	First	300–1000	Control
2	1 year	20s	First	300–1000	Experimental
3	1 year	20s	First	300–1000	Control
4	1 year	20s	First	300–1000	Experimental
5	No	20s	First	n/a	Experimental
6	No	20s	Second	n/a	Control
7	No	20s	Second	n/a	Control
8	No	20s	Second	n/a	Experimental
9	No	20s	Second	n/a	Experimental
10	5–10 years	40s	Second	100–300	Control
11	5–10 years	30s	Second	50–100	Experimental
12	3–5 years	30s	Second	1000–	Experimental
13	3–5 years	20s	Second	50–100	Control

belongs, and four employees of actual security staff members recruited through social media were asked to participate in the experiment (Table 2).

The experiment was divided into two phases. The first phase was conducted using four individuals with experience in a security-related job and one in a non-security-related field, and the results were analyzed. The second phase was conducted using four people who did not have security knowledge and four people of an actual security staff. We added 37 new questions with greater statistical relevance.

2.3 Study Design

The experiments were conducted as shown in Fig. 2. All experiments, including the interview sessions, were conducted in Japanese. Study

We applied two research approaches alternately using one self-learning session, namely, an interview to capture the changes in the mental model through self-learning (2.3.1) and a test to measure the change in learning effectiveness (2.3.2).

The pre- and post-questionnaires and the test and interview scripts, translated into English, are shown in Tables 8, 9, 10, and 11.

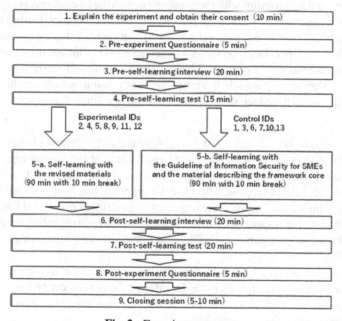

Fig. 2. Experiment process

Pre- and Post- Semi-structured Interviews. We conducted semi-structured interviews that included listing and organizing the components of the security measures using sticky notes placed on a sheet to capture changes in the mental model for the overall security measures determined through the learning process (Fig. 3).

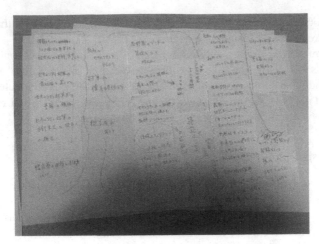

Fig. 3. Task results of ID-6 after self-learning

We asked the participants to list the elements/components of the security measures and to explain each relationship with the grouping or linking of each component. During this phase, they could add new notes but are asked to use other colors. During the remote interview, we asked them to use a drawing software with screen sharing instead of sticky notes and a sheet of paper. Two interviews were conducted before and after the self-study to compare the mental models assumed before and after the self-study. The interviews were recorded. During the post-self-learning interview session, we allowed them to reuse the listed sticky notes to reduce the workload but did not allow the reuse of a full sheet of paper.

Pre- and Post-Test. We created a test to measure the effectiveness of the learning by asking true-false questions and the degree of confidence of the learner regarding their response. The content of the exam was quite basic, allowing the answers to be derived by guesswork. We applied this approach because we supposed that analogies and judgments based on a basic understanding are more important in practice than detailed knowledge. In addition, we had the participants state their degree of confidence regarding the application in an actual business environment. The defined degree of confidence for each question is shown in Table 3.

In addition, we added 37 new questions in the second phase of the experiment, in which security measures contribute to the features of the cybersecurity framework core. These are questions in which one or two of the five functions, i.e., identify, protect, detect, respond, and recover, are chosen.

Self-learning Session. To examine the effect of the revised documents, the participants were divided into two groups: an experimental group and a control group. We were careful to divide the groups evenly based on the profiles of the participants. For the experimental group, we used the materials scribed in Sect. 2.1. For the control group, the experiments were conducted using the Guideline of Information Security for SMEs,

Table 3. Definition of the degree of confidence

Degree of confidence	Expression	Action as security staff member in your workplace
5	Have strong confidence	If you are asked a question, you will be able to respond on the spot without any hesitation
4	Have confidence	If you are asked a question, after some hesitation and anxiety, you can answer it on the spot without reviewing the material, though mentioning your hesitation and anxiety in some cases
3	Have some confidence	If you are asked a question, you can answer it on the spot by guessing, but will create a formal answer after checking the material later
2	Have slight confidence	If you are asked a question, you cannot answer it on the spot, but if you take the question home you can answer it after reviewing the material. However, it does not take much time to investigate because it sounds familiar
1	Have no confidence at all	If you are asked a question, you are unable to answer on the spot, but if you take the question home you can answer it after reviewing the material. However, it takes time to investigate because you do not have an answer in mind

and the supplementary materials, which contain the same description as the part of the revised materials regarding the cybersecurity framework.

We instructed the participants to read all items and gave them a check sheet listing the items and asked them to fill it out to ensure that they did not leave anything unread. If they did not have a sufficient time, we extended the learning phase by approximately 30 min at most. The checklist was common to both the experimental and control groups because the learning items of both materials were the same.

Ethical Consideration. This experiment was approved by the Research Ethics Committee of the Faculty of Engineering, Information and Systems at the University of Tsukuba. The participants were assigned IDs, which were used throughout the experiment. All participants signed consent forms prior to participating in our study. The consent form described the goal of our research, what we expected from the participants, and how the collected data were to be used. The signed consent forms were stored separately and did not contain the assigned IDs to avoid making them linkable to the real identities. We paid 3400 yen to each participant following the Committee's criteria, which is equivalent to the minimum wage in Ibaraki Prefecture, Japan. For each inter-section, we had a break of a few to several minutes in length and allowed the participants to take a rest if they required by stopping the experiment.

2.4 Data Analysis

We conducted the analysis mainly based on the results of listing and organizing tasks for the components of the information security measures. The recorded audio data were transcribed and used in the open coding of the task results.

We imagined three structures through the following steps: 1) A component was treated as a leaf node, 2) a group was treated as a parent node of components included in this group, and 3) a sheet was treated as a root, as a parent node of the group, and as an overview of the security measure: For example, with participant ID-6 post-learning (Fig. 3), the nodes and leaves are as follows (Table 4).

We applied two rounds of open coding to assign codes to each component, and the transcript was used to understand the context of each component. Cohen's kappa was calculated as 0.68 and is considered to be in "substantial" agreement [12] or have a "tentative conclusions" [13]. The conflicts were resolved, and the reconciled codes were used for all analyses. The final set of codes is listed in Appendix Table 12.

Components assigned to the same code were summarized to one; this caused a break in the tree structure in certain cases (the result of participant ID-6 after learning is shown in Fig. 4). In addition, we considered the acquired structures, the meaning of each group name, and the lines and arrows in the sheet, and categorized them into four types.

For the results of the individual tests, the calculations are as follows: For the test scores, 1 point was given for a correct answer and zero points were given for an incorrect answer. For the total degree of confidence, if the question was answered correctly, the degree of confidence was added to the total, and if it was answered incorrectly, the degree of confidence was subtracted from the total. This is because we supposed that it is insufficient to simply give a score of zero because following a false and strong conviction can lead to erroneous actions.

In the case of the 37 questions newly added during the second phase, 2 points were given for a completely correct answer, 1 point was given for a partially correct answer, and zero points were given for an incorrect answer. For the total degree of confidence, if the question was answered correctly (even partially), the degree of confidence was added to the total, and if it was answered incorrectly, the degree of confidence was subtracted.

Table 4. Nodes and leaves created from the task of ID-6 after learning

Node	Leaf
Management's understanding and actions for security	Understand the importance and the risk of information security
	Appoint a person/people responsible for security measures
	Prepare the budget for security measures
	Establish security policies and direct them
Considering and actions of a person/people responsible for security measures	Company Security Assessment
	Prioritization of security measures
	Clear rules of data management for each department
	Creating response manuals for security incidents
	Creating recovery guidelines for security incidents
	Conduct training/simulation
	Periodic inspection and improvement of measures
	Exposure to security-related news
Actions of employees	Regular internal training sessions
	Understanding the need for security measures
	Avoiding using same password or writing down it
	Limitations of external hard drives, etc
	Keeping updated software
	Confirmation of the suitability and security initiatives of the services to be used
	Installing security software
	Establishing an access level for information
	Keeping a record of users
Out of groups	Outsourced security measures
	Regular Security Check of 3rd party

3 Results

3.1 Interview Analysis Based on Mental Model

During this experiment, we identified four different types of mental models through an overview of information security measures: role-based, timeline-based, framework-based, and unstructured (or partial) models.

Role based Model. This model structures security measures based on the perspective of who should implement what. In our pre-self-learning interviews, we confirmed that the participant ID-6 applied this model. The participant categorized the measures into "company-wide initiatives," "security personnel initiatives," and "departmental initiatives," and tried to structure the components listed.

During the post-self-learning interviews, we confirmed that participants ID-5, -8, and -9 also applied this role-based model. Participants ID-6, -8, and -9 attempted to structure the security components from three perspectives; "management," "security personnel," and "employee (individual)," whereas the participant ID-5 only mentioned two; "management" and "management and employee (individual)" (Fig. 4).

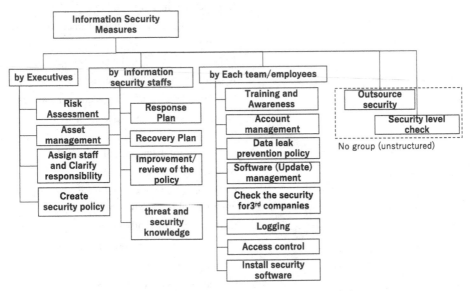

Fig. 4. Role based model of ID-6 after self-learning

Timeline/Phase Based Model. This model organizes the security measures according to the phases or timeline. Through the pre-self-learning interviews, we found that participants ID-1, -2, -3, -7, -11, and -13 applied this model.

The components of the security measures are divided into phases and listed. The results of the pre-learning interviews with participant Pre-1 were slightly different because the components were listed in a row according to the timeline. However, even in this case, we decided to treat them as the same model because they can be arranged on a timeline. Arrows were often written into a diagram to show the flow or timeline. Because some security measures require an improved process, a loopback may occur when ordered in a time series (Fig. 5). This was mentioned by participants ID-1, -3, -11, and -13. During the post-self-learning interviews, participants ID-1, -7, and -10 continued to use this model to describe the relationship and grouping.

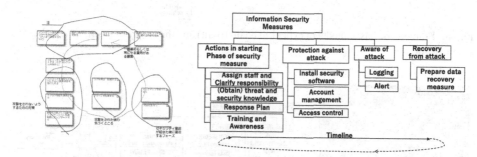

Fig. 5. Timeline/phase-based model (right) and the task result (left) of ID-3 before self-learning

Framework-based Model. Two framework-based mental models are found, one based on the cyber kill chain in a pre-self-learning interview, and the other based on the cybersecurity framework core through a post-self-learning interview.

Cyber Kill Chain. Participant ID-4 used the cyber kill chain framework to list the components and explain their relationship during the pre-learning interview session. The participant first stated that "I will list the components based on the cyber kill chain" and started the listing task but actually used a simpler model than the cyber kill chain, i.e., seven phases, reconnaissance, weaponization, delivery, exploitation, installation, C and C, and actions on objectives, were reorganized into three phases and renamed "intrusion prevention," "prevention of the spread of infection," and "recovery from attack" and the reconnaissance and weaponization disappeared (Fig. 6).

Cybersecurity Framework Core. Participants. ID-2, -3, -4, and -11 tried to use the cybersecurity framework core to list the components and explain their relationship during the post-self-learning interview session.

ID-2, -3, -4, and -11 mentioned that the cybersecurity framework core can be used for this task and tried to first list the categories and then combine the original components they listed during the pre-self-learning interview session (Fig. 7). Red sticky notes were added in the pre-interview grouping phase and reused in post-interview.

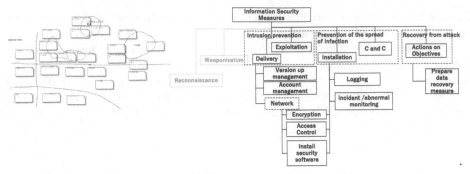

Fig. 6. Framework-based model of cyber kill chain (right) and the task result (left) of ID-4 before self-learning

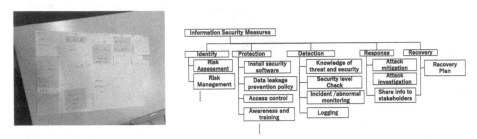

Fig. 7. Framework based model of the framework core (right) and the task result (left) of ID-2 after self-learning (Color figure online)

Unstructured Model (Partial Model). Some participants without education in information security (participants ID-5, -8, and -9) were unable to list the components of the security measures well or failed to organize the components. Grouping could be held partially, but they were unable to find any relationship between groups and/or components. This model was only observed during the pre-self-learning interview session (Fig. 8). Red stickies mean a technical part and yellow stickies mean a knowledge part.

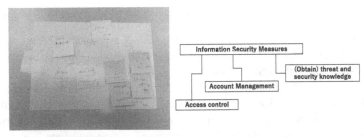

Fig. 8. Unstructured model (right) and the task result (left) of ID-5 before self-learning (Color figure online)

Change of the Mental Model with Self-learning. Table 5 shows the types of mental models the participants had before and after self-learning. We found that several participants changed their type of mental model, and those who had unstructured mental models also acquired a structured mental model through learning. In addition, when the mental model was not changed, learners enriched their details of the model, adding new groups and components. Only changes to the role- and framework-based (cybersecurity framework) models were observed because the original published material is written in a role-based manner and we added the framework information there.

Table 5. Change in the type of mental models

Mental model	Pre-learning	Post-learning
Framework based (Cybersecurity Framework)		2, 3, 4, 11
Framework based (Cyber Kill Chain)	4	
Timeline/Phase based	1, 2, 3, 7, 10, 11, 13	1, 7, 10
Role based	6, 12	5, 6, 8, 9, 12
Unstructured	5, 8, 9	

3.2 Test Analysis

The results are shown in Table 4. Learning led to a significant increase in the mean test scores based on a paired t-test (P-value $= 0.042 < 0.5$; shown as*). However, there were no significant differences in the comparison between the test scores of the experimental and control groups using Welch's t-test. The same trend was observed in the tally based on the degree of confidence.

After confirming the results of the first phase of the experiment, we added 37 new questions in the later phase of the experiment, asking which security measures contributed to which function of the cybersecurity framework.

Although the sample size was small, significant differences were detected between the experimental and control systems using Welch's t-test for the total test and total confidence scores; the P-value of the score was $0.012 < 0.05$, and that of the confidence was $0.002 < 0.05$ (shown as **in Table 6).

Approximately 25 participants may be required as a sample size to detect a significant difference in the degree of confidence with this result.

Table 6. Test score and degree of confidence

| ID | 30 questions (Common, all phases) | | | | 37 questions (2nd phase) | |
| | Pre | | Post | | Pre | Post |
	Test score	Confidence	Test score	Confidence	Test score	Confidence
1	25	87	30	138	N/A	N/A
2	29	110	29	133	N/A	N/A
3	27	113	28	134	N/A	N/A
4	29	117	28	130	N/A	N/A
5	28	129	28	130	N/A	N/A
6	27	66	27	108	32	17
7	29	90	30	108	30	23
8	27	68	30	144	46	78
9	27	115	29	128	46	103
10	25	100	26	110	17	-14
11	27	73	30	122	48	82
12	27	105	29	136	45	93
13	28	90	29	132	36	40
Experiment avg.	27.7	107.8	28.6	131.9	46**	90.5**
Control avg.	26.8	89	28.8	121.6	31**	20**
All avg.	27.3*	98.4*	28.7*	126.7*	38.5	55.25

4 Discussion

As indicated in the previous section, changes in the mental model occurred before and after the current experiment, but we need to consider their triggers.

Only those with information security work experience changed to a framework model, which occurred regardless of whether the participant was in the experimental or control group. This fact suggests that changes in the mental model were not triggered by the improved learning materials, and that those with experience in information security measures might be able to attempt to change the mental model by knowing that the framework core exists.

We suppose that the effects of the materials and pre-testing led the learners to shift their mental unstructured model to role-based model because we took care not to mention any security measures in the interviews. The shift to a role-based mental model may have been influenced by the structure of the original standard documents, which were first divided into an Executive Section and a Practical Section; this requires the "role existence" and descriptions to be written based on the role based perspective.

Related to a mental model shift, we confirmed the difficulty of adapting the new framework. Even if the participants tried to change to a framework-based mental model, they could not always use the framework correctly. For example, ID-4 attempted to use the cyber kill chain based model, but forgot to mention the reconnaissance, and integrated some steps into a single category; indeed, it seems to be far from the original cyber kill chain. The same issue occurs in the cybersecurity framework core case. In particular, when they tried to link their components to a function or category, they sometimes did so improperly. We believe it may have been difficult to resolve this problem using a one-time learning approach. Long-term observations and resolutions are therefore required.

Although the sample size was small, significant differences were detected between the experiment and control systems using a Welch's t-test for the total test and total confidence scores. The experiment group tended to obtain/keep role-based and framework-based model but the control group tended to keep trimline-based model even after self-learning. Participants of role or framework-based model tended to get high scores and those of timeline-based model tended to get low scores. We suppose this is because the improved material shows the relationship between role model and framework model but do not contain the information based on timeline model and the relationship between timeline and framework models. This possibly shows that the improved material is effective for changing or tweaking their mental model and for linking the specific security measures to the cybersecurity framework, which integrates several security guidelines and security measures and helps them obtain a comprehensive and appropriate mental model.

5 Limitation

The mental models observed are those that evolved during the interview. This is particularly true for the experiments on those participants without information security education or experience. We tried not to evolve the mental model too much, which caused some of results of the unstructured model, but the participants still had a chance to evolve their mental model. For example, in the pre-learning interview of participant ID-5, the model is still categorized as unstructured, although the participant remembered the isolated network used in the office and created a new component and group of access controls.

The pre-test might have had an impact on the learning strategy, focusing on specific sections that the participants answered incorrectly; however, we mitigated this with a checklist. Adding 37 new questions during the second phase may have had an impact on the test score but should be limited because we cannot see a gap in the post-test score on 30 questions between the first and second phases.

From a statistical perspective, there was a bias in age and community, and the sample size was small. Thus, the conclusions of this study, both in the test and interview analysis results, might only be replicated and applicable in a limited environment. In particular, the interview data were qualitative in nature and self-reported and were analyzed using a coding approach. It may be possible that other researchers will have different conclusions.

6 Related Studies

6.1 Education in Information Security

The education and training used in the information security field have been studied, although their main research targets are the education and training of employees and education for information security specialists.

Yoo et al. investigated how the flow and psychological ownership affect the effectiveness of security education, training, and awareness (SETA); self-efficacy; and attention to security compliance. Feeling of the "flow" in SETA improved the effectiveness of SETA, and a sense of ownership was found to improve the attention to security compliance [14]. Moneer et al. questioned the effectiveness of SETA and proposed its use as an alternative to the behavioral transformation subscription framework of the behavior change wheel used in the medical field [15].

Live competitions such as the CTF have been studied for the development of security specialists. Katsantonis et al. conducted an analysis, feasibility, and evaluation for the development of a new live competition for educational purposes. They identified the conditions for designing educational gamification and game-based learning methods [16].In addition, to educate workers on OT security, a gamification method was proposed by Yonemura et al. [17].

In a study conducted in Japan on the development of experts who can connect management and field specialists within a company, Son et al. studied the curriculum of universities and graduate schools for the education of experts [18]. They analyzed the curriculum based on the Cybersecurity Workforce Framework [19] defined by The National Initiative for Cybersecurity Education under the National Institute of Standards and Technology.

6.2 Mental Model in Usable Security

In the field of usability security, the mental model is one of the key elements and has been investigated in several fields of information security. In recent studies, Krombholz et al. showed differences in the mental model of HTTPS between administrators and users through interviews that include illustrative work [20]. Wu et al. found through interviews that there are four types of user mental models of encryption, including illustrative work [21]. Fulton et al. identified the impact of media on mental models and described recommendations for not instilling false mental models [22]. However, there have been no studies conducted on the relationship among the mental models used in information security measures, and our study will offer a contribution from this perspective.

7 Conclusion

To improve the learning efficiency and install a comprehensive and appropriate mental model used by information security staff members, we revised materials that explicitly express the relationship with the framework core.

A preliminary experiment was conducted using a group who had not received any systematic education on information security, a group of individuals who had participated in security-related work for approximately 1 year, and a group of actual security staff members.

The experiment aimed to answer what occurs to the learner's mental model during self-learning and how the efficiency changes.

To research the possible mental models for the security measures and their change in learning, we interviewed the participants regarding the work listing and organized the components of the information security measures. We confirmed that there are four models for an overview of the security measures: a role-based model, a time-line/phase-based model, a framework-based model of the cyber kill chain and the cybersecurity framework, and an unstructured model (partial model).

Some of these change by self-learning; individuals who have some experience with information security tend to adopt a cybersecurity framework or keep the original mental model, and those with no experience in information security measures obtain a role-based model upon which the original standard material was based. Those with no experience in information security measures have difficulty recognizing the existence of the framework or their own mental model and will acquire a simple role-based model that is more specific and built into the original document. We suppose that instilling a mental model based on the cybersecurity framework core for those with no security experience may require changing the structure of the materials to that of the cybersecurity framework core, rather than simply showing the relationship and connections.

We also tried to estimate whether an improvement in learning efficiency can be detected statistically in the revised learning materials when applying the current experimental design.

Based on Welch's t-test regarding the question of which security measures contribute to which security functions, we found statistically significant differences in the test and confidence scores in the experimental and control groups; the improved materials may be effective for a comprehensive understanding.

The participants of timeline-based model after self-learning tended to get low scores. We suppose this is because the improved material shows the relationship between role model and framework model but do not contain the information based on timeline model and the relationship between timeline and framework models.

This preliminary experiment was conducted with a small sample size, and calculating the required sample size using the result of this experiment, approximately 25 participants will be required for statistical validity. In a future study, based on the results of this preliminary experiment, we will re-consider the design of the experiment and conduct an additional experiment for approximately 25 information security staff members to ensure that it has made the learners' mental models more comprehensive, appropriate, and efficient in their learning.

Appendix

Table 7. Table of mapping between the categories and sessions of the standard material.

Section	Related categories	Related subcategories	Section	Related categories	Related subcategories
Part1. Executives			2. Develop a response system	RS.CO, PR.IP	
1. Disadvantage of insecurity	ID.RA	ID.GV	2. Make a budget for the security	ID.AM	
1. Loss of money	ID.RA	Pr.AT, ID.GV	3. Create a information security policy and regulations	ID.GV	
2. Loss of customer	ID.RA		1. Identify risks	ID.RA,ID.RM	ID.AM,ID.GV
3. Business stagnation	ID.RA		2. Determine security measures	ID.RM	ID.RA
4. Impact on employees	ID.RA		3. Create a policy and regulation	ID.GV, PR.IP	
2. Responsibility of Executives	N/A		4. Security measures for outsource	ID.SC	PR.AT, ID.AM
1. Liability	ID.GV	ID.RA, PR.AT	5. Check and improvement	PR.IP	
2. Responsibility to society	ID.RA	ID.GV, PR.AT	**5. Strategies for Improvement**	N/A	
3. What executives must do	Pr.AT		1. Information gathering and sharing	N/A	
1. Three principles	N/A		1. How to gather information	ID.RA	
1. Executives shows leadership	ID.BE, PR.AT		2. Information sharing framework	PR.IP,RS.CO	
2. Consider the security of subcontractors	ID.SC	ID.BE, ID.AM	2. Website security	N/A	
3. Communicate with stakeholders	ID.SC, RS.CO	PR.AT/IP	1. Consideration about the website management	ID.AM	
2."Seven important initiatives" to be implemented	ID.GV		2. Constriction of the website	ID.RA, ID.RM	PR.IP
1. Define a security policy	ID.GV		3. Manage the website	PR.PT/DS	PR.AC/IP
2. Make a budget and retain staff/team for information security	ID.GV	PR.IP	3. Cloud service security	N/A	

(*continued*)

Table 7. (*continued*)

Section	Related categories	Related subcategories	Section	Related categories	Related subcategories
3. Consider security measures	PR.IP	PR.IP	1. Choose cloud services	ID.AM,/SC	
4. Check the policy regularly	PR.IP	DE.DP, RS.IM, RC.IM	2. Use cloud services	ID.RM/RA	ID.SC/GV/AM
5. Establish a system of security response and recovery	RS.RP, RC.RP	PR.IP	3. Security measures for cloud services	ID.SC/GV	ID.AM, PR.IP
6. Clarify responsibilities of outsourcing and external services	ID.SC	ID.AM	4. Use of information security services	N/A	
7. Stay up to date on trends	ID.RA	PR.IP	1. Information security consultation	ID.GV,PR.IP	ID.RA/RM
Part2. Practice			3. Information security audit service	PR.PT	
1.Implement and management of security measures	ID.GV	PR.AT	3. Information security audit service	ID.RA/RM	
2. Start with what you can do	N/A		4. Vulnerability diagnosis service	PR.IP	
1. 5 basic items	ID.GV	PR.IP	5. Digital forensics service	RS.AN	
1. Update OS and software	IP.IP		6. Security monitoring and operation services	DE.CM	DE.DP/AE
2. Introduce antivirus software	DE.CM		5. Examples of technical measures	N/A	
3. Use strong passwords	PR.AC		1. Network threat countermeasures	PR.PT	PR.DS, PR.AC
4. Review sharing setups	PR.AC		2. Content security	DE.CM,DE.AE	
5. Know threats and attacks	ID.RA		3. Access control	PR.AC	
3. Organizational initiative	N/A		4. System security management	PR.MA	PR.IP
1. Create a security policy	ID.GV	PR.AT	5. Encryption	PR.DS	

(*continued*)

Table 7. (*continued*)

Section	Related categories	Related subcategories	Section	Related categories	Related subcategories
2. Grasp implementation status	PR.IP		6. Discard data	PR.IP	
3. Decision and dissemination of security measures	ID.RA/RM	ID.GV/AM, PR.AT	6. How to conduct a detailed risk analysis	ID.RM/RA	
4. Work in earnest	ID.GV	ID.RA, ID.BE	1 Identification of information assets	ID.AM	ID.RA
1. Build a management system	N/A		2 Calculate the risk score	ID.RA	
1. Clarify stakeholders	ID.AM, PR.AT		3 Decide on information security measures	ID.RM	

Table 8. Questions and answer options of pre- and post-questionnaires

Questions	Answer options
Pre-questionnaires	
1 What field of business does your company work in?	The list of Japan Standard Industrial Classification
2 Please indicate the number of employees in your company	1–5/5–20/20–50/50–100/100–300/300–1000/1000 or more
3 Please tell us about your current job	Dedicated Security Staff / non-dedicated security staff/other
4 How long have you been in charge of security?	Less than 1 1–3/3–5/5–10/10 or more (years)
5 Is there anyone else in charge of information security?	Yes (persons dedicated and persons non-dedicated)/No
6 How many hours of self-study do you do per week?	Less than 1/1–7/7–14/14 or more (hours/week)
7 What percentage of this is related to information security?	Less than 10/20–30/40–60/70–80/ 80 or more (percent)
8 What do you use as a reference when considering and implementing security measures?	Free answer
Post-questionnaires	
1 What fields do you want to learn about security measures in the future?	Free answer
2 1) Were you aware of the "Guidelines for Information Security Measures for SMEs" issued by the IPA before the experiment?	Used it before/Read it before/Knew its name/Did not know

(*continued*)

Table 8. (*continued*)

Questions	Answer options
2 2) Were you aware of the cybersecurity framework published by the National Institute of Standards and Technology (NIST) before the experiment?	Used it before/Read it before/Knew its name/Did not know
3 1) This time, we conducted the experiment using two patterns of teaching materials. Do you want to obtain these materials?	Yes/No
3 2) Would you like to know your results of the pre-test and post-test?	Yes/No
4 If there is anything that you noticed or were concerned about throughout the experiment, please write it down	Free answer

Table 9. Pre- and post-test questions

Question	True or false
Common 30 questions in both pre- and post test	
1 In the personal information leakage, the information system is not affected and not stopped because the system is not attacked	F
2 Since information leakage by the internal team is caused by the morals of the employees, the executives are not responsible	F
3 Security incidents (information leakage etc.) affect not only customers and their own companies, but also the stakeholders	T
4 They could face imprisonment for leaking personal information	T
5 Since security measures are an issue for IT staff, there is no need for executives to make decisions on them	F
6 You may be held accountable for the security of your subcontractors	T
7 Executives need to be able to adequately explain their company's security initiatives and responses to security incidents to external stakeholders	T
8 Executives do not need to decide the incident response policy on security because they assigned a person in charge	F
9 There is no need to set aside resources (budget and personnel) for information security measures	F
10 The executives need to have those in charge consider the necessary measures and instruct them to implement them	T
11 It is necessary to review information security measures from time to time to keep up with threat trends	T
12 In the case of outsourcing or using external services, there is no need to give instructions to the person in charge in order to select with an awareness of the scope of responsibility	F

(*continued*)

Table 9. (*continued*)

Question	True or false
13 It is not necessary to be prepared with emergency contact information and what to do in the event of an incident	F
14 There is no problem even if you don't use the lock function of your PC, because it can be used by people in your company	F
15 When sending important information by e-mail, it is better to include the information in the body	F
16 In sending important information, it is better to double-check with some peoples to ensure the address is not wrong	T
17 We need to have regular opportunities to explain the importance of information management	T
18 The stakeholders are mentioned in the contract, so there is no need to check their security roles and responsibilities again	F
19 In talking about the information management, it is enough to mention the handling of IT equipment and software	F
20 The management of information assets is carried out in terms of confidentiality, integrity and availability	T
21 Loss of integrity means that the information asset has not been properly handled and may have been altered or corrupted	T
22 There will be no business impact if availability is compromised	F
23 Risk is calculated in terms of two factors: the importance of the asset itself and the likelihood of its damage occurring	T
24 There are three ways to respond to risk: reduction, avoidance, and metastasis	F
25 Risk transfer is the substitution of the company's risk by a service more effective measures (or compensation capacity)	T
26 Installing anti-virus software on a computer is "avoidance" in response to the risk	F
27 The respective roles of executives and employees do not change in normal times or during security incidents	F
28 In checking the security policy, we need to explain the purpose is not to accuse the failure to implement the measures	T
29 If the policy is not consistent with field operations, the policy should be changed as necessary	T
30 Policies need to be changed to keep pace with new information security threats and changes in internal systems	T
10 questions only included in post-test (not used analysis on this study)	
31 You need to collect the latest trends in information security and to share this info with industry organizations and contractors	T
32 Keeping important information in a designated place, such as a stack, instead of leaving it on a desk is effective	T

(*continued*)

Table 9. (*continued*)

Question	True or false
33 Better to introduce a mechanism such as electronic signatures so that they are aware important information is changed	T
34 The hardware with important information is backed up so that it can be restored if something happens	T
35 When hiring employees, they should be informed that there are confidentiality and penalties provisions	T
36 The information assets ledger should contain the least important of the company's information assets	F
37 The policies need only be observed by full-time employees and do not need to tell part-time employees	F
38 It is necessary to prepare and summarize in advance how to respond in case of a security incident	T
39 The scope of the audit and logging should be determined according to policy	T
40 If detection occurs with anti-virus software, there is no need to investigate because it has already been deleted	F

Table 10. 37 questions added from the second phase of the experiment in post-test.

Question	Function	Question	Function
25 action items for basic security		**20. Inform and Train employee about security**	PR
1. Update OS and software	PR	**21. Have a security policy for BYoD**	ID, PR
2. Introduce antivirus software	DE	22. Have NDA for important information	ID
3. Use strong passwords	PR	23. Choose safe and reliable outsource service	ID
4. Review sharing setups	PR	24. Have a response plan and recovery plan	RC, RS
5. Know the threats and attacks	ID, PR	25. Make security policy and inform it to employees	ID, PR
6. Pay attention to the link in E-mail or attached file	PR	6 technical measures	
7. Have any SoP to avoid the wrong transmission	PR	1. Network threat countermeasures	ID, PR
8. Protect an important file with password on e-mail	PR	2. Content security	PR
9. Use secure encryption form for wireless LAN	PR	3. Access control	ID

(*continued*)

Table 10. (*continued*)

Question	Function	Question	Function
10. Prepare and train for SNS troubles	PR	4. System security management	PR
11. Make backup copies	PR	5. Encryption	RS
12. Store important information in secure place	PR	6. Discard data	DE
13. Theft and loss prevention measures for important information	PR	6 information security services	
14. Use screen lock	PR	1. Information security consultation	PR
15. Do not allow unauthorized entry	PR	2. Information security education service	DE
16. Store PC and equipment in secure place when leave office	PR	3. Information security audit service	PR
17. Have a prevention measure not to forget to lock the office	PR	4. Vulnerability diagnosis service	PR
18. Discard the data in an unrestorable way	PR	5. Digital forensics service	PR
19. Keep confidentiality	ID, PR	6. Security monitoring and operation services	PR

Table 11. Pre- and post-test questions

Script for semi-structured interviews
Common pre- and post- interview
1 What elements do you believe are necessary for security measures and what measures and methods do you believe are necessary to achieve security measures? Please list them up with sticky notes (square cards; in remote case)
(Task1. List up the components of information security measure)
2 Could you explain how the components relate to each other and how they structure the security measures? You can use new stickies to add elements, or you can write lines on the board
(Task2. Grouping and linking task)
3 Could you name that group? (if they don't name)
4 Could you explain any relationship between the groups?
5 Do you remember any element, component, measures in grouping? You can add them into the list (ask to use other color note)
Only post- interview
6 Which groups or components did you think learn in your self-learning mainly?

Table 12. Coding result

Codes	Codes
Attack Mitigation	Improvement/Review of the policy
Attack Investigation	Training and Awareness
Share information to stakeholders	Security management of 3rd party
(Have/Create) Response Plan	(Obtain) threat and security knowledge
(Have/Create) Recovery Plan	Assign staff and clarify responsibility
Security with external services	Account management
Install Security Software	Access control
Data leakage prevention policy	Asset management
(Use strong) Encryption	Risk management
Prepare data recovery measure	Risk assessment
Incident /abnormal monitoring	Create security policy
Logging	Security level check

References

1. Fundamental research for education of security human resources. https://www.ipa.go.jp/security/fy23/reports/jinzai/ Accessed 12 Feb 2021
2. Report of questionnaire survey on information security incidents. https://lab.iisec.ac.jp/~hiromatsu_lab/sub07.html. Accessed 12 Feb 2021
3. New type APT. https://www.ipa.go.jp/files/000024542.pdf. Accessed 12 Feb 2021
4. Measures for Developing Cybersecurity Human Resources Inter-Group Working Report. https://www.nisc.go.jp/conference/cs/pdf/jinzai-sesaku2018set.pdf. Accessed 12 Feb 2021
5. Report of cyber security human resource development study group. https://cyber-risk.or.jp/cric-csf/report/CRIC-CSF-2nd-Final-Report.pdf. Accessed 12 Feb 2021
6. NICE Cybersecurity Framework. https://www.nist.gov/cyberframework Accessed 12 Feb 2021
7. Vicente, K.J., Rasmussen, J.: Ecological interface design: theoretical foundations. IEEE Trans. Syst. Man Cybernet. **22**(4), 589–606 (1992)
8. Vicente, K.J.: Ecological interface design: progress and challenges. Hum. Fact. **44**(1), 62–78 (2002)
9. Furukawa, H.: A learning method to support user's understanding about complex systems based on functional models: an empirical study on young and elderly users of mobile phones: In: Proceedings of the UK Sim 13th International Conference on Computer Modelling and Simulation, Cambridge, March, pp. 370–375
10. Guideline of Information Security for SMEs, 3rd edn. https://www.ipa.go.jp/security/keihatsu/sme/guideline/index.html. Accessed 12 Feb 2021
11. Ozaki, S.: Improving the training material of the information security based on Cybersecurity framework. In: HCII Proceedings, Heidelberg (2020)
12. Landis, J., Koch, G.: The measurement of observer agreement for categorical data. Biometrics **33**(1), 159–174 (1977)
13. Krippendorff, K.: Content Analysis an Introduction to Its Methodology. Sage Publications, Beverly Hills, CA (1980)

14. Chul, W.Y., Sanders, L., Cervenya, R.P.: Exploring the influence of flow and psychological ownership on security education, training and awareness effectiveness and security compliance. Decis. Supp. Syst. **108**, 107–118 (2018)
15. Alshaikh, M., Naseer, H., Ahmad, A., Maynard, S.B.: Toward sustainable behavior change: an approach for cybersecurity education training and awareness. In: 27th ECIS 2019 Proceedings, AISeL, Hawaii, USA (2019)
16. Katsantonis, M., Fouliras, P., Mavridis, I.: Conceptual analysis of cyber security education based on live competitions. In: EDUCON Proceedings, IEEE, USA (2017)
17. Yonemura, K., Yajima, K., Komura, R., Sato, J.: Practical security education on operational technology using gamification method. In: ICCSCE Proceedings, IEEE, Malaysia (2017)
18. Son, Y.K., Yamaguchi, Y., Shimada, H., Takakura, H.: A curriculum analysis for information security curriculum development enforcing on technical competencies. IPSJ J. **58**(5), 1163–1174 (2017)
19. NICE Cybersecurity Workforce Framework. https://www.nist.gov/itl/appliedcybersecurity/nice/resources/nicecybersecurity-workforce-framework. Accessed 12 Feb 2021
20. Krombholz, K., Busse, K., Pfeffer, K., Smith, M,. Von Zezschwitz, E.: If HTTPS were secure, I wouldn't need 2FA-end user and administrator mental models of HTTPS. In: IEEE Symposium on Security and Privacy (SP) Proceedings, IEEE, USA (2019)
21. Wu, J., Zappala, D.: When is a tree really a truck? Exploring mental models of encryption. In: 40th SOUPS Proceedings, pp. 395–407, USENIX, Boston, USA (2018)
22. Fulton, K R., Gelles, R., McKay, A., Roberts, R., Abdi, Y., Mazurek, M.L.: the effect of entertainment media on mental models of computer security. In: 41th SOUPS Proceedings, pp. 79–95, USENIX, Boston, USA. Conference Name: ACM Woodstock conference (2019)

Gaming Apps' and Social Media Partnership: A Privacy Perspective

Tian Wang[✉] and Masooda Bashir

University of Illinois at Urbana-Champaign, Champaign, IL 61820, USA
tianw7@illinois.edu

Abstract. As mobile devices and social media presence are becoming ever more integrated into daily lives, mobile games are also becoming increasingly more popular and replacing computer or handheld games. While mobile games provide convenient and timely entertainment, gaming apps also raise privacy concerns, especially when they are linked to users' social media accounts. This connection between gaming apps and social media often allows the gaming apps to access users' personal information. In this study we aim to address the privacy violations that may occur in this context. To conduct this study, twenty gaming apps from the Apple Store were selected and analyzed for the types of access and information exchange between social media and the gaming apps. In particular, it was alarming to learn that social media service providers were granting that access to the third-parties as well. Our analysis reveals that all twenty of the gaming apps collected users' personal and sensitive information, while nine of the apps not only collected personal information but also were able to modify users' information on their profile or timeline. Therefore, the goal of this study is to identify these potential privacy violations, raise gaming app users' awareness of these privacy invasive practices, and propose initial recommendations for social media service providers and gaming app developers to provide better user privacy protections.

Keywords: Privacy concerns · Social media · Mobile games

1 Introduction

As the development of smartphone technologies and mobile gaming apps continues to evolve and become ever more connected so do the privacy violations that may occur as these partnerships tend to share a lot of their users' personal data. Nowadays, mobile games have a significant advantage over computer games or handheld games because they are more convenient to play. People can play games at any time or place once they have gaming apps installed on their smartphones. As a result, many people are addicted to mobile gaming apps. According to Go-Globe [1], mobile gaming apps account for more than 43% of total time users spent on their smartphone in 2018. Currently, there are 1.36 billion mobile gamers worldwide [22]. Given the number of mobile game users, many tech entrepreneurs and mobile app developers invest heavily to create mobile gaming apps since these apps seem to be a good investment and provide huge profits [15].

© Springer Nature Switzerland AG 2021
A. Moallem (Ed.): HCII 2021, LNCS 12788, pp. 475–487, 2021.
https://doi.org/10.1007/978-3-030-77392-2_30

However, privacy in relation to online gaming environment has been a serious concern as well, not only because game companies may sell users' information collected to advertisers or use it for their own purposes [3], but also the popularity and market size for gaming apps make individual users ideal targets for cybercriminals who see games as a platform for stealing users' information or invading their privacy [4]. Online gaming apps usually contain users' personal information, such as the player's name, birthdate, address, mobile number, email address, and even social network ID or credit card account [4]. Leaks of user information will lead to serious privacy violations and negative impacts on building trust between service providers and users.

Meanwhile, since many mobile games have multiplayer options that allow players to communicate with each other, a lot of these gaming apps also ask users to link the app to their social media accounts and to give the app permission to access their social media information. By accessing a user's social media, gaming apps may collect a variety of information, including a user's profile, content posted, and friends list, in order to create and build a community around the game. For example, according to Twitter, when users connect a third-party app to their Twitter accounts, the authorized app may be able to obtain information from and use their accounts in various ways, such as reading Tweets, updating their profile, posting Tweets on the user's behalf, or accessing the user's Direct Messages [16].

While social media provides a faster and easier means of communication for people around the world, it also enables the sharing of massive amounts of personal information that may lead to serious privacy violations. The data sharing practices of social media companies are not limited to social networking environments, but also extend to their third-party applications. In 2010, The Wall Street Journal published a study revealing that many popular apps based on Facebook have been transmitting both users' personal information and their friends' information to various third parties, such as advertising and data tracking firms [12]. Though social media service providers are beginning to consider privacy violations that may occur in their data access and sharing practices with third-party apps, it is still unclear what measures they have taken to protect users' information over third-party apps. In 2019, Twitter updated its privacy policy, stating that the revised language was to ensure users' understanding and enable them to give permission for third parties to access their data and sharing practices [2]. Therefore, Twitter placed the responsibility and protection decisions on the users themselves although numerous studies have shown that users do not read privacy policies and may not even be able to make such informed decisions.

Given the privacy concerns in both gaming apps and social media platforms, the goal of this study is to examine the intersection of these two environments and determine the severity of the privacy violations that may occur in the context of this partnerships between gaming apps and social media. The study aims to identify privacy violations and to propose initial recommendations for both social media service providers and gaming apps for how they may provide better privacy protections for their users. The specific aims for this study are as follows.

- Identify potential privacy invasive practices of gaming apps when they are granted permission to users' social media accounts by the users. In particular, examining the types of personal information that gaming apps access when a user's social media account is linked to the gaming app. Therefore, we will investigate the following questions:

- What kind of permission/s does the social media service provider allow to gaming apps once the users link their social media accounts to the gaming app?
- What kinds of personal information do gaming apps request when the users link their social media accounts to the gaming app?

- Considering these potential privacy violations, we recommend interface design strategies as well as privacy protecting data practices to both social media and gaming apps.
- Raise public awareness about the privacy violations that could occur when users link their social media accounts to third-party applications, especially gaming apps.

We believe that the results from this study will provide an important step in identifying privacy violations that may occur when gaming and social media apps are partners in sharing users' personal data and the extent of these violations when such sharing is offered to third-party apps. This research aims to raise users' awareness of privacy violations and to provide recommendations for social media service providers and gaming app developers to appropriately consider and address privacy protections, as well as to develop effective approaches to minimize data access and data sharing with third parties to better protect their users' privacy in the future.

2 Literature Review

2.1 Privacy on Social Media

Studying privacy involving social media is complex because it involves different parties, such as users, social media service providers, and third-parties, as well as how data is shared and disclosed on social media platforms. A previous study revealed that users are aware of privacy issues when they interact with social media-enabled apps, and such privacy concerns may influence users' behaviors on social media. The study found that users who frequently use these apps are more likely to have concerns about social privacy, and they tend to minimize their engagement on the apps [5]. With existing privacy concerns about social media, users begin to try to protect their private information. For example, some users may choose to limit the disclosures of their private information by reducing the amount of information they disclose publicly or limiting the content of their disclosures to certain topics. They may also carefully choose their friends on social media to control who can view their content [6]. As more users join social media, it is important to pay attention to privacy protection for vulnerable groups, such as children and teenagers. A 2013 Pew Research Center study found that teens are sharing more information about themselves on social media sites than they did in the past [7].

While a previous study showed that most teens are very confident about managing their Facebook privacy settings [7], threats and violations of privacy on social media platforms are still urgent issues that are yet to be resolved. For example, a prior study discussed four causes of privacy leaks on social networks: users' limitations, design flaws and limitations, implicit flows of information, and clashes of incentives [8]. Specifically, social media users might be targeted and manipulated by other individuals or third parties with harmful intentions using the information they shared online publicly. One example of harmful social media events was a series of self-harming tasks called the Blue Whale Challenge, which was being propagated on platforms like Facebook [9]. Also, an attacker can map users' email addresses to their real names by using the account recovery service provided by social media, or re-construct the user's friend list even though the user chooses to protect such information in the settings [10].

2.2 Privacy Concerns on Third-Party Apps

In recent years, many third-party apps have accessed users' information through social media platforms. For example, Facebook allows third-party developers to deploy applications on the Facebook site, but the original codes are still run from the app creators' sites. Associating with Facebook, these third-party apps could collect users' information from their social media accounts, but it is uncertain whether users are aware that their profile information is shared with a party external to Facebook [11]. When accessing third-party apps on social media, users will be asked to give their consent to these apps to access their personal data, but currently no generally applicable policy model effectively specifies the terms or purposes for user data collection and processing [13]. Moreover, even when laws or regulations specify how personal data are supposed to be handled, app permission requests still lack transparency [13]. While third-party apps typically allow users to enable or disable their permissions for the app, this process still has several shortcomings that lead to lack of transparency. A prior study explained two of the problems with third-party apps. First, users may remain unaware that their personal information on social media will be harvested by third parties after they grant permission. Second, many users do not know that apps share the same third-party services, which causes them to be unaware of the potentially rich data that third-party services aggregate [14]. Therefore, social media service providers must take responsibility to notify users about access by third-party apps and for users to understand how their information on social media is collected and shared with third-party apps.

3   Method

This study' first step is to understand what types of access permissions are provided by social media service providers to gaming apps. As a preliminary study, Twitter, Facebook, and Snapchat were selected as the examples of social media providers for this study. Table 1 shows the third-party app permissions provided by these three social media service providers. From the preliminary analysis, some of the social media services do not specify the types of information accessed by third-party apps with users' permission. For example, the statement "more data may be asked by developer from the connected third-party app" by Snapchat is ambiguous and does not include any detailed explanation. Also, even if the social media services have clear statements on third-party app permissions, they are not taking responsibility to protect users' personal data or making any restrictions to the third-party apps once the users choose to give permission to those apps.

Table 1. Examples of social medias and their permission to third-party apps

Social media	Third-party app permissions
Twitter [16]	● **Read:** View profile information (name, location, description, profile photo), view posts from the timeline including protected posts, view account settings, see the following/mute/block accounts, view list and collections. ● **Read and write:** Update profile information, post/delete content on user's behalf, manage account settings, create list and collections. ● **Read, write, and direct message:** Besides the access described above, also have ability to send direct message (DM) for the user, view, manage, and delete DMs on user's behalf.
Facebook [17]	● **Active:** Have access to the user's name, username, user ID (account number), profile pictures, networks connected to, other public information on the profile, friends list, gender, age range, and locale, and publish posts on user's News Feed, timeline or in a group with user's permission. ● **Expired/Removed:** if the user has not been active on the app for more than 90 days or the app is removed by the user, the app will no longer have access to additional private information, but it can still see the accessible data (name, profile picture, cover photo, app user ID).
Snapchat [18]	● **Authorized apps:** Access to the Display Name and Bitmoji. More data may be asked by developer from the connected third-party app. ● **Unauthorized apps:** Access to login information (username and password), but such app is not authorized by Snapchat and will result having trouble logging in or getting locked.

To analyze how gaming apps access to users' social media, we selected 20 apps from the top free games lists on App Store (iOS) that link to social media. The Apple Store has a list of the top 200 free games (including all categories), as well as the top 200 free game for each category. While Apple does not publicly disclose the algorithms identifying the top games, the top-games list is supposed to be an estimate of popularity based on download times, number of users, usage of the app, ratings, and number of reviews. Although many news websites have their own rankings for the top games on App Store, in this study, we used the rankings from App Store itself since it is the official source. Also, not all the gaming apps require users' social media accounts. For example, High Heels!, which is a racing game ranked #1 in the top free game, does not include the option to link to users' social media accounts. Since this study focuses on how gaming apps access social media information, only apps with the option to link to social media accounts were selected. For each selected app, we recorded general information, including the name of the app, category, ranking (if applicable), rating score, and number of ratings.

Specifically, we want to learn if the app requires users to link their social media accounts in order to use the app, and what types of information (i.e., profile, posts, friend list) from the users' social media does the app ask for access. In general, when accessing users' social media accounts, gaming apps will ask for permission to read users' social media information, including their profile information (i.e., name, gender, location) and the content of their posts. Some of the gaming apps will even ask for both read and write permissions, which means the gaming app will not only view the user's social media information but will also have permission to update the user's profile information, post or delete content on the user's behalf, and manage the user's account settings. To analyze how the gaming apps get access to users' social media information, we recorded the social media platform (if the gaming app involves connection with multiple social media platforms, we recorded only one of them as an example), the message from the gaming apps when asking users to authorize the app, and the permission displayed on the social media platforms to see if there is any mismatch between access asked for by gaming apps and access provided by social media services.

4   Results

4.1   Basic Information on the Gaming Apps Selected for This Study

Table 2. List of 20 selected gaming apps and basic information

Name	Category	Ranking (in the category)	Number of ratings	Rating
Call of duty: mobile	Action	#5 (#12 overall)	1.3 M	4.8
Madden NFL 21 mobile	Sports	#3 (#38 overall)	204 K	4.7
Genshin impact	Adventure	#3 (#45 overall)	111 K	4.6
PUBG mobile	Strategy	#3 (#48 overall)	1.1 M	4.3
Animal restaurant	Simulation	#135	46 K	4.9
Love unholy	Simulation	#189	1 K	4.4
Dragon Raja	Role playing	#26	23 K	4.6
Identity V	Role playing	#109	78 K	4.7
Mr Love: Queen's choice	Role playing	#166	17 K	4.8
Life after	Adventure	#54	14 K	4
Astracraft	Adventure	#66	2.7 K	4.7
Onmyoji arena	Strategy	#131	14 K	4.7
Creative destruction	action	#65	162 K	4.6
Maybe: interactive stories	Role playing	#132	5.7 K	4.6
Dead by daylight	Role playing	#43	21 K	4.1
World of tanks blitz	Strategy	#87	75 K	4.6

(*continued*)

Table 2. (*continued*)

Name	Category	Ranking (in the category)	Number of ratings	Rating
Shadowgun War games	Adventure	#95	33 K	4.7
Critical ops	Adventure	#100	22 K	4.4
Risk: global domination	Board	#59	100 K	4.7
War robot mobile	Action	#131	367 K	4.7

Table 2 lists the basic information for the 20 selected gaming apps from the Apple Store. All the gaming apps were selected from the top categories (i.e., Adventure, Board, Role Playing, Simulation). Results showed that all the gaming apps requiring connections to social media accounts are multiplayer games. In other words, these gaming apps involve interacting with other players (in contrast, some mobile games can be played by single player, and there is no need to collect additional information). As a result, they ask for users' social media information to understand users' networking and then try to attract more users based on the information collected. It is also proven by the category of the selected games. As shown in Fig. 1, most of the 20 selected gaming apps were from role playing, adventure, action, and simulation. Games from these categories involve a large number of users interacting (i.e., teamwork, communication, competition).

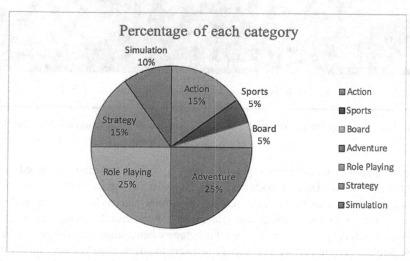

Fig. 1. Percentage of each category for the 20 selected gaming apps.

4.2 Access to Users Social Media Information

All the selected gaming apps ask for information from users' social media profiles. Figure 2 shows the types of information from Facebook asked for by the gaming apps. For the 14 gaming apps asking for connections to Facebook, four of them also ask for the user's email address, and three of them ask for the user's friends list. It is noticeable that although the apps require users to grant permission for them to access the username and profile picture, they do not require users to grant permission for access to email addresses and friends lists. Users could choose to stop sharing this information by changing their settings on Facebook. However, Facebook and gaming apps do not alert users to this option, so users are unaware of the option unless they check the Facebook settings by themselves.

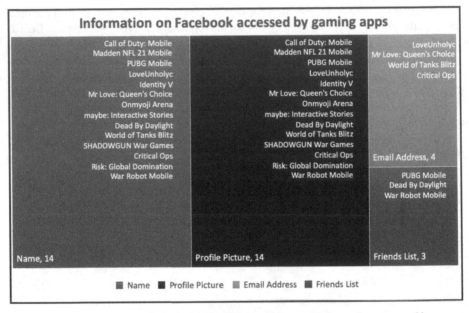

Fig. 2. List of gaming apps linked with Facebook and types of information accessed by apps.

Figure 3 shows the different types of access to Twitter information asked for by gaming apps. For the six apps asking to connect to Twitter, most of them (four out of six) ask for read and write permissions. Only one of them restricts its access as read-only, and one of them asks for all the permissions (read, write, and direct message). Unlike Facebook, which only displays a very brief message when authorizing the gaming apps, Twitter displays detailed information to allow users to check what types of information are accessed by the connected app. In addition, a list of details for read, write, and direct message permissions granted by Twitter is shown in Table 3.

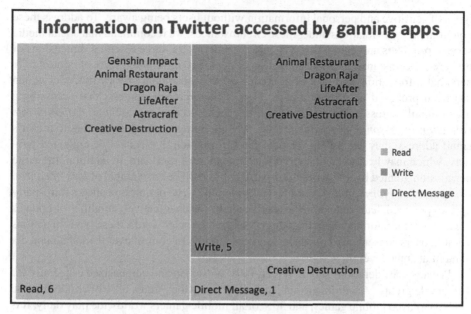

Fig. 3. List of gaming apps linked to Twitter and types of permissions asked by apps.

Table 3. Details on types of permissions granted by Twitter

Permission	Details (messages displayed when authorizing the app)
Read	See Tweets from your timeline (including protected Tweets) as well as your Lists and collections
	See your Twitter profile information and account settings
	See accounts you follow, mute, and block
Write	Follow and unfollow account for you
	Update your profile and account settings
	Post and delete Tweets for you, and engage with Tweets posted by others (like, unlike, or reply to a Tweet, Retweet, etc.) for you
	Create, manage, and delete Lists and collections for you
	Mute, block, and report accounts for you
Direct message	Send direct messages for you and read, manage, and delete your direct messages

5 Discussion

Results showed that privacy violations may occur when users link their social media accounts to third parties like gaming apps. Given that gaming apps could collect a variety of personal information from social media, it is possible that the apps also collect other types of sensitive and personal information without users being aware. To address these potential privacy violations under these circumstances, we recommend that social media service providers and gaming apps should consider users' three essential dimensions of privacy concerns: inappropriate collection of personal information, lack of control over personal information, and lack of awareness of organizational privacy practices which has been proposed by Malhotra et al. [19]. This approach suggests that accessing a user's email addresses on social media (i.e. Facebook) may represent an *inappropriate collection of personal information*. Thus, when gaming apps ask for access to a user's email address, they are asking for personal information that cannot be collected publicly, which may lead to the inappropriate collection of user data. In addition, the write permission granted by Twitter to third-party apps could be an example of *lack of control over personal information*. According to Twitter, the write permission allows third-party apps to post or delete content on the user's behalf, which effectively modifies or updates the user's information without their direct consent. In other words, these types of actions without users consent and knowledge may lead to loss of control over their social media content at some level.

Privacy considerations should be carefully addressed and emphasized especially for vulnerable groups. According to statistics from a previous study, 63% of children in the US have played mobile games, and 30% of all mobile gamers worldwide play daily. It is understandable that the gaming apps are more attractive to young users because they are affordable, interactive, and easy to manage comparing with traditional computer games [20]. While young users like teenagers have become one of the majority user groups for gaming apps, they are also more likely to be targeted and manipulated with their information being shared and disclosed to third-parties if they link their social media accounts to gaming apps. Reports showed that one of the major online risks for teenagers is privacy breaches or personal information shared without permission [21]. Linking social media accounts to third parties like gaming apps would potentially increase the level of risk for privacy breaches. Therefore, because young users are not mature enough or even able to take full responsibility for their online behaviors (especially teenagers), it is necessary for service providers to build safe online environments with minimized privacy issues and protect their personal information.

With the goal of providing better privacy protections for users, this study proposes initial data practices to both social media service providers and gaming app developers. For social media service providers, it is important to advise users with detailed information on what types of data will be collected and accessed by gaming apps before users give permission. Users do not frequently check the status of third-party apps or even remember if they granted access to such apps, but third-party apps will continue collecting data from users unless users manually remove or decline permission. We suggest that social media service providers routinely notify users about any third-party apps actively linked to their accounts. Also, we strongly recommend that social media service providers apply techniques to detect suspicious information access or activities by gaming apps and warn users. Since all the information accessing and collecting activities rely on social media platforms, it is the social media service providers' responsibility to take action to protect users' data. Meanwhile, gaming app developers should also emphasize privacy protection when they access users' information on social media. When asking for social media access, gaming apps should alert users with clear messages to ensure users understand what information will be accessed after linking their social media accounts. Also, we recommend that gaming apps send in-game notifications to users if they take any actions on social media on the user's behalf.

The results from this study is to also raise the public's awareness of online privacy violations that may occur. Besides social media service providers and gaming app developers, individual users are also encouraged to take accountability to better understand how their personal information is collected and shared. For example, individual users are advised to think about what types of information they will share with third parties like gaming apps when linking their social media accounts and granting permission. It is also suggested that users read privacy policies and review details on the access requests to ensure they understand how their information is shared and collected, to minimize the risk of possible privacy violations.

6 Limitation

One of the limitations for this research study is that it only considered and analyzed gaming apps based on the iOS system. Although gaming apps from the Apple App Store and Google Play are similar, it is possible that some of the most popular gaming apps were missing in this study. Also, while there is no major difference in the gaming apps' functionalities, especially related to social media connections, some of the minor functionalities might be different in iOS and Android, which leads to the possibility of differences in permissions granted by social media.

7 Conclusion

In this study, 20 gaming apps were evaluated for privacy violations when the user allowed it to be linked to their social media accounts. Our results revealed that privacy violations such as inappropriate collection of personal data and lack of control over personal information should be carefully considered during the process of granting social media access to gaming apps. Users should be aware of any privacy violations when giving permission to gaming apps to access their social media, but as service providers, social media and gaming apps should also take responsibility for protecting users' data. We believe the results from this study will not only raise public awareness of privacy protection limitations on social media and gaming apps, but also serve as an initial step to develop new techniques that will help protect users' information privacy and provide safer online gaming environments in the future.

Acknowledgements. This research study is supported and funded by Cisco Systems as part of a privacy project.

References

1. The State of Mobile Gaming Industry – Statistics and Trends: Go-Globe (2018). https://www.go-globe.com/mobile-gaming-industry/
2. Hutchinson, A.: Twitter updates permissions to clarify which third-party apps you approve for DM access (2019). https://www.socialmediatoday.com/news/twitter-updates-permissions-to-clarify-which-third-party-apps-you-approve-f/561140
3. The complete guide to online gaming privacy. ProtonVPN (2020). https://protonvpn.com/blog/online-gaming-privacy/
4. Data privacy and online gaming: why gamers make for ideal targets. Trend-Micro (2015). https://www.trendmicro.com/vinfo/us/security/news/online-privacy/data-privacy-and-online-gaming-why-gamers-make-for-ideal-targets
5. Jozani, M., Ayaburi, E., Ko, M., Choo, K.K.R.: Privacy concerns and benefits of engagement with social media-enabled apps: a privacy calculus perspective. Comput. Hum. Behav. **107**, 106260 (2020)
6. Ellison, N.B., Vitak, J., Steinfield, C., Gray, R., Lampe, C.: Negotiating privacy concerns and social capital needs in a social media environment. In: Privacy Online, pp. 19–32. Springer, Berlin, Heidelberg (2011). https://doi.org/10.1007/978-3-642-21521-6_3
7. Madden, M., Lenhart, A., Cortesi, S., Gasser, U., Duggan, M., Smith, A., Beaton, M.: Teens, social media, and privacy. Pew Res. Cent. **21**(1055), 2–86 (2013)
8. Mahmood, S.: Online social networks: Privacy threats and defenses. In: C, Richard, B, Bechara Al (eds.) Security and Privacy Preserving in Social Networks, pp. 47–71. Springer, Vienna (2013). https://doi.org/10.1007/978-3-7091-0894-9_2
9. Khattar, A., Dabas, K., Gupta, K., Chopra, S., Kumaraguru, P.: White or blue, the whale gets its vengeance: a social media analysis of the blue whale challenge. arXiv preprint arXiv:1801.05588 (2018)
10. Mahmood, S.: New privacy threats for facebook and twitter users. In: 2012 Seventh International Conference on P2P, Parallel, Grid, Cloud and Internet Computing, pp. 164–169. IEEE, November (2012)
11. King, J., Lampinen, A., Smolen, A.: Privacy: is there an app for that? In: Proceedings of the Seventh Symposium on Usable Privacy and Security, pp. 1–20, July (2011)
12. Steel, E., Fowler, G.: Facebook in privacy breach. Wall Street J. October 18 (2010)
13. Tsavli, M., Efraimidis, P.S., Katos, V., Mitrou, L.: Reengineering the user: privacy concerns about personal data on smartphones. Inf. Comput. Secur. **23**, 394–405 (2015)
14. Vallina-Rodriguez, N., et al.: Tracking the trackers: towards understanding the mobile advertising and tracking ecosystem. arXiv preprint arXiv:1609.07190 (2016)
15. Mobile gaming apps: how to develop and make them succeed. July 7 2017. Adoriasoft. https://medium.com/@Adoriasoft/mobile-gaming-apps-how-to-develop-and-make-them-succeed-488f49cb229
16. About third-party apps and log in sessions. Twitter. https://hclp.twitter.com/en/managing-your-account/connect-or-revoke-access-to-third-party-apps
17. App Visibility and Privacy. Facebook. https://www.facebook.com/help/1727608884153160
18. Snapchat Support. https://support.snapchat.com/en-GB/a/remove-connected-app
19. Malhotra, N.K., Kim, S.S., Agarwal, J.: Internet users' information privacy concerns (IUIPC): the construct, the scale, and a causal model. Inf. Syst. Res. **15**(4), 336–355 (2004)
20. Lynkova, D.: How many people play mobile games in 2020 – everything you need to know. https://techjury.net/blog/mobile-gaming-demographics/#gref

21. Haelle, T.: Online risks are everyday events for teens -- but they rarely tell their parents. https://www.forbes.com/sites/tarahaelle/2017/02/28/online-risks-are-everyday-events-for-teens-but-they-rarely-tell-their-parents/?sh=1862fb523861
22. Williams, R.: Mobile games sparked 60% of 2019 global game revenue, study finds. https://www.marketingdive.com/news/mobile-games-sparked-60-of-2019-global-game-revenue-study-finds/569658/

Correction to: Testing Facial Recognition Software for Young Adults and Adolescents: An Integrative Review

Aimee Kendall Roundtree (iD)

Correction to:
Chapter "Testing Facial Recognition Software for Young Adults and Adolescents: An Integrative Review" in:
A. Moallem (Ed.): *HCI for Cybersecurity, Privacy and Trust*, LNCS 12788, https://doi.org/10.1007/978-3-030-77392-2_4

The original version of this chapter was revised. Several mistakes have been corrected:

- Section 2: The year has been corrected from "2007" to "2008".
- Section 3.1: The number of older adults has been corrected from "n=12" to "n=10".
- Section 3.2: "Six studies" has been corrected to "Some".
- Section 3.3: "five studies that tracked ... Six that tracked" has been corrected to "six studies that tracked ... Four tracked".
- Section 3.6: "The other were published in relatively ethnically homogeneous countries." has been corrected to "Others were published in relatively ethnically homogeneous countries."
- Caption of table 1 has been corrected to "Inclusion/Exclusion".

The updated version of this chapter can be found at
https://doi.org/10.1007/978-3-030-77392-2_4

Author Index

Printed in the United States
by Baker & Taylor Publisher Services